# Working with Young Children

**Dr. Judy Herr**

Professor, Early Childhood Education
College of Human Development
University of Wisconsin-Stout
Menomonie, Wisconsin

Publisher
**The Goodheart-Willcox Company, Inc.**
Tinley Park, Illinois

Library of Congress Catalog Card Number 2002029740
International Standard Book Number 1-59070-128-3

4 5 6 7 8 9 10    04    09 08 07 06 05 04

Library of Congress Cataloging-in-Publication Data

Herr, Judy.
  Working with young children / Judy Herr.
    p.    cm.
  Includes index.
  ISBN 1-59070-128-3
  1. Child care services--United States. 2. Child care workers--United States. 3. Early childhood education--United States.
I. Title.
HQ778.63.H47    2003
362.7'0973--dc21
                                                    2002029740

Cover photo: ©Camille Tokerud/ImageState

2

# Introduction

*Working with Young Children* is designed to help you prepare for a career in early childhood education. It teaches practical techniques to guide children through a variety of daily experiences in safe, educational ways.

Success in working with children begins by understanding children. This book starts with an overview of the physical, intellectual, social, and emotional characteristics of young children. Using this information will help you plan for and react to children with confidence that your actions are developmentally appropriate.

Once you understand children, you are ready to develop and build your guidance skills. This text teaches you practical techniques for guiding children as you establish rules and handle daily routines. It also gives helpful suggestions for dealing with guidance problems.

An important part of working with young children is creating a safe, healthy learning environment. As you read this text, you will learn techniques for keeping children safe, healthy, and nourished. In addition, you will learn to provide experiences that build children's enthusiasm for learning.

*Working with Young Children* prepares you for other important aspects of nurturing young children. These include planning developmentally appropriate curriculum and developing strategies for involving parents in child care programs. The book also prepares you to handle special concerns related to infants, toddlers, school-age children, and children with special needs. Finally, the book prepares you to launch a career in child care, helping you explore the types of programs and refine your job hunting skills.

# About the Author

The quality of this textbook reflects Judy Herr's intense dedication to early childhood education, with over 30 years of experience in the field. Judy previously supervised and administered seven children's programs at the University of Wisconsin-Stout. She also served as the early childhood program director and Associate Dean of the College of Human Development.

Judy has published numerous books, manuals, and articles on early childhood education. Her articles have been printed in such noted journals as *Young Children, Journal of Family and Consumer Sciences, Early Childhood News,* and *Texas Child Care Quarterly.*

Judy has been a guest speaker at local, regional, national, and international conferences. She is active in professional associations including the National Association for the Education of Young Children. Judy has received many awards, including the Shirley Dean Award for Distinguished Service to the Midwestern Association for the Education of Young Children. She was also named a Dahlgren Professor. Judy participated in the prestigious Management Development Program at Harvard University.

# Contents

# Part 2 Creating a Safe and Healthy Environment

# Part 4  Learning Experiences for Children

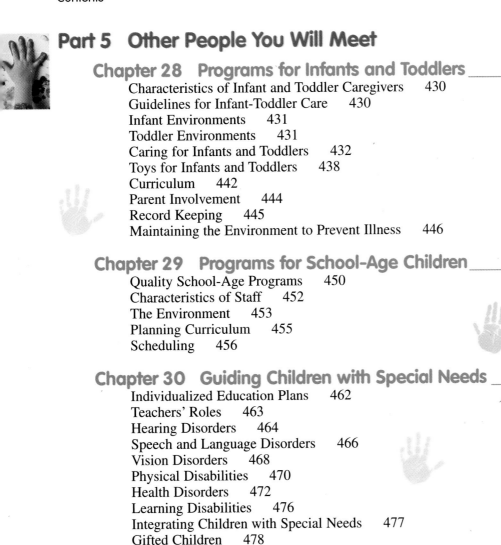

# Part 5 Other People You Will Meet

# Part 1

# The Children and You

Who you are and what you know affects your ability to work with young children. In this part, you will explore current career opportunities in the early childhood field. You will also examine the responsibilities and characteristics of successful early childhood teachers. Various types of early childhood programs will be described.

This part will help you understand the characteristics of children at different ages. It will give you an overview of their physical, cognitive, social, and emotional development. You will learn how to change your teaching skills to fit the developmental needs and interests of children at different ages.

One of the best ways to learn about children is to observe them. Techniques for objectively observing and recording children's behavior will be described in this part.

Working with young children is challenging, but rewarding.
Do you have the characteristics needed to have
a successful career in child care?

# Chapter 1

# You: Working with Young Children

After studying this chapter, you will be able to

- explain how social and economic changes will increase the need for child care services.

- describe career opportunities in the early childhood field.

- describe the CDA Credential.

- list responsibilities of the early childhood teacher.

- explain how certain personal characteristics can help early childhood teachers care for and educate young children.

## Terms to Know

early childhood
nanny
au pair
licensing specialist
entrepreneur
Child Development Associate (CDA) Credential
ethics

Mary takes care of toddlers, 1-1. Suzie, who has been a preschool teacher for two years, has taken a position as a center director. Her friend Marko is the parent coordinator in a local Head Start center, while Tom, who was another classmate, is a parent educator. Two other classmates,

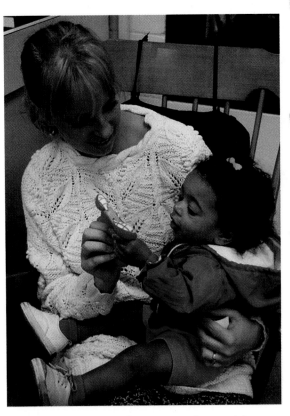

1-1 Taking care of toddlers is one of many job opportunities for people who study early childhood.

Sung Jee and Sally, recently opened a children's clothing store. Each of these individuals studied early childhood. These are just a few of the many challenging and rewarding career opportunities within the early childhood field.

Already you may be asking yourself, "What is early childhood?" **Early childhood** covers the period from birth to nine years of age. During this time, growth is very rapid. The child develops a sense of self as well as language, social, emotional, problem-solving, and motor skills. These accomplishments are an important foundation for later learning.

People who are considering careers in the field of early childhood often have at least three main questions. First, they want to know whether there will be a need for people trained in early childhood. They also want to know about the job responsibilities of early childhood educators. In addition, they ask about the personal characteristics needed to be successful in this field.

This chapter reviews social and economic changes that will continue to create a need for child care teachers. It also gives an overview of teachers' responsibilities and characteristics of successful teachers.

# Social and Economic Changes

The social and economic changes in society will continue to create a need for child care services. These changes occur in families, employers' attitudes, and educators' attitudes. Career opportunities change along with these factors.

## Changes in Families

Most families no longer have a mother as homemaker and a father as wage earner. This traditional family structure exists only in a small percentage of families. An even smaller percentage is expected in the future. Several trends support this prediction.

- Women are becoming more highly educated.
- Married couples are having fewer children.
- Nearly 75 percent of children have parents working or attending school outside the home. Thus, the majority of children need child care or are enrolled in early childhood programs.

- Today, two-thirds of women with children younger than six years work outside the home. This represents a growth of 33 percent in the last two decades.
- Many working women are widowed, divorced, single, separated, or married to men earning a salary that is too low to support the family.

In the next decade, the under-five population is expected to continue to increase. Consequently, there will be an increasing need for early childhood teachers, 1-2.

## Changes in Employers' Attitudes

Corporate or employer-sponsored child care is growing. A recent study found employers contribute about one percent of the total spent on child care. Some employers provide child care assistance as an optional employee benefit. These trends will present many career opportunities for child care professionals.

By providing some type of child care benefit, companies have reported tangible payoffs. Included are positive effects on recruitment, morale, and productivity. Turnover and absenteeism are reduced. Other positive results are better public relations, tax benefits, ease of scheduling, and improved quality of the workforce.

In addition to on-site child care, employers may offer other means of child care assistance. Included may be a resource and referral service for locating quality child care. Lists of child care providers, maps, and brochures may be provided to parents. This type of service respects the employee's right to choose a suitable arrangement.

Some corporations may even hire early childhood specialists to provide sick child care. They can provide emergency back-up arrangements for limited time periods. The average child is ill ten days each year. As a result, many parents are forced to stay home from work. This helps reduce the parents' stress, guilt, and worry that occur when their children are ill.

Intergenerational care is another service being provided by some corporations. This model is often called dependent care. It provides services for the elderly as well as young children.

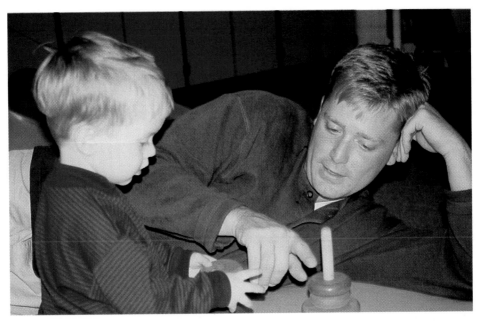

1-2 Young children rely on caring teachers to nurture and protect them while their parents are working.

## Changes in Education Attitudes

Most three-, four-, and five-year olds are enrolled in early childhood programs. In addition, many younger and older children receive child care while their parents work or attend classes. In the 1970s, only 6 percent of children were cared for in child care centers. Today, more than 33 percent of children with working parents attend child care centers. These children spend an average of 30 hours per week in such care.

At the same time, most parents are becoming more aware of their children's developmental needs. As a result, they are seeking quality environments that will promote their children's growth and development. Many working parents search for child care programs that are licensed and accredited.

Ninety-five percent of the nation's five-year-olds attend kindergarten programs for at least half the day. Studies show children who attend full-day versus half-day kindergarten programs do better academically and socially during the primary years. In addition, most parents prefer full-day kindergarten programs because these programs create fewer transitions for their children. Thus, there is a continuing push toward full-day kindergartens. Some school districts are also introducing prekindergarten programs for four-year-olds, as well as preschool programs for children with special needs.

Early childhood advocates are working toward even greater allocation of public education dollars for the youngest children. Their goal is to remedy current problems in education for young children. The demand for quality child care and other early childhood programs has never been greater. More trained teachers are needed. Recent studies show there are not enough quality programs for infants, toddlers, and school-age children. For preschoolers, the majority of programs are mediocre at best. Thus, most children in child care do not receive quality care.

## Career Opportunities in Early Childhood

Never have there been more career opportunities in early childhood. Early childhood programs occur in a variety of settings. Schools, homes, apartment buildings, centers, businesses, parks, and houses of worship are examples. As a result, early childhood specialists may find themselves choosing from many alternatives. Nannies, au pairs, kindergarten teachers, child care teachers and directors, and licensing specialists will be needed. You may find additional possibilities in business settings. See 1-3.

## Nannies and Au Pairs

There is currently a great demand for trained nannies and au pairs. A **nanny** provides care in a child's home. Depending on the parents' needs, some nannies may live in the child's home. In addition to their wages, they may receive meals and housing. Other nannies live on their own.

The dual-career family has contributed to the increasing demand for nannies. One employment service reported that it received over 50 requests for nannies per day. Due to a lack of trained personnel, the placement officers were able to place only 50 nannies in an entire year. Since many nannies have come from other countries, tighter immigration laws have decreased the supply of nannies in the United States. This has created new opportunities for nannies who are trained in the United States.

An **au pair** (pronounced *oh pare*) is a person from a foreign country who lives with a family and performs tasks similar to a nanny. In exchange for room, board, and transportation, the au pair provides child care and may do housework.

## Kindergarten Teachers

The opportunity to attend kindergarten is now provided in most states. Thus kindergarten teachers are needed in public as well as private schools. Even many child care centers hire kindergarten teachers. These centers provide full day kindergarten programs for children of working parents.

---

### Career Opportunities

**Careers in Child Care and Early Childhood Education Programs**

- Au pairs
- Curriculum specialists
- Directors of early childhood and school-age child care programs
- Family child care providers
- Nannies
- Teachers: child care centers, early childhood programs, elementary schools, and school-age child care programs
- Assistant and associate teachers: child care centers, early childhood programs, elementary schools, and school-age child care programs

**Related Careers in the Early Childhood Industry**

- Child care resource and referral specialists
- Early childhood consultants
- Early childhood educators (high school teachers, vocational and technical school instructors, community college instructors, and university professors)
- Early childhood researchers
- Licensing specialists
- Safety specialists
- Sick child care specialist for corporate child care
- Special education specialist
- Staff trainers

**Child-Related Careers in...**

**Business**
- Designers of children's products: clothing, computer hardware and software, furniture, school supplies, sports equipment, toys, and more
- Salespeople of children's products
- Playground designers
- Safety testers for children's products

**Community Service**
- Children's librarians
- Children's art, dance, music, and sports instructors
- Health care: pediatricians, pediatric nurses, pediatric surgeons, pediatric dentists
- Social services: family or children's therapists, counselors, social workers, caseworkers
- Parent educators
- Recreation directors
- Religious education directors or instructors

**Publishing and Art**
- Authors of books and magazines for children and parents
- Editors of books and magazines for children and parents
- Children's artists, illustrators, and photographers

**Entertainment**
- Entertainers: actors, singers, clowns, magicians, puppeteers
- Writers, producers, and directors for children's TV shows, movies, and theatre productions

1-3  A variety of career opportunities exist in the field of early childhood.

## Early Childhood Assistant and Associate Teachers

In addition to the lead teacher, state licensing requirements may require an additional staff member. To achieve the required adult-child ratios for a group of young children, an early childhood assistant or associate teacher may be hired. The role of the early childhood teacher or associate is to provide support for and assist a lead teacher in providing a developmentally appropriate curriculum.

These positions do not require a degree in many states, although specialized coursework or training in child development or early childhood education may be a requirement. For example, the associate teacher may have a CDA credential or an associate degree from a community or technical college. The assistant teacher is typically an entry-level position. Assistants may have earned a high school degree and participated in a professional development course or training program. This position may help the individual gain experience needed to advance to a lead teacher position. Many students work in these positions while working toward an early childhood education degree at a university.

## Child Care Teachers and Directors

With the number of children attending child care centers growing, the need for educated, qualified professionals is also growing. The U.S. Bureau of Labor Statistics predicts an increased number of job openings for early childhood educators. Usually the teacher is responsible for planning curriculum and teaching children. The director's responsibilities are broader. Marketing the program, recruiting children, hiring and supervising staff, and managing the budget are all included. Building maintenance is also the responsibility of the director in some centers.

## Family Child Care Home

Family child care homes provide child care for children ranging in age from 6 weeks to 12 years. This type of care allows a child care provider to work from home. Parents may be attracted to this type of program because of the longer hours of operation and homelike atmosphere. Likewise, child care providers may prefer this arrangement because they can also care for their own children.

## Licensing Specialists

Due to the rapid increase in child care centers, the number of licensing positions are expanding. The **licensing specialist** is usually employed by the state. The role of this person is to protect and promote the health, safety, and welfare of children attending centers.

Licensing specialists generally make regularly scheduled on-site visits to assigned centers. During each visit, the licensing specialist observes whether the center is following state licensing guidelines. He or she may check the number of children in the center, adult-child ratio, size of the facility, food service, and curriculum provided. Building safety, health practices, educational preparation of staff, and physical space are monitored, also.

## Other Career Opportunities

Many other career opportunities exist for you in the field of early childhood. With this background, you will be qualified to hold a variety of positions. For example, a career as a parent educator might appeal to you. In this position, you would work with parents to help them learn parenting skills, 1-4. You might work days, evenings, or weekends. You could design materials or produce visuals to help parents better understand their roles and the nature of young children. You might even produce materials to be shared on the Internet.

Knowledge of child development is also needed for community recreation leaders and children's art, dance, music, and sports instructors. This knowledge is helpful for those creating television shows, books, toys, music, and magazines for young children, too. Social workers, counselors, and therapists must know about children's development in order to provide appropriate help. This is also true of health care providers who treat children. Indeed the demand for workers educated in early childhood far exceeds the current supply.

Finally, you might enjoy a career as an **entrepreneur**. This is a person who creates and

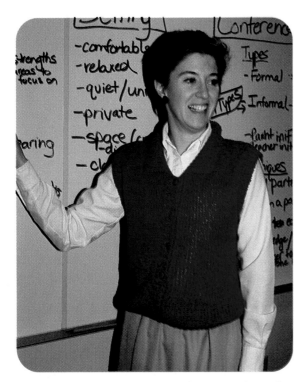

1-4  Parent educators present information that will help parents improve their child care skills.

runs his or her own business. The most common early childhood entrepreneurship is a family child care home. Family child care providers run their business from their homes. They put in all the work, take all the risk, make all the decisions, and earn all the profit associated with their businesses. Consultants, store owners, designers of children's products, and entertainers are other examples of entrepreneurs.

The work available to you as an entrepreneur is limited only by your imagination. If you can shape your ideas into a career that meets a need of children and families, you will likely succeed. For example, you could start a business that specializes in providing substitute staff for child care centers. When a center needs personnel to cover an absent staff member's job, the director could call you. Your responsibility would be to furnish a substitute teacher, cook, janitor, or office assistant.

## Education and Training Needed to Work with Young Children

As you can see, there are many opportunities for people who are interested in working with young children. What education and training is required for these jobs?

A few entry-level positions require little training or experience. For instance, a person with a high school education might work as a teacher's aide or playground supervisor. A teacher's aide would assist the teacher, help the children with their snacks, or supervise play activities.

Most child care jobs require training and education beyond high school. A first step for many is to obtain the **Child Development Associate (CDA) Credential.** Those who have this national credential have taken postsecondary courses in child care education and have demonstrated their ability to work with young children. The six CDA Competency Goals identify the skills needed by early childhood professionals. These goals are divided into 13 functional areas, which describe major tasks caregivers must accomplish to satisfy the competency goals. To be eligible for this credential, a person must be 18 years of age and have a high school diploma. In addition, the candidate must have a minimum number of hours of child care experience and have taken courses in early childhood education.

Most of the jobs described in this chapter require at least a two-year associate degree in child development or a related area. Some states are requiring that early childhood teachers have a CDA Credential to be licensed. The credential is not required, however, if the teacher has an associate or bachelor's degree in early childhood education, child development, or a closely related field. A bachelor's degree usually requires a minimum of four years of college. Directors of child care programs generally need a bachelor's degree.

Some jobs require a graduate degree. These include consultants, researchers, and early childhood instructors or professors. Some large early childhood programs require director candidates to have earned a graduate degree.

Each state establishes its own qualifications for staff who work in child care centers. There is no uniform standard established by the federal government. The qualifications will depend on the job you are seeking and the state in which you plan to work. It is important to know the minimum requirements for your state. You can ask the local agency that licenses child care centers what those standards are.

## The Teacher's Responsibilities

Many career opportunities exist in early childhood. The majority will be as teachers or teacher's aides. These professionals are needed for child care centers, preschools, Head Start programs, and in early childhood programs in public and private schools. Because of this need, this book will focus on the knowledge and skills needed to teach young children.

Your responsibilities as an early childhood teacher will be complex and demanding. You will have both direct and indirect influences on children. Directly, you will interact with children. Indirectly, you will influence children through the arrangement of space and activities. As an early childhood teacher, you will serve a dual role. Often you will play both the teacher and parent-educator role. Usually, the younger the child, the more support you need to provide to the parent in the transition from home to center. The parent may also seek advice on such aspects of child development as toilet learning, biting, and thumbsucking.

You will also need to be a friend, colleague, counselor, janitor, nurse, decorator, safety expert, and even a cook on some days. Not all your tasks will be pleasant. Sometimes your work may be unpleasant, such as changing messy diapers and cleaning up after a sick child. Noses have to be wiped and messes, such as spilled milk, dumped paint, or a leaky sensory table, must be cleaned.

*Challenging* and *rewarding* are two words that can best describe the responsibilities of an early childhood teacher. You will be challenged planning developmentally appropriate curriculum, designing class materials, and coping with behavior problems in the classroom. At times you may become discouraged, particularly when behavioral changes are slow. Once the changes occur, however, the rewards are well worth the time and effort. Early childhood teachers usually feel useful, needed, and important, 1-5. Working with young children is an act of hope for a better future. Most teachers also usually feel loved by the children. For these reasons, most early childhood teachers thoroughly enjoy their profession.

## To Know How Children Grow and Develop

Teachers need to know what children are like. Regardless of your position, you will need a thorough understanding of child growth and development. You will need to understand the abilities and interests of children at particular ages. This understanding will help you prepare inviting and developmentally appropriate environments for young children. Likewise, it will help you design educational experiences that promote children's growth in knowledge, skills, and self-confidence. Moreover, knowing the principles of child development will assist you in developing curriculum that is challenging and interesting without being difficult or discouraging.

1-5 Love from children helps make teaching in early childhood a rewarding career.

Understanding children's behavior will help you work effectively with individuals and groups of children. You will learn that children behave the way they do because their behavior brings them pleasure. That is, what happens to the child after he acts determines whether this behavior will be continued. A child who throws a temper tantrum to get a second turn on a bike (and gets a second turn) will usually repeat this behavior. Thus, you teach children to behave the way they do. Most of what they learn, they will learn from other people and you.

Working with young children, you will notice differences in behavior. Children can learn to be friendly, and they can learn to be aggressive. As a teacher, you will be responsible for teaching children to interact positively. Thus, you will teach them to be cooperative and skillful in getting along with others. To do this, you will need to learn and use developmentally appropriate guidance and group management techniques.

## To Plan a Developmentally Appropriate Curriculum

Teachers are responsible for planning a developmentally appropriate curriculum. Quality programs focus on the "whole child." Physical, social, cognitive, and emotional development are all emphasized. Such programs can provide long-term, positive differences in the lives of young children.

Physical development is stressed in a quality early childhood curriculum. Young children develop a variety of skills through physical experiences that are a foundation for later learning. Coordination, stamina, flexibility, strength, and sensory awareness are all included. See 1-6.

Social development is another important aspect of a quality curriculum. Young children must learn to interact positively with other children and adults. Likewise, they need to learn to adapt to the expectations that are established in the center.

Young children need to acquire information to be able to understand and function in the world. As a result, cognitive development is an important area of the child's development. Thus, problem solving through hands-on activities will be an important part of the children's learning.

Emotional development is also an important element of a developmentally appropriate cur-

1-6  Curriculum should include activities that help improve muscle strength and coordination.

riculum. Young children need to understand themselves. Feelings need to be understood in order to develop self-awareness and self-knowledge. Children need help in learning to recognize, label, and accept their feelings. They need to learn to assert their rights in culturally accepted ways without hurting others.

Your curriculum will need to be designed for the children. A broad knowledge of all the curriculum areas outlined in this book is important. You will find that an understanding of science, math, music, social studies, art, dramatic play, and storytelling will influence what you do with children.

## To Prepare the Environment

A large part of the teaching process involves preparing an inviting and stimulating learning environment. Learning is an active process whereby children gain knowledge and develop new skills. The environment that you provide must encourage children to independently experiment, explore, and manipulate, 1-7. Interaction with materials is an important learning vehicle.

As a teacher, you will need to provide a variety of materials. These materials will encourage children to engage in positive social activities. They also will promote physical, social, cognitive, and emotional development. Lack of variety or quantity can lead to lags in development. For instance, if there are not enough interesting materials, children may fight over the few that

1-7 It is up to you as a teacher to make learning an active process.

they enjoy. Chapters have been included in this book to teach you how to arrange space and select toys, equipment, and supplies.

## To Communicate Effectively

To be an effective teacher, you need to have good communication skills. These skills are important for ease in expressing ideas and gaining trust with children, their families, and your peers.

As a teacher, positive communication skills will help you form and maintain a close relationship with the children in your care. Your words will inform, explain, and guide them. Listening actively to what the children share is just as important as speaking.

Effective communication with parents is also vital. Most child care teachers have daily contact with the children's parents or guardians. Thus, information is usually exchanged on a continuous basis.

Early childhood teachers must also be able to form meaningful relationships with their colleagues. To provide a quality educational program for young children, all staff must work cooperatively. This requires open communication.

## To Demonstrate Teamwork

An important part of any job is getting along with your coworkers. Staff in early childhood programs need to work as a team, 1-8. To be a team member, you will need to help make your coworkers feel important. Everyone enjoys feeling important and valued.

To work well as a team member, you need to support your coworkers through your actions and words. Empathize with them by recognizing and reflecting their feelings. Share ideas with them. Tell them when they have planned interesting activities. Praise them for meaningful interactions with the children. Furthermore, accept their style of caregiving.

Even when team members work well together, conflicts will arise. Thus, knowing how to resolve conflicts effectively is important. Being able to talk through a situation and work together to find a solution can be challenging. With practice, however, you can look at conflict resolution as just a regular part of working on a team.

## To Manage Time Wisely

Rarely does an early childhood teacher have time to do everything he or she wants to do. Thus, time management skills are important. Time management skills help teachers work smarter, not harder. They help you organize your time, set priorities, and distinguish between important and urgent matters.

No matter what you accomplish, there is always more that could be done. You might want to make one more bulletin board, write a letter to a parent, or develop new materials. Time management skills will help you make choices and use your time wisely.

## To Participate in Professional Organizations

The field of early childhood constantly changes. Joining a professional organization can help you keep up with current developments in the field. To enjoy the full benefit of membership, you must be an active participant.

The largest professional organization in early childhood is the *National Association for the Education of Young Children (NAEYC)*. This

1-8  When staff members take and give suggestions on curriculum, they are able to give children the best care possible.

organization was founded in 1926 to improve professional practice and preparation. With over 100,000 members, NAEYC is the primary organization for the early childhood field. This organization has state and local affiliates. Membership services include annual state and national conferences. The organization also publishes a journal and other publications. Reading these materials will keep you informed of teaching trends, issues, research, legislation, upcoming conferences, and new publications, including children's books.

## To Follow Ethical Standards

When you work with young children, you will be faced each day with decisions of an ethical nature. You will be called on to choose between conflicting options. To help you make these tough choices, you will rely on your **ethics**, or guiding set of moral principles. Your ethics will help you to choose the option that it most *ethical*, or conforming to accepted standards of conduct.

People who work with young children should practice ethical behavior at all times. They should maintain the highest standards of professional conduct. For early childhood

professionals, these standards are reflected in the Code of Ethical Conduct created by NAEYC. This code establishes guidelines of responsible behavior to follow in relationship to children, families, colleagues, and communities. It is based on a set of core values for the profession set forth by NAEYC. (See the Appendices of this text to learn more about NAEYC's *Code of Ethical Conduct.*)

Professionals who follow the *Code of Ethical Conduct* ensure that programs for young children are based on the most recent knowledge of child development and early childhood education. In their communities, these professionals serve as advocates for children, families, and teachers. They recognize that biases, opinions, and personal priorities can alter professional judgment. As a result, these professionals are always open to new ideas and suggestions.

Sometimes choosing ethical behavior is not easy. You might be called upon to make a decision that is unpopular with parents, children, or coworkers. A professional who behaves ethically follows the right decision no matter what others do. Being ethically responsible might also mean taking action in some sticky situations. For instance, if you know a coworker is stealing supplies from the center, you may feel a strong pull to report this unethical behavior to the director. You will have to weigh the importance of telling against the consequences of telling. For many professionals, violating their ethics just to avoid conflict is too great a price to pay.

In a sense, much of this text deals with ethics. The chapters of this book will teach you the best practices for working with young children. Following these best practices will bring you into alignment with the *Code of Ethical Conduct*. As you study the chapters that follow, think about ethical dilemmas that might arise and ask yourself how you would handle these situations.

## To Continue to Learn

Professional development is an ongoing process, 1-9. A teacher never finishes learning. In order to keep up with happenings in the field, you need to be a committed, lifelong learner. Conferences, in-service training, course work, journals, study groups, and books all help teachers learn more about their field. In addition, participating in

one or more professional organizations is essential to learning new developments in the field.

## Characteristics of Successful Teachers

Working with young children requires a special kind of person. As an early childhood teacher, you will need to build on your own strengths and develop your own style. Each teacher is different. Some teachers are outgoing and lively. Other teachers may be reserved and naturally quiet. Both styles can be effective. Simply copying the style of another teacher will not necessarily make you a successful teacher. You must develop a style that best suits your personality. When your style suits your personality, you will feel more comfortable working with children and adults. You will also find more enjoyment in your profession.

Although teachers may use very different styles, successful teachers tend to have some common characteristics. See 1-10. These traits help teachers deal effectively with the day-to-day situations that are naturally part of their work.

### Fondness for Children

The most important trait of an early childhood teacher is fondness for children. The rapport established with each child determines the program's success. Every child needs to be understood and accepted. Each child's family background, interests, and desires also need to be respected.

As an early childhood teacher, you will need to show love for each child with whom you work. You need to be kind, firm, and understanding with each child. These actions affect how children feel about themselves and show children how to treat each other. As part of their social development, young children need to be taught that people and feelings are important.

Feeling loved, safe, and emotionally secure helps children develop intellectually and emotionally, 1-11. As you show children they are important, children have confidence in themselves. They are more willing to try new activities.

1-9 Reading is an important part of continuing education for early childhood teachers.

## Characteristics of a Successful Teacher

- Has a positive attitude and a sense of humor.
- Is fond of children.
- Relates easily and spontaneously to others.
- Is patient, confident, and caring.
- Is creative and resourceful.
- Is dependable and reliable.
- Is a keen observer.
- Solves problems well and makes sound decisions.
- Is flexible and adapts well to the requirements of others.
- Is compassionate, accepting children's strong emotions such as anger, love, and wonder.
- Enjoys challenges and is willing and able to grow.
- Takes initiative in the classroom.
- Has knowledge in curriculum, child growth and development, and child guidance.
- Keeps abreast of changes in the field by reading, attending conferences, seminars, and courses.
- Desires continuous learning.
- Becomes an active member of professional organizations.
- Can juggle several activities at once.
- Feels rewarded by even minimal progress.
- Communicates and resolves conflicts well.
- Has lots of energy.
- Has a strong sense of ethical behavior.

1-10  Teachers who have these characteristics tend to have high success in teaching and caring for young children.

## Patience

Effective teachers are also patient, allowing children time to explore, solve problems, and create. Young children often need extra time to complete tasks. Children also need the opportunity to repeat tasks. Much of a child's learning occurs as the result of repetition.

Children are naturally curious and may constantly repeat simple questions. Children do not always remember everything they have been told. Repeating information and reminding children of limits may seem tedious at times. When these situations are handled patiently, however, teachers help children grow and learn while building their self-esteem.

## Compassion

Compassionate teachers are able to accept others without prejudice. Being compassionate requires self-knowledge and self-acceptance. It involves accepting any emotion from others such as grief, joy, fear, love, or even hate.

A compassionate teacher does not simply observe a child's feelings. He or she is sensitive to both positive and negative feelings the children express.

Teachers show compassion by complimenting children for their successes. They also avoid actions that make children feel worthless, such as punishment and shaming. Compassionate teachers work to help children understand the feelings of others and motivate children to respect each other.

## Confidence

Having confidence in your abilities helps you relax in the classroom. Teachers who are relaxed and natural tend to be more successful with children. Children, especially the younger ones, can become easily excited. By remaining calm and self-assured, you will have a calming effect on the children.

Your confidence is affected by your ability to make sensible decisions. You need to feel sure the choices you make are in the best interest of the

1-11  Children who feel loved are more receptive to learning.

children. For instance, when it is raining, children should not be taken outside. Children may not always understand such decisions. If you stand by your choices with confidence, children will accept them.

## Sense of Humor

A sense of humor is helpful when working with children. Children enjoy adults who can laugh. Laughter helps children relax and feel content. When children see a teacher with a positive, cheerful attitude, they are more likely to be positive and cheerful. See 1-12.

Keeping a sense of humor also can make your work more enjoyable. Seeing the funny side of children can be a rewarding experience. Seeing the humor in situations can also help you cope with some of the daily stresses of teaching. Of course, you must be careful to laugh with, not at, children.

## Commitment

In many ways, the job of an early childhood teacher is anything but easy. Demands on your energy will be high. You will be expected to be an expert in child development, child guidance, and curriculum. Parents will ask your advice on

such issues as toy selection, toilet learning, and guidance.

You will find that meeting the demands of this field requires a serious commitment. To keep up with current developments in the field, you must constantly study. This can be accomplished through reading books and attending seminars,

1-12  A teacher who smiles and laughs encourages children to smile and laugh.

classes, and conferences. Participating in professional organizations and talking with other teachers are also helpful.

Preparing for daily teaching is also time-consuming. To be a successful teacher, you must be prepared. You, as a teacher, must fully understand the purpose of each activity. You also need to be sure the activities planned for the day address all areas of a child's development. You must also balance the pace of activities so that children are not constantly active or quiet. Providing a developmentally appropriate curriculum that meets children's needs and is inviting takes time and careful thought, 1-13.

## Personal Desire

Knowing that you really want to teach young children is important to your success. Although you may have doubts, you need to feel that working with young children is rewarding for you. Hearing children make comments, such as I love you or you're pretty, should boost your self-esteem. Otherwise, you will not feel enthusiastic enough about your work to do a good job.

Questioning a career choice is not unusual. You will discover that even experienced teachers have days when they wonder why they chose this career. These questions are healthy. If they help

you determine that you belong in early childhood education, you will feel more confident and committed to your career choice.

Only you can decide whether teaching is really for you. You will need to carefully examine your own interests, feelings, and satisfactions. See 1-14. Studying the chapters in this book can help you. Each chapter contains important concepts. Explore possibilities for applying these concepts to a group of young children.

Working with children will increase your insights. However, provide yourself sufficient time. Until you understand how children grow and develop, how to guide them, and how to develop appropriate curriculum, you might not feel much self-satisfaction. Given time, however, you are bound to discover the real joys and rewards of working with young children.

## Physical and Mental Health

Teaching young children is demanding physically and mentally. It requires you to be constantly alert and handle multiple tasks. Meeting these demands requires you to take care of yourself. Eating nutritious meals and getting enough sleep is important. You will also need to stay physically active and find ways to reduce stress. Seek counseling or other professional help if you notice problems with your mental health, such as stress, depression, or lasting anxiety. Keeping yourself physically and mentally healthy allows you to meet the challenges of your job.

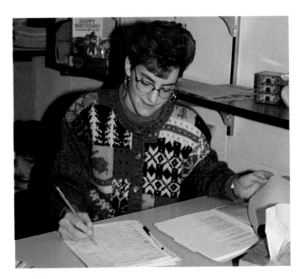

1-13 Spending the time needed to plan an effective curriculum takes a strong commitment from a teacher.

**A Letter to a New Teacher**

Dear Teacher:

As you begin working with young children, you will meet new challenges and find new answers. This process will continue throughout your teaching career. Like friendship, you will find being a good teacher is a matter of caring for yourself, the children you teach, their families, and your colleagues.

There will be many exciting and fulfilling days. The children will be experiencing many new discoveries. Many times over they may tell you that you are beautiful or you have a pretty voice.

You will also have discouraging days. Teaching is not an easy job. It is physically and mentally exhausting. At times, the costs may seem to exceed the rewards. Luckily, the majority of the time you will find that teaching is rewarding and personally satisfying.

When you leave the center at night, often you will reflect on the day's happenings. Replaying in your mind something a child said or did is not uncommon. Thinking about your responses is a method of preparing for the next time.

Remember you will only get out of a career what you invest in it. You must be willing to work overtime if needed and to seek new answers. You must also take advantage of opportunities to improve professionally for the benefit of the children and their families.

Try learning as much as you can about child development, child guidance, and curriculum. Talking to your colleagues, reading professional journals, joining professional organizations, and attending conferences are several methods. Taking additional coursework and obtaining advanced degrees will also strengthen your understanding of young children and improve your competence. Chances are, if you are actively involved, you will never lose your love of teaching.

1-14 Deciding whether you want to be an early childhood teacher is an important step in having a successful career.

# Summary

Many social and economic changes are creating new opportunities in child care. With fewer traditional families and more dual-career families, the demand for quality child care services is high. Employers are becoming more willing to offer child care benefits for their employees. Child care advocates are working to expand the availability of early childhood programs. Job opportunities are being created and expanded. Most jobs in child care require a CDA Credential, an associate degree, or a bachelor's degree. Qualifications vary from state to state.

Most career opportunities in early childhood are as teachers or assistant teachers. The main focus of this book is to prepare you for a career as an early childhood teacher.

Teachers have many important responsibilities. They must understand principles of child growth and development. Teachers develop curriculum and create classroom environments that meet children's developmental needs. They need to communicate effectively and develop teamwork skills. Teachers must manage time wisely and be lifelong learners. Joining professional organizations and following ethical standards are also important.

A successful teacher develops a style that works well for him or her. However, most successful teachers have many traits in common. If you are interested in becoming an early childhood teacher, you will want to have many of these same qualities. Some may come naturally to you while others may need to be developed.

# Review and Reflect

1. _____ covers the period from birth to nine years of age.

2. True or false. Social and economic changes have created a need for more child care services.

3. Why do companies provide child care?

4. _____ or _____ provide care for children in parents' homes.

5. A _____ is responsible for enforcing state child care rules and regulations.

6. Give two job opportunities in which education in early childhood is helpful. Explain how a background in early childhood is helpful in those jobs.

7. Describe the CDA Credential.

8. How does the environment affect a child's development?

9. In teaching, _____ skills are needed to help teachers work smarter, not harder.

10. What is the name of the primary professional organization for teachers of young children?

11. True or false. People who are naturally quiet and reserved cannot be effective early childhood teachers.

12. Give two common characteristics of successful early childhood teachers and explain why these characteristics are helpful.

# Apply and Explore

1. Look through the want-ad section of a newspaper. Write down jobs listed in which early childhood training would be helpful.

2. Take a survey of early childhood teachers. Ask them to share the advantages and disadvantages of teaching. Share your findings with the class.

3. Review the qualities of a successful teacher given in chart 1-10. Make a list of qualities from the chart that you possess.

4. Design a bulletin board displaying characteristics of successful teachers.

5. Survey parents of young children to find out what qualities they value in teachers.

6. Write a one-page paper on why you want to teach children.

7. Visit the Web site for the Council for Professional Recognition (cdacouncil.org) to learn more about the CDA Credential. Use a computer to summarize your findings in a brief written report. **C**

8. Explore the National Association for the Education of Young Children Web site (naeyc.org) to learn more about the association. **C**

# Chapter 2

# Types of Early Childhood Programs

After studying this chapter, you will be able to

■ list and describe the various types of early childhood programs available to parents and their children.

■ explain the advantages and disadvantages of each type of program.

■ name the three types of center sponsorship.

■ explain steps a parent may take in choosing quality child care.

■ list the components of center accreditation.

## Terms to Know

family child care

custodial care

child care centers

Montessori approach

Head Start

school-age child care programs

checking-in services

parent cooperatives

laboratory schools

accredited

Today, many young children attend early childhood programs. The number of children in these programs continues to grow. Parents place their children in early childhood programs for two main reasons.

First, many parents like the rich learning environment of a high-quality early childhood program. Brain research shows that children learn from the earliest moments of life. Their learning is most rapid in the first five years. High-quality programs stimulate learning in this period, 2-1. Studies show that children from

2-1 A challenging environment can help children develop cognitively, emotionally, socially, and physically.

high-quality programs did better in primary grades than other children in reading, math, and social skills.

Second, parents who work outside the home must provide for their children's needs during working hours. For this reason, parents may enroll their children in early childhood programs. Parents pay to have the program to care for children and meet the children's basic needs. In high-quality programs, learning needs will also be met.

Distinct differences exist among the many types of early childhood programs. These programs may differ in their philosophies, ownership, and program offerings. Programs also vary in size, staff qualifications, hours of operation, facilities, and fees. Finally, programs may differ greatly in terms of quality, even when they are of the same type.

Some types of programs are more common than others. However, all of them serve a very important purpose by meeting the needs of young children.

## Family Child Care

The most common type of child care in the United States provided other than by a relative or parent is called **family child care**. In this type of program, child care is provided in a private home. Most states require these homes to be licensed. This, however, is rather difficult to enforce. Some caregivers are not aware of licensing. Others ignore licensing rules.

### Program

Programs provided in family child care settings reflect state rules and the skills of the caregivers. Some homes mainly provide **custodial care**. This type of care focuses primarily on meeting the child's physical needs. The emphasis is on a safe and healthy environment. Meals are usually provided.

In a home where the caregiver has received early childhood training, a developmental curriculum may be planned. This involves planning and equipping the environment to complement the children's developmental needs and interests. For instance, a curriculum for two-year-old children would focus on language and large

motor development and social and emotional growth. Ample space would be needed for these children to move around. Developmentally appropriate puzzles, storybooks, push and pull toys, large blocks, housekeeping equipment, and other toys would also be provided.

## Child Care Centers

Facilities that offer full-day children's programs are often called **child care centers.** The focus of most of these centers is to provide care and education. The care is designed to meet the child's basic nutrition, health, and safety needs. The curriculum emphasizes the whole child including his or her social, emotional, cognitive, and physical needs, 2-2.

Most child care centers open early in the morning and remain open until six or seven o'clock in the evening. Some centers provide care for children 24 hours per day. For parents whose children need care during the evening or early morning hours, this service is most convenient.

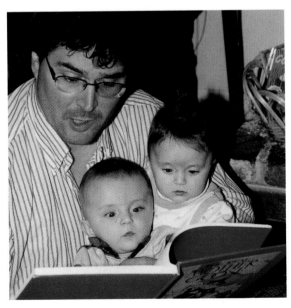

2-2 Many parents rely on the skilled staff of child care centers to provide for the basic needs of their children.

## Program

The program provided by a child care center depends upon the educational background and skills of the staff. State licensing rules also influence the program. Like family child care, some centers simply provide custodial care.

Ideally, the program should meet needs in all areas of development. The focus should be on the whole child and include a balance of engaging activities. Brain development is fostered in an environment that offers a variety of learning experiences.

# Montessori Schools

In the early 1900s, Maria Montessori developed her own method of education. She was the first woman in Italy to receive a degree in medicine. Early in her career, she was an assistant doctor at a clinic that served children with mental disabilities.

While working with these children, Montessori developed her theory of education. This theory stated children learn best by being active. Montessori soon learned these methods could also be used with other children. This led to the development of the first Montessori school in Rome.

Montessori's methods became known all over the world. After a short period of popularity, however, interest in this method declined for the next 40 years. In the 1950s, there was a rebirth of the Montessori method. Magazines and television helped make this method known.

## Montessori Approach

In her first schools, Montessori stressed proper nutrition, cleanliness, manners, and sensory training. Children also worked with equipment she designed. See 2-3. These materials were self-correcting and required little adult guidance. The materials were organized from simple to complex. By handling and moving the materials, the children's senses were trained and they learned to think. They also learned number concepts as well as motor, language, and writing skills.

Montessori believed in self-education. The primary goal of the **Montessori approach** was for children to "learn how to learn." This

2-3  Materials used in a Montessori school are designed to help children learn with little adult guidance.

approach allowed the child to explore materials that were meant to instruct. Certain materials were given to the child by the teacher in a prescribed sequence. This sequence was related to the child's physical and mental development. Montessori felt that this approach would provide the child freedom within limits.

Independence is stressed in Montessori schools. Children must learn to care for themselves. Teachers provide little help. As a result, children learn to button, zip, tie, and put on coats and boots. These experiences are called *practical life experiences* in the Montessori curriculum.

The purpose of *sensory training* is to help children learn touch, sound, taste, and sight discrimination. One piece of equipment for this training is a set of sandpaper blocks that vary in texture. The children are told to rub their fingers across the blocks. Their goal is to correctly match blocks with like textures. Musical bells with varying tones are used in the same way. Based on tone, children match like tones.

Academics are also stressed in the Montessori program. However, before a child is introduced to these experiences, sensory training must be mastered. Then, to teach letter recognition, sandpaper letters are used. After the teacher introduces a letter, children are encouraged to trace the letter with their fingertips. Numbers are taught in the same manner. When a child demonstrates knowledge of and interest in letters, reading instruction may be started.

## Head Start

In the 1960s, the federal government designed the **Head Start** program to overcome the negative effects of poverty on young children. The program mainly provides child care and education for four- and-five-year-olds from low-income families. More recently, it has added some programs for infants and toddlers. Today, Head Start is one of the most successful preschool and family support programs in the country. Head Start operates year-round. Most children attend Head Start for half the day. Before- and after-care is provided at some of these programs.

### Education

The curriculum in a Head Start program is designed to meet the needs of each child. One goal is to build self-esteem that will lead to future success in school. Staff encourage self-confidence, curiosity, and self-discipline.

A variety of learning experiences are designed to meet the children's needs in all four areas of development. Staff and the child's entire family work as a team to plan curriculum and teach children. Parent involvment is the heart of the program.

On preschool achievement tests, Head Start children perform equal to or better than their peers. Once they enter school, these children are more likely to be successful.

### Nutrition

Many children who take part in Head Start do not receive nutritious meals at home. Nutrition then is a vital part of the program, 2-4. Federal rules require the center to provide at least one snack and one hot meal every day. The nutrition program serves foods that reflect the child's ethnic and cultural preferences. The goal is to help children make healthy food choices and develop good eating habits.

2-4 A well-organized, sanitary kitchen is an important link in providing sound nutrition for children.

### Health

All children who attend a Head Start program are given a total health plan. Dental, medical, and mental health services are provided. Prior to enrollment, many of these children have never visited a dentist. Children who have not already received childhood immunizations are given them while they are enrolled.

### Parental Involvement

Head Start recognizes the parent as the child's first teacher. Supporting parental involvement is vital to the program's success. Parents are encouraged to help recruit new children, assist in the center, and take part in policy meetings. Thus, Head Start parents are able to influence administrative decisions.

## Kindergarten

In 1837, the first kindergarten was opened by Frederick Froebel in Germany. The kindergarten curriculum stressed play. Froebel believed that self-development took place through creative activities such as play. The children in this kindergarten, like many today, engaged in painting, stringing beads, blockbuilding, and clay modeling. The children also cared for pets, sang songs, and gardened.

The first American kindergarten was opened in Watertown, Wisconsin, in 1856. It was held in the home of Margerenthia Schurz. This mother and teacher had studied under Froebel. Mrs. Schurz first opened the kindergarten for her own children and four of their cousins.

Today, kindergartens are part of most public and many private school systems. They are usually restricted to children who are at least four years old.

## Schedules

There are three basic scheduling patterns in kindergarten: half-day, full-day, and full-day/alternating day sessions. The half-day session usually runs from two and one-half to three and one-half hours per day. Full-day sessions run from six to eight hours per day. Full-day/alternating day programs vary. Some programs meet every other day. Others require children to attend on Tuesday and Thursday the first week, and on Monday and Friday the next week. Other alternating programs have children attend two full days and one-half day. To illustrate, one group may attend all day on Monday and Wednesday, plus on Friday morning. The other group might attend all day on Tuesday and Thursday, as well as Friday afternoon. For some children, these alternating schedules may be confusing. Studies show that children thrive on predictable schedules.

## Goals

Goals for a kindergarten program permit variety. Basic objectives of most kindergarten programs include
- respect for the contributions, property, and rights of other children.
- development of positive feelings about school.
- development of a positive self-concept.
- growth in language, social, and physical, and creative skills.
- achievement of problem-solving and cognitive skills.
- development of independence, shown by working alone on a task or developing self-help skills.
- development of interpersonal skills.
- appreciation of objects of beauty.

Similar to preschools, most kindergartens emphasize the growth of the whole child.

## Curriculum

Kindergarten curriculum may vary from school to school. Some schools stress certain preacademic skills, such as learning the names and sounds of alphabet letters. Other programs focus more on social development. These programs are less structured than those that stress preacademics.

Kindergarten teachers, unlike most elementary teachers, have more freedom in planning curriculum. Studies show that in most kindergarten programs, about 50 percent of the day is spent on creative activities. Included are art, woodworking, blockbuilding, storytelling, and music. Free play, self-care, and rest fill the remaining time, 2-5. The teacher provides social studies, mathematics, language, and science activities, as well.

2-5 Free play and creativity are important in kindergarten programs.

## School-Age Child Care

**School-age child care programs** provide care for children before and/or after school. These programs are often sponsored by schools, houses of worship, or child care centers. Children from 5 to 10 years old most often attend. These children do homework, play games, and take part in other activities.

As an alternative, some parents use **checking-in services**. These services hire workers who call the home to check whether the child has arrived safely. This is a good option only for children who are mature enough to provide self-care until parents arrive.

## Parent Cooperatives

**Parent cooperatives** are formed and run by parents who wish to take part in their children's preschool experience. Member control allows parents to prepare budgets, hire teachers, set program policies and goals, and assist in the classroom.

Cooperatives provide developmental experiences for adults as well as children. Specifically, parents

- obtain guidance in their jobs as parents.
- learn what children are like at different ages and stages.
- gain several free mornings each month.
- become familiar with creative activities, materials, and equipment.
- gain a more objective picture of their child's development.

Due to all of these experiences, many parents have reported feeling a greater sense of self-satisfaction in their parenting roles.

### Advantages and Disadvantages

There are many advantages to teaching in a parent cooperative. Since the parents make the administrative decisions, collect fees, and order and repair equipment, the teacher can devote more time to the children and curriculum. Another advantage can be the special relationships that many times develop between parents and teachers.

A major disadvantage of a parent cooperative is the lack of control on the teacher's part. Although the teacher acts as an adviser, parents are usually responsible for making rules. At times, there may be differences of opinion between teacher and parents. For instance, parents may feel that children do not have to help return toys to the storage place. The teacher may feel differently. This can cause problems for many teachers.

### Sessions

Parent cooperatives usually operate for two or three hours, two to five days each week. Sometimes these groups are structured by the children's ages. For example, on Tuesday and Thursday mornings, a group of two-year-old children will be scheduled. On Monday, Wednesday, and Friday mornings, three-year-olds may attend. Other centers may prefer to use the "family-type" grouping. In this type of setting, children of mixed ages may all be included in one group.

### Fees

Due to the parent's involvement, fees charged at a parent cooperative are often less than at other programs. Costs are reduced by hiring only a head teacher. Parents serve as the classroom aides. Generally, each parent will assist in the classroom several times each month. In addition, parents volunteer to perform many of the service activities. They may clean and maintain the building, prepare snacks, type newsletters, and do some special jobs, such as painting the classroom.

## Laboratory Schools

**Laboratory schools,** or campus schools, are located on a postsecondary or college campus, 2-6. Although they provide excellent programs for children, their primary purpose is to train future teachers and to serve as a study group for research. Most of these schools have a highly qualified staff, a well-planned curriculum, and excellent equipment.

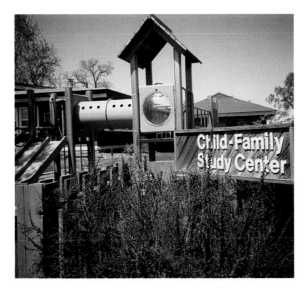

2-6 Laboratory schools generally have highly qualified staffs, well-planned curriculum, and excellent equipment.

# High School Child Care Programs

In the last two decades, many high schools have started providing vocational training for child care occupations. Like the laboratory schools, these programs train future child care professionals. Many high schools have their own child care laboratory facilities where students can work with preschool children. The preschool program may operate two or three days a week. Preschool children of high school students, faculty, and community members usually attend the program.

The high school students plan and present the curriculum under the supervision of a teacher. Some high school students may observe the children while others work directly with the children. The following week, the students who observed the preceding week then work with the preschoolers while the other students observe them.

# Sponsorship of Early Childhood Centers

Early childhood centers can be grouped based on sponsorship. Basically, there are three kinds of sponsorship: public, private, and employer-sponsored centers.

## Public Sponsorship

*Publicly sponsored programs* are funded by federal, state, or local governments. Some of these funds come through school districts. Other funds may come through social service agencies.

An example of a publicly sponsored program is Head Start. Most parents pay no fee for their child to attend Head Start. However, a fee is required if their income exceeds the federal guidelines for the program. Most of the expenses for the program are covered through grants received from the federal government. Funding is usually provided on an annual basis.

State funds may help support programs designed for educational purposes. These programs may be housed in a university, college, secondary school, or vocational school. Examples include child care centers, preschool centers, laboratory schools, and high school child care programs.

Publicly funded child care centers, preschools, and laboratory programs may receive several forms of financial support in addition to parental fees. For instance, a publicly funded child care center may also receive funds from the United Way, community donations, and tuition. Likewise, a laboratory school on a college campus may receive tuition donations or scholarships through alumni groups.

## Private Sponsorship

The largest group of privately sponsored programs is the privately owned center. These centers rely on parent fees to cover most of the operating expenses.

A *privately sponsored program* may be operated by a house of worship, hospital, or charitable organization. Many of these child care centers are nonprofit. They may be governed by a voluntary board of community members and operated as a service to the community.

Most private programs are operated by independent owners. Many of these centers are operated by families. Their motivation in operating a center is to provide a service that makes a profit.

## National Child Care Chains

Some child care centers are a part of chains operated by large national corporations, although some chains are privately held. Midsize chains typically operate on a regional basis. Often these centers are built and located in large cities and suburban areas. To make a profit in these centers, the enrollment must be high. The chains are managed by a central administration that furnishes the financial backing and sets policy. Curriculum guides may be developed by curriculum specialists hired by the organization and provided to the center staff in each of the locations.

## Employer Sponsorship

The number of companies providing their employees with some type of child care assistance is growing. The employer may pay part or all of the costs of the services.

Employers sponsor child care to reduce the conflict between family and work responsibilities. Studies show that there is less employee turnover and absenteeism at companies that provide some form of child care. At such companies, employees have better work attitudes, new employees are attracted, community relations improve, and good publicity is received. Moreover, there are tax incentives for companies who sponsor child care.

Companies can provide child care assistance in several ways, 2-7. The company owned, on-site child care center is one option. Such a center may be located at or near the work site. With this type of program, the company may hire a director to run the program. Other companies

contract with child care chains or firms specializing in child care to operate the center.

There are advantages and disadvantages to an on-site child care facility. One advantage is that parents can spend breaks and lunch hours with their children. In large cities, however, this model may not work. Employees who commute long distances to work may find it difficult to travel with children on public transportation or in car pools.

The off-site center is another option. This model is often used when several companies form a group. Each company may not have enough need for their own child care center. By sharing a facility, the costs and risks are shared by all the companies in the group.

The off-site location may be closer to the parents' homes. Therefore, transportation times are shorter. If space is available, this type of model may also serve other children from the community.

The vendor model allows companies to purchase space in a child care center or several centers. This model is ideal for small companies. It is not as costly as opening a center. There are no costs for start-up, investment in a building, or center administration.

Companies respect parental choice when the voucher model is provided. Parents receive a voucher or coupon worth a certain amount of money from the company. Some companies will pay for all child care costs, while others pay only a portion. This model may be preferred by parents who do not live close to the work site. Thus, it is a useful model for companies in large cities.

One disadvantage of the voucher model is that the money received must be declared as income on tax returns. However, the employee can deduct the cost of child care from federal taxes (and state taxes where allowed).

Child care for ill children is provided by some companies. This benefit can take two forms. A center may provide services for children who are ill and cannot attend school. When this is done, the health department as well as the state licensing agency must be notified. This works best for children who are recovering from an illness, but are not well enough to return to school. The second form allows for a nurse to be sent to a sick child's home to provide care. This allows the parent to go to work.

| **Types of Employer-Sponsored Child Care Assistance** |
|---|
| • Company owned, on-site center. |
| • Off-site center sponsored by one or more companies. |
| • Company sponsored, vendor provided centers. |
| • Vouchers provided by company to subsidize care. |
| • Sick child care. |
| • Referral services. |

2-7 Companies may assist families with child care in many ways.

Finding a quality child care program near home is a problem for many parents. To assist parents in this process, some companies provide a referral service that matches the parents' needs with centers. The company may hire their own resource specialist or contract a resource and referral agency.

Generally, parents are given a list of community child care centers. Specific information on each center is collected and given to the parents. Included are the center's location, fees, hours of operation, goals, enrollment capacity, policies, curriculum, staff qualifications, and special services. Maps showing the location of the centers are often provided to help the parents in the selection process.

## Selecting a Child Care Program

Selecting an early childhood program is one of the most important decisions that parents make. Comfort with the children's care and education can greatly affect the quality of family life, 2-8. For this reason, parents need to take their time in making this decision.

Parents consider many factors as they search for the right program. Each family makes this choice based on its own needs, priorities, and goals. Many parents do consider some common factors, however. See 2-9 for a list of questions parents can use to compare programs.

First and foremost, parents want their children to be safe and comfortable. They want a program that welcomes their child and promotes all areas of the children's development. Cost and location are important, too. Working parents prefer the convenience of a program near their home or job. Parents must choose a program they can afford, as well. For example, parents with lower incomes may need to use a public program or a private program with low fees.

Quality of the program is a key factor. Parents are interested in the program's goals, activities, and schedule. Variety and balance among activities is desirable. Quality programs offer ample materials, equipment, and space. These programs also offer smaller group sizes and more adults within each group. This allows children to receive more attention and personal care. See 2-10

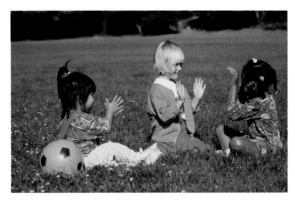

2-8 Parents are greatly comforted when they see their children playing happily in the early childhood program they have chosen.

for the adult-child ratios recommended for various age groups by the National Association for the Education of Young Children (NAEYC).

Many parents ask about the training and experience of the staff. Studies show staff members with early childhood education and experience are often more sensitive to children's needs. They provide more stimulating, child-centered care.

Asking about staff turnover rates can help parents in choosing a program. Parents should avoid choosing programs with high staff turnover. First, frequent staff changes may be a sign of low staff wages or poor working conditions and may indicate problems with the quality of the program. High staff turnover also interferes with children's sense of security. To feel secure, young children need to form close relationships with one or two caregivers. They also need a predictable environment. Staff turnover disrupts the environment and prevents children from forming close relationships with caregivers.

Parents want a facility that is safe for their children. For example, many centers have a security system that helps them monitor who enters and leaves the building. The building should also have smoke detectors, fire extinguishers, and evacuation plans. Parents desire a facility that is clean and in good repair.

### The Selection Process

Most parents follow the same process in selecting a child care program. As a teacher, you need to understand this process and your role in it. Parents need to know much about a program

| Selecting Quality Child Care | Yes | No |
|---|---|---|
| 1. Is the center accredited by the National Academy of Early Childhood Programs? | | |
| 2. Do the children appear to be happy, active, and secure? | | |
| 3. Are all staff members educationally qualified? | | |
| 4. Do staff members attend in-service training, professional meetings, and conferences on a regular basis? | | |
| 5. Are staff meetings conducted regularly to plan and evaluate program activities? | | |
| 6. Do staff members observe, assess, and record each child's developmental progress? | | |
| 7. Does the curriculum support the children's individual rates of development? | | |
| 8. Do the staff and curriculum celebrate diversity? | | |
| 9. Is the indoor and outdoor environment large enough to support a variety of activities? | | |
| 10. Is the environment inviting, warm, and stimulating? | | |
| 11. Is equipment provided to promote all four areas of development: physical, cognitive, social, and emotional? | | |
| 12. Are safe and sanitary conditions maintained within the building and on the play yard? | | |
| 13. Are teacher-child interactions positive? | | |
| 14. Are teachers using developmentally appropriate teaching strategies? | | |
| 15. Are parents welcome to observe and participate? | | |
| 16. Is sufficient equipment available for the number of children attending? | | |
| 17. Does the climate in the center "feel" positive? | | |
| 18. Do teachers meet with parents regularly to discuss the child's needs, interest, and abilities? | | |

2-9  In order to help ease the burden of choosing child care for their children, you may wish to supply interested parents with this questionnaire.

before they can choose it. Your role will be to help parents gain the needed information.

As parents begin a search, they want to identify options. Some parents start by contacting a child care resource and referral agency for a list of licensed programs in their community. Other parents search the telephone book for available programs. Parents also ask people they know about experiences with the available programs. Many parents seek the advice of other parents who use early childhood programs. Parents often trust this more than information given by the program itself.

Next, parents often begin calling available programs. First questions often involve what age groups the program serves, whether openings exist in their child's age group, and what the hours of operation are. Then, parents might ask about fees and location.

Parents who are still interested will ask about the program, staff, and activities. From there, they may arrange a visit to the program. A visit during program hours lets parents observe the environment and meet the staff. Parents may want to see the whole facility, including the kitchen, restrooms, classrooms, and outdoor play areas. They will often ask to see the daily and weekly schedules as well as the menu for meals and snacks. Parents also want to observe the interactions of staff with children and other adults in the program.

After the visit, parents may have additional questions. They may need to visit a program several times before making a final decision. Parents may also want to bring their child to see how the child responds to the environment. With all of this information, parents can decide which available early childhood program will best meet the needs of the child and family.

## Center Accreditation

The best indicator of high-quality child care is accreditation. Being **accredited** certifies that a set of standards has been met by a child care center. The National Academy of Early Childhood Programs, a division of NAEYC, administers a voluntary accreditation system. This system has been designed for child care centers and preschools serving children from birth through age five. It is also designed for programs that serve school-age children in before school and after school care.

The purpose of this system is to improve the quality of programs for young children in group care. It assists parents in their search for high quality programs for their children. In addition, it helps assure parents that their children are receiving quality care. Public recognition is the main benefit of achieving accreditation status.

To be eligible for accreditation status, a center must conduct a self-study. The self-study is an evaluation process designed by the National Academy of Early Childhood Programs. The evaluation provides valuable professional development experiences for all involved–directors, staff, and parents. Part of the self-study involves evaluating the 10 component areas identified as goals of quality early childhood programs, 2-11.

A recent study shows that accreditation has improved program quality. Center directors reported the greatest gains in the areas of curriculum, followed by administration, health, and safety. Most directors also reported that accreditation had increased the visibility of their programs.

| Recommended Adult-Child Ratios | |
|---|---|
| **Age of Children** | **Recommended Ratio** |
| 6 weeks to 1 year | 1 adult to 3 children |
| 1 to 2 years | 1 adult to 5 children |
| 2 to 3 years | 1 adult to 6 children |
| 3 to 5 years | 1 adult to 8 children |
| 5 to 6 years | 1 adult to 10 children |

2-10  These adult-child ratios are recommended by NAEYC for quality child care programs.

**Ten Component Areas of Quality Early Childhood Programs**

- Evaluation
- Curriculum
- Administration
- Health and safety
- Physical environment
- Staff qualification and development
- Staff-children interactions
- Staff-parent interactions
- Staffing
- Nutrition and food services

2-11  A quality early childhood program will meet the developmental needs of children. It also fosters positive interactions between parents, staff, and administrators involved in the program.

## Summary

Many types of early childhood programs are available. These include family child care, child care centers, Montessori schools, Head Start, kindergartens, school-age child care programs, parent cooperatives, laboratory schools, and high school child care programs. Each type of program takes a unique approach to meeting children's developmental needs.

Programs may be sponsored in a variety of ways. The type of sponsorship may affect goals and philosophies. Programs may be publicly or privately funded. Chain child care centers can be privately or publicly held. Employer-sponsored programs are designed to reduce some of the burdens of child care for working parents. Employers are using a variety of ways to provide these benefits for their employees.

With the variety of child care programs available, parents consider many factors in choosing the best program for their child. Some of the factors that parents consider include the type of program, quality of program and staff, adult-child ratio, group size, and condition of facilities. As a teacher, you will need to know what parents look for in a program. Then you can strive to make your program one that parents choose for their children.

Parents may look for programs that have been accredited by NAEYC. Accreditation certifies that a program meets a specific set of standards. Obtaining accreditation involves participation in a self-study, which is designed as an evaluation tool. Center directors, staff, and parents participate in this process. Public recognition is one of the main benefits of achieving accreditation.

## Review and Reflect

1. What is the most common type of child care in the United States?

2. True or false. Child care centers offer full-day programs for young children.

3. Montessori's theory of education stated that children learn best when they are _____.

4. What are "practical life experiences" according to Montessori?

5. Describe the purpose of Head Start.

6. True or false. Nutrition is a vital part of the Head Start program.

7. Name the three basic kindergarten schedules.

8. List five objectives for a kindergarten program.

9. Describe how a checking-in service works for school-age children.

10. _____ are formed and run by parents who wish to take part in their children's preschool experiences.

11. What is the primary purpose of a laboratory school?

12. Publicly sponsored programs are funded by _____.

13. Describe one way employers can provide child care assistance for their employees.

14. Why might a high staff turnover be a concern to parents?

15. Why might parents want to select a child care program that was accredited?

16. For children ages 3 to 5 years, NAEYC recommends the adult-child ratio of one adult for every _____ children.

## Apply and Explore

1. Visit a family child care home. Ask the provider to outline the daily schedule.

2. Arrange a visit to a school-age child care program. Ask to review the curriculum.

3. Discuss the advantages and disadvantages of teaching in a parent cooperative.

4. Discuss the value of center accreditation.

5. Visit the Web site for Effective Parenting (parenting-ed.org) to find information for parents on selecting child care.

6. Search the American Montessori Society Web site (amshq.org) for a position paper on Montessori schools.

7. Use the Web site careguide.net to search for licensed and registered child care programs by state, city and region.

# Chapter 3

# Observing Children: A Tool for Assessment

After studying this chapter you will be able to

- list purposes of assessment.
- contrast initial and ongoing assessment.
- list the factors to consider in choosing a method of assessment.
- list the advantages and disadvantages of various assessment tools.
- compile a list of contents for a child's portfolio.
- summarize guidelines for observing children.

## Terms to Know

assessment

developmental norms

anecdotal record

checklist

participation chart

rating scale

portfolio

Young children are fascinating to watch. Just ask any new mother, father, or proud grandparent! A young child's awkward attempts to try new skills or early efforts at conversation can be captivating. Observing children is something everyone enjoys doing.

Observation also serves another purpose. It is one of the oldest and best methods for learning about children. Most of what is known about child growth and development is the result of some form of observation. Many behaviors of children cannot be measured in any other way. A one-year-old, for instance, cannot answer questions orally or in writing, but the child's behavior can be observed, 3-1.

As a student of child development, much of what you will learn about children will come from observing them. You may be asked to observe the children in your school's child care center. At times you may be assigned to observe a specific aspect of a child's behavior or development. You will also be encouraged to observe children informally outside of school.

Jafar, a student majoring in child development, was assigned his first observation. He was amazed at the developmental differences he saw within the group of three- and four-year-olds. Jafar noticed that Ben was doing an 18-piece puzzle. Sitting next to him was Hunter. He was asking the teacher for help with a puzzle that had only four pieces. Standing at the easel, Wyatt was printing his name across the top of his art project. Next to him was Wendy. She drew a circle in an upper corner of her work and exclaimed with a smile, "That's my name!"

3-1 Teachers observe largely through their eyes and ears.

Each of these children is unique. If you were the teacher in this classroom, how would you plan a curriculum that would meet the needs of each of these children? To begin the process, you would need to gather information. This, too, involves observation. You would need to determine each child's developmental stage. With this information, you could then determine the group's developmental status. The data gathered would help you plan a curriculum that was sensitive to the needs of the group.

## Assessment

**Assessment** is the process of observing, recording, and documenting children's growth and behavior. To be an authentic assessment, observations must be done over time in real life situations. This type of assessment is best because it is the most accurate. It is used to make decisions about children's education. Information is obtained on children's developmental status, growth, and learning styles. Sometimes the terms *assessment* and *evaluation* are used interchangeably, but they are two different processes. Assessment is the process of collecting information or data. Evaluation is the process of reviewing the information and finding value in it.

### Purposes of Assessment

Assessment is important for several reasons. The information collected is used in planning developmentally appropriate curriculum. Assessment keeps the teachers and the curriculum responsive to the needs of the children. An authentic assessment involves gathering information on each child's physical, social, emotional, and cognitive development. It provides information on each child's unique needs, strengths, and interests. It also charts progress over time.

During the assessment process, you, as teacher, gain insights into children's learning styles and needs, 3-2. What are their strengths and weaknesses? What does the group know? What are they able to do? What are their interests and dispositions? Finally, what are their needs? Teachers who have good assessment skills will make better decisions.

Individual and classroom problems can often be identified through the assessment process. When specific examples of a child's behavior are observed and recorded, behavior patterns become more clear. Answers to behavior problems can more easily be found when the specific behavior is observed and noted.

Classroom problems can be identified through assessment. When a problem arises, plans can be made to remedy the problem. To illustrate, perhaps there have been many instances of pushing and shoving in the dramatic play area. By observing and evaluating, you may realize that more classroom space should be provided for this activity. If this is impossible, you may decide to limit the number of children in this area at one time to prevent the undesirable behavior.

Assessment also allows you to identify children who might have special needs. Perhaps a child has a hearing or vision impairment. Maybe a child has an emotional or behavioral problem that requires counseling. These needs can be identified and specialized services obtained.

3-2 Each child has unique strengths, needs, and interests.

Through assessment, you will be able to find out where the children are in their development. Information on each child should be recorded at regular intervals. In this way, you can see how each child is progressing in his or her development. This information will help you make better cirriculum planning decisions. It will also help you decide how to set up the environment and stimulate each child's development.

The information gained through assessment can also be useful during parent conferences. Parents want to know how their children are progressing. You will be able to give them concrete evidence on their child's progress. Parents will also be assured you know and understand their child.

A final purpose for assessment is in evaluating your program. Information obtained through assessment can help your staff determine if your program is effective in meeting its goals.

## When to Do Assessments

As a teacher beginning a new year, you will need to do an *initial assessment*. You cannot assume all children of a given age are alike. Developmental differences will exist. Culture, economic status, and home background will impact each child's development. Therefore, the purpose of an initial assessment is to get a "snapshot" of the entire class. Observing the children is the most common way to gather this information.

You will want to learn as much about the children as possible during your initial assessment. Study the existing folders on each child. Review home background forms. Read the notes from past parent conferences. If possible, visit each child's home. An alliance with parents is important. Parents can give you useful information on a child's learning needs and interests.

In addition to this initial assessment, you will need to do *ongoing assessments* on individual children, as well as the group. A single assessment is not an exact assessment of ability or performance. It is just an indicator.

Ongoing assessment may take more time, but it will also provide more in-depth information. The information gained will be useful in tracking each child's progress and change over time. It should provide evidence of a child's learning and maturation. This information will also be helpful in making decisions for enriching or modifying the curriculum when necessary.

You can gather assessment data during classroom activities. Watch children as they work on art projects and listen to them as they tell stories, 3-3. Observe children as they construct puzzles or build with blocks. Listen in on children's conversations. Discreetly take notes on individual children, especially during free-choice activities. This is when children are most likely to reveal their own personalities and development. These notes will provide important assessment information.

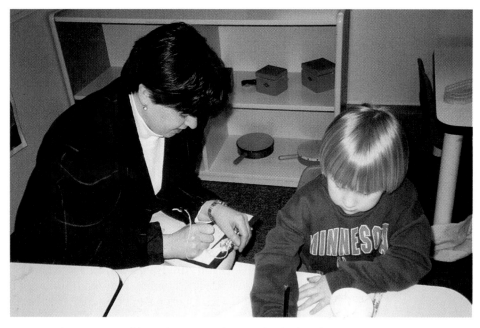

3-3  Teachers can quickly make notes about individual children during classroom activities.

## Formal and Informal Observation

Two different methods of observation are used for assessing young children–formal and informal. They differ in how controlled the conditions are for using them. Formal methods include standardized tests and research instruments. As a result of such research, developmental norms for children have been identified. **Developmental norms** are characteristics and behaviors considered normal for children in specific age groups.

Developmental norms will assist you in comparing and noting changes in the growth and development of children in your care, 3-4. They will also help you as you observe young children in preparation for your career working with young children. Examples of developmental norms are included in the Appendix of this book. They are useful tools for assessing children's developmental status. They also form the basis for planning developmentally appropriate curriculum.

While formal observation methods provide important information, they require specialized training for recording data on carefully designed forms. Training is also needed for analyzing and interpreting the data.

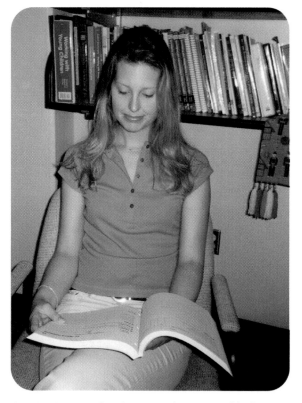

3-4  Reviewing developmental norms will help you assess the progress of children in your care.

Preschool teachers usually use informal observation methods to collect data. These methods are easier to use and more appropriate for program planning. They include observing children in the classroom, collecting samples of their work, interviewing parents, and talking with children.

## Choosing a Method of Assessment

There are three considerations for choosing a method of assessment. First, the method chosen depends on the type of behavior you want to assess and the amount of detail you need. Another consideration is whether the information needs to be collected for one child or the entire group. Finally, the amount of focused attention required by the observer needs to be considered.

Some methods of assessment will require more of your attention. For example, it is difficult interacting with children when you are in the process of writing an anecdotal record. Checklists, videotapes, and participation charts are easier to use while working with the children.

Usually teachers use a variety of methods for gathering information about the children. Since no one method is the most effective or reveals everything, several methods are used. More complete information is obtained by using several types of assessment. Multiple sources of information also reduces the possibility of error when making evaluations.

## Assessment Tools

There are several types of assessment tools that are used in early childhood programs. These include anecdotal records, checklists, participation charts, rating scales, samples of products, photographs, and tapes. Teachers can also interview parents to obtain information.

### Anecdotal Records

The simplest form of direct observation is a brief narrative account of a specific incident called an **anecdotal record**. Anecdotal records do not require charts or special settings. They can be recorded in any setting and require no special training. All you need is paper and a writing tool to record what happened in a factual, objective

manner. The observation is open-ended, continuing until everything is witnessed.

The process of recording the incident requires a careful eye and quick pencil to capture all of the details. You will need to note who was involved, what happened, when it happened, and where it occurred. It needs to be done promptly and accurately. Figure 3-5 shows the contents of an anecdotal record.

When you use the narrative form of observation, your eyes and ears act like a video camera. You will be recording pictures of children playing, learning, and interacting. During your observations, you will record how children communicate, both verbally and nonverbally. You will record how they look and what they do. Physical gestures and movements should be noted. You will also detail children's interactions with people and materials.

### Anecdotal Records Must Be Objective

During the observation process, it is important to record only objective statements. To be objective, a statement must pass two tests. First, it must describe only observable actions. Thus, generalizations about the motives, attitudes, and feelings of the children are not included. Secondly, the recorded information must be nonevaluative. It should not include an interpretation of why something happened, nor imply that what happened was wrong, right, good, or bad. Labeling should be avoided. No judgments or conclusions should be inferred at this point. The example on the following page is a narrative observation:

| Contents of Anecdotal Records |
| --- |
| • Identifies the child and gives the child's age. |
| • Includes the date, time of day, and setting. |
| • Identifies the observer. |
| • Provides an accurate account of the child's actions and conversations. |
| • Includes responses of other children and/or adults, if any are involved in the situation. |

3-5 Anecdotal records should include the items listed.

Sally arrived at school holding her mother's hand. She slowly walked over to her locker, removed her coat, and hung it on a hook. She turned to her mother and said, "You go to work." Sally's mother hugged her and said, "After work I'll take you to the dentist." Sally looked at her mother and started to cry. She said, "I'm not going to the dentist. I'm staying at school." Sally's mother reached out and hugged Sally. Sally continued crying and hung onto her mother. The teacher walked over to Sally and whispered in her ear. Then the teacher put out her hand and said, "Come and look, Sally. We have a new friend at school today. Jodi brought her new hamster." Sally stopped crying and took the teacher's hand. Together they walked over to see the hamster. Sally's mother watched her for a moment and then left the room.

Notice that only an objective description of the observed behavior is recorded. The statements do not include any of the following: causes, emotions, explanations, feelings, goals, motives, desires, purposes, needs, or wishes.

### Interpretation of the Data

Once the narrative data is recorded, a second process begins. This process involves the interpretation of the data. An attempt is made to explain the observed behavior and to give it meaning. Why did the child behave as he or she did? What might have been the child's motives? Did someone or something cause the child to act in this way? This interpretation takes knowledge and skill. It should not be attempted without a thorough understanding of how children grow and develop. The observation itself serves no purpose without the interpretation of behavior to give meaning to the data.

Though an observation may be factual and unbiased, various interpretations are sometimes made. Since no two people are exactly alike, no two people will interpret facts in the exact same way. Each person who interprets a child's behavior may determine different motives for the behavior based on their own personal experiences. Their personal feelings, values, and attitudes may also influence the interpretation of behavior.

To illustrate, an observer wrote the following about Tony:

Tony picked up the pitcher of milk. He moved the pitcher toward his glass. He hit the glass and tipped it over. The milk spilled.

In reviewing the observation of Tony, his behavior might be interpreted in several ways:

- Tony was careless.
- Tony was inexperienced in handling a pitcher.
- Tony wasn't paying attention to what he was doing.
- Tony lacked the strength needed to lift the pitcher.
- Tony lacked the hand-eye coordination necessary to pour from the pitcher.

To decide which interpretation is most accurate, you will need to observe Tony on several occasions over a period of time. You would also need a thorough understanding of how children grow and develop.

Figure 3-6 shows a form for an anecdotal record, although many teachers just use a file card or plain piece of paper. Teachers who record incidents throughout the year have a means of assessing progress. A series of records over time can provide rich details. The records can be extremely valuable in noting progress, strengths, needs, and interests.

### Advantages and Disadvantages of Anecdotal Records

There are advantages and disadvantages in using the anecdotal record. An important advantage is that it is the easiest method of use since it requires no special setting or time frame. Anecdotal records can provide a running record over time showing evidence of a child's growth and development. Therefore, teachers who record incidents throughout the year have a means of assessing progress.

There are also disadvantages with using anecdotal records. Because the incident observed is based on the observer's interest, a complete picture may not be provided. Records may not always be accurate. If the observer decides to write down the incident at the end of the day and is poor at recalling details, important information may be missed.

**SUNSHINE CHILD CARE CENTER ANECDOTAL RECORD**

Child's Name: _____Carrie_____ Date: _10/9/xx_

Child's Age: ___3___ Years ___9___ Months

Setting: __Dramatic Play__ Time: _8:30_ to _8:45_

Observer: __Geneva Peterson__

Incident:

Carrie went directly to the dramatic play area when she arrived at the center. She placed the cash register on a table. After this, she displayed empty food containers on a table. Tony entered the area. He stepped behind the cash register and said, "I want to play with this." Carrie said, "No, it's mine. I had it first." Then using her arm she hit Tony and began pushing him. Tony looked at Carrie, shrugged his shoulders, and walked away. As Tony walked away, a smile came across Carrie's face.

Interpretation:

3-6 You may want to use a form such as this one to record anecdotal events.

## Checklists

Another form of assessment is the checklist. **Checklists** are designed to record the presence or absence of specific traits or behaviors. They are easy to use and are especially helpful when many different items need to be observed. They often include lists of specific behaviors to look for while observing. Checklists may be designed for any developmental domain—physical, social, emotional, or cognitive.

Checklists may be developed to survey one child or a group of children. The targeted behaviors are listed in logical order with similar items grouped together. Therefore, you can quickly record the presence or absence of a behavior.

Typically, a check indicates the presence of a behavior.

Checklists require structuring. You may be able to purchase commercially prepared checklists. Most teachers working in child care centers structure their own. A typical checklist for use in observing an individual child is shown in 3-7. The developmental norms found in the Appendix of this book may be adapted as checklists for assessing individual children or groups of children. Figure 3-8 shows a checklist for assessing the gross motor skills of a group of children.

### Advantages and Disadvantages of Checklists

One of the advantages of a checklist is that there are no time constraints in collecting the data. The information can be quickly recorded anytime during program hours. In addition, checklists are easy to use, efficient, and can be used in many situations. Data from checklists can be easily analyzed.

A disadvantage, however, of using a checklist is the lack of detailed information. Because of the format, only particular behaviors are

Name: __Wyatt Anderson__

Program: __Sunshine Child Care Center__

Age: ___3___ Years ___6___ Months

Date of Observation: __2/9/xx__

Observer: _Sally Olm_

**Fine Motor Skills**

| | Yes | No |
|---|---|---|
| Cuts paper | ✓ | |
| Pastes with a finger | ✓ | |
| Pours from a pitcher | ✓ | |
| Copies a circle from a drawing | ✓ | |
| Draws a straight line | ✓ | |
| Uses finger to pick up smaller objects | ✓ | |
| Draws a person with three parts | | ✓ |

3-7 Checklists are efficient to use and require little effort.

| Gross Motor Skills Group Assessment Three-Year-Olds | | | | | | |
|---|---|---|---|---|---|---|
| | Henry | Ed | Jo | Vicki | Cari | Deb |
| Catches ball with arms extended | ✓ | ✓ | ✓ | | ✓ | |
| Throws ball underhanded | | ✓ | | | ✓ | |
| Completes forward somersault | ✓ | ✓ | | ✓ | ✓ | ✓ |
| Rides tricycle skillfully | ✓ | ✓ | | ✓ | ✓ | ✓ |
| Throws ball without losing balance | | ✓ | ✓ | | ✓ | |
| Hops on one foot | | ✓ | | | | ✓ |

3-8  You can evaluate the gross motor skills of a group of children using a form such as this one.

noted. Important aspects of behaviors may be missed, such as how a behavior is performed and for how long. Only the presence or absence of a behavior is noted in a checklist.

## Participation Chart

A **participation chart** can be developed to gain information on specific aspects of children's behavior. Participation charts have a variety of uses in the classroom. For instance, children's activity preferences during self-selected play can be determined. See 3-9.

Richard O'Grady, an experienced teacher, uses participation charts to record the time each child falls asleep at nap time. He also charts the length of time each child sleeps. He records this information several times a year. After collecting the data, he decides if a change should be made in the scheduled nap time. Likewise, the length of the nap time can be adjusted to reflect the children's needs.

Sometimes teachers find that children's preferences do not match their needs. To illustrate, Randy has weak hand-eye coordination skills. A participation chart shows he spends

| Activity Preferences During Self-Selected Play | | | | | | | | | | |
|---|---|---|---|---|---|---|---|---|---|---|
| | Bryce | Tina | Saul | Ting | Bergetta | Tanya | Hunter | Shawn | Janus | Vida |
| 9:00 - 9:10 | b | dp | a | st | m | dp | a | b | st | s |
| 9:10 - 9:20 | b | dp | a | st | m | dp | a | b | st | s |
| 9:20 - 9:30 | b | dp | m | m | dp | dp | s | b | st | s |
| 9:30 - 9:40 | b | st | m | m | dp | dp | b | b | m | a |
| 9:40 - 9:50 | b | m | m | m | dp | dp | b | b | m | a |
| 9:50 - 10:00 | b | m | s | m | dp | dp | b | b | m | a |
| a=art; b=blockbuilding; dp=dramatic play; m=manipulatives; s=sensory; sc=science; st=storytelling | | | | | | | | | | |

3-9  A participation chart is quick and easy to use, but can give you important information.

most of his time listening to stories and music and watching other children play. To meet Randy's needs, the teacher could introduce him to interesting art activities, puzzles, and other small manipulative learning aids. These materials will help advance Randy's skills in hand-eye coordination, which will be necessary for reading and writing.

## Rating Scales

**Rating scales** are used to record the degree to which a quality or trait is present. Rating scales require you to make a judgment about behavior. Where a checklist only indicates the presence or absence of a trait, a rating scale tells how much or how little is present.

### Advantages and Disadvantages of Rating Scales

Rating scales are easy to use and require little time to complete. Some scales contain only a numerical range. Others define the behaviors more specifically.

A disadvantage of the rating scale is that only fragments of actions are included. In order to choose a rating, the observer should have a good understanding of the behavior he or she is rating. Figure 3-10 shows a typical rating scale.

## Collecting Samples of Children's Products

Collecting samples of children's work systematically over time is another assessment tool. These products can provide valuable information regarding the child's developmental status and growth. Products collected may include artwork, stories dictated or written, photographs, and records of conversations. Over time, these samples can be collected and compared. To illustrate, Chuck could make only random scribbles on paper at the beginning of the year. When Chuck's teacher asked him to tell her about his work, he explained it. She discovered the sample showed more than Chuck's scribbles. He said, "There is my name. That is how to write it. I wrote my mother's name and my sister's." Now he is able to draw a circle. A comparison of the two samples shows the progress Chuck has made in fine-motor and hand-eye coordination skills.

A child's products can be stored in a folder or portfolio. Whenever possible, store materials

### Social/Emotional Rating Scale

Child: _Jo Ellen_                                                        Date: _4/6/xx_
Age: _4_ Years _1_ Months
Observer: _Mark Zenk_

| Behavior | Never | Sometimes | Usually | Always |
|---|---|---|---|---|
| Shows increased willingness to cooperate | | | ✓ | |
| Is patient and conscientious | | ✓ | | |
| Expresses anger verbally rather than physically | | | | ✓ |
| Has strong desire to please | | ✓ | | |
| Is eager to make friends and develop strong friendships | | | ✓ | |
| Respects property rights of others | | | ✓ | |

3-10  On a rating scale, teachers record the degree to which a quality or trait is present.

and items in chronological order. This will save you time when evaluating progress or sharing the materials with parents.

Records may be kept in different forms. Samples may be preserved by photographing, sketching, or diagramming children's products. These methods are especially useful for large structures such as block displays and three-dimensional artwork that cannot be stored conveniently.

# Using Technology for Assessment

Technology is a very useful tool for recording children's development. Making videotapes and audiotapes are excellent ways to preserve information. Tapings may focus on an individual child, a small group of children, or an entire class. Videotapes can preserve both action and speech. Recordings may be made of children telling stories, acting out stories, or explaining their projects. Dramatic play interactions and music experiences can be recorded. By viewing or listening to the tapes, you can note progress in language and speech. The children might also enjoy viewing or listening to the tapes.

Be careful that the presence of the videocamera does not become intrusive. You may want to ask other adults, such as teacher aides or parent volunteers, to assist with the taping. This will allow you to be included in the taping. By reviewing the tape, you can do a self-evaluation of your own interactions with the children.

The digital camera is also a convenient way to record children's development. Pictures taken by the digital camera are stored inside the camera as electronic image files that can be downloaded to a computer. Once the files are downloaded, they can be printed or saved onto the hard drive or a CD for later use. Teachers can use a digital camera to taking pictures of classroom activities. They can download and print these photos for use in a portfolio. Teachers might want to feature photos on the bulletin board before filing them.

# Portfolios

Materials you have collected as a part of ongoing assessment should be placed in each child's portfolio. A **portfolio** is a collection of materials that shows a person's abilities, accomplishments, and progress over time. Portfolios you create for the children in your care summarize each child's abilities. A portfolio includes items that show the child's growth and development over time. Documenting learning is an important skill for teachers to develop.

Depending on the materials collected, the contents of a portfolio can be stored in a variety of forms. Some teachers prefer three-ring binders. Others prefer to use boxes or large folders to store the portfolio contents.

## Contents

A child's portfolio needs to be carefully planned and organized. It should be more than a file of anecdotal records, checklists, and questionnaires. Most teachers include product samples as well. Examples include art projects, audiotapes of conversations, and child-dictated stories. In addition, the portfolios include summaries of parent conferences and parent questionnaires. Figure 3-11 shows the contents of a typical portfolio.

Teachers include samples for each child that reflect unique skills and interests. If Thomas

---

**Portfolio Contents**

A portfolio may contain . . .
- Teacher observations and other records gathered through assessment.
- Developmental rating scales or checklists.
- Parents' comments and completed questionnaires.
- A dated series of the child's artwork or writing.
- Photographs of the child demonstrating skills or engaged in activities.
- Audiotapes or videotapes of the child speaking, singing, and telling stories.
- A list of favorite books, songs, and fingerplays.

3-11 A portfolio contains a wide variety of materials.

built a complex and interesting block structure, his teacher might sketch or photograph it for inclusion in his portfolio. Likewise, teachers may record stories that children dictate to them.

A portfolio should be continually evolving and provide for ongoing assessment. It should be a summary of a child's development. Information gained from evaluating the portfolio can guide teachers in designing curriculum, structuring interactions, and setting up the classroom. Parents, too, will gain from reviewing the child's portfolio with the teacher.

By reviewing the portfolios of children in a program, you should be able to identify unique characteristics of each child. For instance, according to Mark's portfolio, he remains in the cooking area until the entire snack is prepared every day. Often he provides the teachers with other methods of preparing the foods. Cory develops elaborate and imaginative buildings in the blockbuilding area. During self-selected play, Maria always chooses the same theme. She dresses as a ballerina in the dramatic play area. Blake is fascinated with the hamster and rabbit. He wants to learn more about different kinds of animals, their eating habits, and behaviors.

## Guidelines for Observing Children

During your study of young children, you will observe them in many situations. Whether on the play yard, in a classroom, or on a field trip, your behavior as an observer is important. Whether you are in an outside child care facility or in your school's own laboratory, certain guidelines must be followed.

Whenever you gather data about children, you must use special care. The information you collect must be kept confidential. This is perhaps the most important guideline for you to follow. Though you can discuss a child's behavior in your own classroom, you must refrain from doing so outside that setting. Whenever you are talking, other people are listening. The information you share could be embarrassing or even damaging to a child, parent, or teacher.

To protect confidentiality, your teacher may request that you avoid using a child's name during classroom discussions. First names only are permitted in other classrooms. Both practices

will help protect the real identity of a child. These practices will also prevent information about a particular child from leaving the classroom.

While you are observing, coats, books, and other personal belongings should not be brought into the classroom. Young children are specially curious about purses and bags. Such items may cause an unnecessary distraction. Cosmetics and medications could endanger their safety.

During your observation time, avoid talking to the children, other observers, or the staff. However, it is likely that your presence will spark the curiosity of some of the children. A child may ask you what you are doing. If this happens, answer in a matter-of-fact manner. You might say that you are watching the children play or that you are writing notes on how children play.

One of the best ways to learn about young children is to observe them and to make note of their behavior, 3-12. By sharing your observations with other class members, you will be able to see children as they really are. These records will help you understand children and become a better child care professional.

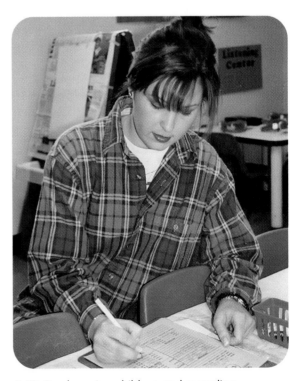

3-12 By observing children and recording their behavior, you will become a better child care professional.

# Summary

Assessment is the process of observing, recording, and documenting children's growth and behavior over time in order to make decisions about their education. Assessment has many purposes, but it is primarily used in planning developmentally appropriate curriculum. An initial assessment is made of all children when they enter a program, but ongoing assessment continues as long as a child remains enrolled in a program.

Most assessment methods involve observing children. Formal observation by researchers has led to the creation of developmental norms. Preschool teachers usually use informal observation methods to collect data.

There are several types of assessment tools that are used in early childhood programs. These include anecdotal records, checklists, participation charts, rating scales, samples of products, photographs, and tape recordings. All of these methods have advantages and disadvantages. Materials that have been collected during the assessment process should be placed in a portfolio for each child.

When observing children, it is important to record only objective statements. Once data is recorded, it may be interpreted. This interpretation takes knowledge and skill. It requires a thorough understanding of child development. Information you collect on children must also be kept confidential. This is perhaps the most important guideline to follow.

# Review and Reflect

1. List three purposes of assessment.

2. What is meant by the term *authentic assessment*?

3. Which of the following is considered a formal method of assessment?
   A. checklists
   B. standardized tests
   C. rating scales
   D. anecdotal records

4. List three considerations for choosing a method of assessment.

5. Which of the following are objective statements?
   A. Pours milk.
   B. Rocks the doll.
   C. Gets even.
   D. Feels lonely.

6. Why is the anecdotal record considered the simplest form of direct observation?

7. Which assessment tool would you use to determine the degree to which a quality or trait was present?

8. List one advantage and one disadvantage in using a checklist.

9. What three methods could you choose to add information on a three-dimensional project to a child's portfolio?

10. List five items that might be included in a child's portfolio.

11. Name three guidelines to keep in mind when observing children.

12. Describe how technology can be used as an assessment tool.

# Apply and Explore

1. Prepare a checklist for a group of children to assess color recognition skills.

2. Using the Appendix, develop a rating scale to assess the motor skills of four-year-olds.

3. Videotape a group of children interacting. Show the tape to classmates. Have each class member write a narrative of what he or she sees. Compare the contents of the narratives.

4. Interview an early childhood teacher about how she or he develops and uses portfolios.

5. Develop a participation checklist for the use of outdoor play equipment.

6. Have each student in the class observe a child for 15 minutes and write an anecdotal record of the observation. Compare and discuss the results. Which records contained the most detail? Which records contained only objective statements? Did any of the records contain interpretive statements? If so, what were they?

7. Use a search engine to find information on the observation of young children.   **C**

# Chapter 4

# Understanding Children from Birth to Age Two

After studying this chapter, you will be able to

- describe the areas and characteristics of development.
- chart the physical development of children in the first two years after birth.
- describe how children develop cognitively in the first two years after birth.
- explain how children in the first two years after birth develop socially and emotionally.

## Terms to Know

development
infant
toddler
preschooler
physical development
gross motor development
fine motor development
cognitive development
social-emotional development

maturation
reflex
motor sequence
object permanence
deferred imitation
telegraphic speech
temperament
attachment
separation anxiety

Studying and understanding child development is an important part of teaching young children. No two children are alike. Children differ in physical, cognitive, social, and emotional growth patterns. They also differ in the ways they respond to play, affection, objects, and people in their environment.

Think of the children that you know. Each is different from the others, 4-1. Some may always appear to be happy. Other children's personalities may not seem as pleasant. Some children are active. Still others are typically quiet. You may even find that some children are easier to like. To help all of these children, you need to understand the sequence of their development. Knowledge of child development is essential to guiding young children and planning a developmentally appropriate curriculum.

## Child Development

**Development** refers to change or growth that occurs in a child. By studying child development, you will develop a profile of what children can do at various ages. Understanding growth and development will help you plan appropriate programs for children. For instance, you will learn that two-year-old children like to run. This means that you should provide space for them to move freely. Likewise, you will learn that infants explore through their senses, often mouthing objects. Knowing this, you will need to make sure that all toys for infants are clean and safe.

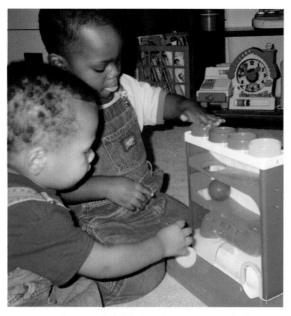

4-1 Knowledge of child development can help you understand how to work with children who have very different personalities.

Different names are often used to describe young children at different ages. For the first year after birth, a child is called an **infant**. From the first year until the third birthday, children are often called **toddlers**. (The name toddlers was given to this age group because of their awkward style of walking.) The term **preschooler** is often used to describe children ages three to six.

Child development is a relatively recent area of study. Researchers are continually discovering new information on how children grow, develop, and learn about their environment. Therefore, studying the basics of child development should just be the beginning for you. Throughout your career, you will need to update your knowledge of the latest research and trends in the field through seminars, courses, professional articles, and conferences. Professional development is a lifelong process.

## Areas of Development

The study of child development is often divided into three main areas. These include physical, cognitive, and social-emotional development. Dividing development into these areas makes it easier to study.

**Physical development** refers to physical body changes. It occurs in a relatively stable, predictable sequence. Therefore it is orderly, not random. Changes in bone thickness, vision, hearing, and muscles are all included. Changes in size and weight are also part of physical development. See 4-2.

Changes in physical skills, such as crawling, walking, hopping, and writing, are another part of physical development. These skills fall into two main areas of development. **Gross motor development** involves improvement of skills using the large muscles. Such activities as running, skipping, and riding a bike fall into this category. **Fine motor development** involves the small muscles. Grasping, holding, cutting, and drawing are some activities requiring fine motor development.

Environmental factors, such as proper nutrition and appropriate toys and activities, also affect what a child can do physically.

**Cognitive development**, sometimes called intellectual development, refers to mental

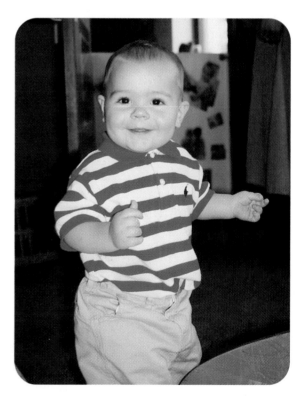

4-2 Changes in height and weight are two of the most obvious signs of physical development.

processes used to gain knowledge. Language, thought, reasoning, and imagination are all included. Identifying colors, and knowing the difference between *one* and *many*, are examples of cognitive tasks.

Language and thought are a result of cognitive development. These two skills are closely related. Both are needed for planning, remembering, and problem solving. These skills develop with maturity and experience.

The third area of development is called **social-emotional development**. These two areas are grouped together because they are so interrelated. Learning to relate to others is social development. Emotional development involves refining feelings and expressions of feelings. Trust, fear, confidence, pride, friendship, and humor are all part of social-emotional development. Other emotional traits include fear, timidity, interest, and pleasure. See 4-3. A person's self-concept and self-esteem are also part of this area.

These three developmental areas are interrelated. Development in one area can have a strong effect on development in another area. For instance, both fine motor development and cognitive development are needed to write words. Language, a part of cognitive development, is needed to communicate with others and develop socially and emotionally.

## Characteristics of Development

Although each child is different, the basic pattern of development is predictable. Development tends to proceed from the head downward. This is called the *cephalocaudal principle*. According to this principle, the child first gains control of the head, then the arms, then the legs. Therefore, infants gain control of head and face movements within the first two months after birth. In the next few months, they are able to lift themselves up using their arms. By 6 to 12 months of age, infants start to gain leg control and may be able to crawl, stand, or walk.

Development also proceeds from the center of the body outward according to the *principle of proximodistal development*. This means that the spinal cord develops before outer parts of the body. The child's arms develop before the hands, and the hands and feet develop before the fingers and toes. Finger and toe muscles are the last to develop.

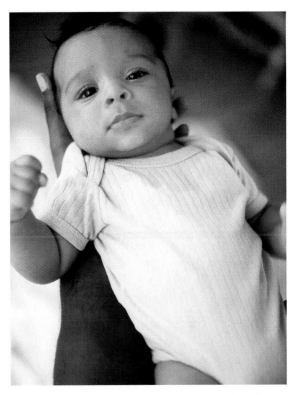

4-3 Learning to trust and show affection for others is a part of social-emotional development.

Development also depends on maturation. **Maturation** refers to a sequence of biological changes in a child. These changes give children new abilities. Much of maturation depends on changes in the brain and the nervous system. These changes allow children to have improved thinking abilities and motor skills.

Children must mature to a certain point before they can gain some skills, 4-4. For instance, the brain of a four-month-old has not matured enough to allow the child to use language. By two years of age, with help from others, the child will be able to say and understand many words.

The characteristics of development help you understand the order or sequence of development in children. However, each child develops at his or her own rate. You may find children the same age who have developed to different levels in each developmental area. Knowing the patterns of development will help you understand what abilities each child already has gained. It will

4-4 Improved muscle strength and coordination are needed to walk and push a wheeled toy.

also help you plan activities that will help the children develop new skills successfully.

## Physical Development in the First Two Years

Growth is rapid during the first two years of life. The child's size, shape, senses, and organs change. Some changes are rapid; others are more gradual. With each change, children gain new abilities. Much of the first year of life is spent coordinating motor skills. Through the repetition of motor actions, infants gain physical strength and motor coordination.

As a caregiver, you need to be aware of physical changes in the first two years. Activities, diets, sleep schedules, and safety policies need to be adjusted as children grow. For instance, infants less than four months old do not have much muscle strength. Typically, these children enjoy being rocked or held for most of

the day. They also enjoy sitting in infant seats. However, by twelve months, the infant's large muscles are more developed. At this time, these children need time and space for crawling and walking.

### Size and Shape

An infant's weight may change almost daily. The average weight at birth is 7½ pounds. Five months later, the infant will have doubled in weight. By one year, the typical child weighs about 22 pounds—about three times the birthweight. By two years of age, most children weigh almost four times their birthweight.

The infant's length also changes rapidly. The average newborn measures 20 inches. Twelve months later, the infant has usually grown 10 to 12 inches. During the second year of life, most children grow 2 to 6 inches more. By 24 months, most children measure 32 to 36 inches in height.

There are weight and height differences between boys and girls by two years of age. At this age, most boys are slightly heavier and taller than girls. Most boys reach about half of their adult height by two years of age. At the same age, girls will have passed their halfway mark by one or two inches.

## Reflexes

At birth, the infant's physical abilities are limited to reflexes. A **reflex** is an automatic body response to a stimulus. The person does not control this response. Blinking when something is coming toward your face is an example of a reflex. Some reflexes, such as blinking, continue throughout life. Others appear in infants and disappear after a few months.

Doctors and others who work with children check reflexes to assess brain and nerve development. When normal reflexes are not present in infants, it may be a sign of brain or nerve damage. If these reflexes continue past the time they should disappear, brain or nerve damage may again be suspected. Professionals often test infants for the reflexes listed in figure 4-5. Infants do not all acquire or lose these reflexes at exactly the same time. The chart shows the age range when each of these reflexes generally disappears.

### Rooting Reflex

The infant's reflexes are needed for survival. See 4-6. This reflex causes infants to turn their heads toward anything that brushes their faces. This action helps them find a food source such as a nipple. Once an object is near an infant's lips, the child will immediately start to suck. This reflex helps the child get food and usually disappears by three to four months of age.

### Moro Reflex

The Moro reflex is sometimes referred to as the "startle reflex." It occurs when a newborn is startled by a noise or sudden movement. The infant will react by flinging the arms and legs outward and extending the head. Then the infant will quickly draw the arms together, crying loudly. This reflex peaks during the first month and usually disappears by five to eight months.

### Palmar Grasp Reflex

The grasp reflex is easy to observe. When you touch the infant's palms, the hands will grip tightly. The grip is tight enough that you can lift

| Some Newborn Reflexes | |
|---|---|
| **Reflex** | **Age of Disappearance** |
| Rooting | 3 months |
| Moro | 5 to 8 months |
| Palmar Grasp | 3 to 12 months |
| Babinski | 8 to 12 months |
| Stepping | 2 to 3 months |

4-5 Continuation of these reflexes after the time they should disappear may be an indication of nerve or brain damage.

4-6 The rooting and sucking reflexes help an infant get food.

the infant into a sitting position. However, do not try this. Since the infant has no control over this response, he or she may let go suddenly. This reflex can also be seen if a rattle or another object is placed across the palm. This reflex weakens after the first three or four months after birth. It disappears totally late in the first year.

### Babinski Reflex

The Babinski reflex is present at birth in babies who were born at full term. To test for this reflex, stroke the sole of the foot on the outside from the heel to the toe. The toes will fan out and curl and the foot twists in. This reflex usually lasts for the first year after birth.

### Stepping or Walking Reflex

A stepping or walking reflex can be observed in full-term babies. When an infant is held so the feet are flat on a surface, the infant will lift one foot after another in a stepping motion. This reflex usually disappears two to three months after birth. Infants learn to step voluntarily late in the first year.

## Motor Sequence

**Motor sequence** refers to the order in which a child is able to perform new movements. Each new movement builds upon the previous abilities. Motor sequence depends on the development of the brain and nerves. For this reason, movements tend to develop in areas closest to the brain and spinal cord first.

In the first months after birth, head and trunk control develops. When this occurs, the infant can lift the head from a surface. The infant also can watch a moving object by moving the head from side to side.

By four or five months of age, an infant can roll over. Most infants are first able to turn from the stomach to the back. Soon after, the child will be able to roll from back to stomach.

Most infants can sit upright at four to six months of age. The infant needs to strengthen the neck and back muscles to accomplish this feat.

Gradually, infants are able to pull themselves into sitting positions. After this, crawling is the next skill in the motor sequence. This skill occurs shortly after the child learns to roll onto the stomach. To *crawl*, the child pulls with the

arms and wiggles the stomach. Some infants may even push with their legs. Many people confuse the terms *crawling* and *creeping*. Crawling occurs when the infant's abdomen is on the floor.

*Hitching* is another movement used by infants. Before they can hitch, infants must be able to sit without support. From this position, they move their arms and legs, sliding their buttocks across the floor.

As the arms and legs strengthen, infants are able to creep. *Creeping* is a movement in which infants support their weight on their hands and knees. See 4-7. They then move their arms and legs to go forward. As arms and legs become stronger, infants are able to stand with help from an adult. Soon after, they are able to stand while supporting themselves with furniture.

With better leg strength and coordination, infants are able to walk when led by an adult. Soon after, they are able to pull themselves up

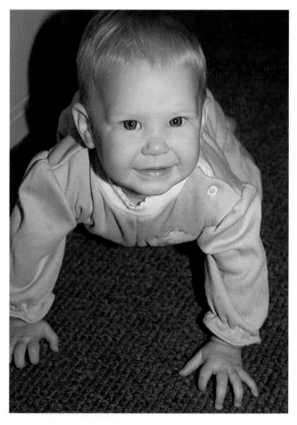

4-7 Creeping requires stronger leg muscles and better leg control than crawling.

into a standing position. Next, infants are able to stand without any support. Finally, they become true toddlers—able to walk without support or help.

There are stages of development for each skill that involves movement. To illustrate, when progressing toward mature motor skills, children show changes in movement. Picture the child's first attempts at walking. These actions are awkward. At first, it is difficult to maintain an upright posture. Next, there is an unpredictable loss of balance. Short steps are taken and the toes are pointed outward. The child keeps the legs spread to have a wide base of support.

Gradually the walking pattern appears smoother. The step length increases and the arm swinging decreases. The child also brings the legs closer together, decreasing the base of support. See Figure 4-8.

Earliest hand movements are reflexive. By three to four months, infants enjoy swiping at objects. At this age, they are still unable to grasp objects because they close their hands too early or too late. By nine months, hand-eye coordination improves and infants can pick up objects.

Infants can begin scribbling with a crayon by about 16 months of age. Simple figures composed of vertical and horizontal lines can be made by

the end of the second year. By two years of age, the child typically is showing a preference for one hand or the other. For some children, hand dominance is not established until age four.

Many other motor skills are gained in the first two years. These skills are listed in the Appendix. The skills listed are norms for each age group. They are considered norms because about half of infants at that age can do the skills. For this reason, you should not worry if a child cannot do every skill listed for his or her age. However, you should seek help for a child who is way behind the norms. For instance, if a 17-month-old cannot roll over, help should be sought.

## Cognitive Development in the First Two Years

At birth, most of an infant's movements are the result of reflexes. As infants grow, they begin to learn how to make things happen for themselves. Soon they are able to coordinate the movements needed to grab a bottle and suck milk from it. They also begin to react differently depending on their needs. A baby may spit out a pacifier if he or she is not hungry. However, a hungry baby may be content to suck on the pacifier.

Two main forces—heredity and environment—influence a child's cognitive development. Heredity determines when a child's brain and senses will be mature enough to learn certain skills. Environmental factors also affect learning. Children need opportunities to use their senses and try new things, 4-9. As a caregiver, you need to provide an environment that allows children to develop to their full potential intellectually.

Being able to see, hear, feel, taste, and smell are important to learning. Through these senses, children learn about many objects and concepts. All of the senses develop during the first two years of life. Sight and hearing develop especially quickly.

### Birth to Three Months

A newborn's vision is blurry at birth. During the first few weeks after birth, infants appear to focus on objects in the center of their visual field.

| Walking Sequence |
| --- |
| **Immature Stage** |
| • Upright position difficult to maintain |
| • Rigid appearance |
| • Loss of balance occurs frequently |
| • Short steps taken |
| • Toes turned outward |
| • Legs spread wide as base of support |
| • Arms held above waist |
| **Mature Stage** |
| • Upright position and balance maintained |
| • Step length increases |
| • Legs closer together, narrow base of support |
| • Relaxed appearance |
| • Arms held at side |

4-8  Changes in movement cause the walking pattern to gradually become smoother.

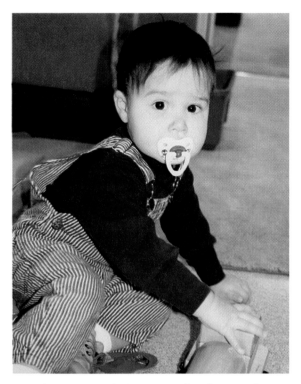

4-9 The activities that you provide infants and young toddlers help them develop cognitively.

source of sound. Newborns are startled by loud noises. They often react to these noises by crying. These same newborns are lulled to sleep by rhythmic sounds such as a lullaby or a heartbeat. They also react to human voices while ignoring other sounds. By three weeks, a newborn can distinguish between the voice of the mother or father and that of a stranger.

During the first three months after birth, infants do not distinguish between themselves and the objects around them. If infants see their hands moving, they do not think of themselves as making this movement. In their thinking, it could easily be someone else's hand.

Children this age start to experiment with reflex actions. Newborns suck everything that touches their lips. They even make sucking motions in their sleep. Gradually, these children adapt such reflexes to objects in their environment. They learn to suck the breast, bottle, pacifier, and their own fingers in different ways, 4-10.

Their near vision is better developed than their far vision. They like to look at objects held 8 to 15 inches in front of them.

As their vision improves, infants show preferences for certain objects. Studies show that infants will gaze longer at patterned disks, such as checks and stripes, than at disks of one solid color. Infants seem to prefer bold colors rather than soft pastels. They also pay more attention to faces than to other objects. In fact, by two months of age, an infant will gaze longer at a smiling face than at a face with no expression.

As infants grow older, they tend to shift their attention on the face. At one month of age, infants appear to focus on the hairline. By two months, infants show more interest in the eyes. The adult's facial expression is most interesting to a three-month-old child. These changes show that children are giving thought to areas of the face that interest them.

Hearing also develops early in life. From birth, infants will turn their heads toward a

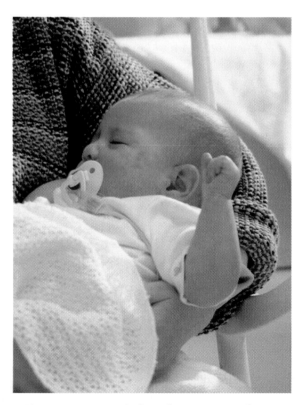

4-10 For very young babies, learning to suck a pacifier differently than the breast or bottle is a cognitive skill.

## Three to Six Months

During this time, children start to focus on their surroundings. Before this age, a child would just gaze at objects. The infant now begins to examine objects more closely. By six months of age, the child can distinguish between familiar and unfamiliar faces.

Infants also start to learn that they can touch, shake, and hit objects that they see. They notice toys make sounds. Memory, foresight, and self-awareness are all developing. The child learns that hitting the crib gym makes a noise. The infant also learns that his or her own movement caused the noise.

Infants from three to six months of age also start to show judgment. For instance, they prefer the smell and voice of a parent to that of a stranger. As early as three days after birth, infants will respond to noise. Infants in this stage also try to locate noises by turning toward them. The infant will look around to explore sources of sounds such as a doorbell, a dog barking, or an oven timer. Many times, though, they will turn in the wrong direction.

From birth, an infant makes noises. During this stage, vocalizations begin to increase. You will find that children this age make many noises when you hold and play with them.

Infants in this stage also respond in new ways to touch. If you blow on or kiss the baby's stomach, the child may smile or coo in response. Children this age also respond happily to light touches and tickling.

Infants in this stage think with their senses and movements. By four months, an infant will start using a predictable pattern to learn about objects. If you give a child at this stage an object, you will see this pattern. The child will first look at the object. Then he or she will mouth it and try shaking it, 4-11. The child may also try banging the object on the floor. This is the infant's way of learning what the object can do or how it can be used.

Toward the end of this period, body awareness begins to develop. The infant may bite his or her toe while playing. If the child has a tooth, he or she may be surprised by the hurt this causes. This does not stop the child, however, from making the same mistake with other toes or fingers.

4-11 Mouthing is a major way that infants learn about objects.

## Six to Nine Months

The concept of **object permanence** begins to develop at this stage. This concept is the understanding that objects continue to exist even if the infant cannot see them. Before this time, anything out of sight was out of mind for the infant. For instance, if a rattle was placed under a blanket, the young infant would not search for it. Now, the child begins to understand that the rattle is still there even though it is covered.

Beginning to understand object permanence shows that these infants are developing memory and goal-oriented thinking. The child will search under a blanket for a rattle that has been covered. This means that the child remembers that the rattle was there. It also means that the child takes actions with the goal of finding the rattle. At this time though, infants give up within a few seconds if they do not find the rattle.

You can test for object permanence by showing the infant an interesting toy. Then cover the toy with a towel or blanket while the child is looking. If the child attempts to uncover the toy, the child shows an understanding of object permanence. This child also shows goal-oriented behavior.

Part of object permanence involves understanding that other people exist all the time. Before this stage, children would simply cry if uncomfortable and stop crying when needs were met. Now, children begin to understand that they can cry as a call to parents or other caregivers. They know that even if a person is not within sight, the person still exists. Their cry will call the person to them.

Crying to call a person is also a sign that infants are learning to communicate. The child learns that making noises can get an adult to understand the child's needs. At this point, the child starts communicating in other ways. When the infant makes a noise, he or she will often listen for a response. If you make a noise in return, the infant will answer back. Usually the infant will listen when spoken to and look up when his or her name is spoken.

## Nine to Twelve Months

During this stage, infants become more intentional about their goals. The child has definite ideas about what he or she wants. If confined to a playpen, the child may cry to be taken out. Once out, the child may crawl across the room to get a forbidden object. At the same time, the child may ignore many interesting objects along the way.

These infants also begin to anticipate certain events. A child at this stage may cry when a parent puts on a coat. The infant has learned that when this happens, the parent will leave. When the child sees the parent enter the child care center, he or she may become excited and happy.

## Twelve to Eighteen Months

Between twelve and eighteen months, infants' hearing and speech continues to develop. They enjoy playing pat-a-cake and peekaboo games. Children at this stage like trial-and-error problem solving. They experiment with objects to find new ways to use them, 4-12. These might include rolling, tossing, or bouncing. These children express joy when they find that toys can make noise. They begin to understand that the force they use affects the loudness or softness of noise in a toy.

Relationships between cause and effect fascinate these young toddlers. For instance, the child loves to hit water and watch it splash. Children also learn ways to use cause and effect to

4-12 Young toddlers often look for new ways to use objects.

reach goals at this age. For instance, the child may learn that by pulling on a tablecloth, he or she can reach a plate of cookies.

Language is a change of behavior that occurs as a result of experience and maturation. It is also related to the child's environment. In Spain, for instance, children learn to speak Spanish, while children in Italy learn Italian. Language becomes a bigger part of communication at this stage. Before this time, some children may say a few words, such as daddy or mommy. Now, children learn to say many new words. Children's first words usually include objects that move and familiar actions. Included are words such as *car*, *truck*, *dig*, *ball*, *up*, *down*, *bye-bye*, *wet*, *dirty*, and *hot*. Mostly, children use one or two words to communicate during this stage. They do not yet understand how to combine a series of words to form sentences.

Books become more important to children at this time. A child in this stage will love to sit on your lap and have you read a story. Young toddlers may be able to identify many pictures in simple books. As you point to the pictures, the child may give the names of the objects. Most children at this age can understand even more words than they can say.

## Eighteen to Twenty-Four Months

As children near their second birthday, there is a change in how they approach their environment. During this stage, children start to think before taking action. They are able to apply what they know about objects to solve problems without as much trial-and-error. For instance, the child may know that standing on a stool in the bathroom helps the child reach the sink. This same child may apply this knowledge to get a cookie on the kitchen counter. Instead of a stool, the child may use a chair or even an open drawer. Children in this stage still tend to think in terms of actions.

Improved thinking skills and motor skills can make caring for toddlers in this stage exhausting. These children want to actively explore everything. They want to find out as much as they can about new places and objects. However, these children are not old enough to understand the dangers that may be involved in exploring. For instance, they may step in an open drawer to reach something without realizing that the drawer may fall. Therefore, you must continually watch toddlers and try to make sure their environment is as safe as possible.

Pretending starts to be part of a child's world at this stage. A young toddler's pretending is often a form of deferred imitation. **Deferred imitation** is watching another person's behavior and then acting out that behavior later. For instance, a father may tuck his child into bed each night and give him or her a kiss on the forehead. At the center the next day, the child may tuck in a doll and give it a kiss on the forehead. Children may also pretend to be animals they have seen, such as dogs.

These children now understand that symbols may represent other real objects. For instance, a younger child might play with a doll by swinging it around and hitting things with it. Now, however, the child will hold the doll like a baby and cover it with a blanket, 4-13.

4-13 This child holds her doll like a baby and wraps it in a blanket.

Children are learning more and more words. At first, toddlers only add one to three words to their vocabularies each month. Between 18 to 24 months, however, as many as 10 to 20 new words may be added each month. When their vocabularies reach about 200 words, they begin to combine two words. The term used to describe these two-word phrases is **telegraphic speech**. For instance, the child might say "doggie bark" to let you know that he or she hears a dog barking. Figure 4-14 shows typical two-word phrases used by toddlers during this stage.

Children like to share what they know with you. As you read to them, they may point to objects to tell you what they are. They enjoy pointing to things that you name. For instance, you may say to the child "Touch your nose." Children at this age are quick to respond by pointing to parts of their bodies. Later, you may get them to point to other objects in the room.

## Social-Emotional Development in the First Two Years

At birth, infants do not show a wide range of emotions. They seem to be basically comfortable or uncomfortable. To communicate this, they use movements, facial expressions, and sounds. By cooing, they show their comfort or delight. By crying, they show discomfort.

In the first few months of life, you will observe a range of emotions. The most reliable clues are infants' facial expressions. Happiness is shown when the corners of the mouth are pulled

back and the cheeks are raised, 4-15. Between six and nine months, the infant will begin to show fear, anxiety, and anger. Signs of fear are the mouth opened with the corners pulled back, eyes widened, and eyebrows raised. By the end of the second year, children are expressing their emotions in many more ways.

Socially, young children tend to focus on a few adults who are close to them. This is especially true of infants. After the first birthday, children may take more interest in other toddlers, 4-15. However, adults are still most important to children in this age group. As a caregiver, you need to realize that your actions will have a strong effect on children's social-emotional development. These children are ready for relationships. They need to be able to count on caregivers who will respond immediately to their distress signals. Healthy social-emotional development is a foundation for learning.

### Temperament

Even from birth, children differ in temperament or the ways that they react to their environment. **Temperament** refers to the quality and intensity of emotional reactions. Such factors as passivity, irritability, and activity patterns are part of a child's temperament.

| Toddlers' Typical Two-Word Phrases |
|---|
| Johnny hit. |
| Big ball. |
| Give milk. |
| My bear. |
| Hi daddy. |
| No milk. |

4-14 Toddlers often use two-word phrases.

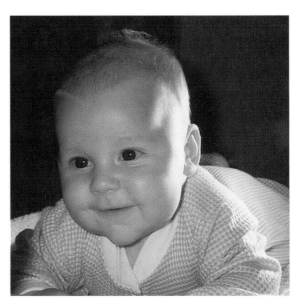

4-15 You can tell by his facial expression this young baby is content.

*Passivity* relates to how actively involved a child is with his or her surroundings. A passive infant withdraws from a new person or event. An active infant does something in response to a new person or event.

Children also differ in their level of *irritability* or tendency to feel distressed. Some infants cry easily. They may be difficult to comfort, even if you hold them and try to soothe them. There are other infants who rarely cry. These infants do not let changes bother them as much. Caring for these infants is usually easier for adults.

*Activity patterns* or levels of movement also vary in infants. Some infants can be described as quiet, making few movements. When asleep, these infants may hardly move. Others are constantly moving their arms and legs. These infants may even sleep restlessly.

If you care for infants, you need to adjust to the temperaments of different children. All infants need loving attention. If given patient, tender care, most children will grow to be happy and well-adjusted. This is even true of very irritable infants.

## Attachment

**Attachment** is the strong emotional connection that develops between people. Most infants become attached to a small group of people early in life. They mainly become attached to the people who care for them. Included may be mothers, fathers, caregivers, or older siblings. Young infants learn that when they are hungry, wet, or frightened, they can depend on these people to make them feel better. The quality of attachment depends on the adults.

Several early attachment behaviors are shown by infants. These behaviors show that infants care for and respond to certain people who are important to them. Infants will single these people out for special attention. When approached, the infant may break into a broad, warm smile. Other examples of attachment behaviors are cooing, kicking, gurgling, and laughing. Crying and clinging are also attachment behaviors. These behaviors show that the child is signaling to others.

Attachment begins early in life. Studies show even young babies show signs of anxiety if they are cared for by an unfamiliar person. These distress signs appear as irregular sleeping or eating patterns.

**Separation anxiety** is another attachment behavior shown by infants. This happens when a child protests because a familiar caregiver is leaving. The child often cries as a sign of distress. The first signs of separation anxiety appear at about six months of age. The reaction becomes clearer by nine months of age. By 15 months of age, separation anxiety is very strong. After this point, this distress gradually weakens.

As a caregiver, you need to be prepared for the attachment behaviors of children in this age group. Children between 9 and 18 months of age will usually have the most difficulty beginning a child care program. To make the transition easier, you should encourage parents to bring the child's favorite toy or blanket.

As children show separation anxiety, you need to remind yourself not to take the reaction personally. These children are simply fearful because their familiar caregivers are leaving them. They do not know what to expect next, and they are in an unfamiliar surrounding with strange people. As children become more familiar with the center, its people, and its routine, they will show less distress.

## Changes over Time

During the first two years after birth, you will see many changes in children socially and emotionally. As a caregiver, your actions will affect how these children change. Establishing trust is a key factor in social-emotional development. Trust develops when there is predictability. If you meet children needs and encourage them to interact with others, children will learn to trust and care for others. They will feel safe and happy.

### Birth to Three Months

At birth, newborns do not have very refined emotions. General excitement and general distress are the only emotions shown. The child may show excitement by looking alert, smiling, or wiggling. Distress is shown by crying. Observing a child in this stage, you may notice that there are no tears when the child cries.

### Three to Six Months

By three months, children respond to people with smiles and laughter. They may make happy sounds as adults play with, hold, or feed them. During this stage, infants start to notice and smile at other babies. Crying is still used to show distress. Early in this stage, tears begin to appear. Later, children start to use different cries to signal different types of distress.

### Six to Twelve Months

Infants in this stage become actively involved with their caregivers. As adults play with and care for them, these children express happiness, joy, and surprise. They also make sounds in response to the speech of others. Infants in this stage also begin to develop fear. You should not be surprised if a child this age cries at the sight of a stranger. By this age, children have also developed attachment to their caregivers. They may cry and even show anger when their caregivers leave them.

This stage may be the most difficult for the child's parents and for you. Separation anxiety starts to show. As a result, a child may start crying and clinging upon entering the center. When you try taking the child from the parent, the child may attempt to push you away. After the parent leaves, the child may continue to cry. Most children, however, will stop crying within a few minutes. This behavior may continue until 14 to 16 months of age.

### Twelve to Twenty-Four Months

Early in this stage, children still show separation anxiety. Children in this stage also show anxiety. In other words, they become upset because of something they think will happen in the future. For instance, this child may cling to a parent who will be leaving soon.

These children become more interested in exploring. Although they still fear the unfamiliar, they are curious about new places and objects, 4-16. Children who feel secure are more likely to explore than those who feel unsure of their surroundings. By this age, children start to take more interest in other children. They like to play next to other children, but they do not interact much with them.

Children start to become more aware of their own abilities at this point. This self-awareness is a source of joy and anger for children. Toddlers are proud and happy when they can do things for themselves. However, sometimes they insist on doing things for themselves that they can't do yet. This can cause frustration and anger for the child.

Children who are becoming self-aware also like to say "no." These children like to know that they can make things happen, and they do not always want to do what adults want. Sometimes they may say no to you just to see what will happen. You will need to be kind but firm with these children. You must help them understand that there are rules that must be followed. At the same time, you need to reassure these children that their wants and needs are important.

4-16 Curiosity helps toddlers explore new places and objects.

## Summary

Understanding child development will help make you a successful caregiver or early childhood teacher. The study of child development is divided into three main areas–physical, cognitive, and social-emotional development. Growth in the first two years of life is rapid. Physically, children start with many reflexes that are eventually replaced with voluntary movements. As they become bigger and stronger, infants are able to roll over, crawl, creep, and eventually walk.

Cognitive growth shows in children's reactions to the environment. As infants, children will mouth and hit with objects to learn how they work. With growth, children begin to understand how different objects work. They also begin to understand that objects exist even if they are not seen. Children begin to think about how they can reach goals. They also learn to communicate, first by crying, and later by using words.

Each child is born with a temperament that sets the stage for social-emotional development. Young infants tend to show two main emotions–distress and excitement. As infants grow, they become attached to caregivers. They express joy, happiness, surprise, and fear. These children may experience separation anxiety when loved ones leave them. As children grow older, they show interest in other children. They also become interested in their own abilities. These children may often test adults by saying no to rules and suggestions. However, they also take pride in their own achievements. These children still look to adults for love and attention.

## Review and Reflect

1. Changes in bone thickness, vision, and hearing are part of _____.

2. True or false. Trust, fear, and pride are part of cognitive development.

3. List and explain three characteristics of development.

4. True or false. Reflex testing can be used to detect whether an infant has brain or nerve damage.

5. Why are infants able to crawl before they are able to creep?

6. If you place a toy car near an infant who is three to six months old, what is the child most likely to do?
    A. Ignore the toy.
    B. Cry.
    C. Put the toy in his or her mouth.
    D. Slide the toy along the floor making car noises.

7. Describe how to test a child for an understanding of object permanence.

8. If a toddler sees his or her mother mowing the lawn one day and then pretends to mow the lawn at the child care center, the toddler is practicing _____.

9. Describe telegraphic speech and provide an example.

10. Describe three factors that affect a child's temperament.

11. True or false. Children do not start to show attachment behaviors until after their first birthday.

12. How would the social-emotional development of a three-month-old differ from that of a one-year-old?

## Apply and Explore

1. Visit a child care center serving infants. Observe differences among them.

2. Observe a parent playing with or caring for an infant. Record the child's age in months. Write an anecdotal record describing the child's interactions with the parent. Share your observation with the class.

3. Visit the Web site for the National Network [C] for Child Care (nncc.org) to review the developmental stages for infants and toddlers and articles on child development.

4. Read the information provided at the Web [C] site for Zero to Three (zerotothree.org) about creating a relationship with an infant through touch, voice, movement, and vision to stimulate the infant's developing brain.

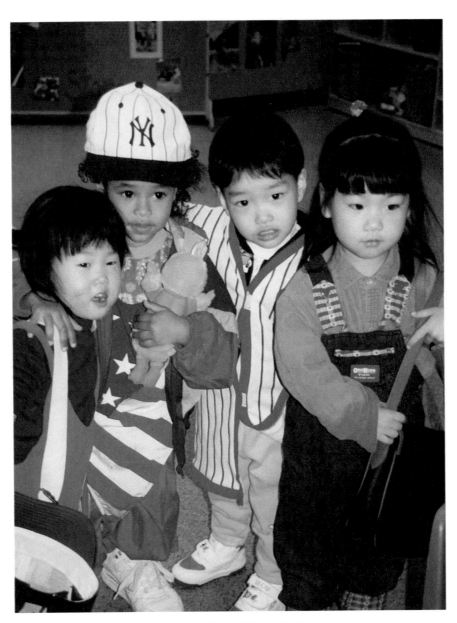

By age three, children begin to form friendships with their peers.

# Chapter 5

# Understanding Two- and Three-Year-Olds

After studying this chapter, you will be able to

- describe the physical, cognitive, and social-emotional development of two-year-olds.

- explain how three-year-olds develop physically, cognitively, socially, and emotionally.

- relate how the development of two- and three-year-olds will affect your role as a teacher.

## Terms to Know

language comprehension

expressive language

egocentric

gender roles

self-concept

To better understand two- and three-year-olds, you need to develop a mental picture. You need to understand how children in these age groups behave. Generally, two-year-olds are active, demanding, and curious. Three-year-old children tend to be more calm. Generally, they try to please and conform. Understanding these differences will help you plan programs that best meet the needs of each child.

## Physical Development of Two-Year-Olds

Two-year-old children continue to grow physically, but the rapid growth that occurred during infancy tapers off. A typical two-year-old will grow two to three inches in height and add about five pounds in weight during the year. Organs, such as the eyes, stomach, heart, and lungs, become stronger.

The digestive system matures slowly in children. The appetites of two-year-olds vary from day to day. Some days they may be excited about eating at snack time; other days they may reject their snacks. Likewise, what they eat at mealtimes may vary.

The coordination of two-year-olds' bodies is improving. They are less top-heavy and their center of gravity shifts downward. Provided equipment, space, and support, these children can master a variety of gross motor skills, 5-1. They can usually run and jump without falling. The fine motor skills of these children are also improving.

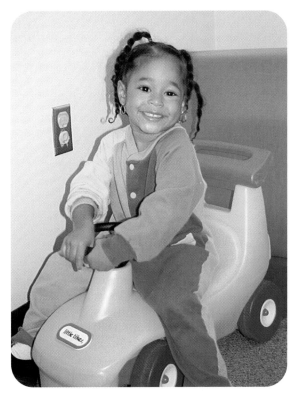

5-1 Two-year-olds have improved muscle strength and coordination.

## Gross Motor Development

Improved coordination and body control makes playing with balls great fun for active two-year-olds. They can pick up a ball by bending at the waist. Likewise, they can kick a large ball. These children are usually able to throw a ball without falling.

Two-year-olds have more control in leg and foot muscles than before. They can walk up and down stairs placing both feet on each stair. (Most children this age need to hold on to a rail as they step.) They also are able to stand with both feet on a balance beam. These children have the skill to walk on their toes. From a standing position, they can balance on one foot. Jumping is also possible. They can jump several inches off the floor with both feet. Most children this age can do a standing broad jump of about eight and one-half inches. In addition, most two-year-olds can sit on a riding toy and move it by pushing with their feet.

## Fine Motor Development

Two-year-old children are rapidly developing finger dexterity and control. They are able to insert keys into a lock and turn pages in a book one at a time. Most children this age also can string large beads or spools and lace cards. They also can hold scissors properly. By two years of age, they can open and close scissors.

Hand preference is fairly developed by this age. Many children will use the same hand for most fine motor activities. However, these children still switch hands for some activities. Alex, for example, draws with his right hand, but eats and throws a ball with his left hand.

You will see children using writing tools at this age, 5-2. At about 24 months of age, children can scribble. At first, these scribbles look like tangles of lines. By about 30 months, children can draw horizontal lines, vertical lines, and circles. Most children draw by holding the tool, crayon, or pencil, in their fist.

Two-year-olds become skilled at building with blocks. They can build towers of six to seven blocks. They can also use two or more blocks to make a train and push the blocks along.

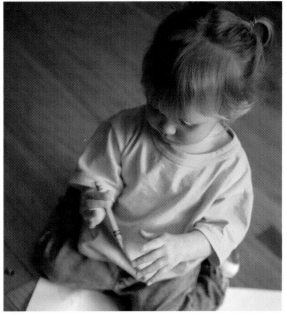

5-2 Using crayons helps two-year-olds refine their fine motor skills.

## Self-Help Skills

With a little help, two-year-olds can accomplish many self-help skills. At this age, they begin to cooperate in dressing. First, they can undress themselves. They are able to remove simple items of clothing such as socks, shoes, and pants. Snaps can be opened successfully. Next, they begin to dress themselves. At first, this involves pulling on simple garments. Zippers can be zipped and unzipped. By 30 months, most children can unbutton large buttons, close snaps, and put on their socks. However, you will need to help children as they try these skills.

By this age, children can drink from a cup or glass without help. They may spill fairly often, but their drinking skills improve with practice. Two-year-olds are also able to drink using a straw. They can use a spoon to feed themselves, but may revert to eating with their fingers if hurried.

Strides are usually made in toilet learning during this time. At two years of age, most children start to use the toilet or potty chair with reminders. However, accidents are common. Between 24 and 35 months, children seldom have bowel accidents. They may still have problems with wetting for several months. By 33 months, many children can use the toilet without help.

# Cognitive Development of Two-Year-Olds

The two-year-old's cognitive development focuses on three main areas. These include language comprehension skills, expressive language skills, and math readiness skills. All of these areas reflect the child's intelligence.

## Language Comprehension Skills

A person's understanding of language is called **language comprehension**. Some experts refer to this as receptive or inner language. This form of language is more advanced than expressive language skills in children. For instance, a 20-month-old child may be able to follow directions. However, this child may not be able to say more than a few words.

Language comprehension grows rapidly in two-year-olds. These children can understand and answer routine questions. While reading a story, you may point to a picture and ask "What is that?" The child may respond by saying "Baby." See 5-3.

By 24 months of age, most children can identify at least six body parts. Children can point to these parts on themselves, others, or dolls. They enjoy playing games in which you state "Find your toes" or "Where are your eyes?"

Many other new skills develop around 24 months. Children can comprehend the pronouns *I, my, mine,* and *me.* They also can provide appropriate answers to yes and no questions.

By 30 months of age, other milestones are reached. When asked, children can give you one cookie. They also can follow two-step commands. For instance, you can tell a child "Take off your coat and put it in your locker."

5-3 Two-year-olds will answer questions about pictures in the stories you read them.

These children can also give answers to *where* questions. For instance, you may ask a child "Where is your locker?" or "Where do you wash your hands?"

Understanding the meanings of words continues through the second year. When picking up objects, two-year-olds can tell the difference between soft and heavy. Size concepts are also developing. Children understand such words as *big* and *tall*. Children also start to understand words related to space. These include such words as *on, under, out of, together*, and *away from*.

## Expressive Language Skills

**Expressive language** is the ability to produce language forms. It is a tool that can be used to express a person's thoughts to others. For most two-year-olds, expressive language quickly develops. Like other aspects of development, it follows a sequence. The child's experiences affect the rate and content of expressive language development. Therefore, it is important you provide an environment that stimulates language development.

Speech usually involves simple sentences by two years of age. In the beginning, only two words may be used. "Johnny hurt" or "Tom dog" are examples. Later, the child will begin to put three-word sentences together. Examples include "Tom go home," "I eat corn," or "See my truck." Sentences follow the word order of the native language.

There are two language strategies that are important when you work with two-year-olds. These are called feeding-in and expansion. *Feeding-in* is a strategy where you provide the child's language. For example, if a child is building with blocks, the teacher might say "You are building with blocks."

*Expansion* is a strategy used to expand the child's language. Typically this is accomplished by reframing the child's utterance into a sentence. For example, if the child says "car" the teacher might say "This is a blue car." If the child says "wheels" the teacher could say "The car has wheels."

The vocabulary of the average two-year-old is 50 to 200 words. You will notice that children at this age often use words without fully understanding them. You might also observe that girls generally develop language skills faster than boys.

Two-year-olds do not understand how to use grammar to form questions. Instead, they use the tone of their voice. They may ask in a questioning tone "Grandma go?" or "Milk all gone?"

Two-year-olds often make negative sentences. They do this by adding the word *no* to positive sentences. For instance, a child may say "No milk" meaning that he or she does not want any milk. The child may say "Teacher no here" meaning that he or she cannot find the teacher.

Between 27 and 30 months, children may begin to use prepositions. For instance, children may say "Cookies in jar." Around this age, children also begin using plurals. They may request "cookies" or "candies."

Modifiers are also added to the vocabulary. *Some, a lot, all,* and *one* are used as quantifiers. *Mine, his,* and *hers* are used as possessives. *Pretty, new,* and *blue* are some adjectives that might be used as modifiers.

Between 31 and 34 months of age, children may begin adding *-ed* to verbs to show past tense. At about the same time, present tense verb helpers appear. These include such terms as *can, are, will,* and *am*.

## Math Readiness Skills

Math skills are developed as children interact with others and with objects. When you ask, a child can give you "just one" of something. Children also understand size concepts such as big and small. Awareness of shapes, forms, and colors is also developing during this stage. They begin to sort objects by shape and color.

# Social-Emotional Development of Two-Year-Olds

Two-year-olds continue to grow socially and emotionally. At this age, children tend to show many negative attitudes. Children like instant gratification and find it difficult to wait. These qualities make patience an important quality as you work with two-year-olds.

## Social Development

At the beginning of this developmental stage, children play next to each other. However, they do not play cooperatively with each other, 5-4. Children in this stage still tend to be more interested in adults. Therefore, they tend to act out adult experiences as they play. These might include driving a car, making a bed, and talking on the phone.

The average two-year-old tends to be possessive. Usually these children do not want to share. There typically is competition for toys. They tend to use body language to let people know how they feel about their possessions.

Two-year-old children can be very physical in their responses. They may push, hit, or shove another child who approaches their toys. Although they have difficulty understanding the concept of sharing, two-year-olds may return a toy that belongs to someone else.

In spite of their negativism and possessiveness, two-year-olds are usually affectionate. They may hug you and hold your hand. Two-year-olds thrive on love and caring from adults. They also enjoy helping you. Whether you are setting the table for lunch or picking up blocks, they are eager to participate.

## Emotional Development

These children like to be able to control their surroundings. Because they can't always do that, they tend to get frustrated and angry at times. Trying to do a task that is too hard for them may cause anger, 5-5. Not being allowed to do or have something may stir angry feelings as well. Two-year-olds may have temper tantrums if they do not get their way. They may scream, cry, stamp, or kick. Their anger is not usually at any

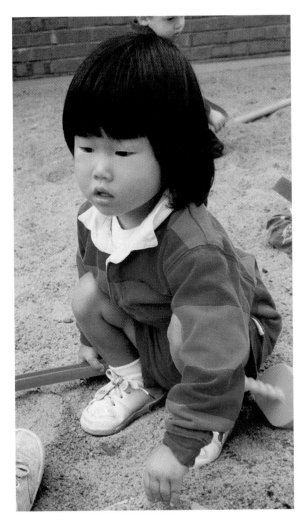

5-4 Two-year-olds do not interact much as they play.

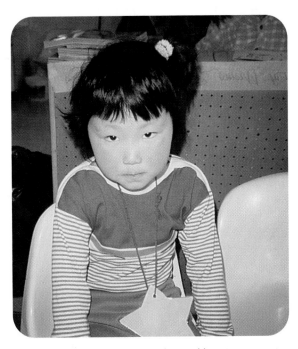

5-5 Being able to meet goals quickly is important to two-year-olds. If they do not get instant results, they often become angry.

one person or object; they are simply frustrated. Children this age still have not learned more appropriate ways of expressing anger.

Fears become common at this age. Two-year-olds are often afraid of being hurt or harmed. Many of their fears have to do with their imagination. Two-year-olds can't always separate pretend from reality, so they may be afraid of a monster from a story. A dream may frighten them because they think the characters are real. As a teacher, you need to comfort children when they are afraid. Even imagined fears are real to toddlers.

Love and caring are shown often by these children. They need to receive love and caring in return. Two-year-olds need to know that people still care for them even if they get angry. They also need to know that they can depend on others. To build trust and security, these children need regular routines. For instance, they may need to sit next to the same person or group of people at every meal or snack time.

## Teaching Two-Year-Olds

The development of two-year-olds has a strong effect on the way you teach and work with them. You need to be prepared to handle those situations that are typical with these children.

If you were to observe a group of two-year-olds, your first observation might be that they are negative. Two-year-olds often use the word "no." At times, they may even mean "yes" when they say "no." For instance, you may ask "Do you want more milk?" The child may say "no" while extending his or her glass toward you for more milk.

You may find yourself becoming impatient with two-year-old children at times. They always seem to want their own way. Whether you want to read a story or take the children on a field trip, you are bound to find a two-year-old who refuses. The child may refuse to leave his or her present activity or to put on his or her coat. Working with two-year-olds requires gentle, but firm, guidance.

Two-year-olds are very **egocentric**. This means that they believe everyone else sees, thinks, and feels like they do. This does not mean they are selfish. They believe that you will think exactly as they do.

Prepare yourself for the dawdling behavior of the typical two-year-old. These children insist on doing things at their own pace. Because of this, routines take longer. When planning a schedule, be aware of this type of behavior. Two-year-olds need plenty of time to move from one activity to the next. Therefore, you will need to be flexible and patient.

Upon entering a classroom of two-year-olds, you will first notice the noise. This is very common. When a child discovers a drum, the child will hit it over and over again. Likewise, they may repeat a new vocal sound many times. If one child starts clapping and stamping his or her feet, the other children may join in. You will need to be prepared for high noise levels and be able to control that noise from time to time.

Curiosity is another trait of two-year-olds. Children of this age enjoy exploring. When new materials are brought into the classroom, the children will carefully inspect them. If you ask them what toy they want, they may have difficulty choosing. Therefore, you should add only a few new items at a time.

Gross motor activity is a favorite of two-year-old children. They delight in movement and are not afraid to try out new equipment. They love to run and chase others. Therefore, adequate supervision is crucial. On field trips, these children like to run ahead. For this reason, you may want to have extra adults on the trips to help supervise.

Two-year-olds like to act out life experiences. They especially like to imitate the activities of adults, 5-6. Therefore, they need a dramatic play corner. Housekeeping equipment, mirrors, dolls, dress-up clothes, toy telephones, trucks, and cars should all be included.

Two-year-olds need some routine in their day. They like to have things done the same way. These children look forward to certain parts of the day, such as story time. Therefore, you need to be careful to follow a similar schedule from day to day. A few changes add interest, but children need to rely on a predictable schedule.

Two-year-olds may also have temper tantrums, but this is normal behavior. It has nothing to do with your skill as a teacher, although you may be embarrassed by a toddler's outburst. What is important is how you handle the tantrum. It is vital that you remain composed.

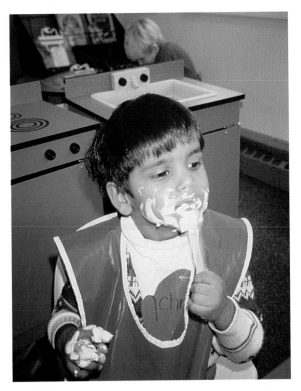

5-6 Teachers should provide many dramatic play materials so two-year-olds can act out such everyday experiences as shaving.

Use a calm voice when speaking to the child. If the child is kicking, you may have to immobilize the child by holding the legs. If the child is a threat to the other children, move the child to another area of the room.

# Physical Development of Three-Year-Olds

For three-year-olds, playing is exploring. They are constantly moving, tasting, smelling, and touching. As a result, their body coordination shows great improvement. You will notice that the arms, hands, legs, and feet are all becoming more coordinated. Likewise, their bodies are becoming less top-heavy and more streamlined. To stay upright, three-year-olds no longer need to keep their legs spread apart. Their walk appears more natural as their toes point forward and their feet move closer together.

## Gross Motor Development

Throwing, jumping, and hopping skills improve as a result of better coordination. The improvement of body coordination is also reflected in the climbing skills of three-year-olds. Now these children can climb and descend stairs easily. In fact, these children can walk up stairs with alternating feet. Their balance is improving.

By 36 months of age, children can catch large balls with their arms. Their catching skill gradually becomes more refined. Eventually, they can catch bouncing balls with their hands. This skill usually emerges toward the end of the third year.

Leg coordination and balancing skills also improve. Three-year-olds can ride and steer tricycles. They can walk heel-to-toe for four steps. They can balance on one foot for up to eight seconds. They can hop on one foot up to three times.

## Fine Motor Development

The fine motor skills of three-year-olds continue to develop. Cutting skills become more refined. The two-year-old could only hold and work scissors. However, a three-year-old can use the scissors to cut paper, 5-7. They can cut five-inch squares of paper into two sections. Young three-year-olds can cut across the paper, but they cannot cut along a line. By 42 to 48 months, children can cut along a line straying no more than one-half of an inch away from it.

Three-year-olds have better drawing skills. Making use of their improved fine motor skills, they often reproduce simple shapes as they draw. If you show these children the shape of a cross, they can copy the shape. They also can trace the shape of a diamond. They enjoy drawing faces. The faces usually include the mouth, eyes, nose, and/or ears. These features are not drawn in proportion, but they are usually placed in the correct position on the face. They lack the fine motor coordination needed to create complex figures.

Three-year-olds also enjoy manipulating blocks and puzzle pieces. They can build towers with nine to ten cubes. They can also construct simple puzzles.

5-7 This three-year-old can use scissors to cut paper.

## Self-Help Skills

Three-year-olds become increasingly self-sufficient. Daily care routines now require little adult assistance. These children can turn the water faucet on and off as long as they can reach it, 5-8. As a result, they can attend to routines such as washing and drying their hands and face. They also can brush their own teeth.

Three-year-olds become better at dressing themselves. They can now open buckles and put on shoes that do not tie. Three-year-olds need little adult help when their clothing has elastic waists or large button openings. They still are not able to work small buttons and hooks. Three-year-olds have trouble telling the front from the back on clothing, too. They do better with clothing that has a design on the front or a label in the back.

At snack and mealtime, these children are now able to use knives. They can spread butter, jelly, and soft peanut butter on bread. They also can pour liquid from a small pitcher. As a result, these children may enjoy assisting at snack time.

Another step toward independence is mastered at this age. Three-year-olds have almost full

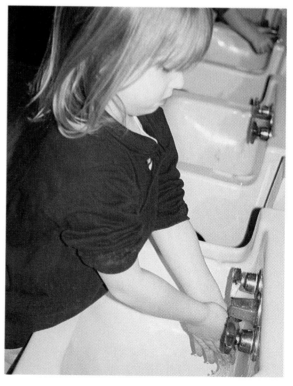

5-8 Being able to turn water on and off increases this three-year-old's ability to help herself.

control over toilet routines. They are even able to get through a night without wetting. This accomplishment is made possible through improved motor control.

## Cognitive Development of Three-Year-Olds

By the third birthday, the ability to think matures. Children move away from thinking only in terms of actions. They are able to solve simple problems. For instance, if you place an object under a cup and place nothing under another cup, the child knows which cup the object is under. If you switch the cups while the child is watching, the child still knows where the object is.

Children at this age still do not think logically. They are still egocentric as they have not yet learned to see things from more than one perspective. For instance, they do not realize that something that seems tall to them might actually seem short to an adult. They get confused about time concepts. These children may also become confused about cause and effect. For instance, if a bell rings before each snack is served, children may think the bell causes the snack to appear.

Even though thinking is still flawed, these children learn quickly. Their language comprehension skills, expressive language skills, and math readiness skills continue to improve.

### Language Comprehension Skills

Understanding of language continues to grow in three-year-olds. On request, the child can now give you two objects. These children can also remember and follow three-part instructions. For example, you might say "Go to the sink, wash your hands, and dry them with a towel." See 5-9.

Three-year-olds begin to understand the pronouns *you* and *they*. They also understand such words as *who, whose, why,* and *how.* They are able to provide answers to questions based on these words. For instance, you may ask the child "Who lives at the North Pole?" Another question might be "Whose teddy bear is this?" While reading a story you may ask "Why is the girl crying?" These children will be able to answer such questions as "How will your mother bake the pie?"

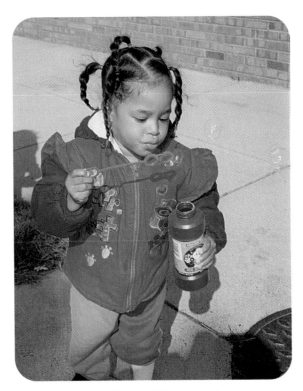

5-9 Three-year-olds can follow your three-part instructions.

Space concepts become clearer. While moving objects, children will understand your instructions that include such words as *toward, up, top,* and *apart.* Toward the end of the third year, children master more space concepts. They understand such ideas as *around, in front of, in back of,* and *next to.*

### Expressive Language Skills

Children's ability to produce language continues to increase. By now, children may use more than 900 words. Three-year-olds also have improved grammar. They may make sentences of four or five words. They may even join sentences together with a conjunction. For instance, the child may say "The bunny died and we don't have it."

Three-year-olds begin to understand the difference between past and present tense. They like to make verbs past tense by adding *-ed* to them. These children make statements such as "I talked" or "Daddy walked." However, they do not yet understand that there are exceptions to this rule. They may use such past tense verbs as "runned" and "goed." They may even use the correct form, but still add -*ed*. For instance, they may say "ranned" or "wented."

Children start to understand possessive nouns. Three-year-olds may refer to mommy's car, daddy's hammer, and teacher's coat. Negatives are not fully understood by three-year-olds. They understand that such words as *no, not, can't, don't, nothing*, and *never* are negative. However, they use all negative terms when they form negative statements. For instance, a three-year-old may say "Kelsie can't do nothing" or "Jackson can't never go nowhere."

During this stage, children start to use question words, especially *why* and *when*. These children tend to add on the question word to a regular sentence. For instance, they may ask "When Daddy is coming?" or "Why the cloud is moving?"

As these children play, they frequently talk out loud to themselves. For example, three-year-old Jenny is painting at the easel and saying, "Jenny is painting a picture. I need red. Where is the red? Now I need yellow. I need to paint with yellow."

## Math Readiness Skills

Three-year-olds continue to learn concepts basic to math. They start to understand the concepts *full, more, less, smaller,* and *empty*. By 42 months of age, most children understand the concept of *largest*. These children like to constantly compare objects, saying one object is bigger or another is smaller.

Counting skills also begin at this stage. If you ask, a three-year-old can give you two objects. These children can also count to three while pointing to corresponding objects. They may be able to recite numbers in order higher than three, but they are not able to count that number of objects.

Children in this age group can distinguish between *one* and *many*. To check for this skill, place one chip on the table. Nearby, place a pile of chips. Ask the child to point to one chip. Repeat the question asking the child to point to many chips. Children who respond correctly have learned the difference between one and many.

## Social-Emotional Development of Three-Year-Olds

After the third birthday, children start to grow out of the temper tantrums, and contrariness of the two-year-old stage. They become cooperative, happy, and agreeable, 5-10. By this time, children start to learn socially acceptable ways of expressing their feelings. They can use language more effectively to communicate with others. Also, they start to form friendships with their peers.

### Social Development

Three-year-olds are eager to help others, especially adults. They like to help with such tasks as passing out crayons and pouring juice. They are learning new ways of showing concern for others. They are learning positive ways to get attention from others. These children are more willing to accept attention from adults and children who are not well-known. They adjust to new people more easily than two-year-olds do.

5-10 Three-year-olds tend to be more content and agreeable than two-year-olds.

By the third birthday, children begin to play with, rather than next to, other children. See 5-11. Although these children interact with each other, their play is not truly organized. For instance, they may play house and each child playing may be the daddy.

Children this age are not as possessive as two-year-olds. They will share with others, but they do not like to share too much. For this reason, three-year-olds usually play with only one or two main friends. These children use language more to communicate with friends. For instance, they may say to a friend "You play with the baby." To another child, they may say "You can't play with us."

Children this age also begin to learn **gender roles**. These are behaviors that are expected of girls or boys. Gender roles are not as clearly defined as they once were, but they are still an important part of learning. Children this age realize that there are physical differences between boys and girls. With the proper role models, they begin to learn how to treat members of the opposite sex with respect.

## Emotional Development

Three-year-olds have strong visible emotions. They get excited. They get angry. They get discouraged. However, they are beginning to understand that there are appropriate ways to express these emotions. They realize that adults do not approve of such actions as temper tantrums. Also, they are eager to act in ways that please others. Therefore, these children are developing control over their strong feelings. Instead of striking another child, they may scream "Stop it!"

Unlike two-year-olds, many situations no longer lead to angry outbursts among three-year-olds. Because they have improved coordination, three-year-olds are less likely to become frustrated when they cannot do something. They also have improved language skills. When children can understand why something is happening, they are less likely to get angry. For instance, a child may want a drink just prior to lunch. You can explain, "It's only a few minutes until lunch. You can have a drink then." When the child understands that he or she will have a drink soon, he or she is less likely to get angry.

Three-year-olds are likely to become angry when things do not go their way. However, they begin to direct their anger at objects. For instance, they may be angry at a pitcher if they spill their milk. Children this age are more likely to express their anger in words. They do not hit, stamp, or cry as much as two-year-olds do.

5-11 Although their play is not organized, three-year-olds will play with each other.

The three-year-old is beginning to develop a self-concept. Your **self-concept** is the way you see yourself. A child's self-concept includes a set of beliefs about himself or herself. Ask three-year-olds to tell you about themselves. They will likely provide you with their names, possessions, and physical appearance. As a result, you might hear something like this: "I'm Kelly. I have a dog. I have a brother. I have black hair."

By this stage, children are not as likely to be frightened by objects that they know. For instance, they are not frightened by the noise from a car. However, they are quite fearful of imagined dangers. They may be especially afraid of the dark. These children also become more fearful of pain. They may be scared that a dog will bite them or that they will be hurt during a doctor's visit.

Three-year-olds are affectionate, and they tend to seek affection in return. They may follow, cling to, or help an adult in an effort to get attention, approval, or comfort. Three-year-olds still do not think in terms of the feelings of others.

Children learn to express their own feelings by watching the adults around them. When you express surprise and happiness, they will also show these emotions. Likewise, if you give a hug to comfort someone who is sad, they will imitate your behavior.

## Teaching Three-Year-Olds

Three-year-olds are typically happy, sociable, and agreeable. Furthermore, they are very eager to please. As a result, they are likely to accept your suggestions, 5-12. They also adjust easily to new adults, classmates, and situations. For these reasons, you will find that most adults enjoy working with these children.

Three-year-olds enjoy playing. They still like playing alone, but they also enjoy playing in groups of two or three. You can introduce themes to their play. Some themes include treating and

healing others. One child will help another who is injured or ill.

The objects that you supply in the classroom will influence a three-year-old's dramatic play. Cooking supplies, tools, phones, and suitcases are popular. These children enjoy pretending to be cooking, making repairs, calling others, and taking trips.

Three-year-old children are becoming increasingly independent. They feel a need to do things for themselves. Signs of independence include such statements as "I can do it" or "Let me do it." These statements are healthy signs that the children are gaining confidence in their abilities.

Some three-year-olds need encouragement to become more independent. They may make such statements as "You do it" or "I can't." When these words are spoken, you need to provide encouragement. These children need to know that you value their independence. They need to feel that they can do things for themselves.

5-12 By the third year, children are more willing to accept and try suggestions from teachers.

## Summary

Two-year-olds grow and change in many ways. Their motor skills improve so that they can run, jump, and balance. They also can scribble, drink, and undress. These children are learning to control their elimination.

Two-year-olds are able to understand and say many words. They can answer simple questions and follow simple directions. They are beginning to learn basic math concepts related to size, number, shape, and color.

Socially and emotionally, these children are striving to be independent. They want to do things their own way, and when they can't, they may have temper tantrums. These children still need affection and attention from adults.

Three-year-olds grow out of many of the problems of two-year-olds. They have better muscle control and coordination. These children can draw, cut with scissors, and work simple puzzles. They can dress themselves without much help from adults.

The thinking abilities of three-year-olds is improving. These children have a growing understanding and use of language. They have a better understanding of questions and instructions. They are using more complex sentences to communicate. They are beginning to learn grammar rules for past tense. These children are also developing more refined concepts of number and size.

Socially, three-year-olds are beginning to reach out. They seek and favor adults, and they are starting to make friends with other children. These children have strong emotions, but they are learning appropriate ways to express these emotions.

## Review and Reflect

1. List three motor skills of two-year-olds.

2. True or false. Most two-year-olds can dress themselves without help from adults.

3. Language comprehension is _____ advanced than expressive language in two-year-olds.

4. Compare the language strategies of expansion and feeding-in.

5. Which sentence is typical of a two-year-old?
   A. "Mommy."
   B. "Mommy go."
   C. "Mommy go and I go too."
   D. "Is Mommy going?"

6. How do most two-year-olds express their anger?

7. When working with two-year-olds, why do you need to allow plenty of time for transitions between activities?

8. True or false. Three-year-olds can climb and descend stairs easily.

9. Describe two self-help skills of three-year-olds.

10. Most three-year-old children can count to _____ while pointing to corresponding objects.

11. Why are three-year-olds less likely to become angry than two-year-olds?

## Apply and Explore

1. Visit a child care center and observe the motor skills of two- and three-year-olds. Write a report comparing the motor skills of the two age groups based on your observations.

2. Design a toy, activity, or teaching aid to help improve the self-help skills of a two- or three-year-old.

3. Interview a child care teacher about the differences in expression of emotions between two-year-olds and three-year-olds.

4. Visit a children's library and find books designed to help young children express their feelings in positive ways. Write a report on one of these books.

5. Visit the Web site for the National Network **C** for Child Care (nncc.org) to review the development of two- and three-year-olds.

6. Review the developmental milestones for **C** preschool children at the Web site for Early Childhood Development (ecdgroup.com).

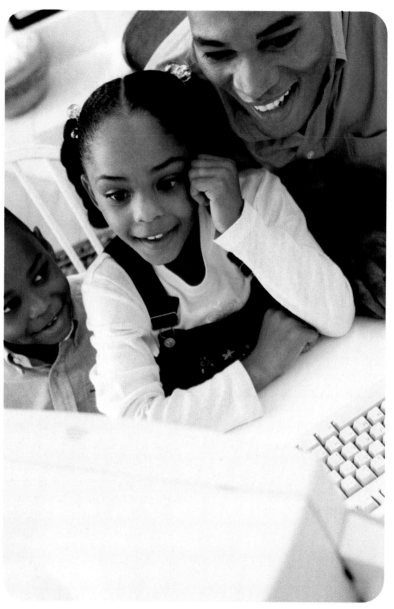

Four- and five-year-olds enjoy new experiences and challenges.

# Chapter 6

# Understanding Four- and Five-Year-Olds

After studying this chapter, you will be able to

- describe the physical, cognitive, and social-emotional development of four- and five-year-olds.

- explain how you as a teacher can plan programs and relate to four- and five-year-olds in developmentally appropriate ways.

## Terms to Know

articulation

stuttering

rote counting

Your days with four- and five-year-olds will be filled with fun and challenges. Preschoolers (as four- and five-year-olds are referred to in this chapter) are capable of handling many basic self-help skills. However, to keep growing and learning, they need new experiences and challenges. Preschoolers have many questions about the world around them. Helping them answer these questions can be a rewarding part of teaching.

## Physical Development of Four- and Five-Year-Olds

Increased body strength and coordination makes movement great fun for preschoolers, 6-1. Physical skills become easier partly because body proportions are changing. Compared to their total height, toddlers have fairly short legs. But by five and one-half years, most children's legs are about half the length of the body. Their proportions are more similar to adult proportions. This makes running, jumping, and balancing easier for preschoolers.

Preschool children are growing in more than just size. Their bones are becoming harder and stronger. Their permanent teeth are forming beneath their gums. Some children in this age group may begin losing their baby teeth. These children need good nutrition to assure that their bones and permanent teeth form properly. Their diets should include foods that are good sources of calcium and vitamin D, such as milk and other dairy products.

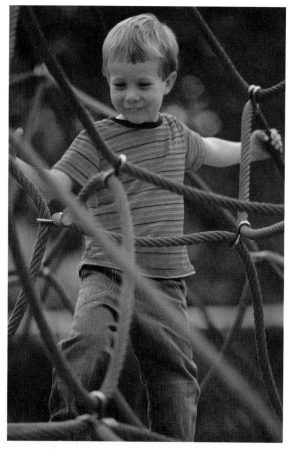

6-1 Preschoolers enjoy such gross motor activities as climbing.

## Gross Motor Development

Four- and five-year olds are using previously acquired skills to perform more complex movements. They improve their skills as their bodies becomes stronger and larger. At four years of age, children can hop on one foot. They also can walk down stairs with alternating feet. Four-year-olds can balance on one foot for about 10 seconds. They can walk backwards, toe-to-heel, for four consecutive steps.

Late in the fourth year, many children may begin learning how to skip. Most five-year-olds have developed this skill. Older four-year-olds may also be riding a bike with training wheels. If they have the opportunity, most children have developed this skill by five years of age. Five-year-olds also can walk forward and backward on a balance beam. See 6-2. They can climb fences and march to music. They also can jump from table height and land on both feet.

Throwing and catching skills also improve during these years. Most four- and five-year-olds are capable of throwing overhand. As they grow, they are becoming better at using their bodies to direct a ball as they throw. When throwing, they rotate their bodies and shift their weight from the back foot to the front foot, using both hands and visually tracking the ball. These children are also able to catch a ball. A five-year-old is able to keep the hands close to the body until just before catching the ball. As the child's brain matures, there is better coordination of motor and visual systems.

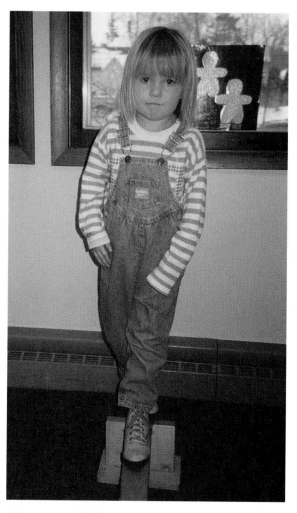

6-2 Improved balance allows this five-year-old to walk forward and backward on a balance beam.

Children this age enjoy working to improve their physical skills. They try to use their skills to the fullest. Sometimes, they may even become reckless. For instance, they may try to ride scooters as fast as they can.

## Fine Motor Development

Children's fine motor skills improve rapidly during the preschool years. They find it easier to string beads and work with small game or puzzle pieces. See 6-3. When they build towers from blocks, the towers are straight and tall. By four years, most children can complete a 12- to 18-piece puzzles. By five years, children can put together puzzles with 18 to 35 pieces. Five-year-olds are also becoming skilled at working clay. They may sculpt simple forms and figures.

Writing and drawing skills also improve quickly. By four years of age, children's drawing forms are more refined. As a result, you will have an easier time recognizing what they are drawing.

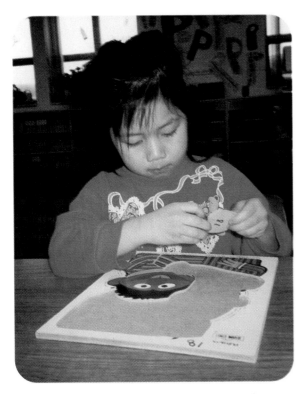

6-3 Four-year-olds have an easier time working puzzle pieces than younger children do.

Preschoolers are beginning to recognize letters. They can tell writing from nonwriting. They can also copy a square and print a few letters. Often the letters are printed improperly, though. Letters that are mirror images are especially difficult for preschoolers. For instance, the child may print *b* for *d* or even for *p*. The child may place five or six horizontal lines on an E.

Five-year-olds show marked improvement in controlling a writing tool. They delight in copying triangles and tracing diamond shapes. They are also fairly skilled at staying within the lines when they color. Most five-year-olds enjoy printing their first names. Preschoolers are capable of copying most letters and printing some simple words, but they may still be having problems printing some letters properly. They are beginning to understand that letters and sounds are linked.

## Self-Help Skills

Preschoolers become more and more self-sufficient. They are dressing and undressing themselves with very little help. Most of these children are capable of telling the front from the back of clothing. However, you may need to give them reminders from time to time. By four years of age, most children can buckle belts and close zippers. By five years, many children can even button and unbutton fasteners on the backs of garments. They also can put shoes on the correct feet. Some five-year-olds can even tie their own shoelaces.

Self-feeding is easier for preschoolers, too. They enjoy helping with serving. They can use spoons and forks with ease. By four years of age, children are using their forks to cut some large pieces of food. They may even try cutting foods with a knife. Most five-year-olds are able to cut fairly soft foods with knives. Preschoolers are also able to clean up their places after they finish eating.

Preschoolers are also better able to take care of their own hygiene. They become more skilled at handling a toothbrush and brushing their teeth. They also can use a washcloth for wiping their hands and faces. Preschoolers become more skilled at brushing and combing their hair, too.

# Cognitive Development of Preschoolers

Children in this age group make many gains in understanding the world around them. They become more skilled in thinking without having to act things out. As a result, they have a better understanding of symbols than younger children. Four- and five-year-olds also have increased language comprehension and expressive language skills. Language is a tool that can help children solve problems mentally.

Four- and five-year-olds now have the language skills to describe what they see and remember. You can test a child's recognition and recall skills. Show the child ten small, familiar toys. Then place the toys in a bag or box. Ask the child what items are in the bag. To recall the items requires the child to create a mental image. Although the child can recognize all ten items, she or he probably will only recall four or five. Children have better recognition than recall skills.

Children start creating their own symbols at this age, 6-4. This is reflected in their play.

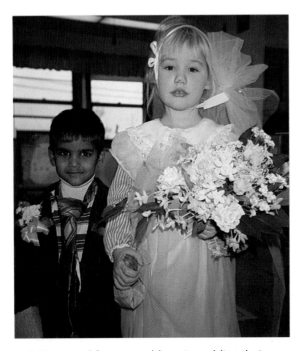

6-4 Four- and five-year-olds enjoy adding their own ideas during cooperative play.

Instead of just imitating the actions of adults, preschoolers add their own ideas. For instance, instead of using a bowl for mixing, they may pretend the bowl is a hat. New symbols also appear in art. Before the fourth year, children tend to scribble or just draw simple shapes. Now children make drawings that represent real objects. These drawings are simple and do not always look like what the child really sees. For instance, a hand may have six or even ten fingers. Four-year-olds often make drawings and then name them. By five years, children decide what they want to draw and then draw it.

Understanding symbols is important for developing more advanced cognitive skills. Symbols are a part of learning in language, math, science, social science, and many other areas of education. Therefore, cognitive development during the preschool years helps prepare children for future learning during the school years.

Preschoolers are eager to learn about why things happen around them. They may ask "Why do dogs bark?" or "Why do boats float?" With their endless string of questions, they are trying to make sense of their world. They still have flaws in their thinking, as three-year-olds do. Through asking questions again and again, their thinking becomes more and more logical.

Your curriculum should help promote the children's cognitive growth. As you provide new experiences, the children's vocabularies will grow. They will learn new concepts. For instance, you may show the children a live bunny. These children will explore concepts about the bunny, such as size, color, and method of eating. Children may also learn new vocabulary words as you show the animal. For instance, you might explain that the bunny is "timid." Each new experience helps the children grow intellectually, 6-5.

## Language Comprehension Skills

The language comprehension skills of four- and five-year-olds are constantly growing. New words related to space concepts increase their understanding. These include such words as *beside, bottom, backward*, and *forward*. They also understand such words as *down, low, different*, and *thin*. By the fifth year, the words *behind, ahead of, first*, and *last* are added to

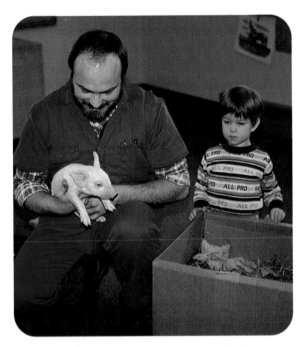

6-5 A visit from a resource person can help children's intellectual growth in many ways.

children's understanding. As you instruct children using these words, children will be able to understand and follow directions. For instance, you may tell a child "Place the green block *behind* the blue block."

Children this age become even better at following three-step commands. These children will be able to follow the directions in the order that they are given. For instance, you may tell a child "Pick up the puzzle, put it on the table, and wash your hands." However, if you do not sequence the directions correctly, the child can become confused.

Children have a better understanding of the difference between plural and singular nouns at this age. For instance, you may tell a child to take a sandwich at lunch time. The child understands that he or she is to take only one sandwich. If you tell the child to take cookies, the child knows that he or she can have more than one.

Children start understanding the passive voice at this time. In a *passive voice* sentence, the object of the sentence is placed before the subject. An example of a passive voice sentence would be "The orange was eaten by Brock." Three-year-olds do not usually understand this

word order. They think the sentence means that the orange ate Brock. Four- and five-year-olds understand that Brock ate the orange.

Because many words and phrases have more than one meaning, preschoolers may become confused about some statements. They tend to take literally such comments as "Wanda just flew out the door." See 6-6. You need to be careful about the phrases that you use around these children. For instance, a phrase such as "I'm dying of hunger" may frighten children.

## Reading

Most four- and five-year-olds cannot read, but they are developing abilities that lead to reading skills. These abilities are made possible as children begin to understand symbolism. Before children learn to read, they need to understand that a group of letters on paper can symbolize any object, from a ball to an airplane.

Four- and five-year-olds can recognize and name many letters of the alphabet. They also can recognize their own names. Children in this age group enjoy having stories read to them over and over again. As you reread stories, these children may be able to pick out and say words that they

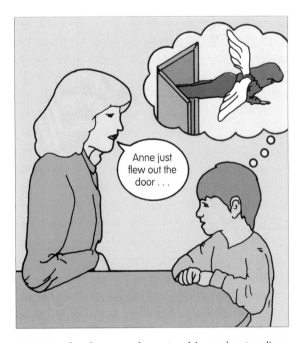

Anne just flew out the door . . .

6-6 Preschoolers may have trouble understanding figurative speech.

recognize. The children will also try to guess words they do not recognize. They tend to look at the first letter of a word and name any word that begins with that letter. For instance, they may point to the word *ball* and say *baby*.

## Expressive Language Skills

Preschoolers become quite talkative. As their vocabularies and grammar skills improve, they enjoy talking to others. See 6-7. At this age, children tend to talk to you rather than converse with you. When you talk about one subject, a child may interrupt to tell you about something entirely unrelated. The child may even make two or three unrelated comments to you in the same conversation. The children can answer your questions. In later years, these children will become better at true two-way communication.

### Articulation

**Articulation** is the ability to speak in clearly pronounced sounds. Articulation improves in many ways at four and five. These preschoolers

6-7 Four- year-olds like to talk with you about anything that interests them.

can make most of the sounds needed to form words. Many children still have trouble making the *ch* sound and the *th* sound in words. Others may have trouble with the *S* sound, causing a lisp.

Some preschoolers also have stuttering problems. **Stuttering** includes repeating sounds or words and pausing for unusually long times while speaking. For most preschoolers, stuttering is a result of thinking faster than they can talk. As children's speech ability catches up to their thinking ability, the stuttering problem tends to disappear.

### Vocabulary

Vocabulary grows quickly over these two years. Most four-year-olds have about 1500 words in their vocabularies. Five-year-olds have about 2000. Children do not always have clear ideas of the meanings of all the words they use. They may make up their own meanings to some words.

Preschoolers have mainly concrete nouns and action verbs in their vocabularies. They are beginning to add some modifiers and adjectives. However, words related to ideas or thoughts are still not a big part of their vocabularies. For instance, children this age would be unlikely to use the words *freedom* or *unfair*, unless they were simply imitating the words of adults.

Children this age do imitate phrases that they hear from adults or television. See 6-8. After a meal, a child may say "That was simply delectable!" This child is most likely imitating a statement heard at home or on television. If you ask, the child could not tell you what delectable means. Children might also use such words as *bionic, biodegradable*, and *computer chip*.

### Grammar

Children's grammar improves during these years. Children start to learn that there are exceptions to rules for past tense. They use such irregular verbs as *ate, ran*, and *went* properly. These children still put *ed* at the end of these words occasionally.

Children also learn how to properly form questions. The three-year-old would say "Why the sky is blue?" Four- and five-year-olds know to say "Why is the sky blue?"

Some grammar rules still give four- and five-year-olds problems. They especially have

6-8 Children may imitate a phrase from television such as "My teeth feel minty fresh and tingly." These children do not always understand the meaning of the phrase.

trouble using the proper forms of pronouns in sentences. For instance, a child may say "Him and me are going to the zoo." They also have trouble with noun and verb agreement. For instance, a child may say "Tommy don't have a crayon."

## Math Skills

Number concepts become easier for children in this age group. Rote counting skills increase quickly. **Rote counting** is reciting numbers in their proper order. This skill is gained by most children before they fully understand that each number represents a certain amount. At four

years of age, most children can rote count from one to nine. By the end of the fifth year, most children can rote count to 20. Rote counting skills develop at different rates for children in this age group. Therefore, you need to observe these children to make sure your curriculum fits their skill levels.

True counting, in which an object is counted for each number named, develops more slowly. For instance, a child may try to count ten objects. The child may touch one object and say "one," another and say "two," and another saying "three." However, the child may then point to another object three times in a row, saying "four, five, six." Children in this age group may be able to count three or four objects. However, they have trouble counting more objects.

Children start to recognize numerals in this stage. A four-year-old usually recognizes the numerals 1, 2, 3, 4, and 5. Five-year-olds learn to recognize 6, 7, 8, 9, and 10 as well. By five years of age, many children can dial their own telephone numbers.

Other math skills develop at this age. Children become better at recognizing shapes. About 80 percent of five-year-olds can recognize the square and rectangle shapes. Four- and five-year-olds also understand more terms related to size and number. These include *short, fat, tallest, same size, first,* and *last.*

Children start to understand money concepts in this stage. Most preschoolers can identify a penny, a nickel, and a dime. These children do not yet understand the true value of money, though. If you ask a child this age whether a nickel or a dime is worth more, the child is likely to choose the nickel. Since it is bigger, children think that it is worth more. They do not yet realize that a nickel is worth five pennies and a dime is worth ten.

Time concepts become more clear at this age. The children start to understand the difference between today, tomorrow, and yesterday. However, many time concepts are still confusing for these children. They don't really understand how long an hour or a minute takes. They also get confused because time is described in so many ways. An adult may tell a child that puppet time is at 3:30, at half past three, this afternoon, or in a few hours.

# Social-Emotional Development of Preschoolers

Preschoolers continue to be helpful and cooperative, 6-9. With improved language skills, children become more involved with each other. Friendships become more important. They know that a friend is a person who "likes you." Emotions are changing in these children. As they learn and grow, the causes of happiness, fear, anger, and sadness change. The ways children react to these emotions change, too.

## Social Development

Companionship is important to preschoolers. Friendships, attention, and approval are important as well. However, they are also becoming more independent of adults. They like to play on their own or with other children. They may not always want you or other adults to participate in play. They may still need your help to get materials or settle disputes.

Children this age start to value their friendships with others. They tend to have only a few friends. They also prefer friends of the same sex. Children in this age group become more willing to cooperate as they play with others. They are more likely than younger children to offer a favorite toy to a friend. Many children in this age group choose best friends. They tend to change best friends fairly often, though.

For four-year-olds, over one-third of a child's play is solitary play. However, by age five, play involves more and more interaction and cooperation. Play groups are still small—only two or three children, but children talk to each other more and do more as a group, 6-10.

Children this age accept supervision. They know their own abilities, and they realize that adults have reasons for rules. These children will accept your instructions, and they will ask your permission before doing certain activities.

6-10 Play becomes more cooperative for four- and five-year-olds.

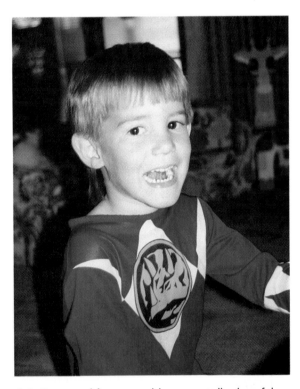

6-9 Four- and five-year-olds are usually cheerful and cooperative.

## Emotional Development

Four- and five-year-olds begin to realize new ways of showing love and caring. They still understand hugs and other physical signs of affection. They may hug another child who is sad. However, they are starting to realize that helping others is a way of showing love. These children may show love for others by sharing something or helping with a task. They may also seek this sign of love from others. For example, children may ask for help with a task even if they don't need it. These children are looking for assurance that you care.

Children in this age group start to develop a sense of humor. See 6-11. Laughter becomes a way of expressing their happiness. These children do not yet understand most verbal jokes, but they laugh at funny faces or actions. They also laugh at things that they know are unusual. For instance, they may laugh at a dog that says "meow" in a story. These children also need good role models to learn that harm done to others is not funny.

6-11  Children this age enjoy humor.

### Fear

Fears are still common, but most only last a few months. Causes of fears change during this stage. These children are still afraid of imagined creatures, such as monsters and ghosts. They may be especially fearful of dreams, because they seem so real. However, they also start to realize that there is a difference between the real and the imagined. This helps children deal with some of these fears. For this reason, you may hear preschoolers state firmly "There's no such thing as dragons." They may ask you repeatedly "Was the story just pretend?"

Other fears may be created by the new knowledge of preschoolers. They are aware of more dangers. However, they do not know enough to fully understand what is and is not dangerous. Their imaginations are vivid. For instance, a child may learn that sharks live in the ocean. This may cause fear of being hurt in the ocean. The child may also become afraid of sharks in rivers, pools, and even bathtubs.

Five-year-olds are also more afraid of being hurt than are younger children. They know of more things that can hurt them. They may be afraid of doctors and dentists. This is because they are aware of pain or injuries associated with these professionals. They may also be afraid of high places and dogs because of prior experiences.

These children sometimes work through fears in play. For instance, a child who is afraid of dogs may pretend to be a fierce dog. A child who is afraid of heights may pretend to be a bird. For these children, play is therapeutic. It helps them act out some of their intense feelings and deal with their fears.

### Anger

Like three-year-olds, children in this age group do not have as many causes for anger as toddlers do. However, they can become angry if they are unable to reach their goals. Four- and five-year-old children are more likely to use words and yelling rather than hitting or kicking to express anger. If they do express anger physically, they are more likely to take out their anger on objects or other children. They do not usually respond to adults physically because they know this action is not accepted.

Some preschoolers respond more physically to anger than others. They may become angry more easily than others also. They may use pushing, hitting, or kicking to show anger. They may not have learned better ways of expressing anger from adult role models or they may want attention.

### Jealousy

Jealousy may be a problem for some children in this age group. These children are most likely to become jealous of a new brother or sister. They may resent the fact that their parents are spending so much time with a new child. They may fear that their parents do not love them as much.

Jealousy may surface in children in many ways, 6-12. The child may regress to earlier behaviors, such as crying or having toileting accidents. The child may also develop physical problems such as stomachaches or nightmares.

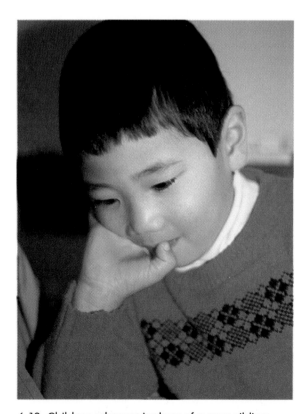

6-12 Children who are jealous of a new sibling may become withdrawn or show regressive behaviors at the center.

These children need to be reassured that they are still loved. Sometimes, they may need a little extra attention away from home to make them feel special. Showing these children that their sibling needs help from a "big sister" or "big brother" can make them feel better, too.

### Sadness

Four- and five-year-olds start to learn that some situations are sad. They become aware of the concept of death. Their first experiences with death may be the loss of a pet. Preschool children do not understand that death cannot be reversed. As a result, it may take children a while to realize that the pet will not come back to life. However, once they understand this, they often become sad.

Children are not always sure how to express sadness. Children may deal with sadness in play. They may pretend to be the lost pet or to talk to the lost pet. Frequently, they need help from adults to learn that it is okay to cry and to talk about their feelings. They also need adults to model appropriate responses to sadness and to provide clear explanations.

Some children must also deal with the death of a close family member. These children need to have as much explained about the situation as they can understand. They also need help from adults in dealing with the loss and sadness.

## Teaching Four- and Five-Year-Olds

Like three-year-olds, four- and five-year-olds tend to be cooperative and helpful. These children are eager to please you, 6-13. If you ask a child to help you, the child feels complimented. These children enjoy feeling needed and important. They may even ask "Can I help you?"

Because these children like to help, you need to carefully select helpers. Choosing the same few helpers time after time can make others feel unimportant. Even children who do not volunteer need to be asked from time to time. These children may be too shy to ask, or they may not feel confident in their abilities to help. By choosing them, you can help build their self-esteem.

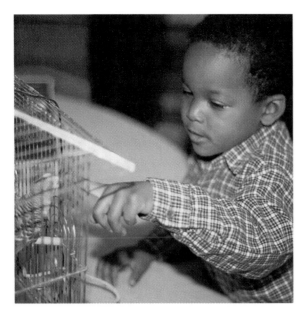

6-13 Preschoolers are eager to help you in such ways as caring for pets.

By this age, children become quite talkative. They still enjoy physical play, but they like to spend more time talking. You will enjoy carrying on conversations with these children. These conversations may become a part of learning activities or story time. After you read a story, these children may enjoy retelling the story. They are usually capable of retelling the story in detail and in the proper sequence.

You will notice that children in this age group will imitate your speech. You may hear one child tell another "Christopher, we walk, we don't run, when we are in the hallway." For this reason, you need to be careful of your statements. You should never use words or statements that you would not want the children repeating.

Children are now more content playing with each other. You do not need to function as a playmate as much. However, you will need to handle more disputes among children. These children may have conflicts over group rules. They will look to you for advice on settling these problems. You may also want to add new ideas to play. Preschoolers enjoy playing some simple, organized games that you may lead.

Some children may have imaginary playmates. A child may come to school explaining that Ralph, his playmate, asked to come with him. He may provide space for Ralph on his cot at nap time. He may have conversations with Ralph throughout the day. This kind of play does not necessarily indicate problems. It is simply a way of using the imagination and having fun.

Children in this age group are often proud of their possessions and family members, 6-14. They may like to bring favorite toys to the center. They may also call attention to new shoes or a new jacket. They may beam with pride when their parents visit the center. Children enjoy talking with you and others about their belongings. Asking children questions about something of theirs can help build their self-esteem.

Children in this age group also enjoy working on projects. Their attention spans and goal-setting abilities are improving. Children's ideas for projects may come from play with peers or from adult activities. Such projects as woodworking, cooking, and sculpting clay may be fun for these children. As they get older, they will engage for longer periods of time in these activities. The average time spent in most activities at this age is about seven minutes.

6-14 Preschoolers are proud to have their siblings visit the center.

# Summary

The growth of four- and five-year-olds helps them become more independent. These preschoolers become stronger and more coordinated. Their changing body proportions help them improve their balance and motor skills. These children also have improved dressing, eating, and hygiene skills.

Four- and five-year-olds' thoughts become more and more adultlike. These children begin to understand and use symbols in play, drawing, and learning. Language skills improve quickly. These children understand and use more words. Their grammar improves also. Much new knowledge helps prepare children for later math learning. These include rote counting and understanding of size and number concepts.

Children become more social with their peers at this age. Their play becomes more cooperative. Children still seek favor and approval from adults. They like to help and talk to adults. Children are learning acceptable ways of expressing their feelings. They are also experiencing feelings for different reasons.

As a teacher, you will enjoy working with four- and five-year-olds. These children can be independent in terms of self-care. They are eager and able to help you, and they enjoy talking with you and learning about new ideas.

## Review and Reflect

1. Why is it important to include foods high in calcium and vitamin D in the diets of four- and five-year-olds?

2. True or false. Four- and five-year-olds stand perfectly still when they throw a ball.

3. Describe the writing skills of four- and five-year-olds.

4. Which of the following dressing skills do most five-year-olds have?

   A. They know the front from the back of garments.
   B. They can buckle belts.
   C. They can put shoes on the right feet.
   D. All of the above.

5. At what age do children make drawings and then decide what they are?

6. Describe the reading abilities of four- and five-year-olds.

7. True or false. A four-year-old who uses the word "imitation" probably does *not* know what the word means.

8. Why are time concepts confusing for four- and five-year-olds?

9. True or false. Five-year-olds prefer friends of the opposite sex.

10. Describe a situation that is likely to cause fear in a five-year-old. Explain why this situation would cause fear.

11. Typically, what is the teacher's role in the play of four- and five-year-olds?

## Apply and Explore

1. Play catch with a four- or five-year-old. Make sketches or written descriptions of the movements used by the child to catch and to throw. Report your findings to the class.

2. Interview an early childhood teacher about the artwork of four- and five-year-olds. Ask to see samples that show the types of symbolism these children use.

3. Make a bulletin board based on phrases that might be misinterpreted by four- and five-year-olds. The bulletin board could contain drawings of preschoolers' interpretations of the phrases.

4. Write a research report on recommended ways of helping four- and five-year-olds deal with death.

5. Visit the Web site for the National Network [C] for Child Care (nncc.org) to review the development of four- and five-year-olds.

6. Review the developmental milestones for [C] preschool children at the Web site for Early Childhood Development (ecdgroup.com).

# Chapter 7

# Middle Childhood

After studying this chapter, you will be able to

- describe the physical, cognitive, and social-emotional development of school-age children.

- summarize potential health concerns of middle childhood.

- explain moral development during childhood.

## Terms to Know

middle childhood
farsighted
nearsighted
obesity
rehearsal
operation
concrete operations
conservation
seriation

classification
social comparison
self-esteem
empathy
compassion
moral development
morality

**Middle childhood** refers to the span of years between ages 6 and 12. Since this time period begins with the onset of formal schooling, it is often referred to as the *school-age years*.

During middle childhood, children become more self-sufficient and independent. They are interested and involved in many new activities. Peers and teachers play an increasingly important role in their lives. Their circle of friends and acquaintances expands far beyond their own family members. These friendships and school-related activities are taking more and more of their time. As a result, they are learning to adopt new social rules and expectations.

Though developmental changes continue to occur throughout middle childhood, the changes are not as dramatic as they were during infancy and toddlerhood. During the school-age years, the brain undergoes changes that allow more highly developed thinking skills. As a result, the children are becoming better problem solvers. They are also growing in self-knowledge and understanding.

School-age children are beginning the process of entering the adult world and are attending more to their own needs. They are becoming better able to get themselves up in the morning, bathe, dress, and eat without adult assistance. Most families expect more of their school-age children because of their improved skills. Often they assist with cooking, dishwashing, and laundry chores. They are also capable of helping with younger siblings.

# Physical Development

Physical development during middle childhood is not as rapid as during the first years of life. Between the ages of 6 and 12, children experience steady physical growth, 7-1. There are gradual and consistent increases in weight and height. Heredity and environment account for most differences in physical growth. Health care and nutrition are environmental factors that can affect both weight and height.

During this period, children are interested in their physical growth. They care more about what other people think of them. Thus, their body size, shape, and physical abilities can influence how they feel about themselves.

At the beginning of this stage, children have much better control of their large muscles than their small muscles. During the six-year span, children show continued improvement in skills learned earlier. They show gains in motor skills,

7-1 Children do not grow as rapidly during middle childhood as they do in the first years of life.

agility, and physical strength. These skills are helpful for participation in games and sports.

## Height

Boys are usually slightly taller than girls at the beginning of this stage. Until age nine, boys retain this edge. Then the reverse occurs as girls begin to grow more rapidly. At 10 years of age, most girls experience a growth spurt. This growth spurt occurs two years later in boys. At ages 11 and 12, most girls have surpassed boys in height. This difference can be a source of embarrassment for some children.

The typical six-year-old is almost four feet tall. During middle childhood, children usually grow about two to three inches per year. By the age of 12, the average child is about five feet tall. By the end of middle childhood, girls may reach 90 percent of their adult height. At the same time, boys may be about 80 percent of their adult height.

Body proportions change during the school-age years. The upper part of the head grew fast during the first six years of life. Now the arms and legs grow more quickly. Children look less top-heavy now than during the earlier years.

## Weight

At age six, the average child weighs about 47 pounds. By age 12, this weight may double. Children gain about five to seven pounds per year during middle childhood.

There are weight differences between girls and boys. From birth through the preschool years, girls usually weigh slightly less than boys. Girls catch up with boys in weight by age 11. By 12 years of age, girls usually weigh about three pounds more than boys.

## Gross Motor Skills

By watching school-age children on the playground, you can see how their motor skills are improving, 7-2. Physical growth contributes to these changes. Gains in height and weight help with coordination. These children possess greater speed and accuracy of movement, with faster reaction times. Movements are more refined and fluid. Moreover, balance has improved.

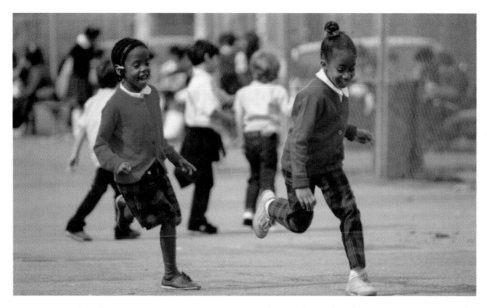

7-2  Motor development continues to improve during the school-age years.

Younger school-age children are constantly practicing and perfecting six skills. These are jumping, balancing, throwing, catching, running, and sequencing foot movements. Their running is faster. With practice, they are more accurate in throwing, catching, and kicking. They can throw balls greater distances.

As they grow older, both boys and girls improve their large motor skills. Even though girls usually surpass boys in height and weight, boys have more physical strength. They have an advantage in muscle mass. As a result, boys may outperform girls in jumping, catching, throwing, and batting. They can usually run faster and for greater distances.

Girls outperform boys in motor skills that require balance, coordination, flexibility, or rhythmic movement. Some examples include playing hopscotch, dancing, and skipping. Girls also have an edge in skills involving the use of the small muscles.

## Fine Motor Skills

Children show improvement of their fine motor skills throughout middle childhood. They have better control of the small muscles in their fingers and hands. Their writing is much better since they are using more wrist movement. Letters and words are more uniform and neater. Moreover, the spacing between letters and words has improved. The improvement of these fine motor skills is also reflected in their drawings, 7-3.

7-3  With better control of the small muscles and hands, children's artwork also improves.

Improved finger dexterity allows school-age children to play musical instruments, such as a piano, guitar, or flute. Their hand-eye coordination skills are also improving. While grasping tools, they can control the motion and speed. This allows them to learn such skills as sewing and assembling models with small pieces.

## Health Concerns

Middle childhood is often one of the healthiest periods for children. The lowest illness rates are for children between 5 and 12 years of age. Therefore, there are fewer sore throats, upper respiratory diseases, and middle ear infections than during the preschool years. One of the reasons for this reduction is the body's developing immune system, which offers protection against disease. School-age children, however, are not illness-free. Many school-age children still have several upper respiratory illnesses each year.

Several chronic illnesses may surface during middle childhood. Ulcers, asthma, and diabetes are examples. In addition, many school-age children develop headaches and acne as they approach adolescence. Some children may develop hearing and vision problems. Lack of exercise is another problem. Others exercise too much, placing their bodies under stress. For these children, overuse can cause sprains, tendinitis (inflammation of a tendon), and even broken bones. A variety of other health problems occur even though most children are at their healthiest.

### Hearing

Children's hearing is usually well developed by middle childhood. Awareness of midrange sounds develops first, followed by high-range and low-range awareness. By 11 years of age, most children have the auditory awareness of adults.

Ear infections can be a health problem. If left untreated, they can cause permanent hearing loss. For most children, the number of ear infections decreases due to structural changes within the body. The eustachian tube, which connects the middle ear to the throat, has changed position. This change helps prevent bacteria and fluids from moving from the mouth to the ear.

### Vision

By age six, most children are ready to read. They can see an object with both eyes at the same time. Their ability to focus improves. Many preschool children are somewhat **farsighted**. This means they can see objects in the distance more clearly than those that are close. During the middle years, their close-up vision improves.

Throughout middle childhood, nearsightedness is the most common vision problem. Being **nearsighted** means being able to see close objects more clearly than those at a distance. The more time children are engaged in reading and close-up work, the greater their chances of becoming nearsighted. With corrective lenses, nearsightedness can be overcome, 7-4. It is estimated as many as 25 percent of children will need to have their vision corrected by the end of the school years. It is important that children's vision be checked regularly to detect any problems.

7-4 Corrective lenses can overcome most vision problems.

## Teeth

During middle childhood, children begin losing their primary or "baby" teeth. First and second graders often have toothless smiles! The first teeth to fall out are the central incisors, which are the lower and upper front teeth, 7-5. By the age of 12, all of the 20 primary teeth will be replaced with permanent teeth. At first, these permanent teeth appear to be out of proportion to the child's face. Gradually the facial bones grow, causing the face to lengthen and the mouth to widen. These changes accommodate the larger, permanent teeth.

Tooth loss can have a psychological effect on some children. They become self-conscious. Calling attention to the change in their appearance may cause them to be uncomfortable.

A common health problem for school-age children is tooth decay. Children with poor dental hygiene habits are most susceptible to cavities. Also at risk are children who are in poor health and who have diets high in sugar.

As a teacher, you should promote good dental health. Begin by modeling proper care of your own teeth. Brush your teeth with the children after each meal. Eat a well-balanced diet, and avoid foods high in sugar. Encourage parents to have their children receive regular dental checkups.

## Obesity

Obesity is becoming a common problem among school-age children. **Obesity** is characterized by excessive bodily fat. A person is considered obese if he or she weighs 20 percent more than other people of the same sex, age, and build. Obesity affects about 25 percent of school-age children.

Being obese can seriously impact a child's emotional health. Obese children are often teased and ridiculed by their peers. They may have fewer friends, and they are often the last to be selected for group projects and teams. As a result, overweight children may lack self-esteem.

Several factors contribute to obesity in children. Some obese children have overweight parents. For them, the tendency to be overweight may be inherited. For other children, environment can be a contributing factor. If the parents

7-5 As you can tell by the missing teeth, two of these three brothers have entered middle childhood.

and other family members overeat, the children will likely do the same. Still other children overeat due to family stress. Children's eating habits can be affected by abuse, the death of a family member, alcoholism, or divorce. Any of these traumatic events can trigger overeating.

Many children are obese as a result of physical inactivity. They may also watch more television than other children. Studies show that those children who spend more time watching television and playing video games get less physical activity. As a result, they are more likely to be overweight.

Research shows that overweight children often are overweight as adults. Adults who are obese may develop high blood pressure, heart disease, or diabetes. Treating childhood obesity, however, is difficult. Obesity is often a family disorder. Behaviors need to be changed that involve both the child and the parents. Obese children need help in making healthier food choices. They need to learn which foods are lower in fat and calories. They need to be shown how to control the portions they eat. They should be encouraged to exercise more. These children may also need help in overcoming emotional problems.

## Cognitive Development

During middle childhood, children begin to think mentally using logic and symbols. They no longer rely only on what they can see or perceive. They begin to use logical thinking instead of only perception. In addition, their memory improves and their attention span is longer. They can process and recall information more readily. These improved thinking skills allow them to engage in academic tasks. Their reading, writing, science, and math skills develop continually throughout the school-age years, 7-6.

The desire to achieve is an important influence on cognitive development during middle childhood. Achievement is often related to motivation. Some children have an internal desire to work hard and achieve. Others are motivated by the prospect of rewards or recognition. Whether the desire to succeed comes from within the child or externally, the motivation to do well influences performance.

### Attention and Memory

Critical to cognitive development is attention and memory. Memory becomes more controlled

7-6 Children learn to read during middle childhood.

than during early childhood. The child's age, motivation, health, and attitude determine the effectiveness of memory. Attention also improves. Children now have the ability to ignore unnecessary information. They are able to focus their attention on the important aspects of a task. They can scan detailed tasks and decide what must be done first. These changes allow thinking skills to become more refined. School-age children are better at processing information. As a result, they are better problem solvers.

To remember information, school-age children often use a technique called rehearsal. **Rehearsal** involves the repetition of information after it is used. The following example will illustrate rehearsal. Bobby is a typical six-year-old. He is able to tell you his address and telephone number. In addition, he knows his grandmother's telephone number and those of several of his friends. His neighbor, Alice, cannot understand how Bobby can remember all of this information at his age.

Bobby uses rehearsal. Bobby usually writes the phone numbers down. While recording the numbers, you can see his lips moving. Then he repeats the numbers many times. His memory is improved by this type of organization and process.

## Mental Operations

There are changes in reasoning and thinking during middle childhood. Gradually, school-age children change the way they process information. During the preschool years, children relied totally on what they saw or perceived. Sometimes their perceptions were flawed. Now their perceptions are more accurate because they begin to use logical thinking. An **operation** is defined as the manipulation of ideas based on logic rather than perception. Between seven and eight years of age, children enter the stage of **concrete operations**. This means they use logic, but it is based on what they have experienced or seen.

Because they can now use logic in their mental operations, children learn several new concepts during the middle years. These include the concepts of conservation, seriation, and classification.

## Conservation

Children gradually acquire the concept of conservation. **Conservation** means that change in position or shape of substances does not change the quantity. If nothing is added or taken away, the amount stays the same. Such properties as weight, length, mass, and volume do not change. The appearance, however, may change. A child's understanding of the principle of conservation can be tested with liquids, a series of objects, and pliable substances.

To illustrate the conservation of liquids, show a child two identical glasses. Fill each glass with the same amount of liquid. Ask the child if the two glasses have the same amount of liquid, and the child will say that they do. Next, pour the liquid from one glass into a taller, thinner glass. Again ask the child if the two glasses have the same amount of liquid. Until about seven years of age, the child will probably say that the taller glass contains more liquid. Between seven and eight, when children enter the stage of concrete operations, they will say that the amount of liquid has not changed. Their logic has overruled their perception.

You can test a child's understanding of the conservation of length by using a series of identical objects, such as pennies. Place 10 pennies in two rows of 5 each. Place the rows side by side. Ask the child if the number of pennies in each row is the same. The child will agree that the two rows contain the same number of pennies. Next, spread the pennies apart in one of the rows. If the child is at the concrete level of operations, the child will say that the longer row still has the same number of pennies. If the child says that the one row has more pennies, the child is focusing only on the dimension of length. Rather than using logic, the child is relying only on perception.

A child's understanding of the concept of mass can also be tested. Show the child two balls of modeling dough that are the same size and shape. Ask the child if the two balls have the same amount of dough. The child will say yes. Then flatten one ball of modeling dough, and repeat your question. The child who understands conservation will note that the amount of dough is still the same.

Figure 7-7 shows several conservation tasks. It lists the questions to ask children to test their understanding of conservation. Those children who have not reached the stage of concrete operations will respond by saying no. If the children respond by saying yes, they have reached the concrete operations stage.

## Seriation

**Seriation** is the ability to arrange items in an increasing or decreasing order based on weight, volume, or size. Like conservation, seriation typically emerges between the ages of six and eight years of age. To illustrate, you may provide a child with a set of sticks of different lengths. Then ask the child to arrange the sticks from the shortest to the longest. Preschool children will lay the sticks haphazardly. Most school-age children will lay the sticks in an orderly fashion from shortest to longest as requested.

Seriation also can involve sequencing the events in a story. After hearing a story, the child should be able to recall the sequence of events. As a result, the child will be able to retell the story. Likewise, following a recipe involves seriation. After preparing a simple recipe, the child should be able to recall the preparation steps.

## Classification

Simple **classification** is the ability to group objects by common attributes, such as size, color, shape, pattern, or function. The typical preschooler can group objects by one attribute only. For instance, if given a group of different-colored shapes, the preschooler could sort by either color or shape. During the early school-age years, children can mentally handle two aspects of the problem, such as color and shape. For instance, they can sort blue squares into one pile and blue circles into another.

## Language

The ability to communicate improves gradually throughout middle childhood. Comparing language development to the preschool years, changes are more subtle. The child's vocabulary doubles between the ages of 6 and 12. As they learn to read, they learn many new words each day. Grammar skills improve. They learn sentence structure, using pronouns, plurals, and

| Conservation Task | | |
|---|---|---|
| **Present** | **Change** | **Ask** |
| liquid | | Is there still the same amount of water in each glass? |
| number | | Are there still the same amount of dimes? |
| substance | | Is there still the same amount of play dough? |

7-7 You can determine a child's understanding of conservation by asking these questions.

tense properly. Children during this stage are also moving from using only oral expression to using both oral and written expression.

One form of language play for school-age children is telling riddles and jokes. Cognitive development is linked to humor. Language skills can improve through the use of humor, 7-8.

# Social-Emotional Development

School-age children are growing in self-understanding. Their self-concept is forming, which affects their self-esteem. They are experiencing many new emotions, and becoming more aware of the feelings of others.

Social relationships become more complex during middle childhood. By choice, children in this stage are spending less time with their parents and more time with peers. Friendships are becoming more important. The family, however, still plays an important role in supporting the child's development.

## Self-Concept

As children enter school, they start to take a closer look at the world around them. They begin to make social comparisons. **Social comparison** is a process where people define themselves in terms of the qualities, skills, and attributes they see in others. Personal strengths and weaknesses are identified as a result of this comparison. A self-concept is formed. Self-concept is the view a person has of himself or herself. Though the child's self-concept has been forming since infancy, school-age children are more aware of who they are.

School-age children can describe their strengths and weaknesses in very concrete terms. To illustrate, Luis is seven years old. Recently, his teacher asked him to describe himself. He said, "My name is Luis. I am a boy, and I live in Breckenridge, Colorado. I have brown eyes, black hair, and am tall. My hobbies are biking and skiing. I am good at them. I am not as good using the computer. I swim at the recreation center with my friends. My friends like me. I try to be helpful to them. My teacher says that I am a good speller, so I help my friends with their spelling."

Luis's self-description refers to his sex, physical appearance, and some social comparisons. Luis, like other children his age, has extended the number of people he is looking to

7-8  School-age children begin to develop a sense of humor.

for information. During the preschool years, his references were primarily his family. Now his reference groups include classmates and teachers. The feedback he receives from these individuals influences his self-concept.

### Self-Esteem

**Self-esteem** is the belief that you are worthwhile as a person. While preschool children usually have very high levels of self-esteem, this sometimes changes in middle childhood. To have healthy self-esteem, school-age children need to believe in themselves. By continually evaluating themselves, some children lose their confidence. Subtle messages echoed by adults and peers can promote or undermine self-esteem. Figure 7-9 shows areas in which children evaluate themselves.

As a teacher, you can play an important role in promoting children's self-esteem. A warm, nurturing attitude is important. Avoid making comparisons among children. By avoiding comparisons, you will be helping children develop confidence in their own abilities. Children feel better about themselves.

Accomplishments need to be viewed in relation to a child's efforts and ability. In almost every classroom, at least one child has learned helplessness. These children think, no matter how hard they try, they cannot be successful. You will spot them immediately. When faced with new experiences or challenges, they give up quickly. Before they make an effort to try, they say "I don't know how" or "I can't do that."

Help children during middle childhood to avoid feelings of helplessness. Encourage them to persist at difficult tasks. Make them believe that with more effort they can overcome failure. Say "I know you can do this if you try harder." Likewise, celebrate when these children do succeed, even in small ways. Provide them with additional feedback on why they were successful.

## Understanding Others

With experience and maturity, school-age children make major advances in understanding others. They are developing **empathy**—the ability to understand the feelings of others. At the same time, they are feeling compassion towards others. **Compassion** is being aware of others' distress and wanting to help them, 7-10.

7-10 School-age children are becoming more aware of the feelings of others.

| Children's Judgments of Self-Worth Are Based Upon: |
| :---: |
| Academic Competence |
| Athletic Competence |
| Physical Appearance |
| Behavior |
| Social Acceptance |

7-9 School-age children judge themselves on these factors.

School-age children can describe another person's feelings and personality traits. Prior to this time, children used only physical descriptions of others. For example, when Ben was a preschooler, his grandmother asked him to describe his teacher. He said, "She has brown hair and brown eyes. She wears glasses and she is pretty." When Ben's grandmother asked him to describe his teacher as an eight-year-old, the description went beyond physical traits. He said, "He is really a happy person. He smiles a lot and says things like 'good job.' Sometimes he gets mad, like when Brian is being a jerk. Then he gets angry with him."

Ben has developed the ability to see another's viewpoint. His ability to imagine what his teacher was feeling or thinking is developing. This is an important developmental milestone. Getting along with others throughout life is dependent upon being able to understand another person's point of view. Studies show that children with poor social skills have trouble identifying other people's thoughts and feelings.

## Friendships

During the school-age years, friendships take on greater importance. During preschool, a friend was a convenient playmate who shared toys. Now, choosing friends becomes a more selective process. Gender often influences the selection of a friend. Most school-age children choose close friends of the same sex. Children with common interests usually become friends.

These friendships are important to children. A friend is a person who shares important thoughts and feelings. A friend offers companionship and emotional support. Emotional commitment is learned through these early friendships.

Some children seem to be particularly well liked by other children. These children are friendly to others. They also show sensitivity and have good communication skills. During middle childhood, peer acceptance can be influenced by appearance and behavior.

Other children are rejected and avoided by their peers. They are not included in after-school functions or invited to parties. They also tend to be ignored during recess and lunch. These children often lack self-control and act aggressively toward others. They may be disruptive or hostile.

Without friendships, the child does not receive the important benefits of interacting with peers. This can be traumatic for some children. Lack of self-esteem, the inability to develop social skills, and loneliness are a result. These children often lack confidence in their abilities. They need special help to recognize and overcome their behavior problems.

## Peer Group Activities

Peer group activities play an important role in the social development of school-age children. They may join 4-H clubs, religious groups, Girl Scouts, or Boy Scouts. In these groups, they learn how to cooperate with others to achieve goals, and they learn rules of group behavior.

### Gender Differences

Informal groups are often single-sex during the early school-age years. See 7-11. The girls cluster with other girls. The boys, too, prefer other boys. Mixed-sex groups may form for talking, eating, or working on projects in the classroom. Boys and girls may enjoy playing kick ball or other games together.

Teasing frequently occurs between boys and girls. Boys love to interrupt the girls' play. When this occurs, the girls respond by chasing them away or tattling to adults.

At school, gender often creates boundary differences in play areas and space. Boys tend to control large fixed spaces that are used for team sports. Studies show they control almost 10 times more space than girls. Space occupied by girls is usually located closer to the school building.

Activity preferences between girls and boys exist. While girls enjoy jumping rope, playing hopscotch, and doing tricks on the jungle gym, boys prefer competitive sports, such as basketball, football, and baseball.

Girls' play involves more taking turns and cooperating with others. Compared to boys, they are often interacting in pairs or small groups. Girls are not as open as boys. They have more select relationships in which they share secrets.

7-11  Friends tend to be of the same sex.

## Games with Rules

Can you remember your middle childhood years? Chances are you were enjoying organized games with rules. If you were like most children, during recess you were playing hide-and-seek, red rover, and blind man's bluff. You probably played tag, jump rope, and hopscotch. Basketball, soccer, and softball were played during physical education classes.

These games are important for children's development. They encourage children to take another person's perspective. From this, children learn why rules are important. Children often spend as much time working out the rules for a game as playing the game.

In recent decades, there has been a decrease in the amount of time children spend in child-organized games. More time is being devoted to television, computers, video games, and adult-organized sports. As a result, children are not as physically fit. In addition, they do not have as many opportunities to learn to follow rules.

## Team Sports

With improvement in their physical skills, both girls and boys enjoy participating in team sports. Soccer, football, softball, swimming, gymnastics, and basketball are common. The most popular team sport is baseball, 7-12.

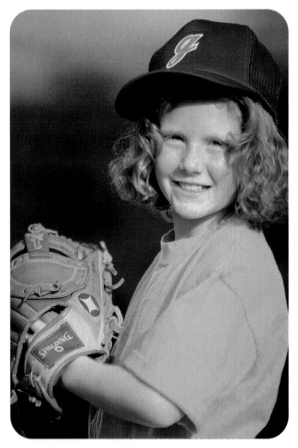

7-12  School-age children enjoy participating in team sports.

Through participation in team sports, children often develop lifelong habits that contribute to a healthy lifestyle.

By participating in competitive sports, children benefit in many ways. These include the following:

- They learn teamwork skills.
- They learn to get along with their peers.
- They benefit from the exercise.
- The activities bring enjoyment.
- A pattern for a healthy lifestyle begins to form.

There are also drawbacks to participating in team sports. There is no safe sport. School-age children can be injured. Bumps, bruises, and scrapes are common injuries. The most serious injuries are head and neck injuries, which usually result from playing football. To reduce injuries, children need to be instructed on the safe use of equipment. They also need to be taught the importance of conditioning activities, such as stretching and warm-up exercises.

Critics of adult-organized sports teams claim they resemble more work than play for children. As the focus is often on winning, children feel pressure from their peers, parents, and coaches to win at all costs. Since adults often control the game, children may not be developing decision-making and leadership skills.

## Moral Development

**Moral development** is the process of acquiring the standards of behavior considered acceptable by a society. **Morality** involves understanding and using accepted rules of conduct when interacting with others. Standards of behavior become internalized.

Children learn moral behavior by interacting with others, 7-13. Preschoolers begin to learn acceptable behavior through the use of rewards and punishment. Some behaviors bring rewards, such as praise or attention. They learn to repeat these behaviors. Other behaviors bring punishment. They have not yet internalized any standards of behavior, but they learn how to avoid punishment.

Children in middle childhood are more aware of the world around them and more sensitive to the feelings of others. As they become more concerned about others' needs, they want to help them. This desire influences their moral development. They begin to internalize rules of conduct.

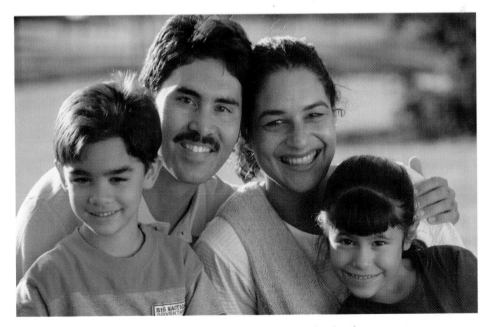

7-13 Children during middle childhood internalize standards of behavior they learn from their parents and others.

# Summary

Middle childhood refers to the span of years between ages 6 and 12. Physical development during middle childhood slows down from the rapid pace of earlier years. Children grow about two to three inches per year during this time period and gain about five to seven pounds per year. Gross motor skills are improving, including greater speed and accuracy of movement. Fine motor skills improve the neatness and accuracy of writing.

Though this is often one of the healthiest periods for children, several chronic illnesses may surface during middle childhood. Ulcers, asthma, and diabetes may develop. Vision and hearing need to be checked regularly so that any problems can be corrected. Obesity is becoming more common among school-age children.

Cognitive development continues as children begin to think mentally using logic and symbols. They no longer rely only on what they see or perceive. They can process and recall information more readily. Memory improves and their attention span is longer. Because they can now use logic in their mental operations, children learn several new concepts during the middle years. These include the concepts of conservation, seriation, and classification. Vocabulary and grammar skills also improve dramatically.

As children take a closer look at the world around them, they begin to make social comparisons. Their strengths and weaknesses become more apparent to them. Children's self-concept forms, which affects their self-esteem. They also begin to develop feelings of empathy and compassion towards others. Friendships and group activities take on greater importance during the school-age years. Most of these relationships are with friends of the same sex.

Morality begins to develop during middle childhood as standards of behavior become internalized.

## Review and Reflect

1. True or false. By 12 years of age, most girls have surpassed boys in height and weight.

2. List the motor skills in which girls generally outperform boys.

3. True or false. A person who is nearsighted can see close objects better than distant objects.

4. List three factors that may lead to obesity in children.

5. Explain how the way children process information changes from the preschool years to the school-age years.

6. Describe a test that you could use to check a child's understanding of the concept of conservation.

7. How does language change during the school-age years?

8. Explain the relationship between self-concept and self-esteem.

9. School-age children begin to develop empathy. What does this mean?

10. Describe the gender differences in play areas and space.

11. Why are team sports important for children's development?

12. True or false. Morality involves the internalizing of accepted rules of behavior.

## Apply and Explore

1. Visit a local elementary school during recess and observe the motor skills of school-age children.

2. Visit an after-school program. Observe the children's social interactions and peer groups.

3. Visit an after-school program. Bring along 10 pennies and two balls of play dough. With six- and seven-year-olds, assess their ability to conserve number and mass.

4. Compile a list of resources for school-age children in your community.

5. Visit the Web site for the National Network for Child Care (nncc.org) to review development during middle childhood.

# Part 2

# Creating a Safe and Healthy Environment

Your primary goal as a child care teacher is to keep children safe and healthy. Creating a safe, healthy environment requires careful planning and preparation.

As you read this part, you will discover how to arrange the space in a center to promote safety as well as learning and fun. You will also learn criteria for choosing toys and equipment that will safely help meet your program goals.

This part gives safety objectives to help you prevent accidents and illness. It also makes you aware of your responsibilities in detecting and reporting child abuse and neglect.

Guidelines for planning and serving nutritious meals and snacks are provided in this part. Also, procedures are given for handling such medical emergencies as wounds, burns, and fevers.

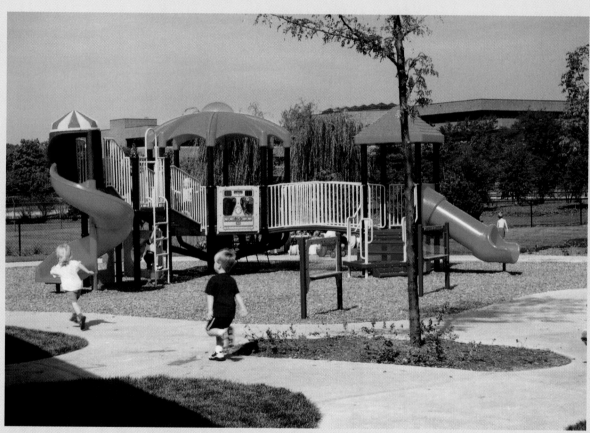

Teachers are responsible for preparing both indoor and outdoor areas for children.

# Chapter 8

# Preparing the Environment

After studying this chapter, you will be able to

- ☐ explain the value of planned indoor and outdoor space.

- ☐ name the basic activity areas in a center, along with the functions of each area.

- ☐ list criteria to consider when choosing playroom furniture and color schemes.

- ☐ summarize factors that affect the organization of space in a center.

- ☐ organize basic activity areas of the classroom and outdoor play yard.

## Terms to Know

isolation area

staff room

audiovisual board

acoustic material

cubbies

cool colors

warm colors

traffic pattern

sensory table

stationary equipment

Michiko is running. Susie is hiding. No one saw Mary take the fish out of the bowl. There is no place for Jose to play with the blocks. The behavior of children in this classroom is affected by the way the space is arranged.

In another classroom, the space is carefully organized. All the children are involved in constructive play. The layout encourages independent learning and communication. There are few, if any, behavior problems. Heather is smiling. Fred is looking at books in a quiet corner of the classroom. At the same time, Wong and his friends are building a large block structure.

In a developmentally appropriate, well-organized environment, children grow and learn. The teacher is responsible for creating an environment that is shaped by the needs and interests of the children.

Classroom arrangement reflects program quality. It also provides clues about expected behavior. A well-planned setting usually promotes interesting play, provides children with choices, and reduces behavior problems. It should encourage interaction with other children and adults, as well as active exploration. Well-planned space is arranged based on the children's temperaments, developmental needs, interests, and program goals. The classroom should also be attractive and inviting.

A nurturing, safe environment is critical for children's social, emotional, physical, and cognitive development. Children need space to build, move, sort, create, pretend, spread out, work, and interact with friends. They need diverse materials in sufficient quantity to keep them actively involved. They need a place to be quiet, to be active, to talk, and to move. Space affects the activity level of children. The choices children make and the way they carry out their choices are also affected by space. Space can even affect the children's concentration and the length of time they will remain with one activity. Therefore, space should be arranged according to children's needs and interests. However, the space should also be convenient for the staff. See 8-1.

## Value of Planned Space

The early years are crucial for the cognitive development of children. Before arranging a classroom, review the developmental objectives of the program. For example, two-year-old children do not have refined large motor skills. To promote safety and motor development, they need large, open spaces. The classroom should be planned with these goals in mind.

An attractive, well-arranged classroom conveys a sense of order. It encourages children to use materials and to do things for themselves. It also molds their behavior. Boundaries found in this type of classroom make the children more

responsible. They know where to find classroom materials. They also know where to return them when they are finished.

Safety is an important concern in planning space. When children feel safe, they feel free to learn. Open spaces must be provided so adults can supervise the entire room. The ratio of caregivers to children also affects safety. If the number of caregivers is low, the room arrangement should be simple to make supervision easier.

Studies have shown that the arrangement of space greatly affects teachers' behavior as well as children's. In centers with well-planned space, teachers were more friendly, sensitive, and warm to children. These teachers taught their children to respect others' rights and feelings. In centers with poorly-planned space, teachers were often more insensitive to their students.

The goals for a well-planned space include
- providing a physically safe environment for the children.
- providing children with areas that promote cognitive, emotional, social, and physical growth.
- providing adults with a space that is easy to supervise.

8-1 Quality early childhood programs have ample space for children and teachers.

- providing space that is pleasing to the eye for both adults and children.
- providing easy access to materials when needed so children are able to direct themselves, 8-2.
- providing space where children can work and play comfortably.

## Physical Space

The physical space of a center may be divided into seven main areas. These basic areas include the following:

- entrance
- director's office
- isolation area
- kitchen or kitchenette
- staff room
- bathrooms
- classroom or playroom

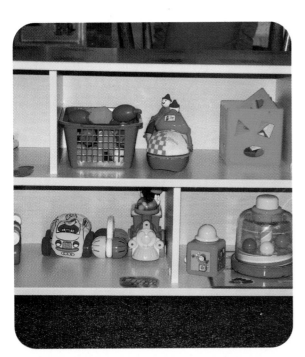

8-2  This infant-toddler classroom features low shelving units that allow children to choose their own activities and clean up after themselves.

### Entrance

The entrance to the center should be attractive and appealing to children and adults, 8-3. Plants, the children's artwork attractively displayed, and a bulletin board for parents will enhance the appearance. If space permits, chairs and a sofa are welcome additions for parents who need to wait.

### Director's Office

The director's office should be just inside the center's entrance. School records, children's records, and public relations material can be stored here. This office can also be used for parent interviews and conferences. Some directors also have a small table in their offices for teachers' meetings and planning sessions.

### Isolation Area

Most states require centers to provide a special room or space for children who become ill or show signs of a communicable disease. This room, often called an **isolation area**, should contain a cot and a few toys. If the space

8-3  This child care center has an entrance area that helps parents feel welcome.

is not available, a cot may be placed in the director's office when needed.

## Kitchen

The size of a center's kitchen depends on the amount of daily food preparation. Even if meals are not served, most centers have a small area with a sink, refrigerator, and stove for preparing snacks. Regardless of the kitchen's use, the local health department personnel should inspect it. They can tell you if all legal requirements are being met.

Floor coverings in the kitchen should be easy to clean. Vinyl coverings and ceramic tile are recommended floor coverings for the kitchen.

## Staff Room

Adults need an area for their own use. This **staff room** should contain a locked storage space for personal belongings. A coat rack, sofa, and tables or desks should also be available. Most staff members prefer having a computer, telephone, professional journals, and curriculum guides available, too. Privacy is also important for the staff area. This area may be used for meeting with parents or other staff members.

## Bathrooms

Most states have laws requiring a certain number of toilets and sinks for a group of young children. Some states require at least one toilet for every 10 children. However, a higher ratio is more convenient. There are many times during the day that several children may have to use the bathroom at the same time.

The size of the toilet fixture will vary with the size and age of the children. A group of two-year-old children would be comfortable with toilet fixtures 10 inches from the floor. Five-year-old children would find 13-inch toilet fixtures more comfortable.

If small toilets are unavailable, a sturdy wooden step can be used for smaller children. This same wooden step can be used in front of the sinks that are too high for children to reach.

For safety purposes, the water heater that supplies water to the children's bathroom should be set on low heat.

Bathroom flooring should be easy to clean. Tile is recommended. Also, it should not be slippery. Avoid having wax applied to the flooring in this area.

## Classroom or Playroom

The classroom or playroom should be on the ground floor close to an exit. A rectangular room is the best shape as it allows for optimal supervision. This shape also allows for many more space arrangements than other shapes.

Studies show that aggression increases in programs that lack adequate space. Quality child care centers need to have enough space for children and a variety of materials and equipment. The recommended amount of space varies from state to state. It can range from 35 to 100 square feet of indoor space per child. The National Association for the Education of Young Children (NAEYC) recommends at least 35 square feet of free indoor space per child. This amount should not include hallways or space taken up by equipment, built-in cabinets, closets, or toilets.

### Walls

All walls should be durable and washable. Many teachers like to attach bulletin boards to the walls. This provides space to hang artwork and papers, as well as absorb sound, 8-4.

8-4 A brightly decorated bulletin board is a welcome addition to any classroom.

Chalkboards can also be attached to walls. They should be installed at the children's eye level.

Instead of bulletin boards and chalkboards, some centers use audiovisual boards. An **audiovisual board** can serve as a bulletin board, chalkboard, and movie screen. It is usually white, off-white, or beige. The disadvantage of the audiovisual board is that magnetic strips must be used to hold up objects when used as a bulletin board. These strips can be costly.

## Floors

A recent trend for playroom floor coverings has been carpeting. Carpeting is easy to maintain. It also provides a sound cushion. Carpeting can also add visual appeal, comfort, warmth, and softness to a room. Use a tightly woven carpet that has a flat, firm surface. This will minimize balance problems for children while stacking blocks.

## Windows

Windows in the playroom should be placed so that children can see outside. Screens should be installed outside all windows. All windows should open in case of a fire.

Drapes or blinds may be used to help control light. They also add interest, softness, and color to a room. Drapes or blinds reduce glare, heating bills, and noise. One disadvantage of drapes is that they become soiled easily. This is caused by children brushing by them with dirty hands or art supplies.

For a different effect, you might wish to hang a valance above each window. This can be a nice addition to a classroom if the colors complement the decor. If you use valances instead of drapes, also use miniblinds or pleated shades to reduce glare.

## Doors

Doors should be lightweight. To guard against injury, the doors should push out to open. Doorknobs should be low enough so children can reach them.

## Acoustics

Studies show that noise affects children's behavior. For this reason, make an effort to use materials that reduce or eliminate noise.

**Acoustic material** is used to deaden or absorb sounds. Carpets, drapes, bulletin boards, pillows, stuffed toys, and sand are examples. Due to the physical makeup of these materials, noise can be reduced or eliminated. For instance, carpeting will absorb the sound of footsteps.

If the classroom is still noisy after the addition of draperies, carpeting, and bulletin boards, acoustical tile may need to be installed on the classroom ceiling. If possible, the ceiling should be 10 to 12 feet high to reduce noise and provide a feeling of spaciousness.

## Temperature

Temperature is important in planning a comfortable environment for young children. They cannot attend to or process information in an uncomfortable environment.

Usually a temperature range of 68 to 70 degrees Fahrenheit will be comfortable. When vigorous physical activities are planned, the temperature should be decreased. In order for children to be comfortable, adults may have to wear a sweater.

## Humidity

Humidity, like temperature, influences the comfort of the environment. Usually a 40 to 60 percent relative humidity range is considered comfortable. To maintain comfort, the relative humidity should be decreased as the temperature rises.

## Electrical Outlets

For safety purposes, electrical outlets should be above the children's reach. When outlets are not being used, safety caps should be inserted for protection. Many times a room arrangement will be influenced by the location of electrical outlets. For example, the music area would be located near an outlet so a record, tape, or CD player could be used. For the safety of the children and staff, do not use long electrical cords. These can cause someone to trip or fall. Because of this danger, many states ban the use of long extension cords in the classroom.

# Furniture

Classroom or playroom furniture should be durable, washable, and stackable. Tables and easels should be adjustable. Then they can be adjusted to fit each child who may use them. To check if an easel is the proper height, have the child stand next to it. Ask the child to touch the middle of the easel pad. If the child has to bend or reach to touch the middle of the pad, adjust the easel.

Chair and table heights are checked in a different manner. Ask the child to sit on a chair. Then push it under the table. If the table and chair are suited to the child, there will be room between the bottom of the table and the child's knees. The child should be able to place his or her feet flat on the floor.

## Chairs

Children's chairs are often used in the art, dramatic play, and dining areas. Chairs should always be the proper height for the children. Plastic, stackable chairs are preferred by most teachers. Plastic chairs have other advantages. They are light enough for the children to move, and they do not require refinishing. An adult-sized rocking chair may be used by children in the library or dramatic play area. The chair may also be used by adults as a special place to hold or comfort a child.

## Tables

Classroom tables should be hard, smooth, and washable. The tables should be light enough to move. Most preschool teachers prefer tables that are large enough to seat four to six children. Rectangular tables are often preferred over round tables. The rectangular shape allows children to have their own space. This reduces the chance for aggression. Low, round tables are sometimes used in the library and dramatic play area.

## Storage Units

Storage units should be organized for easy access of equipment and supplies. Blocks, books, art supplies, games, and other classroom materials are kept in storage units, 8-5. These units should be arranged to encourage children to independently remove and return materials. For flexibility, all storage units should have casters so they can be moved easily. The casters should be equipped with locks so they do not move accidentally. For units without casters, hardware can be bought and easily installed. Keep in mind that pegboard or corkboard can be attached to exposed sides and backs of units. These can serve as bulletin boards.

8-5 Blocks and other toys are well-organized on this shelving unit.

Storage units should match the height of the children. The children must be able to reach the materials. Therefore, choose small, lightweight sections of cabinets.

If doors are needed on the storage units, sliding doors are best. When opened, swinging doors can cause safety hazards.

## Lockers and Cubbies

Children can learn responsibility for their own belongings when they are provided personal storage space. Each child enrolled in the program should have a locker, 8-6. Most lockers for preschool children are 10 to 12 inches wide and 10 to 15 inches deep. Each locker should contain a hook for hanging a coat.

The primary purpose of lockers is to store children's clothing. Finished artwork, library books, parent letters, and other valuable items must also be stored. For storage of these items, many lockers have a top section. These are often called **cubbies**. If the lockers do not have cubbies, containers can be stacked to store the children's belongings. See 8-7.

Lockers and cubbies should have a coat of varnish or paint. This coating will help prevent staining from muddy boots or wet paints. If lockers are painted, use a washable enamel paint.

Lockers should be placed near the entrance. This will save parents time when picking up children. It will save the class from being disrupted when someone must go to his or her locker. It will also save clean-up time during bad weather.

## Color Choices for Child Care Centers

An attractive environment appeals to the senses. The use of color can affect how teachers and children feel about their classroom. Colors can either calm or stimulate young children.

8-6 Use symbols on lockers to help young children identify their space.

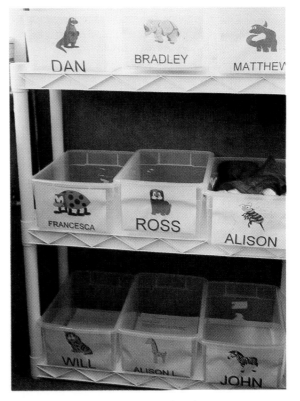

8-7 Empty containers can be used to store children's small personal belongings.

Because of the emotional effects of color, select colors carefully. The goal should be to create a room that looks pleasant and feels spacious. This can be done using **cool colors**, such as blue, green, and purple. Cool colors make a room appear larger. They create a feeling of openness. **Warm colors** make a room seem smaller. These colors include red, yellow, and orange. Studies show that children prefer warm colors until about age six. After the age of six, they start to prefer cool colors.

Other factors affect color selection. These include the amount of available light in the room and the amount of time spent in the room. For example, if the room does not have much light available, a warm color will help the room appear brighter.

Since child care centers are active places and contain a lot of colorful materials, white is often used in classrooms. Children respond well to white. White rooms are perceived as clean and cool. White is an excellent color for the eating, isolation, administration, and reading areas. It is also a good color for the bathroom.

Light blue is often used in child care centers. Children respond to this color by feeling comfortable, soothed, and secure. Therefore, light blue is useful in the nap, reading, eating, and isolation areas.

Light green, like light blue and white, creates a positive response. It makes children feel calm, refreshed, peaceful, and restful. It is useful for isolation, nap, reading, and eating areas.

Yellow makes people feel happy and cheerful. It is a good color in art and music areas. Playground equipment is often painted yellow.

Orange is a welcoming, forceful, energetic color. Its use should be limited. Clearly, an orange room can be overwhelming. However, orange can be used effectively in small areas, such as an entrance.

As with orange, the use of red should be limited, 8-8. Overuse of red can be too stimulating for children. Children may become overactive. Red is best used on indoor gross motor equipment, outdoor equipment, and teaching aids designed to stimulate children.

The color purple can have a mournful effect. It is best used only as an accent color on equipment, bulletin boards, and teaching aids. When used as a wall color, limit its use to reading areas.

8-8 The use of red on this decoration creates interest without being overpowering.

# Factors That Affect Space Organization

An organized classroom can inspire children to take part in the activities of the day. The space should be arranged to define the scope and limits of activities. Space will also affect the children's use of and care of materials. Therefore, the space must provide for proper learning experiences.

When planning classroom space, many factors should be considered. These factors will greatly affect how the classroom is organized. They include licensing requirements, program goals, group size, scale, and traffic patterns.

## Licensing Requirements

All states have their own licensing requirements for child care centers. You will need to know these your state's requirements before you begin planning classroom space. Requirements vary from state to state. However, some common requirements exist. For example, they all require a minimum number of fire extinguishers. Also, all exits must be clear, and entrance doors must open to the outside. In addition, a minimum number of square feet of space must be available for each child.

## Program Goals

A program's goals should be based on the children's abilities, age, and skills. The goals a teacher selects should represent the major stages of development and growth. (These stages were discussed in Chapters 4, 5, 6, and 7.) The environment, as well as planned classroom activities, should stimulate growth and development.

Caregivers concerned with all developmental areas might select the following program goals:

- To promote a positive self-concept.
- To promote independence.
- To promote problem-solving skills.
- To promote fine-motor coordination.
- To promote gross-motor coordination.
- To promote self-control.
- To promote language skills.
- To promote prosocial behavior.
- To promote an appreciation of cultural diversity.

After the goals for the children are listed, review each goal. Decide how each goal will be supported by the classroom environment. For instance, most teachers set a goal to develop independence in children. The arrangement of the room can help children achieve this goal. Materials, locker hooks, and shelving units should all be within easy reach for the children. This will encourage children to act without help from adults in many cases. Chart 8-9 lists a number of ways to meet various program goals.

Program goals should also reflect state licensing requirements. Therefore, if the state requires that children receive one meal and two snacks each day, a program goal might state that children receive nutritious meals and snacks.

## Group Size

Group size is an important factor to consider when arranging space. A large number of children crowded into a small area will cause problems. Children are likely to become upset and fight more when crowded. Likewise, a small number of children with too much space will also cause problems. Too much open space encourages children to run. You must strive to create an arrangement that will be the proper size for the group.

The more children, the more empty space is needed. A good rule of thumb is to plan between one-third and one-half of the classroom for open space. Also, the room arrangement needs to be fairly simple. Children will feel safe and secure in this arrangement.

Arrange shelving units and other furniture with group size in mind. A good arrangement allows teachers and children to move easily through the room. It also allows for teachers and children to see and be seen easily. This will promote a relaxed setting.

## Scale

The classroom environment must be scaled to the size of its occupants. Child-sized furniture should be purchased or built. Bulletin boards, toilets, water fountains, sinks, pictures, and other items should all be at the children's level. One method to judge if the setting is scaled for children is for an adult to walk on his or her knees through the entire classroom. Anything positioned too high for the children should be noted and adjusted.

## Traffic Patterns

The arrangement of a classroom centers around the **traffic pattern**. This is the way people move through the classroom area. Furniture should be arranged to create a useful traffic pattern. For instance, children should be able to walk from the art area to the block-building area without going through the middle of the library area.

Program activities will affect traffic patterns. For example, most child care centers provide breakfast and lunch. These meals may be prepared on site or contracted. Whichever plan is used, the food will likely be made in or delivered to a kitchen. For this reason, the kitchen should be near a delivery door and near the eating area of the classroom.

| How Goals Are Supported by the Environment | |
| --- | --- |
| **Goal** | **How Goal Is Supported by Environment** |
| To promote independence. | Similar materials are stored together. Drawers, shelves, and containers are labeled with outlines of contents. Materials and equipment are easily accessible to children. Coat hooks are low enough for children to hang their own clothing. Individual storage is provided for each child. |
| To promote a positive self-concept. | Equipment is developmentally appropriate. Children's work is displayed. Unstructured materials are available in each area. A variety of materials are available for children to choose. |
| To promote problem-solving skills. | Equipment is developmentally appropriate. Open-ended materials, such as blocks, are available. A variety of materials are available for children to choose. Materials are rotated to create interest. |
| To promote fine-motor coordination. | A classroom area is devoted to manipulative equipment. Enough material to maintain children's interest is available. Materials are easily accessible to children. Materials are changed frequently to create interest. |
| To promote gross-motor development. | A classroom area is devoted to gross-motor activities. An adequate amount of space is provided to encourage play. The traffic flow does not interfere with the children's use of materials. The area is located away from quiet activities. |
| To promote self-control. | Enough space is provided for children to use materials in each classroom area. The classroom traffic flow permits children to work without interruption. Noisy areas are located away from quiet areas. Sufficient variety and quantity of materials are available in each area. |
| To promote language skills. | A book display space is placed at children's eye level. Classroom materials are labeled. A wide variety of materials, including books, puppets, and tapes are available. |
| To promote social skills. | Boundaries between areas are defined with low shelving units. A sufficient amount of materials are available to encourage cooperative play. |
| To promote an appreciation of cultural diversity. | Dolls, puppets, puzzles, picture books, posters, and bulletin board figures represent various cultural and ethnic groups. Music and musical instruments reflect various cultural and ethnic groups. |

8-9  Defining program goals is the first step toward well-organized space.

# Organizing Basic Activity Areas

Classrooms arranged according to activity areas provide an ideal environment for active learning. Each activity area should clearly convey to the children what those choices are. For example, the art area should have an easel and art supplies. By displaying these materials in an inviting manner, the children will be aware of what is available to them. This gives them the chance to make their own choices.

Each activity area is a space of its own, and each area supports the program goals. Each area should be defined, but the space should be flexible. Shelves placed in U or L shapes can create boundaries for classroom areas. The shelves can be moved when the shape of the space needs to be changed.

Arrange activity areas by function. Think carefully of each area as wet or dry, active or quiet, 8-10. Wet and dry activities should be placed far away from each other. Sensory and science activities are examples of wet/active activities. Art, eating, and cooking are types of wet/quiet activities.

Active activities should take place far from quiet activities. Woodworking, blockbuilding, music, and dramatic play are all active activities. Each of these could disrupt a quiet activity. Sleeping, reading, and small manipulative play are all examples of quiet/dry activities.

Most teachers prefer to map out two or three possible area arrangements. This helps them see what will work best and why. Some room arrangement principles are shown in 8-11.

Remember that rather than being static, room arrangements must be dynamic. Rearranging the classroom areas is necessary when the children's interests change. With changing interests, the addition and elimination of equipment and materials needs to be considered.

## Introducing Activity Areas

Children require an introduction to the activity areas in the classroom. They need to learn what materials are in each area. They need to learn what activities take place in that area. They also need to learn the safety and cleanup rules of the area. In programs that operate for nine month sessions, the children can be introduced to the areas at the start of the session.

| Basic Activity Areas |
|---|

8-10 Planning space requires that you consider each activity as it relates to other activities that take place in the same area.

| Principles of Room Arrangement |
|---|

- Whenever possible, arrange areas around the edges of the room. This allows the center of the room to be used for traffic flow.
- Arrange shelving units so that the teacher can clearly view the entire room.
- Store objects together that are used for the same activities.
- Place the art area near a water source.
- Place quiet activities far away from active activities and traffic areas.
- Place dry activities far from wet activities.
- Provide open space for blockbuilding and group activities.
- Define areas by arranging storage units into U- or L-shapes.
- Provide a private space where children can be alone.

8-11 Keep these principles in mind when planning space. Would you add any guidelines to this list?

In programs that operate throughout the year, children can be introduced to each area when they first enroll in the program. Children who have been in the program for a time may help the teacher introduce the areas to new students.

Children need to learn the routine for using and replacing materials. Carefully arranging materials will enable the children to help maintain the learning environment. To help children feel comfortable in using and moving about the areas, use labels and signs, 8-12. Labels and signs direct children's attention. This then helps children become self-directed learners. Labels and signs also encourage children to return materials to storage areas. Tape pictures to the storage areas to serve as reminders.

## Blockbuilding Area

Blocks give children practice sorting, grouping, comparing, arranging, making decisions, cooperating, and role-playing. Therefore, this area should be well-equipped and well-defined. See 8-13.

The best location for blockbuilding should be on a carpeted area. Carpeting helps by reducing the noise level. Define the area with low cabinets. Allow enough room for building. Children will need room to build structures that go around, up, and out.

8-13 Blockbuilding areas are very popular. Make sure this area is well-equipped and spacious.

To stimulate play, provide items other than blocks in the blockbuilding area. Examples include plastic zoo and farm animals, people, traffic signs, wheeled toys, pulleys, and boxes.

Use the low cabinets that define the area for storage of materials. Make sure there are enough shelves to arrange the blocks according to shape. Place all blockbuilding materials at the children's eye level and within their reach.

Large, heavy blocks (and other heavy materials) should be placed on a bottom shelf or on the floor to avoid accidents. Save higher shelves for lightweight items. Label each shelf with the shape of the block that can be found there. Labels help children return the blocks to the correct shelf. Labels also provide matching practice and reduce clean-up time.

## Art Area

Place the art area near a water source. Arrange the space so either groups or individuals can use the area. Use tables, chairs, easels, drying racks, and shelving units that are easy to clean and maintain. See 8-14. Label the shelves with the materials found there.

8-12 With the help of labels and signs, children will learn to move around their environment easily.

8-14  Make efficient use of space by placing a drying rack for artwork overhead.

8-15  This sand table has extra built-in features to increase the children's enjoyment.

## Dramatic Play Area

The dramatic play area is also known as the home living or housekeeping area. For younger children, this area should be arranged to look like a real home. A stove, refrigerator, table, chairs, sink, and doll bed are basic furniture you may wish to provide. Other props may be added. For instance, you may wish to provide dolls, kitchen utensils, cleaning tools, and dress-up clothes. For older children, other props may be added to help them extend their understanding of the world. For example, the area could be set up as a hair salon, bakery, fast food restaurant, or post office.

## Sensory Area

The key piece of equipment in the sensory area is the **sensory table**. It is also known as a water or sand table, 8-15. The size of the table will depend on the amount of space available and depend on the age of the children. Two- and three-year-old children love the sensory appeal of water and sand. A sensory table can give the children practice in social situations.

Not all centers have sensory tables. Some centers use plastic wading pools or washtubs. Whatever container is used, it should be placed near a water source. Children and teachers enjoy adding water to the sand to change the feeling.

Other items are often used in the sensory table. Provide rustproof spoons, shovels, sand pails, measuring cups, funnels, strainers, and other kitchen items. Place shelving units near the table for storage or store items in plastic buckets or laundry baskets.

## Woodworking Area

After building wood sculptures, many children enjoy decorating them with paint. For that reason, locate the woodworking area near the art area, 8-16. For the children's safety, place this area outside the line of traffic.

Items you may wish to provide at the woodworking bench include tools, wood scraps, and styrofoam pieces. Hang a pegboard next to the wood bench, within children's reach. It can be used to hold tools. To encourage the return of tools, paint outlines of the tools on the pegboard. The children can replace tools by matching them with outlined shapes.

## Sleeping Area

Most preschool children rest or nap after lunch. Not all programs, however, have separate sleeping areas. For those that do not, a flexible room arrangement is key. Such an arrangement can be quickly and quietly altered during or

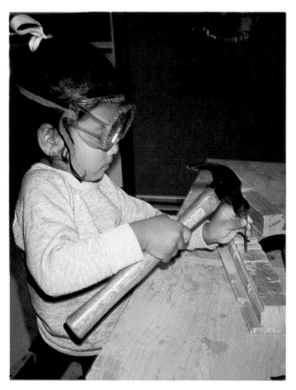

8-16 The woodworking table can hold the attention of children for extended time periods.

immediately after lunchtime into a sleeping area. Allow sufficient space for sleeping. Some states require that two feet of open space exist between cots. Check your state's regulations.

### Small Manipulative Area

The small manipulative, or small motor, area should be located in a dry, quiet area of the playroom. Table blocks, puzzles, plastic building pieces, parquetry blocks, stringing beads, lotto boards, sewing cards, and color cubes with pattern cards are some items you may wish to provide. These materials should represent various levels of difficulty. Many teachers also include math materials and equipment in this area. A table, chairs, and shelving unit are also useful in this area.

### Library Area

The library area should be located in the quietest part of the classroom. Often this is next to the manipulative area. In addition to providing books and magazines, you may want to promote language arts. For example, paper, pens, pencils, and felt-tip markers encourage writing skills. Shelving units, a table, and chairs are all useful in this area. See 8-17. For comfort, pillows may also be added. Many centers also carpet this area or add an area rug.

### Music Area

Rhythm instruments; tapes, records, CDs and players; puppets; and scarves are found in almost all music areas. When space permits, some centers have a piano. For other centers, an Autoharp® or guitar is an option. Space should be provided in the music area for movements and dancing.

### Private Space

Provide a private area in the classroom where children can be alone. Children then have the option of limiting contact with others when they choose. This reduces the pressure of being around others when they wish to be alone. Set a classroom rule stating that children who go to the private space will not be disturbed by others.

8-17 Display books at the children's eye level in the library area.

A loft is one unique way to provide private space, 8-18. In programs where a wooden loft is not in the budget, large cardboard boxes and wooden crates can serve the same purpose.

The private space should be small, allowing room for only one or two children at a time. The children in the private space should not be visible to other children in the room. However, the teacher must be able to see into the private space.

## Science Area

Place the science area in the wet, active area of the classroom. Most science areas contain at least one table. A shelving unit may be placed here. Small caged pets and project materials would be also found in the science area of the classroom. When possible, place this area near a light and water source for growing plants.

## Technology Area

The technology area should be in the quiet, dry part of the classroom. A technology area might be a small area with just one computer and printer or a larger, lab-type section. Electrical outlets are needed for computers and printers. If Internet access is desired, a phone jack will also be needed in this area.

Where you place the computer affects how often children will use it. Keep the monitor visible throughout the classroom. This placement increases children's curiosity about the computer and encourages children to interact. It also helps the teacher supervise from anywhere in the classroom. Store software near the computer. For older children, keep software easy for them to access on their own.

Finally, choose computer furniture designed for young children. Injuries or strains can occur if children must adjust their bodies to reach the mouse or keyboard from adult furniture. Position the top of the work surface two inches below the children's elbows. When seated, children should be able to see the center of the monitor by looking directly ahead. Having a few extra chairs in the area encourages the children to use the computers together.

## Eating Area

When space is available, provide a separate eating area. This area could also serve as a special interest area for cooking activities. It should be located near the kitchen. This allows for easy service and clean-up.

If space is limited, have children sit at tables in other areas of the classroom. The daily schedule will have to be arranged to allow for this.

Chart 8-19 summarizes each classroom area and the furniture, materials, and equipment you may wish to supply in each. In each of the activity areas, include ethnic and cultural materials and artifacts whenever possible. Items such as artwork, fabric, jewelry, tools, utensils, toys, and children's books should be included.

## Displaying Children's Work

The work of the children should be displayed throughout the activity areas. Bulletin boards, wall hangings, clothesline, or appliance boxes can be used for display purposes. Display areas should be placed at the children's height, allowing them to mount and view their own work.

8-18 Children sometimes like to be alone. This loft provides a perfect setting.

| Classroom Area | Furniture | Materials and Equipment |
|---|---|---|
| Blockbuilding | labeled shelving units | large hollow blocks; solid unit blocks; wheeled toys: cars, buses, trucks, fire engines, tractors, planes; small toy people of various ethnic backgrounds; small, colored wooden blocks; zoo animals; farm animals |
| Art | adjustable easels<br>shelving unit<br>tables and chairs<br>drying rack | clay, pencils, crayons, colored chalk, ink markers, paper, tempera paint, scrap paper and fabrics, tape, glue, paste, brushes, scissors, painting smocks |
| Dramatic Play | child-sized refrigerator, stove, sink, cupboard, and doll bed<br>trunk or tree to hold clothes<br>tables and chairs | child-sized cleaning equipment: broom, dustpan, and mops; doll clothes; telephones; mirror; dishes and cooking utensils: tubs, buckets, and pans; dress-up clothes, costumes; purses, backpacks, suitcases; dolls of both genders and various ethnicities |
| Sensory | sensory table<br>shelving unit (optional) | funnels, pitchers, spoons, sponges, containers, strainers, rotary beaters |
| Woodworking | woodworking bench | saw, screwdrivers, hammers, vice, nails, screws, scraps of wood and foam, glue, protective goggles |
| Sleeping | cots<br>mats | blankets, pillows, soft music |
| Small Manipulative | shelving units<br>table (optional depending on space)<br>chairs (optional depending on space)<br>shelving unit | hand puppets, blocks, puzzles, plastic forms for joining, Lego® plastic building blocks, parquetry blocks, stringing beads, board games, sewing cards, colored cubes with pattern cards, bingo games, rods and blocks of different sizes, flannel board numerals, number puzzles, wooden numbers, magnetic numbers, measuring containers, scale, rulers, Tinkertoy® building blocks |
| Library | table<br>chairs<br>rug<br>soft pillows (optional)<br>bean bag (optional)<br>shelving<br>shelving unit<br>flannel board<br>chalkboard | picture books, children's magazines, child-authored books, charts, games, alphabet letters, pencils, felt-tip markers, paper, chalk, |
| Music | piano (optional)<br>shelving unit<br>cassette, record, or CD player | rhythm instruments; tapes, records, or CDs; silk scarves for dancing; puppets for song activities |
| Private Space | loft<br>TV box<br>wooden crates | pillows |

8-19  Providing materials and equipment for activity areas is a thought-provoking process. Many everyday materials can be used for learning.          (Continued)

| Classroom Area | Furniture | Materials and Equipment |
|---|---|---|
| Science | aquarium<br>table<br>shelving unit<br>terrarium | magnets; scissors; prism; measuring instruments; jars and other empty containers; collections of related objects such as leaves, nuts, rocks, and insects; magnifying glasses; small pets; scales; mirrors |
| Eating | tables<br>chairs | vases and centerpieces, placements, plates, eating utensils, cups |
| Writing Center | table<br>chairs | photographs, different colors of lined and unlined paper, pens, pencils, felt-tip markers, alphabet letters, word lists, picture dictionary |
| Technology Center | child-sized computer workstations or tables and chairs<br>extra chairs<br>computer<br>printer | software, printer paper, manuals for computer and software, typing stand, mouse and wrist pads |
| Gross-Motor | balance beam<br>steps<br>walking boards<br>jungle gym | balls, ropes, hula hoops, fabric tunnels, tumbling mat |

8-19  Continued.

A wall hanging can be made from a 36- or 52-inch wide piece of felt, burlap, or sailcloth. The length of the hanging can vary. Hem each end of the hanging. Then insert a dowel through each hem.

Colored yarn or a piece of clothesline can also be used to display work. Colored plastic clothespins can be used to clasp work to the line.

A large appliance box can provide a free-standing display area. The advantage of this type of display is that it is portable. It can be used in any area of the center. Even after it is assembled, it can be moved.

Recognize the work of all the children when putting displays together. To keep displays interesting, set a time limit for each display. Change the work often.

## Outdoor Play Area

Children need to take part in both indoor and outdoor activities. Many classrooms do not have the proper amount of space for large muscle activities. Other activities such as science, art, and music can also take place outdoors during pleasant weather. The outdoor play yard can fill these needs, 8-20.

8-20  The play yard is an exciting and fun place for children.

In outdoor areas, the required number of square feet per child varies from state to state. Usually the requirement ranges from 75 to 200 square feet per child. A rectangular space is most functional. Such a play yard can be seen from end to end. U- or L-shaped play yards are more difficult to supervise and arrange, 8-21.

## Planning the Play Yard

The play yard, like indoor space, needs to be studied in terms of use and then broken into areas. A well-planned play yard usually has empty space and a wheeled vehicle path. These two items aid movement through the yard.

The wheeled vehicle path divides the activity areas of the play yard. This path creates space between areas and makes moving about easier. Without a path, children may constantly be bumping into each other.

To determine where a path should be laid, the teacher should kneel down to be at the children's eye level. The path should be wide enough and clear enough so children can see all areas of the play yard, even when outside school grounds.

Empty space should be located in the center of the yard. Activity areas can be placed around the outside of the yard, around the empty space. You may also need to leave empty space around some pieces of equipment.

When planning play yard space, consider the following guidelines:

- Equipment should be far enough apart so a child using one piece of equipment cannot touch a child using another piece of equipment.
- All equipment should be visible to the teacher from any spot in the yard.
- Children should not have to walk through one area to get to another.
- Between one-third and one-half of the yard should be used for play equipment and the remainder should be open space to allow for ease of movement.

In addition to paths and empty space, there are other factors to consider when planning an outdoor play yard. Among items to be considered are fences, the play yard surface, landscaping, storage, wheeled toy paths, stationary equipment, a water source, and animal shelters.

### Fencing

Most states require play yards be fenced for safety of the children. Fences prevent children from wandering away or strangers from entering the play yard area. This makes outdoor supervision easier for teachers.

Selecting the proper fence requires careful thought. The goal is to purchase a fence that can

8-21 This play yard is designed to be completely visible from this angle. This allows for better supervision.

keep children safe. The fence should fasten securely at the gate. There should be no sharp metal pieces or splintered wood to hurt children.

Two types of fences are commonly found in play yards: chain link and wood. Each type of fence has its good and bad points. For instance, because chain link is an open design, it is possible for the children to observe activities outside of the play yard. This gives the play yard an open feeling. However, some children are able to climb chain link fences. This can be dangerous. In addition, many people feel that chain link fences are unattractive.

Wood fences that complement the center design are very pleasing to the eye. However, the fence must also be designed with the children's safety in mind. Children should not be able to climb over or through a well-designed wood fence. The boards should be sanded to prevent children from getting splinters.

## Surfaces

A portion of the play yard area should have grass. This is best for running and organized games. Under equipment, the best surface for safety is loose material such as bark nuggets, shredded bark, or sand. When children fall on such material, they receive fewer and less severe injuries than when they fall on hard surfaces. A good cushion requires 9 to 12 inches of loose material.

The drawback to loose materials is that they tend to pile up in one spot. They shift under weight placed on them. In high traffic areas they will thin out and pile up around the edges of the area. Therefore, the material must be raked or shoveled back into position fairly often.

## Landscaping

A well-landscaped play yard makes for pleasant surroundings. In addition, landscaping can also be used as part of the science program by encouraging observation skills and promoting learning. Trees, shrubs, and flowers in a variety of sizes, colors, and growing cycles will interest children. Trees are also a good source of shade, beauty, and sound control. A well-landscaped yard gives children a place to be alone, as well as corners for play.

Hills in the yard can be used to develop large muscle skills.

Before choosing flowers or shrubs, consult a landscape architect. Some plants are poisonous. Any landscape architect can tell you which plants to avoid. The architect can also recommend shrubs and flowers from a number of growing cycles. This will ensure children will always have a seasonal plant to study and view.

## Storage Shed

Tricycles, wagons, scooters, shovels, rakes, balls, plastic wading pools, and gardening tools are just some of the items you may want to keep in a storage shed. See 8-22. The materials stored will vary with the climate of the area.

Storage space should be arranged so children can return materials themselves. Painted lines on the floor of the shed can be used to outline parking spaces for wheeled toys. Large barrels or baskets can be used to store many types of materials. Rakes and shovels can be hung on hooks from the wall.

## Wheeled Toy Paths

A path that children can use to push or ride wheeled toys is key for two reasons. The first reason is safety. A path with one-way traffic will prevent children from riding into each other. The second reason is protection of the outdoor play area. A path gives children a place to ride so they do not destroy grassy areas, 8-23. Set limits regarding the use of wheeled toys and paths, and enforce these rules.

The path should be joined to the storage shed. Children can then drive their toys directly into or out of the shed. The path should be designed with curves instead of sharp right angles. This will allow children to make easy turns on curves, keeping them from tipping over on sharp turns.

## Stationary Equipment

Jungle gyms, slides, and tree houses are all **stationary equipment** that are set permanently in the ground for stability. For added appeal, place large pieces of stationary equipment in different corners of the play yard. For safety reasons, spacing is also needed for pieces of

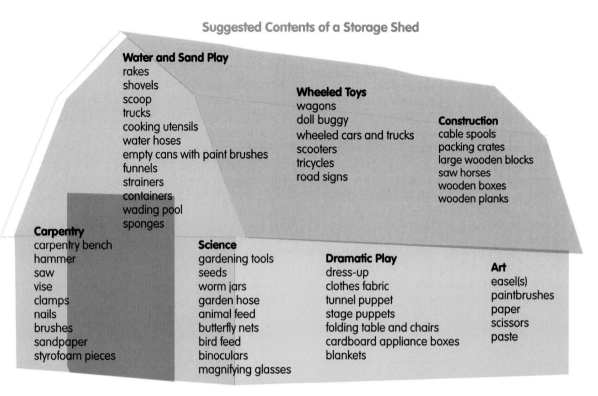

**Suggested Contents of a Storage Shed**

**Water and Sand Play**
rakes
shovels
scoop
trucks
cooking utensils
water hoses
empty cans with paint brushes
funnels
strainers
containers
wading pool
sponges

**Wheeled Toys**
wagons
doll buggy
wheeled cars and trucks
scooters
tricycles
road signs

**Construction**
cable spools
packing crates
large wooden blocks
saw horses
wooden boxes
wooden planks

**Carpentry**
carpentry bench
hammer
saw
vise
clamps
nails
brushes
sandpaper
styrofoam pieces

**Science**
gardening tools
seeds
worm jars
garden hose
animal feed
butterfly nets
bird feed
binoculars
magnifying glasses

**Dramatic Play**
dress-up
clothes fabric
tunnel puppet
stage puppets
folding table and chairs
cardboard appliance boxes
blankets

**Art**
easel(s)
paintbrushes
paper
scissors
paste

8-22  The contents of storage sheds varies from center to center.

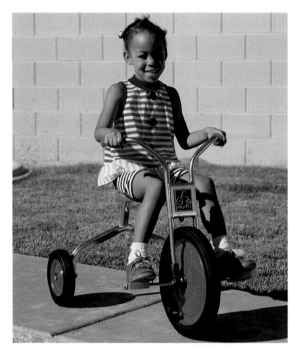

8-23  Wheeled toy paths should have a hard surface.

stationary equipment that are designed for different age groups.

### Sandbox

Children will play in sandboxes for long periods of time. If the sandbox is in a sunny area, children are at risk for sunburn. Therefore, place sandboxes in shady areas. If there is little or no shade in the play yard, build a roof over the sandbox for protection. Also, place the sandbox near a water source. By adding water to dry sand, children can build more detailed structures.

To prevent cats from using the sandbox as a litter box, build a cover for the sandbox. When the sandbox is not being used, place the cover over it, 8-24.

### Water

Water play is a pleasant activity for children during warm weather. For this reason, some centers have built-in wading pools. Other centers use plastic, aboveground wading pools when licensing permits. Regardless of the type of pool, constant supervision is necessary. For reasons of safety, pools need to be emptied at the end of each day.

A garden hose is also useful in the play yard. Attach it to a sprinkler so the children can play in the water during hot weather. The hose can also be used to water gardens and other plants.

## Animal Shelter

Play yards for young children often have a number of animals. The type of animals may be determined by city zoning laws or state child care licensing rules.

To shelter animals, use cages. These should be large enough for the animal, have a mesh floor to keep the cage tidy between thorough cleanings, and have a quality padlock to protect against vandals. Place the cages where animals will be protected from wind, sun, and rain. Provide adequate protection from extreme heat and cold, too.

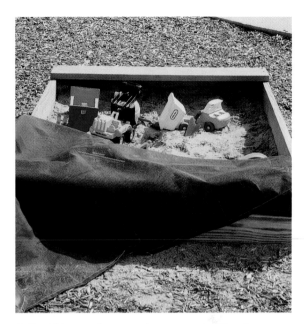

8-24 This sandbox can be covered with a tarp when not in use.

## Summary

Properly organized space is a key to promoting children's learning. It provides children with the option of working alone or cooperatively. It defines expected behavior for children. Properly organized space frees the children to play without interruption. They will stay with activities for longer periods of time, increasing their attention spans. Properly organized space also provides children with choices.

Space should reflect children's developmental needs and interests, as well as program goals. In such a space, children are more relaxed and positive. They feel good about themselves. As a direct result, teachers can spend more time nurturing and less time redirecting children's behavior.

## Review and Reflect

1. Properly planned space is arranged based on _____.
    A. children's developmental needs
    B. children's interests
    C. program goals
    D. All of the above.
2. True or false. Teachers are affected by the arrangement of their classrooms.
3. List four goals for well-planned space.
4. What is the purpose of an isolation area?
5. A _____ room is the best shape for a classroom.
6. Name three uses for an audiovisual board.
7. List four examples of acoustic materials.
8. Storage units should be selected based on the _____ of the children.
9. The top part of a locker is often called a _____.
10. Until about age six, children prefer _____.
    A. warm colors
    B. cool colors
    C. plaid
11. Organized space should define the scope and _____ of activities.

12. List two ways to promote
    A. self-control through the classroom environment.
    B. social skills through the classroom environment.
13. Are problems created when a small group of children have too much space? Why or why not?
14. _____ are the paths people follow through an area.
15. Activity areas are best defined by arranging storage units into _____ or _____ shapes.
16. What activities should be placed in the active/dry area of the classroom?
17. True or false. Children do *not* need to spend time alone.
18. Give two guidelines for a technology area in the classroom.
19. _____ and _____ in the play yard divide activity areas and make moving about easier.
20. What is the safest surface to use under play yard equipment?

## Apply and Explore

1. Draw a room arrangement that includes each of the basic activity areas. Include a center of interest for each area.
2. Read your state's licensing requirements as they apply to classroom space. For instance, how many square feet of space is required per child? How many toilets are required for a group of 40 children?
3. Interview child care teachers about space arrangement. Ask them what they like best about their classroom space. Ask them what they would like to change.
4. Plan a color scheme for a classroom. Be prepared to explain the reasons you chose the colors you did.
5. Check your state's child care licensing **C** requirements by using the Web site for the National Resource Center for Health and Safety in Child Care (nrc.uchsc.edu).
6. Design a classroom at the Childcraft Web **C** site (childcraft.com) by clicking on *Classroom Designer*.

# Chapter 9

# Selecting Toys, Equipment, and Educational Materials

After studying this chapter, you will be able to

- explain guidelines for selecting developmentally appropriate toys, equipment, and educational materials.

- describe safety factors to consider when purchasing toys and play yard equipment.

- explain how to report unsafe toys and equipment to the appropriate agencies.

- list sources and methods for purchasing toys and equipment.

- identify toys and educational materials that teach children appreciation for people of all cultures.

## Terms to Know

spectator toys

physical age

chronological age

developmental age

multicultural

co-op (cooperative)

consumable supplies

Children learn about their world by playing with toys, exploring materials, and interacting with other people. They learn best when provided with a wide range of toys and educational materials. This allows them to make choices. Toys play an important role in facilitating the learning process. For instance, children can learn speech and dressing skills while playing with toys. Children can learn about other people through the use of toys. When playing with toys, children often interact with others. They make choices, solve problems, and apply some control over their environment, 9-1.

Developmentally appropriate toys motivate and engage children as active learners. Simple toys like building blocks can promote cognitive growth. For example, if children do not build a strong foundation under their block building, the building will topple. Thus, they learn physics concepts. If they join two semicircular pieces, they make a circle. In this way, they learn math concepts.

## Selection Criteria

In early childhood programs, selecting toys and equipment for children is often the teacher's responsibility. In preparation, you will need to determine what the children's needs, interests, and abilities are. You will then need to choose the materials that would best meet those needs. As you can see, this is an important job. Careful planning is required.

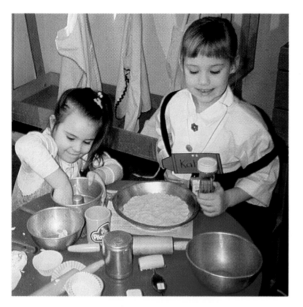

9-1 Toys help children build many skills. By playing together, these children learn important social skills.

The program goals, budget, and curriculum will influence which materials you buy for the classroom. The number of children in the program and the available space and storage should also be considered. You will want to choose toys that are safe, appropriate, and interesting for the children. Guidelines for choosing educational toys are described in the sections that follow.

## Program Goals

Classroom toys and equipment should reflect program goals. If a program goal is to have the children develop language skills, then language materials should be placed in the classroom. Books, pictures, cassettes, CDs, alphabet cards, puppets, pencils, and paper can all be used to promote language skills.

Write your program goals on paper. Then make a list of items that promote each goal. Review the goals and lists. Take count of items you already have in the classroom. Then decide in which areas more toys and equipment are required. You may find a planning sheet helpful for this task, 9-2.

## Budget

When purchasing items for your class, you will need to stay within your budget. To do this, first purchase the basics, such as tables, chairs, and shelving units. You can continue adding items as your funds permit.

Teachers are often surprised at the cost of toys, equipment, and materials. The major portion of the budget for a new program will go toward furniture. The average cost of a classroom furnished with the basics is $700 per child. A well-equipped classroom may cost more than $1100 per child.

| Toy Selection Planning Sheet | | |
|---|---|---|
| **Program Goals** | **Available Toys** | **Toys Needed** |
| To encourage sensory exploration | water table, shovel, cups, pitchers, scoops, clay, egg beaters, feely box, harmonica, kazoo, guitar | bells, drum, texture matching games, pumps, funnels |
| To promote gross-motor skills | low climber, wagon cart, large rubber balls, planks, boxes, jungle gym | low slide, balance boards, bicycle |

9-2 Committing program goals to writing can make the selection of proper toys an easier task.

## Balance

Examining program goals helps you decide what toys and equipment might be purchased. Before buying, however, review each item to decide if it will add balance to the items already available. Ask yourself the following questions: Can the item be used with other toys? Will it help children reach goals that are not being met sufficiently with current toys? Will it promote interaction with peers? Will it help balance toys for all areas of development—physical, cognitive, emotional, and social?

## Space

Keep in mind the space and storage needed for any new items you are thinking about buying or building. This is especially true for large pieces of equipment. For instance, an indoor jungle gym is a useful item in many centers. However, if the space for storing it is not available, it is a poor investment. It may end up being stored in another part of the building. If the location is inconvenient, the jungle gym will not be used very often.

## Supervision

Consider the number of staff available for supervision when selecting toys and equipment. You must think about how each item will affect your ability to properly watch over children. You will have to consider each item individually, balancing safety and developmental needs. Safety is a primary concern. For example, you may want to buy swings for the play yard. The state may require one adult supervisor for every 10 children. You can comply with state guidelines for ratios, but you might feel that more supervision is needed for safety. You may decide, in this case, that the swings would be an unwise purchase.

The developmental stages of children also need to be considered when choosing toys and equipment. This will affect the amount of supervision required. For instance, many five-year-old children can use blunt-nosed scissors with some guidance. However, four-year-old children require much more supervision for the same task.

## Maintenance

All toys and equipment require maintenance. The care required varies with the type of toy or equipment and the amount of use. For example, a plastic jungle gym needs less upkeep than a wooden or metal one. Upkeep of equipment can become costly.

## Durability

Children's toys need to be durable. Children bang, drop, stand on, sit on, and lie on toys. When angry, they may even throw toys. Broken toys can pose a danger to children. For instance, a broken toy can have sharp edges that cut. It is usually best to buy toys and equipment that are well built. You want to buy quality toys that will last through much use.

Wood and cloth are two materials that are durable, 9-3. Wood toys can withstand many years of use by many children. When buying wood toys, look for those made of hardwoods such as maple. The toys should also be split-resistant. The corners of the toy should be rounded.

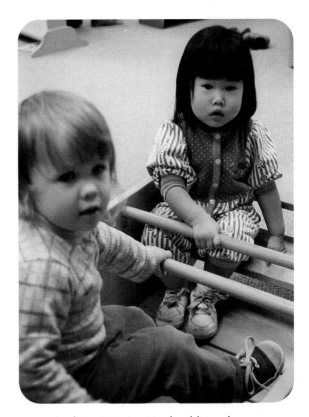

9-3 Wooden equipment is durable and can withstand rough play from children.

## Quantity

The quantity of toys can be as important when purchasing materials as the quality. In most classrooms, it is common to find two or more children playing with the same toys. To promote this type of cooperation, supply an ample amount of toys and materials for children. If there is a shortage of play materials, undesirable behavior can result. Therefore, be certain that any toys you wish to add to the classroom can be purchased in the needed amounts.

Variety should also be considered along with quantity. Is the item you wish to add to the classroom similar to existing items? Studies show that children who have been exposed to a wide variety of toys are more imaginative and creative. In order to provide variety, rotate toys and equipment regularly.

The chart in 9-4 lists suggested toys and equipment for a class of 15 children. These items represent a varied group of toys and equipment.

| Suggested Equipment and Supplies for a Class Unit of 15 Children | |
| --- | --- |
| **Type of Materials and Equipment** | **Select** |
| **Indoor blockbuilding** | • 400 hardwood unit blocks, including such shapes as units, half units, double units, quadruple units, pillars, large and small cylinders, curves, triangles, ramps, Y switches, X switches, floorboards, roof boards |
| **Floor play materials** | • 24 cars, airplanes, boats, fire engines, wagons, tractors, trains of assorted sizes<br>• 30 rubber, plastic, or wooden figures of farm and zoo animals; community workers: police officers, firefighters, and doctors; family members: mother, father, boy, girl, baby, grandparents<br>• 1 rocking boat |
| **Family living and dramatic play** | • 8-10 rubber dolls of all cultures and both genders; doll clothes; chest for doll clothes; baby bottles<br>• 2 doll carriages<br>• 1 doll bed, big and sturdy enough for a child to crawl into<br>• 1 smaller doll bed or crib<br>• Blankets, mattresses, pillows for doll beds<br>• Furniture for household play: wooden stove, cupboard for dishes, sink, small table and chairs<br>• Kitchenware: plastic dishes, tea set, small cooking utensils, silverware<br>• Housekeeping equipment: broom, mop, dustpan, brush, iron, ironing board, clothesline, clothespins<br>• Full-length mirror<br>• Dress-up clothes: men's and women's shoes, handbags, jewelry, hats, belts<br>• Supplies for other dramatic play: office equipment, telephones, cash registers, firefighters' hats, badges, play money, stethoscope, doctors' bags and white coats, nurses' hats |
| **Table and perceptual activities** | • Bingo and lotto games<br>• 12 wooden inlay puzzles of varying degrees of difficulty<br>• 1 puzzle rack<br>• Pegs and peg boards<br>• Matching games<br>• Sets of small blocks (cubes, parquetry, interlocking, snap-in, number)<br>• Large table dominoes: picture sets, number sets |

9-4 The toys and equipment in this list comprise a well-stocked classroom. You may have ideas for further additions.　　　　　　　　　　　　(Continued)

| Suggested Equipment and Supplies for a Class Unit of 15 Children | |
|---|---|
| **Table and perceptual activities (Continued)** | • Nested blocks<br>• Color cone<br>• Pounding peg board<br>• Cuisenaire rods, counting frames; abacus<br>• Hammer and nail sets with fiber insulation boards<br>• Cards: geometric shapes |
| **Art activities** | • 2 easels<br>• Drying rack for art materials<br>• 24 easel paint brushes with ½ in. and ¾ in. handles<br>• 75-100 quarts liquid tempera paint of various colors*<br>• 8000 sheets white manila paper, 4000 sheets newsprint 24 in. by 36 in.<br>• Paste and paste brushes<br>• 20 packages finger paint paper or glazed shelf paper<br>• 24 packages construction paper of various colors*<br>• 4 clay boards, 2 plastic covered pails for storing clay, and clay<br>• 100 lb. flour and 40 lb. salt for dough<br>• 18 blunt scissors, including some left-handed and training<br>• 5 aprons or smocks<br>• Miscellaneous supplies: orange juice cans, baby food jars, drying rack, florist wire, pipe cleaners, armature wire, colored toothpicks, macaroni pieces, transparent colored paper<br>• 5 dozen crayons*<br>• Rolling pins<br>• Transparent tape<br>• Stapler and staples |
| **Music** | • CD/casette player, CDs, casette tapes<br>• Autoharp®<br>• Xylophone<br>• Scarves, streamers<br>• Rhythm instruments: kazoos, shakers, maracas, sticks<br>• Drums, triangles, tambourines, cymbals, tom-toms<br>• Sleighbells for hands and feet<br>• Balls, hoops |
| **Woodworking** | • 1 sturdy, low workbench with 2 vises<br>• Tools: four 7 oz. claw hammers, two 12" crosscut saws, 1 hand drill, 1 rasp, 1 file, 2 screwdrivers, assorted nails with large heads, screws, 2 large C clamps<br>• Soft wood scraps, doweling<br>• Sandpaper<br>• Miscellaneous: buttons, washers, corks, wire, nuts, hooks and eyes, spools, bottle caps |
| **Furniture** | • 15 chairs, 8 in. to 12 in. in height<br>• 3 tables, 18 in. to 22 in. in height, for snacks, meals, and tablework activities<br>• 2 room dividers<br>• 15 cots for resting<br>• 15 lockers for hanging coats, hats, boots, extra change of clothes |
| **Science and special projects** | • Bar and horseshoe magnets<br>• Children's cookbook<br>• Magnifying glass<br>• Large indoor and outdoor thermometers<br>• Tubes<br>• Seeds |
| | *Include colors and hues of art materials and supplies to reflect skin tones. |

9-4  Continued.                                                                                    (Continued)

| Suggested Equipment and Supplies for a Class Unit of 15 Children | |
|---|---|
| **Science and special projects (Continued)** | • Animals: hamsters, mice, rabbits, fish, ducks, and gerbils (where permitted by law)<br>• Magnets<br>• Picture collection: machines, animals, plants, and geography<br>• Books with science concepts<br>• Tape measure, yardstick, rulers<br>• Scales<br>• Measuring cups and spoons<br>• Dry cell batteries, flashlight bulbs, electric wire<br>• Pulleys and gears<br>• Hand mirrors<br>• Hot plate and electric frying pan<br>• Aquarium and terrarium<br>• Cages for pets |
| **Water play (indoor and outdoor)** | • Small pitchers, watering cans, measuring cups, bowls of various sizes, plastic bottles, medicine droppers<br>• Funnels, strainers, egg beaters, ladles, straws, lengths of hose, brushes<br>• Soap and soap flakes<br>• Sponges |
| **Outdoor equipment** | • Sandbox, cans, buckets, spades, spoons, small dishes, colander<br>• Jungle gym<br>• Ladder box<br>• Horizontal ladder<br>• 5 tricycles<br>• 3 four-wheeled cars or "horses" manipulated by a child's feet<br>• 2 sturdy doll carriages<br>• 2 sturdy wooden packing cases (42 in. by 30 in. by 30 in.)<br>• 2 sturdy wooden packing cases (35 in. by 23 in. by 16. in.)<br>• 24 hollow wooden blocks (5½ in. by 11 in. by 11 in.)<br>• 12 hollow wooden blocks (5½ in. by 11 in. by 22 in.)<br>• 12 low sawhorses<br>• 8 small wooden kegs<br>• Wooden ladders<br>• Walking boards (balance beam) and flexible jumping boards<br>• Lengths of sturdy rope and garden hose<br>• Automobile and airplane tires and rubber inner tubes<br>• Rubber balls of different sizes; beanbags |
| **Language arts** | • 50 picture storybooks appropriate to the age, culture, and special interests of the children; books should include a range of poetry and prose, humor, fiction, and nonfiction<br>• Alphabet books |
| **Audiovisual aids** | • Chalkboard, erasers, chart paper<br>• Lotto and picture games<br>• Tape recorder or CD player<br>• Slide projector<br>• Video cassette recorder (VCR)<br>• Computer<br>• Video camera<br>• Television<br>• Felt board and felt figures |

9-4 Continued.

Adapted from Project Headstart, Equipment and Supplies—
Guidelines for Administrators and Teachers in Child Development Centers.

## Child Involvement

Choose toys that will actively involve children. Toys should move children to explore, manipulate, invent, and problem solve. In this way, children learn for themselves. They learn to use their imaginations.

**Spectator toys** such as battery-powered cars and talking dolls require little action on the child's part. Avoid purchasing these types of toys. Besides being costly, their appeal with children is quite often brief. Children will leave these toys for others that involve more imagination.

Choose simple toys, 9-5. Too much detail limits imagination. Open-ended materials free children to use their minds and express their creativity.

Blocks, play dough, paint, sand, and construction sets are open-ended toys. Using these items, children build structures, make designs, and play games. Children find endless ways to use such toys.

Use the checklist in 9-6 to define what skills can be learned from a specific toy. This task will help you see in what ways a toy will affect children. This knowledge can then be used when deciding on a purchase.

## Developmentally Appropriate Toys

Children's physical age and developmental age are often quite different. **Physical age** is an

| Checklist for Skills Learned from Toys | | |
|---|---|---|
| **Will the children learn or improve:** | **Yes** | **No** |
| auditory discrimination? | | |
| balance? | | |
| color concepts? | | |
| counting? | | |
| fine-motor skills? | | |
| gross-motor skills? | | |
| hand-eye coordination? | | |
| hearing-doing skills? | | |
| language concepts? | | |
| matching? | | |
| number concepts? | | |
| patterning? | | |
| seeing-doing skills? | | |
| self-esteem? | | |
| sensory discrimination? | | |
| sequencing? | | |
| social skills? | | |
| space perception? | | |
| strength? | | |
| throwing-catching skills? | | |
| visual discrimination? | | |

9-6  What other skills might you add to this list?

9-5  Cardboard blocks can be the source for a variety of unstructured play. What is built with them is limited only by a child's imagination.

age determined by a birth date. It is also known as **chronological age**. **Developmental age** refers to a child's skill and growth level compared to typical skills for that physical age group. For example, Kathy may be four years old physically, but only functions as an eighteen-month-old child. A child who functions as a four-year-old would be able to string beads. However, Kathy would only be able to do those tasks that an eighteen-month-old child can do. She lacks the hand-eye coordination needed to string beads. As you choose toys, remember the difference between physical and developmental age, 9-7.

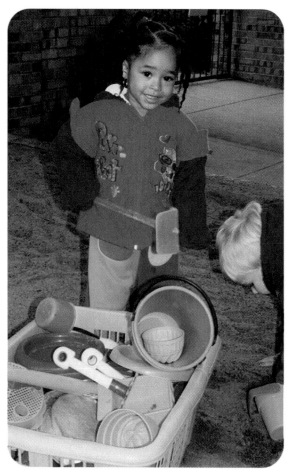

9-7 Toys that are appropriate for children's developmental ages are challenging for those children.

Toys that suit children's developmental ages help them build self-esteem. For instance, Leon will feel powerful as he learns to ride a scooter, or as he pushes a wagon up a hill. As he masters this skill, he gains a sense of control and builds an "I can do it" feeling.

Toys that do not match the child's development can cause frustration. This does little for a child's self-esteem. Lack of success with a toy can have a negative effect on a child. For instance, it is not likely that a two-year-old child would be able to put together an 18-piece puzzle. The child may make a number of attempts at the puzzle. Soon the child will become frustrated and move on to a toy that is more rewarding.

Chart 9-8 lists a number of toys and equipment pieces that are appropriate for various age groups. The ages on the chart refer to developmental ages.

## Violence and Toys

Children should not be taught to handle conflict with aggression or violence. Instead, they need to find useful ways to vent their feelings. One way to prevent aggressive behavior is to avoid giving children superhero or monster toys, toy guns, and war games. Children learn very little from these toys. The play that revolves around such toys is most often aggressive and destructive. For instance, when a child plays with a toy gun, he or she does little more than pull the trigger. Research shows that violent behavior increases when children play with action toys and replicas of weapons. Children who played with toy guns were more likely to destroy other children's work.

Many parents and teachers are opposed to the presence of these toys in the classroom. Therefore, it is best to simply avoid buying these toys.

## Nonsexist Toys and Materials

Nonsexist toys and materials provide children with the opportunity to explore nontraditional roles. Children are not locked into play that is common of their sex. For instance, boys can be nurses, preschool teachers, and stay-at-home fathers. Girls can be airplane pilots, truck drivers, and plumbers. This type of play will also help children form early ideas about careers.

As a teacher, it is important to set up an environment that is free of gender bias. Your attitude about toys will affect what children learn about sex roles. Make a conscious effort to use or suggest a variety of toys to all children. At the same time, however, be matter-of-fact. For instance, you might suggest for Omar to try playing in the kitchen. You can explain to him that there are many fun things to do in the kitchen.

| Developmentally Appropriate Toys and Equipment (Ages 6 months to 5 years) | | | | | | | |
|---|---|---|---|---|---|---|---|
| **Age Group** | **Block and Dramatic Play** | **Gross-Motor Equipment** | **Housekeeping** | **Sensory and Science** | **Creative Art and Books** | **Classroom Furnishings** | **Miscellaneous** |
| **Six months to one year** | grasping toys foam blocks soft animals bucket and blocks | beach balls push/pull toys activity gym | soft dolls stuffed animals puppets acrylic plastic mirrors | tub tub toys sensory mat | wall hangings mobiles | infant seat crib changing counter adult rocking chair cubbie high chair | soft balls stroller standard crib and mattress music boxes mirrors rattles |
| **One-year-old** | Add: large trucks interlocking blocks | Add: toddler stairs driving bench large foam blocks toddler barrel tire swing | Add: doll bed doll blankets doll mattress unbreakable doll wooden telephone | Add: sponges buckets funnels pitchers measuring cups scoops | Add: large crayons hard books cloth books tapes or CDs tape or CD player | Add: clothing lockers storage shelves book display cots | Add: stacking and nesting toys pull toys simple puzzles pop beads stacking cones pegboards |
| **Two-year-old** | Add: unit blocks wooden figures people zoo animals farm animals | Add: doll wagon hollow blocks rocking boat small jungle gym simple climber and slide tricycle | Add: simple doll clothes doll carriage child-sized sink, stove, pots, pans, aprons | Add: sand table water table | Add: picture books blunt scissors paste finger paints play dough | Add: bookcase block cart play table and chairs | Add: more complex puzzles large wooden threading beads small cots rest mat & cover sheet |
| **Three-year-old** | Add: dollhouse small dolls furniture | Add: walking board large wooden nesting boxes scooter wheelbarrow | Add: ironing board iron rocking chair broom, dustpan | Add: balance scales magnets ant farm prisms water pumps spray bottles sand molds | Add: easels paints brushes glue scissors | Add: work and library tables and chairs | Add: increasingly complex puzzles portable screens (room dividers) cots plants |
| **Four-year-old** | Add: puppets puppet theater more unit blocks | Add: planks swings slide shovel, pail, and rake triangle set coaster wagon large climber and slide | Add: chest of drawers washbasin clothesline and pins basket child-sized bed/cradle, carriage, wardrobe | Add: thermometer incubator plastic tubing | Add: clay modeling wax | Add: storage cart chalk/peg and bulletin boards | Add: aquarium pets |
| **Five-year-old** | Add: derrick | Add: balls roller skates | Add: tepee balance scale microphone | Add: microscopes tape measures motors | Add: sewing machine camera video camera | Add: woodworking bench tool cabinet tools | Add: giant dominoes construction sets |

9-8 Plan toy selection well. In this case, the toys from one age group blend into the next age group.

## Multicultural Toys and Materials

Toys and materials that are **multicultural** represent a variety of cultural and ethnic groups. These items are an essential part of a multicultural curriculum that teaches respect for people of all cultures. Multicultural toys and materials encourage children to explore the world's diversity. This helps them learn to appreciate others.

In addition, the early childhood environment needs to help each child develop a sense of identity. The child needs help to understand and appreciate his or her cultural and ethnic heritage. Each child needs to feel welcome and supported in the classroom. Thus, children need to see their heritage reflected among the program's toys and materials.

By choosing multicultural toys and materials, you communicate respect and appreciation for all cultures. A checklist for evaluating a classroom for multicultural toys and materials is given in Figure 9-10.

Puppets, dolls, and people figures should reflect cultural diversity. Puzzles, books, and

| Multicultural Checklist | | |
|---|---|---|
| Does your classroom provide the following multicultural items? | Yes | No |
| • A variety of books containing accurate information about many cultures. | | |
| • A culturally diverse collection of puppets, dolls, and people figures. | | |
| • Puzzles and small manipulatives representing people from around the world. | | |
| • Musical instruments from various cultures, such as maracas, drums, and flutes. | | |
| • Musical recordings in various cultural styles and languages. | | |
| • Art materials and supplies that reflect various skin tones. | | |
| • Multicultural posters, pictures, and decorations. | | |
| • Culturally relevant dress-up clothes, food, kitchen items, and furnishings for the dramatic play area. | | |

9-10  Use this checklist to choose multicultural toys that reflect diversity.

other toys should also be chosen with multiculturalism in mind. Pick items that show people of various cultures in positive and accurate ways. Art supplies should reflect a range of skin tones. Classroom decorations and bulletin boards should show people of all cultural and ethnic groups. Recorded music and musical instruments should represent various cultures, too.

## Using Technology in the Classroom

A critical issue teachers face is the use of technology in the early childhood classroom. Computer use should foster the children's learning, imagination, and creativity. It should compliment other activities and social interaction.

9-9  Include multicultural toys and materials in all areas of the classroom.

Computer use cannot replace physical activity or play with puzzles, blocks, and other materials.

For the most part, computers are considered inappropriate for children younger than three years. Very young children need to focus on learning fine- and gross-motor skills through body movements. They also need one-to-one interaction to develop language and cognitive skills. Most software programs require cognitive skills these children have not yet developed.

Studies have shown benefits for children older than three years who use the computer, however. These benefits are greatest when developmentally appropriate software is used with supporting activities. In studies, children who used the computer had gains in nonverbal, verbal, problem-solving, and conceptual skills as compared to other children.

Adults should use discretion in choosing children's software. Many programs exist, but not all are equal in terms of benefits for children. For instance, programs that model aggression are not appropriate for early childhood programs. Software that promotes learning is often preferred over programs that merely entertain. Two factors are vital—the program must be age-appropriate and easy to operate. Other qualities to look for include

- clear, user-friendly directions that children can follow without adult help
- colorful, animated, realistic graphics to hold children's attention
- logical sequences
- interactions with the child, including feedback
- promotion of problem-solving skills by offering choices
- investigation of concepts, such as numbers, colors, shapes, letters, or counting

By six years of age, most children can operate simple programs and follow instructions from a picture menu. They like showing others how to use the computer.

## Selecting Safe Toys

To promote safety, choose toys carefully. Serious injuries can result from poor toy selection. Many hazards cannot be seen at a glance or with normal use. For this reason, you must study each toy thoroughly before buying it. The safest toys are not always those that appeal most to adults. Rather, the safest toys are those that meet the standards outlined in this chapter.

Several federal laws regulate the manufacture and labeling of children's toys. Two of these laws are the Child Protection and Toy Safety Act and the U.S. Child Safety Protection Act. Passed in 1969, the Child Protection and Toy Safety Act sets basic standards for toy manufacturers. In 1995, the U.S. Child Safety Protection Act was passed. Among other provisions, this law mandates warning labels on toys that indicate whether the toy poses choking hazards to children younger than three years. Manufacturers must make sure toys and other children's products comply with all federal laws.

The government agency that issues and enforces these laws is the *U.S. Consumer Product Safety Commission (CPSC)*. Its mission is to reduce the risk of injuries and deaths associated with consumer products. The CPSC is heavily involved in the safety of children's products. The CSPC also recalls or bans unsafe products, conducts product research, and informs and educates consumers about product safety.

In addition to laws, many manufacturers follow the voluntary toy safety standards known as ASTM F963, which were published in 1997. ASTM F963 was based on standards the Toy Industry Association, Inc. (known then as Toy Manufacturers of America) set in 1971. While toy makers are not legally bound to follow ASTM F963, many do so in order to make their products safer. Toys that conform to ASTM F963 often indicate this on their packaging or labels, 9-11.

As a result of laws and standards, most new toys are developed with safety in mind. When used by children of an appropriate developmental age, these toys are generally safe. For example, small stringing beads are safe and useful for many four-year-old children. In the hands of a two-year-old, however, they present a risk of choking. Keeping inappropriate toys away from younger children is important.

Older toys are much more likely than newer toys to present safety hazards. This is because the toys were made prior to the most recent standards. They may contain the hazards addressed by these standards. Check older toys (or toys of an unknown age) very carefully for potential

## FOR AGES 3 & UP

**WARNING**

This toy contains small parts that may be hazardous to children under 3 years of age. For safety's sake, remove all tags and plastic loops before giving this toy to your child. These attachments are not part of the toy.

9-11 Labels now must indicate which toys present a choking risk for children under three years of age.

9-12 The safest toys for children under age three years have small parts that meet these size standards.

risks. Discard any items you find that contain any of the following safety hazards:

- **Breakable pieces**. For children under three years of age, toys must be unbreakable and able to withstand use and abuse.
- **Sharp edges or points**. Toys made with sharp edges or points are dangerous. Also hazardous are older toys that break and expose internal sharp edges or points. An example is a stuffed toy with sharp wires inside to stiffen its ears, legs, paws, and tail. Dolls that have hair or clothing held in place by straight pins are also dangerous.
- **Small parts**. For children under three years of age, toys and all parts of toys smaller than 1⅝ inches in diameter or 1½ inch long present a choking hazard, 9-12. Check product labeling to verify whether a toy is appropriate for children under three years of age. For toys with no label attached, use a plastic form or empty cardboard tube (from a roll of toilet tissue) to test the size. Any toy that fits inside the form or tube presents a choking risk for children under three years of age. Of particular risk are balls with a diameter or 1¾ inches or less and rattles that are small enough to be lodged in the throat or with pieces that can separate.
- **Toxic materials in or on toys**. For example, older toys may be painted with lead paint, which can be poisonous

if ingested. Older art materials may contain toxic materials.
- **Electrically operated toys with heating elements**. These toys can cause burns, fires, or electrocution. Any electrical equipment should have a seal from a safety testing organization, such as Underwriters Laboratories, Inc. (UL).
- **Battery covers with no locking mechanism**. Children can remove these covers, which exposes the batteries. Batteries present a choking risk and are poisonous if placed in the mouth or swallowed. Also dangerous are battery covers with removable screws. If these tiny screws are lost during battery changes, a child might later find and swallow them. Instead, look for covers that incorporate the screws or other locking mechanisms as part of a single-piece. Even safer is a single-piece cover that is attached to the toy. An attached battery cover eliminates the risk of choking on the cover itself.
- **Fabric products or toys that are not flame retardant or flame resistant**. The label will indicate whether a product is made to resist or slow the rate of burning.
- **Balloons**. Many children each year die from choking on uninflated balloons or

balloon pieces. Inflated balloons can also be hazardous if they pop and are swallowed.

- *Toys with small beadlike objects inside them*. If these toys are broken, the objects can fall out and pose a choking risk.
- *Pull toys with long cords or strings*. Cords and strings on toys should be too short to wrap around a child's neck, preventing the chance of strangulation.
- *Plastic climbing equipment used indoors without proper surfacing*. Carpeting does not provide adequate protection from falls from indoor climbing equipment. The CPSC reports these falls are the leading cause for significant injuries in child care settings. For indoor climbing equipment, approved rubber flooring or tile is needed.

If you have a safety problem with a product, you have an ethical obligation to report it. Your report can help protect other children from the same danger. Call the CPSC or visit the CPSC Web site to report an unsafe product. The CPSC investigates the reports it receives from consumers. If the CPSC finds the product to be unsafe, it may issue a product recall or ban. The CPSC can also set new standards in response to reports of consumer safety problems.

# Selecting Play Yard Equipment

In Chapter 8, you learned about planning for an outdoor play yard. In this chapter, you will learn about selecting the equipment that will be used on the play yard. This equipment may consist of stationary equipment, wheeled toys, wading pools or sprinklers, a shaded resting area, and animal shelters. Stationary equipment is the most costly and difficult to choose.

Selecting play yard equipment may be the job of the director. Teachers are often asked for suggestions to help in this process. In other programs, a committee of parents, teachers, and directors choose the play yard equipment. Everyone involved in the decision needs to know key points to consider.

## Safety

When it comes to play yard equipment, safety should always be the main concern. Many children are injured each year on outdoor play yards. Choosing equipment with safety in mind can reduce the number of serious injuries. Visit the CPSC Web site for detailed information about specific kinds of equipment.

Avoid choosing new equipment that is unsafe and check existing equipment for dangers. Repair or remove any dangerous equipment at once. General hazards to avoid include

- *Exposed pinch-crush parts on seesaws or gliders*. Children's skin or clothing can be caught in these areas. In addition, a child might lose a finger or toe if pinched here. Remove equipment with exposed pinch-crust parts from the play yard at once.
- *Head entrapment openings*. Measure the exercise rings or space between parts of equipment, such as rungs in a ladder. Openings should be smaller than 3.5 inches or larger than 10 inches. Children can get their heads caught in openings between these sizes. Remove any rings or close in any risers on ladders of unsafe sizes.
- *Open-end S-rings on swing sets*. These rings can pinch skin or catch clothing. You can close the S-ring pinching the ring shut with a pair of pliers.
- *Hard swing seats*. Children can be injured if hit by a hard swing seat, such as those made of wood, metal, or hard plastic. Replace any hard swing seats with those made of rubber or canvas, 9-13.
- *Exposed screws, bolts, or sharp edges*. Cuts and scrapes can result from these hazards. Use your hands to feel all the equipment. Cover bolts, screws, or sharp edges with layers of duct tape. Recheck the area often and reapply tape as needed. In addition, exposed screws and bolts are a danger because a child's hair or clothes can catch on them.

Even if a piece of equipment is free from safety hazards, it still may not be safe for use by

9-13 The safest swings have closed S-rings, rubber or canvas seats, steady anchoring, and adequate surfacing.

children in a particular program. Adults should consider each piece of equipment in terms of the following:

- Is the equipment safe for the children's ages and level of development? Some pieces of stationary equipment are designed for older children. Others are made for younger children. Programs with children of mixed ages need separate equipment for each age group.
- Is there enough room for the equipment on the existing play yard? This includes room required around the equipment for safety. Pieces of play equipment should be spaced at least 6 feet apart. Equipment should not be placed to close to sandboxes, wheeled toy paths, fences, or sidewalks.
- Is there appropriate surfacing for the equipment? If not, can it be added? Play equipment should never be installed over blacktop, brick, or cement. The space under and around all play yard equipment must be covered with an impact-absorbing material. Examples include resilient tiles, wood mulch, sand, and fine gravel. To absorb impact, loose-fill material must be kept 9 to 12 inches deep.
- Can the equipment be anchored properly? Equipment must be stable to avoid overturning, tipping, sliding, or moving in any way. The equipment needs to be anchored in concrete below

ground level before it is used. The anchoring process needs to comply with manufacturer's specifications.

## Appeal

If the equipment does not appeal to children, they will not use it. Before choosing equipment, teachers might ask children what they want to do on the playground (such as climb, swing, run). Then equipment can be chosen to allow children to meet their goals.

Equipment needs to be able to accommodate several children at once, 9-14. It should also be accessible for children with special needs. Colorful and interesting design attracts children's interest. Children prefer having a variety of equipment. They enjoy being able to push, pull, balance, swing, and slide. Children also like equipment on which they can climb or crawl in, out, under, and around. What they seem to like least is equipment with just one use.

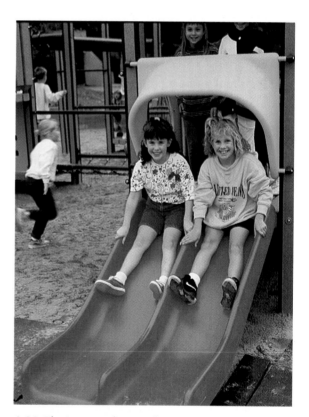

9-14 Playing together on the equipment enhances children's social skills and enjoyment of active play.

## Maintenance

When shopping for playground equipment, keep maintenance in mind. The program's staff will be responsible for repairing or replacing broken equipment. For safety reasons, children must not use or play near broken equipment.

Choose equipment that is durable. This equipment will withstand many years of heavy use. It will be less likely to break and need repair, which lowers maintenance costs.

For durability and safety, many of the newer playgrounds are constructed from plastic with metal and wood supports. This type of equipment combines the best features of each type of material. All-metal equipment is too hot in summer and too cold in winter. Over time, this equipment will also rust. All-wood equipment will weaken, splinter, and rot.

## Cost

Of course, programs must follow their budget when making playground purchases. Some programs plan a fundraiser to help meet the cost of expensive items. Staff should search catalogs and Web sites of several companies to learn what is available. Programs should receive cost estimates from each company. They should ask about costs for delivery, assembly, and installation. Knowing the final cost helps the program set goals for obtaining the money needed.

## Sources for Toys and Equipment

Before you begin selecting new toys and equipment, take an inventory of materials that are on hand. After this is done, compare the inventory with program goals. For example, you may note that there are too few manipulative toys. These then should be at the top of the list for purchase. See 9-15.

Using your list, browse through catalogs to find items you need. Take time to look through all the catalogs at the center. Catalog prices can vary a great deal. Consider all costs before ordering. For instance, does the shipping cost for an item make the purchase price too high? Some companies will not charge a shipping fee if the order is large.

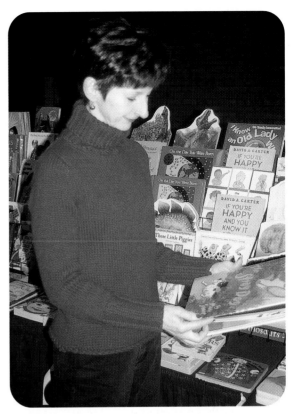

9-15 The exhibit area at an early childhood conference is a good source for toys and equipment.

Equipment can also be bought through a co-op. A **co-op** (cooperative) is a group of people or organizations who join together for the mutual benefit of more buying power. Co-ops are sometimes formed by directors of several small centers. One of the goals of the co-op is to purchase toys and equipment at the lowest cost. Companies will often give a discount on large orders. The directors share the savings with all those who are making purchases.

If time is available, you may wish to visit flea markets, garage sales, and discount stores. Materials can often be purchased at reduced prices. When buying used items be extra cautious regarding safety. Check for product recalls and know the safety standards for the objects you seek.

Toys can also be designed and built at the center. Senior citizens, Girl Scout and Boy Scout troops, and others may volunteer to help. Many of these people are skilled in making puppets, doll clothes, dramatic play clothes, and wooden toys.

## Buying Consumable Supplies

Clay, paper, paint, paste, glue, and other art materials are called **consumable supplies**. Once a consumable supply is used, it cannot be used again. In order to save money, some centers order these materials only once or twice a year. There are many ways to purchase these supplies.

If the order is large, the center may ask vendors to make bids on the sale. *Vendors* are the people who sell the supplies. Their bid is the price at which they will sell the items.

The center might also contact a vendor when placing a large order and ask for a 10 percent discount, plus free shipping. Many directors are surprised to learn that this can be done. This is very useful for stretching the center budget.

Another approach is to make a list of the supplies needed. Mark those items that could be donated, 9-16. Note who is in charge of securing what items. For example, the head teacher may be in charge of getting newsprint. Another teacher would be in charge of getting wallpaper. In some centers, the director is solely responsible for securing all donations.

| Consumable Supplies | | | | | |
|---|---|---|---|---|---|
| **Quantity** | **Item** | **Purchase** | **Solicit Donation** | **Source** | **Person Responsible** |
| 1 roll | Newsprint | | X | Dunn County News | Anna |
| 10 cans | Red tempera paint | X | | ABC School Supply | Jodi |
| 10 cans | Yellow tempera paint | X | | ABC School Supply | Jodi |
| 5 rolls | Wallpaper | | X | Menomonie Paint Store | Anna |
| 2 buckets | Sawdust | | X | Peterson Lumber Co. | Anna |
| 4 gallons | Dried corn | | X | Hardy's Elevator | Jodi |
| 4 yards | Fabric scraps | | X | Northwest Fabrics | Anna |
| 2 gallons | Paste | X | | ABC School Supply | Jodi |
| 1 box | Foam packing pieces | | X | James Jewelers | Anna |
| 24 boxes | Crayons | X | | ABC School Supply | Jodi |

9-16 Many groups are often eager to donate materials to worthy programs such as child care centers.

## Summary

Selecting toys and equipment is an important task. There are several guidelines that should be followed before purchases are made. Key factors to be considered are program goals, budget, balance, space, supervision, maintenance, durability, quantity, child involvement, and developmental age. Toys should also be nonviolent, nonsexist, multicultural, and safe.

Safety is a key consideration when buying toys and play yard equipment. Laws and guidelines have been developed to help you choose safe products for the children in your care. Report any defective or unsafe products to the U.S. Consumer Product Safety Commission.

Once guidelines are reviewed, purchases can be made. The teacher must know where and how to make these purchases. In this way, the teacher will be able to use the center budget wisely.

## Review and Reflect

1. True or false. Toys can promote the development of specific skills.

2. Why is budget an important consideration when buying items for the classroom?

3. Classroom toys and equipment should reflect the _____ the center has developed.

4. How does available space affect toy and equipment selection?

5. True or false. Maintenance is not an important factor in choosing equipment.

6. Toys must be durable because _____.
   A.  children will sit on, stand on, and drop them
   B.  broken toys can be dangerous
   C.  it is expensive to replace broken toys
   D.  All of the above.

7. Why is the quantity of toys an important consideration in toy selection?

8. _____ toys require little action on the part of children.

9. Explain the difference between physical age and developmental age.

10. Why is it important to choose toys that are appropriate for a child's developmental age?

11. Play that revolves around violent toys is often _____.
   A.  constructive
   B.  aggressive and destructive
   C.  a good learning experience

12. What are multicultural toys?

13. Give two guidelines for setting up a technology area in the early childhood classroom.

14. List two characteristics that are vital in selecting developmentally appropriate software programs.

15. The age at which most children can comfortably operate simple computer programs is _____ years.

16. List three safety guidelines to follow when purchasing toys.

17. Describe the dangers of each of the following:
   A.  Rings.
   B.  Wooden swing seats.
   C.  Screws and bolts.

18. Name three impact-absorbing materials that would be appropriate to use under outdoor play equipment.

19. What is a consumable supply?

## Apply and Explore

1.  In small groups, make a basic list of equipment for a classroom.

2.  Discuss favorite childhood toys and the value of each.

3.  Ask an early childhood program director about toy and equipment selection criteria.

4.  Cut pictures of toys from equipment catalogs that would be safe and appropriate for most two-year-old children.

C  5.  Check the age-by-age toy guidelines as well as tips for choosing toys for children with disabilities at the web site of the Toy Industry Association, Inc. (toy-tia.org).

6.  Search the Web site for the U.S. Consumer C Product Safety Commission (cpsc.gov). Check the warning related to playground hazards that can endanger children.

7.  Check the Web sites for online catalogs for C the following vendors: eichild.com; kaplanco.com; and lakeshorelearning.com. Prepare a brief written report describing offerings from each of these vendors.

8.  Visit the Web site C childrenandcomputers.com to review software recommendations for young children.

# Chapter 10

# Promoting Children's Safety

After studying this chapter, you will be able to

- list objectives for maintaining a safe environment for children.
- describe guidelines for promoting children's safety.
- name ways to promote and practice fire safety in an early childhood program.
- outline the procedures for treating poisonings.
- recognize the signs of child abuse.
- teach children how to resist child abuse.
- explain types of liability as a child care provider.

## Terms to Know

| | |
|---|---|
| limits | sexual abuse |
| emetic | incest |
| nonaccidental physical injury | molestation |
| neglect | statute |
| emotional abuse | privacy law |

"Please give me that broken toy," teacher Tina Goldstein said to the child. She immediately saw the danger of the unsafe toy. At the same time, Gloria Hernandez, the center director, was checking the art supplies. In the kitchen, the cook was filling out the monthly safety and sanitation checklist. All these staff members were showing their concern for the children's safety by checking the safety of their surroundings.

Dangers can be found everywhere in a child care center, 10-1. Electrical outlets, cleaning

10-1 Young children are active and adventurous. They can get themselves into dangerous situations in seconds. Supervision is necessary at all times.

supplies, woodworking tools, outdoor climbing equipment, and cooking tools can all cause injuries. Staff members must closely watch for and remove these dangers. Failure to do so may result in accidents. Most of these accidents can be avoided.

Accidents are more likely to occur when the children's routine is disrupted. Accidents also occur more frequently when staff are absent, busy, or tired.

Children can also be put in danger through abuse. Teachers must be aware of the signs of physical and emotional abuse. By law, teachers must report known or suspected child abuse.

As an early childhood teacher, you will need to be alert to any dangers that threaten the safety of your children. In addition, your program must have safety limits and procedures. The staff must also be aware of their legal responsibilities for protecting the children in their care.

## Safety Objectives

The staff is responsible for providing a safe environment for children. The following are basic objectives toward this goal:

- Supervise the children at all times.
- Maintain at least the minimum adult-child ratio as required in your state.
- Develop safety limits.
- Provide a safe environment.
- Practice fire safety.
- Know emergency procedures for accidental poisoning.
- Develop plans for weather emergencies.
- Recognize signs of child abuse and report any known or suspected cases.
- Teach children how to protect themselves from sexual assault.

The following sections will summarize procedures for meeting each of these objectives.

### Supervise the Children at All Times

"It happened so fast—I just left them for a moment or two," said the child care teacher. This teacher did not understand that children cannot be left alone for even a moment. A teacher who is responsible for a group of children should supervise constantly. Young children do not always understand the concept of danger. As a result, child care teachers must protect the children until they can protect themselves.

Young children are unpredictable, quick, and fearless. They lack sound judgment because they lack experience and cannot see from another's viewpoint. They may bite, throw, push, or shove. All these actions can endanger others as well as themselves. Young children may not recognize behaviors or actions that can cause injuries.

To properly supervise a group of children, keep your back to the classroom wall. Focus on the interior of the classroom. The entire room should be visible. Move closer to an area if you observe children who need assistance or redirection. Likewise, constantly observe children who are not involved in an activity. These children are more likely to create potential safety problems.

Bumps and bruises can occur in overcrowded classrooms. Make sure there is enough space for furniture and equipment. Observe children as they play. Can they move from area to area without bumping into furniture or other children? If sufficient space does not exist, remove some furniture or rearrange the classroom.

### Maintain Minimum Adult-Child Ratios

Adult-child ratio relates directly to safety. A classroom should never have fewer adults than required by state law for its age level and group size. Having more adults than the minimum is even safer. These extra adults can step in quickly to protect children when unsafe situations arise.

At least the minimum number of staff members set by your state's licensing rules must be present at all times. Failure to comply may result in the center's license being revoked or a citation indicating the center was not in compliance. Remember, too, if a child is injured, and staff/child ratios are not being met, center staff may be held liable.

### Develop Safety Limits

**Limits** are guides to actions and behaviors that reflect the goals of a program. Limits have also been called *rules*. The most important limits set by early childhood teachers involve safety issues. These limits protect the children in the classroom. Make safety limits clear, simple, and easy for children to understand, 10-2.

Some typical safety limits include:

- Walk indoors. Do not run.
- Use blocks for building, not for hitting.
- Wipe up spills right away.
- Tell the teacher when equipment breaks.
- Always fasten your seat belt when riding in the center van, 10-3.
- Climb the ladder to go up the slide. Do not walk up the slide from the bottom.

Remind children about the limits. Otherwise, they may forget or ignore them. For example, Eino may walk in front of moving swings. When this happens, say, "Eino, walk around the swings, not in front of them." Usually, this reminder will redirect a child. If Eino still fails to comply, you may have to say, "Eino, you need to stay away from moving swings." Do not allow anyone to continue swinging until Eino moves a safe distance away from the swings.

Teach children to wipe up spills promptly. Always keep paper towels within the children's reach. When children forget to wipe up a spill, remind them. Likewise, it's important to praise children who remember. Say, "Gerald, thank you for wiping up that spill. Now no one will slip and fall." Praise will encourage all the children to remember the limits. In time, you may hear the children remind each other of the limits.

10-2  Use bulletin boards to teach children about safety.

10-3  The driver of the center van should require children to fasten safety belts before each ride.

## Provide a Safe Environment

Closely observing children and setting safety rules for them to obey helps create a safe center. This is only part of the process. You must also keep watch for hazardous situations. Toys, equipment, electrical appliances, hot water, and cleaning supplies can pose danger to children. Center vehicles and the building itself can also be hazardous to children.

### Toys and Materials

A teacher's first job regarding toy safety is to choose items wisely. Picking safe toys and materials greatly reduces the risk of serious injury. (Refer to Chapter 9 to review toy selection safety.)

Selection is just the start, however. As a teacher, you must supervise children using the toys. Children often use toys in ways for which they were not designed. While most times this play is harmless, sometimes you must step in for safety reasons. For instance, a wooden mallet for use with a pegboard might be dangerous if children use it to hit each other. A metal toy car can be used safely for driving on the floor. This same car poses a safety risk if thrown, however. You must teach children about safe toy use and repeat safety limits often. Be firm but pleasant when enforcing the limits.

Remember, a toy can be safe for one child, but dangerous for another. Accidents can occur when children use toys that are too advanced for them. For instance, five-year-old children love to play with large marbles. These same marbles are a choking hazard for younger children.

Check toys frequently for safety. To illustrate, check the seams of cloth toys for tearing and weak threads. Tug at the different parts of the toy to test its strength. If the toy lacks durability, remove it from the classroom. Depending upon the condition and value, it can either be repaired or discarded.

Toys should also be examined for sharp or splintered edges. Observe to see if any small pieces have broken off or splintered. If a toy needs repairs, immediately remove it from the classroom.

As a teacher, you must also stay informed about changes in safety standards. When new standards are issued, check current toys to be sure they conform. Discard items that do not meet the new standards.

## Playground Equipment

Staff members have several duties when it comes to playground safety. First, they must be sure to plan the play yard with safety in mind. (Refer to Chapter 8 for guidelines about planning play yards.) For example, proper surfacing is a key safety concern, 10-4.

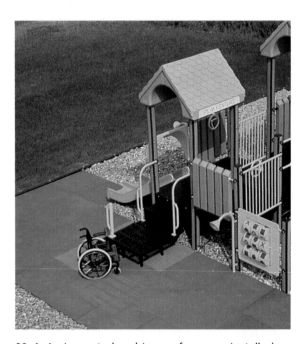

10-4  An impact-absorbing surface was installed under this playground equipment to prevent serious injuries related to falls.

Second, staff members must select safe play yard equipment. Safer equipment eliminates many preventable accidents. (Refer to Chapter 9 for more on this topic.) Many products are available today to help children enjoy safe outdoor play.

Third, staff must evaluate existing equipment for safety. Older equipment may not meet current safety standards. This equipment often contains hazards not found on newer equipment. These hazards include head entrapments, sharp edges, hard swing seats, and all-metal slides. Staff should research laws on play yard equipment safety. They must be sure their program complies with these requirements. Next, staff can seek tips from professional organizations regarding play yard safety. These tips can offer extra protection by exceeding legal requirements.

As equipment ages, it is likely to need upkeep and repair. For this reason, all play yard equipment must be checked often for dangers. Many programs devise a safety checklist to guide teachers in inspecting the play yard. Teachers conduct weekly checks, fill out the checklist, and give it to the director. The director must then arrange for needed repairs or maintenance.

Finally, and perhaps most importantly, staff are responsible for supervising children on the play yard. Even the safest equipment can cause accidents when it is not used properly. Limits must be set and enforced regarding equipment use. Children can be involved in setting these limits, if developmentally appropriate. Teachers must closely watch children using the equipment and step in when needed. Staff should praise children who are practicing safety.

## Center Vehicles

Motor vehicle accidents pose the greatest threats to children's lives. Vans, buses, and other vehicles owned by the center should have safety door locks and seat belts. For younger children, car safety seats that meet standards for the appropriate age should be installed. Train all staff and parent volunteers on the proper use of safety seats. While riding in any center vehicles, children should be fastened in a properly adjusted seat belt or safety seat. Do not allow children to put their arms or heads out of the vehicle's windows. When a number of children are riding in a vehicle, extra adult supervision may be required.

Center vehicles should be equipped for emergency situations. A first aid kit for treating minor injuries should be located in each vehicle. Moreover, a fire extinguisher and tools for changing tires should also be present in each vehicle. Vehicle drivers should be informed how to use these items.

## Building Safety

Many accidents that occur in centers involve the building and building fixtures. Windows, floors, and stairs all may cause injuries.

Keep windows closed at all times, unless gates or sturdy screens are in place. Keep floors dry. If wax is used, use a nonslip type. Cover stairways with carpet or rubber treads. Make sure stairways are well-lighted and free of clutter. Install railings at the children's level on both sides of the stairs.

Sliding patio doors, doors with glass panels, and storm doors can all be dangerous. The Bureau of Product Safety estimates that over a quarter of a million people are injured by glass each year. To protect the children, use only safety glass. Decals applied to sliding glass doors at their eye level warn children of glass they might not otherwise see.

Cover all unused electrical outlets in the building. Avoid using extension cords, particularly if they are placed under carpets or rugs. If the cord becomes worn, a fire may occur.

## Practice Fire Safety

To promote fire safety, check the center regularly for fire hazards. The best protection against fires is prevention. For instance, store matches where children cannot reach them and accidentally start fires. As a teacher, you need to find and correct fire hazards. A fire safety checklist is shown in 10-5. Study this list so you will be able to spot hazards and take action quickly.

| Fire Safety Checklist | | |
|---|---|---|
| | Yes | No |
| 1.  Exit passageways and exits are free from furniture and equipment. | | |
| 2.  Locks on bathroom and toilet stall doors can be opened from the outside, and can be opened easily by center staff. | | |
| 3.  Protective covers are on all electrical outlets. | | |
| 4.  Permanent wiring is used instead of lengthy extension cords. | | |
| 5.  Each wall outlet contains no more than two electrical appliances. | | |
| 6.  A fire evacuation plan is posted. | | |
| 7.  Fire drills are conducted at least monthly, some of which are unannounced. | | |
| 8.  Flammable, combustible, and other dangerous materials are marked and stored in areas accessible only to staff. | | |
| 9.  Children are restricted to floors with grade level exits (no stairs). | | |
| 10.  The basement door is kept closed. | | |
| 11.  There is no storage under stairs. | | |
| 12.  Fire extinguishers are in place and checked regularly. | | |
| 13.  Smoke alarms and fire alarms are checked at least once a month. | | |
| 14.  Matches are kept out of the reach of children. | | |
| 15.  Toys, chairs, tables, and other equipment are made of flame-retardant materials. | | |
| 16.  Carpets and rugs are treated with a flame-retardant material. | | |

10-5  A fire safety checklist may include many items. Would you add any items to this checklist?

Check smoke alarms at least once each month to make sure they are working. If smoke detectors are battery powered, change batteries when indicated.

### Fire Extinguishers

Each child care center needs several fire extinguishers. One fire extinguisher should be placed in or next to the kitchen. Place an extinguisher in or near each classroom. Another extinguisher is needed in the laundry area. Check your state's licensing regulations for the placement of fire extinguishers.

The director is often in charge of buying fire extinguishers for the center. Before buying an extinguisher, contact your local fire department. The fire chief can tell you which type of extinguisher is best suited for your center's unique needs. You will want one that fights the types of fires your center is most likely to have. In addition, ask the fire chief how to maintain the extinguisher and recharge it after use.

Schedule an in-service on fire extinguisher use prior to the opening of the center. Some directors prefer to have a local firefighter conduct this in-service. After this orientation, update all staff members yearly (and newly hired members) on fire extinguisher use.

Check the condition of each fire extinguisher monthly. Note any problems you find. Replace immediately any extinguisher with any of the following conditions:

- pressure gauge indicating the higher or lower pressure than recommended
- blocked nozzle or other parts
- missing pin or tamper seal
- dents, leaks, rust, or other signs of damage

### Fire Drills and Evacuation Procedures

Most state licensing rules and regulations require fire and disaster drills. Most states also recommend drills be scheduled on a regular basis, such as once a month. These drills will prepare staff and children for a real fire or other emergency. During drills, use the daily class roster to take roll. It is an important tool for checking on the evacuation of all children and their safe return indoors.

Every center needs to have well-planned evacuation procedures. The procedures should include escape routes, staff assignments, and location of alarms. The evacuation procedures should be posted in every room where they can be easily seen. Emergency phone numbers should also be posted. In case of blocked routes, alternative evacuation routes should be planned. An example of procedures to be used is shown in 10-6.

If a fire is discovered in the center, sound the alarm immediately. Stay calm. If you panic, the children will panic as well. Evacuate children from the building at once, even if you do not see flames. Smoke, not fire, is responsible for more deaths. Leave the classroom lights on and close the doors. Do not lock the doors, however. Lights allow firefighters to see better in a smoke-filled structure.

Take roll as soon as the children and staff have cleared the building. When firefighters arrive, inform the chief whether anyone is still in the building.

When making evacuation plans, remember that infants are more difficult to remove than older children. This is because infants cannot walk. Most adults cannot carry more than two infants at one time. Therefore, when ratios are higher than one caregiver to two infants, a careful plan needs to be made. Some centers practice by placing several babies in a crib and rolling it out of the building. Wagons can be used for evacuating older children.

Plan and introduce fire and burn prevention into the curriculum, if developmentally appropriate. Teach the children what to do if their clothing catches fire. Chart 10-7 shows the stop, drop, and roll technique.

| Evacuation Procedures |
|---|
| 1. Sound fire alarm. |
| 2. Evacuate the building. |
| 3. When leaving the building, leave lights on and close doors. Do not lock doors. |
| 4. Call the fire department after leaving the building. |
| 5. Take roll as soon as the children are together in a safe place. |
| 6. When the firefighters arrive, report whether all children and staff are out of the building. |

10-6 Review evacuation procedures with children. Post the procedures in a noticeable place.

**Stop, Drop, and Roll**

**2. DROP:**
Drop to your knees.

**3. ROLL:**
Cover your face with your hands, and then roll over and over to smother the flames.

**1. STOP:**
Don't move. Stop where you are.

10-7  If clothing catches fire, the stop, drop, and roll technique should be used.

## Weather or Disaster Emergencies

Blizzards, hurricanes, floods, electrical storms, tornadoes, and earthquakes are examples of weather or disaster emergencies. All these conditions pose safety threats for the children and staff. Therefore, it is important to have an emergency plan for possible weather or disaster emergencies. The plans you formulate will depend on the geographical area in which you are located.

In areas where natural disasters occur more often, evacuation drills should be practiced with the children on a monthly basis. Evacuation procedures need to become routine for the children.

In some weather emergencies, you may decide to close the school. You need to have a plan in place for notifying parents of such an emergency. Special arrangements may need to be made for transporting the children.

Be prepared for weather emergencies. Always keep battery-operated flashlights and a radio in a convenient spot. For some weather emergencies, blankets, water, food, and a first aid kit should also be available.

## Poisonings

Studies show that children under five years of age account for almost two-thirds of poisonings that occur each year. Nearly any substance can, under certain conditions, be poisonous. The National Safety Council claims that the average residence contains over 40 poisonous products. Chart 10-8 lists many of these poisonous products.

Children eat many things adults would not think of placing in their mouths. There may be times when you are not sure whether a child has eaten something. For instance, you see a child playing with an empty aspirin bottle. The child has powder around the mouth. When in doubt, always assume the worst. If the child has eaten the aspirin, failing to act may result in great harm.

If you suspect that a child in your classroom has eaten something poisonous, remain calm. Telephone the nearest poison control center. If your area does not have a poison control center, call the nearest emergency room. Ask for instructions on treating the child.

| Poisonous Substances | | | |
|---|---|---|---|
| Batteries/battery acid<br>Candle wax<br>Cleaners: ammonia,<br>   bleach, dishwasher<br>   detergent,<br>   dishwashing liquid,<br>   disinfectants, drain<br>   cleaner, dusting<br>   spray, lemon oil,<br>   spot remover, | toilet bowl cleaner,<br>   window cleaner<br>Cosmetics and personal<br>   care items: after-<br>   shave lotion, hair care<br>   products, makeup,<br>   mouthwash, nail<br>   polish and nail polish<br>   remover, perfume,<br>   sunscreen | Flowers and plants:<br>   many varieties-<br>   consult a greenhouse<br>   for names<br>Glue<br>Lighter fluid<br>Matches<br>Medications: many<br>   prescription and over-<br>   the-counter drugs | Mouse poison<br>Paint and paint thinners<br>Pesticides<br>Plant food<br>Shoe polish<br>Soap<br>Vitamins |

10-8 These common household items are all poisonous and should be kept out of the reach of children.

## Emergency Procedures for Poisonings

Poisoning emergencies often involve swallowing toxic substances. Other types of poisoning emergencies can occur, also. These include breathing toxic fumes and chemical injuries to the eyes or skin.

If any type of poisoning emergency occurs, follow the procedures given below. Do not rely on first aid information, antidote charts, or product information. Often this information is outdated or incorrect. The child may experience additional injury if the wrong action is taken.

Always contact your local poison control center for all cases of poisonings. When you call the center, be prepared to provide specific information. You will be asked to describe the child's symptoms. You will also be asked to identify any first aid procedures you have already administered. Report the time at which the substance was taken and the child's age and weight. Then provide the name of the poisonous substance. If the child removed the substance from a container, have the container with you when you call. Report the amount of substance the child consumed. Unless the exact amount is known, overestimating the amount consumed is better than underestimating it.

All first-aid stations at child care centers should have an emetic available for poisoning emergencies. An **emetic** is a substance that induces vomiting when swallowed. Syrup of ipecac is an example of an emetic. Use extreme caution before giving a child syrup of ipecac. *Never give a child syrup of ipecac unless the physician at the poison control center advises this treatment.* Some poisons, such as drain cleaner or lye, can cause serious damage to the child's esophagus if vomiting is induced. These substances are called caustics. They burn going down the child's esophagus. If vomiting is induced, they will also burn coming up.

One of the leading causes of poisoning in young children is plants. When eaten, certain plants can cause skin rashes, upset stomachs, or even death. Many common household plants are poisonous. To prevent poisoning, check with your florist before purchasing a plant for the classroom. Finally, teach children never to put any leaves, flowers, or berries into their mouths.

## Child Abuse

As a child care professional, you are very concerned about the health and safety of the children in your care. You do everything you can to see that the center is a safe place for them to be. However, the children are not in your care all the time. When they are away from the center, some children are abused. Because you are with the children for several hours a day, you may be the one to notice signs that a child is being abused or neglected. It is your responsibility to report known or suspected cases of child abuse to a department of social services, child protective services, or the police.

There are four types of child abuse: nonaccidental physical injury, neglect, emotional abuse, and sexual abuse. Be aware of the signs of each type of abuse.

## Nonaccidental Physical Injury

The most visible type of child abuse is **nonaccidental physical injury,** 10-9. This is physical abuse inflicted on purpose. Children being abused in this way often come to school with bruises, bites, burns, or other injuries. They may have frequent complaints of pain.

Physically abused children often refuse to discuss their injuries. This may be because their abusers threaten them with further harm if they tell someone. Other children may talk about harsh punishment they have received.

Often these children come to the center wearing clothing to hide their injuries. Their clothing may be unsuitable for the weather.

As a result of being physically abused, some children may show an unusual fear of adults. Katrina is one example. She was abused by her father for two years. A teacher at Katrina's child care contacted authorities with her suspicions. Katrina had an unusual fear of adults, especially her father. Whenever he came to pick her up, she backed away and avoided eye contact with him.

Child abuse was suspected for other reasons as well. Katrina often arrived at the center with visible bruises. She also wore long-sleeve turtleneck tops in warm weather. One hot summer day, her teacher was concerned that Katrina might be too warm. When she was changing Katrina's top, the teacher found many bruises. Katrina could not explain the injuries.

| **Signs of Possible Physical Abuse** |
|---|
| Child has unexplained or repeated injuries (bruises, bites, cuts, burns, fractures). |
| Child and parent provide illogical or conflicting explanations for injuries. |
| Child complains frequently of pain. |
| Child displays fear of adults, including parents. |
| Child avoids giving or receiving affection. |
| Child wears clothing that can hide injuries, even when unsuitable for the weather. |

10-9  These signs may indicate a child is being abused.

## Neglect

When children are not given the basic needs of life, they suffer from **neglect**. Neglect takes many forms. A neglected child may be deprived of proper food, medical care, shelter, and/or clothing. Children who have been unsupervised may also be neglected. Neglect may or may not be intentional on the part of the abuser. However, the potential for harm is possible.

Children who wear clothing that is too small or dirty may be neglected. Neglected children may also wear clothes that are inappropriate for the weather. They may lack coats, gloves, or hats for the winter. Children who are poorly groomed may also be neglected.

Other signs of neglect may appear in a child's health. Neglect may result in children who are too thin or malnourished. Constant fatigue, illness, or poor dental care may be other signs of neglect.

Alert teachers should observe for signs of neglect. They must be sensitive to different child-rearing practices as well as cultural expectations and priorities.

Derek is a neglected child. His teacher observed he appeared small for his age. After observing him for several more months, she noted developmental lags. He appeared to be lagging behind many of his same-age peers. Often he would ask when snack or lunch would be served. During cooking activities, he would try to eat or take food. He also complained of being hungry. Derek lacked proper nutrition.

Observing these signs, Derek's teachers suspected neglect. They compared information and shared their concerns. As child care teachers, they knew they were required to report suspected child abuse. They knew Derek would never reach his full potential without proper nutrition.

## Emotional Abuse

**Emotional abuse** is abuse of a child's self-concept through words or actions. Children lose self-esteem due to emotional abuse. Excessive or inappropriate demands may be made on the children by parents or guardians. This can cause emotional harm to children. Emotional abuse is the result of insufficient love, guidance, and/or support from parents or guardians.

Children who are emotionally abused may repeat certain behavior over several months. Look for the following signs:

- refusal to talk
- unusual or unpredictable behavior
- excessive clinging or crying
- withdrawn behavior
- destructive behavior
- poor motor coordination for age
- fear of adults

## Sexual Abuse

**Sexual abuse** is forcing a child to observe or engage in sexual activities with an adult. Rape, fondling, and indecent exposure are all forms of sexual abuse. Each of these acts involve adults using children for their own pleasure. **Incest** is sexual abuse by a relative. **Molestation** is sexual contact made by someone outside the family with a child.

There are many signs of sexual abuse. A child may have problems when walking or sitting. The child may complain of itching, pain, or swelling in the genital area. Some sexually abused children have bruises in the genital or anal areas. They may also have bruises in their mouths and throats. Some may complain of pain when urinating.

Sexually abused children commonly have poor peer behaviors. They may show extremely disruptive or aggressive behaviors. Often they will regress to infantile behaviors, such as baby-talking, thumbsucking, or bed-wetting. Some will show a lack of appetite. These children often express affection in improper ways.

Annabelle is a sexually abused child. She refused help with clothing and toileting needs. She would not allow teachers to help her remove her outdoor clothing. Her teachers thought Annabelle's behavior was unusual. After observing another incident, they suspected she was sexually abused. Annabelle liked Richard, one of the children in her group. They saw her rubbing his crotch with her hand during group time.

After observing Annabelle's behavior, the teachers reported their suspicions of abuse. They realized if they continued waiting for more proof, there could be greater risk to the child.

## Reporting Child Abuse

Health care workers, social workers, school administrators, and teachers are *mandated reporters* of child abuse. This means they are required by law to report any known or suspected cases of child abuse or neglect. As a mandated reporter, you should read your state's **statute**, a formal document drawn up by elected officials. The statute will explain your legal responsibilities and the penalties for failing to make a report. To receive a copy of the statute, contact your local law enforcement office.

Follow your program's procedure for reporting child abuse and neglect to the proper authorities. Your program must comply with the law, but may also have other guidelines in making a report. For instance, you might need to complete certain paperwork and report the abuse to the director. Some programs designate one employee to make all reports of child abuse for the program. In other programs, each staff member reports these cases himself or herself.

If you must make a child abuse report, do so immediately by telephone. Include the name, age, and address of the child and his or her parents. Report the facts that led to your suspicion. After the telephone conversation, confirm the report in writing. Make a copy of the written report for the program and one for yourself. As long as you make the report in good faith, you will not be subject to legal action if your suspicions are found not to be child abuse or neglect.

Should a child abuse case result in a trial, you may be required to testify in court. This may make you feel nervous, but focus on telling the truth. Your legal and ethical responsibility is to tell the court what you know about the case that will help the court protect the child.

## Protection Education

Planning for children's safety goes beyond the classroom. Children need to learn how to deal with dangers outside the classroom. They must learn about sexual abuse and how to protect themselves from it.

Warning children about strangers has been a common practice for some time. However, only 10 to 15 percent of child abusers are strangers to the children they abuse. The other 85 to 90 percent are people known to the children. These people may be neighbors, relatives, friends of the family, scout leaders, siblings, or parents. Most offenders are men. However, women are also reported.

Before age eight, 3 to 4.6 percent of all children are sexually assaulted. About 10 percent of these children are assaulted by the time they are five years old. Girls are reported as victims far more often than boys. Studies show that race, intelligence, family income, and social class do not appear to affect the occurrence of sexual assault.

Teach children to resist sexual attacks. They must first resist the offender by saying no. Then they must tell a trusted friend or relative about the attack. Role-play this process with the children. Give them phrases to use if they find themselves in trouble. For example:

- If someone tries to give you a wet kiss, shake hands instead.
- If someone tries to get you to sit on his or her lap and you do not want to, say "No, not now."
- If someone wants to give you a hug and you do not want it, say "No thanks."
- If someone tries to touch your genitals, say "Stop. That is not okay."
- If someone rubs or pats your bottom, say "Do not do that."

Children may have trouble identifying sexual abuse. This is especially true with people they know. To combat this problem, explain to the children the difference between good touch and bad touch. A *bad touch* is any of the following: a touch the child does not want or like, a touch that hurts or makes the child uncomfortable, a secret touch, or any touch to a child's private parts (genitals). A *good touch* is wanted and appropriate. It does not make the child uncomfortable.

Suggest various scenarios and ask the children whether these are good or bad touches. In the classroom, encourage children to tell the other person when they don't want to be touched or don't like how a touch feels. Help them put these feelings in words. Intervene if a child persists with a touch after being asked to stop.

Children also need to learn how and who to tell if someone assaults them. Use puppets, charts, movies, or other materials to teach children this lesson.

# Liability

By law, young children are not expected to care for themselves. This is the primary role of the staff at the center. The staff must ensure the children's safety and health. Education is a secondary function.

Center directors are liable for the acts of their employees. *Liable* means having a responsibility that is upheld by the law. Having *liability* means you can be punished for failing to uphold your legal responsibility. The extent of liability may vary, however. As a result, only individuals who are safety- and health-conscious should be hired, 10-10. The director needs to observe newly hired people to ensure they use good supervision techniques.

## Types of Liability

Child care staff can be punished by law for failing to follow state licensing rules and regulations. Center staff can be liable for *not* doing the following:

- Obtaining a signed health form from a licensed physician for each child.
- Requiring a staff member to have an approved physical before working with children.
- Providing safe indoor and outdoor equipment.
- Operating a center with the required adult-child ratios.
- Providing proper supervision.
- Providing proper food storage.
- Maintaining fence and door locks in proper condition.
- Providing staff with information about children's special needs.
- Refraining from corporal (physical) punishment.
- Providing a safe building.
- Removing children who lack self-control and are a hazard to themselves as well as others.
- Covering electrical outlets.

Center directors and staff must keep constant watch over the center environment. They must ensure that it is safe as well as healthy. New teachers will need constant support from the staff and director.

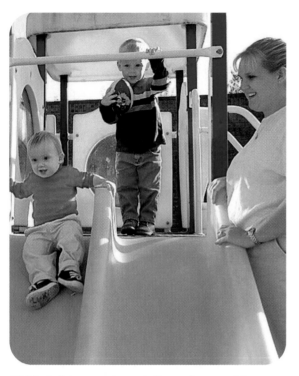

10-10  Safety-conscious staff members watch for danger in all situations.

## Forms

Every center should develop a number of forms related to the health and safety of the children. Many of these forms direct the staff in the care of the children and protect staff members from possible liability. Two forms commonly used by centers are injury report forms and various types of release or permission forms.

Every center should have a standard injury report form. Any information recorded on this form is useful if legal action is brought against the center. Parents also need to be informed about the details of a child's accident. A sample form is shown in 10-11.

Various permission forms should also be on file. These forms should be filled out at the time of the child's enrollment. Permission is usually required for such items as special screening tests or walks around the neighborhood. To protect children from being picked up from the center by a stranger, unauthorized person, or even a noncustodial parent, a transportation form should be used. This form should contain the names, relationship, telephone numbers, and driver's license numbers of people who have permission to transport the child to and from the center. Staff should check the identification of anyone other than the parents who comes to pick up the child from the program. In the event a parent wants to add or remove an individual from the list, a new form needs to be completed.

### Privacy Law

The **privacy law** is designed to protect children. It states that a child's records cannot be given to anyone other than parents, without the parents' permission. Give a child's records only if the parents have made the request in writing. After receiving the request, the materials must be released within 45 days. A form that can be included in each child's file is shown in 10-12.

Parents are given unlimited access to all of their child's records kept by the center. Included may be screening information, developmental

---

**Injury Report Form**
**Child and Family Study Center**

Child's Name _____

Date of injury _____Time of injury _____A.M./P.M.

Staff members present: _____

Witness(es): _____

Description of the incident: (Include specific information, such as where the child was playing, with whom, and with what.)



Description of injury: (Include specific information, such as type, location, size, and severity of injury and symptoms noted following injury.)



Action taken by staff: (Include all actions, such as treating injury, seeking medical advice or care, comforting child, and notifying director and parents.)



_____
(staff signature)

_____
(parent signature)

10-11  The information in an accident report form is useful for parents and teachers.

evaluations, and parent meeting planning sheets and summaries. Many teachers share all this information during parent meetings. These meetings will be discussed more in Chapter 31, *Parent Involvement*.

The information contained in this file is confidential and is not to be circulated outside the center without the prior written consent of the child's parents.

Under Public Law 93-380: Parents have access to all educational records. According to this law:

(1) You are not allowed to provide the information contained in this file to anyone without the written consent of the child's parent or guardian.

(2) You must advise parents of their rights concerning their child's file

(3) Parents have the right to read and review the file. Moreover, they may request a revision of information in their child's file.

(4) Within forty-five (45) days, you are required to respond to a parent's request.

File reviewed by:

| Name and Title | Address | Reason | Date |
|---|---|---|---|
| | | | |
| | | | |
| | | | |
| | | | |
| | | | |

10-12  Use a form such as this to record reviews of children's files.

## Summary

Providing a safe environment for children requires a great deal of time and attention to details. Danger can be found in every corner of the center. These dangers can threaten both the physical and mental well-being of children. Protecting children from these dangers is the most important job of a teacher.

Child care professionals need to be prepared for any emergency. You should know how to use fire extinguishers and how to safely evacuate the children in case of a fire or other disaster. You should know how to handle accidental poisonings. Child care workers also need to recognize signs of possible child abuse and know how to report suspected cases.

Child care staff can be held responsible for failing to follow state licensing rules and regulations. It is important to know what those rules are and to know the extent of any possible liability.

## Review and Reflect

1. Name four basic safety objectives.

2. What is the primary role of the staff at a center?

3. True or false. Most accidents in a child care center can be avoided.

4. Usually, younger children require _____ staff supervision than older children.

5. Name three ideal places to keep fire extinguishers in a child care center.

6  True or false. Smoke claims more lives than fire does.

7. Applying _____ at eye level to glass doors makes glass visible to children.

8. True or false. Nearly any substance, under certain conditions, can be poisonous.

9. What is an emetic?

10. Name the four types of child abuse.

11. List three behavior patterns exhibited by emotionally abused children.

12. Explain what is meant by a *bad touch*.

13. List three unsafe situations for which a center is liable.

14. True or false. Parents are allowed only limited access to records kept by the center concerning their child.

## Apply and Explore

1. Design an evacuation chart for the classroom.

2. Using the poisonous substances chart in this chapter, conduct a safety check of your home. List the poisonous substances you found.

3. Arrange a visit to a center to learn about their safety objectives. Ask to view any safety checklists they might use.

4. Interview the local fire chief concerning the proper use of fire extinguishers.

5. Arrange a visit to the emergency room of a local hospital. Ask the doctor on duty to discuss emergency procedures used for poisonings.

6. Create a puppet play using phrases that children may use if ever faced with sexual abuse.

7. Check the Web site of the National Resource Center for Health and Safety in Child Care (nrc.uschsc.edu) for safety tips for child care centers.

8. Review the Web site for the National Program for Playground Safety (uni.edu/playground) to learn more about planning a safe play yard.

# Chapter 11

# Planning Nutritious Meals and Snacks

After studying this chapter, you will be able to

- list goals for a good nutrition program.
- explain the importance of a healthful diet.
- describe nutritional problems that can result from a poor diet.
- name the food groups in the Food Guide Pyramid for Young Children and the main nutrients they supply.
- plan nutritious and appealing meals and snacks for children.

## Terms to Know

nutrition

nutrients

undernutrition

malnutrition

diabetes

insulin

allergy

anaphylactic shock

Food Guide Pyramid for Young Children

It was lunchtime at the New Horizons Child Care Center. Nidda asked for a second serving of spinach, a food being served for the first time. Maria said the potatoes were yummy. Geneva said her mother was sending oranges for her birthday treat. Throughout her meal, the teacher talked with the children and ate portions of the foods served.

The lunchroom was decorated with 12 large paper ice cream cones. Each cone represented one month of the year. The children's names and birthdays were written on paper scoops of ice cream. These scoops were placed in the cone that matched their birthday month.

On the other side of the lunchroom was a large carrot cut out of tagboard. A cloth measuring tape was pasted down the center. Each child's height was marked next to the tape.

In this classroom, children learn about nutrition both directly and indirectly. For instance, the variety of foods served and the teacher's comments about the food are direct learning experiences. Children learn about many types of food and that mealtime is a pleasant time. The positive attitudes and pleasing surroundings of the lunchroom are indirect learning experiences. By watching friends and teachers, children develop habits and attitudes about food. Many of their food attitudes and behaviors will last into adulthood. Hopefully, they will establish a lifelong pattern of eating a nutritious diet.

Teaching children about nutrition will be an important responsibility for you as a teacher. Proper nutrition is needed for children's health, growth, and development. Behavior and learning ability is related to nutrition. Some studies suggest that young children who have learned healthful food choices may experience lifelong health benefits.

Teaching nutrition concepts requires a good nutrition program. A good program centers on the needs of the children, including their ethnic backgrounds. These nutrition concepts should be integrated into all subject areas. Program goals should include the following:

- Providing nutritious meals and snacks.
- Introducing new healthful foods.
- Encouraging healthful eating habits.
- Involving children in meal activities.
- Providing nutrition information to parents.

To meet these goals, you will need to understand how food is used by the body. In addition, you must know the various nutrients and their sources. Meal plans and food experiences for the children are also needed to meet program goals.

## Nutrition

**Nutrition** is the science of food and how the body uses the foods taken in, 11-1. **Nutrients** are the chemical substances in food that help build and maintain the body. Certain nutrients are needed to build a strong body and mind. There are six groups of nutrients needed for growth and maintenance of health. These are proteins, carbohydrates, fats, vitamins, minerals, and water. Chart 11-2 lists some of the most important nutrients, their functions, and sources.

Food also provides the body with energy. Each food has its own energy value. This value is measured in calories. Energy from food supports body processes, such as breathing and blood circulation. All your organs and body systems need energy to function. Your body's physical and mental activities require energy, too.

The amount of calories a person needs depends on age and activity level. Children need more energy than adults, in relation to body weight. For instance, a four-year-old boy weighing 42 pounds needs about 1800 calories per day. A 45-year-old man weighing 160 pounds needs about 2700 calories per day. Thus, the child needs about 43 calories per pound while the man needs about 17 calories per pound. Children's physical growth is greater than adults' growth. Children are also very active. All their physical activities use a great deal of energy.

11-1 Knowledge of nutrition is needed for planning healthy meals and snacks.

### Nutritional Problems

Undernutrition, malnutrition, and overeating are problems that affect children's health and development. The effects of poor nutrition on cognitive abilities have been proven in several studies. In order to plan nutritious meals and snacks, you need to know the effects of these problems.

**Undernutrition** means not eating enough food to keep a healthy body weight and activity level. The person gets too few nutrients because not enough food is eaten. This often results from poverty. **Malnutrition** is a lack of proper nutrients in the diet. It happens when a nutrient is absent or lacking from the diet. An unbalanced diet, poor food choices, or the body's inability to use the nutrients properly can be the cause.

Children with these problems often are shorter than their peers. Long-term deficiencies can slow, or even stop, growth. Other signs of poor nutrition include irritability, bowed legs, sunken eyes, decaying teeth, and fatigue.

*Overeating* is the intake of more food than is needed by the body to function properly. Many factors contribute to overeating. There is a larger

| Nutrient | Functions | Sources |
|---|---|---|
| **Proteins** | Build and repair tissues, antibodies, enzymes, and hormones.<br>Regulate fluid balance in the cells.<br>Regulate many body processes.<br>Supply energy, when needed. | Meat, poultry, fish, eggs, milk and other dairy products, peanut butter, lentils. |
| **Carbohydrates** | Supply energy.<br>Provide bulk in the form of cellose (needed for good digestion).<br>Help the body efficiently digest fats. | Sugar: Honey, jam, jelly, sugar, molasses.<br>Fiber: Fresh fruits and vegetables, whole grain cereals and breads.<br>Starch: Breads, cereals, corn, peas, beans, potatoes, pasta, rice. |
| **Fats** | Supply energy and carry fat-soluble vitamins.<br>Protect vital organs and body from shock and temperature changes. | Butter, margarine, cream, cheese, marbling in meat, nuts, whole milk, olives, chocolate, egg yolks, bacon, salad oils and dressings. |
| **Vitamins**<br>*Vitamin A* | Helps promote growth.<br>Helps keep skin and mucus membranes healthy.<br>Helps prevent night blindness. | Liver, egg yolk, dark green and yellow fruits and vegetables, butter, whole milk, cream, fortified margarine, cheddar cheese. |
| *Thiamin (Vitamin B-1)* | Promotes normal appetite and digestion.<br>Helps keep nervous system healthy.<br>Helps body release energy from food. | Pork, other meats, poultry, fish, eggs, enriched or whole grain breads and cereals, dried beans, brewer's yeast. |
| *Riboflavin (Vitamin B-2)* | Helps cells use oxygen.<br>Helps keep skin, tongue, and lips healthy.<br>Aids digestion. | Milk, cheese, yogurt, liver, meats, fish, poultry, eggs, dark leafy green vegetables, enriched breads and cereals. |
| *Niacin (B-vitamin)* | Helps keep nervous system, skin, mouth, tongue, and digestive tract healthy.<br>Helps cells use other nutrients. | Meat, fish, poultry, milk, enriched or whole grain breads and cereals, peanut butter, dried beans and peas. |
| *Vitamin C* | Helps keep gums and tissues healthy.<br>Helps heal wounds and broken bones.<br>Helps body fight infection. | Citrus fruits, strawberries, cantaloupe, broccoli, green peppers, raw cabbage, tomatoes, green leafy vegetables, brussel sprouts, cauliflower. |
| *Vitamin D* | Helps build strong bones and teeth in children.<br>Helps keep adult bones healthy. | Fortified milk, butter and margarine, fish liver oils, liver, sardines, tuna, egg yolk, sunshine. |
| *Vitamin E* | Acts as an antioxidant. | Liver and other variety meats, eggs, leafy green vegetables, whole grain cereals, salad oils, shortenings, other fats and oils. |
| *Vitamin K* | Aids in blood clotting. | Organ meats, leafy green vegetables, cauliflower, other vegetables, egg yolk. |
| **Minerals**<br>*Calcium* | Helps build bones and teeth.<br>Helps blood clot.<br>Helps muscles and nerves function properly.<br>Helps regulate the use of minerals in body. | Milk, cheese, other dairy products, leafy green vegetables, fish without bones. |

11-2  Each nutrient performs a specific function and can be found in several sources.      (Continued)

| Nutrient | Functions | Sources |
|----------|-----------|---------|
| Phosphorus | Helps build strong bones and teeth. Helps regulate many body processes. | Protein and calcium food sources. |
| Iron | Combines with protein to make hemoglobin. Helps cells use oxygen. | Liver, meats, egg yolk, dried beans and peas, leafy green vegetables, dried fruits, enriched and whole grain breads and cereals. |
| Water | A basic part of blood and tissue fluid. Helps transport nutrients and waste. Helps control body temperature. | Water, beverages, soups, and most foods. |

11-2 Continued.

and more available supply of food. There also is a trend toward more snacking. Unfortunately, overeating can cause many health and emotional problems. A major health problem caused by overeating is obesity.

Obesity can lead to many other health problems in adult life. These include hypertension (high blood pressure and related problems), diabetes, heart disease, hardening of the arteries, and many other diseases.

Obesity can also cause emotional problems. Many obese children lack self-esteem. They may be treated poorly by classmates and lack friends.

Obesity is easier to prevent than to treat. First, note the activity level of any heavy children. Encourage them to join in gross motor play. Second, discuss your concerns about a child's nutrition with staff and parents.

## The Food Guide Pyramid for Young Children

To ensure good nutrition, children need to eat a variety of foods. Their nutritional needs differ from those of adults, however. The U.S. Department of Agriculture (USDA) developed the **Food Guide Pyramid for Young Children**. Use this model as a guide for planning meals and snacks for children ages two to six years, 11-3.

Children need foods from the bottom five groups of the Pyramid daily. Fats, oils, and sweets (the tip of the Pyramid) should be limited in their diets. Chart 11-4 lists foods that are included in various groups of the Pyramid and the number of servings needed for each group.

### Milk Group

Children need two servings from this group daily. The most important nutrient provided by this group is calcium, 11-5. Riboflavin, protein, and phosphorous are also provided. Fortified milk and milk products also contain vitamins A and D.

Milk is considered the best source of calcium in this group. Milk products such as cheese, pudding, and yogurt are also good sources. Children ages two years and younger

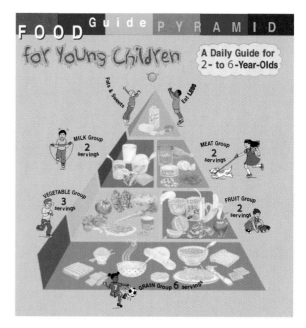

11-3 The Food Guide Pyramid for Young Children can help you see how the different food groups work together to form a nutritious diet.

| Food Groups, Sources, and Daily Needs | | |
|---|---|---|
| **Food Group** | **Number of Servings for Young Children** | **Sources** |
| **Grain** | 6 | Enriched or whole grain breads, buns, bagels, muffins, rolls, cornbread, tortillas, biscuits, pita bread, pancakes, waffles, cereals, crackers, rice, macaroni, noodles, rolled oats |
| **Vegetable** | 3<br>Serve one vegetable rich in vitamin C daily.<br>Serve several vegetables rich in vitamin A each week. | **Rich in vitamin C**: tomatoes, cauliflower, green peppers, broccoli, brussel sprouts; tomato and mixed vegetable juices<br>**Rich in vitamin A**: asparagus, greens, broccoli, brussel sprouts, cabbage, lettuce, green and black-eyed peas, red and green peppers, pumpkin, spinach, squash, and sweet potatoes, vegetable juices<br>**Other vegetables**: potatoes, onions, mushrooms, eggplant, corn, cucumbers, beets, green beans |
| **Fruit** | 2<br>Serve one fruit rich in vitamin C daily.<br>Serve several fruits rich in vitamin A each week. | **Rich in vitamin C**: strawberries, papayas, oranges, tangerines, grapefruit, kiwifruit, orange, grapefruit, and other fortified juices<br>**Rich in vitamin A**: apricots, avocado, cantaloupe, nectarines, papayas, peaches, prunes, tangerines<br>**Other fruits**: apple, banana, blackberries, blueberries, cherries, dates, figs, grapes, pears, pineapple, plums, raspberries, watermelon |
| **Meat** | 2 | Beef; pork; turkey; chicken; eggs; fish; shellfish; tuna; lamb; frankfurters (hot dogs); veal; variety meats such as heart, kidney, and liver; lima, navy, pinto, great northern, kidney, and garbanzo beans; lentils; peanut butter |
| **Milk** | 2 | Milk: whole, reduced fat, lowfat, fat free, buttermilk, evaporated, and nonfat dry; yogurt; cheese; cottage cheese; pudding |

11-4 Nutritious meals can be planned using the Food Guide Pyramid for Young Children.

need the fat whole milk contains. For children over two, reduced or lowfat milk is a better choice. It contains less fat, but otherwise has all the same nutrients.

## Grain Group

A child's diet should include six servings of grains daily. Carbohydrates, iron, and B-vitamins are the chief nutrients in these foods.

Foods in the grain group include whole grain and enriched breads. Also included are pancakes, pastas, crackers, and hot and cold cereals. Only whole grain and enriched products should be served to children. Check labels on products to be sure. Also, if you make bread products at the center, be sure to use whole grain or enriched flour.

## Meat Group

Two servings from this group should be included in a child's daily diet. Protein is the most important nutrient supplied by foods in this group. Meats are also good sources of B-vitamins, iron, and phosphorous.

Animal products in this group provide the highest quality of protein. These include beef, pork, veal, lamb, eggs, seafood, and poultry. Dried beans, dried peas, and lentils are also

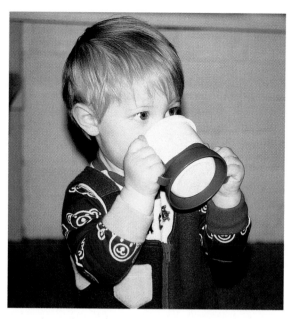

11-5 The calcium found in milk helps build strong bones. This is very important for the body of a growing child.

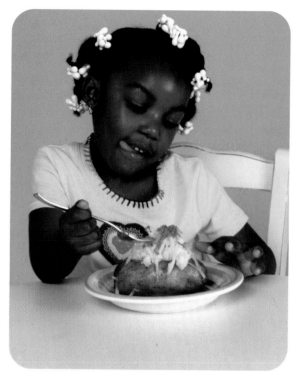

11-6 Serving a fruit or vegetable at snack time gives children one of the servings they require.

included in this group. The proteins in these foods are not as high-quality as the proteins in animal products. However, they are good sources, especially if they are served with milk, milk products, breads, or cereals.

### Vegetables

Preschool children should receive three servings from this group daily. Foods in this group are major sources of vitamins C and A, 11-6.

Rich sources of vitamin C include green peppers, brussel sprouts, broccoli, and tomatoes. Rich sources of vitamin A are found in deep yellow and dark green vegetables. Carrots, pumpkin, and winter squash are examples of deep yellow vegetables. Spinach, broccoli, and asparagus are deep green vegetables.

When planning meals for children, be sure to include sources of vitamin A and vitamin C. At least one source of vitamin C should be served daily. A good source of vitamin A should be included several times a week. Other vegetables are important, too. Vegetables should be served raw or cooked as little as possible. This is because cooking in water can lower the vitamin content of foods.

### Fruit Group

Preschool children should receive two servings from this group every day. Like vegetables, fruits are major sources of vitamins C and A. Serve fruits raw or slightly cooked to retain nutrients.

Rich sources of vitamin C include citrus fruits such as lemons, limes, oranges, and grapefruits. Strawberries and kiwifruit are other sources. Deep yellow fruits, such as apricots, peaches, and cantaloupe, are rich sources of vitamin A. Serve at least one source of vitamin C each day and one source of vitamin A several times a week. Other fruits are important, too.

### Fats and Sweets Group

Foods in this group do not have very high nutritional value. They mainly provide calories. Such foods as butter, margarine, jellies, syrups, and salad dressings are included. Pastries, candy bars, doughnuts, and many other sweets and snack items are included, too.

Eating large amounts of fats and sweets can lead to weight gain and obesity. If children fill up on fats and sweets while refusing other foods, they can be deprived of needed nutrients. That is why it is important to limit foods from this group. Instead, offer such items as fresh fruit or crackers with cheese for snacks. Of course, it is okay for children to have foods from this group from time to time. However, be sure you also offer enough servings from the other food groups that day.

## Meeting Special Nutritional Needs

As a teacher, one of your tasks is helping each child in your care meet his or her nutritional needs. Most children of a certain age share similar nutritional needs, but some children have unique needs. These special needs are often created by a health condition, such as diabetes or allergies. When you understand the special nutritional needs of the children in your care, you can plan appropriate meals and snacks for them.

**Diabetes** is a condition in which the body cannot properly control the level of sugar in the blood. People with diabetes do not produce **insulin**, the hormone that regulates blood sugar level. Many children with diabetes take insulin injections to keep their blood sugar level within a healthy range. When blood sugar is too high or too low, the child will feel sick.

According to the American Diabetes Association, there is not a specific "diabetic diet." People with diabetes need to follow the same basic eating guidelines as other people. They need a varied diet with plenty of fruits, vegetables, and grains. Keeping the diet low in saturated fat and cholesterol is important. Moderating sugars and salt is advised.

Blood sugar fluctuates with food intake and physical activity. For this reason, the foods chosen and portion sizes eaten should reflect balance. Eating at regular intervals also helps the blood sugar remain steady.

Managing the planning and scheduling of snacks and meals for a child with diabetes can be challenging for a teacher. The child's parents can provide specific instructions. Chances are they have worked with a registered dietitian (RD) to develop a personalized meal plan for the child.

Parents also need to tell you about the best spacing of meals and snacks for their child. With practice and communication, you can work together with parents to meet the special food needs of a child with diabetes.

Special nutritional needs may also exist among children with allergies. An **allergy** is the body's negative reaction to a particular substance. The offending substance is called an **allergen**. Sometimes the allergen is a substance in the environment, such as pollen, dust, or mold. Other times the allergen is a food. Food allergies are more common among children than adults. Children often outgrow food allergies by six years of age.

Wheat, soy, peanuts, tree nuts, fish, shellfish, eggs, and milk cause 90 percent of food allergies. Corn, beans, and berries are other foods that can produce an allergic response. Most allergic reactions to foods occur within hours after contact with the allergen. Some occur within minutes.

An allergic reaction can range from mild to severe. Symptoms might include sniffles; abdominal pain; diarrhea, nausea, and vomiting; and swelling of the lips, face, tongue, throat, or eyes. Hives and nasal or respiratory congestion may also occur. The most severe allergic reaction, called **anaphylactic shock**, is potentially fatal. Shock symptoms develop quickly. These symptoms include weakness and collapse. Other signs include problems breathing, a drop in blood pressure, and severe itching and swelling. Abdominal cramping can also occur accompanied by diarrhea and vomiting. Seek immediate medical help for anyone with signs of anaphylactic shock.

A child with food allergies needs to have a restricted diet. The child must not eat even a trace amount of the food that is an allergen. You should offer a safe substitute that provides similar nutrients. In some cases, just the smell of the offending food can cause a severe allergic reaction. This child cannot even be in the same room with the allergen, which means you must eliminate this food from the classroom. Food allergens can make meal and snack planning difficult for teachers.

Again, parents are your best resource for meeting a child's special nutritional needs. Include a question on your enrollment forms regarding food allergies. This will remind parents to share the information with you. If a child has food allergies, get detailed notes from the parents about what foods to exclude from the diet, which foods to offer as substitutes, and what steps to take if an allergic reaction occurs. Always check enrollment records of a newly enrolled child before serving the child any food or drink. Read product labels to check the ingredients of foods. Be mindful of children's food allergies as you plan menus for meals and snacks.

In addition to diabetes and allergies, the children in your care may have other special food needs. Your menu must meet the nutritional needs of every child. Talk with parents about any special needs their children might have. Find out what, if any, modifications are needed. Make sure all staff members who will feed the children are aware of these needs.

# Planning Meals and Snacks

Nutrition is the most important part of a well-planned menu. However, many other factors also contribute to a well-planned menu. For instance, scale serving sizes to the children's appetites. Children manage best with small servings. Their appetites often vary from day to day. Suggested serving sizes for specific age groups are listed in 11-7.

## Food Appeal

Children will eat more if the food appeals to them. Variety, texture, flavor, color, form, temperature, and food preferences all affect how much a child enjoys a meal.

### Variety

Children like variety in the foods served to them. A meal with all the same texture or color could be boring for children. Children also enjoy trying new foods. A new food should be added with a meal of familiar and well-liked foods. This is because children may be overwhelmed if given too many new foods at once.

### Texture

Soft, hard, chewy, mashed, chopped, crisp, creamy, and rough are all textures. It is wise to combine textures when planning meals and snacks for young children. This makes the meal more interesting for the children. For instance, at mealtime, serve one soft food, one crisp food, and one chewy food. See 11-8. Combine contrasting textures for a pleasing effect. This also provides you with an opportunity to include language concepts during meals and snacks.

Dry foods are hard for children to eat. Serve dry food only in combination with two or more moist foods.

| Food | Ages | | |
| --- | --- | --- | --- |
| | 1 Year | 2-3 Years | 4-6 Years |
| Milk | 1 cup | 1 cup | 1 cup |
| Bread | ½ slice | ½-1 slice | 1 slice |
| Cereal | ¼ cup | ⅓ cup | ½ cup |
| Vegetable | | | |
|   Vitamin A source | 2 tablespoons | 3 tablespoons | 4 tablespoons |
|   Other | 2 tablespoons | 3 tablespoons | 4 tablespoons |
| Fruit | | | |
|   Vitamin C source | ¼ cup | ⅓-½ cup | ½ cup |
|   Other | 2 tablespoons | 3 tablespoons | 4 tablespoons |
| Meat, lean cooked without bone | ½ ounce | 1-½ ounces | 1½-2 ounces |
| Egg | 1 egg | 1 egg | 1 egg |
| Dried peas or beans, cooked | 1 tablespoon | 2-3 tablespoons | 3-4 tablespoons |
| Peanut butter | 1 tablespoon | 2-3 tablespoons | 3-4 tablespoons |
| Cheddar cheese | ½ ounce | 1-1½ ounces | 1½-2 ounces |
| Cottage cheese | 1 tablespoon | 2-3 tablespoons | 3-4 tablespoons |
| Butter or margarine | ½ teaspoon | 1 teaspoon | 1 teaspoon |

11-7 Consider the age of children as you plan meals and snacks.

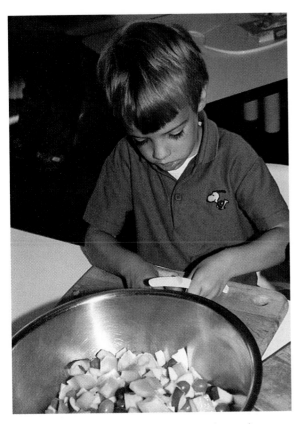

11-8 The crisp apples, soft pears, and squishy grapes in this fruit salad provide an appealing texture combination.

Some meats are difficult for young children to chew. Their teeth cannot grind meat as easily as adults' teeth. Because of this, children usually prefer hamburgers. Chili, spaghetti, and casseroles are other ways of serving meat with varied textures.

### Flavor

In general, children prefer mildly seasoned foods. One rule of thumb is to use only half as much salt as noted in a recipe. Whenever possible, enhance the natural flavor of the food. This means that only small amounts of sugar and spices should be added.

### Color

Children enjoy color in their meals. If the foods you are serving are not very colorful, add color to one or more of the foods. For example, tint the applesauce pink. For St. Patrick's Day, you might color vanilla pudding green.

### Food Forms

Serve most foods in bite-sized pieces. Children have poorly developed fine motor coordination skills. They find it difficult to use spoons and forks well. Therefore, slice cooked carrots and other vegetables in large pieces rather than dicing them. Try adding diced vegetables to another food. For instance, add diced carrots to mashed potatoes.

Soup is also difficult for many young children to eat. They become tired from spooning. Children may get frustrated if they spill on clothing or the table.

Two methods can be used to make soup easier to eat. One method is to thicken the soup. This can be done by adding solid ingredients or a thickener, such as flour. The second method is to let the children drink the soup from a cup.

Whenever possible, prepare foods so they can be eaten with the fingers, 11-9. For example, serve chopped raw vegetables instead of a tossed salad.

### Temperature

Variety in the temperature of foods served can be appealing, too. For snack, offer a cold glass of milk with a room-temperature food, such as crackers. At mealtime, serve a cold fruit or pudding with a warm casserole. For safety reasons, be sure to serve each food at its proper temperature (hot foods hot and cold foods cold). Keep in mind, however, children are more sensitive to temperature extremes than adults.

## Food Preferences

Children differ in their individual food preferences. For example, while some children enjoy spicy foods, others prefer milder flavors. Most children have at least a few foods they strongly like and some they strongly dislike. Although food preferences are personal, they are also influenced by home life. One family may eat many vegetables, while another family might eat them less often.

As a teacher, you will quickly learn about the children's likes and dislikes. When possible, honor the child's preferences unless they are unhealthful. Suppose Cortney likes her sandwiches cut diagonally. Accommodating this food

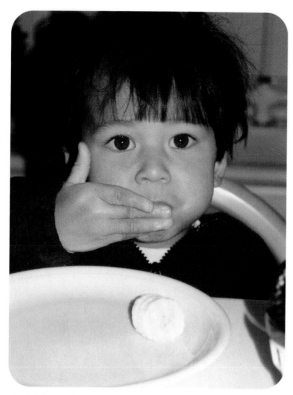

11-9  These large slices of banana will be easy for children to pick up with their fingers.

preference when possible will help mealtimes run more smoothly.

## Multicultural Experiences

Children need to be exposed to healthful foods from various cultures. This will help create community among a diverse group of children. Through repeated experiences, children will learn how food relates to social and cultural customs. Including foods from the children's cultures helps promote cultural identity and self-esteem. Foods from other cultures help children learn to taste new dishes and respect cultural differences.

Family members can help you promote a multicultural approach to the food program. Encourage them to share recipes for snacks, meals, and holiday celebrations. Invite parents to prepare for the class special foods from their culture. Some parents may enjoy teaching children to help prepare the foods.

## Serving Meals

Licensing requirements outline how often and how much food must be provided for young children in child care centers. These requirements vary from state to state. As a rule, the number of hours a child spends at a center governs the number of snacks and meals served. In most states, children who attend less than four hours a day must be served a fruit juice or milk and a snack item. Children who attend five or more hours must be served both a meal and a snack.

The decision to serve breakfast is often based on two factors. These are the length of the program day and the distance the child travels to reach the center. Centers with full-day programs or children who travel long distances often serve breakfast.

### Breakfast

The purpose of breakfast is to break the 10- to 14-hour overnight fast. Breakfast provides energy for morning activities. Studies show that children who eat a nutritious breakfast perform better mentally and physically.

A good breakfast should include foods from at least four of the five required food groups. The USDA Child Care Food Program recommends:
- fruit or juice
- protein-rich food
- milk
- bread or cereal

Fruit drinks or punches are not juice substitutes, even when fortified with vitamin C. Fruit juices have fewer additives and less sugar.

### Self-Serve Breakfasts

Self-serve breakfasts are popular with center staffs. This is because children can eat their breakfasts as they arrive. They can choose what and how much to eat, based on their own appetites. The self-serve breakfast gives children the chance to prepare their own breakfasts.

Many prepackaged breakfast foods come in child-sized servings. These include dry cereals, yogurt packs, and muffins. Juice and milk are also available in child-sized servings.

### Snacks

Most children eat small amounts of food at one sitting. They may not be properly nourished by just eating three meals a day. Therefore, provide snacks between meals. Snacks satisfy hunger and help meet daily food requirements.

In most centers, snacks are served mid-morning and again in mid-afternoon. Snacks should not interfere with a child's appetite for meals. Because of this, it is best to schedule snacks at least 1½ hours before meals.

Choose snacks according to the Food Guide Pyramid for Young Children. Plan a snack based on the menu for the day. Consider the nutrients, colors, and textures of the meals. Then choose snacks that complement the meals. Avoid fats, sweets, and highly salted foods such as potato chips, pretzels, and corn chips. Chil-

dren usually enjoy simple snacks they can eat with their fingers. Suggestions for snack ideas are shown in Figure 11-10.

## Lunch

To ensure children receive the proper nutrients, be sure to include the following types of food in their lunches:

- whole grain or enriched bread, rice, or pasta
- protein-rich food
- two vegetables or one fruit and one vegetable
- milk

---

### Snack Ideas

**Grain Group**

Granola
Rice cakes
Dry cereal mixes (not presweetened)
Roasted wheat berries, wheat germ, bran as roll-ins, toppers, or as finger food mix
Variety of breads (tortillas, pita breads, crepes, scones, pancakes, English muffins, biscuits, bagels, cornbread, popovers) and grains (whole wheat, cracked wheat, rye, oatmeal, buckwheat, rolled wheat, wheat germ, bran, grits)
Toast (plain, buttered, with spreads, cinnamon)
Homemade yeast and quick breads
Waffle sandwiches
Whole grain and spinach pastas
Pasta with butter and poppy seeds
Cold pasta salad
Rice (brown or white)

**Vegetable Group**

Vegetables (with or without dips): sweet and white potatoes, broccoli, cauliflower, radishes, peppers, mushrooms, zucchini, squashes, rutabagas, avocados, eggplant, okra, pea pods, turnips, pumpkin, sprouts, spinach, carrot sticks
Kabobs and salads
Vegetable juices and juice blends
Vegetable soups
Stuffed celery, cucumbers, zucchini, spinach, lettuce, cabbage
Vegetable spreads

**Fruit Group**

Fruits (use variety): pomegranates, cranberries, apricots, pineapples, tangerines, kiwifruit, apples, strawberries, cantaloupe, banana, cut grapes
Kabobs and salads
Fruit juices
Fruit in muffins, yogurts, and breads
Stuffed dates or prunes
Dried fruits (banana chips, prunes, apples, dates, figs)

**Meat Group**

Meat strips, chunks, cubes
Meatballs, small kabobs
Meat roll-ups (cheese spread, mashed potatoes, spinach as stuffing)
Meat salads (tuna, chicken, turkey)
Sardines
Fish sticks and chicken nuggets
Hard boiled eggs
Deviled eggs
Egg salad spread
Beans and peas mashed as dips or spreads
Bean, pea, or lentil soup
3-bean salad
Chopped nut spreads
Nut breads
Peanut butter on, in, around, over, or with anything

**Milk Group**

Dips (yogurt, cottage cheese)
Cheese (balls, wedges, cutouts, faces, strips, slices)
Milk punches made with fruits or juices
Yogurt or pudding
Cottage cheese with vegetables or pancakes
Cheese fondue (preheated, no open flame in classroom)

11-10  Plan snacks to coordinate with the Food Guide Pyramid for Young Children.

Grains, protein-rich foods, and vegetables are often served together as one dish. They might be used in a casserole or soup, for instance. Combining food groups can make mealtimes more interesting than always serving each of these groups separately.

Try including foods from various cultures. This will help the children develop an appreciation of other foods. The children will learn that people have different food preferences. Where rice is an important staple in some cultures, bread is in others.

Desserts are optional. They need not be served with every lunch. Plan desserts carefully. Many are high in fat and sugar and low in other nutrients. For example, plain cookies and cakes have little nutritional value, but are high in calories. Instead, plan to use carrots or pumpkin in recipes to provide vitamin A. Custards and puddings are considered good desserts since they contain calcium and protein.

When included, desserts should be part of the meal, like the vegetable or bread. They should not be treated as a special part of the meal. Never tell children they must eat everything on their plates in order to get dessert. This will only make desserts appear special.

Chart 11-11 contains sample daily food plans for one meal and a snack. Note how each meal-snack pair complement one another.

## Serving Safe Meals and Snacks

When planning nutritious meals and snacks, keep safety in mind. Remember that young children are learning how to chew and swallow. When they are in a hurry, they may gulp their food. This can create a risk of choking. To prevent choking, avoid serving foods that, if swallowed whole, could block children's windpipes. Foods to be avoided include cherries with pits, hard or sticky candies, marshmallows, nuts, peanut butter by the spoonful, gum, raisins, popcorn, pretzels, raw celery, whole raw carrots, whole grapes, and hot dogs (unless sliced lengthwise, then crosswise into bite-sized pieces).

| Sample Menus for Lunch and Snack | | | | | |
|---|---|---|---|---|---|
| **Pattern** | I | II | III | IV | V | VI |
| **Snack** | Orange juice<br>Whole wheat<br>  bread<br>Butter | Apple wedge<br>Cheese | Milk<br>Banana | Hard cooked<br>  egg<br>Tomato juice | Celery stuffed<br>  with peanut<br>  butter<br>Apple juice | Milk<br>Peanut butter<br>  and cracker |
| **Lunch** | Ground beef<br>  patty<br>Peas<br>Carrot strips<br>Enriched roll<br>Milk | Roast turkey<br>Broccoli<br>Mashed<br>  potatoes<br>Whole wheat<br>  bread<br>Milk | Fish sticks<br>Scalloped<br>  potatoes<br>Stewed<br>  tomato<br>Whole wheat<br>  bread<br>Milk | Black-eyed<br>  peas with<br>  ham<br>Mustard<br>  greens<br>Purple plums<br>Corn bread<br>Milk | Scrambled<br>  eggs<br>Spinach<br>Fried apples<br>Biscuit<br>Milk | Oven fried<br>  drumsticks<br>Corn-on-the-<br>  cob<br>Sliced<br>  tomato/green<br>  pepper rings<br>Whole wheat<br>  bread<br>Milk |
| **Pattern** | VII | VIII | IX | X | XI | XII |
| **Snack** | Apple juice<br>Cheese toast | Milk<br>Pineapple<br>Cottage cheese | Grapefruit<br>  juice<br>Finger-size<br>  pieces of<br>  leftover meat | Raw carrot<br>  strips, green<br>  pepper with<br>  dip<br>Milk | Tomato juice<br>Flour tortilla<br>  with melted<br>  cheese | Fresh fruit in<br>  season<br>(strawberries,<br>  melons,<br>  tangerines) |
| **Lunch** | Meatloaf<br>Green beans<br>Baked potato<br>Carrot strips<br>Enriched<br>  bread<br>Milk | Tuna<br>  sandwich on<br>  whole wheat<br>  bread<br>Tomato juice<br>Raw cabbage<br>  (small pieces)<br>Apricots<br>Milk | Pinto beans<br>  with melted<br>  cheese<br>Chili peppers,<br>  chopped<br>Tomato, onion,<br>  lettuce<br>Flour tortilla<br>Milk | Meatballs in<br>  tomato<br>  sauce over<br>  spaghetti<br>Zucchini<br>Peaches<br>French bread<br>Milk | Lunchmeat<br>  roll-ups<br>Sweet potato<br>Apple,<br>  banana, and<br>  orange salad<br>Rye bread<br>Milk | Swiss steak<br>  cubes<br>Cauliflower<br>Cooked<br>  carrots<br>Whole wheat<br>  roll<br>Milk |

11-11  Planning menus is the first step toward teaching nutrition concepts.

## Summary

Teaching children about nutrition is an important responsibility. Children who learn healthful food choices can use the information their entire lives. Good nutrition promotes children's growth and development.

In order to teach about nutrition, you must first understand how food is used by the body. You must also understand how nutrients fuel the body. You can then use this information to plan nutritious meals and snacks. The Food Guide Pyramid for Young Children is a useful tool for planning menus. Food will appeal more to children if you consider the texture, flavor, color, form, and temperature of the foods you plan to serve.

## Review and Reflect

1. True or false. Children who have learned healthful food choices may also experience lifelong good health.

2. List four goals of a good nutrition program.

3. Define nutrition.

4. What are nutrients?

5. Name the six groups of nutrients.

6. The energy value of food is measured in _____.

7. Describe the difference between undernutrition and malnutrition.

8. What are the six food groups in the Food Guide Pyramid for Young Children?

9. Milk is a good source of _____.
   A. calcium
   B. riboflavin
   C. phosphorus
   D. All of the above.

10. What are the chief nutrients found in breads and cereals?

11. A good source of vitamin _____ should be served several times a week, and a good source of vitamin _____ every day.

12. Good sources of _____ include cream, olives, egg yolks, and nuts.

13. Describe the eating guidelines for children with diabetes.

14. True or false. Ninety percent of food allergies result from wheat, soy, peanuts, tree nuts, fish, shellfish, egg, and milk.

15. Why should food be served to children in bite-size pieces?

16. List the recommended foods for a nutritious breakfast outlined by the USDA.

17. True or false. It is a good idea to tell children to eat everything on their plates in order to get dessert.

18. Name four foods that should not be served to young children because they might cause choking.

## Apply and Explore

1. Plan a breakfast, lunch, and snack menu for one week for a group of three-year-old children.

2. Interview a dietitian about the importance of a nutritious diet for children.

3. Observe a group of children at lunchtime. Describe their food preferences. Note what is or is not lacking in their lunch menu based on the recommendations given in this chapter.

4. Prepare a list of desserts. List the nutritional information for each of these desserts. Are they nutritious? Why or why not?

5. Discuss why obesity is easier to prevent than treat.

6. Use a search engine to find information on snack ideas for toddlers and preschoolers.

7. Connect to the Web site for the American Diabetes Association (diabetes.org) and search for *Diabetes Food Pyramid*. Compare this with the Food Guide for Young Children. How are they alike and different?

# Chapter 12

# Guiding Children's Health

After studying this chapter, you will be able to

- develop a workable health policy for a child care center.
- list steps for controlling the spread of foodborne illnesses.
- explain the importance of first aid training.
- identify various injuries and outline procedures for treating them.
- explain how to care for children who become ill while in your care.
- describe your responsibility when caring for children with special illnesses.

## Terms to Know

policy

communicable diseases

foodborne illness

wound

abrasion

rabies

burn

first-degree burn

second-degree burn

third-degree burn

head lice

asthma

epilepsy

human immunodeficiency virus (HIV)

acquired immunodeficiency syndrome (AIDS)

Tu-Ling's health affects his performance, ability to learn, and behavior. Tu-Ling has a constant inner ear infection, and he is having trouble hearing. This hearing loss may affect his development of language skills, contact with peers, and general behavior.

A child's health is a key concern when planning, preparing, and maintaining a classroom environment, 12-1.

A healthy environment for young children starts with sound health policies. To avoid the transmission of disease, stress personal hygiene

12-1 Contact parents on health issues when appropriate.

and safe food handling practices. Plan for emergencies such as control of head lice. Also plan for sudden illnesses. In addition, obtain the knowledge and skill to provide first aid treatment.

## Objectives for Guiding Health

It is your responsibility to protect, maintain, and improve children's health. Thus, you will need to create a healthy environment. The following objectives should be considered:

- Develop center health policies.
- Review the children's health records to ensure that they receive immunizations.
- Recognize ill children when making daily health observations.
- Isolate children who may have an illness from the group.
- Contact parents on health issues when appropriate.
- Plan a safe environment to prevent accidents.
- Provide first aid treatment.
- Take part in health-related in-service training.
- Include health in the curriculum.

## Health Policies

A **policy** is a course of action that controls future decisions. It is important for your center to have health policies. These policies will help you make consistent decisions regarding the health of the children in your care.

In most states, the health of children in child care is regulated by state licensing rules and regulations. Their purpose is to protect young children. These rules and regulations address only the basic health requirements. Your center may have additional health policies that are more specific.

### Medical Examination

All children enrolled in your program should have a preadmission medical examination. This exam will help you learn

- whether the child is free from **communicable diseases**. (These are illnesses that can be passed on to other people.)
- if immunizations are current.
- if the child has any health problems that need special attention.

To provide the best environment for children, the staff must also be in excellent physical, mental, and emotional health. They should have an examination prior to their first day of work. A record of these examinations should be maintained in the employees' files.

### Immunizations

To protect all children, each child attending the center must have the proper immunizations. The only exception to this policy is when a child is exempted by state laws for religious or medical reasons. Children who are not properly immunized or exempted must be excluded from the center. Partial immunizations do not provide protection against many diseases. The American Academy of Pediatrics suggests the following immunizations: hepatitis B; diptheria, tetanus, and pertussis (DTaP); measles, mumps, and rubella (MMR); inactivated polio vaccine (IPV); Haemophilus influenzae type b (Hib) vaccine; varicella (chicken pox) vaccine; and pneumococcal conjugate vaccine. See 12-2. Find

| Immunizations for Young Children | |
|---|---|
| **Immunization** | **Age** |
| Hepatitis B vaccine | Birth; 1 to 4 months; 6 to 18 months |
| Diptheria, tetanus, and pertussis (DTaP) | 2 months; 4 months; 6 months; 15 to 18 months; 4 to 6 years |
| Tetanus (td) | After 4 to 6 years, every 10 years |
| Polio vaccine (IPV) | 2 months; 4 months; 6 to 18 months; 4 to 6 years |
| Haempohilus influenzae type b vaccine (Hib) | 2 months; 4 months; 6 months; 12 to 15 months |
| Measles, mumps, and rubella vaccine (MMR) | 12 to 15 months; 4 to 6 years |
| Varicella (chicken pox) vaccine | 12 to 18 months |
| Pneumococcal vaccine | 2 months; 4 months; 6 months; 12 to 15 months |

12-2 Proper immunization is a health policy required by most state licensing agencies.

out which immunizations are required by law in the state where you live.

## Attendance Policy

For the safety of all the children, centers need a policy stating when an ill child should be kept at home. For example, your policy might state that a child should be kept at home if he or she has shown any of the following symptoms within the past 24 hours:

- A temperature over 100°F, unless the child's normal temperature is above the average.
- Intestinal upset along with diarrhea or vomiting.
- Severe cough or cold.
- Drainage from open sores, eyes, nose, or ears.
- Rash.

Parents should be advised to keep a child home for 24 hours after a fever subsides, 12-3. Instruct parents to report all sickness to center personnel.

## Administering Medications

To protect staff against lawsuits, most centers have policies for medication. These policies must adhere to, but can exceed, your state's licensing requirements. For instance, your state may require that only a doctor-prescribed medication may be given to a child. You must follow this rule. Always record the child's name, time, and date, and the type and amount of medication given.

Medicines should also be stored appropriately. Refrigerated medications should be stored in a secure, labeled container. Nonrefrigerated medicines should be stored in a locked place out of the children's reach. It is important that medications contain a label specifying the child's name, physician's name, name of medication, dosage, and how often to administer.

Always use caution when giving medications. Give the exact amount prescribed at the prescribed time. If you do not know the child well, verify his or her name before giving the medicine. This is especially true in programs where one person, such as the director, administers all medications. Always read the label on the medication at least three times. First read the

label as you remove the medication from storage to be sure you have the right medication for the right child. Read it again as you dispense the medicine into the measuring device. Look at the label one last time before giving the medicine to double check it is the right amount of the right medicine for the right child. If you have any questions about the medication, call the parents or the prescribing doctor *before* giving the medicine.

## Napping

One health policy that is needed to help prevent the spread of illness is related to napping. Children should not share cots or beds. Rather, each child should be provided with a washable cot or bed and clean sheets. Clean sheets should be provided on a weekly basis. At times, it may be necessary to change sheets more frequently, such as when a child is ill, has perspired a great deal, or has soiled the sheets.

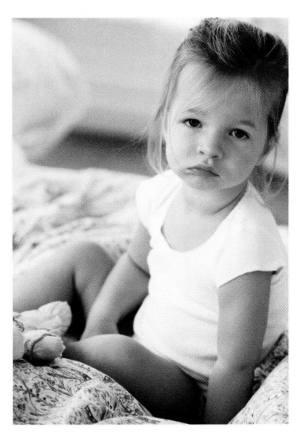

12-3 Even after a fever subsides, it can take up to 24 hours for children to feel well enough to attend child care.

## Daily Health Inspection

To protect children's health, conduct an informal health inspection each day. This inspection is best conducted as soon as each child arrives at school. Observe for rashes, sores, swelling or bruising, changes in appearance of eyes, runny noses, flushing of skin, coughing, sneezing, and a sweaty appearance.

Even after the health inspection at arrival time, observe the children throughout the day for symptoms of illness, 12-4. If a child appears sick, contact the parents.

Preschool children are prone to communicable diseases. These include chicken pox, conjunctivitis (pink eye), influenza, and measles among others. Observe for symptoms of each of these diseases. Make this information known to all staff. Post a communicable diseases chart in the staff room, 12-5.

## Contacting Parents

Children may arrive at the center in good health, but later show symptoms of illness or infection. When do you decide to contact a parent to pick up a sick child? The answer to this question depends on the illness and the center's policies. Most states require centers to have an isolation area for sick children. A sick child should be removed from the classroom and wait with an adult in the isolation area until a parent arrives.

Always contact parents when a child shows signs of illness. Describe the symptoms to the parent. If the child is very ill, the parents should be responsible for picking the child up within a reasonable amount of time. Programs need to have this clearly stated in their policies.

Each child's folder should contain emergency information. Record parents' or guardians' home, cell, and work telephone numbers. Also note phone numbers of the family doctor and dentist. An example of an emergency information sheet is shown in 12-6.

Parents should also be notified if their children have been exposed to a communicable disease. Send notices home to all parents if even one child has been infected with head lice. An example of a notice is shown in 12-7. Provide space to include the child's name, illness exposed to, and the date.

## Personal Hygiene

Personal hygiene is an important component of a healthy environment. When cleanliness is stressed, fewer children and staff become ill.

Stress the importance of cleanliness to all new employees, as well as volunteers. This can be done through an in-service training, employee handbook, or orientation. Each person should follow basic habits of cleanliness. They should bathe or shower daily and keep their hair clean. A hairnet should be worn while working in the kitchen. Use disposable tissues and discard them after use. Cover the mouth when coughing or sneezing.

Emphasize to staff members the importance of proper hand washing while working with children. Hands should be washed before and after eating, handling food, or feeding a baby. Also wash after using the toilet or diapering a child. Wash hands after coughing, sneezing, rubbing the nose, or handling handkerchiefs. Hand washing helps prevent the spread of contagious diseases in a child care center. Studies show that many illnesses, such as diarrhea, can be greatly reduced when proper hand washing policies are followed.

Hand washing is also important for children. Require children to wash their hands before and after eating; after handling pets; after coughing,

| Symptoms of Illness |
| --- |
| • atypical behavior: more quiet, tired, fussy, or aggressive than usual |
| • breathing difficulties |
| • diarrhea |
| • fever |
| • frequent scratching of body or scalp |
| • change in color of urine or stools |
| • headache or stiff neck |
| • infected skin patches |
| • loss of appetite or refusal to eat |
| • redness or discharge from eyes |
| • severe coughing |
| • congested or runny nose |
| • sores |
| • sore throat or difficulty swallowing |
| • achiness |
| • rashes |
| • vomiting |

12-4 Watch the children for these signs of illness.

## Communicable Diseases

| Disease | Incubation Period (Time from Exposure to First Signs) | Signs and Symptoms | Period of Communicability Precautions and Restrictions | General Information |
|---|---|---|---|---|
| Chicken pox (Varicella) | 2 to 3 weeks, commonly 13 to 17 days | Sudden onset, slight fever, lesions often appear first on scalp, then on face and body. Successive crop of lesions remain 3 to 4 days, leaving crusts. | Keep patient home until all lesions are crusted over, usually 5 to 6 days after onset of rash. | Mild disease in children. May be more severe in adults and in children with cancer, leukemia and other high risk conditions. Vaccine is available. |
| Conjunctivitis (Pink Eye) | 24 to 72 hours | Redness in the white of the eye. May or may not have pus discharge. Eye irritation. | The communicable period depends on the cause, but is usually while inflammation or drainage is present. Keep patient home during communicable period, and refer for medical diagnosis and treatment. | Most infections are viral by cause; some are bacterial. May spread person to person through hand to eye contact. Also an early symptom for measles. Some symptoms may be an allergy, and are noncommunicable. |
| Viral hepatitis type A (formerly infectious) | 15 to 50 days Average 25 days | Usually abrupt onset with fever, fatigue, loss of appetite, nausea, and abdominal pain. Jaundice is less common in children than in adults. | Most communicable during first week of illness and up to 1 week after jaundice. Keep patient home and no food handling or patient care while communicable. | Vaccine not available in all areas. May be confused with Hepatitis B. Differential diagnosis is important for prevention and control. Household contacts should be given immune serum globulin as soon as possible. |
| Influenza | 24 to 72 hours | Rapid onset with fever, chills, headache lack of energy, muscle ache, sore throat, cough. | Communicable for 3 to 7 days after clinical onset. Keep home until symptoms disappear. | Vaccine is available and should be given to all children or persons with greatest risk of serious complications from the disease: the chronically ill and the elderly. |
| Measles (Rubeola) | 8 to 13 days | High fever (101 F or more), with cough, runny nose and /or conjunctivitis. Blotchy rash appears 3 to 5 days after early signs, beginning on face and becoming generalized, lasting 4 or more days. | Communicable from onset or respiratory illness until 4 days after appearance of the rash. Keep patient home until 5 days after the appearance of rash. | A very serious, highly contagious but vaccine-preventable disease. |
| Mononucleosis, Infectious | 2 to 6 weeks | Characterized by fever, sore throat, and inflamed posterior lymph nodes. | Keep patient home, at the discretion of physician. | In children the disease is usually mild and difficult to recognize. |
| Mumps | 12 to 26 days, commonly 18 days | Fever, pain and swelling about the jaws involving one or more salivary glands. Many infections occur without symptoms. | Keep patient home until salivary gland swelling has subsided, or other symptoms have cleared. | Infectious early. May cause complications in adults. Vaccine available. |
| Pediculosis (Lice) | Eggs hatch in a week; reach maturity in about 2 weeks | Excessive scratching on head or other parts of body. Light gray insects lay eggs in the hair, especially at the nape of the neck and around the ears. | Keep patient home until treated (should not need to miss more than 1 day of school). | Avoid sharing personal belongings such as clothing, head gear, combs, brushes, and bedding. |

12-5  Awareness of the symptoms and treatment for communicable diseases and illnesses is important in order to control the spread of sickness through the center.

(Continued)

| Communicable Diseases | | | | |
|---|---|---|---|---|
| Disease | Incubation Period (Time from Exposure to First Signs) | Signs and Symptoms | Period of Communicability Precautions and Restrictions | General Information |
| Ringworm (scalp, skin, feet) | Variable, 1 to 3 weeks | Scalp: Scaly patches of temporary baldness. Infected hairs are brittle and break easily. Skin: Flat, inflamed, ringlike sores that may itch or burn. Feet: Scaling or cracking of the skin, especially between the toes or blisters containing a thin watery fluid. | Communicable as long as active lesions are present. Keep patient home until adequate treatment is begun. | Preventive measures are largely hygienic. All household contacts, pets, and farm animals should be examined and treated if infected. Ringworm is spread directly by contact with articles and surfaces contaminated by such infected persons or animals. |
| Rubella (German Measles) | 14 to 21 days | Mild symptoms, slight fever, rash lasting about 3 days, enlarged head and neck glands common (particularly in back part of neck, behind ears.) | Keep patient home until 4 days after appearance of rash. | Highly communicable, but vaccine-preventable disease. Complications are mild except in pregnancy when fetal infection or damage may occur. If contacts include a pregnant woman, she should consult her physician immediately. |
| Pertussis (Whooping Cough) | 5 to 10 days | Begins with upper respiratory symptoms. An increasingly irritating cough develops with a characteristic "Whoop" and frequently occurs in spasms accompanied by vomiting. | Keep patient home for 21 days from beginning of "Whoop," or 5 to 7 days after onset of appropriate therapy. | Most dangerous to preschool children. Immunization is not recommended for children over 6 years of age. Susceptible contacts should be treated and observed for respiratory disease. |
| Scabies | 4 to 6 weeks with first infections several days with reinfection | Small raised reddened areas or lesions with connecting grayish-white lines. Marked itching. Most commonly found in the folds of the skin, finger webs, wrists, elbows, thighs, beltline, abdomen, nipples, buttocks. | Keep patient home until under adequate treatment and no open lesions can be observed. | All cases, family members, and other close physically contacts should be treated for scabies simultaneously. |
| Streptococcal Infections including Scarlet Fever (Strep throat) | 1 to 3 days | Fever, sore throat; tender swollen glands with a fine, red rash present in Scarlet Fever. | Keep patient home for 7 days from onset if untreated; with adequate medical treatment, 24 hours. | Medication for symptomatic patients is recommended because of possibility of complications, including rheumatic fever. Culture survey rarely recommended. |

12-5  Continued.

sneezing, or blowing their noses; and after messy activities. Careful hand washing can keep germs and illnesses from spreading among the children. To remind children to wash their hands, some teachers post hand-shaped signs near the table, art area, pet cages, bathrooms, tissue box, and snack tray.

## Controlling Foodborne Illness

**Foodborne illness** is caused by eating food that contains harmful bacteria, toxins, parasites, or viruses. People who eat these foods can become very ill. They can have painful symptoms, including stomach pain and cramps, diarrhea, bloody stools, nausea, vomiting, severe headaches, or fever.

Young children and pregnant women are at high risk if they get these diseases. As a teacher or center director, you should take precautions to prevent these illnesses among your staff and the children. Foodborne illness often results from improper food preparation, handling, or storage. Using safe food handling techniques will prevent many of these illnesses.

When preparing foods, keep your work area clean. Avoid transferring harmful bacteria from

## Emergency Information

### Child and Family Study Center

Child's Name _____   Birthdate _____

Home Address_____   Home Phone _____

**Mother**

Home Address_____   Home Phone _____

_____   Cell Phone_____

Work Address _____   Work Phone _____

_____   E-mail _____

**Father**

Home Address_____   Home Phone _____

_____   Cell Phone_____

Work Address _____   Work Phone _____

_____   E-mail _____

### In Case of Emergency, Who Should Be Notified?

Name _____   Phone _____

Relationship _____

Name _____   Phone _____

Relationship _____

Family Doctor _____   Phone _____

Address _____

Family Dentist_____   Phone _____

Address _____

12-6 Always have the information needed to contact parents in an emergency.

one food to another. This can occur when you or your utensils touch a contaminated food and then touch another food. It can also occur when foods touch a contaminated counter, appliance, or towel. Keeping these items clean will prevent spreading contaminants, 12-8.

Cook all meat, poultry, seafood, and egg dishes thoroughly. This will kill any harmful bac-teria in these foods. Learn federal recommendations and your state's requirements for institutional food preparation. Other policies may be set by your center or the agencies that fund your center.

Store foods at safe temperatures, too. Foods that are cold (below 40°F) or hot (above 140°F) are safest. Temperatures between 40°F and 140°F

Dear Parent:

This is to notify you that your child,

_____, was exposed to

_____ on _____

at the Child and Family Study Center.


Signed _____
                  (Head Teacher)

Date _____

12-7  It is important to inform parents when children are exposed to a communicable disease.

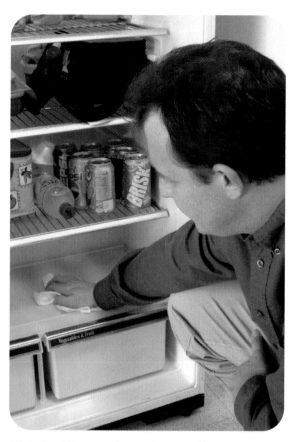

12-8  A refrigerator that is clean and kept at 40 F helps control transmission of foodborne illness.

promote bacteria growth. Never leave perishable foods out at room temperature for more than two hours. Discard foods left out longer than this. This applies to plates of food, baby food, formula, and breast milk, too.

If foodborne illness should occur at your center, seek medical help for those affected. Alert any parents whose children may have eaten the contaminated food.

# First Aid

In every preschool, injuries and illness occur. Sometimes, it may just be a scratch or bumped knee. At other times, it may be a sudden high temperature.

First aid training provides the knowledge and skill needed to handle emergency medical care. With the proper training, you will know how and when to treat illnesses and injuries. You will also know when professional medical help is required.

All employees in child care should be certified by the American Red Cross. This certifica-

tion may have been acquired through prior course work or past employment. If an employee is not certified, he or she should be required to obtain certification in order to be employed.

Conduct a first aid in-service training session for all center personnel each year. Include secretaries, janitors, cooks, and bus drivers in the training session. Training should focus on updating personnel on first aid procedures of the American Red Cross.

## First Aid Supplies

In order to administer first aid, you will need some basic supplies. Most drugstores, department stores, and school supply catalogs sell first aid kits that would include these basic supplies. You may also purchase your supplies separately and put them together in a kit.

Store all first aid items in one area. Keep them out of children's reach. However, do not

**First Aid Kit Inventory**

| Quantity | Item | Quantity | Item |
|---|---|---|---|
| 1 | Quick reference first aid manual. | 1 pair | Scissors for cutting tape and bandages. |
| 15 | Individual adhesive bandages in ½-inch, ¾-inch, and round sizes. | 1 package | Safety pins. |
| 10 | 2 by 2 inch sterile first aid dressings, individually packaged for burns and open wounds. | 1 tube | Hydrocortisone cream for insect bites. |
| 10 | 4 by 4 inch sterile first aid dressings. | 5 | 1 ounce bottles of syrup of ipecac. |
| 1 roll | Gauze bandage, 2 inches by 5 yards. | 1 | Flashlight. |
| 2 rolls | Adhesive tape or surgical tape, 1 inch wide. | 1 | Synthetic ice pack. |
| 20 | Disposable paper tissues. | 1 box | Box of temperature strip thermometers for use on the child's forehead or digital thermometer. |
| 1 bar | Mild soap, for cleaning scratches, wounds, etc. | 20 | Alcohol wipes. |
| 1 pair | Tweezers for removing splinters. | 20 | Cotton swabs. |
| | | 1 package | Absorbent cotton balls. |
| | | 1 bottle | Antibacterial skin cleaner. |

12-9  Make sure the first aid kit is well-stocked at all times.

keep first aid supplies in a locked cabinet. During an emergency you may not have time to search for a key.

Each month, check the contents of the first aid kit. Make sure all first aid kits have the necessary supplies, 12-9. To do this, check the contents against a list. Many programs have one person responsible for this duty. Replace any supplies that have run out.

If some children have special health needs, you will need additional supplies. An antihistamine or bee sting kit may have to be added for children with allergies. Children with diabetes may need sugar or honey. For emergency preparedness, always take a first aid kit on field trips.

# Wounds and Their Treatment

A **wound** is damage to the surface of the skin or body tissue. Basically, there are two types of wounds. A *closed wound* is an injury to the tissue directly under the skin surface. It does not involve a break in the skin. An *open wound* is a break in the skin.

## Closed Wounds

Children usually get closed wounds from falling, being struck, or running into some object. Most closed wounds involve the soft tissues under the skin. The most common type of closed wound is a bruise.

Common signs of a closed wound are discoloration, tenderness, and pain in the damaged area. To help control the pain, apply a cold cloth or pack to the injured area, 12-10.

## Open Wounds

Cuts and scrapes that break the skin are called open wounds. Two first aid problems are caused by open wounds. First, there may be rapid blood loss. If this is the case, the injured child may go into shock. Second, exposed body tissue may become contaminated and infected.

Some open wounds bleed freely. This reduces the danger of infection. Other wounds bleed very little. These are more likely to become infected.

12-10 Cold packs help reduce swelling in closed wounds.

Open wounds on the top skin layer require simple treatment. To clean the wound, wash it with soap and water. If the wound is deep or does not stop bleeding in a short amount of time, seek medical attention.

## Abrasions

An **abrasion** is a scrape that damages a portion of the skin. Children usually get abrasions from falling and handling rough objects. It is common to have several children in a classroom with skinned knees, scratched arms, or rope burns.

Bleeding from an abrasion is often limited to blood flow from broken capillaries (small veins). However, bacteria or dirt may still enter the wound and infection can still occur. Dirt particles may actually slow down the healing process. Sometimes, abrasions heal around the particles, forming a permanent scar.

## Cuts

Cuts, or incised wounds, on body tissues are often caused by broken glass, metal, or sharp edges. Bleeding can be heavy if a blood vessel has been cut. Nerves, muscles, or tendons can also be damaged if the cut is deep enough.

## Puncture Wounds

Puncture wounds are made by sharp objects such as nails, splinters, thumbtacks, and even sticks. In order to puncture the skin, the force at which the object meets the skin must be strong.

Bleeding is often light. As a result, the wound is not flushed out. Infection may set in. Harmful bacteria such as tetanus may grow in the presence of moisture and warmth. This can then be carried within the body.

## Bites

Bites are a type of puncture wound. They can be inflicted by humans and animals. In the case of a mild human bite, you may need only to thoroughly wash the injured areas. However, if the skin is broken, consult a doctor at once. This is especially important if the bite was from an animal. This is because there is a danger of an infection such as rabies.

**Rabies** is a disease caused by a viral infection of the nervous system and brain. Humans who are infected are not able to swallow. This is a result of the tightening of throat muscles.

Rabies is transmitted through the saliva of a rabid animal. It can be contracted by a human when animal saliva enters an open cut. The infection is most often spread to humans when the rabid animal bites and breaks the skin.

Call a doctor at once if a child is bitten by an animal. Report the animal's size and color to the police. If the animal cannot be caught and tested for rabies, the child will need to undergo rabies immunization. This is a very painful series of shots. Without the immunization, the child can die.

All animal bites are dangerous. They carry great risk of infection. Most animals carry a wide variety of bacteria in their mouths, not the least of which is rabies. For that reason, take immediate action when a child is bitten by an animal.

## Open Wound Care

Some open wounds require medical attention. See 12-11. As the teacher, you can usually treat minor wounds such as abrasions and small cuts. First, wash the area with warm water. Then, as you apply a bandage, bring the wound edges together. This will help prevent scarring.

Assume that any loss of blood is harmful. To control severe bleeding, place a sterile gauze over the wound. Press on the wound with the palm of one hand. The object is to control the bleeding by pressing the blood vessels against something solid such as a bone or muscle.

## Open Wounds That Require Medical Attention

- An animal or human bite that has broken the skin.
- Bleeding that cannot be stopped in five minutes despite all effort to control it.
- Deep cuts on the face or some other part of the body where scar tissue will be noticeable.
- A wound that goes deeper than the outer layer of skin.
- Wounds with foreign objects such as dirt deep inside the tissue.
- A wound with foreign matter that cannot be removed.
- Puncture wounds if child is not current on tetanus immunizations.

12-11 Recognizing the severity of wounds can help you determine if medical care is needed.

If there is no sign of a fracture, elevate open wounds of the leg, arm, neck, or head. To elevate, raise the injured area above the level of the child's heart. The force of gravity will help reduce blood pressure in the injured area, thereby slowing blood loss.

## Burns and Their Treatment

A **burn** is an injury caused by heat, radiation, or chemical agents. Burns vary in size, depth, and severity. Burns are generally classified by degree or depth. There are three classes: first-degree burns, second-degree burns, and third-degree burns. A person can have more than one type of burn from a single accident.

Children are commonly burned by hot liquids, cooking and electrical equipment, open fires, matches, chemicals such as strong detergents and acids, and overexposure to the sun. See 12-12. When developmentally appropriate, you should teach children to stop, drop and roll in case their clothes catch fire.

### First-Degree Burns

**First-degree burns** are burns to the top layer of skin. They are the least severe of all burns. They may result from brief contact with hot objects, overexposure to the sun, or scalding by hot water or steam. Common signs include redness or mild discoloration, pain, and mild

swelling. Healing is normally rapid because the burn does not go deep.

Special medical treatment is not needed for first-degree burns. Applying cold water to the burn will often help relieve some pain.

### Second-Degree Burns

**Second-degree burns** cause damage to underlying layers of skin. These burns are more serious than first-degree burns. They are caused by extreme overexposure to the sun, contact with hot liquids, and contact with flash fires from gasoline, kerosene, and other products.

Second-degree burns are marked by pain, blistering, swelling, and discoloration. Over several days, the burn is likely to swell a great deal. Due to the severity of these burns, they require medical treatment. Do not treat the burn by breaking blisters or by placing an ointment on the burn. This may cause infection. If infection arises in the wound, a second-degree burn can quickly become a third-degree burn.

12-12 Care must be taken to keep children safe around items that cause burns.

## Third-Degree Burns

**Third-degree burns** destroy the skin layer and nerve endings. They can be caused by open flames, burning clothing, immersion in hot water, contact with hot objects, and contact with live electrical wires.

Third-degree burns are very serious. They require prompt medical attention. An ambulance should be called at once.

## Sunburn

Children can get first- or second-degree burns from exposure to the sun's ultraviolet rays. There is usually a 3- to 12-hour lapse in time between exposure and development of sunburn. Sunburn does not usually require a hospital stay. However, sunburn can cause a child to be out several days due to swelling, pain, headache, and fever. Sunburn also raises the risk of skin cancer later in life.

Protect the children in your care from sunburn. Babies younger than 6 months should not be exposed to direct sunlight. Keep these babies in the shade. For children older than 6 months, apply a children's sunscreen with a sun protection factor (SPF) of 15 or more. Sunscreen should be applied to all exposed areas of skin 30 minutes prior to sun exposure. Reapply sunscreen after swimming, heavy sweating, or 2 hours of sun exposure. Hats and sunglasses also protect children from the damaging rays of the sun. Schedule outdoor play periods to avoid sun exposure from 10 a.m. to 4 p.m.—the time when the sun's rays are most intense.

## Splinters

Children often get splinters. It will be your job to remove them. A pair of sterilized tweezers is the best tool for this process. To sterilize tweezers, store them in a jar of rubbing alcohol. You can also soak them in alcohol or boil them for 10 minutes. A third option is to hold the tip of the tweezers in a flame and wipe the carbon away with a clean cloth before using.

First wash the area with soap and water. Then remove splinters at the same angle they entered the skin. Do not put any ointment or antiseptic on the wound. Cover with a sterile bandage until a doctor can see it. If you cannot remove a splinter, consult a doctor.

## Insect Stings

Wasps, bees, hornets, yellow jackets, and fire ants are all stinging insects. The stings are painful to all children. For children who are allergic to insect stings, a sting can be fatal. React quickly when a child has been stung. Most deaths from insect stings occur within two hours of the incident.

If a child is stung, scrape the stinger away with your fingernail. Avoid using tweezers to pull the stinger out. This might squeeze the stinger and release more toxins into the skin. After removing the stinger, watch for signs of an allergic reaction.

A rash or swelling usually indicates a mild allergic reaction. Anaphylactic shock can result from an extremely allergic reaction. Watch the child closely for signs of anaphylactic shock. If you notice any of these signs, get prompt medical help.

Children who are allergic to stings and have been stung before may have their own medication and injection equipment. Make sure it is available for emergencies. When you leave the classroom, take the equipment.

## Choking

While choking can occur among people of all ages, children are at highest risk. Young children are more likely than adults to put small objects, such as toys, buttons, and coins, in their mouths. Children younger than four years are more likely to choke on hard or round foods. They are less likely to chew food well or sit still while eating. Children are also more likely to stuff their mouths with too much food. All these actions increase the risk of choking.

The best way to prevent choking is to protect children from choking hazards. Keep small toys and other objects that pose a choking hazard out of the reach of children younger than four years. Avoid offering foods that are known choking hazards. (Refer to Chapter 11 for a list of these foods.) Have children sit while eating and eat only a small amount at a time.

When choking occurs, however, program staff must respond quickly. All staff members need to know what techniques to use to treat choking and how to perform them. For example, treating an infant differs from treating an older child or adult. Helping a conscious victim is not done in the same way as helping someone who is unconscious. As a result, staff members need training to learn which steps to use in each situation. They also need to see the techniques demonstrated and have a chance to practice.

Newly hired staff should be required to attend first-aid training that includes techniques for the abdominal thrust and cardiopulmonary resuscitation (CPR). Staff members who successfully complete the course will be certified to provide these procedures. All staff must complete refresher courses for these techniques yearly to keep their certifications current. The director can arrange to have these trainings offered as a yearly in-service.

## Dental Emergencies

Dental emergencies include cut or bitten tongues, lips, or cheeks, knocked out permanent teeth, and broken teeth. With any of these problems, take quick action and remain calm.

12-13  When given by a trained person, the abdominal thrust can save the life of a choking child.

If a child complains of a toothache, help the child rinse the affected area with water. Apply cold compresses if the face is swollen. Urge the parents to take the child to a dentist.

If a child has a cut or bitten lip, tongue, or cheek, apply ice to the injured area. If you see blood, hold a clean gauze or cloth over the area. Gently apply pressure. Contact the child's parents if the bleeding does not stop in 15 minutes. If the cut is severe, take the child to an emergency room.

To provide emergency care for a knocked out permanent tooth, first find the tooth. Pick it up by the crown, not the roots. If the tooth is dirty, rinse it gently with milk. Do not use water. However, avoid unnecessary handling. Keep the tooth moist. If the tooth is not broken, put it back in its socket and gently hold it in place. If you cannot put it back, place the tooth in a container of cool, clean milk. Call the child's dentist and parents immediately. In order to save the tooth, the child must see a dentist at once.

If a child breaks or chips a tooth, report it to the parents. They can decide whether a dentist should be consulted. Gently clean the injured area with warm water. Use a cold compress to reduce swelling.

## Head Lice

To maintain a healthy environment, you will need to recognize head lice. **Head lice** are small insects that live on people's hair and scalp. They are about one-tenth to one-eighth of an inch in length. They have no wings and do not fly. They have six pairs of hooks in their mouths. With these hooks, they attach themselves to the hair shaft. Short legs and large claws help them keep their grip on hair. They produce small round eggs, called nits. These nits look like grains of sand.

It is difficult to see head lice with the naked eye. However, there are several signs you can recognize. Look for the following:

- A constant itch of the scalp, especially behind the ears and at the base of the scalp. Often the child will have infected scratches or a rash on the scalp.
- Small, silvery eggs attached to individual hairs. Usually a magnifying glass will help reveal these.

■ In severe cases, lymph glands may swell in the neck or under the arm.

Head lice can spread through direct contact with the hair. Combs, brushes, hats, and bedding are key sources of transportation. Head lice can also crawl from person to person.

If one child in your classroom has head lice, other children and staff members may get it, too. Send notices home to all parents if even one child has been infected with head lice. In some areas, a county or city nurse will conduct daily inspections at a center that has had an outbreak.

The best way to get rid of head lice is to seek medical help. Most physicians prescribe a medical shampoo or lotion. All family members should be treated. Doctors also suggest boiling or dry-cleaning all hats, combs, brushes, clothing, bedding, and furry toys. Items that cannot be washed or dry-cleaned should be sealed in a plastic bag for 30 days, which is the life cycle of a louse. Rugs, upholstered furniture, and mattresses should be vacuumed. Combs and brushes should be boiled for 10 minutes or soaked for one hour in a bleach solution.

# Caring for Children Who Become Ill

Whenever a child becomes ill, he or she should be moved into a separate area at once. An isolation area or room is needed in every early childhood center. Some states require that centers have isolation rooms.

Due to a lack of space, some centers do not have a special room for this purpose. Instead, a cot in the director's office is used for these emergencies.

When children become ill, they may vomit, develop diarrhea, or develop a fever. Child care workers need to know how to handle these signs of illness.

Children often vomit when ill. After the child has vomited, he or she will need to rest and keep warm. Remove the child from the group and contact the parents.

The child may request food or drink. However, only provide sips of water. Any other foods may prompt more vomiting. Record the number of times the child vomits and the amount thrown up. Report this information to parents when they arrive.

Diarrhea may be caused by a virus, food-borne illness, or allergies. Many illnesses cause diarrhea that lasts for two or three days. Chronic diarrhea may be a symptom of infection, inflammation of the intestines, or allergies. Chronic diarrhea may last for up to 10 days.

With diarrhea, a child will have an increased number of stools compared to the child's normal pattern. The stool may be loose, watery, and unformed.

Children who have diarrhea need to be isolated. Remove them from the classroom and contact their parents. They should be diarrhea-free for 24 hours before returning to the center.

## Temperature Emergency

The human body normally maintains an average internal temperature of 98.6°F. Normal temperatures range, from 97°F to just under 100°F. For this reason, it is important to have each child's normal temperature recorded on a health form.

A slight change in a child's temperature is a signal that the body is preparing against illness. A temperature at least two degrees above normal is significant. Most, but not all, young children will run a higher fever than adults.

A child may have a slight rise in temperature for several reasons. For example, the presence of infection raises a child's temperature. Too much physical activity will also raise a temperature. Temperature also may vary depending upon the time of the day. Temperatures are somewhat lower in the morning than the evening.

To take a child's temperature, you have a few options, including
■ traditional mercury thermometers
■ digital thermometers
■ single-use temperature strips (for forehead)

Experts now advise against using mercury thermometers, especially with children. If this type of thermometer breaks, mercury can spill or evaporate into the air. Inhaling, touching, or swallowing mercury can damage the brain, spinal cord, kidneys, and liver. For this reason, it is best to keep these thermometers out of early childhood programs.

Although they are more expensive than other types of thermometers, digital thermometers are preferred. They are easy to use and give a quick and accurate reading. Some digital thermometers are designed for the ear, 12-14. Others can be used orally, rectally, and under the arm. Read the directions for proper use of any digital thermometer. Temperature strips are easy to use but less accurate than a digital thermometer.

Call the parents right away if a child has a fever. Report any other unusual behavior.

## Special Health Concerns

If a child with a special physical condition is enrolled in the program, you will need to make plans for this child's health and well-being. Begin by discussing the child's condition with the parents. Be certain you understand what the condition is and what type of emergencies may arise. Find out what approach the center needs to take. Does the child require a special diet, medications, or specific exercises? Also ask the parents how to help the child feel comfortable.

You will likely encounter several common health concerns among the children in your class. Some of the most common of these include the following:

- *Allergies.* An allergy is the body's reaction to a substance in the environment, which is called an allergen. Smoke, dust, mold, mildew, pet dander, pollen, and certain foods are common allergens. Reactions to an allergen include sneezing, runny nose, coughing, itchy or watery eyes, headache, skin rashes, hives, diarrhea, and vomiting. Some allergies are seasonal, while others are continuous. Ask parents what the allergens are and try to avoid exposing the child to these. Medications may be needed to treat the symptoms of allergies.
- *Asthma.* **Asthma** is a chronic inflammatory disorder of the airways. Symptoms include coughing, wheezing, rapid or labored breathing, shortness of breath, and chest tightness. Ask parents what conditions trigger their child's attacks and try to prevent these conditions. Examples include smoke, cold

12-14  At many centers, digital ear thermometers are used to get an accurate temperature reading quickly and easily.

air, exposure to an allergen, and overexertion. Find out what medications should be given and when. For older children, ask the child to tell you right away when an asthma attack is starting so you can administer medications. For younger children, you will need to observe carefully for signs of an attack.
- *Diabetes.* For a child with diabetes, the body cannot properly control the level of sugar in the blood. Having too much or too little sugar in the blood can cause serious health problems. Children with diabetes cannot regulate blood sugar because they do not produce insulin. They must balance their food choices, intake, and activity levels. Many children with diabetes must also monitor their blood sugar throughout the day and take insulin injections as needed. You will likely need to help with these procedures. Ask the child's parents about your

role in managing the disease. Learn the signs of an insulin reaction, the body's response to an imbalance of insulin. If a reaction occurs, offer juice, sugar, or candy to help adjust the blood sugar level quickly. Keep these items handy at all times just in case. In severe cases, a child may pass out. Take the child to an emergency room or call an ambulance at once.

■ *Epilepsy.* **Epilepsy** is a condition in which a person has periodic seizures. There are two types of seizures. *Grand mal seizures* consist of repeated convulsions or jerking over the entire body. *Petit mal seizures* are milder than grand mal seizures. They consist of a few brief muscle twitches and a sense of confusion. Ask the child's parents what medical treatment should be given to prevent seizures. Have them describe the seizures and how they can be prevented. In the case of a grand mal seizure, protect the child from injuring himself or herself. Help the child lie down and monitor the child's breathing. Contact the child's parents and doctor after every seizure. Describe what occurred before, during, and after the seizure.

■ *Human immunodeficiency virus (HIV).* **HIV** breaks down the body's immune system. This virus eventually leads to the disease **acquired immunodeficiency syndrome (AIDS).** AIDS

further destroys the immune system and over time can be fatal. Most children with HIV got the virus from their mothers during pregnancy, birth, or breast-feeding. It can also be acquired through contact with the blood of an infected person. Hugging, touching, or being near someone with HIV does not spread the disease. Children with HIV can attend child care unless they have open sores, uncontrollable nosebleeds, bloody diarrhea, or are at high risk for exposing others to blood-contaminated bodily fluids. Ask parents about the treatment, diet, and activity level recommended for children with HIV. These children have a weakened immune system and have trouble fighting even common illnesses. Alert the parents about communicable diseases of other children in your class right away.

More information about most of these illnesses is given in Chapter 30, *Guiding Children with Special Needs.* Children may have other special health concerns, too. Have all parents complete a health questionnaire upon admitting their children to the center. Talk to parents about how to manage these concerns. Follow parents' instructions and keep careful records about diet, medications, physical activity, and rest. These records give the child's parents and doctor a more complete picture about how the child is doing or what changes should be made.

## Summary

Children's health can be protected, maintained, and improved in many ways during each day at the center. This is a very important part of the job of a teacher.

The best way to begin guiding children's health is by setting health policies. Policies might include requiring all children enrolled to have medical exams and immunizations. Contacting parents about health-related issues might also be addressed in your health policy.

The second step in guiding health is having knowledge of various illnesses and diseases. You will need to know how to control transmittable illnesses and diseases. You also will need to know what steps you should take in caring for children who are injured or become ill while at the center.

Protecting, maintaining, and even improving health is a major responsibility of a teacher. The teacher is trusted with the well-being of many children.

## Review and Reflect

1. What will a preadmission medical exam help you learn about a child being enrolled?

2. List the immunization(s) needed for children at the following ages:
   A. 0 to 4 months
   B. 12 to 18 months
   C. 4 to 6 years

3. True or false. Each child should be provided with a washable cot or bed and clean sheets for napping.

4. Name four signs of illness you should watch for daily.

5. True or false. Parents should be contacted whenever a child shows symptoms of illness.

6. What is foodborne illness?

7. In order to prevent the growth of bacteria, keep foods at a temperature above _____ F or below _____ F.

8. A _____ is damage to the surface of the skin or body tissue.

9. The most common type of closed wound is a _____.

10. Skinned knees, scratched arms, and rope burns are examples of _____.

11. Why should a doctor be contacted immediately if a child is bitten by an animal?

12. Which is the most serious burn, a first-degree burn or a third-degree burn?

13. How should you treat a burn caused by a child touching a hot object?

14. Most deaths from insect stings occur within how long of the incident?

15. What is the best way for a child to get rid of blockage in the windpipe?

16. List two symptoms of head lice.

17. _____ is a hormone that keeps sugar in the blood at a proper level.

18. What is epilepsy?

## Apply and Explore

1. Prepare a handout listing the health policies of a center for preschool children.

2. Interview a child care center director about food safety requirements and policies followed by the center. Ask if the center has ever had an outbreak of foodborne illness and if so, how this was handled.

3. Write a research paper on a serious illness that can affect children. Explain the illness itself and dispel any commonly believed untruths about the illness. Explain various treatments for the illness.

4. Check online at the National Resource **C** Center for Health and Safety in Child Care Web site (nrc.uchsc.edu) for health tips suggested for child care centers.

5. Visit the Web site kidshealth.org to learn **C** more about allergies and asthma. Use the computer to write a brief paper on your findings.

6. Use the Web site of the American Red **C** Cross (redcross.org) to search for the chapter nearest you. Contact this chapter to learn what resources are available near you for first-aid training.

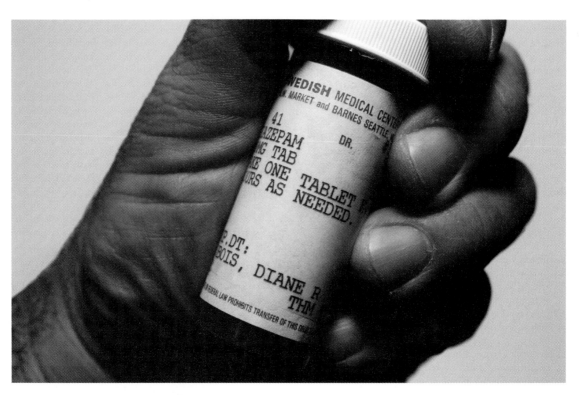

Read each medicine label three times before administering medicine to a child.

# Part 3
# Guiding Children

As you work in child care, guidance will be a routine part of your experiences with children. Children need positive guidance to learn how to get along with others and to stay safe.

In this part, you will study and practice techniques for guiding children throughout the day. You will gain insight into methods for handling such guidance problems as negativism and fear.

You will learn guidelines for establishing and enforcing limits throughout the classroom. This part will also teach you ways to guide children through such daily routines as dressing, eating, and napping.

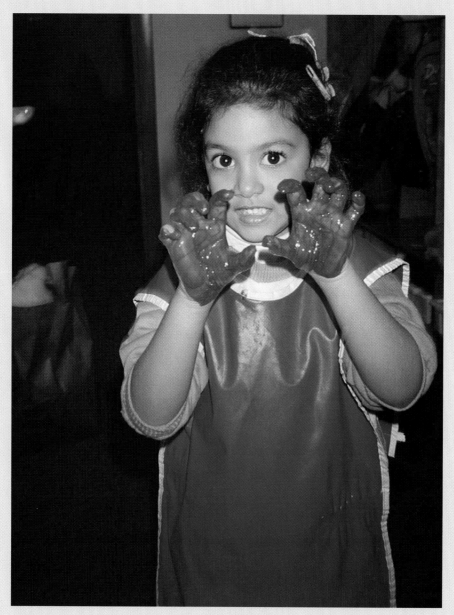

Understanding children's behavior is an important part of guidance.

# Chapter 13

# Developing Guidance Skills

After studying this chapter, you will be able to

- identify goals of effective guidance.
- list personality traits of effective early childhood teachers.
- describe principles of direct and indirect guidance.
- explain various techniques for effective guidance.
- summarize ways to promote a positive self-concept in each child.

## Terms to Know

| | |
|---|---|
| guidance | artificial consequences |
| prosocial behaviors | time out |
| indirect guidance | I-message |
| direct guidance | prompting |
| positive reinforcement | redirecting |
| consequence | modeling |
| natural consequences | active listening |

Alicia sat in the corner looking at a library book. Slowly she ripped a page from the book. On the other side of the room, Wyatt knocked Hunter's block tower over. Then she sped to the art table and grabbed Ryder's play dough. At the same time, May entered the room, greeted another child, and threw her coat on the floor.

How will you, as a teacher, guide each of these children? Guiding children is a complex process. Understanding and guiding children's behavior requires knowledge of child growth and development. It also requires the ability to understand each child's behavior. This is a constant process that never ends. As a teacher, you will continually learn more about your role in guiding young children.

## Goals of Guidance

**Guidance** consists of direct and indirect actions used by an adult to help children develop appropriate behavior patterns, 13-1. Effective guidance should maintain children's self-esteem and produce a desired change in behavior. Self-control is the long-term goal of guidance. That is, the children should learn to direct their own behavior without outside control.

Another goal of guidance is to promote prosocial behaviors among the children. **Prosocial behaviors** are acts of kindness that benefit others. They are behaviors that demonstrate cooperation and helpfulness. The following are examples of prosocial behaviors:

- accepting others' feelings
- verbally and physically comforting others

13-1 Younger children often require more guidance than older children.

- helping others
- cooperating with others in play and cleanup time
- sharing toys and materials
- sharing affection
- showing concern

## Guidance and You

As a teacher, your personality will affect the behavior of the children in your care. Many studies have been conducted to determine the effect that specific personality traits have on children's behavior. These studies show that effective early childhood teachers encourage and show interest in children. These teachers use more suggestions than commands. Children respond faster to suggestions than commands.

According to research, teachers should interact often with their children and ask open-ended questions. These questions require more than one-word answers. Children in this type of environment will show certain positive characteristics. These include independence, verbalization, cooperation, task persistence, and high self-esteem. See 13-2.

Model prosocial behaviors. Children will imitate your example, so let it be a positive one. Studies also note that uncooperative teachers have more hyperactive, disruptive,

13-2 This child will learn a great deal through interaction with the teacher.

and bored children. On the other hand, children in the classes of talkative teachers tend to be more shy. Nurturing teachers have children in their classes who interact easily with others.

Aggressive and attention-seeking behavior on the part of the children is also influenced by the teacher. This behavior occurs most often with permissive teachers. Such teachers often fail to get involved with or stop aggressive and attention-seeking behavior. The children who behave this way may see the teacher's lack of involvement as permission to engage in such behavior.

## Preparing for Guidance

There are some general guidelines for developing effective guidance skills. Study these guidelines. They will help you become an effective teacher.

One of the first steps toward effective guidance is observation of the children. Watch and note how individual children behave in certain situations. This will help you understand the children in your class. Review the observation techniques described in Chapter 3.

Ask yourself how you respond to each of the children in your class. Do you have any biases?

Are you expecting certain behaviors from children based on culture, gender, personality, or appearance? The stereotypes you hold may affect your perception of a child. For example, do you expect Clarice to be better behaved because both of her parents are doctors? Being honest about your own attitudes and how they may influence your interactions will allow you to be more objective.

Another important guideline is to plan with other teachers. Sharing observations, feelings, and suggestions will help you fully understand the children. One teacher may be able to add to your observations, 13-3. As a result, you will better understand why a child refuses to take part in art activities.

Next, do not talk to other adults when you are teaching, unless it is important. The children's needs should always come first. Being alert to these needs requires your full attention. Make a practice of talking with other teachers only if necessary. Save other comments for after program hours.

Finally, sit with the children whenever possible. You will be closer to the children's level. As a result, they will find it easier to approach you and gain your attention. Do not interrupt an activity unless you can add to knowledge or

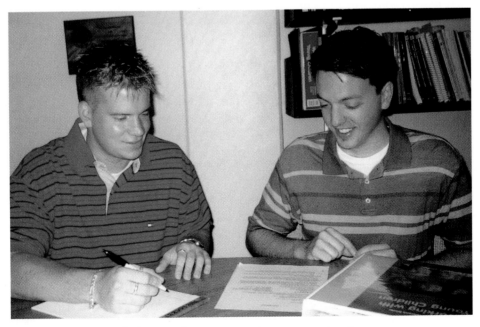

13-3 With the help of other teachers, you can learn more about the children in your center.

safety. Let the children begin interaction with you. Remember that to develop independence and self-confidence, never do for the children what they can do for themselves.

# Direct Guidance

Child guidance may be direct or indirect. **Indirect guidance** involves outside factors that influence behavior. The layout of the center is a form of indirect guidance. Indirect guidance will be discussed later in the chapter.

**Direct guidance** involves nonverbal (physical) and verbal actions. Nonverbal actions include facial gestures such as eye contact, a smile, or even a surprised look. Your words are also a form of direct guidance.

Facial expressions can communicate a variety of messages ranging from disapproval and sadness to approval and reassurance. Body gestures are another type of direct guidance. Putting your arm around a child is one form of direct guidance.

Young children gain much information from nonverbal actions. They might learn the caregiver's mood and expectations. Infants and toddlers focus most of their attention on what they see and feel rather than on verbal clues. Even as children begin to pay more attention to words, they still rely on nonverbal actions to help them understand messages.

Your nonverbal actions need to reinforce what you are communicating verbally. Watch that your words match your nonverbal signals. For example, if you are asking a child to stop a behavior, your facial expression should also convey disapproval. Children become confused when adults' words give one message and their actions another.

Direct guidance principles are shown in 13-4. Following these principles will help you develop direct guidance skills.

## Use Simple Language

Using simple language is important. Young children have limited vocabularies. To communicate clearly, use language they can understand. Consider the ages of the children. Adjust your vocabulary to fit those ages. For instance, two-

| Direct Guidance Principles |
|---|
| Use simple language.<br>Speak in a relaxed voice.<br>Be positive.<br>Offer choices with care.<br>Encourage independence and cooperation.<br>Be firm.<br>Be consistent.<br>Provide time for change.<br>Consider feelings.<br>Intervene when necessary. |

13-4 These direct guidance principles outline the verbal and nonverbal skills you will need for effective guidance.

year-olds usually learn the word *big* before they learn *large*. Therefore, use the word *big* with these children. Working with three-year-olds, you might use the word *large*. This depends, however, on their level of development. With four- and five-year-olds, again adjust the level of your vocabulary. With these children, you might say *huge*.

## Speak in a Relaxed Voice

Speak in a calm, quiet, relaxed tone of voice. Children will listen to this type of voice. Save loud voices for emergencies. At those times, you will gain the children's attention with a loud voice. If you raise your voice during the normal course of the day, children will become used to this level. When an emergency occurs, you may not be able to gain their attention. In addition, when you raise your voice, the children will also raise their voices. The classroom will become a very noisy place.

## Be Positive

Guide the children by telling them what to do, as opposed to what not to do. Children will feel more comfortable with a positive comment. For example, instead of saying "Don't put that puzzle on the floor," say "Put the puzzle on the table." See 13-5. This will remind the children of the rule that puzzles are used on a table.

| Using Positive Guidance | |
|---|---|
| **Negative** | **Positive** |
| "Do not put the puzzle on the floor." | "Put the puzzle on the table." |
| "Do not touch anything!" | "Place your hands in your pockets." |
| "Do not run." | "Please walk." |
| "Quit screaming." | "Use your indoor voice." |
| "Do not drip paint." | "Wipe your brush on the container." |
| "Do not get paint on your clothes." | "Put on a painting smock." |
| "Do not rip the pages." | "Turn the pages carefully." |
| "Do not walk in front of the swing." | "Walk around the swing, please." |
| "Do not use your fingers." | "Use your fork." |

13-5  Be aware of negative comments you make and try to replace them with positive comments.

## Offer Choices with Care

New, unskilled teachers sometimes confuse offering a choice with giving a direction. For example, when it is lunchtime, the teacher may say "Do you want to go in for lunch?" By asking this question, the child is given a choice. If the child is not interested in eating lunch then, he or she may answer by saying no.

Children should be offered a choice only when you want them to have a choice. In this case, a better direction would be "It is time for lunch now," or "We need to go inside for lunch now." Make sure that once you offer a choice you allow the child to carry through with his or her choice. For example, you might ask a child if she or he prefers watering the plants or feeding the fish. If the child chooses feeding the fish, accept the choice. Do not try to get children to change their minds. When you do this, you are telling them that there really was not a choice.

## Encourage Independence and Cooperation

Give children the least amount of help they need. In this way, they will have opportunities to learn independence. For instance, encourage children to dress and feed themselves. Encourage them to share responsibility for keeping the classroom clean and orderly.

Some children begin school dependent on others. At home, these children have an adult or sibling to attend to their needs. As a result, they come to school expecting the teacher to dress them, pick up after them, and intercede for them. Encourage independence from the start in order to change this behavior. For instance, when Eugene reports that Tommy is teasing him, ask Eugene how he feels when this happens. If he says he does not like it, tell him to share his feelings with Tommy. Likewise, if Talia does not want to share her clay, Eugene needs to tell Talia he is mad because she will not share.

Children only become independent if allowed the opportunity. Many people are surprised at the competence of three-, four-, and five-year-old children who are provided the chance to do for themselves. See 13-6.

These children also must learn to help each other. Encourage children to work with each other. When Toby tells you he cannot zip his coat, say "Ask Joanne if she can help you." If Marlene cannot tie her shoe, say "Ask Luis to help you tie it." These experiences help the children to learn prosocial behaviors.

## Be Firm

Be firm when disciplining children. At the same time, speak in a quiet voice. Some children are very demanding. When you tell them that

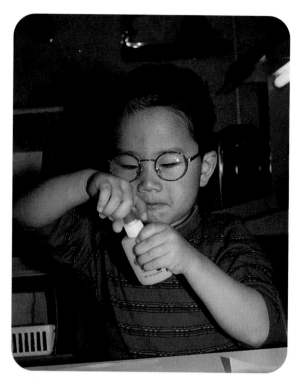

13-6 Young children are good at doing tasks for themselves, if given a chance.

they cannot do something, they may cry. Some may even throw temper tantrums. If it is behavior that you cannot allow to continue, you must stand firm.

When a child throws a temper tantrum, you may feel like giving in. If you do, the child will likely use the same method again when he or she wants his or her own way. Effective guidance requires firmness.

## Be Consistent

Children are good at testing adults. If they feel an adult is not firm in disciplining, they will repeat their unacceptable behavior. In fact, they may want to find out what will happen if they continue to repeat their unacceptable behavior. For this reason, discipline and approval should be given consistently. For instance, do not discipline children one day and praise them the next for running to the door at playtime.

Make sure that you are also consistent from child to child. Children quickly develop a sense of fairness. If you tell one child to pick up the toys at cleanup time, all children should have to clean up. When you are not consistent, children will challenge your requests.

## Provide Time for Change

Young children need time to change activities. It is important to provide them with ample time for change. Without this time, children can become confused. By allowing time, you will provide children with an adjustment period. For instance, when children are preparing to go outside during cold weather, allow them time to put on their coats, hats, and mittens. This time will allow them to prepare themselves for new activities and new surroundings.

## Consider Feelings

Although it is not always included in daily lesson plans, learning about feelings and emotions is an important part of any day at the center. Children need to recognize, understand, and express their feelings.

Young children often have strong feelings. These feelings often center around control of their environment. Such feelings often relate to their bodies, siblings, eating, friendship, and toileting.

Feelings are best discussed in small group settings or alone with a child. For some children, talking about feelings and emotions is difficult. It is your responsibility to help them understand their feelings. See 13-7.

Facing someone else's pain is also difficult for young children. You will observe that children do not know how to deal with the pain of others. When a new child begins school and cries over separation from parents, the other children do not usually get involved. Some may pretend to not see or hear the child. Others may have a pained look on their faces. This shows sensitivity. Although they may feel sympathy, they tend not to get involved. Usually, if a child is bleeding, only then will they get involved. They will bring the child to you for a bandage. However, they will not usually console the child.

You can show them how to help these children. For instance, if Patrick is crying, put your arm around him. By doing this, you will teach the children a way to comfort each other. They will learn that crying can be mended with a hug.

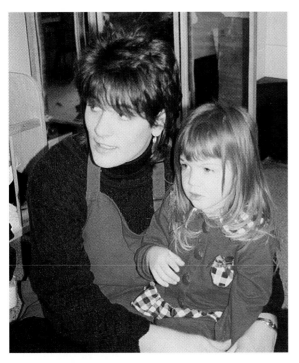

13-7 Many children do not know how to handle their feelings. They may require your help in order to feel good about themselves.

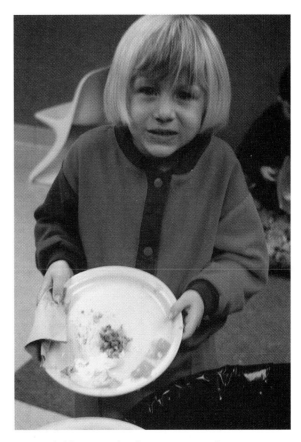

13-8 Children need to be encouraged to help with cleanup.

Young children also need to learn how to handle mistakes. When a child spills milk or breaks a toy, do not overreact. Instead, show the child how to handle the mistake. The child will then know not to fear mistakes. See 13-8. For example, remind the child who spilled the milk that the milk must be cleaned up. Show the child how to do this. Depending on the situation, you may wish to help clean up.

## Intervene When Necessary

To be an effective teacher, you will need to know when to intervene. Allow children to explore on their own. Interrupt only when you can add to their knowledge or promote their safety. For example, if a four-year-old says "Cows give eggnog at Christmas," clarify this statement. Unless you intervene, children who are listening may believe this comment.

Safety intervention will often require words and action. If James is not careful climbing up the slide, you will need to walk over and review the limits with him. Make clear the dangers of

falling. Intervention would also be required if you were observing a group of children and noticed that a child was in danger of being hurt. It is important to intervene before this happens by redirecting the play or providing assistance.

You may also need to intervene for health purposes. Remind children to dress properly for outdoor play in the winter. Encourage children to cover their mouths when they cough. When cooking, remind children not to use the cooking utensils to taste the food.

Children need to learn to be friends with all the children. Thus, do not allow children to be excluded from play because of age, culture, or gender. When Erica says "Only girls can come into the playhouse," it is important for you to intervene. One way to handle this is to say "This school is for everyone." By doing so, you will give the children the words they need to defend their right to participate.

You must also intervene when children are impolite. Sometimes you will hear a child say "I do not like you," or "You are ugly." When this happens, you need to intervene. Point out to the child that such words can hurt another's feelings. With young children, that may be sufficient to end the behavior.

Property arguments may also require intervention. Center property does not belong to the children, but to the school. Therefore, the children must share it. During a property argument, remind the children to share. If this does not work, give the equipment to one child for a set time period. Then give it to the other child for another time period. For instance, tell Mandy that she may play with the truck in the morning and Mark may play with it in the afternoon. Then make sure each child has a turn.

It is important for children to learn that they cannot grab materials from others. No matter how strong the child's feelings, others have rights, too. Children need to take turns painting at the easel, participating in cooking activities, and watering plants, 13-9. While children learn and develop, you will need to intervene. That is why in many early childhood classrooms, you will hear a teacher saying many times a day "You can have a turn next," or "After she is finished, you can paint."

## Indirect Guidance

You will recall that indirect guidance involves outside factors that influence behavior. The physical setup of a center is a form of indirect guidance. It can indirectly influence both the children's and teacher's behavior. For example, a well-planned facility makes supervision easier. If you can supervise properly it will help you to feel relaxed and in control. The children will feel safer knowing they are being protected.

In order to carefully supervise young children, an open classroom is best. Stand with your back toward the classroom wall. You should be able to view the entire room. Such an arrangement will allow you to observe and give help when needed. It will also reduce your own fatigue, since you will have to run back and forth between areas less often.

A healthy, safe environment can be promoted through the physical setup of the facility. In one large room, you will be able to see everything that happens, 13-10. Therefore, you can step in when dangerous situations arise. For instance, the behavior of two-year-old children needs close monitoring. Many two-year-olds will hit another child instead of saying "I do not like that." With the proper physical arrangement, you

13-9 These children have learned that they must take turns as they participate in activities.

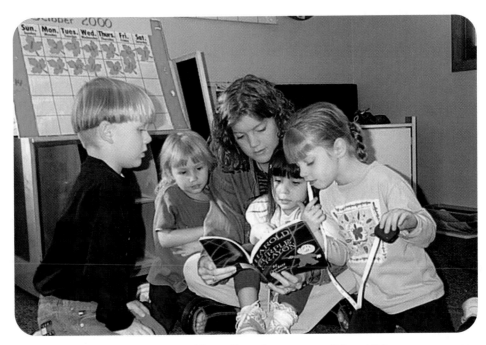

13-10  This teacher has positioned herself so she can see all the children.

can see such situations occurring and step in immediately.

Young children, and especially two-year-olds, often do not have well-developed gross motor skills. They often stumble, trip, or fall. To reduce the number of these accidents, large, open areas are best. Shelving units should be placed around the outside walls of the room.

Children's independence can also be encouraged through the physical setup of the facility. Independence should be a learning objective of every early childhood program, no matter the ages or abilities of children in the program. For example, you should encourage toddlers to use the washroom if they have developed control of their bowels and bladders. For this reason, the washrooms should be easy to find and use. Sinks, toilets, and hand dryers should be set at the children's level.

Children can also be encouraged to hang up their own coats and assist with cleanup. To encourage this, provide low hooks for hanging coats and hats. Low shelf units and sinks will encourage children to help with cleanup. All toys and materials should have a designated place in the classroom. Placing a picture of the item on a shelf or container is one way of assisting the children. When containers are marked, teachers are usually more successful in having the children replace toys and equipment to the proper storage place.

Through these arrangements, you will save time and energy assisting the children. This will allow you more time to observe and work with the children and plan meaningful activities.

## Techniques for Effective Guidance

As an early childhood teacher, you will teach children acceptable behaviors. Likewise, the children in your classroom will also teach each other. Whatever effect you have on the children's behavior, the children, in turn, will affect others.

There are specific guidance techniques that can be useful in guiding children's behavior. These techniques include positive reinforcement and the use of consequences. In addition, you will want to include warning, time out, I-messages, praising, affirming, suggesting, prompting, persuading, redirecting, modeling, listening, ignoring, and encouraging.

## Positive Reinforcement

Children's behavior can often be molded by rewarding positive behavior. This technique is called **positive reinforcement**. For instance, if you thank a child for holding the door, the child will most likely hold the door again. You have provided a positive reinforcement of the child's behavior. Positive messages will encourage the child to repeat the behavior. Repeated positive reinforcement will result in repeated behavior.

You must be careful when using positive reinforcement that you are rewarding behaviors you want the child to repeat. Teachers sometimes do not realize they are rewarding children for unacceptable behavior. For instance, laughing at a child who is acting silly at group time is reinforcing the child's behavior. This reaction is seen by the child as a reward. It encourages the child to repeat the behavior.

## Using Consequences

Consequences are important in molding children's behavior. A **consequence** is a result that follows an action or behavior. Consequences can be very effective in shaping behavior. There are two types of consequences: natural consequences and artificial consequences.

**Natural consequences** are those experiences that follow naturally as a result of a behavior. They do not require anyone's intervention. For example, the natural consequence of forgetting to put away an art project is that it might be thrown away during cleanup time. The natural consequence of forgetting to put on your gloves is that your hands will get cold. Natural consequences can be very effective in guiding children's behavior, but they cannot be used if a child's safety is at risk. For instance, if a child runs into the street without stopping to look for cars, the child could be hit by a car. In this case, an adult must intervene to make sure the child stops and looks before crossing a street.

When natural consequences cannot be used to guide behavior, artificial consequences may be established. **Artificial consequences** (also called logical consequences) are those that are deliberately set up by an adult to show what will happen if a limit is not followed. The consequences should be related to the behavior as much as possible.

When using artificial consequences, the children must first be made aware of the limits.

Then they need to know the consequences of choosing not to follow the limits. For example, if Brad drives his scooter into Lawrence, tell him to stop. Remind him of the consequence if he does not stop. The consequence might be that he will have to give up his turn on the scooter. If Brad runs into Lawrence again, enforce the consequence. Thus, Brad will learn that driving into others is not acceptable behavior.

## Warning

When children fail to follow a limit, you must remind them that they are misbehaving and their behavior will have consequences. You are *warning* the children. Warn only once. If the behavior continues, proceed with the consequences. Effective warnings contain only two parts. First, state the misbehavior. Then state the consequences. Examples include:

- "Joel, sand needs to be kept in the sandbox. If you throw it again, you will lose your turn."
- "Tunde, either choose a place in the circle, or I will choose one for you."
- "Mandy, blocks are not to be used like guns. If you use the block as a gun again, you will need to leave the block area."

When warning children, use a firm voice. Your voice should reflect your displeasure with the child's behavior.

## Time Out

**Time out** is a guidance technique that involves moving a child away from others for a short period of time. Time out is used when a child's disruptive behavior cannot be ignored. The child needs time to calm down. In some classrooms, this technique is used when a child is out of control with anger. To protect the other children, the teacher moves the angry child to a quiet place away from the group. This is one way of allowing the child to gain self-control. However, time out should never be used as a form of punishment.

Time out can be an effective guidance tool for some children. Four- and five-year-olds usually understand the purpose better than younger children. By this age, most children have the ability to understand their behavior can have negative consequences. Time out is an example of an artificial consequence.

To be effective, tell children in advance what behaviors will result in time out. If you decide to use time out, carry it out in an unemotional, direct way. Simply state the limit that has been broken and say "Time out." Promptly remove the child to an area away from the group, but within your vision. Nothing further should be said. You do not want to reward the child with added attention. Limit the time to three minutes. If the child returns to the group and the behavior continues, add another minute to the original time.

Not all teachers agree with the use of time out. These teachers feel the technique should seldom be used, if at all.

## I-Messages

When a child misbehaves, use an I-message to communicate your feelings. An **I-message** tells the child how you feel about his or her behavior. It does not place blame with the child, which would cause the child to feel he or she was a bad person. Rather, it helps the child learn how others view his or her actions.

Your I-message statement should include three parts: (1) the child's behavior, (2) your feelings about the behavior, and (3) the effects of the behavior. After you state the I-message, you should then say what you want done. For instance, you may say "When I see you hitting Yasser, I am unhappy because you are hurting him. I want you to stop hitting Yasser." Note that in this example, the behavior is hitting, it makes you feel unhappy, and the effects cause another child to be hurt. An I-message shows the child how his actions are perceived by others.

## Effective Praise

Studies show that not all praise is equally successful. *Effective praise* is specific and individualized to fit the situation and child. It acknowledges the child's actions or progress. It is thoughtful and does not interrupt the child's activities. Effective praise recognizes the child's positive behaviors and encourages the child to persist at a task. This type of praise may compare a child's progress to past performance. The goal is to make the child feel capable and valued. Young children thrive on effective praise. When

you say "I like the way you helped, Cedric," you tell the child he is important. This is a form of verbal praise. See 13-11. Nonverbal praise can also be used successfully. A smile, wink, or pat on the back are all types of nonverbal praise. Displaying a child's work on a bulletin board is also a form of praise. Some teachers paste a star or sticker on paperwork or artwork that a child has done. This is also nonverbal praise.

When praising young children remember the following:

■ Make praise age appropriate.
■ Give praise immediately. It is most effective to praise children while they are still in the act.
■ When praising, always establish eye contact.
■ Do not overuse praise. If you do, it will not be as effective.

Affirming helps the children by identifying and labeling positive behavior. Like adults, children love to be acknowledged, and they repeat behaviors that are acknowledged. A teacher might use such affirmations as "You enjoy helping others" or "Raul likes having you share the toys with him." When behaviors are affirmed, they are likely to be repeated, 13-12.

Ineffective praise may be more damaging than helpful. This type of praise is often called *empty praise* because it is repetitive and not genuine. Frequent use of ineffective praise can lead children to base their feelings of self-worth on adults' opinions of them. Examples of ineffective praise include sayings such as *good job, super, terrific,* and *fantastic.*

## Suggesting

*Suggesting* means placing thoughts for consideration into children's minds. This, in turn, often leads to action. For instance, after Candy spills her milk at the table, you may have to suggest she clean it up. To do this, say "Candy, here is a sponge." This will likely be enough to encourage Candy to wipe the spill. If not, you may have to add, "You need to wipe up the milk." During snack time, you may suggest to the children that they try a new fruit. This can be done directly or indirectly. Simply stating "This fruit is delicious," is enough to encourage some children to try the food. A more direct approach

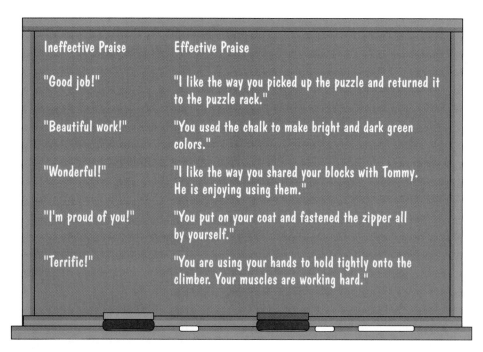

| Ineffective Praise | Effective Praise |
|---|---|
| "Good job!" | "I like the way you picked up the puzzle and returned it to the puzzle rack." |
| "Beautiful work!" | "You used the chalk to make bright and dark green colors." |
| "Wonderful!" | "I like the way you shared your blocks with Tommy. He is enjoying using them." |
| "I'm proud of you!" | "You put on your coat and fastened the zipper all by yourself." |
| "Terrific!" | "You are using your hands to hold tightly onto the climber. Your muscles are working hard." |

13-11  Effective praise is specific and acknowledges the child's actions or progress.

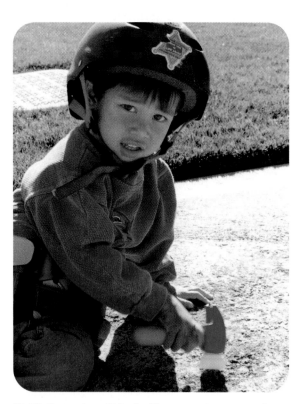

13-12  By saying, "It looks like you enjoy pretending to build," a teacher could encourage this boy to continue this play.

may work for other children. For example, you may say "Tammy, try this fruit today. It is delicious."

Always make suggestions positive. Lead children's thoughts and feelings in a desirable direction. If you tell the children to listen carefully to the story, they will probably follow your advice. However, if you tell the children that they are noisy and behaving poorly, they will probably continue to act this way. Negative suggestions usually produce negative behavior.

Effective teachers use suggestions many times each day. You will have many daily opportunities to mold behavior through suggestion. For example, Darlene may forget to put the blocks back on the shelf. A suggestion may work here. Corinna may drop her coat on the floor as she enters the room. A suggestion may work here, also.

## Prompting

Children often need **prompting** either to stop an unacceptable action or start an acceptable one. Prompting can also be used to prepare children for transitions. Prompting differs from suggesting because a response is required of a prompt. Examples of verbal prompting include:

- "Moses, do you remember where we keep the play dough?"
- "Glenda, what must we remember when riding bikes?"
- "Michelle, do you remember where you put your painting?"

Prompting can also be nonverbal. You may place a finger over your lip at group time to signal "Quiet, please!" Limits printed on a poster board (if age appropriate) are nonverbal prompts. Frowning can show your disapproval. Even turning a child around to attend to group activities is a form of prompting.

Generally, make prompting simple and noncritical. Prompt in a calm, impersonal manner. You may ask a child "What are you supposed to be doing?" or "What should we be doing before we have a snack?"

Prompting may need to be repeated often before acceptable behavior is developed. A child who is new to the center may need to be prompted for several days to hang his or her coat on the hook before this behavior is developed. Once the child complies, praise this behavior.

## Persuading

By *persuading*, you encourage children to act or behave in a certain way by appealing to their basic wants and needs. Seeing things from their point of view will give you an idea on the best way to approach a situation.

Link behavior with the children's feelings. For instance, a child who hangs back from an activity might be persuaded to join by appealing to his or her need to belong. You might say, "We are having such fun, Elizabeth. Will you join us?"

A child who interferes with another child's activities also needs to be persuaded. You can persuade the interfering child by helping him or her understand the other child's feelings. For instance, you may say, "Kenny, Joanie is afraid that if you keep jumping, you will knock her building down."

## Redirecting

Children often need redirecting to a substitute activity. When **redirecting**, you divert, or turn, their attention in a different direction. One way to redirect is through distraction. A child who cries when his or her parent leaves may need to be distracted. Choose an interesting toy or book to distract the child's interest away from the parent.

Redirection encourages children to express themselves in more socially acceptable ways. For example, an active child may constantly push other children. To help this child release energy, provide activities that are physically demanding. Playing with a punching bag, carpentry tools, or play dough will provide an outlet for extra energy. The key to redirecting is providing an appealing substitute.

## Modeling

Children learn by imitating others. Whenever you speak or move, you are **modeling** behavior. Modeling involves both verbal and nonverbal actions. It is a powerful tool when working with young children. At an early age, children become aware of the actions of the adults around them. Thus, it is important to set a good example. Social development is an important part of the early childhood curriculum. Much of what children learn is the result of watching others and imitating their behavior. Set an example by modeling prosocial behavior, 13-13.

## Listening

*Listening* involves giving children your full attention. It is more effective when you are at eye level with the child. Nodding also conveys your attention. One type of listening is called active listening. Through **active listening**, you first listen to what the child is saying to you. Then you respond to the child by repeating what was just said. This lets the child know you have heard what he or she said and you accept it. It does not mean, however, that you solve the problem. See 13-14.

For instance, Jerome was playing in the housekeeping area. He wanted to use the broom that Sherry was using. He asked Sherry, "May I have the broom?" Sherry responded, "No, I am using it. Besides, I had it first." Jerome got angry. He ran over and shared the incident with the teacher's aide. The aide listened carefully to what Jerome was saying. Then the aide repeated what Jerome had just said to make certain she heard

13-13  Modeling can be used in many situations at the center.

13-14 Active listening is a nonverbal skill that helps children develop self-esteem.

correctly. The aide said, "You are angry because Sherry will not let you use the broom." Jerome learned that people will listen to him and his feelings will be accepted. However, he will have to solve the problem himself.

## Ignoring

Do not encourage inappropriate behavior. When a child is able to gain your attention by whining, crying, or throwing a temper tantrum, you have reinforced the child's behavior. The child will likely continue this behavior rather than control it.

If a child's inappropriate behavior is not dangerous, avoid giving the child attention. Do not look directly at the child. Avoid acknowledging the behavior. This is called *ignoring*. On the other hand, praise the child when he or she models acceptable behavior.

Ignoring is inappropriate when the child's behavior is harmful, either verbally or physically, to the child or others. Likewise, it is inappropriate to ignore a child who is damaging property. If you choose to ignore the behavior, you should tell the child what the behavior is that you are ignoring. Also, tell the child the

behavior you desire. Then, do not look at the child. Be sure you do not acknowledge the behavior in any way through your actions or words. When the child models acceptable behavior, praise him or her.

For example, Mrs. Garcia has noticed that whenever Miranda wants something she whines and uses baby talk. Mrs. Garcia tells Miranda that she will not pay attention to her until she uses her "big girl" voice. Mrs. Garcia also demonstrates for Miranda what she means. Miranda continues to whine and use baby talk, so Mrs. Garcia ignores Miranda's requests. Eventually Miranda uses the appropriate words, and Mrs. Garcia answers Miranda's request.

Changing a young child's behavior is usually not a quick process. In fact, the behavior may actually become worse before it improves! It is important to be patient. Unless you ignore unpleasant behavior 100 percent of the time, it is likely to reoccur.

## Encouraging

Encouraging is a guidance technique that helps children believe in themselves. By *encouraging* children, you are recognizing their efforts and improvements. You may observe that successful teachers often use this technique. They want children to feel good about themselves. Examples of encouraging phrases you may use include:

- You can do it all by yourself!
- You know how it works.
- I know you can fix it.
- You were able to do it last week.
- You must be pleased.

## Promoting a Positive Self-Concept

When guiding children's behavior, your actions should always promote a positive self-concept in each child. A child's self-concept includes the qualities the child believes he or she possesses. It is a result of beliefs, feelings, and perceptions a child has of himself or herself, 13-15. Children's self-concepts reflect the feelings others have for them and the confidence they have in themselves.

13-15 A child with a healthy self-concept is not afraid to explore new and different types of play.

Children's self-concepts are mirrored in their behavior, 13-16. A child who lacks confidence may reveal feelings of inadequacy. For instance, the child may not be willing to try new activities, may withdraw from an experience, show little curiosity, or appear overly anxious or overly dependent. This child may also be hostile, seek attention, or perform poorly.

Children with positive self-concepts perceive themselves as able and important. They accept and respect themselves as well as others. These children are often able to judge their own skills and cope with problems they confront. Typically, they are more objective and understand other people's behaviors.

| Checklist for Evaluating a Child's Self-Concept | | |
|---|---|---|
| | **Yes** | **No** |
| Does the child speak positively about himself/herself? | | |
| Does the child appear to feel proud of his/her appearance? | | |
| Is the child proud of accomplishments? | | |
| Does the child accept failure? | | |
| Is the child willing to try new experiences? | | |
| Does the child make decisions on his/her own? | | |
| Is the child independent? | | |
| Does the child share his/her possessions? | | |
| Is the child willing to vocalize thoughts? | | |
| Is the child naturally curious? | | |
| Does the child usually appear calm and controlled? | | |

13-16 Observation is an important tool in social studies. Not only is it used to determine skill level, it can also be used to evaluate a child's self-concept.

| Teacher Checklist for Promoting a Positive Self-Concept |
|---|
| ☑ Do I observe children carefully before speaking? |
| ☑ Am I an open-minded person? |
| ☑ Do I recognize and value differences in children? |
| ☑ Do I constantly strive to gain more knowledge about the world and share it with the children? |
| ☑ Do I provide the children with choices so that they may become independent decision makers? |
| ☑ Am I constantly trying to increase my human relations skills? |
| ☑ Do I state directions in a positive manner? |
| ☑ Do I encourage parents to share their attitudes with me? |
| ☑ Do I avoid showing favoritism? |
| ☑ Do I listen to the children? |
| ☑ Do I help children sort out their mixed emotions? |
| ☑ Do I plan developmentally appropriate activities? |
| ☑ Do I respect cultural differences in young children? |
| ☑ Do I permit enough time to complete activities? |
| ☑ Do I call attention to positive interactions between and among children? |
| ☑ Do I make expectations clear? |
| ☑ Do I acknowledge the child's attempts at tasks as well as accomplishments? |
| ☑ Do I encourage children to use self-statements of confidence? |
| ☑ Do I use praise effectively? |

13-17 The teacher's behavior can promote or hinder development of a positive self-concept.

You can promote or undermine a child's self-concept by your words and actions. In many subtle ways, a teacher affects how children feel about themselves. Your reactions may give children the feeling they are bad or annoying. For instance, you may need to ask children to be quiet. Consider the message the children will receive. If you ask them to be quiet because they are too noisy, they may feel they are bad people because they make too much noise. If you ask them to make less noise because it is disturbing you, the children see they can help you by being quiet. They do not feel they are bad, noisy people.

If a child spills juice, do you call the child clumsy or react negatively by scowling? Instead, do you accept this as common behavior for a young child and help wipe up the spill? Caring adults are able to separate children's needs from their own. Clearly, they are able to see the difference between adult's needs and children's.

Every day you provide subtle messages in the form of verbal and nonverbal feedback. These signals can either promote or decrease children's sense of self-esteem. You can make children feel appreciated, worthy, loved, and secure by being accepting, concerned, and respectful. Helping young children grow to respect themselves, as well as others, is not easy. Listen carefully to what you say and how you say it. Consider the impact your words have on the children. Watch the subtle ways you interact with them. Your message should always convey that they are important. Review the checklist shown in Figure 13-17 to see if you are promoting positive self-concepts.

There are many ways you as a teacher can promote the development of positive self-concepts. You can plan activities that focus on making children feel good about themselves and their abilities. Several are described in Figure 13-18. You can also provide children with experiences with which they will have success.

## Building Positive Self-Concepts

- After an outing, make an experience chart. Include children's names and their exact words.
- Provide a special chair and crown for each child on his or her birthday. Take an instant photo of the child.
- Make a slide show of the children in action: on a field trip, at a party, at a play, or at the end of an ongoing project. Present the slide show to the children.
- Record children's stories from sharing and telling time on a large piece of posterboard titled *Our News*.
- Make charts of children's likes. For instance, you might chart children's favorite colors or animals.
- Make charts of hair and eye color to reinforce concepts of similarities and differences among people.
- Tape-record children telling their own stories.
- Make height and weight charts.
- Add a full-length mirror to the room.
- Label children's lockers and artwork with their names.
- Make a mobile or bulletin board with the children's pictures or names.
- Provide children with family face puppets of various cultures. Encourage children to act out imaginary family situations using the puppets.
- Outline children's bodies on large sheets of paper for them to decorate and display.
- Provide dramatic play kits to encourage children to try new roles and roles that they find interesting. For example, a carpenter kit could include a hat, an apron, a hammer, nails, and boxes or scraps of wood.
- Display children's pictures at their eye level.
- Use children's names frequently in songs and games.

13-18  These activities are quite useful for helping children build positive self-concepts.

## Summary

Effective guidance skills are necessary for effective teaching. Effective guidance should maintain children's self-esteem and produce a desired change in behavior. Self-control is the long-term goal of guidance. That is, the children should learn to direct their own behavior without outside control. Another goal of guidance is to promote prosocial behaviors among the children.

Child guidance may be direct or indirect. Direct guidance involves physical and verbal actions. The direct guidance principles described in this chapter will help you to more effectively guide children's behavior. Indirect guidance involves outside factors that influence behavior. One important factor that indirectly affects guidance is the physical setup of the classroom.

Guidance techniques will help you put your guidance skills to work. Specific techniques you may wish to use include positive reinforcement, natural and artificial consequences, warning, time out, I-messages, praising, affirming, suggesting, prompting, persuading, redirecting, modeling, listening, ignoring, and encouraging.

When guiding children's behavior, your actions should always promote a positive self-concept in each child. A child's self-concept includes the qualities the child believes he or she possesses.

## Review and Reflect

1. What are prosocial behaviors?

2. Studies show that _____ teachers have more hyperactive, disruptive, and bored students.

3. Why do children of permissive teachers often exhibit aggressive and attention-seeking behavior?

4. Describe one of the general guidelines you should follow for effective guidance to occur.

5. Give three examples of actions useful in direct guidance.

6. Use positive guidance statements to rewrite the following:
    A. Do not scream!
    B. Do not get paint on your dress.
    C. Do not spill the milk.
    D. Quit running!

7. Name the direct guidance principle being used in each of the following examples.
    A. Penny was disciplined yesterday for running through the cooking area. When she ran through the cooking area today, she was again disciplined.
    B. The children are playing in the art area. It will be lunchtime in 10 minutes. Their teacher says to them, "Children, it is almost time for lunch. Please start cleaning up the area."
    C. Henry is running from one end of the teeter-totter to the other. His teacher comes over to him and says, "Henry, stop that. You might hurt yourself."
    D. A teacher says to her children, "On Friday, we will be eating lunch outdoors. You can choose to have either a hot dog or a hamburger for lunch."

8. Give an example of how the physical setup of the classroom can be used to encourage independence in the children.

9. Why would a teacher want to use positive reinforcement?

10. Explain the difference between natural consequences and artificial consequences.

11. True or false. Praise should be given at the end of the day for any positive behaviors observed during the day.

12. How does a prompt differ from a suggestion?

13. The key to _____ is supplying an appealing substitute.

14. Explain the process of active listening.

15. True or false. Ignoring is an appropriate guidance technique when the child's behavior is verbally harmful to other children.

16. List three ways that you can encourage the development of children's positive self-concepts.

## Apply and Explore

1. Observe a teacher interacting with children for one hour. Record all incidences of verbal guidance.

2. Practice verbal guidance techniques by showing a friend how to use a puzzle.

3. Discuss situations in which a teacher may have to intervene in the classroom.

4. Conduct a self-observation. Using a tape recorder, record your interactions with children. Listen to your interactions. Were they positive? Did you help the children in identifying and labeling positive behavior? How would you change some of your interactions with the children to make them more positive?

5. Make a list of children's activities that promote a positive self-concept.

6. Observe in a classroom setting for half an hour. List all examples of praise you hear. After your observation, identify each example as effective or ineffective praise.

7. Search the online catalog for the National Association for the Education of Young Children (naeyc.org) for resources on guidance and discipline of young children. Use the computer to create a bibliography listing these resources.

# Chapter 14

# Guidance Problems

After studying this chapter, you will be able to

- identify situations and feelings that cause tension in children.
- describe behavior problems that result from tension.
- guide children as they learn appropriate behavior.
- describe the effect of family stressors on children and families.

## Terms to Know

overstimulated

frustration

stress

Four-year-old Missy is tattling on the other children. After arriving at the center, she told the teacher that Toby had pushed her the day before. During snacktime, she announced loudly that Hunter did not take the muffin he touched. Later, during clean-up time, she told the teacher that Jafar did not put away his puzzle.

Hoa does not like to take a nap during naptime. He begins crying every day after lunch as naptime approaches. Yolanda, who is normally very cooperative, has been less so in the weeks following the birth of her new brother. Rather than taking turns, she has become bossy on the play yard. The teacher has also seen her hitting other children.

During your teaching career, you will likely have several children in your classes who will have similar behavior problems as Missy, Hoa, and Yolanda. Many times, behavior problems will be disruptive to the class. The behavior may be harmful or it might infringe on the rights of others. Mishandling of classroom pets, equipment, and materials may also occur.

Disruptive behavior often is caused by tension. Overstimulation, changes in routine, and loud noise are just a few causes of tension in children. Because children do not know how to handle tension, they often react with disruptive behavior such as pushing and disturbing other children, running, and yelling, 14-1.

Helping children to deal positively with tension-causing events is an important job of the teacher. You will need to understand situations and feelings that cause tension in children. Recognizing behavior patterns that result from tension is also important. Then you will need to

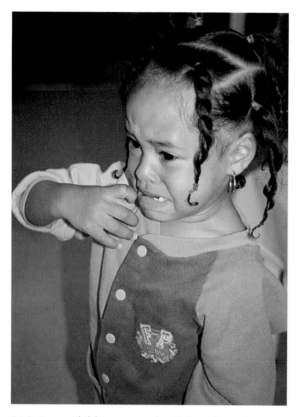

14-1 Some children cry and withdraw from the group when they feel tension.

be able to help children deal with this tension. With this information, you will be able to effectively guide and help these children.

## Causes of Behavioral Problems

There are many causes of behavioral problems in children. These include certain situations and feelings children do not know how to handle. In addition, there are physical problems that can cause tension in children. Being aware of situations and emotions that produce tension is important. This knowledge will allow you to avoid, or at least lessen the effects of, these causes.

### Overstimulation

Children can become overexcited, or **overstimulated**, by many things. For instance, simply playing with other children can overstimulate some children, 14-2. Usually, the larger the group

of children, the greater the likelihood that overstimulation will occur. You may want to limit the number of children that can be in a certain area at any time. This will help prevent the chaos created when a large group of children play together. For example, post a sign in the blockbuilding area limiting the space to four children at any given time. For younger children who do not read, make a simple sign showing four stick people. It will serve the same purpose. Similar signs can be posted in other areas of the classroom.

Some children become overstimulated when there are program changes. Holidays, such as Christmas and Valentine's Day, can be overstimulating times for children. Avoid making holiday plans too early. When this happens, the children may get keyed up long before the event occurs.

Overstimulation can also result from having too many activities planned. When this happens, some children have a hard time making choices. Instead of staying with one activity, they run back and forth between several. Their activity and excitement, in turn, can affect others.

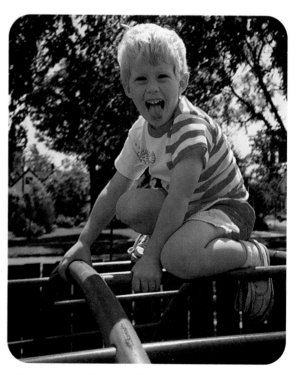

14-2 The combination of being outside and climbing on a jungle gym can cause overstimulation in some children.

## Breaks in Routines

Routines are important to children. They let children know what to expect and when. If routines are not followed, children become confused. Behavior problems can arise. For instance, Jimmy takes a nap at 12:30 p.m. everyday. If this is not done, he may become overtired. This may result in disruptive behavior. If a child's family follows a different routine at home than the center does, this can affect the child's behavior. Parents may notice behavior problems at home because the child does not know what to expect next. In addition you may see more behavior problems after weekends and holidays when the child readjusts after being away from the center for a few days. Talking with parents about these problems may help them adjust their schedule to more closely match the child's routine at the center.

All children need consistent daily schedules. Quiet activities need to be followed by active activities, 14-3. If children sit still too long, they may lose interest in the activity and become disruptive. Likewise, if children remain active too long, they may become overstimulated and disruptive. When changes in routine are necessary, such as a planned field trip, prepare the children ahead of time. Talk to them about what will happen. Also, explain to the children what your expectations are before, during, and after the trip.

14-3 After a quiet activity, such as storytime, children need periods of active free play.

## Noise

Noise affects children differently. Children with very sensitive ears are particularly upset by noise. For example, these children will cover their ears when a smoke alarm goes off. Likewise, if an ambulance drives by with its siren wailing, some children will cringe. While some children may try only to escape the noise, others may react by pushing or hitting others.

To avoid the problems caused by noise, control the volume of tapes, records, and CDs. Also pay attention to the volume of your own voice. In frustration, you may raise your voice or yell. Unfortunately, this causes a chain reaction. As the volume of your voice increases, the children's voices also become louder. This, in turn, will affect children sensitive to noise. The result will be chaos.

## Waiting Time

Children often behave poorly when they have to wait for long periods of time. By nature, they are usually in motion. Therefore, if they are kept waiting too long for a story, they may start pushing or hitting. This behavior is not the children's fault. However, it may gain the teacher's disapproval. If this occurs, it may damage the children's self-concepts.

Manage your time wisely. Cut down on waiting time by being prepared. If you are going to read a book for a large group, choose it in advance. Place it where it will be convenient. Likewise, prepare materials for all group activities in advance. If the children are actively involved in self-selected activities, it will reduce waiting time and resulting behavior problems.

## Frustration

Children sometimes feel they are not in control. They feel defeated or discouraged. These feelings are called **frustration**. They cause tension in children, 14-4. In order to control frustration, carefully plan each day's activities. The activities you choose should be developmentally appropriate. They should reflect the needs, interests, and abilities of the children in the center.

Some children arrive at the center full of energy. These children need to be active. Provide

14-4 Being in control is important for young children. When they are not in control, they may become frustrated.

wheeled toys, blockbuilding, and woodworking activities for these children. Other children prefer quiet activities, such as books, puzzles, stringing beads, or play dough. By observing the children in your program, you can provide the proper materials, supplies, and equipment.

Forcing children into activities they are not prepared to join can result in frustration. A better approach is to allow the children to decide what is best.

Conflict over toys can also create frustration. Therefore, make certain that several kinds of toys are available to the children at all times. Conflicts often arise over toys. When possible, purchase several toys of the same kind. Wise teachers buy more than one wagon, scooter, fire engine, and car.

Select materials and equipment to match children's developmental level. This allows the children to feel success and develop an "I can do it" attitude. Working with mixed-aged groups presents special problems. Include open-ended materials such as blocks, play dough, and sand. Children of all ages will play with these, but in different ways. See 14-5. Provide puzzles and books for a range of abilities.

When necessary, redirect children to materials that match their abilities. Repeated failures will cause frustration, which may lead to anger. An angry child may pinch, hit, push, kick, or bite.

As an adult, you may become angry when the children are uncontrollable due to frustration. When this happens, try to relax. Carefully watch your words and actions. If the children sense you are upset, they, in turn, will become more upset. They need to feel you are calm and in control.

## Physical Problems

Poor health or other physical problems can cause tension and behavioral problems in children. One teacher, Mr. Peterson, had such a problem in his center. During Ethan's first day at the center, Mr. Peterson and several other teachers observed Ethan. They feared he would be a behavior problem. He ignored all directions and suggestions made by Mr. Peterson. Ethan also seemed to have a high anxiety level.

14-5 A sensory table and paints are materials that appeal to children of many ages.

Ethan's behavior became a source of frustration for Mr. Peterson. More than once, he wondered whether Ethan should even be in the center. He feared that other children would copy Ethan's behavior. Mr. Peterson was also concerned about his ability to handle Ethan's behavior. This concern continued for several weeks.

Mr. Peterson finally decided to ask the center director to observe Ethan's behavior. After observing Ethan, the director determined a possible cause for Ethan's problem. First, the director noted that Ethan did not respond to many of the verbal requests made by Mr. Peterson or other children. The director also noted that while interacting with others, Ethan closely watched their faces when they spoke. The director suspected that Ethan had hearing loss. For added information, the director then picked up two wooden blocks, stood behind Ethan, and clapped them together as hard as she could. While several other children either jumped or turned to see what was happening, Ethan did not respond.

Before sharing these observations with Ethan's father, Mr. Peterson repeated the clapping incident. Ethan failed to respond. In addition, other staff members tried speaking to him when they were out of his field of vision. Again, each time he failed to respond. At this point, the center director shared these observations with Ethan's father. She encouraged Ethan's father to have his hearing tested.

Luckily for Ethan, his father, the staff, and other children in the center, the cause of Ethan's behavioral problems was pinpointed. After having his hearing tested, Ethan received a hearing aid. His behavior improved dramatically. At the same time, his speech also improved.

Children may be overly active or tense due to other health problems, 14-6. A child who is in constant pain due to lack of dental or medical care may act inappropriately.

Medications can affect some children's behavior. Observe for symptoms such as dilated pupils, drowsiness, slurred speech, poor coordination, and general irritability. In many states, parents are required to report to the staff when their children are on medication.

Prolonged or recurring illness or hospitalization can cause frequent absences from the center. When this occurs, some children are not able to maintain their friendships. Coming back

14-6  Pain from this child's head injury may cause him to be tense and uncooperative.

to the center is difficult for them. Some of these children may become *onlookers*. This means they watch others, but do not get involved. Other children may become aggressive. By acting out, they hope to gain the other children's attention. Onlookers and aggressive children need your help. Carefully observe them. Focus on their needs.

An onlooker needs to get involved. Encourage this child by suggesting activities he or she might try. If the child does not respond, gently take the child by the hand, and walk him or her to an appealing activity. You may have to play with the child for awhile or involve other children in the activity.

Aggressive children need a calming influence. Direct these children to activities in which they can release energy. For instance, direct the aggressive child to woodworking, sculpting, or water play activities.

Poor or inadequate nutrition can also affect behavior. Studies show that between one-fourth and one-third of preschool children do not receive the caloric intake recommended for them. Children who do not have the proper caloric intake or nutrients may be inattentive and sluggish. Motor skills and motivation are also affected.

# Stress

**Stress** is the body's reaction to physical or emotional danger signals. This reaction often takes the form of tension. Mild or occasional stress is not a problem. However, constant stress, prolonged stress, or the piling up of many stressors can threaten a child's ability to cope.

The foundations for life are laid during childhood. Early in life, children watch how adults cope with stress. Children learn their responses to stress from these adults. As a result, children vary widely in how they handle stress. Children who learn negative coping skills may become more prone to stress. They may become illness-prone, withdrawn, nervous, aggressive, or angry. On the other hand, some children learn positive coping strategies. These children are resilient—they bounce back quickly from all stress.

Stress can be caused by both negative and positive events. One negative event that can cause stress in children is the breakup of a family. Even the most amicable divorce is a major stressor for young children because it disrupts the family stability. Other negative stressors include abuse, neglect, rejection, separation, and fights. Positive events that cause stress may include parties, vacations, overnight visits with friends or relatives, the birth of a sibling, or getting a new pet.

Starting child care or changing to a new child care program can be stressful for children. In many centers, children also move from classroom to another as they get older. Adjusting to new teachers, playmates, and surroundings can take time. Learning a new routine can also cause tension. This stress should subside as the child adjusts to the new center or classroom. Helping children feel safe and welcome is the most helpful way to ease this discomfort.

In poor-quality programs, however, the stress continues. Programs with insufficient adult-child ratios and large group sizes cannot adequately meet children's needs. Adults in these programs often lack the necessary time to nurture each child's development. These programs often lack enough few toys and materials for the number of children enrolled. The facilities may be inadequate in other ways, too.

## Family Stressors

As the primary social unit, the family can serve as a buffer from stress. It can also be a source of many stressors in a child's life. The influences of family can be positive or negative, depending upon how the family operates. Family harmony is important for the health of all the members. Stress within the family disrupts this harmony. All family members, including young children, can be affected. Stress can also strain family relationships. Children can sense this tension.

Family crises cause major stress within a family. See Figure 14-7 for a list of family stressors. What others can you identify? In any of these situations, daily family life will be disrupted, at least for a time. Resulting changes in routine can upset infants as well as older children. These children lose a sense of predictability and security when they do not know what to expect next. This can cause children to become irritable, have problems eating and sleeping, and become clingy or demanding. These are normal responses to stress.

In some families, the stressor is a temporary condition. For example, the loss of a parent's job may be short-lived as the parent seeks a new job. With other stressors, family life is permanently changed, such as with a death or divorce. Extra support from friends, extended family, and the community may be needed to cope with a permanent stressor.

Being constantly active from morning to night causes another, less intense type of stress. In a family with this schedule, a young child's needs may be overlooked as parents and older siblings rush to meet their obligations. Both children and adults need time to unwind and be together as a family. Family time and relaxation help people ward off the harmful effects of stress.

| Possible Family Stressors | |
| --- | --- |
| • Birth or adoption of a sibling | • Friend moving away |
| • Marriage, separation, or divorce of parent(s) | • Parent's loss of employment |
| • Custody, visitation, or child support issues | • Financial or legal problems in the family |
| • Marriage of a parent | • Substance abuse or addiction of family member |
| • Stay-at-home parent entering the workforce | • Exposure to violence (unsafe neighborhood) |
| • Family member moving into or out of home | • Incarceration of family member |
| • Serious illness of self or family member | • Becoming homeless |
| • Death of a friend, family member, or pet | • Arguing, fighting, or violence among family members |
| • Moving to a new home | • Abuse or neglect of self or family member |

14-7 Crisis and changes within the family account for much of the stress children feel.

Handling family stressors of any type is difficult for young children. The intensity of a child's reaction will depend on how threatening the stressor is. Children feel worse if they believe they have caused a divorce, separation, death, or other family crisis. Feeling their behavior caused the crisis leads children to feel guilty. Explaining that a crisis is not a child's fault can be helpful.

## Effects of Stress

Prolonged stress in early childhood can undermine healthy brain development. A child depends on his or her environment for experiences that will promote optimal brain development. Stimulation from caregivers also influences the wiring of the brain. That is why consistent, predictable, and responsive care is needed.

Good beginnings can last a lifetime. Healthy relationships promote brain growth and healthy social attachment. A strong, secure attachment to a nurturing caregiver appears to provide a protective biological structure. It buffers children from the effects of stress. Studies show children with strong, secure attachments have fewer behavioral problems when confronted with stress throughout life.

Neuroscientists describe *windows of opportunity* in the development of a child's brain. These are periods when experiences or the lack of experiences will have the greatest impact. The window of opportunity for learning to control emotions and cope with stress is limited. This period extends only from birth to three years of age.

In addition, abuse, neglect, or constant stress can cause the body to release chemicals that impact the brain's complex wiring. The effects are lasting—smaller brain size and diminished ability to control emotions and behavior. Children with these problems find it harder to form lasting relationships with others.

## Signs of Stress

When family stability is disrupted, this can often be observed in the children's behavior. A frequent sign of stress is regression. *Regression* means showing behaviors that were typical at earlier stages of development. Toileting accidents and thumbsucking are examples. A child who has used the toilet successfully for some time may begin to have accidents. Likewise, a child who had given up thumbsucking might revert to soothing himself or herself with this habit.

In addition to regression, many other behavior changes can indicate children are stressed. Being aware of the common signs of stress listed in Figure 14-8 is also helpful. Sometimes, however, these behaviors can be unrelated to stress. How then can you determine which signs are caused by stress? Knowing the typical behavior of each child in your class helps you note these behavior changes.

| Possible Signs of Stress in Young Children | |
|---|---|
| • Accident-proneness | • Hitting |
| • Anger | • Indigestion |
| • Anxiety | • Insomnia |
| • Baby talk | • Irritability |
| • Bed wetting | • Kicking |
| • Biting | • Nightmares |
| • Crying spells | • Pounding heart |
| • Detachment | • Respiratory tract |
| • Eating problems | illness |
| • Excessive | • Stuttering |
| aggressiveness | • Tattling |
| • Excessive laziness | • Teeth grinding |
| • Fingernail biting | • Temper tantrums |
| • Headaches | • Thumbsucking |

14-8 The problems shown in this list may signal stress.

## Communicating with Families About Stress

A partnership with families is important to support children's development. Two-way communication between teachers and families is vital. Teachers should realize the important role families play in children's lives and vice versa.

Families have a responsibility to support children through times of stress and crisis. Children depend on and turn to family members (especially parents) to protect them from the effects of stress. Parents can often provide the comfort children need to overcome stress. By their example, parents teach children how to cope with stress and handle problems.

As a teacher, you can help children handle stress when you are aware of family situations that could affect the child's behavior. Ask parents to keep you informed of any major family events, such as births and deaths. Also important are events that change the structure of the family, such as marriage, separation, or divorce. Children need the loving support of parents and teachers through these times of adjustment.

If a child's behavior changes suddenly, share with parents the signs of stress you have noticed. Ask if events at home might be causing the stress. Work with parents to plan ways to help the child and address the troubling behavior. As with other guidance issues, children benefit the most when there is consistency of guidance between parents and teachers.

Recognize, however, that crises in the family will affect parents, too. During a divorce, for example, children are not the only ones hurting—parents suffer the loss as well. While your main focus is helping the children, you want to approach this task in the most sensitive and relevant way. Listen to the parents and offer kind words to let them know you understand they must be hurting, too. If the parents seem open to suggestions, you may be able to refer them to community resources that can help.

## Helping Children Cope

Stress affects children as much or more than it affects adults. Unlike adults, however, children lack the skills to understand and handle the pressures. As a teacher, you can help children develop positive responses to stress.

When you note a child's behavior has changed, observe the child more carefully. Calmly accept the child's behavior, if possible. (Of course, hurtful or unsafe behavior would be an exception to this. You must gently but firmly stop these behaviors.) Criticizing a child for his or her response to stress only leads the child to feel more stress. For example, scolding a child for thumbsucking in response to stress may make the child feel badly about himself or herself. Talk to the child about his or her feelings. Reassure the child you care about him or her. Offer comfort, closeness, and encouragement.

Provide a supportive, affectionate environment. Children exhibit less stress when teachers are attentive, 14-9. Observe carefully and really listen to the children. Talk with children about their feelings. Help them recognize, label, and clarify their feelings. Teach them coping behaviors. Use effective praise and acknowledge the child's actions, feelings, and progress. Correct any misconceptions children have about themselves or their feelings to help children see themselves as positive, worthwhile people.

## Specific Problem Behaviors

Young children often behave in a socially unacceptable way when they are tense. Negativism, theft, anger, biting, exploration of the

14-9 Children are better able to handle stress when their teachers care about them enough to listen attentively.

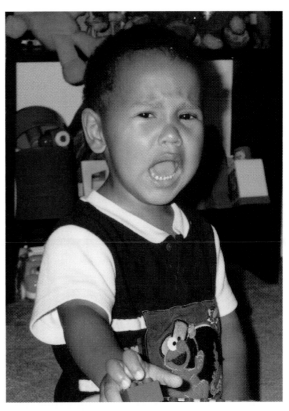

14-10 Young children may resist your requests to end their free play.

body, thumbsucking, and fear are all possible reactions to tension. These reactions remind us children are people, too. You must deal with and guide their behavior, just as you would an adult.

## Negativism

Preschool children can be negative, particularly between two and three years of age. See 14-10. It is not unusual for a child of this age to oppose every request you make. Children at this age are wanting to become more independent. A "no" in many cases is a child's attempt at independence. For instance, you may say "Pick up the block." The child might look at you and say "No."

### Handling Negative Behavior

Accept a young child's negative behavior. However, keep in mind all health and safety regulations. For example, children must wash their hands before eating. If a child refuses to do this, take the child's hands and wash them. Tell the child "You need to wash your hands." Let the child know, through your voice and body language, that you expect cooperation.

A negative child cannot be hurried. If he or she is hurried, opposition will be stronger. Given time, most children outgrow this stage of development.

## Stealing

Preschool children do not understand the difference between *mine* and *yours*. When children under three years of age take something, they are not stealing. At this age, children do not understand the concept of stealing. Before considering the needs of others, preschoolers attempt to meet their own needs. The desire for something appealing may combine with a young child's natural impulsiveness. As a result, they may take items that do not belong to them.

Small objects, such as toy cars and puzzle pieces, may vanish from the classroom. When you notice these items missing, warn the other teachers. Ask them to closely observe the children.

### Handling Stealing

Help children learn to respect the possessions of others. If you see a child take something, do not ask the reason he or she stole it. Likewise, do not lecture about stealing. Instead, make the child return it. Otherwise, the child may keep taking things from others. Remember that preschoolers do not understand ownership.

A useful way to teach children about ownership is to respect their property rights. That is, before trying Jodi's new puzzle, ask her permission to use it. If you see another child looking at Jodi's toy, say "Why don't you ask Jodi if you can use it?"

You should also try to minimize opportunities for stealing. When children bring toys or other items from home, problems can occur. If toys are allowed to be brought to the center, there need to be clear rules. Toys are best left in the child's cubby and only taken out for naptime or show-and-tell. To avoid potential problems, many centers have a policy stating that toys should not be brought from home.

## Anger

A child's anger can serve a useful purpose. Anger draws attention to something that annoys the child. You can then help that child learn to deal with anger. The greatest number of tantrums typically occur at about 18 months of age. After this age, there is a sharp decline. Age also affects how a child will project anger. Young children often use their whole bodies to express anger. By age two, children may hold their breath for as long as they can. Screaming, kicking, hitting, pounding, and hitting one's head against a wall are other ways these children express anger. By the time children turn three, verbal abuse is more common, while four-year-olds often engage in name-calling.

### Handling Anger

Discourage hurting behavior. Young children should not be allowed to hit each other. However, they will try. When they do, stop them immediately. Say "I am sorry, but Jeff does not like that." At the same time, you might have to

hold the child's hand. The child may try to hit you. Stop that action also. For older preschoolers, you may also use comments. For example, you may say, "You are usually kind. I'm surprised you did that."

Ignoring outbursts is also a successful technique when dealing with an angry child. Of course, ignore this behavior only if there is no threat to the health and safety of the children. If children are able to get attention or gain control through outbursts, they will keep using this behavior. For example, if Carrie cries and yells for another cookie and then receives one, she will cry and yell again. On the other hand, if she does not receive the cookie, she will learn that her outburst is unacceptable.

The children need to express their feelings and assert their rights in socially acceptable ways. You can redirect anger through activities such as finger painting, modeling with clay, punching a punching bag, hammering, and playing at the sensory table, 14-11. All these activities involve use of children's hands, arms, and legs. Their anger will be redirected into physical movements. Remember to have enough supplies and equipment for these activities. Use a minimum of rules.

Surprisingly, noise can also help relieve aggression. Yelling, beating drums, dancing to loud music, crying, and making animal noises can all relieve anger. Remember, however, that noise can be catching. If several children make too much noise, the rest of the group may also become noisy.

Whenever possible, catch children before they react angrily. For instance, if you see that Mattie is going to kick over Tommy's blocks, stop her. Then say, "Mattie, would you like Tommy to knock over your blocks?" Mattie will be forced to think about what she was going to do.

## Biting

Young children often bite when they are upset. This is not unusual behavior, particularly with two-year-olds. For many of these children, biting is only a temporary problem. They may bite because they cannot express themselves using words. For them, biting is a form of body language.

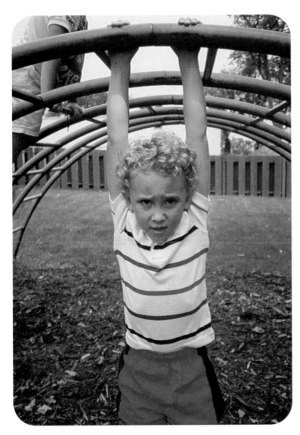

14-11 Children can release energy through physical activity.

## Handling Biting

You need to help children who bite. Start by keeping playtime simple for these children. Limit the number of playmates they may have at any time. Large groups often create stressful situations. Therefore, biters become nervous and then bite.

You need to respond quickly to prevent children from hurting each other. Isolation of a biter sometimes helps to curb this habit. When the child bites another, say, "Paula does not like that." Then say, "I am sorry, but you must sit down over here." Make the child sit for a few minutes, but no longer than five. Then, allow the child to return to the play area.

Do not forget the child who has been bitten. This child also needs to feel secure. To provide security, observe constantly. Never allow a child to bite back. Biting back does not prevent biting. It only creates more aggressive behavior.

## Tattling

Tattling seems to occur in many classrooms and is a typical behavior for many young children. Frequently, the child who tattles is insecure and tattles to get your attention. As a teacher, you may find tattling irritating, but you need to listen to the children. You want the children to be aware that classroom limits are important. You do not need to be told, however, each time a child misbehaves.

### Handling Tattling

To prevent tattling, try to build children's self-esteem. This, in turn, will make them feel more secure. For a child who is insecure, stay close while supervising. Knowing that a caring adult is nearby is helpful.

Try to have a daily one-to-one time for listening and talking with each child. This may be during free play or small group time. During this time, provide the child feedback by recognizing his or her positive qualities. To illustrate, you may say, "Sharice, I like the way you help Marco" or "Eileen, Brian enjoys having you help him with the puzzle." Positive reinforcement will help to prevent a child's need to tattle.

Try ignoring tattling behavior. If Jared tattles to you that Ronnie has taken his scissors, comment by saying "You need to tell Ronnie to return your scissors." This encourages Jared to speak to the child who has misbehaved. Likewise, if Christopher tattles that Julia has taken his bicycle, encourage problem solving. Say "Christopher has taken your bike. What should you do?" If Kelsi always talks about other children, set a limit by saying "I enjoy talking with you, but we shouldn't talk about others."

## Exploring the Body

Children begin to explore their bodies early in life. It is common for one-year-olds to explore their genitals during diaper changing. As children begin to gain control of their body functions, interest in the genital area grows. By three years of age, children are aware of sex differences. Boys may, in fact, become concerned because girls do not have penises. By age four, children who have to use the bathroom may hold the genital area. When this occurs, remind the child to use the bathroom. By five years of age, children may begin to manipulate their genitals. They may do this by rubbing pillows between their legs or squeezing their thighs together tightly. Some children may rub their genitals in an effort to reduce irritation caused by tight clothing.

### Handling Body Exploration

Exploration of the body is normal behavior in development. However, it is not considered proper to engage in such behavior in public. Therefore, it is important to guide children away from public display of body exploration.

During naptime, you might see children touching themselves. Children sometimes rub their genitals while trying to get to sleep. When this occurs, never shame or threaten the child. Remember, whenever possible, use a positive approach when guiding young children. This can be done by firmly telling a child privately that this behavior is impolite in public.

## Thumbsucking

Like adults, children feel certain tensions. To relieve the tension, some children may suck their thumbs. Studies show that almost half of all infants suck their fingers or thumbs. By 18 months, thumbsucking usually reaches its peak. Then the behavior becomes less frequent, especially during the day. By four or five years of age, children who suck their thumbs usually only do so before they go to bed. Children of this age will sometimes engage in thumbsucking if they are tired.

Many parents are concerned about thumbsucking. Reassure them that usually there is no need to worry about this behavior. Encourage them to accept this behavior as a normal stage of growth. Most children outgrow thumbsucking by six or seven years of age.

Parents may be concerned that thumbsucking will affect children's facial appearance or damage teeth. Dentists state that there is no cause to worry if thumbsucking stops before permanent teeth erupt.

### Handling Thumbsucking

Children's urge to suck may be satisfied by supplying a pacifier. One advantage of a pacifier is that it does not place pressure on the roof of the mouth or the jaw. When they're ready, most children give up their pacifiers. In fact, some children may have an intense sucking need for only the first few months of life. When these children stop using their pacifiers, they can be taken away permanently. If, however, a child reverts to sucking fingers or thumbs, return the pacifier.

If you notice thumbsucking, do not pull the thumb out of the child's mouth. This guidance may not be successful. In some cases, it might cause the child to increase thumbsucking. During the first three years, the harder you try to stop thumbsucking, the stronger it becomes. Instead, accept and ignore the behavior. In this way, children will usually stop thumbsucking between four and five years of age.

Attending a child care program may help curb thumbsucking for some children. At the center, the child will find many new interests and friends. As a result, you may not notice thumbsucking. Many times children will only suck their thumbs when they lie down for naps or are tired.

## Fear

Every child experiences fear. By three years of age, most children have many kinds of fear. Some fears will be real while others will be imaginary. As the child grows, real fears will be kept. Imaginary fears will be outgrown.

Common childhood fears include falling from high places, putting faces in water, thunder, the dark, people in uniforms, fire engines, ambulances, and animals. Fear of the unknown is also common in young children. You may see this fear on the first day of school. Children may cry, cling, and refuse to leave their parents. As the teacher, be prepared for this fear. Inform parents in advance about this common fear.

### Handling Fear

Understanding children's fear is important in guiding young children, 14-12. For example, fear of the dark is quite common among young children. You may notice this fear at naptime or when a videotape is being shown. Understand that this behavior is due to unfamiliar surroundings. These children cannot sleep or concentrate on videos. Instead, the children may focus on scary images formed by the shadows in the darkened room. Help these children by keeping a

14-12  Teachers need to be prepared for fears on field trips that may be caused by unfamiliar sights or sounds.

14-13  Playing hospital helps many children deal with their fears of hospitals and doctors.

small light turned on during these times. Then the room will not be totally dark. Also, allow children to keep a familiar stuffed toy or blanket near them.

Accept children's fears. For young children, even the silliest fear is real. When a fire engine passes the play yard and a child cries, give the child immediate attention. You may wish to hold the child's hand, kneel down and put your arms around the child, or hold the child on your lap. When you do this, you are meeting the child's immediate needs. After the crisis, talk to the child about the fear.

Children may need to act out situations in order to conquer their fears. See 14-13. For instance, Toby's grandmother died in the hospital. When Toby came back to the center, he asked two other children to play hospital with him. Toby played the role of a doctor while one of his friends played the nurse. This was Toby's way of handling the fear he felt when his grandmother died at the hospital.

Talking with children can also help them control fear. For example, Mark visited his cousin Chris. When he returned to school, Mark told his teachers that the house had ghosts. As a result, Mark said that he was never returning. Mark's teacher was observant. He talked to Mark about his visit with Chris. He explained that sleeping in strange places is often frightening because it is new.

Jennifer was afraid of the new bunny. Fortunately for Jennifer, her teacher was understanding. She helped Jennifer face her fear by introducing her to the bunny in gradual steps. First, she asked Jennifer to place a carrot in the cage. Then she encouraged Jennifer to watch the bunny eat. The next day she encouraged Jennifer to touch the bunny's fur. Jennifer continued this for about one week. Her teacher did not rush Jennifer. Finally, she asked Jennifer if she wanted to hold the bunny. Jennifer said yes. Jennifer's teacher carefully and slowly took the rabbit from the cage and placed it on Jennifer's lap.

When children feel unsafe or strange, they may reject a person or situation. For example, a child may greet a new aide with "Go away, I hate you." If this happens, do not scold the child. Telling the child that he or she likes the aide will not help either. Instead, accept the child's feelings. You may say "Miss Brown is our new teacher. When you get to know her, you will learn to like her."

Children sometimes will hit others when they are afraid. For instance, a resource person visited a group of four-year-olds. This person brought a large snake to show the children. When Janice saw the snake, she began to act aggressively. She hit Susan and Peggy. The teacher then stepped in. She explained to Janice that her friends might be frightened, too. She then explained to Janice that this type of snake was not dangerous. There was no need to fear it.

## Summary

As a teacher of young children, at times you will experience problems guiding the children in your care. Common causes of guidance problems include overstimulation, changes in routine, and loud noise. Frustration and physical problems can also cause guidance problems.

Knowing how stress affects young children is also important. Stress can have many causes. Changes or problems within the family can cause stress among children and families. Young children do not know how to handle this stress very well. As a result, they most often express stress through their behavior. If adults note that a child shows signs of stress, they can offer the child the help he or she needs. Although family events can be a source of stress, families can also serve as a buffer for children during times of stress.

Your role as a teacher will be to help children and families deal positively with tension-causing events. Knowing more about common family stressors and signs of stress will help. You can help by communicating with families, modeling coping skills, and providing an extra measure of comfort and reassurance for the child.

In addition, you will face other problem behaviors in the classroom. These include negativism, stealing, anger, biting, exploring the body, tattling, thumbsucking, and fear. Handling each of these problem behaviors takes guidance skills and techniques that are unique to the situation.

## Review and Reflect

1. Why do children react disruptively when they experience tension?

2. Name four events that can cause tension in a child.

3. True or false. Usually, the larger the group of children, the greater the likelihood that overstimulation will occur.

4. _____ let children know what to expect and when to expect it.

5. True or false. Noise affects all children in the same way.

6. Name two ways to cut down on waiting time.

7. Describe frustration and list two causes of frustration in children.

8. Frustration can be prevented by _____.
   A. supplying the same materials to all children
   B. letting children choose which play activities they would like to do
   C. forcing children to play with certain materials, regardless of their abilities
   D. planning only one or two activities a day

9. Name four ways that medications can affect children's behavior.

10. _____ are children who watch others participate, but do not participate themselves.

11. What is stress?

12. Name two steps you can take to help a child deal with stress.

13. List four possible family stressors for children.

14. What will happen if you hurry a negative child?

15. Explain how you would effectively guide the children in the following situations.
   A. Philip gets angry whenever you announce cleanup time.
   B. Joanne bites George whenever he takes a toy from her.
   C. Amber runs to tell you every time another child misbehaves.
   D. Martin cries and clings to you when a clown visits the class.

16. True or false. Exploration of the body is a natural stage in development.

## Apply and Explore

1. Prepare a checklist of ways to avoid overstimulation of children.

2. Discuss teacher strategies for reducing waiting time.

3. Visit a child care center. Observe children for any signs of stress. Note what signs you see. Discuss your findings when you return to class.

4. Discuss the advantages of thumbsucking from the child's point of view.

5. Interview four parents to learn what problems they have guiding children.

6. Use the Internet to research common fears among children. Use the computer to compose a report that summarizes your findings.

7. Search the Web site daycare.about.com for guidance tips and resources related to the problems described in this chapter.

8. Check the Web site parenting-ed.org handouts related to guidance problems.

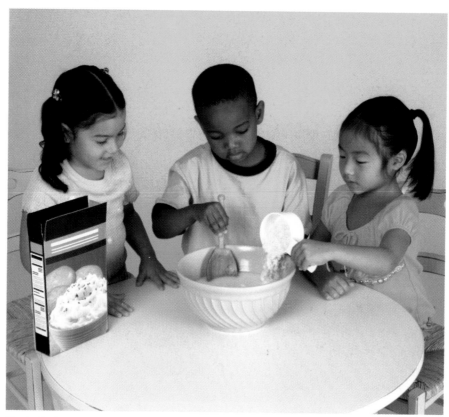

Limits help a small group cooking activity run smoothly.

# Chapter 15

# Establishing Classroom Limits

After studying this chapter, you will be able to

- explain the reasons for having classroom limits.
- list guidelines for establishing classroom limits.
- describe methods for enforcing limits.
- list useful limits for various classroom areas and activities.

## Term to Know

flexible limits

Limits are necessary to help children effectively work in groups. They promote safety, respect, and responsibility. In child care centers, effective limits serve as a kind of shorthand to state the goals of the center. Limits should focus on actions and behaviors that reflect goals. As a teacher, your input in suggesting limits for the center is important.

Every area of the classroom will need to have limits. As the classroom teacher, it is your responsibility to explain and enforce limits. Limits need to be explained at the children's level of understanding. The staff and children should also know the reasons for the limits. In addition, you should make sure that each adult working in the classroom understands the limits. The limits should also be posted in the teachers' lounge and in the classrooms.

## Establishing Limits

There are three reasons for establishing classroom limits. First, according to the law, children's health and safety must be protected. Limits help make the classroom a safe place for the children. Second, children feel free to explore when they know their teacher will stop them if they go too far, 15-1. Thus, they feel protected from mistakes. Finally, limits help children develop self-control. As children learn to accept and obey limits, they gradually come to learn that limits are part of life. One of the center's goals should be to develop socially responsible behavior in young children. Establishing limits will help the center reach this goal.

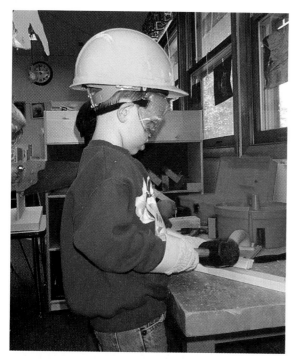

15-1 Enforcing limits about the use of safety equipment allow this boy to explore his woodworking project more freely.

## Guidelines for Setting Limits

When setting limits for children, make the limits short. Focus on one main point. Use familiar language and short, simple sentences the children can understand. You and the children need to have the same understanding of what the limit means. Be sure the words you use describe the exact behavior you desire. Children are often confused by such general words as *be nice, stop it,* or *behave.* These words can have many meanings and do not say precisely what you want. State the limits in terms of the positive behavior you expect.

Set limits that are reasonable. This means that children have the ability to carry out the action. Limits should serve a useful purpose. Give children specific reasons for each limit. If you cannot think of a reason for having a limit, rethink the limit. Try to determine whether your expectations really are that important. Unreasonable limits can cause young children to feel angry.

Avoid making too many limits. Having a few well-established limits is better for the children and for you. If you have too many limits, the

children will forget them. You, too, may have trouble remembering and enforcing them.

Define both acceptable and unacceptable behavior. Decide how to deal with unacceptable behavior. Normally, the best approach is to stop such action firmly and quickly. You may find, however, the child will become angry, 15-2. This anger may show in several ways. The child may resist set limit, cry, yell, or simply stare at you.

Limits need to be re-examined by the entire staff on a regular basis. Children's behavior will change as they grow and develop. Therefore, limits should change as the children change. Any limit changes must be discussed with the entire staff. Discuss what changes need to be made and why. If you determine that a limit no longer fits the group's needs, discard it.

Limit changes also need to be discussed with the children. When an issue arises, invite the children to discuss the problem. Begin by stating the issue. Then ask the children to think of ways of solving it. During the discussion, encourage the children to state the limits in a positive way. Write out each new limit, calling attention to the printed words.

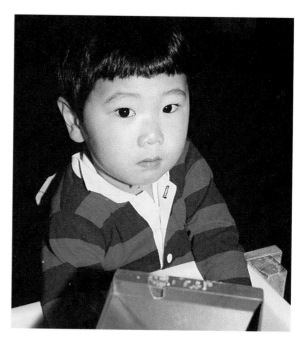

15-2 Undesirable behavior should be stopped, even if the child becomes upset.

## Enforcing Limits

Children follow limits best when the limits are enforced. Children need to know what is expected of them. However, children will often test these well-established limits. You should feel comfortable with this testing process. At the same time you should also maintain your position. Do not be afraid or back down. For example, if you said each child may do only one painting, make sure no child paints two. Friendly reminders may also be helpful, such as "When you are finished, Tommy wants a turn to paint a picture."

Enforcing limits also requires that limits be flexible at times. **Flexible limits** allow you to adapt to the needs of an individual or situation. For instance, your limit states that children are expected to wear smocks in the art area. If an art activity is not messy, you might be flexible about this limit and allow the children to work without a smock. Your limits must be flexible enough to handle such situations, 15-3.

The way you react to children who break limits affects children's feelings of security. Children feel secure knowing the limits protect them. However, when one child violates a limit, another child's security may be threatened. For instance, a child may express his or her anger in a violent way, such as hitting. That child is violating a limit. You must tell the child that hitting is wrong. The child who was hit is also affected. He or she has lost some security. You need to reassure and pay attention to this child. In fact, giving attention to the injured child shows that hitting is not a good way to gain attention.

## Limits for Specific Areas and Activities

The limits you set may be very different from the limits set at another center. This is because no two centers are alike. Equipment, facilities, and staff vary among centers. However, similar activities take place at many centers, regardless of location. For instance, cooking, blockbuilding, and reading occur at most centers. General limits for some of these areas and activities can be used as guidelines for all centers.

15-3 Limits may need to be adapted to the needs of an individual child or situation.

## Sensory Play

In some classrooms, sensory activity is provided each day. A water or sand table is often used for this activity. During a typical week, shaving cream, ice cubes, snow, colored water, or soapy water may be used in the water table. Dried beans, seed corn, oats, rice, or pebbles may be used in the sand table.

Depending on the material being used, the limits may change somewhat. For instance, a child would not need to wear a smock for protection when playing with dried seed corn. With shaving cream, however, the smock may be required.

Limits for sensory play might include the following:

■ Wear smocks for all wet or messy activities, 15-4.

■ Wipe up splashes and spills immediately.

■ Keep sensory materials inside the table.

Eating or throwing sensory materials is not allowed, but this should be stated in a positive manner as shown above. If a child does not follow the limit, he or she must face the conse-

15-4 Wearing smocks during messy activities will keep children clean and dry.

quences. For example, you might say, "Jacques, I cannot let you throw sand. It could get in someone's eyes and hurt them. If you choose to throw sand, you will have to stop playing here." If Jacques keeps throwing sand, stop his play immediately and offer him a choice between more acceptable activities.

## Dramatic Play

The dramatic play area might be called the home living or housekeeping area in some centers. Materials should be provided to help the children gain a better understanding of themselves and others around them. Dramatic play also allows children to work out their own feelings. Thus, to provide the children with the least restrictive environment, limits can include:

■ Wipe up all spilled water.

■ Put materials away after use.

■ Respect the participation of others.

## Small Manipulative Activities

This area of the classroom contains games and small objects. With these materials, children learn to build, compare, sort, arrange, and match. Also, color, number, size, and shape concepts can be mastered. As children use small manipulatives, they also develop fine-motor and hand-eye coordination.

Usually, there are few limits in this area. Suggested limits include the following:

■ Return toys to the shelf after use.

■ Keep games and puzzle pieces in this area of the classroom, 15-5.

■ Take turns with materials.

## Cooking

Children learn about food by participating in cooking activities. Cooking allows children to feel a sense of accomplishment. Tasting, smelling, touching, listening, and seeing help build language, number, sequence, and physics concepts.

Health and safety precautions must be addressed in the limits. Therefore, the following limits are needed:

■ Wash hands before cooking.

■ Wear an apron or smock.

■ Wipe up spills immediately.

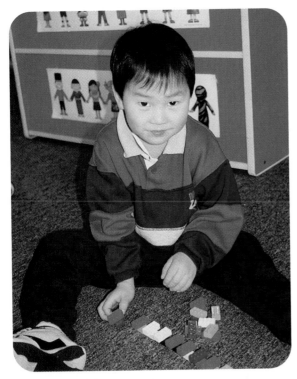

15-5 The limit that small manipulatives cannot leave the designated classroom area makes cleanup much simpler.

- Only teachers pick up hot items.
- Eat prepared foods only during lunch or snack time.
- Everyone assists with cleanup.

Supervision is required during all cooking activities. Whenever electrical appliances are being used, never leave the activity area! If more supplies are needed, signal for another teacher to get them for you. Always use pot holders and hot pads with cooking appliances.

## Blockbuilding

Blockbuilding encourages children to be productive and creative. Blockbuilding also provides children with a way to release energy. The children's safety is important in this area. Limits must stress safety. Close supervision is always required in this area. Because of this need, building activities should be allowed only during a set time period.

Limits for blockbuilding activities might include the following:
- Use blocks for building only, 15-6.
- Keep blocks in the blockbuilding area.
- Return blocks to the storage shelves after use.
- Touch only your own building project unless you ask permission.

## Music

All children enjoy music, 15-7. It is a universal language. By participating in music activities, children can develop self-expression, listening, language, and coordination skills. Music, like other activities, needs specific limits that promote safety, respect, and responsibility:
- Children select the instruments they want to use.
- Return instruments to their assigned places on the shelves after use.
- Use musical instruments only for creating sounds.
- Say only nice words about others' music.

15-6  Blocks are to be used for building only.

15-7 Children enjoy creating music.

15-8 Children can learn valuable pre-reading and language skills in the book corner.

## Art

For children, art is usually a pleasing activity. Therefore, they usually spend a lot of time playing in this area. Art is offered daily in most centers during the self-selected activity period.

Children in this area should be encouraged to explore materials. They should not be told what to make, nor should their artwork be compared. Most centers use only the following limits:

- Cover tables.
- Wear smocks for messy activities.
- Wipe up spills immediately.
- Work only with your own materials.

## Book Corner

In the book corner, children can develop language and pre-reading skills. Children should be encouraged to explore the books in this area, 15-8. In doing so, they will learn about their own family and community. They also will learn about other cultures. Limits for the book corner might be the following:

- Turn one page at a time.
- Give torn books to the teacher.
- Return books to the shelf after use.
- Touch books gently.

In order to encourage the children to explore, change books on a regular basis. Some teachers change books on a weekly basis, leaving several favorites to carry over. Control the number of books available at any given time. When too many books are in the area, it can become cluttered. Likewise, a child may have difficulty locating a favorite storybook.

## Science

All children need science activities. These activities encourage them to discover their own environment. As they observe and question, they will see relationships and draw conclusions.

Teachers need to carefully plan science activities. Include a variety of classroom and outdoor activities. Emphasize hands-on activities that allow children time to explore their surroundings, 15-9. During these activities, encourage the children to participate by observing, touching, holding, and questioning.

As a teacher, you will need to demonstrate some of the limits in this area. For example, you will need to show the children how to hold a bunny, water a plant, or feed classroom pets. Equipment use will also need to be demonstrated

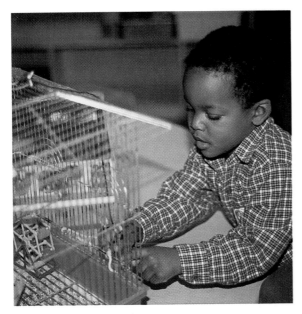

15-9 Hands-on activities encourage children to become involved in the world around them.

for the children. You may even choose to have children assist with cleaning the animal housing.

Limits for the science area might include the following:

- Feed pets and water plants only with a teacher's supervision.
- Keep science equipment in the area.
- Handle pets with care.
- Wash your hands after touching pets.

## Playground Activity

On the playground, children can express themselves in creative ways. They can build ships, houses, forts, and other objects with wooden crates and other materials. Through play, children develop motor coordination skills, social play skills, and a sense of cooperation.

The primary concern of the teacher is the children's safety. Limits must be set and enforced if children are to play happily and safely on the playground. These limits will vary, depending on the equipment being used and the children's abilities.

### Swings

Swings are not found on all playgrounds because they require constant teacher supervision.

If swings are available, specific limits must be set, such as the following:

- Only one child on a swing at a time.
- Sit in the center of the swing.
- Use both hands for holding on.
- Stay on the swing until it has stopped.
- Only teachers push children on swings.
- Keep clear of moving swings.

### Slides

Slides are a source of hazard for young children. Accidents happen when children bump into each other. Some children are injured when they stand up as they go down the slide, or when they slide head first. As a result, set these limits:

- Use both hands when climbing up the steps.
- Wait until the person in front of you is off the slide before you slide down.
- Slide down feet first and sitting up.
- Get off the slide as soon as you get to the bottom.

### Jungle Gyms

Jungle gyms are very appealing to young children. Since children are adventurous, any activity on this piece of equipment has to be carefully supervised. Children must also be taught the correct and safe way to use the jungle gym. Include the following limits for jungle gym use:

- Only four or five children may use the jungle gym at one time.
- Use both hands to hold on.
- Make sure you do not step on another child when climbing.

### Seesaws

Seesaws are another piece of equipment that require constant supervision when being used. Therefore, the limits you establish should stress safety. Include the following:

- Hang on to the handle with both hands.
- Keep feet out from under the board as it goes down.
- Stop before the board hits the ground.
- Tell your partner when you want to get off the seesaw.

### Wheeled Toys

Tricycles, bicycles, and other wheeled toys can pose dangers when not used properly. For this reason, safety limits are needed regarding the use of these toys. These limits include the following:

- Each wheeled toy can have only one rider at a time.
- Always wear proper safety gear when riding, 15-10.
- Sit on the seat to ride.
- Ride only on the wheeled toy path.
- Watch for other riders or walkers.

## Communicating Limits

What method can you use to clearly communicate limits to young children? As you have already read, limits need to be short, simple, and reasonable. Some teachers make this task easier by first dividing their limits into three categories. These categories include (1) be safe, (2) be kind and respectful, and (3) be neat and responsible.

When reminding children about certain limits, the teachers begin by using one of the three categories. Figure 15-11 shows examples of this method.

| Category | Examples |
|---|---|
| Be safe! | Use both hands to hang on to the swing.<br>Sit at the table while using scissors. |
| Be kind and respectful! | Say *thank you* when someone helps you.<br>Hold the door for others. |
| Be neat and responsible! | Hang your jacket in the locker.<br>Wear your smock while painting. |

15-11 Use clear, concise language when communicating limits to children.

15-10 When riding wheeled toys, helmets are a must.

## Summary

Limits focus on actions and behaviors that reflect the goals of the center. Limits must be made for all classroom areas and for all activities. As the classroom teacher, it is your responsibility to explain and enforce limits. Limits need to be explained at the children's level of understanding. The staff and children should also know the reasons for the limits.

Limits that are consistently enforced and fair help create a relaxed atmosphere at the center. Limits may need to be flexible to adapt to the needs of an individual or situation. Limits will be different from one center to another. It is important that all staff members have input into setting limits. These limits should be reviewed on a regular basis and revised as needed.

Having limits teaches good citizenship. Children know what is expected of them. Adults know what to expect. Both groups find the center a pleasant place to be.

## Review and Reflect

1. Explain the importance of having limits in a child care center.

2. List three reasons for establishing classroom limits.

3. Name three guidelines for setting limits for children.

4. Give an example of a limit that is stated negatively. Rewrite the limit so it is stated positively.

5. Should limits ever change? Explain your answer.

6. Why is it important that limits be enforced consistently?

7. _____ limits allow you to adapt to the needs of an individual or situation.

8. Why should children be expected to wipe up any spills they make in various areas of the classroom?

9. List two ways teachers can encourage children to look at the books in the book corner.

10. Name one limit for each of the following pieces of playground equipment: swings, slides, jungle gyms, seesaws, and wheeled toys.

## Apply and Explore

1. Discuss ways in which limits may change as children grow. Give some specific examples.

2. Collect classroom limits from two centers. Discuss the similarities and differences between the two sets of limits.

3. Role-play the following scenes that might occur in early childhood programs. How should caregivers respond?
   A. Toby is in the book corner. While looking at a book, she accidentally tears a page.
   B. Tommy goes down the slide. When he reaches the bottom, he continues to sit there.
   C. Sarah and Frank are on the seesaw. Suddenly, Sarah jumps off.
   D. During a cooking activity, Mark accidentally spills his milk.

4. Cut pictures of two pieces of outdoor play equipment from a catalog. Write limits for each piece.

5. Check the Web site of the National Network for Child Care (nncc.org) for information on guidance, discipline, and appropriate limits for children of various ages.

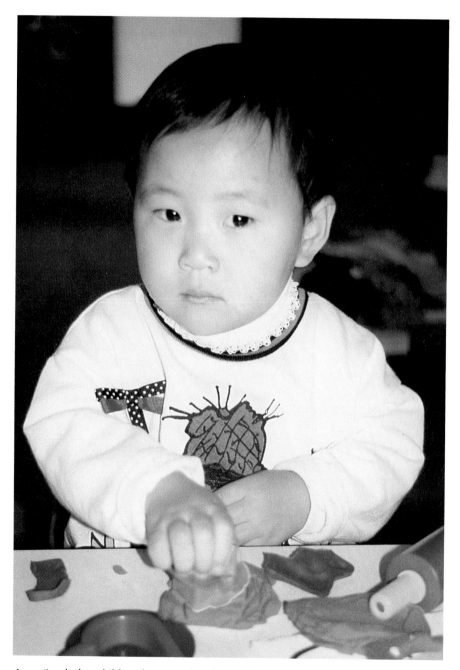

A routine helps children become familiar with daily events.

# Chapter 16
# Handling Daily Routines

After studying this chapter, you will be able to

- explain the importance of a daily schedule.

- guide children successfully through the daily routines of dressing and undressing, eating, napping, toileting, and cleanup.

- explain the use of transition techniques to move smoothly from one activity to another.

## Terms to Know

routines

pica

dawdling

transitions

auditory signals

**Routines**, such as dressing, undressing, eating, napping, and toileting, are everyday experiences. They promote the children's social, self-help, and learning skills. Routines at child care centers reassure children by providing a pattern for each day. By following a schedule, children know the order of daily events. They also know what to expect with each event.

Daily routines provide opportunities for children to develop independence. Young children feel great satisfaction in doing things for themselves. See 16-1.

Daily routines will need your guidance. Otherwise, routine activities may become time-consuming and frustrating. Learning to handle routines helps your classroom run smoothly.

## The Daily Schedule

A well-planned schedule provides the framework for the day's activities. Schedules for early childhood programs vary by type of program. For instance, the sequence of events in an all-day program will not be the same as that for a half-day program. Factors such as the length of the program's day and the time children arrive will need to be considered.

A well-planned schedule should help prevent conflicts. It must also be planned to meet the children's needs. Health and safety are important considerations. To feel comfortable

16-1 Teaching children how to put on outerwear allows them to be more independent.

| Scheduling Segments for a Full-Day Program |
| --- |
| I.    Arrival, greetings, and self-selected indoor activities |
| II.   Cleanup, toileting, and hand washing. |
| III.  Snack, cleanup, and hand washing |
| IV.   Self-selected activities and cleanup |
| V.    Teacher-structured large group activity |
| VI.   Outdoor self-selected activities |
| VII.  Cleanup, toileting, and hand washing |
| VIII. Lunch, cleanup, hand washing, and toothbrushing |
| IX.   Transitioning for nap time: quiet music or story time |
| X.    Toileting, hand washing, nap |
| XI.   Self-selected activites, indoor or outdoor |
| XII.  Cleanup, toileting, and hand washing |
| XIII. Snack, cleanup, and hand washing |
| XIV.  Outdoor free time |
| XV.   Departure |

16-2  A daily routine may give children a feeling of security.

and secure, children need to have consistency and predictable routines.

The daily schedule should be designed to include basic routines. Figure 16-2 shows the segments of a typical schedule. Include time for both indoor and outdoor play. Consider the weather when deciding how much time to allow for outdoor play. Remember to plan time for eating and napping, too.

When planning the daily schedule, include large blocks of open time. At least half of the day should be set aside for self-selected activities. Young children enjoy selecting activities and deciding how long to remain with each activity. Many preschool children have short attention spans. Differences also exist in the speed at which they complete projects. By providing larger blocks of time, you will be meeting these children's individual needs.

There will be differences in each child's response to the schedule. For some children, the pace may be too fast, and they may feel stressed. Other children may become bored if the pace is too slow. Children's reactions often depend on the number of hours they spend at the center. Children attending full time may feel differently than those attending part time.

## Arrival Routines

The arrival of children should follow a regular routine so children know what to expect. The children's arrival requires the teacher's full attention.

A typical arrival routine begins with the greeting of each child. Kneel down to the child's level and make each child feel welcome. Acknowledge any item the child might have brought from home. The children should then be directed to store their outer garments and other belongings in their cubbies. They then can move to a self-selected activity until all the children have arrived.

Children react differently to separation from their parents. Some will remain silent while others cry. Some will refuse to enter the room, and others will bring favorite toys from home. Children vary in the duration of their separation anxieties. Some children will feel comfortable in a day or two. For other children, this may take a week or even several weeks. As a teacher, recognizing and responding to these anxieties is important. Your caring and understanding will be a key in helping the children make this transition.

## Large Group Activities

In most programs, time is included in the schedule for large group activities. Teachers may refer to this segment as group time, story time, or circle time. Often this time is used for stories, songs, fingerplays, and discussions. If developmentally appropriate, teachers also use it for discussions about the weather and calendar.

Schedule large group activities when the children are well-rested and nourished, such as mid-morning. Since not all children arrive at one time, avoid scheduling group time at the beginning of the day. Problems can also occur when large group time is scheduled just before lunch. Usually the children are under the most stress at this time of day. They are becoming tired and hungry, which could impact their behavior.

Group time should take place in an area where there are few distractions. The children should be seated away from books, puzzles, and other materials that they could pick up. Many programs have a carpeted area for group time. Some teachers prefer using individual carpet squares. A teacher or aide may pre-arrange the squares prior to large group activity to make sure the children are not sitting too close together. It will also ensure that the children are sitting near the teacher and not blocking other children's views.

A key to the success of group time is being organized and ready. Immediately capture the children's attention with a fingerplay, puppet, or song. This will encourage stragglers to pick up their pace and join the group. Always end group time before the children lose interest.

## Small Group Activities

Small group activity periods may be scheduled for 10 to 15 minutes. Typically, the four to six children in the group have similar interests or abilities. During this time, the children work with a teacher or aide. The purpose may be to teach specific concepts such as colors, numbers, shapes, or sizes.

## Self-Selected Activities

The largest block of time in the schedule is for self-selected activities. This may also be referred to as center time or free play. The activities may be scheduled for indoors or outdoors. A variety of developmentally appropriate activities should be available.

When longer play periods are available, children engage in more involved activities. Larger blocks of time help lengthen the children's attention spans. These longer time periods are also valuable to you. As a teacher, you can engage in conversations with the children, asking questions and assessing learning.

## Meals and Snacks

A half-day or two-hour preschool program usually provides a 15-minute snack period. Lunch is usually provided in centers that operate full-day programs. Typically a half hour is allowed for lunch. The amount of time needed for snack or lunch will vary depending upon the age of the children and the number in the group.

## Nap Time

Check your state's regulations on rest or nap time. Most states require children enrolled in a full-day program to have a nap time. Usually this is scheduled after lunch. Allow one to two hours for this activity. Nap time routines will be discussed later in this chapter.

# Daily Routines

Throughout the day, many routines take place in the center. As a teacher, you will need to know how to handle these routines. Encourage the children to become as independent as possible in carrying out these basic routines. These routines include dressing and undressing, eating, napping, toileting, and cleanup.

## Dressing and Undressing

As a teacher, you will want to encourage the children to dress and undress themselves as much as possible. Begin by telling the children what you expect of them. This is important. When four-year-old Frankie hands you his coat, refuse to help him put it on. Instead, tell Frankie he is able to dress himself. If needed, prompt him by providing verbal instruction. Once his coat is on, do not forget to praise him for his accomplishment. This will help him enjoy becoming independent. See 16-3.

Children should also be responsible for hanging up their coats. You may notice that many of the children simply lay their coats in their lockers. Do not allow this. For instance, if you see Eileen lay her coat in the locker, say "Eileen, you need to hang your coat on the hook." If she does not understand, show her how to hang it on the hook. Then take the coat off the hook and let Eileen hang it herself.

Label lockers so children can find their own spaces. The labeling method you use will vary with the ages of the children. Names are usually written on the lockers for infants. This helps both teachers and parents. For two-year-olds, use a picture of the child. Names and symbols are helpful to three-year-olds. If children cannot recognize their names, they can find their symbols. Give each child a different symbol. Most four- and five-year-olds can recognize their names.

### Suggestions for Parents

Dressing can be time-consuming and frustrating for teachers and children. For this reason, some centers provide parents with a list of clothing suggestions for the children. The list usually includes the following:

- Send an extra set of clothing for your child to keep at school. These can be used in case of an emergency. For instance, a child might fall in mud, rip a pair of pants, or have a toileting accident.
- Attach labels to the inside of your child's clothing. It is common for several children to have the same style and size of clothes. Labeling helps prevent confusion.

16-3 Letting children know they are capable of dressing and undressing themselves helps children build independence.

- Select clothing for your child with large zippers, buttons, or snaps. This makes dressing easier for children who do not have well-developed small motor skills.
- Boots and shoes should fit properly and slide on and off easily.
- Shoelaces should not be too long because they can be a tripping hazard and are hard for children to tie. You may want to choose shoes with Velcro closings, which are easier for younger children to manage independently.
- Consider buying elastic-waist slacks and shorts instead of snap or button types. They are easier for children to handle during toileting.

## Demonstrating

Buttoning, zipping, pulling on boots, tying shoes, and putting fingers in gloves are all actions that can be demonstrated. Demonstrating at the child's eye level is the most effective. Sometimes verbal guidance is all a child needs. At other times, you may need to start an action. Allow the child to finish the process. He or she will feel a sense of accomplishment. For example, Siri can put on his coat but cannot get the zipper started. Start the zipper and have Siri finish zipping it by himself.

***Tying Shoes.*** Tying is a skill that requires advanced coordination. As a result, most children do not learn this task until five years of age.

There are several methods for teaching children how to tie shoes. One method is to place the child on your lap. From this angle, the child can observe the process. For most children, the easiest technique to learn is to loop each string like a bunny ear. Tie these loops into a double knot. Encourage the child to repeat this process.

Some children will have shoes that clasp with Velcro instead of tie with laces. Bring shoes with ties to the center to teach these children how to tie. Let them use these shoes to practice. This will help them learn tying skills, or you can let them practice on a shoelace box, 16-4.

***Boots.*** Boots that are too small can be hard to put on. When this happens, place a plastic bag

16-4  A shoelace box is useful for teaching tying to children.

over the child's shoes or feet. This will help the boot slip on and off more easily.

Some centers keep a box of surplus boots. When a child is wearing boots that are too small, the teacher can make an exchange. Boots from this box are also handy if a child forgets to bring boots from home.

Children can practice putting on and taking off their own boots, or they may practice using the extras in the box.

***Coats.*** To demonstrate putting on a coat, lay the child's coat, button or zipper side up, on the floor. Have the child kneel at the collar end. Tell the child to place his or her hands and arms into the sleeves. Then tell the child to put it over his or her head. Use your own sweater or jacket to demonstrate this for the children. See 16-5.

## Eating

Nutritional services provided by centers vary. Some centers serve only lunch, while others may also serve breakfast. Snacks may be the only

| 1. The child kneels at the collar end of the coat. | 2. The child puts his or her hands in the coat sleeves. | 3. The child flips the coat over his or her head. | 4. The child puts his or her arms all the way into the sleeves. |

16-5  This technique can be used by children to help them learn how to put on a coat.

food served in centers that do not operate all day. Some centers require that children bring their own bag lunches. While most centers provide older children with meals, they require parents to provide infant formulas, breast milk, or baby foods.

As a teacher, you will have many concerns during mealtime. A main concern is serving nutritious meals that children will like. This concern is addressed in Chapter 11, "Planning Nutritious Meals and Snacks."

You will also want the children to enjoy eating and practice their table manners. Making mealtime pleasant and orderly is another concern of teachers, 16-6. This means making meals appropriate for the ages, abilities, and interests of children. It also means teaching rules of etiquette during meals.

16-6  Proper manners and order contribute to a pleasant snack.

You will notice that children's appetites change. Children's appetites are influenced by illness, stage of development, physical activity, and a body's individual nutrient needs. Emotions can also affect appetite. For example, if Lila has cried since her parents dropped her off this morning, she may not be hungry at lunchtime. Appetite changes will require you to be flexible regarding the children during meals.

### Infants and Toddlers

Infants and toddlers have definite food likes and dislikes, 16-7. It is not unusual for them to spit out or refuse foods they do not like. On the other hand, they will eagerly eat foods they enjoy.

A cup can be introduced as early as six to seven months of age. At first, children may take only a few swallows. Spilling will occur for several months. Later, children will enjoy using cups by themselves. To help these children, provide spill-proof cups.

Once children become mobile, their interest in food may decrease. During this stage, some children are too interested in moving to sit still very long. Even if placed in a high chair or feeding table, they may try to get out and continue with their play.

Provide finger foods to infants and toddlers whenever possible. By picking up small bits of food, the child will develop fine motor skills and hand-eye coordination skills. It also gives them a sense of accomplishment and helps them in developing independence.

Interest in self-feeding using spoons may occur between 15 and 18 months of age. You will need to be patient with children who are learning to feed themselves. You may have to help them fill their spoons. Since spilling occurs often, the children should wear bibs. Also expect food to be spilled on the feeding tray, high chair, and floor. Wipe up the spills immediately so others do not slip on them.

### Two-Year-Olds

Two-year-old children become increasingly skilled at handling cups and spoons. Provide these children with child-sized spoons and small, unbreakable cups. Fill the cups only halfway. Then if a drink is spilled, there is less to clean up.

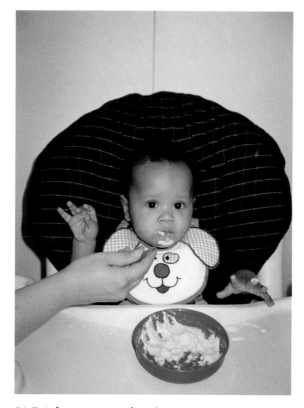

16-7 Infants can use facial expressions to communicate their food preferences.

Use small milk or juice pitchers (16 ounces) with two-year-olds. Encourage the children to fill their own cups. Watch carefully and provide support. See 16-8.

### Three-Year-Olds

By the age of three, children have distinct food preferences. They may refuse to eat certain foods because of their color, shape, or texture. Your attitude will help children accept these foods. In addition, family food attitudes and preferences can influence what children may eat. Other children can also influence food preferences. Some children who flatly refuse to eat vegetables at home may enjoy eating them with their peers.

Three-year-olds are old enough to assist with mealtime. Ask them to set the table. Make place mats containing outlines of the plate, glass, fork, and spoon. These patterns will help children set the table properly with minimal adult assistance.

16-8 Supervise two-year-olds as they pour their own drinks. They may need help handling the pitcher.

Provide forks and spoons to help the children develop handling skills. Use glasses with weighted bottoms to help prevent spills. Use pitchers with lids and pour spouts. Shallow bowls allow the children to see what is in the bowls.

Have children serve themselves. As a rule, tell children to fill their milk glasses only halfway. Keep portions small. A simple guideline to follow is one tablespoon of food for each year of age. If children want more food, they may ask for second portions.

Keep a wet sponge on the table for spills. When children spill, accept this as a normal occurrence. Avoid scolding the child. Rather, guide the child in wiping up the spill.

### Four- and Five-Year-Olds

Four- and five-year-olds like to help at mealtime. They may ask to set the table, serve, and assist with after-meal cleanup. They may also enjoy helping to prepare the meal. Encourage them to do

so. For a classroom activity, have them prepare pudding, rolls, or other simple foods, 16-9. Later, serve these foods for snack or lunch.

Older children enjoy talking at the table. You may wish to help them begin conversations. Mention activities they have seen, heard, or done. They will begin talking with each other and naturally move on to other subjects.

### Limits

Limits for eating depend on the ages of the children. However, general limits might include the following:

- Taste all foods before asking for seconds of food or milk.
- Remain at the table until everyone has finished.
- Wipe up your own spills.
- Eat food only from your own plate.
- Say thank you after someone has served or passed you food.
- Say please when asking to have food passed or served to you.

16-9 Children enjoy helping prepare foods they will eat later.

## Eating Problems

Eating problems are common during the preschool years. These problems usually peak at three years of age. Eating will remain a problem for 25 percent of four- and five-year-olds. In most cases, problems will end somewhere around the sixth birthday. Food refusal, dawdling, pica, and vomiting are all eating problems that can become serious.

***Food Refusal.*** Food refusal problems are related to a lack of interest in food. Food refusal often begins between one and two years of age, 16-10. At this time, children's need for food decreases. Some children may need only one meal a day. Refusing food because it is not needed is not a problem. However, children who do not eat even when they need food have food refusal problems.

Lack of exercise or energy, excess energy (hyperactivity), and illness can all cause a lack of interest in food. These fairly common problems sometimes cure themselves. There are steps you can take, however, to help children with food refusal problems.

To encourage children to eat, serve small portions. Avoid pushing the children to eat. Instead, talk with the parents of children having problems. Find out what these children eat at home. Despite mealtime refusal at the center, these children may be getting proper nourishment at home.

Do not provide extra snacks to children who refuse to eat breakfast and lunch. If you do, they will not be hungry at mealtime.

***Pica.*** **Pica** is a craving for nonfood items. Cravings include paper, soap, rags, and even toys. This condition is fairly uncommon in most preschool children.

If you think that a child may have this problem, ask other staff members to observe the child. Compare your observations. Discuss the problem with the center director. You may want to schedule a conference with the parents to discuss the problem. A combined effort between parents, medical professionals, and teachers may solve the problem.

***Dawdling.*** While one child eats only one or two bites, the other children may have finished

16-10 Toddlers and two-year-olds are especially known for their strong responses to foods they dislike.

an entire meal. It is common to have several children who eat slowly in a group of preschoolers. This is called **dawdling**. Some may hold food in their mouth for a long time, failing to chew or swallow it. Others are so busy talking at the table they forget to eat. Still others may push the food around their plates or play with it. These children lack interest in food.

Many times dawdling is an attempt to gain attention. Therefore, do not urge or threaten dawdling children. Instead, provide these children with small portions of food. After being given a reasonable amount of time to eat, clear the table without comment. Children will learn that if they want to eat, they must do so in a timely fashion.

***Vomiting.*** Young children are able to *induce* (to produce on purpose) vomiting. If a child in your class vomits often, without other signs of illness, he or she is possibly inducing it.

If you are sure a child is not sick, ignore repeated vomiting. Clean up the mess quickly, without emotion. If the child notices any concern, he or she may begin vomiting to get your attention.

You should, however, share the child's behavior with the parents. Find out if this behavior also occurs at home during or right after a meal. If it does, you will need to work with the center director and parents to solve the problem.

## Napping

"Will my child be required to take a nap?" This question is asked often by parents who are thinking of enrolling their child in a center. Some children may have outgrown napping at home. Your response will depend on your state's child care licensing regulations and center policies.

Most states require that preschool children nap at least one hour, 16-11. A center can expand that requirement if they wish. For instance, if a state requires all children under the age of five to have naps, a center may expand that rule to require all enrolled children to have naps. In any case, you should check your state's guidelines for requirements.

Most child care centers have a set nap time. At the end of this time, most children are awake. If not, they are gently woken. You may note that a certain child needs to be woken every day. If this happens, the child may not be getting enough rest at home. This needs to be discussed with the parents. Check with your center director to find out who is responsible for talking to the parents. If you are asked to contact the parents, use a positive approach. Share your observations with the parents. Try to arrive at a solution together.

16-11 Naps are required in many states.

### Nap Time Rituals

Schedule quiet activities prior to nap time. Children often enjoy hearing a story at this time. Select stories that will soothe the children. Four-year-olds may like to look at books until they fall asleep. You may want to play soft music.

Lack of rest can cause irritability in young children. Most preschool children, tired or not, can postpone sleep at nap time. Younger children may simply cry. Older children, however, may make repeated demands for your attention. They may request to go to the washroom or have a drink of water. In most cases, these are only pleas for attention.

Plan ahead to prevent children from making too many demands at nap time. First, have the children use the toilet, brush their teeth, wash their hands, and have a drink of water before they lie down. Ask if anyone needs a tissue or wants to look quietly at a book. Make sure they have their blankets and stuffed toys. After this, begin to cover them. Do not be surprised, however, if a child still asks for another drink of water or trip to the bathroom. These rituals seem natural to most two- and three-year-old children. They sincerely believe their needs are real. However, if you allow these children to meet these needs before nap time, they will have an easier time getting and staying settled. See 16-12.

Not all children will fall asleep at nap time. Their need for sleep varies. It is common for some of the five-year-olds to remain awake. Five-year-olds will cooperate, however, if nap time limits are stated clearly and enforced.

Children who do fall asleep may tell you they had bad dreams while sleeping. Others may cry out in their sleep. When this happens, calmly approach the child. Let the child know you are near. One way to do this is to hold the child's hand or straighten the covers.

As a teacher, it is important to respect the children's need for sleep. Because it is difficult for some children to fall asleep, try to remain as quiet as possible. Avoid talking to other teachers during nap time.

## Toileting

The toileting needs of infants are met through the use of diapers. Infants cannot control

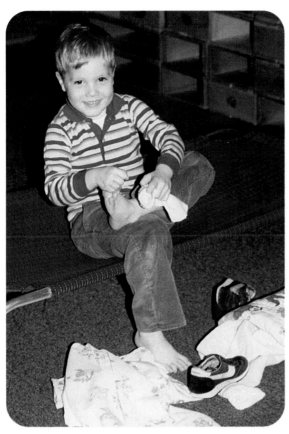

16-12 Allow children to remove shoes and socks at nap time. They will be more comfortable and relaxed.

*elimination*, bowel and bladder release. For them, elimination is a reflex action. The first few weeks after birth, infants eliminate many times each day. They may cry when it happens. The number of eliminations will decrease as the infant gets older. However, the volume increases. By 28 weeks, a child may remain dry from one to two hours. When they do eliminate, however, the diaper is usually soaking wet. It may leak unless it is changed immediately. Diapers need to be checked often and changed when wet to prevent diaper rash.

Children differ in their toilet learning needs and schedule. Some children use the toilet as early as two years. Others may not have full bladder and bowel control until three years or later. For some children, toilet learning will take just a few days. Other children may require several months.

## Toilet Learning Timetable

Children cannot be taught to perform toilet functions until their central nervous systems are ready. As a rule, this does not occur until after two years of age. At this age, most children will express their need to use the toilet. Some may pull down their pants and sit on the toilet. Others will tell you they have to use the bathroom.

Each child in the center will have his or her own toilet learning timetable. Never force children to develop self-regulation. When they are ready, they will master control of their bodily functions. Instead praise them as they become better at keeping themselves dry. Controlling elimination is one step toward independence. It is a real accomplishment for young children.

Certain factors may affect a child's toilet learning timetable. Illness, a new baby in the home, or weather changes are common factors. Remember, too, that toileting accidents are common during a child's first few weeks at the child care center. These accidents may indicate the emotional stress the child is feeling in a new environment. Another factor is the toilet learning attitudes and practices at home. In some homes, adults may overreact to children's toileting accidents by showing their disapproval. These children may feel ashamed by their failure to control elimination. In the center, you need to be sensitive to children's feelings following an accident. Quietly help them change into clean clothes.

## Guidance

As a teacher, keep a matter-of-fact attitude in toilet teaching. Shaming and scolding have no place in helping a child develop control. Instead, provide children with the facilities and encouragement to stay dry.

Have toilet seats or potty chairs available. If you provide a seat for the toilet, also provide a step stool to help the children reach the toilet. Not all children like to sit on the toilet. Some are afraid they will fall in the toilet and be flushed down. These children will prefer the potty chair.

During toilet learning, the child's clothing should be easy to manage. Pants that pull down easily work better than those that are hard to unfasten. Also during this time, it is a good idea to keep several extra pairs of underwear and clothing at the center.

Children often provide clues when they have to use the toilet. Some start wiggling. Others cross their legs. When you notice these signs, provide reminders to the child. You can remind the child by saying, "It is toilet time again," or "Louis, do you need to use the toilet?" After children use the toilet, remind them to flush the toilet and wash their hands. At the same time, be sure to wash your own hands. See 16-13.

## Cleanup

Cleanup is an important routine in early childhood classrooms. Children learn to be responsible for themselves, their belongings, and classroom materials and equipment. Cleanup time can be stressful for a new teacher. Consider Carlos, who recently began teaching in a preschool. He frequently finds himself raising his voice and scolding or nagging the children to help in cleanup. Carlos' frustration is not uncommon. The following suggestions may be helpful.

### Guidance

Try to maintain a positive attitude toward cleanup. Scolding or nagging the children usually is ineffective. You will discover that some children are unresponsive and do not want to participate.

Begin by setting firm ground rules and then follow through. All children should be expected to participate in cleanup. You must deal on an individual basis with the child who refuses to participate. You may say "Tanya, you need to put the

puzzle away." Observe Tanya closely. If she walks away from the table, take her hand. Then say "Tanya, come. You need to return the puzzle to the tray." If Tanya still refuses to put the puzzle away, she needs help in understanding the consequences. Explain that if she fails to put the puzzle away, she will not be able to play with the puzzles.

You will find that some children need encouragement or reminders. You might try saying the following:

- Help me put the blocks away.
- Show me where the puzzles are stored.
- Where do we hang these dress-up clothes?
- Timmy, you worked hard making your block structure. Now show Malcolm how to put the blocks away.

Foster independence by visually assisting the children in seeing where materials and equipment belong. For instance, in the woodworking area, paint a silhouette of each tool on a piece of tagboard. Hooks in the dramatic play area should be available for hanging dress-up clothes. To assist the children, attach an eight-inch loop of string to each item of clothing. On the block shelves, provide separate sections for each shape and size of blocks. The manipulative area needs to have separate, transparent containers for different types of pieces.

Young children enjoy pleasing others. They will work hard to win your approval. Thus, it is important that children's efforts at cleanup be praised. Praise their efforts by saying "Sally, I like the way you are helping Frankie put the blocks away" or "Ampario, I like the way you picked up all of the pieces of your puzzle."

## Transitions

**Transitions** are changes from one activity to another or moves from one place to another. They occur many times during the day. Children may go from self-selected activities to using the bathroom to snack time to outdoor play in just a few hours. Transitions must be carefully planned to help children get through the daily routine without a fuss.

Provide a five-minute warning prior to making the transition to the next activity. This will allow children time to finish what they are

---

**Tips for Guiding Toilet Learning**

- Each child has his or her own toilet learning timetable. Never force children to learn before they are ready.
- Maintain a matter-of-fact attitude.
- Praise children as they become better at keeping dry.
- Do not shame or scold.
- Make toilet seats or potty chairs available.
- Watch for clues that children provide when they need to use the toilet.

16-13 Remember these rules for effective toileting guidance.

doing. You might play the piano for five minutes or use an egg timer.

There are four basic methods for making successful transitions. You may use concrete objects, visual signals, novelty, or auditory signals. You may use several types of transitions in one day. Remember to be consistent. Young children respond better if they know what to expect. Therefore, it is best to use the same transition for individual activities. For instance, play the same cleanup song every day to let the children know it is cleanup time.

## Concrete Objects

Using concrete objects as a form of transition involves children moving items from one place to another. This technique directs a child's attention from one activity to another, 16-14. Examples include the following:

- "Leon, please put your picture in your cubby." This will direct Leon from an art activity to a new activity.

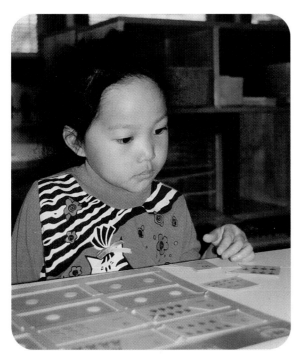

16-14 Putting away toys helps prepare children for the next activity.

- "Rose, hang up your coat." Rose will move from an outdoor activity to an indoor activity.
- "Ting, here is some play dough. Take it to the art table." Ting is directed toward starting an art activity.
- "Shilpa, put these washcloths on the bathroom hook." This signals the end of cleanup.

## Visual Signals

Using visual signals is another transition method. This method involves informing children of a change through signals they can see. For instance, when you show the children a picture of lunchtime, the children move to the lunch table. After story time, you might hold up a picture of outdoor play. This will serve as a signal to the children that it is time to put on outdoor clothing and wait at the door for you. See 16-15 for other examples of visual transitions.

The first few times you use visual signals, you will need to explain them to the children. After you use them several times, the children will know what to expect.

## Novelty

Novelty transitions involve the use of unusual, new actions or devices to move the children from one activity to another.

Locomotion is one type of transition. The children use motion to make their transition. For instance, ask the children to pretend they are elephants. Have them walk like heavy elephants to the snack table, or ask them to tiptoe lightly like tiny monkeys.

Using locomotion is limited only by imagination. Children can march, skip, or walk backwards. Before introducing a transition, however, consider the abilities of the children. For instance, do not ask a group of two- or three-year-olds to skip. They may not have developed this skill yet.

Transportation is another type of novelty transition. The children can move like freight trains, jets, buses, or cars. Each time you introduce a locomotion or transportation transition, get involved with the children. Model the movement you want them to make.

| Using Visual Transition | |
| --- | --- |
| **Visual Transition Method** | **Application of Method** |
| Construction paper | Use to break children into small groups. Place a piece of blue, red, green, or yellow construction paper at each table. Divide children into four groups and assign each group one of these colors. Have groups find their tables. |
| Hand motions | Use on playground to motion children indoors or to a specific area. |
| Blinking lights | Use to gain children's attention or to warn children to complete an activity. |
| Clock | Use with older children by telling them "When the big hand is on the 12, it will be lunchtime." |
| Words | Use to dismiss children from a group. Make a name card for each child. Hold cards up one at a time. Children are dismissed when they see their names. |

16-15  Visual signals can be used many ways for transition.

Identification games are also used for novelty transition. For instance, you may direct the children from one activity to another by asking "Who is wearing red today? You may go into the bathroom and wash your hands before we have our snacks." Continue using other colors that the children are wearing until every child has departed from the group.

Novelty transitions can also be made using single alphabet letters. Direct the children to another activity by asking "Whose name starts with the letter T? You may go outside." Continue calling out letters until all of the children are outdoors.

## Auditory Signals

**Auditory signals** inform the children of a change through the use of sound. A bell, timer, Autoharp®, tambourine, or piano can all inform children of a transition. Some teachers use a simple song or chord of music as a transition signal. For example, when Mr. Andrews plays "Mary Had a Little Lamb" on the piano, the children know it is time to cleanup.

Auditory signals also need to be developed for individuals. There will be times when you may wish to signal only one child. For instance, you may quietly tell a child that he or she needs to cleanup or go to the snack table. This is called an *individual transition.*

Auditory signals are quite useful for providing warnings. For instance, a ringing bell tells the children that playtime will end in five minutes. At the end of the five minutes, they know it is time to cleanup.

# Summary

A daily schedule and routines provide structure to each day. Within this structure, children have the opportunity to develop independence. Having a predictable schedule and helping children to handle daily routines allows the center to run smoothly.

A well-planned schedule provides the framework for the day's activities. Schedules for early childhood programs vary by type of program. Factors such as the length of the program's day and the time children arrive will need to be considered.

The daily schedule must also be planned to meet the children's physical and psychological needs. Health and safety are important considerations. For comfort and security, children need to have consistency and predictable routines.

Dressing, undressing, eating, napping, toileting, and cleanup are all daily routines. Each of these presents its own particular challenges and problems during the course of a day. For instance, asking children to participate with cleanup seems like a predictable activity. However, without the proper guidance, this task may become frustrating for both the children and the teacher. Therefore, it is important for you to learn positive guidance strategies to help children learn responsibility.

# Review and Reflect

1. How do routines and daily schedules benefit young children?

2. Why is it important to provide large blocks of open time in the daily schedule?

3. Describe a typical arrival routine.

4. Why do many programs ask parents to send a second set of clothing for children to keep at school?

5. Name five factors that may influence a child's appetite.

6. List three limits for eating that might be used with young children.

7. Give two suggestions for handling a child who refuses to eat.

8. What is pica?

9. Do child care centers have the right to decide if nap time should be included in the daily schedule? Explain your answer.

10. At what age are most children ready to begin toilet learning?

11. Describe one way you could encourage children to participate in cleanup.

12. List four types of transitions and give an example of each.

# Apply and Explore

1. Practice putting on your sweater or jacket using the technique outlined in the chapter.

2. From a sitting position, practice teaching tying, buttoning, and zipping to one of your peers.

3. Ask experienced teachers for their successful nap time techniques. Present this information as a report.

4. Observe children at cleanup. Record the techniques the teacher uses with the children to encourage them to participate. Discuss your findings with your classmates.

5. Ask parents what clues their children use when they need to use the toilet. Compare these to the clues you observe.

6. Explore the Web site www.smallfolk.com to learn more about how to handle feeding problems for children under age five years.

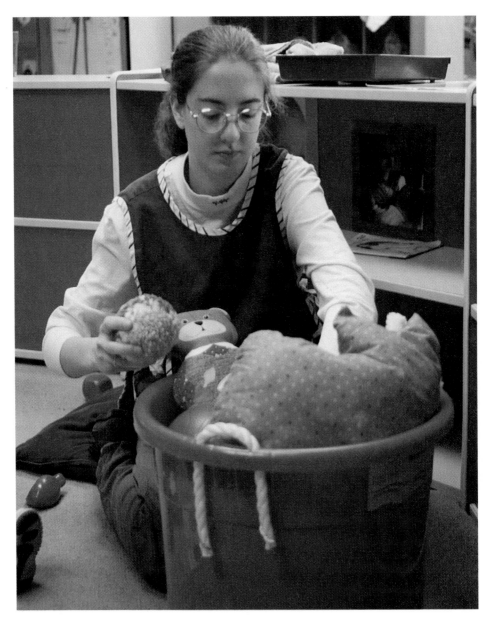

A variety of materials should be included in the curriculum.

# Part 4

# Learning Experiences for Children

Good learning experiences for children are based on careful planning that begins with the establishment of program goals for your early childhood program. Quality programs reflect children's developmental needs and interests. In this part, you will learn how to plan curriculum that is based on the development of the whole child. You will learn appropriate methods of developing and writing program curriculum.

Providing a variety of learning experiences helps children learn and grow in many ways. As you read this part, you will learn techniques for guiding the following types of experiences: art, storytelling, puppetry, manuscript writing, math, science, social studies, food and nutrition, music and movement, and field trips.

Each chapter will give you guidelines for planning and supervising activities. You will read many ideas for specific activities to try with children. You will also discover what types of supplies and resources you will need to conduct these activities.

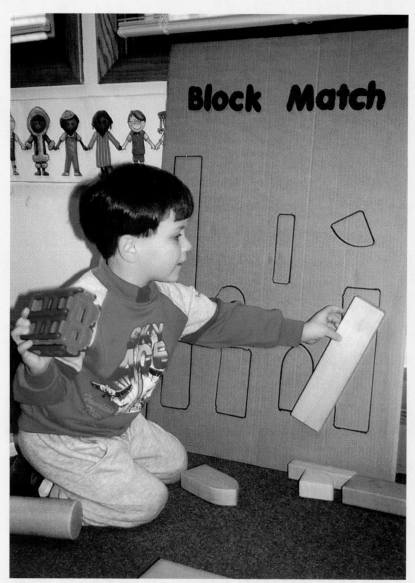

Plan a variety of techniques to use in learning experiences.

# Chapter 17

# The Curriculum

After studying this chapter, you will be able to

- develop program goals.

- indicate who is involved in curriculum development.

- cite the importance of assessment in curriculum planning.

- explain the content and process-centered approach to curriculum development.

- describe factors to consider in curriculum planning.

- illustrate the use of themes as a basis for planning curriculum.

- write a block plan and lesson plan for one week of a program.

## Terms to Know

program goals

content and process-centered approach

direct learning experience

indirect learning experience

field-sensitive

field-independent

visual learner

auditory learner

theme

spiral curriculum

flowchart

concept

block plan

lesson plan

learning objective

motivation

closure

Reading a story, feeding a bunny, singing songs, and playing outdoors are all parts of the curriculum. Cooking, scribbling on paper, building with blocks, and playing in the dramatic play corner are also considered the curriculum. The curriculum includes all the activities, materials, and equipment used, 17-1. Even room arrangements reflect the curriculum.

A good early childhood curriculum is based on how children develop and learn. It consists of a wide range of concepts, experiences, and materials designed to meet the developmental needs of a group of children. These needs include their

17-1 Age-appropriate play materials such as these lacing beads should be part of the curriculum.

social, emotional, physical, and cognitive needs. It involves determining what children need to be able to do and what they need to know. A good curriculum also focuses on children's learning styles and characteristics. It often organizes important concepts into themes.

A good curriculum tailors learning experiences to children's ages and stages of development. It also requires detailed planning. This chapter will describe the factors to consider when planning a curriculum.

## Developing Program Goals

Before the curriculum can be planned, the goals of the center's program need to be determined. In an early childhood program, the program goals outline the philosophy of the center. **Program goals** are broad statements of purpose that state the desired end results—what is to be achieved. Some people describe goals as the "why" of the curriculum.

Program goals based on child development focus on the whole child. Goals for children in an early childhood setting might include the following:

- To develop a positive self-concept and attitude toward learning.
- To develop independence.
- To think critically and develop problem-solving skills, 17-2.
- To respect and understand cultural diversity.
- To develop effective language skills, both listening and speaking.
- To develop fine motor coordination.
- To develop gross motor coordination.
- To develop personal initiative.
- To develop a curiosity about the world.
- To develop positive social skills, including cooperation and inter-dependence.
- To develop respect for one's own rights as well as the rights of others.
- To develop an understanding of the relationship between people, events, and objects.

Each of these goals is broad. The goals include all four areas of development since a developmentally appropriate curriculum considers the whole child.

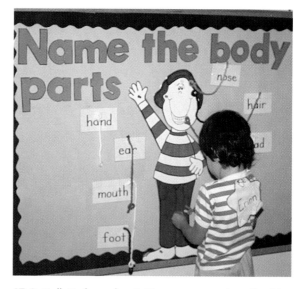

17-2 Bulletin board activities are a good method to teach problem-solving skills.

## Meeting Goals

Teachers, available resources, activities, and the environment all influence whether goals will be met. For example, if one of the goals is to create independence, provide children with a minimum of help. This gives children many opportunities to grow in independence. Classroom activities should require little involvement on the part of the teacher. Children should be able to participate in most activities without an adult's help. The activities, then, will need to match children's skill levels.

The classroom environment, including room arrangement, can also foster the development of independence. Placing coat hooks, paper towels, tables, chairs, and equipment within children's reach is helpful. This allows the children to act on their own. They do not have to depend on teachers for help at all times.

## Who Plans the Curriculum?

Curriculum development can involve one person or several staff members. In small centers, the head teacher is often the person in charge of planning the curriculum, 17-3. Teachers have firsthand knowledge of their children's interests, needs, learning styles, and prior experiences. In

17-3 Using a self-planned curriculum allows teachers to create their own games for the children.

some centers, a wide range of additional people are involved in the process. Directors, teachers, aides, parents, and in some cases even the center cook may all be included at some time. Each of these people can provide helpful information in planning the curriculum. In large organizations, a curriculum specialist may be hired to help plan the curriculum.

The child care director usually plays a key role in curriculum development. In most centers, the director is in charge of supervising all center activities. Therefore, the director's position usually includes curriculum supervision.

Some child care chains provide the directors of their centers with preplanned curriculum units. Each director is responsible for introducing the curriculum to the teaching staff. After modifying it to fit the children's needs, the teachers are expected to use the curriculum.

A preplanned curriculum has both advantages and disadvantages. For a staff with little

training or experience, a preplanned curriculum can be helpful. Activities, procedures, and suggestions are often outlined in detail. Having these curriculum ideas at their fingertips saves teachers time and energy.

A preplanned curriculum has some disadvantages. It may not factor in the individual differences and learning styles of the children in your program. The curriculum needs to be based on the learners' abilities so it can build on what the children already know. Experienced teachers may feel stifled or limited by a preplanned curriculum. Because of their experience, they are more likely to observe a mismatch between children's needs and the curriculum. If this happens, experienced teachers are likely to feel frustrated.

## Assessment: An Important Step in Curriculum Planning

Every child is unique, even though there are many similarities within age groups. For this reason, assessment is necessary in order to plan a curriculum that is both individualized and age appropriate for all areas of learning.

The assessment process should provide you with useful information for planning a curriculum. The first assessment supplies data on what the children already know and what skills they have achieved. This data can help you fit curriculum to individual children. It can also be helpful for informing parents of their children's progress over a period of time.

Assessment should be based on the children's activities at the center. It should highlight what the children know and what they can do. It should include collections of the children's work, such as artwork, stories, and projects. Teachers' observations and summaries may also be included.

## The Content and Process-Centered Curriculum

Though there are a number of approaches to curriculum planning, the most popular method is the **content and process-centered approach**. Learning is seen as a constant process of exploring and questioning the environment. A hands-on curriculum is stressed. All four areas of child development—social, emotional, physical, and cognitive—are included. A wide range of age-appropriate materials, supplies, and experiences are used to enrich the environment, 17-4. Materials and equipment are matched to the children's abilities, cultural background, and development.

Basic learning materials are a key part of the content and process-centered curriculum. These materials are chosen and structured by the teacher. They may include puzzles, games, blocks, sand, water, books, records, and supplies for dramatic play and science study.

The physical environment is carefully planned and prepared with the content for learning. It should be based on an assessment of children's developmental needs and interests. Once established, the children assume responsibility by choosing most of their own activities. As a result, the use of time, space, and equipment is largely determined by the children.

17-4 In this process-centered environment, a child learns more about firefighters by trying on a firefighter's outfit.

A good curriculum includes direct and indirect learning experiences. **Direct learning experiences** are planned with a specific goal in mind. For instance, a carpentry learning activity may be planned to develop fine motor skills and to teach the use of safety goggles. The room arrangement may be planned to foster the independence needed for this task and call attention to the activity.

**Indirect learning experiences** occur on the spur of the moment. For example, while watching Reina, Dwayne may learn how to button his coat. Shelly may learn how to paint by watching Mark. While mixing paint, Kelsie may learn that adding red paint to blue paint makes purple paint.

# Factors to Consider in Curriculum Planning

As you begin planning a curriculum, there are a number of important factors to keep in mind. You must first decide what information should be covered. There are three important questions to ask as the content of the curriculum is determined. The learning activities selected need to be balanced. In addition, various learning styles and learning characteristics need to be considered.

## Choose the Information to Cover

As you begin planning the curriculum, you must decide what information to cover. Three basic questions can help you with this process. First, consider the question: Is the information worth knowing? In order to answer this question, think about the cultural context. In some societies a certain learning outcome may be important. Ask yourself if the outcome will help the child better cope with his or her surroundings.

Children in the United States at some point must learn to read. Our culture places great importance on reading. As a result, children are read many stories in child care centers. Through listening, children learn to enjoy and appreciate literature. In an illiterate society, these skills would not be needed. Other skills important to that culture would be stressed.

A second question needs to be answered: Is the information testable? In other words, the child should be able to see firsthand that the information is true, 17-5. Many times, teachers choose activities based on personal appeal. They like the activity. For instance, activities related to dinosaurs have long been included in the curriculum of many child care centers. Think about the activity based on this question. Will children ever see a live dinosaur? This activity is not testable. Another activity might be more appropriate. Instead of reading a book about dinosaurs, choose one about an animal children know about or may have a chance to see at the zoo.

Here is another example. If you were going to do a unit on foods, making butter would be a testable activity. To begin this activity, tell the children that cream can be made into butter. Then show the children the consistency of cream. After this, give each child a container filled with whipping cream. Show them how to shake the container. Tell the children to keep shaking until the mixture becomes thick. After the cream has turned to butter, let each child taste the butter. This will help them test their knowledge.

The third basic question remains: Is the information developmentally appropriate? A learning activity that requires giving scissors and paper to three- and four-year-olds is appropriate. Children this age can use scissors properly. This activity would be inappropriate for children 18 to 24 months old.

Reading the book *Little Red Riding Hood* might also be inappropriate. You may find that even some five-year-olds are not ready for this book. Many preschool children cannot separate fantasy from reality. As a result, this book could produce fear.

## Balance Learning Activities

An appropriate curriculum contains a balance of learning activities supporting all developmental domains. These activities must be chosen with care. Activities that keep children busy are not always the best activities. Likewise, just because children prefer a certain activity does not mean it must be kept included in the curriculum. You must evaluate each activity to be sure it is right for the children.

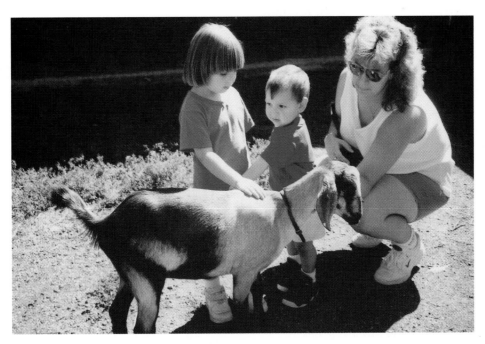

17-5 Information on goats is testable if children can see and touch a goat.

A good curriculum includes a balance of structured as well as unstructured learning activities. Examples of unstructured activities include blockbuilding, collages, water play, and sand play. Children should spend most of their time in self-initiated play with unstructured activities. This type of play allows them opportunities to practice newly developed skills.

Structured, or close-ended, learning activities also need to be included. These activities indirectly prescribe children's actions. Stringing beads, working puzzles, and cooking are all examples.

Whenever possible, also plan a balance of indoor and outdoor learning activities, 17-6. The climate in your area will determine whether this is possible. During extremely hot and cold weather, the children should remain indoors. When this happens, provide children with gross motor activities appropriate for indoors.

In warmer climates, weather permitting, many indoor learning activities can be moved outdoors. Painting, water play, and story and music time can all be done outdoors.

Active and quiet learning activities must be balanced. Planning too many active learning activities in a row may overstimulate some children. The result can be chaotic. To prevent this, follow active learning activities with quiet ones. For example, outdoor activity followed by a story and small group would be a good balance.

Too many quiet learning activities in a row also have a drawback. Children will get restless. The results can be just as chaotic as too many active learning activities. Children may lose interest in the activities and begin to wiggle and talk out of turn.

## Consider Learning Styles

When planning activities for young children, consider the diversity of individual learning styles. Basic learning styles include field-sensitive, field-independent, visual learner, and auditory learner.

### Field-Sensitive

**Field-sensitive** children like to work with others, 17-7. In a group setting, they are helpful. They will volunteer and assist others in picking up blocks, setting the table, and finding a place for a puzzle piece. Field-sensitive children will also try to gain your attention.

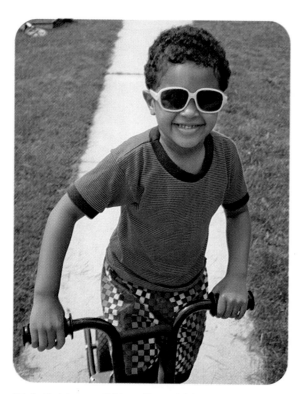

17-6 Outdoor activities allow children to get fresh air and work off excess energy.

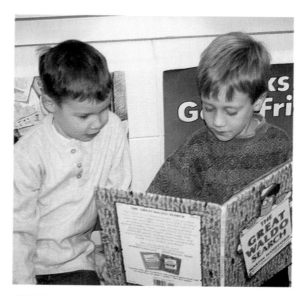

17-7 Field-sensitive children enjoy playing with others.

When introduced to a new activity, field-sensitive children want a model to follow. They may ask to be shown how to do the activity. If there is not a model or demonstration, they may wait. When someone else begins, they will observe. After this observation, they will begin their work.

### Field-Independent

**Field-independent** children like to try new activities. They enjoy discovery. These children do not have to be urged to try new activities. In most cases, they will be the first to try new activities. Children who are field-independent will rarely contact the teacher for help. They enjoy engaging in new tasks without directions or assistance from the teacher.

Field-independent children prefer to work on their own, 17-8. However, they enjoy competition as well as individual recognition. Field-independent children are also task orientated. When engaged in an activity, they generally do not notice what is going on around them.

### Visual Learners

**Visual learners** depend a great deal on the sense of sight. These children notice small changes in the environment. When a plant is added to the science table, they are the first to notice. Visual learners enjoy looking at books and other objects.

### Auditory Learners

**Auditory learners** are those who learn best through hearing. These children are the first to hear a fly in the classroom or a snowplow outdoors. You will find that auditory learners enjoy listening. To meet their needs, music, stories, and poems need to be included in the curriculum.

You may find that learning styles vary from program to program. That is, last year more children might have been field-independent, while this year more children are field-sensitive. The number of children who are primarily visual learners may also vary from year to year. This information is important for planning a program that relates to the children's learning styles.

Most children use a combination of senses. That is, they use both visual and auditory input to learn. To provide for these children's needs, plan activities that involve several senses, 17-9. For example, while reading a book, also show the

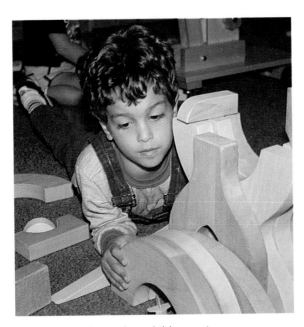

17-8 Field-independent children enjoy working alone.

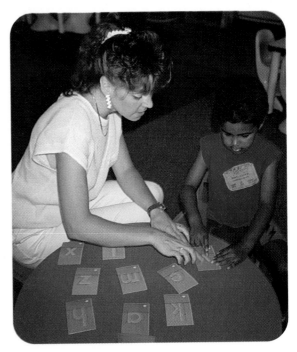

17-9 Showing and talking about a new activity appeals to a child's visual and auditory senses.

pictures. Using this method, children should retain more knowledge. They will also find activities more satisfying.

## Consider Learning Characteristics

The children in each classroom have a wide range of learning characteristics. Some work slowly and others quickly. Some children are attentive, and others bore easily. Some are quick decision makers, while others take more time.

Evaluate children's learning characteristics in relation to your own. If you work quickly, keep this in mind as you plan the curriculum. When demonstrating for children, slow down so

they can understand concepts. Avoid reading or talking too fast.

Use caution when planning group learning activities. If Joey works extremely slow and Tommy works quickly, being in the same group may be frustrating for both. It is better to place children with others who work at the same pace.

Some children have long attention spans. They are able to pay attention and sit still for long periods of time. Other children, however, are easily distracted. To hold the interests of these children, plan novel and interesting group activities. For instance, during story time use a variety of teaching methods. During one week, use at least three types of media. Flannel board

### Activities for a Puppet Theme

**Fine Motor Development**
Handling puppets.
Making puppets.
- Paper bag puppets.
- Peanut puppets.
- Sock puppets.
- Paper plate puppets.
- Stick puppets.
- Milk carton puppets.
- Spoon puppets.

**Art**
Designing and making puppets.

**Social Studies**
Attending a marionette show.

**Language, Storytelling, and Dramatic Play**
Telling a story using a puppet.
Putting on a puppet show.
Telling a shadow puppet story.
Learning new vocabulary related to puppets.
Looking at pictures of puppets at group time.
Setting up a puppet stage with a variety of
    puppets.

**Sensory Table**
Provide a variety of puppets made from
    different materials.

17-10  A brainstorming session among several teachers yielded this list of activities for a puppet theme.

figures, flipcharts, puppets, draw and tell charts, and videotapes could all be used to tell a story.

Children also make decisions in different ways. Some children are quick to make decisions. This type of decision making is called *impulsive*. When given the chance, impulsive decision makers act immediately.

Other children are slower to make decisions. This type of decision making is called *cautious*. These children approach a new activity carefully. They study the environment before they begin.

Remember that not all children complete activities in the same amount of time. Children move and learn at different rates. As a teacher, you will need to be aware of individual learning styles and characteristics when planning the curriculum.

## Themes

As teachers plan their curriculum, they often use themes. A **theme** is one main topic or idea around which the classroom activities are planned. Connecting activities through the use of a theme allows children to build upon previous learning. It helps them build connections and reinforce what they've learned. Successful themes take the children's age, abilities, and interests into consideration. Also consider the time of the year and the availability of supportive resources. Be sure the theme includes some hands-on activities.

Once a theme is chosen, the activities can be developed, 17-10. The number and types of activities will vary with the theme. For example, a theme on apples may include a trip to an orchard. A bulletin board might show the three colors of apples. Books such as *Johnny Appleseed* could be read at group time.

An apple theme also lends itself to cooking. Applesauce, baked apples, apple muffins, and apple butter could be made. An art activity might be making apple prints from sponges cut in the shape of apples. Lotto games could be made using the three colors of apples. Apples of various sizes and colors could be placed on the science table. These can be cut apart and studied under a microscope. Chart 17-11 lists other examples of themes.

Very seldom do the majority of the activities

| Examples of Themes | | | |
|---|---|---|---|
| Alphabet Letters | Costumes | Friends | Seasons |
| Animals | Directions | The Garden | Fall |
|   Farm Animals | Exercise |   Flowers | Spring |
|   Flying Animals | Fantasy and Reality |   Plants | Summer |
|   Pets | Fairy Tales |   Trees | Winter |
|   Water Animals | The Family | Gestures | Shadows |
|   Zoo Animals |   Mother | Hats | Shapes and Sizes |
| Books |   Father | Health | Signs and Pictures |
| Boxes and Containers |   Sisters | Holidays and Celebrations | Telephones |
| Brushes and Brooms |   Brothers | Homes | Toys |
| Bugs |   Grandparents | Hospitals | Transportation and Travel |
| Camping |   Aunts | How I Care for Myself |   Land |
| The Circus |   Uncles | The Library |   Water |
| Clothes |   Cousins | Machines |   Air |
| Colors | The Five Senses | Measuring | Watches and Clocks |
| Community Helpers | Feelings | Money | Water |
|   Doctors | Foods | Music | We Act |
|   Firefighters |   Fruit Group | Our Town | Weather and |
|   Nurses |   Grain Group | The Newspaper |   Temperature |
|   Police Officers |   Meat Group | Numbers and Counting | We Create |
|   Postal Workers |   Milk Group | Puppets | We Dance |
| Computers |   Vegetable Group | Safety | We Sing |
| Cooking and Baking |   Fats and Sweets Group | | Wheels |

17-11 Themes can come from all segments of children's environments.

that are planned relate to the theme. Some themes will have more related resources than others. Stories and bulletin board displays are the only two activities that nearly always relate to the theme.

## Theme Ideas

As a rule, certain themes appeal to certain age groups, 17-12. Very young children's interests center on their immediate surroundings. As children grow, their circle of interests becomes larger, like a spiral. A curriculum based on this concept is called a **spiral curriculum**.

Two-year-old children are interested in their immediate world. Themes such as sight, sound, touch, taste, and smell are appealing to them. Families, colors, shapes, pets, farm animals, and foods are also good themes for two-year-olds. For each classroom area, plan a variety of activities that relate to the theme you choose. This will keep the young children interested.

Three-year-old children are interested in their families. However, they are becoming interested in their neighbors and their community. Themes based on the supermarket, bakery, library, post office, fire station, and police station are of special interest to these children. Their interests are growing in the spiral outside of their immediate surroundings.

Themes related to animals are also enjoyed by three- and four-year-olds. These themes can focus on groups of animals. Groups might include farm, forest, water, and zoo animals. Bugs, birds, dogs, and cats can also have appeal for these young children.

Four- and five-year-old children enjoy themes related to a wider variety of topics. Themes can be grouped into a few broad categories. For instance, broad themes might include *My World, Things I Like to Do, Things that Move,* and *Transportation.*

These categories could be broken down to contain a few sub-themes. *My School, My Home, My Feelings,* and *My Family* are just a few examples of sub-themes in *My World.*

### Holiday Themes

Use caution when planning holiday themes for children. Preschool children lack a clear concept of time. If a holiday theme is introduced too early, children may become too excited. For instance, if Halloween is introduced the first week of October but does not actually happen until four weeks later, children will become confused. They will not know when to expect Halloween.

The activities planned around holiday

| A Spiral Curriculum | | |
|---|---|---|
| **Themes for Two- and Three-Year-Olds** | | |

| | | |
|---|---|---|
| All About Me | Concepts I'm Learning |  |
| I'm Me, I'm Special | Big/Little | |
| My Family | Up/Down | |
| My Friends | Soft/Hard | |
| My Home | Wet/Dry | |
| My Toys | Things That Go | |
| My Senses | Cars and Trucks | |
| Foods I Eat | Trains | |
| Colors in My World | Boats | |
| Shapes I See | Airplanes | |
| Circles | Animals in My World | |
| Squares | Dogs | |
| Triangles | Cats | |
| Rectangles | Farm Animals | |
| Hearts | Zoo Animals | |

17-12  Children's interests widen as they get older. Study this chart for evidence of the spiral curriculum concept.

(Continued)

## A Spiral Curriculum

### Themes for Three- and Four-Year-Olds

People in My World
  My Family
  My Friends
  Police Officers
  Firefighters
  Bakers
  Meat Cutters
  Librarians
  Printers
  Medical Doctors
  Nurses
  Pharmacists
  Ambulance Attendants
  Bankers
  Chefs
  Waiters and Waitresses
  Musicians
  Hair Stylists
  Photographers
  Artist
  House Painter

Zookeeper
Postal Worker
Office Workers
Computer
  Programmers
Clerks
Sanitary Engineers
Pilots and Flight
  Attendants
Gas Station Attendants
Auto Mechanics
Painters
Carpenters
Plumbers
Farmers
Florists
All About Me
  My Senses
  My Feelings
  My Home
  My School

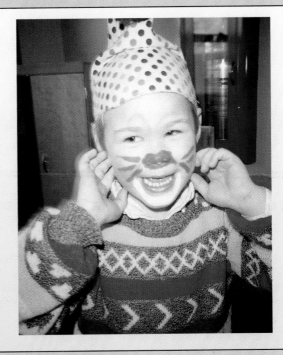

### Themes for Four- and Five-Year-Olds

My Body
  Good Health
  Exercise
  Nutrition
Communication
  Speaking
  Listening
  Reading
  Puppets
  Acting
  Writing
  Radio
  Television
  Computers
Fairy Tales
My World
  Pets
  Plants

Flowers
  Insects and Spiders
  Seeds
Safety
Transportation
  Air
  Land
  Water
Tools at Work
  Gardening
  Carpentry
  Mechanics
  Cosmetology
  Dentistry
  Art

17-12  Continued.

themes are also often quite stimulating for children. If this excitement goes on for weeks, behavior problems could arise. More guidance will be needed. Some teachers prefer to integrate holidays into broader themes. They may include Thanksgiving in a celebration theme, Valentine's Day in a friends theme, or Halloween in a costumes theme.

Children's attention spans, needs, interests, and available resources are major factors affecting theme length.

Some themes can be carried out for a month or longer. A community helpers theme could go on for months by featuring many different community helpers.

## Developing Themes Using Flowcharts

An effective method for developing themes is to use resource books. To make this possible, many centers have a set of encyclopedias to use as references for background information. After using this resource, a flowchart can be drawn. A **flowchart** outlines major concepts related to a theme.

Drawing a flowchart is a simple method for listing concepts related to a theme. For example, when developing a theme on puppets, consult a resource. List all concepts you might include, 17-13. The major headings in a puppet flowchart could be *vocabulary*, *movement*, *types*, *stages*, *materials*, and *characterization*.

After drawing up a flowchart, writing objectives is the next step. Study the flowchart for objectives that can be developed. For instance, based on the flowchart in Chart 17-13, children might be expected to

- identify the six types of puppets.
- develop skill in moving puppets with rods, wires, strings, and hands.
- enjoy a puppet show.
- learn new vocabulary words: marionette, shadow, and dummy.

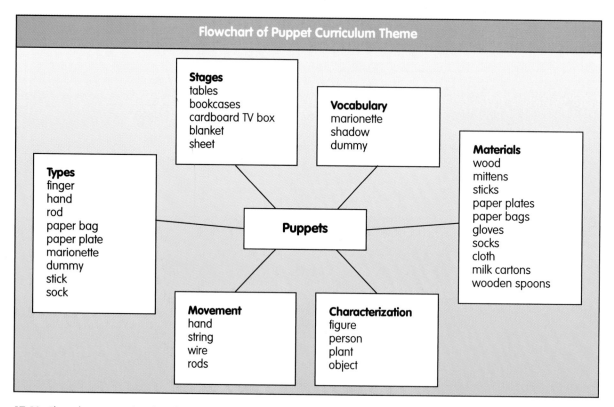

17-13 Flowcharts can be developed using resources such as encyclopedias.

- construct puppets from a variety of materials.
- express their own thoughts and feelings using puppets.
- practice using a puppet behind a puppet stage.

## Concepts Based on the Theme

Curriculum themes are an important vehicle for helping children form concepts. A **concept** is a generalized idea or notion. Learning basic concepts helps the children to understand their world. By forming concepts, children learn to group experiences in a meaningful way.

Concepts can be developed around a theme. To do this, review your flowchart, then write the concepts. For instance, if your theme is birds, concepts might include the following:

- There are many kinds of birds.
- Some birds are pets.
- Birds hatch from eggs.
- Most birds fly.
- Birds live in nests, trees, houses, and cages.
- Birds have a head, body, wings, a beak, and feathers.

# Written Plans

After considering your curriculum approach, theme, concepts, and activities, written plans need to be developed. Many centers require two types of written plans. A **block plan** is an overall view of the curriculum. It outlines the general plans. A **lesson plan** is more detailed than a block plan. It outlines specific actions and activities that will be used to meet goals and objectives.

## Block Plan

A block plan is key to planning a balanced curriculum. Without this written block plan, curriculum areas may be overlooked. You may think these areas were covered, but without a written record, you cannot be sure.

A block plan usually includes days of the week, time periods, and scheduled activities. Figure 17-14 shows a sample block plan.

Block plans should be kept on file. They can be used as a reference to review what has happened during the year. The plans also contain a variety of activities that may be used in future years, if appropriate.

To write a block plan, follow these steps:
1. Review your program goals.
2. Review your observations and assessment of the children.
3. Note the children's interests.
4. Consider the availability of your resources.
5. Select a theme.
6. Develop concepts.
7. Select activities and record them on the block plan.

## Lesson Plans

Lesson plans are more detailed than block plans. While a block plan gives just the title of a book, a lesson plan provides step-by-step directions for sharing the book. Figure 17-15 contains a sample lesson plan. Lesson plans contain the following:

- Developmental goals
- Learning objective
- Concepts
- Materials needed
- Motivation
- Procedures
- Closure/transition
- Evaluation

### Developmental Goals

Developmental goals are statements that tell the "why" of the activity. They are more specific than program goals. Examples of goals for cooking applesauce with a group of four-year-olds are shown in the sample lesson plan in 17-15. To write developmental goals for a lesson plan, think carefully about each activity. Ask yourself, "What can the children learn from this experience?" Then write the lesson plan, as outlined above, including all the learning involved.

### Learning Objective

A **learning objective** describes the expected outcome of an activity. Objectives are used to plan teaching strategies. There are three

## Morning Session: 2-Year-Olds

Week ___ August 27-31 ___   Theme ___ My School ___

| | 9:00-10:10 Free Play/Centers | 10:10-10:25 Large Group | 10:25-10:40 Snack | 10:40-11:00 Small Groups #1 | #2 | #3 | 11:00-11:30 Outdoors |
|---|---|---|---|---|---|---|---|
| **Monday** | • water colors<br>• water & toys in sensory table<br>• tunnel<br>• tennis shoes color match game | My Nursery School story cards / If You're Happy & You Know It | crackers<br>tomato juice | stringing beads | table blocks | stringing beads | • sand toys |
| **Tuesday** | • crayons and markers<br>• goop in sensory table<br>• driving wheel<br>• tuff blocks | Short walk around the neighborhood | banana<br>milk | table blocks | stringing beads | table blocks | • balls |
| **Wednesday** | • play dough<br>• styrofoam pieces in sensory table<br>• balance beam<br>• color clowns | Little Red Wagon song / My Nursery School | apple & cheese<br>milk | book: Where Is It? by Tana Hoban | puzzles | feely box | • painting with water |
| **Thursday** | • soap flake finger painting<br>• water in sensory table<br>• rocking boat | Tour of school / "Little Red Wagon" | veggies & dip<br>milk | feely box | Where Is It? | puzzles | • bubbles |
| **Friday** | • roller painting<br>• sand in sensory table<br>• crawling cubes | If You're Happy and You Know It / Tour of school | peanut butter & crackers<br>milk | puzzles | feely box | Where Is It? | • rocking boat |

17-14 This block plan is for a group of two-year-olds. Notice the theme and the large group activities related to it.

## A Sample Lesson Plan

**Date**: 9/21              **Time**: 10:00 A.M.
**Group**: 4-year-olds
**Activity**: Cooking Experience—Applesauce

**Developmental Goals**:
- To practice following directions.
- To develop cooking safety habits.
- To practice using a knife as a tool.
- To practice personal hygiene by washing hands before and after cooking experience.
- To observe the beauty of an apple.
- To learn the parts of an apple: seed, core, flesh, skin, and stem.
- To taste the ingredients in applesauce.
- To taste cooked apples.
- To observe the changes in texture and color when heat is applied to the apples.

**Learning objective:**
Given apples, knives, measuring cup and spoons, a bowl, a mixing spoon, a microwave oven, sugar, cinnamon, and a recipe chart, the children will help peel apples, measure the ingredients, and prepare applesauce.

**Materials needed:**

6   peelers
12  apples
    recipe chart
    water
2   cups of sugar
3   tablespoons of cinnamon

measuring cup and spoon
kettle
bowl
mixing spoon
microwave oven

**Motivation/introduction:**
Set up the housekeeping area with recipe chart, cooking utensils, and tray with food. Ask "What can we make from apples?" Listen to responses. Tell the children "Today we are going to make applesauce."

**Procedure:**
1. Tell the children to wash their hands.
2. Review the recipe chart step by step.
3. Cut an apple in half. Show the children the parts of an apple: seed, core, flesh, skin, and stem.
4. Demonstrate how to use a peeler as a tool, stressing safety.
5. Pass out apples and peelers, again explaining safety.
6. Encourage children to observe and feel the apples.
7. Peel apples.
8. When apples are peeled, focus children's attention back to recipe chart. Proceed by following directions step by step until the mixture is ready for a heat source.
9. Discuss each of the ingredients, allowing children to taste them, if they wish.
10. Ask individuals to measure the sugar, cinnamon, and water.
11. Direct children's attention to the applesauce as it cooks. Clarify the process by asking questions such as How are apples different?
12. Serve the applesauce as a snack.

**Closure/transition:**
Assign cleanup tasks to the children. Have the children wash their hands. Tell the children the applesauce will be eaten at snack time. Then prepare the children for outdoor play.

**Evaluation:**

17-15 Lesson plans contain much more detail than block plans. Notice all the details needed to write a lesson plan for cooking applesauce.

---

**Learning Objectives**

**Conditions of Performance**: States the conditions under which the child will perform.
 Given a three-piece puzzle...
 Given crayons and a pencil...
 Given a set of blocks...
 Without the aid of a teacher...
 Given farm animals...
 After listening to the story...

**Behavior**: States what the child will be able to do.
 ...the child will cut...
 ...the child will draw...
 ...the child will construct...
 ...the child will sing...
 ...the child will match...
 ...the child will climb...
 ...the child will jump...
 ...the child will skip...
 ...the child will stack......
 ...the child will retell...

**Level of Performance**: States the minimum level of achievement.
 ...four inches...
 ...all...
 ...at least three feet...
 ...two out of three times...
 ...within a five minute period...

17-16 Studying these parts of learning objectives will help you write effective objectives.

---

parts to learning objectives. These parts are the conditions of performance, the behavior, and the level of performance. Figure 17-16 includes examples of each part of the behavioral objective.

The *conditions of performance* list what materials, equipment, or tools the child will use. Included could be puzzles, paper, scissors, beads, or any other materials and equipment found in early childhood settings. The conditions of performance can also include what the child will be denied. For example, they may need to construct a puzzle without the aid of a teacher.

*Behaviors* refer to any visible activities done by the child. It tells what the child will be doing. When choosing behaviors, avoid words that are open to many interpretations. To *know, understand, enjoy, believe,* and *appreciate* are all words that can mean many things. For instance, how will you judge if a child understands? Useful words for writing learning objectives are listed in 17-17.

The *level of performance* states the minimum standard of achievement. It should note how well you want the child to do. The level of performance many times is understood. Therefore, it is not always included as part of the objective.

---

**Behaviors for Objectives**

| | | | | |
|---|---|---|---|---|
| answer | dry | measure | remove | take |
| arrange | feed | mix | replace | tap |
| ask | find | move | return | taste |
| brush | finish | name | roll | tell |
| button | follow | open | run | throw |
| catch | follow directions | organize | say | tie |
| choose | group | paint | select | touch |
| clap | hit | paste | separate | turn |
| climb | hold | pick | sequence | use |
| close | jump | peel | show | use two hands |
| collect | label | place | sing | wait |
| color | list | point to | sit | wash |
| construct | locate | pour | skip | weigh |
| count | look at | print | solve | wipe |
| cut | make motions | put hand on | sort | write |
| describe | mark | put in order | stack | zip |
| draw | match | recall | stand | |

17-17 Learn to use concrete terms such as these when stating learning objectives.

## Materials

Under the materials section of the lesson plan, list everything that is needed for the activity. For example, if you are going to make instant pudding, include milk, pudding mix, bowl, wire whisk, spoon, scraper, and measuring cup. If you are going to do a finger painting activity, list paint, paper, aprons, and wet sponge.

## Motivation

**Motivation** describes how you will gain the children's attention. The best devices are items that interest the children. A picture of a cat may be used as motivation before reading a story about cats. Motivation devices include pictures, puppets, alphabet letters, tapes, resource people, cards, artwork, photographs, animals, stuffed toys, clothing, and masks.

## Procedures

The procedures section resembles a cookbook. Simple, step-by-step directions should be provided. The directions should be in order. If needed, number each step to remember the order. Each of the developmental goals should be included in the procedures. For example, if a goal is to have each child taste the ingredients, this should be a step in the procedures. An example of procedures for an activity is shown in 17-18. The sample lesson plan also contains procedures.

## Closure/Transition

**Closure** refers to how an activity will end. It might include clean-up tasks or sampling of food items at snack time. Transition refers to the movement from one activity to another. In some cases, closure and transition are the same task. For example, at the end of a creative drama activity, you may ask the children to walk like heavy elephants to the snack table.

## Evaluation

A staff who provides a quality early childhood program is continually evaluating the curriculum. In some centers, time is set aside every day for this purpose. Many child care centers, however, do not have the resources to do this with the entire staff. Instead, staff members will evaluate the activities they conducted on their

---

**Procedure Chart**

**Activity: Visual perception** (This type of activity encourages children to see fine differences between and among objects.)

1. Place individual cards face down on the table.
2. Provide each child with one game board.
3. Demonstrate how to play the game, stressing the importance of taking turns.
4. Ask one child to begin by choosing a card from the middle of the table.
5. After the child has drawn the card, ask "Do you have an object like that on your board?"
6. If the object does not match, instruct the child to return the card to the center of the table, face down.
7. Continue with the next player until one child has filled all of the game board spaces.

17-18  Using a procedure chart, you should cover each step of an activity.

---

own. This process involves three steps: (1) evaluating the learning experience, (2) evaluating the children and their responses, and (3) evaluating your own teaching strategies.

When evaluating the learning experiences, ask yourself whether the activity was proper for the age group. If, for example, children had trouble cutting paper there could be several reasons for the trouble. Were the scissors in good repair? Scissors with dried glue on the cutting edge will not cut properly. Left-handed children need left-handed scissors. Paper thickness could also be a problem. Children who are learning to cut need lightweight paper and proper tools.

Successful learning activities give children the chance to test their knowledge. For example, children will learn more about making applesauce by taking part in the activity than if they only watched an adult make it.

Your teaching skills only have meaning if the children learn. Therefore, it is important to study the children and their responses to activities and to you. First, see that the children reach the objective. If they do not, think through the activity. Ask yourself what you could have done differently. Likewise, if there were behavior problems, try to find the cause.

Lack of organization, you will find, can affect the outcome of an activity. If you forget some of the ingredients for a cooking activity, leaving the group to gather them could affect outcomes. During your absence, some child may start to mix the ingredients. The product may not turn out if the ingredients were not measured properly.

Chart 17-19 includes a sample evaluation form for an activity. Your center may have a similar evaluation form, or you can create one using these questions. Completing this form can help you reflect on an activity and evaluate it. After using the form a few times, you may find that you can remember the three parts of the form, including the specific questions. At this point, you may want to start writing your evaluations on index cards. In time, you will be able to go through this process mentally.

At first, you may find the evaluation process time-consuming. You will learn, however, that it is useful. With constant evaluation, you will improve your teaching skills as well as the curriculum.

---

**A Sample Evaluation of an Activity**

**Activity**: Story—"Never Talk to Strangers"
**Group:** Five-year-olds

**I.  The Activity: Selection and Development**
  **A. Was the content (concept) worth knowing?**
    The content is valuable for five-year-old children since it deals with personal safety. With the increased incidence of child abuse, this is an important topic.
  **B. Was it developmentally appropriate?**
    Although fantasy was involved in the story, almost all the children were able to understand the content.
  **C. Was it interesting to the children?**
    All the children but Don listened and responded. During the repetitive sentences, the children repeated, "Never talk to strangers. "
  **D. Did the activity include opportunities for the children to use or "test" their knowledge?**
    After the story, the children were asked questions. These included:
    • Is your grandmother a stranger?
    • Is your neighbor a stranger?
    • Is a man you never saw before a stranger?
  **E. What would you suggest as a follow-up experience?**
    Children's books related to child abuse will be read tomorrow. The game "Good Touch and Bad Touch" will also be introduced.

**II.  The Children: Responses**
  **A. Did all the children reach the objective(s)? If not, why?**
    With the exception of Don, all the children reached the objective.
  **B. Were there behavior problems? If so, do you have any insight as to what caused them?**
    If Don and Ben were separated during the story, Don may have paid attention. Likewise, Ben found Don's behavior disturbing. He tried to move away from him, but another teacher made him sit down.

**III.  The Teacher: Strategies**
  **A. Were you well organized?**
    Yes, the book was placed so I could easily find it. During the outdoor play period, an individual carpet square was laid out for each child. Approximately ten inches were left between each square. This spacing probably helped maintain group control.
  **B. Were you satisfied with the effectiveness of your teaching strategies in reaching the learning objective? If not, why?**
    I should have practiced the story beforehand. In addition, I should have held the book so that all the children could view the pictures.
  **C. Did you effectively guide or manage the group?**
    Yes, with the exception of Don, I managed the group effectively.
  **D. Did you introduce the concepts in a stimulating manner?**
    The cover of the book appealed to the children. After the story, two children asked to have it read again.
  **E. Did you involve the children in the closure of the activity?**
    Yes, I did. The children were involved through a series of questions. Concepts of strangers and safety were both discussed.
  **F. What strategies would you change if you were to repeat this activity?**
    First, I would separate Don and Ben. I would also practice reading the book to myself several times before sharing it. This would make me less dependent on the story lines. As a result, I would feel confident enough to share the pictures with the children.

17-19 Evaluation is the final step in the curriculum development process. It can be used to determine how well your curriculum worked.

## Summary

A good early childhood curriculum is based on how children develop and learn. It consists of a wide range of concepts, experiences, and materials designed to meet the developmental needs of a group of children. Before the curriculum can be planned, the goals of the center's program need to be determined. Program goals focus on the whole child. Assessment is also an important part of curriculum planning. It will identify what the children already know and can do.

The content and process-centered approach to curriculum planning is the method most often used. Learning is seen as a constant process of exploring and questioning the environment. As the curriculum is planned, several factors need to be considered. You first must decide what information you will cover in the curriculum. You will also want to balance the learning activities and consider individual learning styles and characteristics.

Activities are often selected based on a theme. Flowcharts may be used to develop ideas related to the theme. Concepts are formulated for the theme as well. Finally, written plans are developed which include activities for all the classroom activity areas. Both block plans and lesson plans are developed. The final step is evaluation. A staff who provides a quality early childhood program is continually evaluating the curriculum and finding ways to improve their teaching plans.

## Review and Reflect

1. What are program goals?

2. True or false. Curriculum development involves only the teacher who is responsible for the group.

3. List two advantages of a preplanned curriculum.

4. Describe a process-centered approach to curriculum development. Explain how materials and environment relate to this approach.

5. How do direct and indirect learning experiences differ?

6. List three questions to ask when choosing the information to cover.

7. _____ children like to work with others and often volunteer to help.

8. _____ children like to try new activities and work on their own.

9. _____ learners enjoy looking at books and other objects.

10. _____ learners enjoy activities involving music, stories, and poems.

11. Explain the meaning of spiral curriculum.

12. What is a flowchart?

13. How does a block plan differ from a lesson plan?

14. How do developmental goals and program goals differ?

15. Name the three parts of learning objectives. Explain each of these parts.

16. The _____ section of the lesson plan gives step-by-step directions.

17. When evaluating the success of a specific learning activity, what three steps should you follow?

## Apply and Explore

1. Interview a child care teacher about curriculum planning.

2. Review the flowchart for the puppet theme in Figure 17-13. How would you adapt this flowchart for a group of two-year-olds?

3. Write a lesson plan for preparing pancakes.

4. Write five learning objectives. Exchange papers with classmates and evaluate the learning objectives.

5. Discuss strategies for meeting the program goals given in the chapter.

6. Check the Web site perpetualpreschool.com C for a variety of resources related to curriculum planning, teaching tips, and professional development activities.

# Chapter 18

# Guiding Art, Blockbuilding, and Sensory Experiences

After studying this chapter, you will be able to

- explain how art experiences promote physical, social, emotional, and cognitive growth.
- describe techniques for guiding art experiences.
- list the stages of art skill development.
- compile a list of art supplies needed for a well-stocked classroom.
- plan a variety of art, blockbuilding, sensory, and woodworking activities suitable for young children.

## Terms to Know

string painting
mono painting
chalk painting
texture painting
salt painting
spice painting
plasticene
collage
bridging

Preschool children are curious about their world. They thrive on hands-on experiences. For them, art activities can be learning opportunities. Using their imaginations, young children can think, plan, and create their own ideas. Their need for movement, self-expression, and achievement is fulfilled by working with modeling materials. While developing basic skills using art media, young children are expressing feelings and ideas.

## The Importance of Art Experiences

Art promotes physical, social, emotional, and cognitive growth in children. Physical growth is promoted through the movements involved in painting, coloring, drawing, scribbling, and playing with clay, 18-1. All these motions improve fine motor skills. Art activities foster motor and hand-eye coordination. In turn, these skills promote growth in other areas.

Social growth is promoted by art. Children learn responsibility. For example, they learn that they must put on their smocks before painting. They also learn that they must put their work in a safe storage space when they are finished. Learning to work and share with others is stressed. In many programs, several children will share one container of paint or a box of crayons. They learn to respect the property of others. They also learn to value the work and ideas of others.

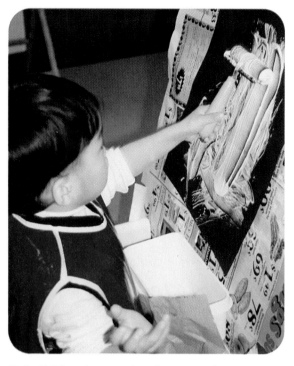

18-1 Children improve hand-eye coordination during art activities that use small muscles.

## Techniques for Guiding Art Experiences

As a caregiver, you must be creative in your approach to art. You must observe in order to find new ways to expand children's learning experiences. Creative growth is promoted through careful choice of various art materials and opportunities to create. A good art program allows children to express their ideas. It also provides them with time to experiment and explore new materials and techniques. These experiences should involve all five senses: sight, smell, taste, touch, and hearing.

Helping children during art sessions is an important task. If done properly, children will accept your help. If done improperly, however, children will come to think of you as an intruder. Tasks done for or forced on children often cause tension and displeasure.

To foster independence, start each session by telling the children what supplies and tools are available that day. Encourage them to use the supplies, 18-2. For instance, if they have never worked

Art experiences also promote emotional growth. Through a creative activity, children are allowed to express emotions. For example, pounding at the woodworking bench, hitting play dough, or scribbling with crayons allows angry children to express their frustrations in an acceptable way. Children also have the chance to choose their own activity. For instance, during a painting session children decide what they will paint. Their choices—a pet, a friend, or a flower—are often expressions of their feelings. Through art, they learn to communicate feelings nonverbally.

Finally, the children's cognitive growth is promoted by exploring, experimenting, and problem solving with many materials and tools. Through this process they use the skills of an investigative scientist. They learn important concepts such as color, size, texture, and shape. By manipulating and controlling tools, skills such as drawing and cutting are learned. They learn that cutting takes things apart while taping and stringing helps put materials together. Visual and tactile skills (skills related to sight and touch) are also developed. For example, rolling, rubbing, pounding, and tearing can change how an object looks and feels.

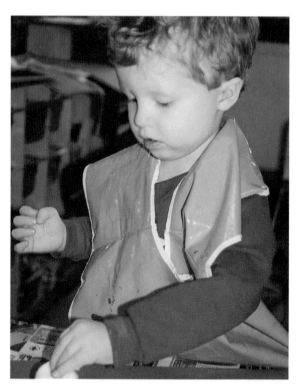

18-2 Devise new supplies to use during sessions and show children how to use them.

with cotton balls, tell them "I think you will enjoy painting with cotton balls. They are very soft."

As you walk through the class, observe what the children are doing. However, it is best not to ask them what they are making. They might just be experimenting with different tools and supplies. In this case, they do not know what they are making. Keep in mind that some children lack the language skills needed to explain their artwork. Asking questions may make them uneasy. Always focus on the process when commenting on the children's art experiences. Your goal is to make the children feel successful and confident. Make comments such as those listed in Figure 18-3.

Let children decide when their work is finished. Take them at their word. Do not urge them to fill up space or add to their work. This decreases their pride and confidence.

Model art appreciation by offering feedback to the children about their work. However, avoid singling out one child's work as being the best. Instead, use praise that invites everyone to respect everyone else's work. For instance, you might say "Mary loves red and blue," or "Mark's colors are happy colors." Hanging the children's work tells them that their work is valued.

In preschool children's artwork, color does not play an important part. Often there is no relationship between the colors chosen and the objects in the artwork. Children choose colors they like as opposed to colors that mirror real life. An apple may be painted bright pink or an elephant red. Studies show children do have color preferences. Beautiful colors, according to young children, include yellow, blue, orange, and green, 18-4. Brown, white, and black are labeled ugly. You may wish to keep a large supply of preferred colors on hand.

18-4  Children prefer painting with bright colors such as yellow and green.

## Stages of Art Skill Development

Children move through three distinct stages as they build art skills. These stages are scribbles, basic forms, and first drawings. Knowing these stages helps child care workers plan activities that reflect children's skill level.

### Scribbles

The first stage in art skills most often occurs between 15 months and 3 years of age. Children's motor control and hand-eye coordination are not well developed yet. However, they can make zigzags, whirls, and circles. In the scribble stage, children do not connect the marks on the paper with their movements. Their scribbles are by-products of the experience. They enjoy the physical sensation of moving a marking tool across the page. See Figure 18-5 to learn how children's drawing movements progress from simple to more complex.

To help children in this stage, make them aware of their movements. Comment on how hard they press their pencils, how fast they move their arms back and forth, or how large they

---

| Commenting on Children's Art |
| --- |
| "You're using a purple crayon." |
| "Your work has interesting lines." |
| "What a nice yellow star you're making." |
| "You must really like green." |
| "That type of brush stroke feels smooth, doesn't it?" |

18-3  Children feel deeply about their artwork; choose your comments carefully.

| Progression of Drawing Movements |
| --- |
| • Dots |
| • Horizontal lines |
| • Vertical lines |
| • Diagonal lines |
| • Curved lines |
| • Multiple lines |
| • Loops |
| • Zigzags |
| • Circles |
| • Crosses |

18-5 A child learns the simple dot movement long before learning to draw crosses.

make their movements. Such remarks help children make the connection between their actions and the art they create.

Comments about the look of children's artwork are also helpful. For example, you may say "This is a long line," or "This line has a curve." As you speak, trace some of the lines with your finger. The children's attention will focus on the form they have created.

## Basic Forms

The second stage in art skill development of children is basic forms. This often occurs between ages three and four. Children learn basic forms such as ovals, rectangles, and circles. They now have more control over their movements and better hand-eye coordination. As a result, they can control the size and shape of a line. During this stage, they are beginning to enjoy their ability to create forms.

At this stage, children also begin to see the connection between their movements and the marks they make. Before this time, children's scribbles were the result of the sheer pleasure of moving their arms and hands. Now children connect those motions to their artwork. Children may even begin to name their drawings at this stage. They also start to feel pride in their work.

As in the scribble stage, you can help the children understand and talk about their work by commenting on their movements. For example, say "You are moving your arm in big circles."

You might describe the end product. Say "You have drawn a big picture."

## First Drawings

The third stage of art development occurs during the fourth and fifth years, 18-6. During this stage, children produce their first real drawings. They attempt to mimic their view of the world. Using their increasing skill with basic forms, they begin to combine shapes to represent objects or people. The drawings are often large. Objects are randomly placed. Color is unrealistic. Crudely drawn human figures with straight lines for arms and legs are common. Later, children often add animals, trees, houses, cars, boats, and airplanes to their artwork.

# Art Supplies and Tools

You have the option of buying or making many of your own art supplies and equipment. Most teachers need to purchase the basic tools: scissors, paintbrushes, cookie cutters, easels, and paper punches. Many of these items can be purchased at school supply stores, catalogs, Web sites, or large discount stores.

18-6 First drawings represent a child's view of the world. Colors are often unrealistic. Notice the sun is blue.

## Tempera Paint

Tempera paint is used in many child care centers. It has a slight odor and tastes chalky. When dry, painted surfaces tend to crack and peel. Tempera can be purchased in both liquid and powdered form. Many teachers prefer liquid over powdered tempera because it does not need to be mixed. Since liquid tempera is much more expensive, however, many teachers still use powdered tempera. Powdered tempera paint is water soluble (dissolves in water). Thickness of the mixed paint varies from a sticky paste to runny fluid. To avoid drips and runs, mix the paint to the consistency of thick cream. Consistency will also affect color.

To reduce costs, many teachers add *bentonite*, a thickening agent, to powdered temper paint. Bentonite can be purchased through landscape and gardening stores. Adding bentonite to powdered paint extends the paint much further.

Some teachers mix enough paint to last for a week or two. Others mix the paint each day. Whichever you prefer, remember to put the powdered paint in the container before you add the liquid. To avoid paint that is too thin, add only a small amount of liquid to the tempera while stirring constantly. This will make a very thick paste. Then slowly add more liquid until you get the desired thickness.

To prepare a large quantity of tempera paint, use the recipe in 18-7. Some teachers prepare paint daily because they are unable to store it. Instead, they make a basic bentonite mixture that can be mixed with any color. The recipe for this mixture is given in 18-8. You will notice that in this recipe, the powdered paint is added to the liquid. This method differs from mixing tempera with a plain liquid (either water or pure bentonite).

## Brushes

Provide children with a number of paintbrushes. They should range in size from ½ - to 1-inch wide. The youngest children should use the widest brushes. As their small muscle coordination improves, they can be given smaller

---

| Tempera Paint |
| --- |
| 7 to 10   tablespoons bentonite |
| A large bowl or jar |
| One-pound can powdered tempera |
| 2   tablespoons soap flakes or detergent |
| 3   cups liquid starch |
| Water |

Place bentonite into large bowl or jar. Add entire can of powdered tempera. Stir in soap flakes/detergent and liquid starch. Add water until desired consistency is obtained.

18-7  This recipe will yield a large amount of one color of tempera paint.

---

| Basic Bentonite Mixture |
| --- |
| ¾   cup powdered detergent |
| 1   cup powdered bentonite |
| 2   quarts water |

Mix all ingredients using a beater or wire whisk. Place mixture into crock or plastic container. Let stand for two or three days. When you are ready to mix paint, remove some basic bentonite mixture from container and add enough tempera to make desired color.

18-8  Use this recipe to make bentonite, a paint extender.

---

brushes. Pieces of string, cotton swabs, sponges, and feathers may be used as paintbrushes by older children.

## Easels

Sturdy, adjustable easels should be provided as a place to paint. Brushes and paint should be placed in an attached tray. Clamps or hooks at the top of the easels should be used to hold the paper in place, 18-9. The easel should be adjusted so that the painting surface is angled or slanted outward. This reduces the dripping and running of paint. Cleanup time is also reduced.

18-9 Easels are useful tools. They can be used to hold paper for painting or drawing activities.

## Crayons, Chalk, and Felt-Tip Markers

Children enjoy using crayons, chalk, and felt-tip markers. However, these items are harder to use than paint. As a rule, these tools need to be pushed hard with small muscles that are not well-developed in young children. Paint, however, flows easily.

Crayons come in regular and kindergarten sizes. Kindergarten-size crayons are round and large. These crayons do not break easily, nor do they roll easily off tables or other surfaces. Crayons can be stored in bowls, baskets, or boxes.

Chalk is available in both an art and chalkboard form. Art chalk comes in a variety of sizes. As with crayons, chalk can be purchased in large, fat sticks. Choose basic colors that are clear and brilliant. Be careful that children do not use art chalk on a chalkboard. Marks from art chalk cannot be erased from a chalkboard. Store chalk in baskets, boxes, trays, or bowls.

Felt-tip markers come with washable or waterproof inks. Always buy washable felt-tip markers for use in child care centers. Be sure that any markers you buy have tight caps. This prevents the markers from drying out. Remind children to replace the caps after use.

## Paper and Painting Surfaces

There are many types of paper and painting surfaces that can be used successfully for art activities. Included are newsprint, manila paper, construction paper, wallpaper, cardboard, and old newspaper. Other alternatives are listed in 18-10.

The least costly paper is newsprint. It is durable and easy to use. Roll ends of newsprint can be bought at little or no cost from local newspaper printers. Cut the large sheets into the size sheets you want. To determine the size of the paper, remember younger children have poorer muscle control. As a result, they need large surfaces on which to paint or draw. A good size for easel painting is 18- by 24-inch sheets.

## Coloring Books

Studies show that coloring books have a negative effect on children's creativity by blocking their creative impulses. For this reason, avoid relying heavily on color books for children under six years old. The value of art as a form of expression is lost when children are limited to designs in a coloring book. Children become self-conscious and doubtful about their art talents. For example, Sara colors in the outline of a kitten in a coloring book. The next time she is asked to draw something, she recalls the perfect kitten from the coloring book page. She knows she could not draw that perfect kitten. She says, "I cannot draw very well."

Some teachers see no harm in using coloring books and feel that their children enjoy working in them. Coloring books are also easy to buy and keep on hand. However, for more enriching art experiences, rely on activities that allow children to explore interesting materials and experience cause and effect.

**Paper Alternatives for Art Activities**

sandpaper

waxed paper

foil

shelf paper

butcher paper

magazines

paper bags

tissue paper

crepe paper

wallpaper

wrapping paper

boxes and tubes

egg cartons

18-10 Paper for use in art activities comes in many forms. Some of these types of paper can be obtained for little or no cost.

## Paste

Library paste works well for adhering lightweight paper. Paste can be prepared or purchased. Many teachers prefer to buy paste by the gallon, which is more economical. Other teachers prefer to prepare their own paste, 18-11. To improve bonding strength, you can add small quantities of glue to your paste. For young children, water-soluble adhesives are the best. They are inexpensive and easy to handle.

## Glue

The best all-purpose adhesive is a white, liquid glue. It can be used on heavyweight paper, cardboard, fabric, plastic, and wood. Glue is more permanent than paste, and often more costly. If purchased by the gallon, it is a better bargain. Many building supply stores carry glue in gallon containers.

**Paste**

1 cup cold water

1 cup flour

2¼ cups boiling water

1 teaspoon powdered alum

¾ teaspoon oil of wintergreen (optional)

Mix the cold water with the flour, stirring until smooth. Continue stirring while adding boiling water. Cook mixture on low heat in a double boiler until smooth. At this time, the mixture should look slightly bluish-gray and shiny. Remove from heat and add oil of wintergreen for an interesting smell. Store in a cool place.

18-11 Making paste is easy and can be a source of budget savings.

Take precautions when using white glue. Glue is difficult to remove from clothes, carpeting, and art tables. Therefore, wipe up spills immediately. Children should wear smocks. Table surfaces should be covered with newspapers. If used, you can provide small squeeze bottles of glue or pour small quantities into shallow pans or jar lids. Wipe the glue bottles immediately after the children are finished using them. Glue cleans up easily while it's still moist. Once it has dried, cleanup is difficult. Use with older preschoolers who are less likely to spill the glue.

## Cleanup Tools

Keep cleanup tools in the art area so they are available when spills occur. Small buckets, sponge mops, and various sizes of sponges are useful. Keep supplies within children's reach. Cut mop handles down so they are child sized. This will encourage children to be responsible for cleaning up.

## Space and Storage

Well-planned space is needed to encourage children to use art areas. Storage and display areas for artwork are part of a well-planned space. Bookshelves can be used to store staple supplies. These supplies include paper, scissors, paste, glue, collage materials, crayons, markers, chalk, tape, and paint.

Containers are needed to store paint, paste, scissors, and collage materials, 18-12. Baby food jars, plastic cups, and plastic bowls are often used to store tempera paint. Shallow dishes, including empty frozen food containers, can be used to hold paint during painting activities. After use, the paint can be covered for storage.

Paste containers may be small enough for one child or large enough for a group to use. The size will depend on the activity. Empty squeeze bottles and baby food jars are useful for individual activities. Foil or small plastic dishes are useful for several children to use together at one time.

Scissors should be stored within easy reach. Special scissor holders may be bought. Scissor

18-12  Store materials in individual containers.

holders can also be made by the staff. Egg cartons, turned upside down, are often used to hold scissors.

Collage materials need to be well-organized to appeal to children. They should be sorted and placed in clear plastic boxes, shoe boxes, plastic dishpans, or baskets. Place these containers on a shelf within eye level of the children.

## Painting Activities

To learn what painting means to young children, listen and watch. You will note that most children find their work pleasing. The artwork of a two-year-old is different than that of a four-year-old. Children's paintings change from simple dots and strokes to crude figures as they move through art development. Some children enjoy moving the tools, 18-13. Other children enjoy the feelings and visual aspects.

Consider some of the children you might meet. Noah, a two-year-old, seems to be fascinated by the painting process. He dips his brush and paints, making large circles over his entire paper. His friend, Renee, delights in moving her brush back and forth. When she dips her brush

18-13 Many children enjoy using different painting tools.

into different colors, she ignores the cleaning process.

Mark, an active three-year-old, makes large dots and zigzags all over his paper. He pays little attention to the paint color but carefully watches his strokes. Heidi, another three-year-old, paints different colors on top of each other. As a result, her paper becomes soaked. At this point, she uses her hand to feel the paint. Then she proceeds to remove her painting from the easel. During this process, it tears. This does not bother Heidi. Like most three-year-olds, she is interested in the process, not the product. She paints one color on top of another and enjoys observing the changes in the layers of colors.

Jon, a highly verbal five-year-old, is comfortable handling the brush. He paints a man by making a circle face. Then he paints straight lines to represent legs. He uses a smaller circle for a mouth, two large round dots for eyes, and a V-shaped figure for a nose. As he paints, he keeps renaming his figure and inventing related stories. First, he tells the child standing next to him that the figure is a police officer. Later, he claims the same figure is a firefighter.

Children like Jon are not unusual. Some comment to themselves as they paint. They appear to be carrying on a conversation with their painting. These comments are useful. They tell you what the child feels and thinks. Sometimes children are eager to discuss their artwork; other times, they are not.

There are many types of painting activities that children will be eager to do. Included are easel, finger, string, texture, salt, mono, spice, and chalk painting. From these experiences, children learn to apply the correct amounts of paint and to recognize color and shapes.

## Easel Painting

Easel painting should be a daily activity in all early childhood programs. Provide an easel, paper, brushes, and paint. Easels should be adjusted to the correct height for the children. Brushes with long handles (about twelve inches) in a variety of sizes should be provided on the easel tray. The size of the paper you give the children will depend on the activity and age of the children. For young children, provide large sheets of newsprint. Sheets of this size will encourage the use of large muscles. On special occasions, you may wish to provide colored paper and white tempera.

To ensure success in easel painting plan the session ahead of time. Provide only a small amount of paint since children often spill. Pour only enough paint to cover the bottom of the container. This will save cleanup time. Make only one color of paint available for early experiences. When a second color is added, provide a brush for each container.

Permit only one child to use each easel. Encourage children to wear smocks. Push long sleeves above their elbows to prevent paint from getting on their clothing.

Teach young children how to use the paintbrush. Gently dip the brush into the paint container, 18-14. Then wipe the brush on the side of the container. This will rid the brush of extra paint. As children gain skill, give them smaller brushes and pieces of paper with which to work. Wash brushes after use. Until they are used again, place them with handles down in a storage container. This allows the bristles to dry.

18-14 Recycle plastic food containers by using them as paint containers.

## Finger Painting

Finger painting is a sensory experience. It promotes expression and release of feelings. It is one of the most satisfying experiences for young children. Some may resist their first experience because they fear getting dirty. These same children, after having the chance to observe, may begin painting with one finger. Later, when they become comfortable, they will use their hands and arms as brushes.

Finger painting requires more supervision than most other painting activities. For this reason, work with no more than four children at a time. Children need to stay at the table until they are finished painting. Hands must be washed immediately after painting.

Finger paint recipes are given in 18-15. Finger paint may also be made from instant pudding, soap flakes whipped with water, partially-set flavored gelatin, and shaving cream. Children enjoy using a variety of paints.

## String Painting

To prepare for **string painting**, cut several pieces of heavy yarn or string. Place a tray, or trays, of colored tempera paint and paper on the table. Show the children how to slide the yarn through the paint and across the piece of paper. Another technique is to place the string in a folded piece of paper and pull it out.

## Mono Painting

A **mono painting** starts with a regular finger painting. After this, an 8 x 12 inch piece of paper is placed over the finger painting. The papers are patted together, then pulled apart.

| Finger Paints |
|---|
| **Speedy finger paint** |
| 1  cup of laundry starch |
| 3  cups of soap flakes |
| 1  cup cold water |
| Mix all ingredients together. If colored finger paint is desired, add food coloring or colored tempera. |
| **Blender finger paint** |
| 1  pound powdered tempera paint |
| ¼  cup liquid starch |
| ⅓  cup water |
| 1  tablespoon of powdered laundry detergent |
| Place in blender. Mix until finger paint is blended well. |
| **Cornstarch finger paint** |
| 1  cup of dry starch |
| ½  cup water |
| 1½  cups boiling water |
| ¾  cup powdered laundry detergent |
| Mix starch and ½ cup water in heat-resistant bowl. Add 1½ cups boiling water while stirring rapidly. Blend in ¾ cup powdered laundry detergent until smooth. |

18-15 Using recipes allows you to make the type and color of finger paint you need.

## Chalk Painting

To make a **chalk painting**, dip chalk into water and draw on construction paper. Use chalk at least one inch thick. Choose paper color based on the color of chalk being used. Add vinegar to the water to deepen the color of the chalk.

## Texture Painting

Make paint for **texture painting** using liquid tempera or mixing powdered tempera with liquid starch. To this mixture, add sand, sawdust, or coffee grounds. For best results, the paint should be thick.

## Salt Painting

Materials needed for **salt painting** include construction paper or cardboard, paste or glue, cotton swabs or tongue depressors, and salt mixed with colored tempera in shakers. Have the children spread paste or glue on the paper. Then have them shake the salt mixture onto the glue or paste. Shake off excess paint and set aside to dry.

## Spice Painting

**Spice painting** results in a scented painting. Prepare the mixture by adding a small amount of water to liquid glue. Give each child enough glue to spread over their piece of paper. They can use their fingers to do this. Then have them shake spices onto the paper. When it dries it will look as interesting as it smells.

Cinnamon, onion powder, garlic powder, and oregano all make aromatic paintings. For texture, use bay leaves, cloves, or coffee grounds. The center budget may dictate which and how many spices you can use. In addition, consideration must be given to any policies toward the use of food. Some directors tend to discourage this type of food use.

## Molding

Play dough, Plasticene®, and clay are materials that can be molded and formed. Children enjoy the tactile appeal of these materials. Because they can be reshaped, they stimulate the imagination and allow children the freedom to change their minds. You will observe them poking, rolling, stretching, pounding, squeezing, coiling, flattening, and tearing the clay or play dough. It can be turned into a ball, snowman, cat, pancake, or snake. Often the children will use accessories such as pans, cookie cutters, and rolling pins to make pies, cookies, and other "baked goods" from these materials.

Children's play with molding materials reflects their level of development. Two-year-old children pull, beat, push, and squeeze. When children are about three years of age, they make balls and snake-like shapes. By age four, children can make complex forms, some of which they name. By age five, children will often announce what they are going to make before they begin.

Clay may be purchased at local art-supply stores and through school catalogs. It is available in two colors, white or red. When wet, the white clay appears grayish in color. Since red clay can stain clothing, most teachers prefer the white. Mixed properly, it should be stored in a plastic bag, diaper pail, or garbage pail to prevent drying. Clay can be used on a vinyl tablecloth or tile to save on cleanup time.

Play dough is soft and pliable, and it has a softer texture than clay. It offers little resistance to pressure and responds easily when touched. Each type of play dough has different features. Provide the children with a number of types by using the recipes in 18-16. You can vary these play doughs even further by adding rice, cornmeal, pebbles, sand, oats, and coffee grounds. Scented oils such as peppermint and wintergreen add a fragrant smell.

| Play Doughs |
| --- |

### Refrigerator play dough

1  cup salt
2  cups flour
1  tablespoon alum (optional, a preservative)
1  cup water
3  tablespoons oil
   Food coloring or tempera (optional)

Mix salt, flour, and alum. Add oil, water, food coloring, and mix. Check the consistency. If sticky, add more flour. Store in a tightly covered container in the refrigerator.

### Sawdust play dough

3  cups flour
3  cups sawdust
1  cup salt

Mix the three ingredients together. Add water as needed to form a soft dough.

### Cooked play dough

1  cup salt
½  cup flour
1  cup water

Mix ingredients together in a pan. Cook over medium heat, stirring constantly. Remove the mixture from the heat when it becomes thick and rubbery. After cooling, the mixture will not be as sticky. Store in an airtight container.

18-16 Varying the types of play dough you make helps give children a variety of sensory experiences.

Many teachers use Plasticene® for modeling. **Plasticene®** is an oil-based, commercially manufactured modeling compound. It is available in many bright colors including blue, green, orange, red, and yellow.

Unlike play dough and clay, Plasticene® does not dry out. It can be rolled up and used over and over again. It needs little care, even when used daily. However, one disadvantage of Plasticene® is that it can leave an oily residue on the children's hands and table surfaces. For this reason, some teachers do not make it available to the children.

## Cutting

Children need time, supplies, and space each day for cutting. Young children learn to cut because they enjoy working scissors. At first, children just snip in a straight line. Provide strips of construction paper or wrapping paper. The paper should be long enough so the children may hold fast to one end of it. Avoid heavy wrapping paper, corrugated paper, or vinyl paper. Children do not have enough small muscle strength to cut through these materials. As children progress, they may wish to cut in curves. This requires good hand-eye coordination skills.

Have children work with one type of paper. This allows them to master handling one type of material and tool. To avoid failure, give children quality scissors. Provide left-handed children with proper scissors. Mark these scissors with colored tape. All scissors should have rounded tips.

## Collages

The term **collage** means a selection of materials mounted on a flat surface. Collages are two-dimensional arrangements of many materials. Making collages gives children the chance to make choices. They can decide what material will be placed where. Two-year-olds may paste layers of materials on top of each other. Collages also introduce many materials of contrasting colors and textures to children. Materials that can be used in collages are listed in 18-17. Consider the children's ages when choosing collage materials. For instance, buttons, beads, or other small objects would be inappropriate for children younger than three. These tiny items can present a choking hazard.

The base for a collage should be a heavyweight material. Construction paper or cardboard are ideal. Arrange collage materials in attractive containers. Children can browse through these containers choosing items for their collages. Remember to provide adhesives. Library paste is a good medium for younger children to use. As children gain skills in making collages, liquid starch, rubber cement, and white glue can be used. Liquid starch works well on tissue paper. Rubber cement or white glue is a better choice for heavier materials, such as buttons. To add interest, tint white glue with tempera paint.

| Objects for Collages | | |
|---|---|---|
| aluminum foil | flower petals | plastic pieces |
| baking cups | gift wrap | rubber bands |
| beads | greeting cards | sandpaper |
| bottle lids | juice cans | scrap yarn, string, & ribbon |
| burlap | lace | seashells |
| buttons | leather | seeds |
| candy wrappers | leaves | sequins |
| can labels | magazine pictures | shoeboxes |
| cartons | netting | shoelaces |
| cellophane | newspaper | small tiles |
| cereal boxes | paper cups | sponges |
| chalk | paper plates | straws |
| clear plastic trays | paper ribbons | suede |
| confetti | paper towel or toilet paper | tape |
| construction paper pieces | tubes | tissue paper |
| corks | pebbles | tongue depressors |
| cotton balls | pinecones | tree bark |
| doilies | plastic or foam packing | twigs |
| egg cartons | material | used gift boxes |
| fabrics | plastic milk jugs | wallpaper samples |
| feathers | plastic or wooden | wooden clothespins |
| felt | spools | wood shavings |

18-17  The types of items used in collages are nearly limitless. Many types of items are listed here. What other interesting items could be used?

# Blockbuilding

Blocks are important learning tools for young children. They are probably the most popular materials in child care centers. While playing with blocks, children are in constant motion, reaching, stretching, and changing body positions. As they build with the blocks, they are improving their eye-hand coordination and strengthening their muscles. Through block play, children also learn many new concepts and skills. Figure 18-18 lists the many ways that block play promotes learning in the four developmental domains.

## Stages of Blockbuilding

Children play with blocks in different ways as they grow older. The following stages of blockbuilding have been identified:

- Stage One. At two years of age, children carry the blocks around and do not engage in construction. They enjoy filling containers with blocks and dumping them out.
- Stage Two. From two to three years of age, building begins. The children will either stack the blocks vertically or lay them in horizontal rows. They strive to build towers higher until they fall down, and their "roads" become longer and longer. They usually keep building until they run out of blocks or space.
- Stage Three. Simple bridging occurs. **Bridging** is a process of placing two blocks vertically a space apart. Then a third block is added. Children build these bridges and tunnels over and over again.
- Stage Four. Children begin to construct enclosures. They enjoy building houses, apartments, barns, stores, caves for animals, and other types of buildings.
- Stage Five. By three to four years of age, children begin to build more intricate buildings. These buildings are now higher, wider, and more elaborate. They are beginning to choose blocks carefully in order to carry out their designs.

| Learning Through Block Play | |
|---|---|
| **Domain** | **Learnings** |
| **Physical Development** | • Developing fine- and gross-motor skills<br>• Building hand-eye coordination skills<br>• Understanding object-space relationships<br>• Increasing motor coordination by lifting, carrying, and stacking |
| **Cognitive Development** | • Understanding balance, weight, and measurement concepts<br>• Exploring shapes, sizes, and proportions<br>• Understanding mathematical concepts, such as *larger than* or *smaller than*<br>• Understanding language concepts, such as *over, under, same different,* and *beside*<br>• Experimenting with gravity and cause and effect<br>• Developing skills in predicting, comparing, sorting, and classifying |
| **Emotional Development** | • Gaining self-confidence<br>• Finding a sense of accomplishment and success<br>• Developing patience and tolerance<br>• Expressing feelings through role-playing |
| **Social Development** | • Improving cooperation skills<br>• Practicing turn-taking and sharing skills<br>• Learning to respect the work of others |

18-18  Children benefit in many ways from blockbuilding experiences.

■ Stage Six. The children begin naming their structures and include dramatic play. They may build an airport for toy airplanes.

■ Stage Seven. By five years of age, children decide what they want to build prior to construction. Their structures becoming more symbolic and are used in dramatic play. They will build airports, garages, houses, and barns. Once built, their play becomes more creative by adding props and accessories. Often the children like to play with the same structure for several days.

## Types of Blocks and Accessories

Blocks come in a variety of materials including wood, cardboard, plastic, rubber, and foam. Square and rectangular blocks made from lightweight materials are best for younger children. Children from three to six years of age prefer wooden blocks in a variety of shapes and sizes.

The children enjoy having accessories to use with block play. Usually they prefer simple figures such as animals and multicultural people. Often they will want to recreate a setting they have experienced. After a field trip to the farm, they may build a barn. Other settings may include airports, fire houses, parking garages, a zoo, racetracks, train stations, and bus stations. To maintain the children's interests, rotate the materials occasionally. To facilitate sharing and cooperative efforts, always purchase two of each item.

## Sensory Experiences: Sand and Water Play

Sand and water play are often referred to as sensory experiences. They are provided in many programs with preschoolers. Both activities can occur indoors and outdoors. Children find pleasure in these unstructured and fluid materials. Working with sand or water is relaxing and relieves tension. Water and sand play also encourage social interaction as children play side-by-side or with others.

## Sand Play

A sandbox should have an 8- to 12-inch ledge around it. This gives the children a place to display their molded sand forms. It will also provide seating for the children.

Outdoors, the sandbox should be placed in a quiet area of the play yard, 18-19. If possible, it should be placed near a water source so the sand can be moistened. Moist sand can be used to pack molds and cans and to create castles. Moist sand is preferable to dry sand because it does not get into the eyes, shoes, or hair as easily. By placing the sandbox far from the building entrance, less sand will be brought into the center. As the children walk across the play yard, some of the sand should fall off.

An indoor sand table should also be placed near a water source. It is usually located in or near the art area on flooring that is easily cleaned. Ceramic tile and linoleum are good choices.

A variety of containers should be provided for stirring, sifting, straining, pouring, smoothing, and molding the sand. Cans, buckets, plastic measuring cups, gelatin molds, cookie cutters, strainers, funnels, basters, muffin tins, bread pans, shovels, sifters, and spoons are examples. With these items, the children can construct roads, caves, tunnels, and castles. They will also enjoy using trucks and cars in the sand. Plastic or rubber animals and people are other accessories children enjoy playing with in the sandbox.

## Water Play

With careful supervision, water play is another activity that is developmentally appropriate for all children. Water play can take place indoors using a water table, plastic bins, laundry tubs, or wading pools. For variety, you can fill the tub with snow. Food coloring and soap can also be added for interest. Occasionally you may want to use shaving cream in the water table. The cream can be colored to correspond with different holidays.

A variety of nonbreakable kitchen utensils can be provided for use in the water table. Sponges, measuring cups, plastic squeeze bottles, egg beaters, and basters are examples. The children may also enjoy playing with boats and washing dolls and doll clothing. Older children may also enjoy using a garden hose outdoors. They can wash the sidewalks, buildings, wagons, and playground equipment.

18-19 This canopied sandbox helps protect children from the sun when they are playing outdoors.

18-20 Proper safety equipment should be provided for woodworking activities.

# Woodworking

Children enjoy woodworking activities. Hammering is usually their first interest. When provided the proper tools, they may pound nails for 20 minutes. Developmentally, woodworking can be a valuable experience. It promotes hand-eye coordination, fine and gross motor development, and creative expression. In addition, it provides the children with an emotional release.

If properly used, tools are safe for children to use, 18-20. Teachers need to demonstrate how to use the tools safely. In some classrooms, teachers demonstrate hammering using golf tees and styrofoam. Some teachers have a large tree stump cut for their classroom. They place a can of nails and a hammer near the stump to encourage participation. Children using a hammer for the first time may want you to start the nail.

Tools for the woodworking area need to be carefully chosen. They should be lightweight and have handles that are easy for the children to grip. Examples of woodworking tools include claw hammers, hand drills, pliers, sandpaper blocks, a vise, and saws. Thin nails with large heads are easiest for children to use. Wood glue should also be available.

## Summary

For young children, art activities are important learning experiences. Through their own creativity, children express their ideas, as well as their emotions. Art promotes physical, social, emotional, and cognitive growth in children.

A good art program fosters independence. Let children decide when their work is finished. Model art appreciation by offering feedback to the children about their work. Use praise that invites children to respect the value of each person's work.

Children move through three distinct stages as they build art skills. Knowing these stages helps child care workers plan activities that reflect children's skills level.

The teacher has an important job in guiding art, blockbuilding, and sensory experiences. The teacher will decide what types of activities will be introduced. A variety of materials and techniques should be used. Knowing how to carry out this task so children benefit from the experience is important for the teacher.

## Review and Reflect

1. How do art experiences promote social growth?

2. Why is it best not to ask children what they are making?

3. Name the stages of art skill development. Explain one stage in detail.

4. True or false. Children are careful to choose colors that mirror real life instead of choosing colors they like.

5. Explain how to mix tempera paint to get the desired consistency.

6. True or false. As children progress in art skills, paintbrushes should become more narrow.

7. Why are chalk, felt-tip markers, and crayons more difficult for children to use than paint?

8. Summarize the controversy concerning the use of coloring books.

9. _____ painting is a sensory experience that promotes the release of feelings and is very satisfying for children.

10. How does a two-year-old's play with clay differ from a five-year-old's?

11. Which molding material would you choose for children to use? Give the reasons for your selection.

12. Name three ways children benefit from blockbuilding experiences.

13. Name three woodworking tools that children might enjoy using.

## Apply and Explore

1. Collect children's drawings. Determine what stage of development each drawing represents. Give reasons for your conclusions.

2. Prepare and use each of the finger paint recipes given in the chapter. Discuss which has the best texture. Suggest methods for storing the paint.

3. Prepare each of the play dough recipes given in the chapter. Compute the cost to make each recipe. Compare these costs to the cost of purchasing commercial play dough products.

4. Review equipment catalogs and prepare a list of the different types of blocks and accessories for this area of the classroom.

5. Explore the Web site for Crayola (crayola.com) to learn more about using art to stimulate creativity in young children.

Storytelling is often part of the daily routine.

# Chapter 19

# Guiding Storytelling Experiences

After studying this chapter, you will be able to

- explain the advantages of storytelling.
- list the four types of children's books.
- discuss the process of choosing children's books.
- outline the steps to follow when reading aloud to children.
- explain a variety of storytelling methods.

## Terms to Know

storytelling
picture books
storybooks
family life stories
animal stories
fairy tales
reviews
props
draw and tell
flipcharts
flannel boards

The words *once upon a time* contain magic for young children. The art of storytelling has delighted millions of children throughout the ages. By inviting children to share in a make-believe world of adventure, the storyteller provides a strong educational tool.

**Storytelling** is an important task for child care teachers. It involves reciting a story or reading from a book. In most centers, storytelling is routine. It is included in the daily schedule, 19-1. Storytelling is a valuable experience for children. They develop a love for both stories and books as a result of daily storytelling sessions.

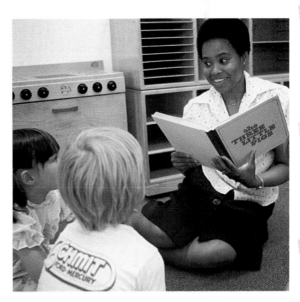

19-1 Storytelling is an enjoyable time for teachers and children.

This in turn enhances their language development. Moreover, children develop an understanding of customs and culture through traditional stories.

## The Importance of Storytelling

Regular storytelling promotes children's cognitive, social, and emotional development. Storytelling helps young children

- understand other people
- develop a positive attitude toward books
- develop listening skills
- build correct concepts of objects and form new ideas
- increase their vocabulary
- associate written and spoken words
- understand that printed words carry meanings
- develop an appreciation of printed words
- develop a desire to read, 19-2
- learn that people read from left to right across a page

Carefully chosen stories are a key part of the storytelling experience. Stories that draw on the children's backgrounds help them understand themselves better. Children learn the words that describe feelings and experiences they have. They learn to think about familiar situations in new ways. Stories invite children to explore and wonder about their world.

Stories also provide models of acceptable behavior and positive relationships. When exposed to a variety of characters, children learn that other people often feel the same way they do. They learn how people express their feelings. They become more understanding of others' needs.

Storytelling helps children learn reading skills. As a teacher reads aloud from a book, children learn to follow the pages from left to right and top to bottom. By watching the storyteller read, children learn the relationship between spoken and printed words. They also learn to listen. Books help children learn alphabet letters, numerals, and language.

Storytelling is also a good form of relaxation. Listening to a story is a quiet activity. Children are not moving about or interacting with other children.

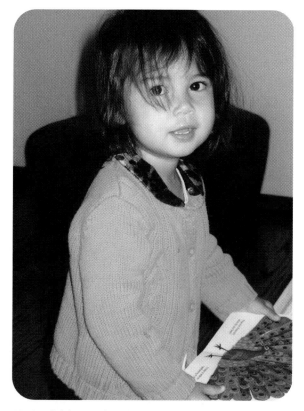

19-2 Children's desire to read is often rooted in early storytelling experience.

## Books as a Source of Stories

Children's books are an important source of stories. Most can be divided into two main groups: picture books and storybooks. **Picture books** have single words or simple sentences and simple plots. These are usually the first books shared with young children.

After picture books, **storybooks** are introduced. Storybooks are often categorized as family life stories, animal stories, and fairy tales. These books also contain pictures, but they have more words and more complex plots than picture books. Most of these books are built around themes of achievement, love, and reassurance. A book that uses all three themes is *Peter Rabbit*. In the story, Peter has an adventure but safely returns home (achievement). His mother tucks him into bed and gives him tea (love and reassurance). Examples of other such stories include *Little Bear, Mike Mulligan and His Steam Shovel,* and *Little Tim.*

**Family life stories** contain the theme of social understanding. The children in these stories usually have problems. Some problems may be funny; some serious. However, all problems are resolved with love and concern. The purpose of these stories is to help children develop social understanding by sharing the problems, troubles, and feelings of others. Examples include *Johnny Crow's Garden, My Dog Is Lost, My Grandpa, Timid Timothy,* and *Will I Have a Friend?*

Young children also enjoy **animal stories**. In these stories, animals have some human qualities. Usually, the animal hero has some unusual success or ability. Examples include *Little Brown Bear; All About Dogs, Dogs, Dogs; Nothing But Cats, Cats, Cats;* and *Angus and the Cat.*

Fairy tales are another type of book enjoyed by older children. **Fairy tales** have a theme of achievement. The characters or heroes perform difficult tasks in order to succeed. They must confront giants, witches, or other obstacles. Kindness and goodness win out over evil. *Three Billy Goats Gruff, Three Little Pigs,* and *Cinderella* are popular examples of fairy tales. These books are predictable. To help children make sense of the stories, obvious clues, pictures, and repeated phrases are included.

## Selecting Books for Children

Storytelling is an art that requires study and practice. The key to a good story is selection. Choose books that have dramatic elements. Children will enjoy "seeing" and "feeling" the events. Stories that mirror the children's emotional experiences will engage their hearts and minds. A story is only good if children enjoy it. If the story is to be an effective classroom activity, the teacher should also enjoy and value it. Otherwise, sharing it in an interesting way will be difficult.

Selecting storybooks is often hard for new child care teachers. Public libraries have many useful lists and descriptions of books. These are called **reviews**. Reviews will help you find titles, authors, and publishers of books. Reviews can also be ordered from the American Library Association Children's Service.

## Fictional Content

Stories should reflect the children's developmental level, backgrounds, and experiences. When choosing books for children, consider the content, illustrations, vocabulary, durability, and length of the book. Familiar objects, people, and situations make stories more interesting to children. Stories about children with backgrounds and activities similar to their own are special favorites.

Most preschool children cannot separate fact from fiction. Therefore, it is important to look for realistic stories. Until children are about five years old, they are often not ready for fantasy, 19-3. Books in which animals or inanimate objects, such as trees and flowers, behave as humans should be avoided for very young children.

## Illustrations

Illustrations create interest and arouse children's imagination. The pictures in a book for young children should almost tell the story by

19-3  Younger children may become confused or even frightened by fantasy stories.

themselves. Children will be more interested if they can "read" the story by looking at the pictures.

Pictures should be easy to recognize and help the children make sense of the story. Good pictures also help the children anticipate what happens next in the story. Too much detail and shading or lack of color will confuse young children. Instead, children respond best to brightly colored pictures with large, clearly defined objects. Illustrations should

- be large, colorful, and plentiful
- represent the written word
- reflect actions
- avoid unneeded detail
- be realistically and attractively colored

## Vocabulary

A good children's book uses words that can be understood by most children of a certain age. Only a few new words should be introduced in a story. Repetition of some words will increase the children's enjoyment. This rhythm of word sounds is one major reason children enjoy stories such as Mother Goose tales.

## Durability

Children should be allowed to hold and carry books as well as turn pages. Therefore, covers and pages must be sturdy. Covers made of strong, washable material are best. Pages should be easy to handle. The page surface should be dull to prevent glare. The book's binding should lay flat when the book is open.

## Length

Appropriate book length varies with children's age. Infants and toddlers may stay with a book for just a few minutes. Their books are often only a few pages long. Two-year-olds will remain interested in a book for 5 to 8 minutes; three-year-olds from 6 to 10 minutes; four-year-olds from 8 to 12 minutes; five-year-olds from 10 to 15 minutes. This interest is reflected in the number of pages in the book.

## Selecting Books Based on Age

Age plays an important part in choosing books for children. Chart 19-4 outlines some factors to consider for different ages.

Infants and toddlers need durable picture books. These books may be made of washable cloth or firm cardboard. Thick pages allow for easier handling. Pictures should be large and clearly defined. Simple items in children's surroundings should be represented in the pictures. Toddlers may enjoy pointing at and touching objects in the pictures.

Two-year-olds prefer books about things they know, do, and enjoy. They respond enthusiastically when favorite activities, such as running, eating, and dressing, are mentioned. Animals and small children are the favored subjects. Books for two-year-olds should still be quite durable with plenty of large, clearly defined drawings. Actions and sounds represented in the pictures should be familiar. The colors should be realistic.

| Considerations for Children's Books | | | | |
|---|---|---|---|---|
| **Toddlers** | **2-year-olds** | **3-year-olds** | **4-year-olds** | **5-year-olds** |
| Thick pages<br>Large, clearly defined pictures<br>Brightly colored pictures of simple, familiar objects and routines. | Imitate familiar sounds<br>Repeat children's own experiences<br>Contain large pages with big pictures<br>Include the familiar<br>Simple plots | Include things and people outside of the home<br>Explain the *who* and *why*<br>Interpret the child's own experiences<br>Contain repetitive sound words | Include humor in reality<br>Contain new words<br>Explain the *how* and *why*<br>Include exaggeration | Add something to their knowledge<br>Take them beyond the here and now<br>Contain new information and relate it to familiar facts |

19-4 Children of different ages each have their story preferences.

Three-year-old children may request stories by title. They show preference for stories about familiar subjects, 19-5. They also enjoy learning about people outside the home. They enjoy stories about community helpers such as police officers, mail carriers, and garbage collectors. Three-year-olds want to know what these people do and why. Pictures should be realistic, simple, and clear. The number of sentences on each page should be limited.

Four-year-old children are less self-centered than the younger group. These children are becoming more curious about the world around them. They want to know how and why things work. At this age, children enjoy short, simple stories that use exaggeration. Four-year-olds often enjoy pranks in books. Looking at the pictures can help them experience the story.

19-5 Children enjoy looking at books that contain familiar subjects.

Five-year-old children like stories that give them added knowledge. They will frequently memorize favorite stories word for word. They prefer stories that take them beyond here and now. These children want new information and relationships along with familiar facts. Fantasy trips beyond the confines of their world are now appreciated. Examples of these books include *Little Red Riding Hood, Peter Rabbit,* and *Goldilocks and the Three Bears.* Children of this age will clearly tell you their likes and dislikes.

## Avoiding Stories That Reinforce Stereotypes

It is important to choose age-appropriate stories. Selecting anti-bias stories that are free from stereotypes is essential, too. *Stereotypes* are preset ideas about people based on one characteristic, such as sex, culture, nationality, religion, or age. Stereotypes are unfair and should be avoided. Read stories and study illustrations carefully before using them. Stereotyping is often easiest to spot in pictures. Pictures should be examined closely since they have more impact on children than words.

Children's stories need to be free of sexism. *Sexism* is any action, attitude, or outlook used to judge a person based only on the sex of that person. In the past, many books did not show women who possess a full range of interests and skills. Most children's books showed women wearing aprons and doing housework. Girls were passive and helped their mothers around the house. Boys, on the other hand, were active and adventurous. Doctors, lawyers, and police tended to be men. Also, few men were shown in roles of teachers and nurses.

Study the ratio of men to women in the illustrations. As a rule, there should be as many men as women or girls as boys. Notice how characters are described and what kinds of activities the pictures show them doing, 19-6. Books that avoid sexism will describe women and girls as lively people who do interesting things. Likewise, men and boys will be shown as caring people who are interested in homes, families, and friends.

Through books, children can also gain an understanding of people who have different skin coloring, food preferences, and languages. Knowledge of the differences among people can

19-6 Books that show men involved with their families and women in interesting jobs do not promote sexism.

promote acceptance. Both illustrations and text should depict people of all ethnic and cultural groups in a positive way.

Finally, search stories for stereotyping of older people. Children must be given a realistic and positive picture of seniors. Stories should describe warm, pleasing relationships between older people and children. In this way, children can learn to know and admire older members of their community.

# Reading Stories to Children

Good oral reading takes time and effort. Three steps need to be taken before reading stories to young children. First, choose stories that both children and you will enjoy. Then become familiar with the story. Finally, decide how you will present the story. The success of the story lies in your ability to be interesting and enthusiastic.

## Preparing to Read

Read the story several times so you know it well. Then a quick glance at the page will remind you of the text. This leaves your eyes free for contact with the children. No one way is best for learning stories. Each person has his or her own method.

Oral reading skills are important when storytelling. One way to build these skills is to practice reading in front of a mirror. Another method is to record yourself as you read. Using these methods, you can correct any problems you notice. For example, tape yourself and then ask the following:

- Did I convey enthusiasm about the story?
- Did I keep the tempo lively?
- Did I suggest different voices for different characters?

After you are familiar with the book, decide whether you want to read or tell the story. Reading the story has its advantages when working with young children. They can look at the drawings as they listen to the story. Reading stories may also get some children interested in reading. As they watch you, the children will learn the link between printed and spoken words. The advantage to telling a story is you are able to better dramatize action and characters.

A comfortable setting is required for a successful reading time. Children must be free from distractions. They should sit in a group to listen. Some teachers like to have children sit on carpet squares or pillows. A colorful quilt may also be used. Such seating arrangements prevent children from moving around and help them focus more on listening.

Story groups should be small, 19-7. You may wish to divide children into two or more groups, based on age and interest. This also allows the children more interaction.

Most children need a settling down time. To help children get ready to listen, some teachers recite a fingerplay. Another technique is to talk to the children using a puppet. Other teachers simply discuss the events of the day.

## Introducing the Story

Begin stories by setting the mood. Ask questions, make personal comments, or show the book cover to get children involved in the story. Ask children to predict what the story is about. Setting the mood should be brief. A few sentences are often enough.

A personal comment is one way to introduce a story. You may share where you learned about the story. For example, "This is a story that my grandmother told me as a child." You can set

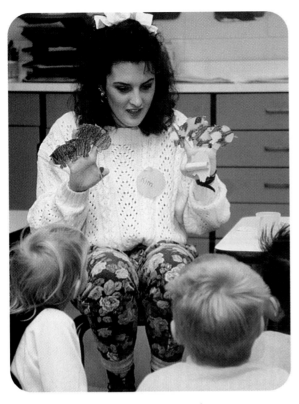

19-7 In small groups, children are free to interact with the teacher.

a humorous mood by asking "How many of you like to laugh?" You might hold the book up and show the cover. The picture on the cover should suggest the story content.

Props are also good for introducing stories. **Props** are any items that relate to the story and would attract children's attention. To introduce *Peter Rabbit*, for example, you may bring in a live rabbit, a stuffed rabbit, or a picture of a rabbit. See 19-8.

Store props in a storytelling apron. As you introduce a story, pull props out of the apron pocket one at a time. A storytelling bag can be used in the same way. The bag is also useful for storing books in the reading area.

Explain any words the children do not know before you begin the story. For example, before reading *The Gigantic Elephant*, define the new word *gigantic*.

Before you start, create a feeling that something special is about to be shared. This feeling can be produced by the enthusiasm in your voice as you introduce the book. Your facial expression can also create excitement.

| Props for Introducing Stories | |
|---|---|
| A red balloon | "The Red Balloon" |
| A red apple | "The Apple is Red" |
| A doll | "William's Doll" |
| A black cat | "The Tale of the Black Cat" |
| A purple crayon | "Harold and the Purple Crayon" |

19-8 Well-chosen props will grab children's attention.

## Reading the Story

Read stories with pleasure and feeling. Maintain eye contact with the children. Pause before introducing a new character or idea.

Read the story in a normal speaking voice. Speaking too softly or at a high pitch may cause the children to lose interest. Think of your voice as a tool. To add interest, you can whisper or shout when appropriate. You may mimic a sound, or adjust your pace to reflect the story. The pitch of your voice can also be changed. An example would be the story of *Goldilocks and the Three Bears*. Project yourself into the characters. Use a high pitch for the baby bear and a low pitch for the papa bear.

## Handling Interruptions

Interruptions happen often when telling stories to young children, 19-9. The children will ask such questions as "Why is baby bear brown?" Accept these interruptions and answer questions patiently. There may be children who continue to ask many questions. If this happens, say "Mark, please save your questions until after the story."

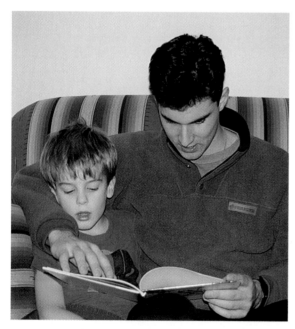

19-9 Do not be annoyed by interruptions. Young children like to ask questions and make comments on stories they are hearing.

Wiggling children can distract other children. Do not make an issue of this. It is best to ignore the wiggling and keep reading. A positive response is to praise children who sit still. For example, you may say "Joellen, I like how quietly you are sitting." This will strengthen Joellen's actions. It will also encourage wigglers to sit still.

## Maintaining Interest

Children's interest in a story can be seen in their laughter, stillness, and expressions. If children do not appear to like a story, talk faster. You might use more emphasis or skip over some details. You can also restore interest by asking the children simple questions about the story. To quiet a bored or disruptive child, ask "Louis, what color is baby bear?" Sometimes, no matter what you do, a book does not have holding power. If this should happen, end the story. You may say, "Boys and girls, this is not the right story for today."

## Ending Stories

Ending a story is as important as introducing it. The children need to know when you are finished. Therefore, the ending should be clear. You may ask a question about the story such as "What did you like best about the story?" You also may ask a question about the characters, the plot, or the setting.

At times, a simple "Thank you for listening" may be enough. You may also wish to give the children something to take home after some stories. This is done most often for special occasions. For example, when reading *Winnie the Pooh*, you may wish to give the children balloons.

Be prepared to read the same story over and over again. You will be pleased to hear "Please tell us that story again." This request tells you the children enjoyed the book.

## Evaluating Your Performance

After reading a story, you will need to evaluate your methods. Children's reactions are good feedback. As a rule, the more children respond to a story, the better your methods. If children lose interest, you may have talked too fast or too slow. In other cases, you may have spoken so carefully that you forgot to add expression and vary tone.

Note your strengths as well as your weaknesses. When children smile, laugh, and watch closely, you have used methods that hold their interest. Build on your strengths as you read stories in the future. In addition, review the tips for effective storytelling listed in 19-10.

# Achieving Variety in Storytelling

In addition to reading stories aloud, there are other methods of storytelling. Guidelines for these methods are like those for reading aloud. First, decide whether you will read from a book or make up your own story. Next, practice the story in front of a mirror using a tape recorder until you know it well. This will help you prepare to perform as a storyteller.

Younger children in particular will stay interested longer when several methods are used during storytime. As a child care teacher, you will need to learn a number of storytelling methods.

---

### Tips for Effective Storytelling

- Choose a book that is developmentally appropriate for the children.
- Use a good introduction to establish the mood of the story.
- Explain unfamiliar words.
- Encourage child participation.
- Tell the story with a conversational tone.
- Use eye contact.
- Convey enthusiasm.
- Demonstrate good posture.
- Use different voices for particular characters to create interest.
- Pronounce words clearly.
- Use a lively tempo.
- Allow comments to be added to story.

19-10 Determining your strengths and weaknesses will help you improve your storytelling skills.

## Draw and Tell

**Draw and tell**, or *chalk talk*, is one storytelling method. Drawings are made on chalkboard, tagboard, or an 18-by 24-inch newsprint pad as the story is told. Textbooks containing draw and tell stories can be purchased from school supply stores or catalogs. Some child care workers prefer to find a storybook and adapt it. Illustrations may be deleted, combined, and added. As a general rule, no more than five sheets of paper should be used.

If you do not have good drawing skills, you may want to use an opaque projector to prepare the stories. Find a book and place it on the projector. Tape a piece of cardboard or paper on the wall. Project drawings from the book onto this paper or cardboard. Lightly trace the drawings with a pencil. Then as you tell the story, use brightly colored markers to retrace the lines.

Draw and tell stories may be prepared so they can be used more than once. Cover original light tracings with clear laminate. Use grease pencils to draw in the outline and fill in the color. After the story is done, clean the clear laminate by wiping it with a piece of felt. Window cleaner may also be used for cleaning.

## Tapes

Audio story tapes have appeal for young children. They contain sound effects and music. Story tape sets often include an illustrated booklet that children can use to follow along with the story. Tapes of many popular stories are available.

Videotapes can hold the interest of most children. One disadvantage is that children may already have seen them on television. Commercially purchased or teacher-made tapes may be used for storytelling. Audio- and videotapes may be purchased through school supply stores, catalogs, or in the exhibit area at early childhood conferences.

To save money, some child care teachers prefer to make their own tapes. To do so, you will need a tape recorder, cassette tape, and story. As you make the tape, read the story clearly. Pause after each two-page spread. At this point, insert a signal. You may want to hit a spoon against a glass or play a piano key. This signal will tell children listening to the tape to turn the page in their book, 19-11.

## Puppets

Puppets have always appealed to young children. Having puppets tell a story is a useful change of pace. Use a puppet as a listener who remarks and asks questions about the story. Puppets can be made from tin cans, tongue depressors, socks, and other inexpensive materials. A mitten also makes a good puppet. Cut eyes, a nose, and a mouth from construction paper and paste them onto the mitten. Use the mitten puppet with the story *The Lost Mitten*. Stuffed animals can be used in the same manner. For example, a brown teddy bear could be used to tell the story of *Little Brown Bear*.

After you tell the story, place the puppet in the library area. Puppets help children in constructing and expressing their understanding of stories, 19-12. (Refer to Chapter 20, Guiding Play and Puppetry Experiences, for more information.)

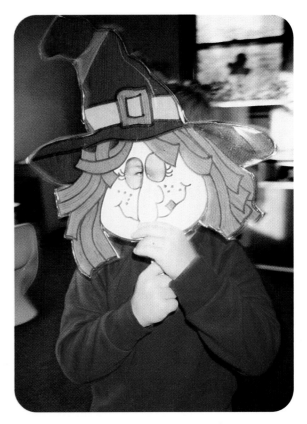

19-12 Puppets help children express their understanding of stories.

## Individual or Group Stories

Given the chance, children can be clever storytellers. After a field trip, guest visit, or other special event, ask children to record a story about that special time. You might have the children work together in small groups. Write down the children's ideas as they tell you their story. Seeing their own words helps children understand the link between spoken and written words. You could write the ideas on a piece of tagboard paper or on the chalkboard. You can also record these stories with a camcorder and play them later for the children to enjoy.

## Flipcharts

**Flipcharts** are stories drawn on large tagboard cards. If you lack drawing skills, you will find the opaque projector helpful. After you finish drawing, tracing, and coloring the cards,

19-11 Even young children who do not yet read can follow along in a book while listening to a tape.

number the back of each card. This will help you keep the cards in correct order for storytelling. You may also wish to print the story for each drawing on the back of each flipchart. To protect the flipchart, cover it with a plastic film.

After telling the story, you may wish to place the flipchart in the book area. Then the children have an opportunity to use the flipchart themselves and retell the story. Some children also enjoy arranging the cards in order of the story.

## Slide Stories

Slide stories usually center around pictures taken on field trips or during classroom events like holiday parties. You might start a slide story at the beginning of the year. Then at the end of the year the slide story can be told. Slide stories involving the children are also enjoyed by parents at special events.

## Flannel Boards

A flannel board story is one of the most popular listening activities for young children. **Flannel board**, or *felt board*, storytelling uses characters and props cut out of felt and placed on a felt background, 19-13. Flannel boards may be purchased from school supply stores and catalogs or made by the teacher. To make a board, you will need a piece of foam insulation board, 27 by 17½ inches. This material can be bought at a lumber supply company. To prepare the board, cover it with two contrasting pieces of felt, 29 by 19½ inches. The two pieces provide different-colored backgrounds for felt figures.

Pieces of paper, cardboard, or felt are used to show major characters or objects. These may be hand drawn, bought, or cut out of storybooks. Flannel board books contain many stories. They also often contain patterns for characters and props. These can be bought from school supply stores.

A quick way to make figures is to use a non-woven interfacing fabric. Hold the fabric in place and trace over the patterns with a black felt pen. Fill in the areas you wish to brighten.

Felt figures may also be made from a storybook pattern. Place a piece of carbon paper behind the paper and on top of a piece of card-

19-13  These felt figures can be placed on the flannel board as the story is told.

board. Trace over the drawing with a paper clip. This transfers the image onto the cardboard. Cut out the cardboard figures to use as patterns. The patterns can be placed on felt and traced. If you need larger figures, use the opaque projector to enlarge the drawings.

### Presenting a Flannel Board Story

Before you present a flannel board story, you will need to do some advance preparation. Practice reading the story script several times. Check your flannel board figures and place them in order of use. Keep the figures on your lap in a flat box or basket when you tell the story. Avoid placing the figures on the floor as a curious child may pick them up. This could interfere with the success of the story.

Place the figures on the flannel board one at a time. Like writing, the figures should follow a left to right sequence. Practice telling the story and placing the flannel figures on the board. For emphasis, look directly at the figure as you place it on the board.

After you finish telling a flannel board story, leave the assembled board in the book area. The children will enjoy using the flannel board figures to retell the story or create new tales. By observing and listening, you will be able to assess their understanding of the story. You may even want to encourage the children to create their own stories by providing them figures from a variety of stories.

## Displaying Books

An important area of a classroom is the library area. Books, flannel boards, tapes, and other storytelling equipment are located in this area. The books should be arranged in an appealing manner. The book covers should be visible to attract the children's interest, 19-14. Books should be arranged so they will not fall after one is removed.

The library area should be located away from traffic. It should also be separated from the rest of the classroom by dividers. This provides a quiet atmosphere. Scissors, crayons, and painting should not be allowed here. These limits should prevent the books from being misused.

The books for the library area should be carefully chosen. Each child's developmental needs should be considered. You may wish to include books on topics children in the group are facing, such as divorce, illness, and death. Some books, such as the children's favorites, can remain in the area continually. Other books can be rotated frequently. Fun books should always be available. Add new books often to stimulate children's interest and enthusiasm. You may want to borrow books from the public library, friends, and parents.

19-14  Displays that show book covers encourage children to look at books on their own.

## Summary

Storytelling can be a useful learning tool for children. Through storytelling, children can develop an enjoyment of books and learn many skills. Some of these skills include learning to form new ideas and increasing vocabulary.

Stories must be selected with care. Content must match the developmental levels and experiences of the audience. In addition, content must be free of stereotypes.

Illustrations should spark interest and be pleasant. The vocabulary and story length must match children's skills. Finally, the books must be durable.

Before reading to children, it is important to prepare ahead of time. There are several ways to present a story. Draw and tell, story tapes, and flannel boards are a few options.

## Review and Reflect

1. Stories that draw on children's _____ help them understand themselves better.

2. True or false. Storytelling is a good form of relaxation.

3. Which types of books are usually the first books shared with young children?
   A. Picture.
   B. Fairy tales.
   C. Animal.
   D. Family life.

4. What theme is used in family stories?

5. In _____, kindness and goodness win over evil.

6. True or false. It is not important if a teacher likes a story as long as the children enjoy it.

7. What are the functions of illustrations?

8. The appropriate length of a book will vary with the _____ of the child.

9. What is sexism?

10. True or false. Teachers should choose books that show people from all ethnic and cultural groups in a positive way.

11. Name three ways to introduce a story.

12. The _____ of a story must be clear.

13. Name two ways to build oral reading skills.

14. Explain one storytelling method.

## Apply and Explore

1. Using one of the storytelling methods explained in the chapter, prepare a children's story. Share it with the class.

2. Prepare a bibliography of children's books you might use in storytelling. Divide the books into groups based on age: toddlers, two-, three-, four-, and five-year-olds.

3. Create an introduction for a story. Use props when reading your introduction.

4. Select several multicultural children's books to add to the book area.

5. Listen to a children's story on audiotape. List the strategies used to hold the children's attention.

6. Videotape yourself reading a book to a group of children. Evaluate your presentation.

7. Visit the following Web site sponsored by the U.S. Department of Education especially for teachers of young children: ed.gov/offices/OESE/teachingouryoungest. Explore the Web site for tips about the importance of reading and storytelling. You might also want to read the document *Teaching Our Youngest—A Guide for Preschool Teachers*.

Puppets are fun, effective teaching aids.

# Chapter 20

# Guiding Play and Puppetry Experiences

After studying this chapter, you will be able to

- describe the stages of play.
- explain the stages of material use in play.
- summarize the benefits of socio-dramatic play.
- prepare the classroom environment and guide socio-dramatic play activities.
- summarize the benefits of puppetry experiences.
- make and use three types of puppets.
- write and tell a puppet story.

## Terms to Know

dramatic play
socio-dramatic play
projection
solitary play
parallel play
cooperative play
personification
manipulative stage
    of play
functional stage
    of play

imaginative stage
    of play
role-playing
coaching
modeling
prop box
puppetry
conflict

Play is an important part of a young child's day. Young children love to pretend and play make-believe. Such fantasy play provides opportunities for growth and development. Play also encourages experimentation and discovery. Young children are actors without stage fright. They say what they feel and feel what they say. By observing children at play, you will gain insight into their cognitive, social, and emotional development. Play is a window into their minds.

**Dramatic play** is a form of play in which a single child imitates another person or acts out a situation. **Socio-dramatic play** involves several children imitating others and acting out situations together, 20-1. It is the most complex form of play seen in child care settings. However, it is seldom observed before age three.

Puppetry is another type of play that allows a child to imitate others. A child's puppet may become a wolf, police officer, or even a witch. Through this play, a child may share his or her inner world. The child places feelings and emotions he or she feels onto the puppet. This is known as **projection**.

## Stages of Play

Children go through several stages of play before they are able to take part in socio-dramatic play. First is solitary play, followed by parallel play. Finally, children learn to engage in cooperative play.

Infants most often play by themselves. This play is called **solitary play** or independent play. Their play is basically exploratory in nature.

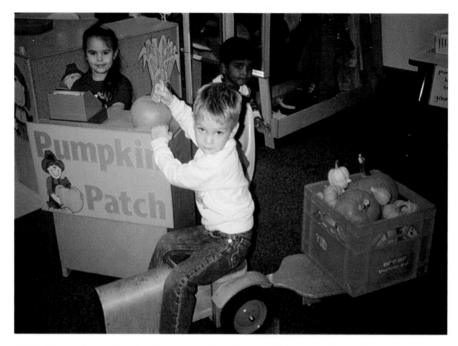

20-1 Socio-dramatic play involves at least two children as they role-play. These children are role-playing workers in a farmer's market.

Solitary explorations involve the child gathering information. Until about nine months of age, infants explore single objects. After this, they can examine multiple objects at once.

Parallel play is typical of two-year-olds. In **parallel play**, children play beside each other, but not with each other. All the children may be involved in similar activities, but there is little interaction among the children. Children in this age group focus more on using play materials on their own.

**Cooperative play** is play between two or more children. As children grow socially and emotionally, they begin playing with their peers for short time periods. Gradually they learn to respect the property rights of others. This is a clue they are gaining social skills, 20-2. At the same time, they are learning that permission is needed to use some materials. They are more willing to share with others.

It is at this stage that socio-dramatic play begins. As children take part in cooperative play, they become more interested in social relationships. As this occurs, they learn how to develop and maintain peer relationships. From this grows socio-dramatic play.

20-2 Children learn social skills such as cooperation in socio-dramatic play.

Children who are aggressive and uncooperative may have problems with cooperative play. To be successful in cooperative play, they need to give affection, be friendly, and consider other children's wishes. They also need to understand the viewpoint of others.

As you observe children in these three stages of play, you will notice that many engage in personification. **Personification** means giving human traits to nonliving objects. For instance, children may talk to dolls or puppets. They act as if the toys can hear what they say. Many everyday situations are acted out. A child may say "Mommy is going to feed you now." While speaking to a puppet, a child may say "You're going to go for a walk now." They will use exaggerated movements and voices. This is typical behavior for most young children.

20-3  Making a hamburger out of play dough is a sign of imaginative play.

## Stages of Material Use in Play

Children move through three stages of material use in their play. Not all young children, however, will reach the second or third stages.

The first stage of material use is called the **manipulative stage**. A child at this stage handles props. For instance, when given a baby bottle, children in the manipulative stage will screw and unscrew the cap.

The second stage is called the **functional stage**. During this stage, the child will use the prop as intended while playing with other children. Using a doll bottle, the child will pretend to feed a doll.

The third stage is called the **imaginative stage**. Children in this stage do not need real props, 20-3. They are able to think of substitutes. Instead of feeding the doll with a bottle, they may use their finger, a stick, a clothespin, or a pencil. Likewise, if a broom is needed to sweep the floor, a yardstick may be used.

Many times children at the imaginative level come up with unique ideas for their socio-dramatic play. They may use a toy to represent a dinosaur, a doll carriage for a grocery cart, or a paper bag as a chef's hat. When dramatizing a restaurant theme, they may make paper money to buy food.

Some children find it difficult to get involved in a role if there are no real props. In a restaurant scene, for instance, some children will play the role of servers. Children at the manipulative or functional stage will say they cannot play the role without paper and pencil. Children who have reached the imaginative stage might use their hand for the paper and use a finger as a pencil. Not all young children are able to reach the imaginative level.

## Socio-Dramatic Play

As children engage in socio-dramatic play, they mimic adult roles. They may play at being a wife, husband, mommy, daddy, doctor, or police officer. This is called role-playing. **Role-playing** allows children to try out a variety of roles, 20-4. As one child plays the role of a hairstylist, another plays the role of the customer. Each role follows social rules determined by the group of children. Children engaged in role-playing often give specific instructions for roles. A child might say "You be the doctor, and I'll be the little girl." Conditions are also common. For example, a child may say "I'll play, but I have to be the bus driver."

20-4  This child is role-playing a nurse.

## Benefits of Socio-Dramatic Play

Children benefit in many ways from participating in socio-dramatic play. From this type of play, children grow cognitively, physically, socially, and emotionally.

Studies have revealed a strong connection between play and cognitive development. Children's roles range from babies to parents to bears to astronauts. Their imaginations allow them to act out what they cannot yet be in real life. During this type of play, children make decisions and choices. By doing so, they learn problem-solving skills, 20-5. Language concepts are also developed as children engage in play. They learn new names for equipment and gain new ideas from other children. As they generate plots and storylines, language skills, creativity, and imagination are fostered.

Physical development is promoted through the play actions of children: sweeping floors, dressing dolls, and pretending to paint furniture. Building structures that enhance socio-dramatic scenes also helps develop physical skills.

Social and emotional development are promoted through socio-dramatic play. Children try out different social roles. Sometimes negative feelings and situations that disturb children are acted out. Through these experiences, children learn about human relationships. They learn what kind of behavior upsets another child. They learn how to get along with others and discover important social skills. As a result, they gradually learn how to balance their play to satisfy and please others.

## Play Themes

Themes for socio-dramatic play vary. The themes of play often focus on everyday situations children experience, 20-6. Children may imitate auto mechanics fixing cars, cooks making dinner, or painters working on a house. Teachers will often provide props that complement a unit of study, as well as the children's interests.

Themes change with age. Three-year-old children's play stresses process. There is no pre-planned plot or theme. Real and pretend are still not firmly separated, so the child becomes what

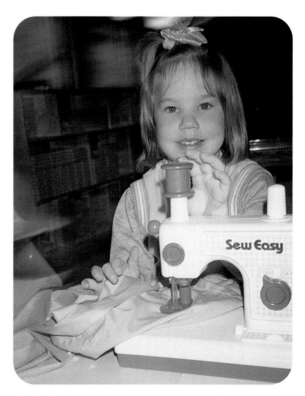

20-5  Cognitive development occurs as this child uses a sewing machine in the dramatic play area.

| Themes for Dramatic Play | | |
|---|---|---|
| **Occupational Roles**<br><br>Artist<br>Baker<br>Barber<br>Builder<br>Bus driver<br>Computer operator<br>Cook<br>Dentist<br>Disc jockey<br>Doctor<br>Farmer<br>Fish catcher<br>Florist<br>Firefighter<br>Garbage collector<br>Gas station attendant<br>Grocer<br>Hairstylist<br>Librarian<br>Mail carrier<br>Mechanic<br>Office worker<br>Pharmacist<br>Pilot<br>Photographer<br>Police officer<br>Post office clerk | Sailor<br>Scientist<br>Shoe salesperson<br>Teacher<br>Truck driver<br>Waiter/waitress<br>Veterinarian<br><br>**Other Themes**<br><br>Airport<br>Beach<br>Camping<br>Circus<br>Costume shop<br>Farm/ranch<br>Gardening<br>Hat shop<br>Hospital<br>Pet show<br>Post office<br>Radio station<br>Restaurant<br>Spa<br>Store<br>Television station<br>Theater<br>Zoo | |

20-6  Many roles and situations can become the theme of play.

he or she imitates. Routines are important. Many three-year-old children always begin their day with the same activity.

Four-year-old children are more likely to take part in socio-dramatic play. Their play no longer centers primarily around the home. Play now involves more aggressive behaviors. Four-year-olds like to imitate ghosts, monsters, or TV action heroes. As you watch their socio-dramatic play, you will often notice feminine and masculine traits exaggerated. For example, to role-play a mother, children need all the props: gloves, hats, purses, high heels, and scarves.

Children's roles change frequently. One moment a child may be a career woman, and the next she may be a helpless baby. Children are included in or excluded from play based on sameness and difference.

The socio-dramatic play of five-year-olds reflects games with rules, as well as fears and hostile feelings. At this age, the child usually can tell the difference between reality and fantasy. As a result, you may hear the child say "This is just pretend."

Real-life roles as well as folk heroes are part of five-year-olds' socio-dramatic play, 20-7. Queens, kings, nurses, teachers, brides, and characters such as Big Bird and Batman are all frequent themes. At the same time, children are quite interested in romance. Thus, they like to act out fairy tales such as *Cinderella*.

## The Teacher's Role

The first role of the teacher is to act as a resource person who provides materials and space. Studies show that in classrooms where

20-7 Five-year-olds enjoy playing roles they see every day.

theme-related props were provided, children spent more time in socio-dramatic play. The quality of toys and activities in the classroom will also affect the time spent in socio-dramatic play. Provide interesting materials, 20-8. Real materials will also enhance play. That is, instead of supplying small plastic firefighter hats, provide real hats from a local fire station. Change materials often to maintain interest.

The teacher's role also includes coaching, modeling, and reinforcing. **Coaching** requires that you provide children with ideas for difficult situations. For instance, a child may not want to be a baker because there is no baker's hat. You may then suggest that the child use a paper bag as a hat. Another child may be hitting a classmate. In this case, you should tell the child to stop because the other child does not like to be hit. You might also remind the child that others will stop playing if the experience is not pleasant.

In **modeling**, you show the children the appropriate behavior to use during their socio-dramatic play. In a shoe store scene, a child may not know how to sell shoes. You may say "Would you like to buy some shoes today?" Watching you, the child has a chance to model this behavior for the other children.

Verbal guidance is helpful. Remaining outside of the play, you may offer comments and suggestions. For example, you may see a child unable to get involved in play. You may say to the child "Your son looks hungry. Shouldn't you go to the store and buy some food?" This statement may encourage the child to take the role of the

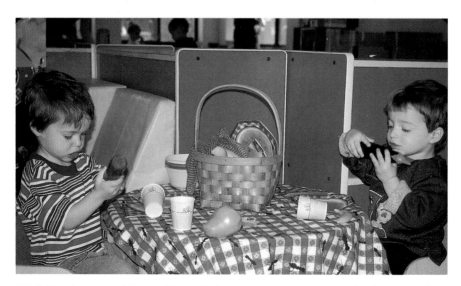

20-8 Teachers need to provide realistic props to encourage socio-dramatic play.

parent. It should also get the child involved in dramatization with the children who have set up the grocery store.

Children's positive behaviors during socio-dramatic play should be reinforced. Comments may be made directly to the children who are using the desired behavior. If Sally just gave Sam a turn to use the cash register in their restaurant, say "Sally, I like the way you are giving Sam a turn."

## Scheduling

Dramatic play is best scheduled during self-selected play periods. These periods must be long enough for the children to carry out their ideas. Many child care programs allow the first hour in the morning for this type of play.

Avoid scheduling too many activities. This affects the number of children who take part in and remain with socio-dramatic play. If few children are playing, too many activities may be scheduled. Reduce the number of activities. Schedule only activities that complement each other. Blocks, woodworking, puppets, and art activities all encourage dramatic play.

## Equipment and Setup for Socio-Dramatic Play

The first decision in arranging for socio-dramatic play is to decide on the location of the play area. Children spend more time in socio-dramatic play when the area is in the center of the classroom. Small areas tend to promote quiet, solitary play. Large, open areas promote more socio-dramatic play.

The quality of socio-dramatic play is promoted through age-appropriate materials. To promote harmonious play, provide plenty of these materials and store them in accessible play areas.

### Prop Boxes

Extend children's play by providing prop boxes. A **prop box** contains materials and equipment that encourage children to explore various roles. Boxes that are the same size, clearly marked, and made of lightweight cardboard can be stored and carried with ease.

Prop box themes might include an office worker, shoe shop owner, painter, hairstylist, post office clerk, baker, grocer, florist, gas station worker, librarian, chef, fast food worker, or carpenter. Each prop box should contain materials for one role, 20-9. Whenever possible, integrate books which can be used to reinforce the theme. In addition, the materials should be nonsexist and multicultural. To illustrate, a prop box for a hairstylist should include styling tools and products for men as well as women. It should also include hair care items for people of various ethnic groups.

### Costume Corner

Every dramatic play area should have a costume corner. Rotate costumes to complement current studies. For instance, if the theme of the week is community service, provide clothing to reflect this. Clothing for firefighters, nurses, doctors, and post office clerks can all be included. If Halloween is the theme, provide a variety of Halloween costumes. Make sure that the costume corner contains clothing from a variety of cultures. For example, you might try to include wooden shoes, grass skirts, and kimonos.

Store these costumes after use. Lightweight, cardboard boxes are good for storage. Mark each box clearly so it is easy to locate.

### Housekeeping Area

Every early childhood classroom should have a housekeeping area. Dramatic and socio-dramatic play often occurs in this area. Supply child-sized furniture and equipment. Kitchen utensils, furniture, and other household items that complement current themes should be included. To keep interest, rotate equipment often.

| Beauty Salon Props | |
|---|---|
| brushes | towels |
| cordless curling iron | aprons |
| cordless hair dryer | emery boards |
| combs | newspapers and |
| empty hair care | magazines |
| product containers | cosmetics |
| mirrors | play money |
| rollers | cash register |

20-9  A prop box for a beauty salon might contain some of these items.

## Outdoor Play Area

The outdoor play area needs equipment that promotes socio-dramatic play. Include a jungle gym, sandbox, housekeeping items, toy cars and trucks, sawhorses, wooden boxes, planks, and boards. Accessories such as tents, large blankets, and hats are also useful. With these materials, children can build forts, houses, and ships.

# Puppetry

**Puppetry** involves the use of puppets in play. A *puppet* is a figure designed in likeness to an animal or human. Puppets come in a number of sizes and shapes. People make puppets move by using their fingers, hands, and wrists. Puppets can appear to express emotions if they have movable mouths, legs, and arms.

Puppets are powerful learning tools for young children. With a puppet, a self-conscious child can act out feelings such as anger and love. While using the puppet, the child often becomes the character and loses himself or herself. All children can learn how to communicate feelings and thoughts using puppets, 20-10. They may say things to a puppet they will not say to a person. By listening, teachers may learn what makes children angry, sad, or happy.

For the teacher, a puppet can be a teaching aid. Puppets can be used effectively in almost every area of the curriculum. Chart 20-11 points out some of the values of puppets. Often, puppets are used to motivate children, to encourage them to share their thoughts, and to spark ideas. Group time can begin with a puppet. The appearance of a puppet may be changed for special occasions. For instance, green can be worn for St. Patrick's Day.

Puppets can be used to help children solve problems. When children fail to cooperate in cleanup, the puppet can say "I feel bad when all the boys and girls do not help pick up the toys." Puppets can also be used to give suggestions, such as "Tell Ricardo you want a turn."

## Types of Puppets

Puppet types include hand, mascot, and "me" puppets. The value of each type depends upon the needs and interests of the children.

### Hand Puppets

Hand puppets are the easiest to use since no strings or rods need to be worked. A hand puppet is worked by placing the second and third fingers in the puppet's head. In this position, the hand is more relaxed and the puppet's entire body can be spread open. The thumb should be placed in one of the puppet's arms and the fourth and fifth finger in the other arm.

Hand puppets can be held in front of the face or over the head. This allows the puppeteer to work the puppet from a sitting, standing, or kneeling position.

### Mascot Puppets

Some teachers choose to have a mascot puppet in their classroom. A mascot puppet is typically large. Therefore, it usually remains in the classroom all year. Therefore, it should be well made to withstand handling from the teacher and children.

Mascot puppets can be used in many classroom routines. It can help introduce new

20-10 Children can use puppets to express their feelings.

| Puppets and Curriculum | |
|---|---|
| **Curriculum Area** | **Value of Puppets** |
| Art | • Offers emotional release<br>• Provides sensory stimulation<br>• Promotes fine and gross motor development<br>• Encourages problem solving and decision making<br>• Provides for exploration of materials |
| Math | • Encourages thinking through problems<br>• Introduces concepts<br>• Promotes the development of classification skills<br>• Encourages measuring, ordering, and counting skills |
| Social studies | • Promotes communication skills<br>• Models sharing and cooperation with others<br>• Models critical thinking skills<br>• Demonstrates concepts, such as friendship and self-esteem |
| Language arts | • Encourages development of language skills<br>• Encourages listening and speaking skills<br>• Promotes the development of concepts such as *above, below, under, in front of,* and *behind* |
| Dramatic play | • Offers emotional release<br>• Promotes listening skills<br>• Encourages problem-solving skills<br>• Promotes decision-making skills<br>• Promotes self-expression and creativity<br>• Provides opportunities to gain self-confidence as group members<br>• Provides opportunities to express feelings |
| Science | • Introduces concepts<br>• Promotes classification of foods, animals, and objects<br>• Explores the value of the five senses<br>• Demonstrates differences and changes in texture, shape, and size<br>• Provides for exploration of animal and nature themes |

20-11 Puppets can be used as a learning tool in many areas of the classroom.

activities and class members. The puppet can also be used as a teaching tool. It can model proper classroom manners. For this reason, the puppet should be given an expressive face and a strong personality. The mascot puppet can also be used to teach classroom rules. If a child neglects a rule, the teacher may have the mascot puppet provide a reminder.

### "Me" Puppets

Children can also be taught how to make puppets using their own hands. These are sometimes called "me" puppets. To make "me" puppets, you will need nontoxic, washable markers, felt pieces, fake fur, construction paper, and double-stick tape. Demonstrate how to make a "me" puppet using your own hand. Line the inside opening between your index finger and thumb with a red marker. This line will be the puppet's lips. Using another colored marker, add the puppet's eyes. Use a piece of construction paper or fake fur for the hair. With double-stick tape, attach the hair to the top of your knuckle.

Show the children how the puppet can open and close its mouth and talk when you move your thumb. Urge the children to make a variety of puppets, including people and animals. School-age children may enjoy making "me" puppets on the first day of school. After making their puppets, each child can share something about himself or herself. This might include age, hobby, grade in school, or favorite stories.

## Making Puppets

Many teachers make their own hand and mascot puppets using store-bought or self-designed patterns. Chart 20-12 contains a list of materials for making puppets. After cutting the fabric, the mouth, eyes, ears, nose, and other parts should be sewn on. It is quicker to attach these parts with glue. However, this method is not durable. In fact, many times the parts will fall off once the glue has dried. All seams should be sewn with a ¼-inch seam allowance. The seams on a hand puppet should be on the outside of the puppet.

| Materials for Making Puppets | | |
|---|---|---|
| terry cloth<br>velvet<br>felt<br>flyswatters<br>dishmops<br>pliers<br>brooms<br>wooden spoons<br>velour<br>suede<br>gloves<br>socks<br>hats | tongue depressors<br>mittens<br>foam packing materials<br>coat hangers<br>plastic packing materials<br>construction paper<br>aluminum foil<br>egg cartons<br>paper bags<br>paper plates and cups | drinking straws<br>pictures<br>paper towel or toilet paper tubes<br>plastic bottles<br>envelopes<br>boxes<br>fake fur<br>ribbons<br>buttons<br>foam balls |

20-12 Items that can be used to make puppets are limited only by imagination.

## Puppet Stage

A puppet stage is not always needed, 20-13. However, most classrooms have a lightweight, portable stage. The puppet stage should be easy to fold and store. In fact, a cardboard cutting board is an excellent puppet stage. These can be bought at fabric shops. If the board is too tall for children, it can be cut to the correct height. To make the stage more interesting, the cutting board can be painted or wallpapered. It can also be covered with contact paper or fabric.

A tension rod can also be used in creating a puppet stage. When covered with a gathered curtain, the rod can be placed across a door as a temporary stage. Use a simple curtain in a solid color that will not be distracting.

Puppet stages can be ordered through most equipment catalogs. Generally, they are made of wood. As a result, they are often quite heavy. Teacher-made puppet stages have the advantage of being more portable and less expensive.

## Writing Puppet Stories

Not all puppet stories are found in books. In fact, most puppet stories are written by teachers. These stories are often contemporary and designed to fit the children's needs and interests.

To begin writing a puppet story, select a theme. Using a theme will help you decide the order of the events in the story. Themes can be based on friends, relatives, or other people. Personal experiences are another useful theme, as are manners, safety, friendships, vacations, holidays, and center experiences. Some other theme ideas for puppet stories are listed in 20-14.

Developing a plot is the most challenging aspect of writing a puppet story. The children must be able to follow the action of the story. The events should occur in a logical manner. Begin with the theme and include the story events and problems. Remember, it is the problems that add interest and tension to the story.

| Theme Ideas for Puppet Stories |
| --- |
| Odin's Broken Tooth |
| My Dog Heidi |
| Kelsi's Hamster |
| My Cousin Pilar |
| Bobby's Friend Eric |
| Christmas at Aunt Sharese's |
| My Favorite Gift |
| A Trip to the Zoo |
| Jeffrey and Eva's Grandmother |

20-14  Children do not require complex themes for stories. Simple, familiar experiences are more interesting to them.

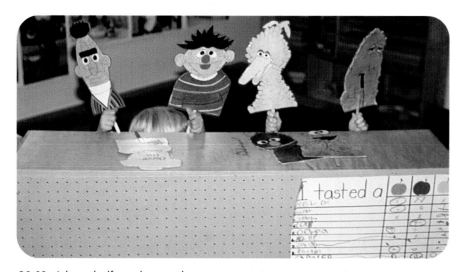

20-13  A low shelf can be used as a puppet stage.

End the story by resolving the conflict. In a story, **conflict** can be described as two or more forces that oppose each other. Conflict adds interest. When developing scenes of conflict, think in terms of synonyms and antonyms. Make a list of opposites. For example, opposite pairs might include: ugly—beautiful; poor—rich; weak—strong; soft—hard; kind—mean.

The ending of a puppet story finishes the picture for the children. The ending should make clear that the story is over. It should leave children with the story's most important point.

## Working Puppets

When using a puppet in the classroom, the puppet should always model proper communication skills for the children. When the puppet speaks, it should move and face the children. When children or you speak, the puppet should be held still, facing the speaker.

Three basic types of movements can be modeled with hand puppets. The fingers, wrists, and arms may be moved. The fingers can create small movements in the puppet's arms and head. Waist movements can be made using the wrist. Arm movements can be used for locomotion movements. Chart 20-15 explains the various finger, wrist, and arm movements that can be used in puppetry.

## Telling a Puppet Story

At this point, you have practiced the story and are comfortable working the puppets. You are now ready to tell the children a puppet story. Begin by creating the story setting and preparing the children.

The room should set the mood for a story. For a circus theme, you might place colorful balloons next to the storyteller. A Valentine's Day event might include a valentine box set next to the storyteller. Likewise, a Halloween story could be enhanced with dimmed lights. The purpose of this preparation is to put the children in the proper frame of mind for enjoying the presentation.

The first few minutes of a puppet story set the tone of the story. Make a special effort to gain the children's attention. This may be done using recorded music, slamming doors, or having the children sing a song. However, keep some surprises for later in the story.

### Puppet Voices

To develop your puppet's character, use a special voice. Since puppets are not people, their voices should not be similar to human voices. Pitch is important. If there are two puppets being used, one should have a low-pitched voice and the other a high-pitched voice.

The children should be able to hear the puppet voices clearly. Voices should also be constant. The puppet should have the same voice throughout the story. If the puppet begins with a high-pitched voice, it should finish with one.

The voice should also match the puppet's size and character. A huge tiger should have a booming voice. On the other hand, a spider should have a tiny voice. A puppet of an elderly person may have a slower voice than that of a child.

## Movements for Puppetry

### Finger Movements

- The puppet's head can nod *yes* by moving the fingers up and down inside the puppet's head. This movement can also mean *I understand* or *I can do it.*
- The idea of *me* or *mine* can be expressed by pointing the fingers inside the puppet's hands toward the puppet.
- The puppet can gesture for someone to *come here* by waving one hand toward the body.
- Clapping and jumping up and down can express joy or enthusiasm.
- Pointing can convey such ideas as *you* or *over there.*
- Waving can be used to say *good-bye* or *hello.*
- Rubbing the puppet's hands together can mean the puppet is cold or thinking of doing something sneaky.
- Thinking can be expressed in a number of ways. The puppet can cross its hands or tap its head lightly.
- The fingers can be used to mimic sneezing, crying, and snoring (move the puppet's head up and down slightly).

### Wrist Movements

- To show a *no* movement, rotate the puppet back and forth.
- To show a seated puppet, pivot the wrist, changing from a front to a side view. After this, the wrist needs to be bent, allowing the puppet to rest on a seat.
- To show a bow from the waist, bend the wrist down. At the same time, use the finger to make the puppet point toward itself.
- To show a puppet reading a book, model left to right progression skills by pivoting the wrist to mimic this action. At the same time, slowly move the fingers in the puppet's head to show reading action.
- To make a puppet appear to be looking for something, move the wrist back and forth. Using some arm movement, the puppeteer can make the puppet look to the sides of the stage and above and below it.

- To show a lifting movement, bend the wrist down as in bowing and grasp objects with the hands using hand and finger movements.

### Arm Movements

- To mimic running, move the wrist up and down in a rapid, choppy motion. At the same time, move the puppet quickly across the stage.
- To mimic walking, hold the puppet upright and straight. As the puppet is moved across the stage, move its arms up and down.
- To mimic hopping, each hop needs to be deliberate. For variety, have the puppet hop in circles, returning to the ground as the last motion for each hop.
- To mimic flying, use broad arm movements. The puppet should always face the direction that it is flying.
- To mimic fainting or falling, use a broad arm movement and have the puppet land on its back. The speed at which the puppet lands depends on the desired effect. The best effect is acquired by freezing the puppet's movements for a few seconds before falling.

20-15  Simple finger, wrist, and arm movements can be used with puppets.

## Summary

Play is an important part of a young child's day. Children go through several stages of play before they begin to take part in socio-dramatic play. These stages are solitary play, parallel play, and cooperative play. Children also move through three stages of material use in their play. These are the manipulative stage, the functional stage, and the imaginative stage. Socio-dramatic play and puppetry experiences are two types of make-believe in which children like to take part. Each offers its own benefits to children's growth.

Socio-dramatic play allows children the chance to try out many roles. Through this play, children grow physically, socially, emotionally, and cognitively. Themes for socio-dramatic play vary. With proper teacher guidance and age-appropriate materials, socio-dramatic play can be an excellent form of play for children.

Puppetry experiences provide children the chance to explore emotions, thoughts, and situations. Children can project their feelings onto puppets. Teachers can help children learn how to handle difficult emotions and situations in a constructive way through puppetry experiences.

Several types of puppets can be used with children, depending upon their needs. Puppets can be purchased or handmade. Most puppet stories are written by teachers.

## Review and Reflect

1. Define *socio-dramatic play*.

2. Play in which children play by themselves but stay close by other children is called _____ play.
   A. cooperative
   B. solitary
   C. parallel
   D. dramatic

3. True or false. Socio-dramatic play is the simplest and first type of play used by children.

4. Children in the _____ stage of material use will screw and unscrew the cap on a baby bottle.

5. True or false. All children reach the imaginative stage of material use.

6. Indicate what age groups use the following play themes:
   A. Imitation of ghosts and monsters.
   B. No preplanned themes.
   C. Real life roles as well as folk heroes.
   D. Filling, emptying, and releasing objects.

7. In _____, the teacher shows correct behavior for children during their socio-dramatic play.

8. _____ requires that teachers provide children with ideas for difficult situations during socio-dramatic play.

9. State two recommendations for scheduling socio-dramatic play.

10. What is included in a prop box?

11. How can puppets help teachers to better understand children?

12. _____ puppets are made using the puppeteer's hand.

13. Why is conflict an effective element in a puppet story?

14. Explain how you would match a puppet's size and character with your voice for the puppet.

## Apply and Explore

1. Brainstorm a list of prop box materials for a zookeeper, painter, baker, and carpenter.

2. Design a hand puppet.

3. Write a puppet story.

4. Visit a local child care center and observe the socio-dramatic play area. What types of play did you notice? What stages were the children in?

5. Observe and compare a group of two-year-old and four-year-old children. Describe the differences in their play.

6. Search the Web site for the National Network for Child Care (nncc.org) for information on children's play.   **C**

7. At the Web site perpetualpreschool.com, review the information on dramatic play.   **C**

# Chapter 21

# Guiding Manuscript Writing Experiences

After studying this chapter, you will be able to

- define manuscript writing.
- list reasons for encouraging the development of writing skills in preschool settings.
- explain activities that help children develop writing skills.
- make letters following the Zaner-Bloser writing system.
- outline the sequence children follow in learning alphabet letters.
- discuss guidelines for helping children develop writing skills.

## Terms to Know

manuscript writing
hand-eye coordination
skywriting

"Writing before kindergarten?" asked a concerned visitor. "Preschool children can't even read yet." This person was unaware that children can informally begin to learn writing at this age. Correct spelling, form, and style are given only minor attention during the preschool years. Instead, the emphasis is on a readiness to develop needed skills and attitudes for writing. As children explore, they learn how symbols and meaning combine. Art and play activities are critical in children's growth as symbol makers. Learning to write is a result of maturation, exploration, and practice.

When children begin to use symbols or drawings to represent ideas or words, they are beginning to write. When observing these children, you will note they use a combination of "sticks" and "circles" in their scribbling. Those children who are ready to create messages in print need encouragement.

For preschool children, learning to write is similar to learning to speak. Children must first observe others in the process and then imitate what they have seen. Children should be immersed in a print-rich environment. Children who are not ready for writing must be introduced to activities that will help them prepare. Activities that promote fine-motor and hand-eye coordination are needed. Eventually children will become interested in writing.

**Manuscript writing**, or print script, is a simple form of calligraphy. These simple strokes look like the printed words seen every day in the children's world in books, in newspapers, on street signs, and on computer screens. Print script does not require the sustained muscle control needed for cursive writing. It involves unconnected letters that are made of simple, separate strokes. Vertical lines (|), horizontal lines (—), diagonal lines (/), and circles (O) are used to compose the strokes. These basic strokes can be made easily by children who lack well-developed fine-motor skills. Because of the separate strokes, this process is also slower to complete than cursive writing. However, manuscript writing is more legible. Children can learn their letters at a faster rate.

Manuscript writing is not taught formally in the preschool setting. Most young children are not developmentally ready for this task. It is included in this book only to introduce readiness activities and the sequence by which children should learn manuscript. It is also included to teach caregivers of young children correct letter formations. All teacher-made materials should be done using proper manuscript writing techniques, 21-1. Your work will then serve as a model for children. It may also stimulate older children to identify individual letters of the alphabet and to write.

## Objectives for Writing

There are many reasons to encourage writing in preschool, especially with children who are ready for the task. Children need to learn

- to note the differences in the formation of letters
- to write the alphabet letters and numerals
- that words are made of letters
- that letters represent sounds
- that letters in the English language go from left to right, and top to bottom
- letter/sound associations
- the spelling of words is related to their sound

Four elements are needed if children are to meet these objectives. Included are interest, enthusiasm, clear instructions, and support given by you to each child.

## Prewriting Skills

Manuscript writing is mainly a perceptual and motor skill. Two skills are needed before

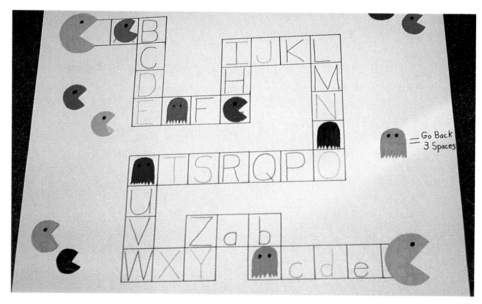

21-1 Teacher-made materials must be carefully prepared to serve as models for children. All letters must be accurately reproduced as shown on this game board.

children are able to use manuscript writing. These include fine-motor and hand-eye coordination skills. Children need enough fine-motor coordination to hold a writing tool and make basic strokes. They also need their hands and eyes to work together. Caregivers need to include activities that promote these skills in the daily routine. This will ensure that children learn the basic skills needed to learn manuscript writing.

## Fine-Motor Activities

Fine-motor activities are those that encourage children to use the small muscles in their hands and fingers. Materials used in these activities are listed in 21-2. Observe the children's interest and success with these materials. Provide interesting developmental materials. Practice should provide the children with the fine-motor coordination skills needed for manuscript writing.

## Hand-Eye Coordination Activities

**Hand-eye coordination** is muscle control that allows the hand to do a task in the way the eye sees it done. Activities that promote this type of coordination are listed in 21-3. These activities will promote the development of writing

### Activities That Improve Hand-Eye Coordination

| | |
|---|---|
| painting | drawing |
| pasting | tracing |
| finger painting | copying |
| stringing beads | stapling |
| weaving | cutting |
| tying | constructing puzzles |
| building with blocks | fastening zippers, |
| placing pegs in | snaps, and buttons |
| pegboards | lacing |
| hammering | |

21-3 Hand-eye coordination activities help train the eye and hand to work together to accomplish a task.

skills. Therefore, they should be available for use at all times.

## Manuscript Writing Systems

There are a number of manuscript writing systems available for teachers to use. The differences in these systems are minor. Included are the directions in which strokes are made and the shapes of the letters. Research does not support one system over another. Whatever system you use, be a skilled and consistent model.

Zaner-Bloser is perhaps the most widely used system. It is the system introduced in this book, 21-4. It was selected because of its common use and the ease by which children can learn to print using it. D'Nealian is another manuscript system that is used in some kindergartens. Since the letter formation is more difficult, it is not popular for preschool children.

### Materials Used in Fine-Motor Activities

play dough
clay
sand
building blocks
puzzles
finger paints
table blocks
small, wheeled toys
snap beads
threading beads
buttons and
   buttonholes
easel paints
rubber stamps
magnetic letters
wooden letters

21-2 Using these materials will require use of small muscles, thus promoting their growth.

21-4 The Zaner-Bloser writing system is easy for children to use and for teachers to teach.

## Graphic Writing Tools

Provide a variety of graphic writing tools for young children. Chalk, crayons, washable felt-tip markers, and colored and lead pencils are examples. Until three years of age, children are interested in making something happen with a tool. They enjoy scribbling and may hold a writing tool in each hand, 21-6. They often use colored felt-tip markers and soft lead pencils. These very young children hold the writing tool in the fist and use their shoulder and arm muscles to produce a marking. With time and practice, they will gain better control of the writing tool.

In addition to moving the shoulder and arm muscles, three- and four-year-old children start to use their wrists to move the writing tools. These children enjoy writing tools including chalk, crayons, and colored lead pencils. Children's controlled scribbling begins emerging into letter-like forms. Circles, crosses, horizontal and vertical lines are produced. Gradually children will use the tools to write the letters of their names. At this stage, children do not use correct spacing or position. They may also invent their own spellings for words.

Between four and five years of age, children begin to use a mature tripod grip on the writing tool. They enjoy writing their names and drawing simple stick figures, suns, and snowmen. Five- and six-year-olds exhibit good control of writing tools and can form both upper- and lowercase letters. They like to draw more complex objects, such as flowers and houses.

## Paper

Provide a variety of paper to encourage children to write. Young children enjoy making choices, so offer colored paper as well as white. Most preschool children lack the muscle control and hand-eye coordination to use lined paper. Use large, unlined pieces of paper such as newsprint instead.

## Manuscript Sequence

There is a sequence in how children usually learn alphabet letters. First children recognize whether a line is curved or straight. Next they learn to distinguish round letters (*O, C*) and curved letters (*S, D*). Then they learn to recognize curved letters that have intersections, such as *B* and *R*. Finally, letters with diagonal lines (*K, X*) and horizontal lines (*L, H*) are recognized.

Certain letters are easiest for children to form. The sequence recommended in the Zaner-Bloser method follows the similarities in lowercase letters. This is because lowercase letters are used more often. Zaner-Bloser's recommended sequence is as follows:

litoadcefgjqusbhprnmvywkxz
1, 2, 3, 4, 5, 6, 7, 8, 9, 10
LITOADCEFGJQUSBHPRNMVYWKXZ

The easiest letters are those made of straight lines or circles. You can follow this sequence as you design written materials.

## Building Writing Skills

Proper writing skills are based on a few basic guidelines. With practice and maturity, children learn the importance of letter size, proportion, spacing, and line quality. You must be able to guide them through common problems, such as letter reversals. Also, you must be able to

work through unique situations faced by left-handed children.

## Size and Proportion

To provide useful models for children to imitate, perfect your own writing skills. You must use the correct letter size and proportion. Lowercase letters are always half the size of uppercase, or capital, letters. This rule holds true no matter how small or how large the writing, and no matter where the writing appears (name tags, charts, chalkboard, or games).

The size of the children's writing reflects development of their fine-motor and hand-eye coordination. First writings are typically large. The letters vary in size and proportion. As the children's coordination skills mature, their writing decreases in size. Within any given classroom, there will usually be a wide range of skill. Look at the writings in 21-5. Kathryn's writing is mature for a four-year-old child. Her letters are similar in size and proportion. Amy's writing shows some variation in both size and proportion. Given time, she will develop the skill to make letters of proper proportion and size. Jena's writing almost looks like a scribble. Even though she is the same age as Kathryn and Amy, she

21-5 These writings show three levels of writing skill. Jena requires extra practice to bring her skills up to a higher level.

still lacks the skills needed to write her name legibly. Jena needs many more hand-eye and fine-motor activities.

## Spacing

Achieving proper spacing between letters and words is difficult for many beginning writers. Proper spacing requires more fine-motor control than most preschool children have. To help children gain control, have them write the letter *O* between words. However, this may still be too difficult for some preschool children. If so, direct them to place their index finger on the paper after the word. Then have them write the first letter of the next word to the right of their finger. Unless a child's fingers are unusually large, this should produce proper spacing.

## Line Quality

Observe the line quality of children's writings. If a line wavers, this usually means immature coordination. Wavering lines can also result from writing too slowly or moving fingers but not the pencil. In this case, the writer is trying to draw rather than write. Most often, wavering lines are a sign the child lacks enough muscular control to apply constant pressure to the writing tool. To remedy this, have children use more arm action and relax their grips. Illegible writing is another common problem. Pencil lead that is too fine or too hard may be the cause of illegible work.

## Reversals

Young children have difficulty learning the direction in which letters face. In the early stages of writing, children often reverse letters. For instance, one letter becomes another letter. Children will print *b* when they intend to write *d*. Some letters are written backwards. A *J* may have the tail reversed. Children may also write the letters of a word in the reversed order. For instance, Mark may write his name *kraM*.

You can guide children with reversal problems by pointing out differences in direction. If the child confuses the letters *b* and *d*, say "*b*, line, then circle." This tells the child that *b* contains a straight line first and then a circle. If the child is having a problem writing *d* correctly, say, "*d*,

circle, then line." After being given these directions, some children will repeat them aloud when writing *d* or *b*.

## Practice

Children need many opportunities to practice their writing. Be selective in what activities you provide to promote this skill. Be careful these practices do not become meaningless drills. For instance, when children are required to write a line of ten letters, they can become bored and tired. Their fingers become tense. The result can be the last letter is not formed as well as the first. The lines will waver. Children usually use the last letter they wrote as a model, so any errors will be repeated.

During practice with writing tools, show children how to hold the writing tool properly. First, ask children to watch the way you pick up a pencil. Place the pencil between your first finger and thumb. Lightly rest your index finger on the top of the pencil. Show the children how the index finger controls the heaviness of the letter. See 21-6.

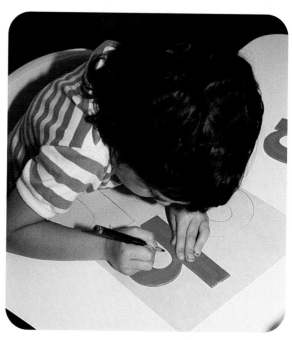

21-6 By holding this pencil properly, this child is successful in the practice activity.

## Left-Handed Children

About 10 percent of all children are left-handed, 21-7. A series of activities can assist you in learning a child's preferred writing hand. Ask children to pick up a piece of paper, throw a ball, pick up a fork or spoon, or place pegs in a pegboard. To avoid stressing the use of one hand over the other, center objects in front of children. If a child repeatedly uses his or her left hand, he or she has shown a preference for that hand. Left-handed children should be placed so the left arm is at the left end of a table for eating and work. Such placement prevents the problem of bumping arms with a right-handed child.

# Early Experiences in Writing

Early experiences often determine whether children like or dislike an activity. For this reason, start slowly and provide activities children will not find frustrating. Since most children

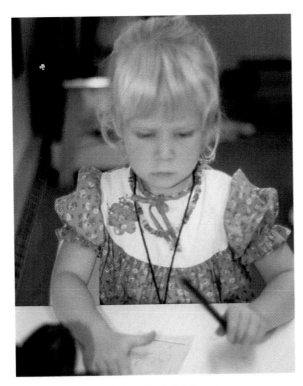

21-7 Work with left-handed children to make sure they are in a comfortable position for writing. This child has been correctly seated with her left arm toward the left end of the table.

have an interest in the letters of their own names, begin by encouraging children to copy their first names. Most children have had experience writing or watching adults write their names. Early childhood teachers should stress that children learn the proper letter forms. Do not capitalize all the letters. Children can become confused if they see their name written in different ways at school and at home. For instance, the name *Tom* should be written using an uppercase *T* followed by lowercase *o* and *m*.

## Techniques for Encouraging Writing

Your major role is to carefully prepare an environment that will encourage children to scribble and write. Children experience more success in developing print awareness in a print-rich environment. Some children will learn to recognize names and other words in their environment. To encourage this skill, you will need to use many teaching tools, 21-8.

Provide children with copies of their names. Then make a bulletin board containing the children's pictures. Under each picture, place the correct name.

Other practices to provide a print-rich environment and encourage writing include using place mats at mealtime. Print the child's first name on the place mat. In addition, print names in the upper-left corner of all papers. Writing can also be encouraged by printing labels for classroom materials and furniture. Label cots, toothbrushes, cubbies, tables, windows, doors, clocks, sinks, shelves, and curtains, as well as other items.

Make children aware of printed names other than their own. Do this by printing all the children's names on tagboard cards. At transition times, place all the cards in a small basket. Then draw one name at a time, allowing the children to identify the name.

Encourage children who are ready to print their name on their artwork. To prepare them for the left to right progression required in reading, tell children to print their names in the upper left corner of their artwork. Gradually the children will learn that letters must be kept in a certain order. They will follow the left-to-right, top-to-bottom patterns of written English.

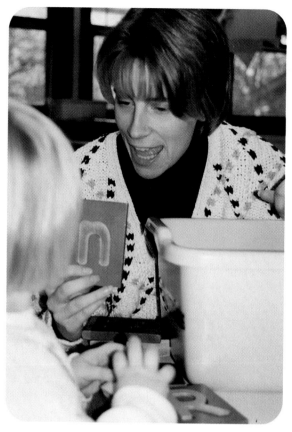

21-8 Letter blocks provide an opportunity to trace and match letters. This helps children become familiar with all letters.

When working with children who are having trouble in writing a particular letter, try **skywriting**. Stand beside the child. Demonstrate the correct way to make the letter by writing it in the air in front of you. Have the child observe your motion, hold up his or her writing hand, and follow the strokes. Observe the child to be sure that he or she is making the correct letter.

Always use the correct terminology. For example, when writing capital letters call them capital or uppercase letters. Do the same for lowercase letters.

Provide children with letters cut out of sandpaper and mounted on tagboard. By feeling a letter, the children learn its form and shape. Another technique is to print the manuscript letters on paper and cover the paper with clear acetate sheets. Give children grease or china marking pencils to trace the letters. Remove their markings with a piece of felt or window cleaner.

The acetate sheets are reusable. You might also develop puzzles that require children to match corresponding uppercase and lowercase letters.

Think of every way possible to create a print-rich environment. Create and place signs around the room, post travel posters in the block area, and have the children dictate stories as well as thank you notes to you. Post them in the classroom. Dramatic play could be made into a literacy event. To illustrate, an office or grocery store could be set up for four- and five-year-olds. The children could be encouraged to print labels and signs. You could also add message pads and pencils in this area to encourage writing.

## Group Experiences

There are many group situations in which writing can be encouraged, 21-9. Write in the children's presence. Have children dictate an invitation, letter, or thank-you note to you. As they dictate, record their message in print. Follow the correct manuscript format. Call attention to the use of an uppercase letter at the beginning of a sentence, a question mark or a period at the end, and an uppercase letter at the beginning of proper names.

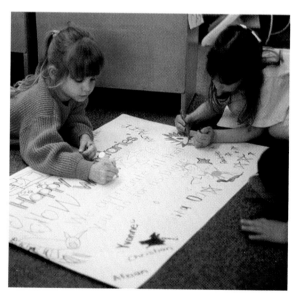

21-9 An oversized thank-you card from the entire class encourages these children to practice their writing skills.

## Space for Writing

A writing center has particular appeal for four- and five-year-olds. This space should be separated from other areas of the classroom by bookshelves, screens, or mobile bulletin boards. This allows the privacy and quiet required for writing. Provide a variety of writing tools such as crayons, pens, pencils, chalk, and markers. Provide paper of many sizes, envelopes, picture dictionaries, and models of the alphabet. Magnetic letters can be used for tracing. See 21-10.

Teacher-made materials can be added to the writing center. Charts containing words related to the current theme can be hung in this area. Display individual photographs of the children with their names written under them. Children enjoy looking at photographs of themselves and their classmates. Their interest will help them develop letter- and name-recognition skills.

Teachers also need to display materials that encourage printing. These materials include alphabet models, sandpaper letters, and sandboxes. Using a sandbox, children can practice tracing various alphabet letters with their index fingers. A large chalkboard can also be useful.

Children can make large, free movements that give writing a smooth quality.

Charts and other labels throughout the classroom can be useful displays for the children to copy. Prepare recipe charts for cooking activities. Attendance, classroom helper, and small group membership can also be recorded on charts.

Watching children's writing progress will be exciting as well as rewarding. Observe the appearance of simple letter shapes in a child's writing. Celebrate these accomplishments by hanging the child's work in a prominent place.

## Documentation Boards

Many teachers use *documentation boards* to display the children's writing artifacts. These can be made using bulletin boards, tagboard, or other types of boards. Each documentation board provides a place to display samples of a particular child's work. By examining samples created over time, progress will be evident. Documentation boards can convey to parents the importance of children's scribbling and the process used to learn writing.

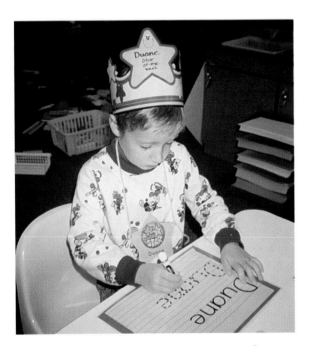

21-10 A well-organized writing center provides a positive learning environment for children to develop their writing skills.

## Summary

Having a print-rich environment encourages children to learn how to write. Learning to write is a complex process. In the preschool setting, children can observe and practice manuscript writing. This type of writing involves unconnected letters made of simple, separate strokes. These skills are an excellent basis for the more advanced writing done at later ages. Taught properly, children can also build basic reading skills.

## Review and Reflect

1. Manuscript writing _____.
   A. is a complicated form of calligraphy
   B. is more difficult to learn than cursive writing
   C. does not require the sustained muscle control that cursive writing does
   D. All of the above.

2. True or false. Manuscript writing should be taught formally in the preschool setting.

3. List three objectives for encouraging writing in preschool.

4. In order to meet these objectives, what four things must the teacher provide to each child?

5. What two activities should be provided to encourage children to build skills in manuscript writing?

6. True or false. The differences in writing systems are minor.

7. Why should lined paper be avoided for young children's writing activities?

8. Arrange the following letter groups in the order in which children learn to recognize them.
   A. Curved letters with intersections (*B, R*).
   B. Round letters (*O, C*).
   C. Straight and curved lines.
   D. Letters with diagonal lines (*K, X*).

9. True or false. Uppercase letters are always half the size of lowercase letters.

10. What is another name for uppercase letters?

11. A common writing problem in which children might confuse *b* and *d* is _____.

12. List three items that can be placed in the writing area to encourage printing.

13. True or false. When a child becomes tired, his or her fingers will tense, causing his or her print to waver.

14. List three items that could be added to a dramatic play area to promote an interest in writing.

15. True or false. A documentation board contains artifacts that show a child's progress over time.

## Apply and Explore

1. Collect, compare, and discuss writing samples from a group of five-year-olds.

2. Practice making the letters following the Zaner-Bloser writing system.

3. Practice writing a letter using manuscript writing. When you finish, check your letter for line quality, spacing, and letter formation.

4. Prepare two sets of tracing alphabet cards that children can use. Make one set using uppercase letters. Use lowercase letters for the second set.

5. Brainstorm a list of all equipment and fixtures in the classroom that could have labels attached. Prepare the labels.

6. Create a writing suitcase. Include a variety of graphic writing tools and paper. Show your suitcase to the class.

7. The Web site school.discovery.com/clipart offers teachers an array of powerful tools to create their own materials. Explore the site to find appropriate clip art for use in a writing center for four- and five-year-old children.

# Chapter 22

# Guiding Math Experiences

After studying this chapter, you will be able to

- list objectives of early math experiences.

- use two basic assessments to determine math skills of children.

- recognize a variety of items that can be used to promote math experiences.

- identify math experiences that promote the development of key math concepts.

- design math experiences that stress specific math concepts.

## Terms to Know

specific task assessment

parquetry blocks

matching

sorting

recognizing

set

empty set

one-to-one correspondence

rational counting

numerals

"One, three, five, two" and similar phrases can often be heard from young children. They are searching for meaning as they echo these words. Reciting numbers is a key step in learning math concepts. Math is sometimes defined as the science of shapes and numbers. For the young child, math is an active process of thinking about and organizing experiences to make sense of their world.

Children create math concepts by relating new experiences and information to what they already know. Meaningful learning requires the ability to see patterns. Classroom equipment, materials, and activities must provide opportunities for the children to understand patterns through play.

Early math experiences for children should focus on exploration, discovery, and understanding. Concepts are developed by the exploration of hands-on materials and the discovery of their relationships. Math concepts are usually taught informally in day-to-day activities in early childhood classrooms. These include art, cooking, games, dramatic play, music, sensory play. and storytelling, 22-1. Almost every activity area in the classroom promotes math exploration.

Children may learn shapes, color, and order (logic) concepts through art activities or by playing with blocks. Cooking activities teach how quantities are related and ordered. For instance, you might tell a child "Beat the eggs first, add the sugar second, and add the vanilla last." Classroom games can teach the concepts of first and last, as well as high and low numbers. If

22-1  Games help children learn many math concepts.

dice are used in games, addition concepts can be taught to the older children. Dramatic play offers many teaching opportunities. For example, as children play store, they can learn about money, 22-2. Songs, stories, and fingerplays can contain numbers and math words.

Other ways to include math concepts in the daily routine include asking "Are there enough chairs?" "Is everybody here today?" or "Is there a cookie for each child?" Math concepts can be used in any appropriate situation. For example, you may introduce counting concepts by remarking "Kelsie brought three kittens to school."

Transitions (time between scheduled activities) are a good opportunity to present new math concepts. For example, you might say "It's two o'clock and time to go to the library." At clean-up time, one-to-one relationships can be taught if there is one puzzle for Juan and one for Nikki to put back on the shelf. After group time, you may have the group of children wearing red use the bathroom first.

## Goals of Early Math Experiences

Well-structured settings provide play experiences that also help promote math skills. These math experiences should help form concepts such as color and shape recognition, classification, measurement, counting, time, temperature, space, and volume concepts. The math experiences should stress the following:

- observing and describing concrete objects
- recognizing colors, patterns, and attributes

22-2  As children play store, they start to form concepts about money.

- comparing objects and using terms that describe quantity, such as "more than" and "lighter than"
- classifying sets of objects
- copying patterns
- recognizing shape concepts
- recognizing and writing numerals
- using logical words such as "all," "none," and "some"
- using one-to-one correspondence
- estimating quantity and measurement
- developing problem-solving skills

## Assessing Math Ability

Before planning math activities for children, first determine the children's skill levels. In order to do this properly, children need to be assessed individually. There are two common forms of assessment: observation and specific task assessment. The information obtained from these processes will help you plan developmentally appropriate math activities.

### Assessment by Observation

Observation involves informal viewing of a child during self-selected activities. Specific behaviors to watch for include the following:
- identifying colors and shapes
- sorting and classifying objects, 22-3
- counting objects
- setting a table correctly
- pouring liquids and carefully watching the amount poured
- constructing patterns
- writing numerals

Through observation, you will be able to determine a child's needs. If you notice a child cannot sort objects, you will need to provide sorting activities. Specific activities are outlined later in this chapter.

### Specific Task Assessment

**Specific task assessment** involves giving children set activities to determine skill and/or needs. Examples include the following:
- Present a child with crayons and say "Tell me the colors." After the child has replied, say "Now count these for me."

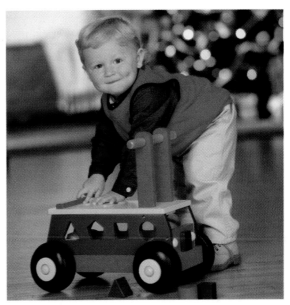

22-3 A teacher can observe this toddler playing with a shape sorter as a way to assess his math readiness skills.

- Show a child one group of four pennies and one group of seven pennies. Then ask the child "What group has more pennies?"
- Present a child with circle, diamond, square, and rectangle shapes. Say "Find the square." Then have the child identify each of the remaining shapes.
- Show a child four different-sized balls. Ask "Which is the smallest ball?" and "Which is the largest ball?"
- Lay 10 blocks in front of the child. Ask "How many blocks do I have here?"

As with observation, the information provides information for use in planning math activities.

## Math Equipment

The physical environment needs to foster mathematical thinking. Provide the children with a variety of materials that promote physical and mental activity. Include collections of items. These items encourage counting, observing, creating, sorting, discussing, constructing, ordering, and comparing. From these activities, children can develop math concepts. Chart 22-4 lists many materials for learning math concepts. If these materials are available in the classroom, children can explore and discover many math concepts.

## Supplies for Math Activities

| | | |
|---|---|---|
| flannel boards<br>felt-covered numerals<br>felt cutouts of various sizes, colors, and shapes<br>scraps of cloth<br>pegboards<br>magnetic shapes<br>calendars<br>lines numbered 0 through 20<br>rules, yardsticks, and tape measures | thermometers: indoor, outdoor, play<br>alarm clock<br>egg timer<br>giant wooden dominoes<br>giant counting rods<br>scales: bathroom and balance<br>light and heavy objects; rocks, pennies, corks<br>measuring containers of various sizes and types | buttons for counting and sorting<br>empty spools<br>puzzles with geometric inserts<br>jigsaw puzzles<br>sequencing puzzles<br>tactile numbers<br>counting frame<br>pattern blocks |

22-4 Many items can be used to stress math experiences.

## Mathematical Activities

Math activities for preschool children should promote the development of many skills. For example, children should learn to identify, classify, and understand the concept of a set. Children should also learn to count and recognize numbers and understand the concepts of space, size, volume, and time. The art of curriculum design is matching children's needs to their interests. This requires good observation skills and a good knowledge of child development.

### Color Concepts

Color is considered a math concept since it helps children learn to discriminate among objects. Using color, children can classify, pattern, and sequence, 22-5. Identifying colors also seems to help language development. It requires the skill to recall a name and associate it with a visual image. Then, as the children's language skills grow, their skill at naming colors improves.

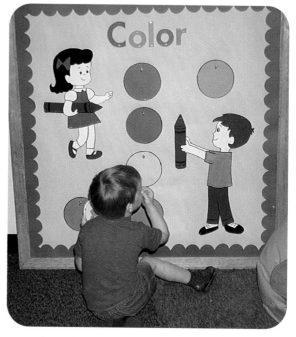

22-5 The color in this bulletin board helps children see differences between the circles, crayons, boy, and girl.

According to studies, children learn to identify colors before shapes. However, it is not uncommon for a preschool child to confuse color and shape. For example, you may ask a child to name a shape, and the child will answer with the name of a color.

By age two, many children can match a color to a sample. However, some three-, four-, or five-year-old children may not be able to match colors. This problem may be caused by color blindness. Color blindness can be discovered through careful observation of children as they try to learn colors. Children who are color-blind see shades of green and red as grayish brown. They may even see all colors as gray. If you notice that a child has a problem, report it to the center director. Often the director can discuss the problem with the child's parents. The parents can then decide if their child should be tested for color blindness.

Color concepts can be taught formally or informally. You can teach children to name colors using different-colored blocks. Hold up a blue block and ask for the name of the color. Continue by asking the children to point out other red objects around the room. Repeat these steps using the rest of the blocks.

Color recognition can also be taught at transition times. For instance, at the end of story time you may say, "All the children who are wearing blue may go to the bathroom." Repeat this, using different colors, until all the children have been excused.

Sorting objects by color can also be used to teach color concepts. Provide each child with a small bag containing several colors and shapes cut from tagboard. The children can be directed to sort by color and then by shape.

Charts are a good way to teach color concepts. Charts also teach children the usefulness of graphing. An example would be a chart labeled "eye colors." Divide a piece of tagboard into four even, vertical sections. Then divide the tagboard into enough horizontal sections for every child in the class. Have each child in the class look at the chart and determine their eye color. If the children are able, encourage them to write their name under the color that matches their own eyes. See 22-6. If the children cannot write, give them pictures of themselves or round faces cut out of tagboard. After all the children

are done, ask "Which eye color is the least common?" Then ask "What eye color is the most common?"

Colored shapes can also be graphed on charts. For example, cut basic shapes from colored tagboard. Using a felt tip marker or pencil, divide the tagboard into four equal horizontal sections. Next, divide the tagboard vertically into five or six sections. Glue different shapes in each box in the first vertical column. See 22- 7. Then give the children shapes to match.

A feely box or bag is useful for teaching color. Place colored buttons, paper, felt strips, or blocks into the box or bag. Have children draw an object from the bag and identify its color.

Color hunts in the classroom are a fun way to teach color concepts. To conduct a color hunt, ask a child to choose a color. Then have other children point out objects of the same color found in the classroom.

Discussion helps children learn to recognize colors. Have a child choose a color. Then ask the child what thoughts the color brings to mind. One child may choose red and say, "Red makes me think of fire trucks and valentines." Another child may choose blue and say, "Blue makes me think of the sky."

| Eye Colors | | | |
|---|---|---|---|
| Brown | Blue | Green | Hazel |
| Pablo | Mark | Sandy | Cory |
| Sally | Chris | Reina | Rose |
| Shawnna | Pouneh | | Ingrid |
| Tom | | | |
| Sung Jee | | | |
| Pedro | | | |

22-6 This chart can be used to help children understand the concept of eye color.

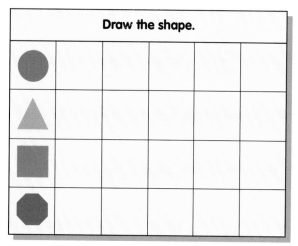

22-7 This chart helps children learn to identify shapes. Children need to focus on the outlines before they can identify the shape.

Other activities you can conduct to teach color concepts include the following:

- Hold up a piece of green construction paper. Ask children wearing green to stand up. Repeat using different colors each time. To add interest for four- and five-year-old children, give more complex directions. For instance, say "If you are wearing blue, stand on one foot."
- Pour all your crayons into a basket or box. Then set out several empty baskets or boxes—one for each color of crayon. Encourage the children to sort the crayons by color.
- Display several identically colored shapes on a flannel board. Then add one that is the same shape, but a different color. Ask the children "Which one does not belong?" This activity can also be done using different shapes.
- Play "I Spy" with a group of children. First, note a brightly colored classroom object. Then say "I spy something yellow." Encourage the children to take turns guessing what object you are thinking about. If they cannot guess it, give them more clues. The next game is started by the child who guesses correctly.

## Shape Concepts

Children are often confused by shape. At first they will say circles and squares are the same figures because both have closed boundaries. Over time they will become aware of the features of the boundaries themselves.

The skills needed to identify and draw shapes do not develop at the same time. Children can most often name shapes before they can draw them. When copying shapes, circles are easiest for children, followed by squares, then rectangles and triangles. Most children cannot copy shapes other than circles until they are about four years of age. Before this, their copies have round corners and distances of uneven length.

To learn basic shape concepts, use a variety of activities that stress touching, holding, and matching of shapes. *Shape* is defined by what "goes around the outside," or the outline of the object, 22-8. To help the child grasp this concept of shape, have them trace around the outside of the shape.

Some teachers prefer to use **parquetry blocks** to teach shape concepts. These blocks are geometric pieces that vary in color and shape. When the children are familiar with the blocks, hold up a block and ask the children to find a block with a similar shape. Next, build a simple design with three or four blocks. Ask the children to copy it.

Other activities to encourage the identification of shape include the following:

- Cut geometric shapes out of one color of tagboard. Ask the children to name and sort the shapes.
- Place a circle on a flannel board. Ask the children to name an object in the classroom of that shape. Repeat this activity using squares, rectangles, and triangles.
- Use jump ropes, masking tape, or chalk to make shapes on the floor. Ask children to name the shapes as they walk, march, or walk backwards on the figure.
- Give each child a shape cut out of tagboard. Then have the children move around the classroom to find another child with the identical shape. This activity is most useful with four- and five-year-old children.

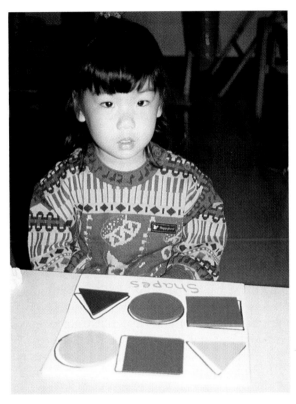

22-8 Children need to focus on the outlines of these shapes before they can identify them.

- Introduce a game called "It's in the bag." The objective of this game is to help children name shapes by touch. Begin by placing a variety of tagboard shapes or blocks in a paper bag. Hold up one shape and ask a child to find its match by feeling in the bag.
- Plan a treasure hunt. Instruct children to find shapes around the room. For example, a round clock can be pointed out as a circle.

Do not teach shape and color concepts at the same time. Wait until color concepts are well understood. Otherwise, some children may confuse color names with shape names.

Shape concepts are harder to teach than color concepts. Since color descriptions are used more often in everyday conversation, they may be easier for children to understand. For example, children often hear phrases such as a black puppy, yellow socks, red shirt, and green room.

## Classification

Classification is one of the first skills displayed by young children. Classification is the process of mentally grouping objects or ideas into categories or classes based on one attribute. Examples include size, color, shape, pattern or function. If the object belongs to a class, it has one or more features in common with another object. Classification allows people to cope with large numbers of objects.

**Matching** is a form of classification. It involves putting like objects together, 22-9. **Sorting** also involves classification. It is the process of physically separating objects based on unique features.

Children begin to learn classification skills in their first few weeks of life. By two months, children begin to classify experiences as pleasant or unpleasant. Eating applesauce may be pleasant. Sitting in an infant seat may be unpleasant.

Infants gather information to make classifications by using their senses through repeated experiences. This gives them the ability to relate past and present experiences. This process is known as **recognizing**. Recognizing is a simple form of classification.

First classroom experiences with classification should involve only one feature. Often this

22-9 The simplest matching activities involve putting two objects that are exactly alike together.

feature is color, size, or shape, 22-10. Provide items with obvious differences. For young children, this might include size, length, height, shape, color, or thickness.

Some useful classification tasks for young children include the following:

- Provide children with a set of black and red buttons. Have them sort the buttons into piles by color.
- Give children toys with and without wheels. Have them sort the toys into two piles based on whether or not they have wheels.
- Give children pictures of known and unknown objects cut from old magazines. Ask them to sort the pictures into "I don't know the name of" and "I know the name of" piles.

- Provide children with a bucket of household items. Fill the water table. Have them put the items in the water, then sort them into "float" and "sink" piles.
- Give children kitchen and bathroom items. Have them sort the items based on use.

As children build classification skills, increase the number of common features in the activities, 22-11. This can be done in two ways. Either increase the number of items to be classified, or increase the number of groups into which items can be sorted.

Advanced activities include classifying classroom items according to function. For example, some items are used for listening, some for talking, and some for writing. As another activity, give children a set of fabric squares. Ask the children to sort the materials into piles of striped, plaid, polka-dotted, and solid fabrics.

Notice that after children learn classification skills, they begin to watch and describe features of objects. First a child may say an apple is round and red. Later the child may classify it as good food. Finally the child may say the apple belongs to a group of foods known as "fruit."

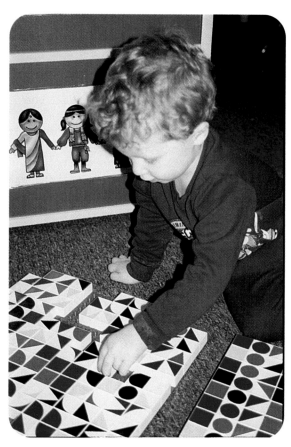

22-10 These blocks are designed to be classified by shape or color.

22-11 This sorting game involves the use of a spinner and familiar classroom objects.

## Sets

Before children learn to add and subtract in elementary school, they need to understand sets. A **set** is a group of objects that are alike in some way and, therefore, belong together. Common features of a set may be color, shape, size, material, pattern, texture, name, or use.

A key objective of early math activities is to have children learn to organize objects. Objects belonging to a set are its members. A set can have a few or many members. A set of glasses is often a certain number, such as four or twelve. A set with no members is called an **empty set**.

In order to understand the concept of a set, children first need to learn about sets that have like members. This is best taught in small groups. Items needed are sets of objects having like members, such as puzzle pieces, blocks, crayons, and squares of colored paper. See 22-12. Introduce one set of objects at a time. Say "What are these? These are all blocks. We call them a set of blocks." Then introduce the remaining sets. Repeat the process. Stress the concept of set. To conclude the activity, ask "What are some other sets in the room?"

The concept of set can be strengthened by asking a small group of children to divide themselves into a set. First divide the children into sets of light- and dark-haired children. Encourage them to regroup themselves into different sets. They might divide by sex, age, color of eyes, or color of clothing.

Teach the concept of an empty set during snack time. Provide each child with a plate holding a banana sliced into five pieces. Tell the children to eat one piece of banana. Explain that they now have a set of four banana pieces. Tell the children to eat another piece. Ask the children how many pieces remain. Tell them that is the number of members still in the set. Keep going until all the pieces are eaten. Then explain that a set without any members is called an empty set. To strengthen this lesson, ask the children to name other empty sets in the room. For example, the set of tables without legs or the set of children with beards are empty sets.

## Counting

Counting is a basic math skill. It needs to be included in the curriculum because it is a key problem-solving tool. The foundation for understanding counting is called one-to-one correspondence. **One-to-one correspondence** is the understanding that one group has the same number as another. It is the most basic part of the concept of numbers.

Children may start developing oral counting skills as early as two years of age. Two- and three-year-olds learn to count at least up to their ages. Four- and five-year-olds can often count higher. These children touch an item each time they say a number. Sometimes they forget which items they have counted. They might skip several items or touch (count) an item more than once.

Children are often first exposed to counting by listening to adults count objects. In time, children repeat these counting words. After they know the names of the numbers, they can later learn to identify written number words (two) and numerals (2).

The ability to count occurs in two stages: rote and rational counting. Rote counting is learned before rational. Rote counting is recitation of numbers in order. This skill involves memory, not understanding. **Rational counting**

22-12 Many common items can be used to teach the concept of set.

involves attaching a number to a series of grouped objects, 22-13. For example, a child has a box of crayons sitting on the table. If you ask the child for some crayons, he or she may place them on the table one at a time. As the child places each crayon, he or she assigns it a number in sequence.

Many children you teach will be able to recite numbers in their correct order. However, they will often not understand the meaning the numbers represent.

Three-year-old Tammy has typical number skills. The following activities illustrate her understanding:

■ The teacher places seven pennies on the floor and asks Tammy to count them. She counts from one to nine before she touches the last penny.

■ The teacher then arranges the pennies in a circle. Again she asks Tammy to count them. She becomes confused several times and has to begin again.

■ Next, the teacher places seven pennies in a pile and spreads out seven pennies more. When asked which pile has more pennies, Tammy points to the pennies that are spread out.

Children should always be exposed to rational counting using concrete objects. The simplest way to do this is through physical guidance. Use buttons, books, disks, table blocks, and crayons. Lay the objects in a straight line. Then

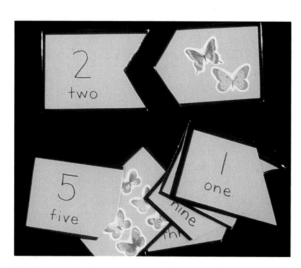

22-13 Rational counting involves attaching a number to a series of objects.

take the child's hand as he or she counts, touching each object as it is counted. At first, you may have to help the child count aloud.

After children have had many counting experiences, test their understanding. Send a child to get four crayons, two pieces of paper, or three blocks.

## Identifying Numerals

In order to read and write, children must be able to recognize written numbers and their symbols. **Numerals** are the symbols that represent numbers. Each numeral represents a quantity. Numerals serve as shorthand for this quantity.

Children gain these recognition skills as they are continually exposed to numerals. Children see numerals at home, at school, and in the community. Numerals can be found in the grocery store, on signs, and on TV programs and commercials. They can also be seen on calculators, clocks, and watches.

A good activity for teaching number symbols is to have the children take part in a number walk. To do this, collect 10 sheets of 9-by-12-inch paper. Number the sheets from 1 to 10. (To increase the durability of these sheets, cover them with clear adhesive sheets.) Then place the papers in a circle on the floor at random. Play some familiar music and ask the children to walk through the path of numbered pieces. When you stop the music, ask they children to tell the name of the number on which they are standing.

Another way to teach symbols is to set up a grocery store in a dramatic play area. Collect empty food containers and attach stickers with price tags from one to five cents. This activity can also include a toy store or drugstore. Look for numbers on measuring tools, calendars, books and puzzles.

A number line is yet another way to teach numbers. This teaching aid is based on units of length instead of objects. Make a calendar using a number line and refer to it daily during group time.

Children should have the opportunity to write numerals in their symbol form. Since children often find numerals hard to form, you may see many reversals. These problems are common and usually are self-correcting in time. You may be surprised to learn that children often prefer to write numbers over alphabet letters. Have children practice by writing in numerals on calendars or charts.

## Space Concepts

Describing the positions of objects in space is an important part of early math experiences. Space concepts that should be introduced are listed in 22-14. You should be aware that prepositions are abstract—they represent a location in space. To best learn the meanings of prepositions, children should be shown concrete examples. Since children's awareness of location and space grows out of their own bodies, have them move physically.

Space concepts can be taught during cleanup time, art time, blockbuilding, and other activities. Some experiences for teaching space concepts include the following:

- Play the game "Simon Says" using the words listed in 22-14. Give directions to the children, such as "Place your finger on top of your nose" and "Raise your right hand above your head." Using simple concepts often works well, even with two-and-a-half and three-year-old children. When using a new concept, you may have to model it for the children. You can also use an animal puppet, stuffed toy, or doll to lead the game. To get the children more involved, allow them to take turns using the puppet and giving directions.

- Place several pictures of fruit on a flannel board. Then ask, "Which piece of fruit is below the orange?" "Which piece of fruit is above the apple?" "Which piece of fruit is beside the grapes?"

- Give each child three different items, such as a block, a penny, and a button. Then give the children verbal directions using space words: "Place the penny on top of the block." "Place the button under the block."

- Use familiar circle games such as "Hokey Pokey" to teach space concepts.

- Stack five familiar items, such as a penny, stick, rock, clothespin, and puzzle piece, on a table. Then ask the children questions about the items: "What item is at the top?" "What item is at the bottom?" "What item is in the middle?" A stack of colored blocks or puzzle pieces can also be used to teach the concepts of top, bottom, and center.

Remember that children need frequent review to maintain any skill. Unlike adults, children do not tire easily from repetitive experiences. Your enthusiasm and support is important.

## Size Concepts

Children develop size concepts only through experience. Introduce and stress the words listed in 22-15 to teach children about size. These words can be used throughout the day.

## Volume Concepts

An early childhood program should offer many opportunities to explore volume. Sand tables and water tables are useful for this task. Provide many containers of varying volumes and shapes for measuring. During the children's play with these materials, introduce volume concepts such as empty, full, little, much, a lot, and some. When children use these concepts, they think about their world in terms of quantity.

## Time Concepts

"Is yesterday Christmas?" Molly, a four-year-old, asked one of the other children. Molly's question is common of a young child. Time is a

| Space Concepts |
|---|
| before, after |
| high, low |
| up, down |
| here, there |
| far, near |
| above, below |
| in front of, in back of, between, beside |
| inside, outside |
| top, center, bottom |

22-14 These word groups stress space concepts.

**Size Concepts**

big, little
large, small
long/tall, short
wide, thin
big, bigger, biggest
small, smaller, smallest
inches, feet, pounds
smaller than, bigger than

22-15 Use of proper terms, along with visual aids, will help children grasp the size concepts.

difficult concept for children to understand, partly because "time" can stand for so many situations. Past, present, future, tomorrow, and soon are all examples of time concepts.

Studies suggest that young children have only a vague concept of time. In fact, the average five-year-old child knows only the difference between afternoon and morning, and night and day. Children usually cannot read the time on a watch or clock until about age seven.

You can use routines to teach time concepts to young children. For example, you might say the following: "After lunch, we take naps." "Your mother will come to pick you up after outdoor playtime." "Before large group time, we need to put our toys away." You can offer time experiences to children by using the correct time words. Include the words such as those listed in 22-16.

Children should also learn about the passing of time. For example, you may ask "Do you remember the clown that came to school?" or "How did we make the play dough last time?"

There are many activities for teaching children time concepts. Included are the following:

- Provide children with a large, month-long calendar. Use the calendar each day during a large group activity.

Review the days of the week and use such words as *yesterday*, *tomorrow*, *last week*, and *next week*.
- Encourage children to play with a toy alarm clock.
- Hang a large classroom clock at the children's eye level.
- Use a cooking timer during cooking experiences. Some teachers also use a

**Time Concepts**

day, night
before, after
minute, second
now, later
morning, afternoon, evening
yesterday, today, tomorrow
early, late
spring, summer, autumn, winter
new, old

22-16 Use terms such as these to describe time. This reinforcement will help children understand time concepts.

cooking timer to give children a warning before they change activities. For example, the teacher may set the timer and say "In five minutes, it will be time to clean up."

■ Provide time-recording equipment, such as a stopwatch, an alarm clock, a wristwatch, and an hourglass, 22-17. Place these items on a table where children will feel free to explore them.

## Temperature Concepts

Cooking and outdoor activities help introduce temperature concepts. (Ideas for cooking activities are given in Chapter 25.) To teach these concepts, include such words as thermometer, hot, cold, warm, and cool.

22-17 Children enjoy using wristwatches and comparing timepieces to help them learn time concepts.

## Summary

Math experiences in the early childhood setting should stress exploration, discovery, and understanding. Young children require these broad, basic experiences. With such a foundation, they can build more advanced mathematical thinking skills as they get older.

Teachers can find many ways to integrate math learnings in the classroom. For younger children, math experiences can be informal in nature. Many daily events and routines lend themselves to informal math experiences. Play experiences can also be a setting for math experiences.

## Review and Reflect

1. List four objectives of early math experiences.

2. Name and describe the two common forms of assessment used to determine math abilities.

3. True or false. Math materials and equipment should consist of only traditional items such as an abacus and flash cards.

4. Why is color considered a math concept?

5. _____ defines "what goes around the outside."

6. Is it a good idea to teach shape and color concepts at the same time? Why or why not?

7. _____ is the process of mentally grouping objects based on some unique feature.

8. What is the difference between sorting and matching?

9. A _____ is a group of objects that are alike in some way, and, therefore, belong together.

10. _____ is a difficult concept for children to develop because the word represents the past, present, and future.

11. List three vocabulary words that can be used to teach temperature concepts.

## Apply and Explore

1. Review a school equipment catalog and list any equipment that can be used to teach space concepts.

2. Discuss methods to use to help young children understand size concepts.

3. Make a list of activities parents or guardians can use to teach counting.

4. Find a recipe that could be used for a cooking activity to teach temperature concepts.

5. Discuss activities that could be used to teach children the concept of set.

6. Research and compile a bibliography of children's storybooks that include mathematics.

7. Use the Web site for Super Kids Educational Software Review: superkids.com to read reviews of educational software for teaching math to young children.

# Chapter 23

# Guiding Science Experiences

After studying this chapter, you will be able to

- explain what is meant by the term science.
- discuss reasons for studying science.
- outline the procedure for planning science activities.
- list a variety of science activities and sources for supplies.
- explain the role of the teacher in guiding science experiences.
- identify methods for developing children's understanding of their senses.
- name and explain various ways to teach science concepts.

## Terms to Know

science
science table
open-ended questions
closed-ended questions
feely box

Two-year-old Ricardo's first contact with a butterfly was accidental. His study of the bug was brief but intense. It involved mainly his senses of sight and touch. Quickly he picked the butterfly up and said, "What's dat?" His mother replied, "It's a butterfly." This experience opened the world of natural science to Ricardo. Later, whenever he saw a butterfly or a moth, he repeated his new word, "butterfly."

Science is everywhere. Much of what children learn relates to science concepts. Their first learnings are often simple but meaningful. You can help form children's science concepts through science experiences. Teaching children science concepts will help them develop respect for their environment, too.

## What Is Science?

**Science** is the study of natural processes and their products. It is a way of viewing the universe. In order for children to understand their world, they must explore and question. As children explore, they actively learn. For this reason, early childhood experiences should use the hands-on approach for both process and products. This approach allows children to be involved in and think about the sights, sounds, and smells of their environment. Your role as a teacher is to provide a rich and inviting environment filled with hands-on activities.

Science is a creative field of study. It requires the development of curiosity and imagination. As children watch, study, wonder, or question, they learn about science.

Science is a way to gain understanding of why events happen the way they do. Studying science inspires children to be aware of, and involved with, their surroundings. The answers to such questions as How will it change? and What will happen if...? can be found.

Science involves observing, exploring, measuring, comparing, classifying, predicting, and discovering. The focus for young children should be on observing and exploring, 23-1. Young children are good at those tasks because they see the world from a fresh point of view. They have no preset ideas of how the world and nature work.

All attempts to gain information about our surroundings begin with observation. By using their senses, children begin to observe relationships between events. They start to group information and make generalizations.

## Why Study Science?

Studies show science activities enhance the curiosity of children, 23-2. Children also build skill in picking out similarities and differences. Vocabulary improves. Children improve their language skills and general knowledge as concepts such as *round*, *triangular*, *big*, and *small* are discussed. This promotes reading readiness skills.

Fine-motor and hand-eye coordination improve as children measure items, collect samples, and handle objects. By weighing and counting items, math skills are also enhanced.

## Planning Science Activities

Some of the most successful science experiences will be unplanned. For instance, you might bring in a flower you found on the way to the center. This can be the starting point to a discussion of flowers. As an ant moves across the floor,

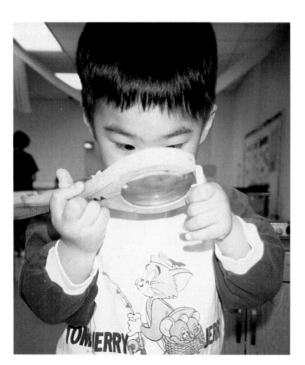

23-1 This child is learning to observe and explore as he views the nature collection through the magnifying glass.

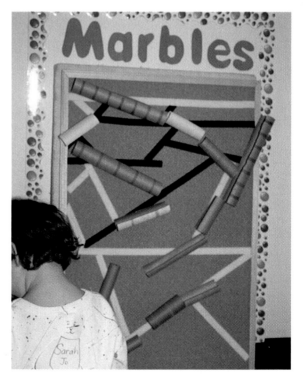

23-2 Developing a marble bulletin board that illustrates the concept of gravity enhances the curiosity of young children.

you can watch, study, and discuss it. If the wind rises suddenly, blowing debris around the play yard, you can discuss the wind.

However, most science experiences need to be planned. Focusing on a theme helps children learn about their world by structuring and organizing information. You will need to schedule events, prepare materials, and arrange the science area. You will find that science activities mesh well with other daily activities. You may plan a food or sensory activity that teaches a science concept. Fingerplays, stories, field trips, math activities, physical activity, and art projects can all teach science concepts.

Give children time to play with, examine, and try the science materials and equipment, 23-3. Science activities should offer children the chance to

- observe and explore
- note differences and likenesses
- make predictions and solve problems
- collect samples
- develop new interests and skills
- listen to sounds
- view videos
- look at books
- collect pictures

## Science Area

The science area is often set apart from other classroom areas. Tables, shelves, and/or storage cabinets can be used. The science area is best located near a kitchen. This allows access to both heat and water sources, which are quite important for many science projects.

An outdoor science area may also be used. This area may contain a garden space and an area for conducting weather tests. Small animals, such as rabbits and birds, may be raised. Store garden tools, insect nets, and water tubes in an outdoor shed to encourage children to use the outdoor area.

## Equipment and Materials

Equipment and materials for a science area need not be costly. Most items can be obtained at little or no cost. Two factors must be given some thought during the selection process. First consider the safety of the item. Then decide whether the children have the skills needed to use it. See Chart 23-4.

Many child care centers have a **science table,** 23-5. This table is used to display science-related items. The teacher often obtains the items to be placed on the table. Whenever possible, the science table should have a focus. The collection of items should provide direction for advancing the children's learning. A group of plastic reptiles may be placed on the science table. Resource books showing pictures of the reptiles should also be placed on the table next to the reptile. This will allow the children to compare the model reptiles with those in the book. Finally, concept-related literature books should be included on the table. Children can also be encouraged to bring their own items for the table. Collections children often enjoy adding include leaves, nuts, rocks, insects, nests, cocoons, and seeds.

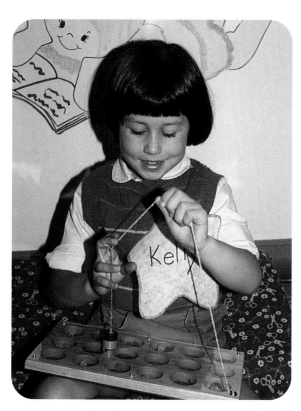

23-3 Having the chance to play with, examine, and use science equipment will promote children's growth in science knowledge.

| Science Supplies | | |
|---|---|---|
| **School supplies** | globes<br>paints<br>clay<br>chalk<br>markers<br>straws<br>colored paper<br>construction paper | chart paper<br>scissors<br>paste or glue<br>string<br>blocks |
| **Scrap items** | pocket mirrors<br>large spoons<br>clocks<br>sawdust<br>locks and keys<br>metal scraps<br>flashlights | watering cans<br>airplane and automobile<br>   parts<br>funnels<br>wood scraps |
| **Classroom pets** | hamsters<br>harmless snakes<br>frogs<br>birds<br>rabbits | spiders<br>fish<br>mice<br>guinea pigs<br>gerbils |
| **Nature items** | stones<br>snails<br>rocks<br>shells<br>soil<br>sand<br>logs<br>pinecones | leaves<br>plant bulbs<br>seeds<br>birdfeeders<br>windsocks<br>flowers |
| **Tools** | hammers<br>nails<br>rulers<br>saws<br>screwdriver<br>screws<br>bolts<br>air pumps<br>trowels | vice<br>pliers<br>levers<br>ramps<br>pulleys<br>wheels<br>magnets<br>magnifying glass |
| **Household items** | jars<br>strainers<br>food coloring<br>salt<br>sugar<br>spoons<br>corks<br>tongs<br>cloth pieces | cardboard tubes<br>flashlights<br>scales<br>measuring cups and spoons<br>pots and pans<br>empty containers and trays |

23-4  Materials and equipment that can be used in science experiences are nearly endless.

23-5  This science table has many interesting items for children to explore.

Children should feel motivated to explore the science table on their own. Therefore, the material on the science table should be changed often. If collections remain on the table too long, children become bored and lose interest. It also helps to house collections in an appealing way. You might display items in a tent, store setting, cave setting, booth, trailer, push cart, or wagon.

The science table should sit away from walls. This allows children to move about the table freely. They will feel comfortable touching, smelling, hearing, and observing as they explore.

Centerpieces at the snack or lunch table also promote children's interest in nature. A bowl of pinecones or gourds or a bouquet of flowers brings the world of science indoors. They also promote discussion during mealtime.

Playground equipment can be used to teach science concepts. For example, pedaling a bike makes the energy needed to move a bike. Using a teeter-totter demonstrates the laws of balance.

## Role of the Teacher

As a teacher, your role is to offer space, materials, and activities that encourage discovery. For safety reasons, you must provide constant supervision. You also want to learn when to let children work alone and when to step in. At times, a simple suggestion can help a child who is frustrated. On the other hand, unneeded

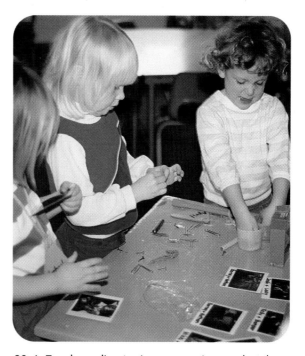

23-6  Teachers direct science experiences, but they must also know when to step back and let children do for themselves.

input can sometimes stifle curiosity. This can destroy the desire to keep experimenting.

The activities you plan should include materials for all children. Children should have ample hands-on activities in which they work with materials. This process allows children to discuss relationships and concepts among themselves.

Activities should promote development of the following five basic process skills:

- observing objects using the five senses
- drawing conclusions from observations based on past experience
- classifying objects into sets based on one or more observable properties
- comparing sets of objects by measuring and counting
- communicating by describing objects, relationships, and occurrences

Provide many chances for children to practice observing. Children enjoy watching and wondering. Going on field trips, viewing filmstrips, looking at pictures, and viewing objects on the science table are all good ways to help children build on powers of observation.

To encourage children to explore, use effective questioning techniques. Asking numerous questions is not always a useful technique. Instead, ask fewer questions that require more thought. **Open-ended questions** promote discussion and require decision-making skills. **Closed-ended questions** (sometimes called *single-answer questions*) demand few decision-making skills and are most often answered with yes or no. See 23-7. Poor questioning techniques encourage children to guess.

Children need time to answer open-ended questions. Positive response should be given to all answers. When a better answer is offered, explain how it adds to other answers. Children

also need to be heard. Being listened to strengthens a child's wish to participate.

The teacher generally sets the tone for learning science in the classroom. A simple rule is to base activities on children's questioning. Do not give answers to questions children have not asked. Let the children use process skills as well as listen, watch, or read about science. Teachers who control the activity do little to promote questions. To create the right climate, provide material for all children, study their interaction with the materials, and listen to them talk to each other. Finally, ask only those questions that add to the child's knowledge.

# Developing the Child's Understanding of Senses

As children learn more about their senses, they become aware of how to explain their surroundings. Help children learn to focus on how they use their senses by peeling an orange. During the experience, children can see and smell the orange. After it is peeled, they can feel it and taste it. By peeling an orange, children can learn the following concepts: we see with our eyes; we smell with our noses; we feel with our skin; and we taste with our tongues.

## Feeling

Feeling is a fun and important sense to explore through science activities. Whenever time permits, provide opportunities to feel a number of objects in the classroom. A **feely box** can be made by cutting a circle in a box large enough for the children to put their hands in. (A feely bag can also be used. It should be opaque and easy to reach into without exposing the contents.) Put different objects and materials inside the box. Let each child reach in the box and try to identify an object. If they are unable to respond, provide clues. For example, if the item is a spoon, you may say "It is something we use to eat cereal with in the morning."

| Open-Ended and Closed-Ended Questions | |
|---|---|
| **Open-Ended** | **Closed-Ended** |
| What are you observing? | What color is it? |
| How could you classify these? | Can you classify these by shape? |
| What happens to hamburger when it is fried? | Has the hamburger changed color? |

23-7 Can you think of other pairs of open-ended and close-ended questions?

Children can also build the sense of touch using fabric samples of varying textures. These may include velvet, leather, flannel, knit, burlap, felt, and cotton. Encourage the children to explain what each piece feels like. You might add other materials such as pinecones, leaves, fake fur, sandpaper, glazed paper, sponge, pebbles, and cork. To add variety, place the materials on the science table where the children can sort them based on like textures.

## Smelling

Preschool children need to learn that objects can be named by their smells. One method for teaching this is to collect items in the classroom that have distinct odors, such as tempera paint, markers, crayons, play dough, bar soap, sawdust, and gerbil food. Place a small amount of each item in a container such as a small paper cup. Explain to the children that the game you will be playing involves naming items by smell.

Food can also be used in the smelling activity. For example, place ketchup, mustard, applesauce, chocolate syrup, orange juice, and other common foods in containers and repeat the same steps.

## Seeing

Experience using sight is just as important as smelling. One game to use is "I Spy." For example, you may say "I spy something green. It is small and round. It is in the art area." After you speak, pause to allow the children to guess. If the children are not able to guess, provide more clues.

An activity that helps children build visual memory skills is naming what is missing from a group. Use this activity for one child or small groups of children. Collect common classroom objects such as crayons, blocks, puzzle pieces, paintbrushes, and toy cans. Gather the children, show them the objects, and explain that you will remove one object. Instruct the children to close or cover their eyes. Remove one object, then have them open their eyes and tell you what object is missing.

There are many variations to this game. You may increase the number of objects. You might place three or four objects in a sequence and ask which objects are out of sequence. You may remove two or three objects from the group and have the children name what is missing.

## Hearing

Hearing is another sense that helps children understand and explain their environment. To help children become more aware of this sense, use a tape recorder.

Teach the concept that each person's voice sounds different from any other. Record the voice of each child. To encourage the children to talk, ask each child to tell you about a family member, a favorite person, or a story. After you have taped all the children in the classroom, play the tape to the group. Ask the children to identify each child's voice by name.

## Tasting

Tasting skills can be built through the use of food. Plan a tasting party using a number of common foods. Blindfold a child and give him or her a small sample of some food. Ask the child to name the food. Repeat the activity with all the children in the group. Some teachers prefer to do this as a group activity, providing a sample of each food for all the children at the same time.

# Using Color to Teach Science Concepts

Color is a part of science that children observe daily. Naming colors is one way children describe their world. Color also serves as a basis for grouping. The primary colors, red, blue, and yellow, can be introduced to the children in the science area. Encourage the children to match red, blue, and yellow toys, such as beads or blocks, with similarly colored boxes. The secondary colors, purple, green, and orange, can be introduced next. Again, using toys, have the children match the color of the toy to the container.

Some teachers have special color days. For example, Monday may be orange day. To prepare for this day, send a note or letter to parents or guardians. Ask that children wear the color of the day. This may be in the form of a hair ribbon, pin, barrette, or any article of clothing. You may also use a nature walk to observe colors, 23-8. Snacks may be coordinated with the color of the day. For example, orange slices, carrots, or cantaloupe may be served on an orange day.

Mixing colors is another way to teach color concepts. By mixing primary colors to make secondary colors, the children learn how colors are made. Thus, as children learn color concepts, they become aware of their surroundings. One way to show mixing of colors is to overlap colored cellophane. Another way is to set up jars or clear plastic glasses in the science area. Have the children fill the jars with water. Using food coloring, place drops in each container. Stress color comparisons by using terms such as *lighter than*, *darker than*, or *same color as*.

## Using Water to Teach Science Concepts

Water delights almost all children. As young children play with water and accessories, they learn about science concepts. Some concepts taught with water include the following:

- Water flows when poured.
- Water dissolves some foods.
- Water takes many forms.
- Water makes objects wet.
- Water can be held in a container.
- Some items float on water.
- Some materials absorb water.

## Equipment and Accessories

In programs without water tables, large washtubs, sinks, photographic developing trays, or plastic swimming pools can be used. A table can also be made, 23-9. Supply water table accessories. Include funnels, spoons, sprinkling cans, nesting cups, plastic containers, egg beaters, measuring cups, strainers, corks, sponges, plastic tubing, soap, and food coloring.

To avoid excessive cleanup, put down a shower curtain or plastic tablecloth to protect the floor. Plastic aprons may be used to protect the children's clothes.

Fill the container with water based on the children's experience and age. (Younger children only need two or three inches.) Provide the children with accessories and allow them to experiment freely.

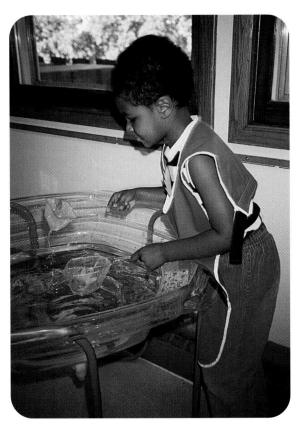

23-9 This water table is transparent allowing children to observe the contents.

23-8 Nature walks are a good time to observe colors, such as the many colors of leaves.

## Activities

Freeze water for the children. From this, the children will learn that

- ice is frozen water
- ice can melt
- melted ice is water
- ice can be picked up
- ice melts in warm places

Teach the children that some materials absorb water. Use sponges, terry cloth, tissues, paper towels, cardboard, plastic wrap, waxed paper, newsprint, finger paint, and plastic. You may wish to make a chart listing the materials and noting whether they absorb water. From using these materials, children should learn that some materials soak up water.

Water can teach children about floating. Fill the water table half full. Provide items such as wooden blocks, pencils, paper, plastic alphabet letters, metal spoons, and aluminum foil. Record each item that floats on a chart. Children will learn that some items float on water.

Through observation and participation, children can also learn what materials dissolve in water. Fill several small pitchers with water. Then have each child fill several baby food jars or plastic glasses. Give each child a material that dissolves in water, such as salt, sugar cubes, or baking soda. Also supply items that will not dissolve, such as cooking oil, rice, or margarine. Then let each child stir the mixture. Ask the children "What happens when you add (salt, rice, etc.) to water?" Encourage the children to discuss the results as each item is added to the water.

Painting with water is an activity best suited to the outdoors. Provide the children with cans of water and wide paintbrushes. Select a cement area that will not be used for walking to avoid accidents. Have the children paint surfaces such as a cement sidewalk. Then ask them what happens to the water. Try this in different types of weather. Children will see that on hot days the water evaporates and on cold days it freezes.

# Using Foods to Teach Science Concepts

Science experiments that can be eaten are both fun and educational. By watching foods as they cook, children learn how solid materials can change. Some foods become softer and some firmer as they are heated. Heat may also change the color and blend the flavors of foods. Many guidelines for using foods in classroom experiences are given in Chapter 25.

Baking bread is a science project that involves both a process and a product. In order to have baked bread, a process must be followed. This process involves

- reading the recipe
- collecting all the ingredients, pans, and utensils
- mixing the correct amounts of ingredients
- setting the correct oven temperature
- checking when the bread should be removed

A number of other cooking projects can be used. Some teachers prefer to tie these experiences to weekly themes or units. For example, they may have a unit on fall, Halloween, or Thanksgiving. Cooking experiences can focus on pumpkins, squash, apples, or cranberries. Activities should include

- preparing food in different ways (boiling, baking, broiling)
- using many kitchen tools (mixers, food processors, blenders)
- examining the insides of foods (peeling a potato, slicing an apple)
- observing the way foods change during preparation

Foods that can be prepared easily in the center are listed in 23-10.

| Foods Children Can Prepare | |
|---|---|
| ice cream | scrambled eggs |
| cookies | cocoa |
| pumpkin bread | butter |
| applesauce | ice pops |
| bread | pudding |

23-10 Making food items such as these will give children the chance to both proceed through a recipe and see the finished product.

Children can learn that food varies in size, shape, and color. Some foods are heavier than others. One way to teach these concepts is to supply children with carrots, celery, apples, bananas, oranges, and pears for snacks. Have them discuss the differences among these foods.

## Using the Child's Own Body to Teach Science Concepts

Children go through rapid physical changes during the preschool years. These changes are more obvious to parents and teachers than to the children themselves. One way to help children understand their own bodies is through science experiences. Using photographs and drawings of the children is quite effective.

One science concept to introduce is that people can be recognized by the way they look. To teach this, take pictures of each child using an instant camera. After the picture is developed, show it to the child. Encourage the child to tell you about the picture. If he or she does not respond, ask specific questions about the photo, such as "What are you wearing in the picture? What color eyes do you have? What color hair do you have?"

Some children may find it hard to link a photo with themselves. For instance, one teacher had a very difficult time teaching this concept to twins. Each time the twins saw themselves in a mirror or a picture, they identified their sibling. Experiences like these are helpful for showing children they have unique physical traits.

A growth chart can be used to teach the concept of measurement, 23-11. A chart can be made by outlining and cutting a shape such as a carrot from a piece of tagboard. Use orange for the carrot and green for the stem. Glue a tape measure vertically down the center of the carrot. Hang the carrot to a door, wall, or bulletin board. Have each child stand next to the tape. Record the children's heights on the tagboard.

The concept of weight can be taught in the same way. Create a chart to record each child's weight. You may want to record weight at the start of the year and again at midyear to show this concept to the children.

Measurements and the concept of growth can also be taught using body shapes. Have each child lie down on two large pieces of paper. Trace around the child's body and cut the shape from each piece of paper. Choose one piece for the front and one for the back. On the front piece,

23-11 Colorful growth charts are a fun way to teach children about measurement.

have the child draw his or her facial features, hair, and clothing. Color clothing and hair on the back piece. Place the two shapes back to back and staple together on one side. Stuff the figure with newspaper and staple the entire figure closed. Hang each child's figure in the room and use it as a frame of reference for the child's growth.

# Using Gardening to Teach Science Concepts

The study of gardening and seeds helps children build an interest in growing things. By five or six years of age, most children can identify common seeds such as watermelon, apple, and peach seeds. However, not many children know they are eating seeds when they eat bananas. Not many children know walnuts, pecans, rice, and peas are also seeds.

## Seeds and Food

Science experiments using seeds can be introduced during snack or lunchtime. Talk about only one type of seed at a time. For example, ask the children "What color is the orange? What is inside the orange?" Then give each child an orange that you have begun to peel. Show them how to peel the rest of the fruit. Show them how to pull the orange apart. Encourage the children to look for seeds. Ask questions about the orange seeds, such as "How many seeds are there in your orange? Are the seeds the same size? How do the seeds look? How do the seeds feel?" When they are through, have them place their seeds on the science table.

Introduce new seeds at snack times or lunchtimes. Use the same steps. Compare the seeds from different fruits in terms of size, color, and texture. Again, collect the seeds. Place them on the science table. Collect seeds from a number of fruits to display on the science table.

### Seed Party

Have a seed party to teach children that some seeds must be shelled before they are eaten. Collect a number of nuts that can be eaten: peanuts, walnuts, pecans, and a coconut. Ask the children to help you crack the seeds and remove the meat. As they sample the meat from each seed, discuss the flavors and talk about which seeds are grown underground.

Pumpkin, sunflower, soybean seeds, and mixed nuts may also be used. You may want to roast or sauté some of the seeds. During the roasting period, ask questions such as "Which seeds are labeled nuts? How does cooking change the taste? How does cooking change the texture?"

## Observing Seeds

A nature or seed walk is another way to teach children that seeds come from fruits of plants. Before leaving on the walk, give each child a paper bag with the child's name on it. You may prefer to wrap a piece of packing tape with the sticky side out on each child's wrist. The children can stick the seeds to the sticky tape as they are discovered. Walk to a park or other area where seeds are plentiful and encourage the children to collect seeds. When the group returns to the classroom, ask each child to choose three seeds to add to the science table. Save the rest of the seeds for an art display.

Place magnifying glasses on the science table next to the seeds, 23-12. Encourage the children to use the glasses to view the shapes,

23-12 This child is using a magnifying glass to study the shape, size, color, and texture of the seeds from a gourd.

sizes, colors, and textures of the seeds. This activity should help the children become aware of the seeds' differences and similarities.

## Planting Seeds

Planting seeds indoors and outdoors is another way to teach children concepts about plants and their growth. Have children plant bean, corn, carrot, and radish seeds in individual containers. Use paper cups, tuna cans, milk cartons, or clay pots. If possible, use transparent recycled containers so the children can observe root growth below the surface. Write the children's names on the containers. Provide soil for the children to use for planting. The best mixture for growth is garden soil, or loam. It supplies nutrients for the plant and provides good moisture and drainage control. Have children fill the containers with soil. Then let the children choose seeds to plant. Show them how to use their fingers to make holes in the soil. Add the seeds and cover with soil. Label each container with the seed name. Then show the children how to lightly dampen the soil using a watering can.

Most seeds will grow when given proper moisture and temperature. When the seedlings emerge from the surface of the soil, place the containers where they will receive sunlight. Encourage the children to check the containers daily. Ask questions such as "What seeds sprouted first? Do all plants have similar leaves? How many leaves does each plant have?" From this experience the children should learn the following:

- Seeds planted in soil and given water, warmth, and sunshine grow.
- Some seeds germinate earlier than others.
- As plants grow, their size changes.

### Dish Garden

Make a dish garden using pineapple, turnip, carrot, or beet tops. First, cut the tops off about one and one-quarter inch below the leaves. Then place the tops in clear, shallow dishes with water and sand. Put the dish on the science table where the children can observe the growth.

### Vase Garden

Collect an onion, potato, sweet potato, or avocado pit and a jar large enough to hold the vegetable. Suspend the vegetable on toothpicks, 23-13. You may have to add small amounts of

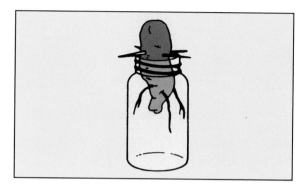

23-13 Many vegetables grow with little care if suspended in this way.

water from time to time. As the vegetable sprouts and evaporation takes place, the water level will decrease. Students can observe the roots and stems as they grow.

### Bulletin Board Garden

Plants can also be grown in resealable plastic bags. Hang one bag for each child on a bulletin board that is decorated like a garden. With help, each child can plant a seed in a bag. Start by folding a paper towel and soaking it. Put the wet towel inside the bag. Place a bean seed between the side of the bag and the paper towel. In time, the seed will sprout and its roots will fill the bag.

You can also grow flowers in these bags. Fill the bags with potting soil instead of a paper towel. Add flower seeds. After the seeds sprout, move the plants to indoor pots or an outdoor garden (if the weather permits).

### Outdoor Garden

When space allows, grow an outdoor garden. The available space as well as the children's ages and interests, may influence what you grow. It might be a flower garden, a simple vegetable garden, or both. Let the children take part in caring for the garden and enjoying its end results.

## Using Air to Teach Science Concepts

Every day children have experiences with air. They watch airplanes and birds, fly kites, and blow up balloons. They feel the wind blow against their bodies and clothing.

**Bubble Solution**

½ cup glycerin (purchase from drug store)
2 cups water
3 tablespoons liquid detergent

23-14 Bubble solutions are very easy to make.

23-15 As children blow bubbles they become aware that the bubbles, and therefore air, take up space.

## Teaching About Air

To help children understand the concept that air takes up space, inflate some balloons. Do this activity in a group. Start by showing the children a deflated balloon. Then tell them to watch closely as you blow up the balloon. After the balloon is inflated, ask "What is inside the balloon?" Pass out balloons to all the children. Encourage them to fill the balloons with air. After the activity, collect the balloons.

Bubble solutions are another way to teach children that air takes up space. You can buy a prepared solution or use the recipe in 23-14. Give each child a straw and a paper cup. Using a pencil point, make a hole about one inch from the bottom of the cup. Have the children place a straw in the hole. Then have them dip the open end of the cup in the bubble solution. Finally, ask them to remove the cup from the solution and, with the cup in an upside down position, blow into the straw.

Encourage the children to blow bubbles. Ask them "What is inside of the bubbles? How did you get air inside of the bubble? How can you make the bubble larger? How can you make the bubble smaller?"

Use a clear container, such as an aquarium or glass mixing bowl, to conduct another experiment. Fill the container with water and pass straws to each child. Tell the children to place their straws in the container and blow, 23-15. Ask "What happens when you blow air through the straw into the water?"

## Teaching About Wind

To teach the concept that the wind makes things move, use thin strips of newsprint or crepe paper streamers. For this activity to work, you need to introduce it on a windy day. Take the children outside and hand out the streamers. Show them how to hold the streamers. Ask "What happens to the streamer when the wind blows? What direction is the wind moving? What happens when you run fast?"

## Using Weather

Develop environmental awareness by focusing on the weather—snow, wind, rain, thunderstorms, and rainbows all appeal to young children. Develop a weather felt board to use at group time. Include figures of children, clothing for all seasons, clouds, sun, snow, and raindrops. Each day a child can select the clothing and symbols to represent the weather.

# Using Magnets to Teach Science Concepts

Children are intrigued by magnets. Concepts about magnets are best learned through a combination of teacher guidance and hands-on activities, 23-16. Therefore, teachers need to buy

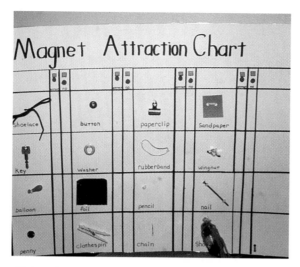

23-16 Charts are also useful for learning magnet concepts.

quality magnets. These can be bought through science equipment or school supply stores. Buy a variety of magnets, including horseshoe, ceramic, bar, disk, and rod-shaped magnets.

As children work and play with magnets, they will observe the following:

- Magnets pull some things, but not others.
- Some magnets are big; others are small.
- Some magnets are stronger than others.
- Magnets pick up objects made of iron.

To aid in building these concepts, place several magnets on a table. Collect objects that magnets will pick up and others they will not. Types of objects magnets attract include metal screws, staples, nails, paper clips, and other small metal objects. A magnet will not pick up objects that do not have an iron content. Such objects include paper, cloth, wooden pencils, crayons, shoelaces, and aluminum dishes.

Place a variety of horseshoe and bar magnets in a small box. In a second box, place chalk, toothpicks, paper, nails, paper clips, plastic spoons, and other objects. Have the children name each object and tell whether the magnets can lift it.

## Using Wheels to Teach Science Concepts

Children see wheels every day. They may travel by car, truck, bus, or train to the child care center or preschool. There they see wagons, tricycles, scooters, and other toys with wheels. At home they might see machines with wheels, such as vacuum cleaners and lawnmowers. Perhaps on a trip to the airport they have seen people pulling suitcases with wheels. All these experiences should help them learn about the uses of wheels.

Children can learn the following concepts about wheels:

- Wheels are round.
- Wheels roll.
- Wheels usually turn on an axis.
- Wheels make work easier for people.

To learn these concepts, children need to be exposed to many types of wheels. You might demonstrate these concepts using wagons and wheelbarrows.

To help children learn to identify a wheel, use a feely box or bag. Place cubes, balls, wooden blocks, and rubber wheels in the box. Ask one child at a time to feel in the box and find the wheel.

Another way to teach children about wheels is to cut out and hang pictures of wheels from magazines. Include fire engines, cars, trucks, tractors, wagons, airplanes, golf carts, scooters, and roller skates. Then cut out and hang pictures of other types of transportation. These might include motorboats, sailboats, skis, rafts, sleds, ice skates, donkeys, elephants, and horses. When you have finished, ask the children to point out the pictures with wheels.

## Using Field Trips and Walks to Teach Science Concepts

Field trips promote curiosity, supply opportunities for discovery, and encourage interaction with the environment. During field trips, children can observe how machines make work more precise, easy, and orderly. For example, on a trip to the fire station, point out the fire alarm system, ladder, ax, hose, and fire extinguisher.

Short walks with a focus can also help the children learn about science. Topics for these walks could include colors, seeds, rocks, footprints, animals, insects, plants, or leaves. On rainy days, it might be interesting to take a walk to study earthworms, puddles, or rainbows. Chart 23-17 lists field trip locations and things to observe there.

## Using Animals to Teach Science Concepts

Some animals can be used as classroom pets. Science concepts can be taught to young children using these pets. For example, children can learn how different animals look and feel, what they eat, how they should be handled, and how they respond to their environment. Pets can help teach responsibility, empathy, and respect for all kinds of life. After having the opportunity to observe and compare animals, children can draw conclusions from their experiences, 23-18.

23-18  Having classroom pets gives children a chance to observe, care for, and learn about pets as a part of their daily routine.

| Science Field Trips | |
|---|---|
| **Location** | **Science Concepts Studied** |
| Lumber company | Nature of wood and sawdust |
| Automobile and bike shops | Workings of motors, gears, chains, wheels; use of tools |
| Grocery stores | Forms of foods |
| Vacant land | Insects, plant life, animal shelters |
| Print shop | Mechanics of the printing process |
| Commercial laundry | Effects of cleaners, heat, starch |
| Produce market | Nature of fresh fruits and vegetables |
| Interior decorating shop | Nature of fabrics, use of colors |
| Television and radio studios | Production and transmission of images and sounds |
| Fire department | Mechanics of trucks, engines, ladders |
| Animal hospital | Care of pets |
| Toy shop | Nature of toy materials, such as plastic, wood |
| Excavation site | Nature of soil, rocks, building materials |
| Zoo | Birds, insects, animals |
| Botanical gardens | Plant life |
| Museum | Rocks, geological formations, other science concepts |

23-17  Field trips can be used to teach a variety of science concepts. For instance, a trip to a fruit market can teach children about plants and seeds.

## Care of Animals

All animals brought into the classroom should receive humane care and treatment. Children should always see animals being handled and cared for properly. Make every effort to provide for the basic needs of classroom animals. These needs include food, water, light, air, proper space for movement, and exercise.

## Value of Animals

Experiences with animals should teach children the following concepts:

- There are many kinds of animals.
- Animals are fun to watch.
- Animals, especially pets, require care.
- Pets depend on humans for proper care.
- There are many kinds of animals; some are small and some are large.
- Animals need water, proper food, shelter, and exercise.
- Animals have different kinds of body coverings, such as feathers, scales, hair, and smooth skin.
- Animals move in different ways. They may fly, swim, walk, run, crawl, creep, or hop.
- Animals have different numbers and kinds of legs. Some have two legs, some four, some six, some eight, and some have none.
- Animals can be identified by the different sounds they make.

## Animals as Classroom Pets

Many animals can be used as classroom pets. Hamsters, snakes, toads, frogs, fish, rabbits, and guinea pigs have all been used in early childhood programs. Other classroom pets might be a gerbil, mouse, or bird. Chart 23-19 lists the average life span of some common classroom pets.

### Hamsters

A healthy hamster is chubby and has a shiny coat and bright eyes. Buy hamsters only from pet stores that handle healthy animals. (One strain of hamster spreads a form of meningitis.)

Hamsters should be housed in a wire, rustproof cage. The cage should have an exercise wheel. Since hamsters are able to chew

| Average Life Span of Classroom Pets | |
|---|---|
| Mouse | 1 to 2 years |
| Hamster | 1½ to 2½ years |
| Gerbil | 4 years or more |
| Guinea pig | 6 years |
| Rabbit | 6 to 7 years |
| Canary | 10 to 15 years |

23-19 When cared for properly, classroom pets have long life spans.

through many materials and escape through small holes, a wire cage prevents escape. Wood shavings should be spread on the floor for cage litter. This litter should be replaced daily. Newspaper should also be placed in the cage for the hamster to shred for nesting. Because hamsters have two pairs of gnawing teeth, they enjoy chewing a piece of soft wood. Gnawing also helps keep the hamster's teeth at a healthy length.

Provide hamsters with nutritious food. You can buy grain for hamsters at a pet store. Hamsters also enjoy almost all greens such as lettuce, clover, alfalfa, and grass. Provide them with fresh water in a special bottle purchased from a pet store. This bottle prevents spilling and ensures that the animal has a constant supply of water, 23-20.

Generally, hamsters have been found to be quite friendly with children if they are treated gently and fed regularly. When they are handled roughly or exposed to loud voices, they have been known to bite. For this reason, you need to make rules for handling the hamster. Supervise this activity closely.

### Snakes

Harmless snakes make good classroom pets. They require little care and, when handled properly, rarely bite. Having a snake in the classroom can also prevent or dispel any fear the children might feel.

Aquariums are good housing for snakes. Spread newspaper on the bottom of the

23-20 Note the water bottle in this gerbil's cage. It is the type used for hamsters and rabbits, too.

aquarium. Then cover the newspaper with gravel and a small piece of wood. For privacy, build a cave in one corner with small rocks. Add a small dish of water. To prevent the snake from escaping, cover the top with a secure screen.

Different types of snakes require different foods. Your local pet shop salesperson or conservation authority worker can help you determine the snake's dietary needs. As a rule, small snakes can exist on insects, worms, and meat. Frogs and mice are required by the larger species. Some teachers prefer to arrange for their local pet store to feed large snakes.

## Toads and Frogs

Toads and frogs are common classroom pets. They can be housed in an aquarium. To avoid odors, clean the housing often. Water should be changed at least twice a week. You will notice that frogs often sit in their water. They do this to moisten their bodies, which is necessary for their survival.

Toads and frogs enjoy eating small earthworms or insects. They will accept raw or chopped beef, or canned dog food. Children enjoy watching these animals use their sticky tongues to catch food such as bugs.

## Fish

Fish are an ideal pet for some teachers because they require less attention than most other pets. If you would like fish as classroom pets, you will need to decide whether to buy tropical or freshwater fish. Freshwater fish are less costly and have easier care requirements. They can be kept in a fishbowl rather than in an aquarium.

Tropical fish require an aquarium. Most teachers prefer 20-gallon aquariums. They are easier to maintain than smaller tanks. Also, children can see the fish more easily. Maintain a water temperature between 70°F and 80°F at all times. To ensure this range, purchase a thermometer and a self-regulating aquarium heater.

The pH balance of the water is important. It should be kept close to neutral. This is especially important if you wish to breed tropical fish. If the pH is acidic, it can be corrected by adding sodium biphosphate or sodium bicarbonate. These products can be purchased at a pet store. You might also buy a kit to test the water.

Fill the tank with water and allow it to settle. There should be a half gallon of water for every inch of fish in the aquarium. Wait one week for the water to reach the correct temperature and pH balance. Then add the fish.

Talk to the salesperson at your pet store to find out exactly what, how much, and how often to feed your freshwater or tropical fish. Chances are a prepared fish food and/or shrimp brine will be recommended.

## Rabbits

Rabbits have always been a favorite pet of young children and their teachers. However, not all teachers enjoy having a rabbit indoors. This is because rabbits must be cleaned quite often.

Rabbits are often kept in large wire cages that allow plenty of room for movement. For shelter, place a wooden box at one end of the cage. Wood shavings or straw should also be placed in the bottom of the cage for bedding.

You may prefer to keep the rabbit outdoors to prevent classroom odor. Make sure the cage is sheltered from the wind and sun. If your play yard is enclosed, you may let the rabbit exercise outside the cage for short periods.

Because rabbits are hearty eaters, they require large amounts of food and water. You can buy rabbit feed at a pet store. Green or leafy vegetables, including lettuce, cabbage, and celery tops, are also enjoyed. You may wish to omit cabbage and other strong-smelling vegetables from their diet. This will help control the unpleasant odor of strong-smelling urine. Use caution when handling the rabbit. Rabbits have sharp toenails and may scratch when they're afraid.

### Guinea Pigs

Most early childhood teachers agree that guinea pigs make good pets for young children. They are easy to handle and they do not bite. Also, guinea pigs are very gentle. They enjoy being held and cuddled by children. In addition, even very young children can easily observe, care for, and handle them. These pets have heavy bodies and tight skins. They can be picked up

easily by placing a hand under the pig's body.

Wire cages provide good housing for these animals. Recommended cage sizes are about two and one-half to three feet in length, one and one-half feet deep, and one and one-half feet wide. Doors on cages need to fit tightly to prevent the animals from escaping. Spaces to hide, exercise, and sleep should be included. A small cardboard box can be placed inside the cage for sleeping.

Food for a guinea pig is similar to that of rabbits. They enjoy pellets or grains including corn, wheat, and oats. Grass, alfalfa, clover, and carrots can be added to their diets for variety. Most teachers who have guinea pigs for classroom pets recommend pellets as the most convenient type of food.

## Care of the Earth

The children need to learn to preserve the earth by keeping it clean, 23-21. Set the stage by recycling in your classroom. To do this, place four bins labeled *paper*, *glass*, *metal*, and *plastic* in a classroom area. Encourage the children to sort items.

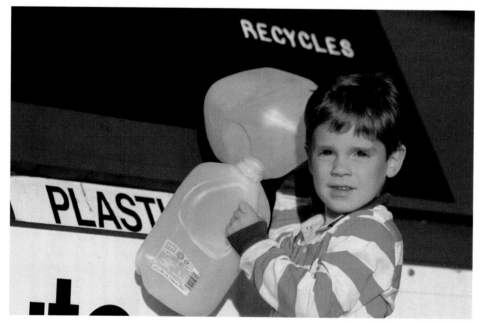

23-21 Children should be encouraged to recycle whenever possible.

## Summary

The nature of modern life makes studying science important. Young children can be introduced to science at the center through simple experiences.

In order to guide these experiences, teachers must know the objectives of studying science. They must also know how to help children reach these goals. This will require planning.

With a solid plan, teachers can then design a variety of activities to teach science concepts. Many methods and items can be used to teach these concepts, including colors, water, food, bodies, gardens, air, magnets, wheels, field trips, and pets.

## Review and Reflect

1. What is the definition of *science*?

2. Because science is creative, it requires the development of children's _____ and _____.

3. List three reasons why science should be studied.

4. True or false. All science projects need to be planned in detail.

5. During their science experiences, children should have many opportunities to _____.
   A. observe
   B. solve problems
   C. collect samples and pictures
   D. All of the above.

6. Why should the science area be located near the kitchen?

7. What is a science table?

8. True or false. Unneeded teacher input can sometimes stifle children's curiosity, thereby limiting their desire to continue experimenting.

9. List the five basic process skills.

10. _____-ended questions promote discussion, but _____-ended questions tend to require only one word answers.

11. Name four ways to teach science concepts. Of these four methods, explain one in detail.

## Apply and Explore

1. Develop a collection of items that could be placed on the science table. Explain how the collection would contribute to the science experiences of young children.

2. Brainstorm a list of centerpieces for the snack or lunch table that would help develop science concepts.

3. Draw a sketch of a science area as you would design it. Include placement of equipment.

4. Review a recipe book. List examples of cooking activities that would involve a process and product.

5. Develop a recipe file of foods that can be prepared by the children in an early childhood setting.

6. Make a dish garden using a pineapple, turnip, carrot, and beet top. Document the amount of time it takes for each to sprout.

7. Explore the Web site of the National Wildlife Federation (nwf.org) for information related to science learnings for children.

8. Search the Kids section of the Kids Health Web site (kidshealth.org) for rules for staying safe around animals.

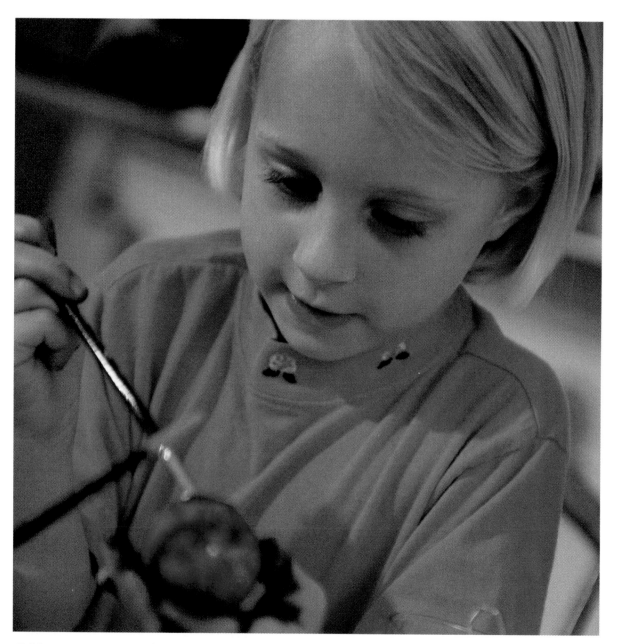

Children enjoy preparing for and celebrating holidays and special events.

# Chapter 24

# Guiding Social Studies Experiences

After studying this chapter, you will be able to

- explain the importance of social studies experiences.
- outline the role of the teacher in designing and guiding social studies experiences.
- describe ways to include multicultural, intergenerational, government, ecology, geography, community living, holiday, and current events concepts in the curriculum.

## Terms to Know

incidental learnings
perceptions
culture
omission
ecology

Young children approach classroom life eagerly and positively. They are interested in everything that goes on and are always full of questions. For instance, they might ask

- Where is Africa?
- How does the police officer help me?
- Why doesn't she have a daddy?
- What is Passover?

Many of these questions arise naturally during daily classroom activities. Children's questions might relate to social skills, cultures, careers, holidays, current events, history, or geography. These questions all revolve around social studies as a curriculum area.

The field of social studies includes many subjects that help children learn about themselves, as well as other people. Children learn about families, peers, and people in the community. In addition, they learn positive group living skills, such as cooperation and responsibility, 24-1.

Young children build social studies concepts as they move through the world around them. For example, children learn key social studies concepts when they walk around the neighborhood. Social studies concepts can also be developed by looking at many types of housing. Role-playing doctors, mail carriers, grocers, or parents also promotes an understanding of social studies. So does the process of making and eating ethnic foods or hearing a story about community helpers. By taking part in tasks for maintaining the classroom, children learn social studies concepts. Watering flowers, feeding classroom pets, and putting blocks away teach children about getting along in their world.

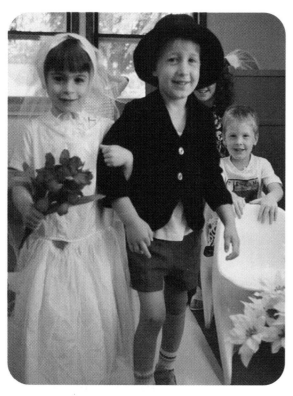

24-1 Through social studies experiences, children learn to accept themselves and get along with others.

24-2 Learning to share ideas helps children build communication skills.

## Importance of Social Studies

Children need to understand and appreciate how other people live—their lifestyles, languages, and viewpoints. Social studies helps children acquire skills for living. By including social studies concepts in the curriculum, children will

- develop self-respect and a healthy self-concept.
- develop respect for others.
- develop self-control and independence.
- learn to share ideas and materials, 24-2.
- develop healthy ways of relating to and working with others.
- gain the attitudes, knowledge, and skills needed for living in a democracy.
- develop respect for other people's feelings, ideas, and property.
- learn about the roles people have in life.
- learn to appreciate the past and its relationship to the present.
- learn the need for and purpose of rules.

The value of the social studies curriculum, then, is that it makes children better able to understand their world and their place in it.

## The Teacher's Role in Social Studies

The key to a good social studies program is your skill as a teacher and the knowledge you bring to the classroom, 24-3. Your interests will determine the degree to which social studies will be included in the curriculum. Through your training, you will understand the need to use community resources, chance learnings, themes, group participation, observation, and evaluation to enrich the social studies program.

To provide quality learning experiences, you need to make daily observations. These routine checks should provide data related to the children's interests, abilities, developmental levels, attitudes, and knowledge. From this data, you can determine what children need to know and what behaviors need to be changed.

24-3 Teachers play a crucial role in quality social studies programs.

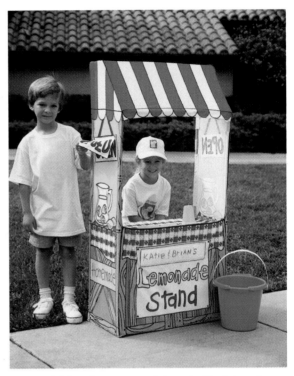

24-4 Children have many interests. To determine individuals' interests, playtime is an excellent time to observe.

## Determine the Children's Interests, Abilities, and Characteristics

Every group of children brings a wide variety of interests to the classroom. Some children may be interested in airplanes, trains, or geography. Other children may prefer to study community helpers. To determine children's interests, you can

- observe them during play, noting the type of play and their use of materials and equipment, 24-4.
- interact with them in a casual way, asking them what they enjoy.
- ask the children's parents to share their children's interests with you.
- observe the children's choice of books.

Like interests, the skills of every group of children should influence the social studies program. In any given classroom, there will be many levels in cognitive, physical, social, and emotional development. As a teacher of young children, you will need to match materials and equipment with each child's ability level.

Determine children's ability levels by

- observing the children's social skills as they play with other children.
- reviewing the children's physical growth and health records.

- structuring a variety of tasks for each child to complete, noting their success.

There is no shortcut for gathering data to determine the children's skill levels. Gathering takes time. The information, however, is essential for planning a developmentally appropriate social studies curriculum.

Developmental characteristics are key to designing a social studies program. These traits can be observed and used as a starting point for planning social studies activities. Characteristics and their implementations are listed in 24-5.

## Develop the Curriculum

Once the children's interests, abilities, and characteristics have been determined, you are ready to plan the curriculum. Encourage children to take part in the planning. This process will help them organize their thoughts, express their ideas, and experience the results.

During the planning process, allow children to make important choices. Involve all children

| Activities Related to Children's Characteristics | |
|---|---|
| **Characteristics** | **Implementations** |
| Interest centered on immediate environment. | Provide opportunities to explore the school, home, and neighborhood. |
| Enjoys opportunities for self-expression. | Provide small group opportunities whenever possible. |
| Shows interest in people with whom he or she is acquainted. | Share resource people with whom the children have indicated an interest. |
| Learns best through direct experiences. | Provide concrete materials and hands-on activities. |
| Enjoys pretending. | Provide many opportunities and props for dramatic play. |
| Tends to be egocentric (self-centered: I or me) | Provide consistent guidance in respecting other's rights and following rules. |

24-5  Watch for children to show these characteristics. Social studies activities can be implemented to either enhance or discourage such traits.

in the group. You may find that some may be quite shy. These children may feel better if given a chance to plan individually in a small group.

Young children are able to plan the following aspects of their activities:

- Whom to play with.
- Materials needed for a project.
- Places to visit.
- People to invite to the classroom.
- How to celebrate birthdays and holidays.

## Themes

Many teachers use themes when planning a social studies program, 24-6. One theme can be used to combine the learning opportunities of many different activities. Therefore, varied experiences help children learn concepts. (See Chapter 17 for additional information on themes.)

## Use Community Resources

Look closely at your community resources for a variety of learning opportunities. Record the names of stores, museums, art galleries, community services, community workers, and housing groups that may be of interest. The people providing these services might also have suggestions for curriculum objectives and goals.

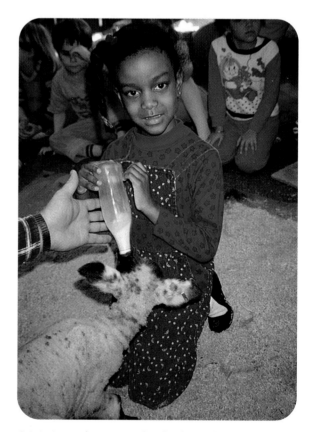

24-6  A pet theme can be the basis for teaching many social studies concepts.

## Incidental Learnings

You should structure the classroom to promote **incidental learnings**. These are learning experiences that happen during the course of a normal day. Watch for everyday happenings that can teach children something. For example, point out the paint that dried out when the lid was left off or the plant whose leaves yellowed when not watered. These situations cause children to question and learn on their own.

Every classroom has unique incidental learning experiences. The following are examples:
- Classroom and playground repairs.
- Classroom rules.
- Roles of center workers such as the janitor, bus driver, or office worker.
- Handling an argument.
- Happenings in the local community.

## Evaluation

Evaluation is a key part of planning the social studies curriculum. The evaluation process will help you see if goals have been met, what new goals are needed, and whether any current goals need modification. This process can be done with the children. For example, you may ask the children the following questions:
- What did you like best?
- Why did you like it?
- What did you learn?
- What do you want to learn more about?
- What would you like to do again?

# Building Social Studies Concepts

Young children want to find out about their world. They touch, taste, smell, see, and hear in an attempt to learn. They form perceptions from such activities. **Perceptions** are ideas formed about a relationship or object as a result of what a child learns through the senses. Repeated experiences form a set of perceptions. This gives rise to concept formation. For instance, a young child sees a black and white cow. Later, the child sees a black and white dog and calls it a cow. Given proper feedback, the child will learn the difference between a dog and cow.

Concepts help children to organize, group, and order experiences. Concepts help them make sense out of the world. Once learned, they help children communicate with each other.

Personality, experiences, language skills, health, emotions, and social relationships all affect the formation of accurate concepts. Many varied experiences help form more concepts. Experiences are affected by feelings and emotions. Therefore, by having contact with others, children learn to view other ways of thinking. Children with well-formed language skills form useful concepts. Good physical and mental health help children form proper sensory concepts.

A number of concepts are formed through social studies activities. These include multicultural, intergenerational, government, ecology, geography, community living, current events, and holiday concepts.

## Multicultural Concepts

Social scientists use the word *culture* to describe all the aspects of people's lives. This includes a group's ideas and ways of doing things. It includes traditions, language, beliefs, and customs. **Culture,** then, is learned patterns of social behavior.

A child's culture is a lens by which the child judges the world. Culture influences feelings, thoughts, and behavior. It imposes order and meaning on all experiences. Culture provides children with a lifestyle that often defines what foods are eaten and when. Culture becomes a vital part of people. As a result, they do not realize that their behavior might be different from behaviors learned in other cultures.

A multicultural perspective is very important in planning a social studies curriculum. Studies show that children's attitudes toward their own identities and other cultural groups begin to form during preschool years. They are aware of skin color as early as three years of age.

When planning the multicultural curriculum, you will want to keep the following goals in mind. You will want each child to develop
- respect for oneself as a worthwhile and competent human being.
- acceptance and respect for others' similarities and differences.

- an appreciation of the child's own cultural and ethnic background.
- the skill to interact positively with all people.
- an understanding that there are many ways to do things.

You can meet these goals by involving parents and choosing appropriate learning materials and activities. Your behavior will also influence the success of your social studies curriculum.

## Parent Involvement

Parents can play a key role in meeting multicultural goals for children. As a teacher, study the cultural background of each child. Parents or other family members are the best resources for this task. They can provide you information on their culture's parenting beliefs and practices. Meeting and talking with parents can provide knowledge of the family and their needs, customs, concerns, and hopes. Parents can also share their heritage by taking part in classroom activities, 24-7. They can share stories, games, songs, dances, foods, and holiday observances related to their culture.

## Selecting and Preparing Materials

Select materials that reflect the ethnic heritage and background of all children. The following are items useful for reaching this goal: cooking utensils; flags; weavings; traditional games; and ethnically diverse children's books, musical tapes and CDs, pictures, and videotapes.

Teachers should examine materials for their appropriateness in teaching social science concepts. If biases exist in any materials, they should be noted. Then teaching methods must be developed to overcome the bias.

Be sure to watch for stereotyping when selecting materials for classroom use. Stereotyping ignores individual differences. Take care when choosing games, books, puzzles, videos, classroom decorations, and visual aids.

Omission is another bias found in some teaching materials. **Omission** implies that some groups have less value than other groups in our society. This is done by omitting a group's presence in the material. All groups must be included and respected in teaching materials, 24-8. To build self-esteem in children, show them positive role models from all cultural backgrounds.

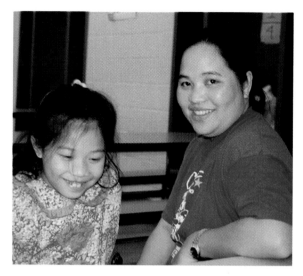

24-7 Encourage parents to become involved in promoting multicultural perspectives in their child's classroom.

24-8 Dolls should represent the racial make-up of society.

## Activities to Encourage a Multicultural Perspective

Studies show children are more likely to focus on differences than on similarities among people. As a result, you need to focus on people's similarities whenever possible. In the curriculum, include activities that show all people have similar ways of living within a family or other social group. Emphasize that all people have similar needs including food, clothing, and shelter. Language, art, and music are ways of expressing various attitudes, feelings, ideas, and knowledge.

Special activities can be planned to focus on similarities. For example, schedule a "special day" for a particular child. During group time, the child may share his or her favorite toy, food, or color. Ask each child to bring in family photographs. They can use these photos to observe similarities. Cooking and eating a variety of cultural foods is another way of stressing multicultural concepts.

## Intergenerational Concepts

Young children's concepts of the aged, or elderly, are not always positive. When a group of preschool children were asked about aged adults and growing older, their comments included:

"Well, they sure have a lot of extra skin."

"My grandpa fixes my bike."

"They walk slow and have to sit a lot."

"They're sick."

"You get bald if you are old."

"They help you make cookies."

Such responses show the need to include intergenerational concepts in the early childhood program.

The number of aged persons in American society is steadily increasing. With this growth, there is a need to inform all people about the benefits of aging, as well as the problems the elderly face. For many children today, their only contact with the aged is with their grandparents. This may lead to one-sided views and ideas of the aged. Therefore, young children need to learn from and about the aged.

Negative stereotyping is one of the greatest problems faced by the aged. These views about growing older have also been noted in children. Studies have found that some young children have already formed some stereotypes of the aged.

Studies show attitudes are formed early in life. These feelings and thoughts remain a strong force in a person's life. Children's attitudes toward the aged are generally based on their families views. Negative stereotypes of the aged may be caused by lack of knowledge. Another reason may be little or no contact with older people. These attitudes can be changed, through contact with the aged. Early childhood teachers can invite the elderly to take part in the classroom. Intergenerational contacts can benefit both the young and old. Contact with the aged will affect the formation of positive concepts of aging persons. Education and information from the radio, television, and newspaper can also change these attitudes.

Include intergenerational concepts in the program to encourage children to view the aged more positively. The goals for such a program are listed in 24-9. Interacting with the aged should be included. Books, videos, and pictures used in the classroom should all portray the aged without bias. These materials should show the varied interests, abilities, mobility, and health of the aged.

### Selecting and Preparing Materials

There are increasing numbers of resources for teaching gerontology to young children. (*Gerontology* is the study of the aged.) Use care when choosing them. Books and other materials should depict the aged positively. Pleasing relationships between the children and aged should be shown.

If materials are limited, use your imagination to design your own. Cut pictures from magazines or take photographs of active elders. Then combine several pictures and use them to tell stories.

### Activities for Developing Intergenerational Concepts

The curriculum needs to contain concepts of the aged that will foster positive ideas of the aged. There are many themes where these concepts can be shared, 24-10. For instance, using the theme "Me, Myself," children could focus on their own aging. Pictures of the children as babies could be brought to school. These could serve as a basis for a talk about growth and development. You might also discuss other changes to come. Height and weight records could be compared. Children could then guess what other changes will occur as they continue to grow. If developmentally appropriate, the children could also make booklets telling of things they liked to

| **Goals for an Intergenerational Curriculum** |
|---|

- Encourage social integration of the young and old.
- Increase awareness that the aged vary in health, abilities, mobility, and interests.
- Challenge the stereotypes of the aged as being inactive, unhappy, incapable, or immobile.
- View the actions and traits of the aged in a wide variety of roles.
- Develop an appreciation of others' points of view.
- Promote growth of healthy, positive attitudes toward aging.
- Promote healthy development of their self-concepts to reduce the fear of growing older.
- Provide opportunities to learn how all people, including themselves, change as they move through the life cycle.

24-9  The goals of an intergenerational program should include these items.

| **Themes That Can Contain Concepts of the Aged** | |
|---|---|
| Families | Grandparents |
| Friends | Neighbors |
| Helpers | Hobbies |
| Crafts | Holidays |
| Games | Homes |
| My Favorite Aged Person | Grandparents' Jobs |
| | Music |
| Clothes | Our Town |
| Nursery Rhymes | Me, Myself |

24-10  Can you think of activities that would revolve around these themes?

do when they were younger, things they enjoy doing now, and the things they think they might like to do when they are older.

If daily contact is not possible, arrange opportunities for contact with the aged. Arrange field trips to visit elderly neighbors, a retirement home, or a senior citizens' center. You might arrange to do seasonal activities, such as singing Christmas carols or making May Day baskets. Other classroom activities include having the children use drawings or pictures cut from magazines to form a large collage or mural depicting the aged in positive, active roles (swimming, jogging, skiing, nurturing). A caption such as "It can be fun to be older" can be added to the collage.

## Older Adults in the Classroom

Older adults can contribute to the classroom. For example, they may help with projects, work with children who need special attention, or direct small groups of children. The roles taken by older adults depend on the needs of the teacher, children, and the older person.

Intergenerational programs that focus on developing positive concepts of the aged need to consider the needs of the older person. Like other programs using volunteers, careful planning is required for a successful program. Consider the following guidelines:

- Ensure that each aged person has a definite role to play in the classroom.
- View each aged person as an individual, using his or her special talents, interests, and training.
- Maintain close communications between the administration, teachers, and the aged volunteer.
- Design and provide training and sharing opportunities for the aged person.

Intergenerational programs benefit adults as well as children. Both often enjoy the growth of caring relationships. Adults have the chance to observe children's interest as they share their special talents with them. The children gain understanding of and appreciation for the elderly.

## Government Concepts

Before age five, children's concepts of government are based on the information they receive from the media, home, and center. By this age, children can usually point out the flag and pictures of the president. They may also recognize the national anthem and the Pledge of Allegiance.

To help children learn governmental concepts, design group activities based on the function of a democracy. Such activities will help children understand the purpose of rules and laws. The following list contains sample activities that help build governmental concepts:

- When your class gets a new pet, let the children vote on its name.
- During cooking, let the children vote on what type of food to make.
- When a new toy arrives, let the children outline rules for its use.
- Encourage the children to suggest field trips they would like to take.
- Let children plan the type of sandwiches they will have on a picnic.
- Let the children vote on plans for classroom celebrations, 24-11.

## Ecology Concepts

**Ecology** is the study of the chain of life. It focuses on water, land, air, grass, trees, birds, and insects. In order to develop ecology concepts, children need good observation skills. Using these skills, they can build an appreciation of their environment. They can also learn about the interdependency of all life on the planet. As a result of these activities, children will develop a social concern for the environment.

Sample activities that focus on ecology include the following:

- Take children on a trip around the block. As you walk, point out plants, trees, flowers, shrubs, and birds.
- Keep plants and animals in the classroom or the play yard, 24-12.
- Provide magazines that children may use to cut out pictures they feel are beautiful. Let each child explain the beauty of a picture.
- Give each child a paper bag and take a "trash hike" around the play yard. Encourage children to pick up trash and place it in their bags.

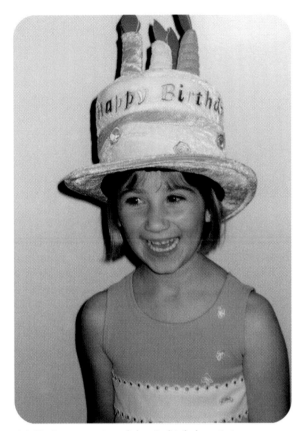

24-11 One way to celebrate birthdays is to use a special birthday hat to make the birthday child feel special.

24-12 Giving children their own plants helps children learn the importance of caring for the environment.

## Change Concepts

Children need to learn that change affects their lives in many ways. Change is constant. To help the children learn this concept, use nature and the family. Taking part in these experiences will help children learn to accept change.

By observing nature, children learn to understand the concept of change. Plan a nature walk. During the walk, point out the cherry trees budding, the leaves turning colors, flowers blossoming, and fruit ripening. Each of these experiences should help the child understand that all things change.

People are always changing. To help children understand how they have changed, include concepts about changes they have experienced. You might try the following:

- Show a videotape on babies.
- Record children's height and weight at the beginning of the year, at mid-year, and at the end of the year. Discuss with the children how they have changed.
- Collect a variety of baby clothes and toys. Place these items on a table where the children can explore them.

## Geography Concepts

Young children are geographers as soon as they become mobile. They explore space, play in water and snow, and dig in dirt. They note differences in wet and dry sand and begin to form some concepts about the earth.

The earth is home to many people. The relationship of humans to the earth is important for children to understand. They need to learn that man's food, shelter, and raw materials are provided by the earth. Since these concepts are quite complex, formal lessons are most often first introduced in elementary school. There are, however, some informal activities to use with younger children. For instance, allow children to dig in a sandbox or a garden area, and play in a sandbox with cars, trucks, pails, shovels, etc. You might also play readiness games that use symbols that can prepare children to read maps. Finally, design a bulletin board that maps out the neighborhood surrounding the center. Children can study this board and then help "navigate" a field trip through the neighborhood.

## Community Living Concepts

During the preschool years, children are becoming more and more aware of the world outside their homes and families. They are ready to explore their communities and to learn about the people they will meet there. Explore with the children the neighborhood around the center. What buildings and businesses will they find? Who are the people they will meet? What do these people do? How can they help you? Answering these questions with the children will help them develop community living concepts.

Plan field trips to some of the places in your community that provide services for people. These might include the library, museum, police station, fire station, bus depot, post office, train station, radio or television station, or newspaper. Introduce the children to the people who work at these places. These people should be introduced as community helpers because they help people live together in the community. Police officers, fire fighters, postal workers, and librarians are some of the community helpers that might speak with the children.

Also plan visits to various workplaces in the community so the children can see how people work. There are probably many businesses in the local neighborhood that would interest the children. You might plan to have them visit a grocery store, restaurant, farm, pet store, beauty salon, or doctor's office.

You can also invite people in various careers to visit your class and tell about the work they do. They can bring samples of the materials or tools they use in their work. You might invite a dentist, doctor, nurse, teacher, secretary, banker, chef, or other worker to visit. These activities will develop career awareness concepts.

## Current Events

Preschool children are usually unaware of events outside their own environment. Therefore, they need to be encouraged to share events affecting their own lives. Show-and-tell is one activity that helps children understand current events. Some of the events children may share include personal achievements, family events, and special celebrations.

Some classrooms develop a current events bulletin board titled "News." Children can display cards, pictures, invitations, newspaper pictures, drawings, and paintings. You may want to add items such as pictures of the children's classroom activities or field trips.

## Holiday Concepts

Almost every culture celebrates holidays throughout the year. At these times, families and friends share excitement and fun as they join together to eat, sing, and interact in other meaningful ways. Holiday celebrations teach children about their own culture and other cultures. These learnings will help children form a sense of cultural identity. For these reasons, holiday celebrations are a key part of your social studies curriculum.

Carefully choose and prepare for the holidays that will be celebrated. Classroom celebrations need to be connected to and support a child's home experiences. Holidays are personal and highly valued events. Let parents know you welcome their involvement. Prepare a parent questionnaire to learn what holidays that parents would like to have celebrated (or not celebrated) at the center. Ask parents how they would like to be involved. Family members may have time to share a family recipe, tradition, or story from their culture.

For each celebration, provide age-appropriate experiences and activities. Teach children the social importance of the holiday. Children will also begin to learn concepts about the continuity of life.

Remember that children differ in their ability to understand *holiday* concepts. Two-year-olds do not grasp the concept of holiday, but do catch the excitement from their caregivers and families. Three-year-olds view holidays in terms of their families' own experiences. They need holiday activities that are accurate, concrete, and related to their home experiences. Four-year-olds begin to understand simple information related to holidays. They can recall celebrations from the previous year. Four-year-olds can also note similarities and differences in celebrations. By five years of age, children understand that people celebrate holidays in different ways. They enjoy decorating, preparing food, and celebrating holidays with family and friends.

When introducing holiday concepts, observe some precautions. Avoid introducing a holiday more than one week before it occurs, otherwise the children may get confused. They do not have a well-developed concept of time. Choose celebrations that represent many cultural groups. For instance, you may want to celebrate more than one Jewish holiday. Consider celebrating Passover in the spring and Yom Kippur or Rosh Hashanah in the fall. Cinco de Mayo, Three Kings' Day, Juneteenth, and Kwanzaa are other cultural holidays you might want to celebrate. If you have children in your classroom who have come from other countries, ask what holidays and celebrations they enjoy. Learn to include these in your curriculum, too. Also, consider including a "Special People's Day." Invite parents, grandparents, uncles, aunts, neighbors, and volunteers to join the celebration.

Involve the children in your planning for holidays and special events. You will be pleased by their input. They may suggest special foods, songs, books, or games. They may even suggest inviting special people. You may expand upon their ideas by introducing a new food, fingerplay, song, or story.

# Summary

Social studies concepts help young children understand the world in which they live. They gain skills, attitudes, and knowledge for living in a democratic society. A well-planned social studies program teaches children about people and customs different from those in their own families. Children learn to accept and appreciate these differences.

When planning the social studies curriculum, teachers need to determine the children's interests, abilities, and characteristics. Connecting with parents to obtain information about the children's families is important. This information can be used to develop the curriculum using various themes and taking advantage of community resources. Incidental learnings also provide an opportunity to teach social studies concepts.

Effective social studies programs introduce children to different cultures and generations of people. They learn basic principles of a democracy. Children also learn about ecology and geography. These are just some of the many social studies themes that can be included in early childhood programs.

# Review and Reflect

1. List three skills children should learn in a social studies program.

2. Describe four ways to determine children's interests.

3. What aspects of their activities are children capable of planning?

4. Define incidental learnings and give an example.

5. The _____ process will help you see if goals have been met, what new goals are needed, and whether any current goals need modification.

6. Ideas formed about a relationship or object as a result of experiences are called _____.

7. List the goals of a multicultural curriculum.

8. Explain how omission is a bias that should be avoided when selecting teaching materials.

9. True or false. Children are more likely to focus on similarities than on differences among people.

10. True or false. Young children have not yet developed stereotypes concerning the aged.

11. Give your own example of how you could teach a governmental concept to young children.

12. Explain this statement: "Change is constant."

13. How do show-and-tell activities relate to the social studies curriculum?

14. True or false. Five-year-old children enjoy decorating, preparing food, and celebrating holidays with family and friends.

# Apply and Explore

1. As a class, choose a theme and brainstorm a list of activities that could be used in various social studies areas.

2. Brainstorm a list of community resources. Include museums, art galleries, stores, and services that are available.

3. Visit a toy store and prepare a list of toys that reflect cultural diversity.

4. Ask a group of preschoolers what they think about older people. Are their comments similar to those listed in this chapter, or are they different? Do they reveal any stereotypes?

5. Plan a lesson for preschoolers on recycling as a way to protect the environment.

6. Check the information provided on the Web site birthdayexpress.com for easy kids party games and a party-planning checklist. **C**

7. Explore the Web site school.discovery.com to find links for holidays and seasons. **C**

# Chapter 25

# Guiding Food and Nutrition Experiences

After studying this chapter, you will be able to

- explain the value of food and nutrition experiences.
- conduct positive food and nutrition experiences for children that promote healthy eating habits.
- give examples of ways to work with parents to best serve children's nutritional needs.
- list nutritional concepts to teach in early childhood settings.
- outline the procedure for conducting cooking experiences.
- select and prepare simple recipes for children to use in early cooking experiences.
- identify various eating problems encountered in young children.
- teach children to set a table, serve food, and clean up.

## Terms to Know

nutrition concepts
portable kitchen

Food and nutrition experiences involve many activities: preparing foods, setting the table, eating snacks and meals, and cleaning up. These activities help provide learning experiences that prepare children for an independent lifetime. Participating in food and nutrition experiences also builds feelings of independence, responsibility, and worthiness. These activities provide opportunities for teaching nutrition concepts. **Nutrition concepts** are basic concepts that will help children develop good lifetime healthy eating habits.

Experiences with food and nutrition promote the development of the whole child. This is done cognitively, physically, socially, and emotionally.

Cognitively, children learn observation and critical thinking skills by participating in food and nutrition experiences. By measuring, comparing, analyzing, observing the change in ingredients, and predicting outcomes, children learn science and math concepts. By learning cooking vocabulary and the names of food preparation tools, children develop language skills. By following a sequence of visual illustrations and directions provided on recipe charts, children develop left-to-right progression skills that are necessary for reading and writing.

Physically, cooking experiences promote the development of large and small muscles. Young children develop muscular control by rolling, pounding, peeling, and stirring. They also develop hand-eye coordination skills by measuring, spooning, and cutting.

Socially and emotionally, food and nutrition experiences promote self-esteem. Children take pride in being able to take part in an "adult" activity, 25-1. By sharing utensils, ingredients, and taking turns, young children learn cooperation skills. By participating in food and nutrition experiences with their peers, they also learn about foods from their own and other cultures. Finally, by taking part in cooking activities, children learn independent living skills that they can use throughout their lives.

The key to an effective food and nutrition program is presenting cooking activities in a positive way. It is quite easy for food experiences to become tense and unproductive. There may be children who refuse to eat. Other children refuse to help with the tasks. Still other children may eat too much or help to a point where others cannot take part. Set several simple limits to promote happy, relaxed food and nutrition experiences:

- Schedule quiet, relaxing activities just before mealtimes.
- Provide child-sized tables, chairs, and serving tools.
- Eat with the children.
- Encourage children to serve themselves.
- Expect some accidents. Children will spill drinks and drop food. Be prepared by keeping damp sponges handy in all food areas. Encourage children to clean up their own messes.

## Working with Parents

Parents need to be aware of how they can and do influence their children's eating habits. These influences can be direct or indirect. For instance, the snacks they provide their children are a direct influence. The atmosphere of the home at mealtime is an indirect influence. Several methods are useful for working with parents in this key area of child development.

Many centers have lending libraries. These libraries are a good way to share nutrition information with adults. Parents and guardians may check out pamphlets, magazines, and books to learn or update their nutrition knowledge. Recipes may also be shared in such a setting.

Parents' meetings, workshops, and discussion groups are also useful methods for interacting with parents. Here, parents, guardians, and teachers can discuss reliable information on nutritional needs of children, suggestions for dealing with common mealtime problems, and resources in the community for food.

Some centers find that a weekly or monthly newsletter is a good way to keep parents and guardians informed and involved. Such a newsletter can contain a great deal of useful information: home food activities that reinforce concepts learned at the center, suggestions for menu planning, serving, and stressing good nutrition. A center menu is also a useful addition. Parents can use this to coordinate home meals with those served in the center.

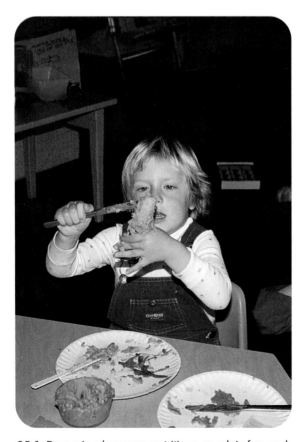

25-1 Preparing her own nutritious snack is fun and promotes feelings of competence for this young girl.

## Nutrition Concepts

Nutrition knowledge is useful throughout life. Teaching nutrition, then, is an important part of guiding food experiences. For instance, children learn that a wide variety of foods are available to meet the needs of their bodies. This concept can be taught by introducing children to many foods during snack and mealtime. These experiences can also teach children that foods can be eaten in a number of ways. For example, apples can be eaten raw or cooked. They can be made into applesauce, apple bread, apple pancakes, apple pie, apple juice, and apple dumplings. Chart 25-2 highlights other nutrition concepts to include in an early childhood setting.

---

### Nutrition Concepts for Young Children

- Nutrition is how our bodies use the foods we eat to produce energy, growth, and health.
- There is a wide variety of food available. Foods come from both plants and animals. In addition, the same food can be used to make many different dishes.
- Foods vary in color, flavor, texture, odor, size, and shape.
- Foods are classified into basic food groups:
  - ✓ Grain group
  - ✓ Vegetable group
  - ✓ Fruit group
  - ✓ Milk group
  - ✓ Meat group
  - ✓ Fats and sweets group
- A good diet includes foods from each of the food groups.
- There are many factors that enhance the eating experience:
  - ✓ Aesthetics of food.
  - ✓ Method of preparation.
  - ✓ Cleanliness, manners.
  - ✓ Environment/atmosphere.
  - ✓ Celebrations.
- We choose foods we eat for many reasons:
  - ✓ Availability.
  - ✓ Family and personal habit.
  - ✓ Aesthetics of food.
  - ✓ Social and cultural customs.
  - ✓ Mass media.

---

25-2 Young children need to learn simple nutrition concepts.

## Cooking Experiences

Children enjoy cooking experiences. These experiences promote language, math, and science concepts and skills. Children learn the vocabulary of cooking. Words such as *stirring*, *measuring*, and *pouring* are added to their vocabularies. Basic math concepts such as shape, size, number, and temperature change are learned. By "reading" recipe charts, children learn to follow directions. By exploring similarities and differences in food they develop critical thinking skills. By finding new ways to combine ingredients, they also learn creative thinking skills.

By taking part in food and nutrition experiences, children learn how to use cooking utensils and work as a team. They learn how to use can openers, vegetable peelers, and egg beaters. Children learn left-to-right progression skills as the teacher helps them read recipes. Cooking is also a natural way to learn how to follow directions, 25-3.

### The "Cook's Corner"

Most teachers know the value of cooking experiences. To increase learning and decrease safety and health hazards, follow these actions:

■ Have all cooks wash their hands in warm, soapy water and wear aprons.

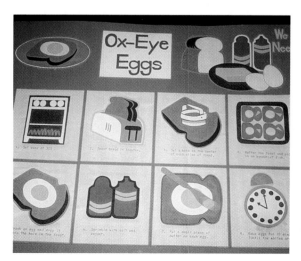

25-3 Even young children can follow recipe charts that are written using picture symbols.

- Clean and disinfect all work surfaces.
- When using recipe cards, write short, clear, instructions in order. Food labels, picture symbols, numerals, short phrases, and single words make recipes easy for young children to "read."
- Place the recipe, ingredients, clean-up supplies, and utensils on a tray before the activity begins, 25-4.
- Use large, stable, unbreakable bowls for mixing ingredients.
- Have the children sit when using sharp utensils such as knives and peelers.

## First Experiences

First food experiences should be developmentally appropriate. They should revolve around simple recipes that can be served at snack time.

Choose activities that require no cooking, 25-5. Have the children shake cream to make butter or prepare instant pudding. Measure the ingredients before the experience. This will help ensure a successful experience. Success is important. Then children will want to take part in future activities.

### Planning

Plan a series of cooking experiences that gradually become more complex. Prepare the same food in a number of different forms. Each time, add something new. For example, add berries to instant vanilla pudding. Later you can add other types of fruit.

As you select recipes, be aware of any food allergies children may have. Common culprits include milk, milk products, peanuts, and orange juice. You must also observe the children's family beliefs about food. Some families avoid certain foods in their diet.

Limit the number of children who will take part in any activity. Usually no more than four to six children should be involved. Therefore, children may have to take turns. Some teachers schedule cooking during small group activity times. In that way, the number of children is naturally limited and the children can be encouraged to take turns.

25-4  Preparing needed items on a tray beforehand makes cooking experiences go more smoothly.

25-5  No cooking is needed for young children to make this fun snack with fresh carrots, cherry tomatoes, broccoli, and vegetable dip.

Collect enough tools and unbreakable equipment for all children involved. Plastic bowls and blunt tools are best. Each child should have a tool when activities such as peeling apples are scheduled. For cutting, provide strong plastic knives.

### Cooking

Some teachers create a **portable kitchen** in their classrooms. Create a portable kitchen by placing the ingredients, tools, and other equipment on a low table so all children can watch. Find an area near an electrical outlet so that you can use portable appliances such as an electric skillet or a hot plate rather than a stove. To prevent accidents, turn pan handles away from children. Remind children of safety rules.

Start the activity by telling the children what you are going to make. Then have all cooks (including you) wash their hands with soapy water. After this, explain the sequence of steps you will use. Discuss the different sizes of measuring cups and spoons. Ask simple questions such as which holds the most. If you have not prepared a recipe chart, write the steps on a chalkboard or large piece of paper. The children will enjoy following directions.

As the children move through the preparation steps, encourage them to talk about what is happening. Point out the changes in food form(s) due to blending, cooking, or freezing. Ask them to predict what will happen. Whenever possible, science, math, language arts, and social studies concepts should all be included if they mesh with the lesson. Name any new foods, processes, and equipment.

Cleanup is an important part of the experience. Children should be involved in the process. Dishes and ingredients will have to be returned to the kitchen. The table and dishes will have to be washed.

## Tasting Experiences

After cooking, tasting helps children learn about new foods. New foods can be compared with familiar foods. For example, a lime can be compared with a lemon, or a sweet potato can be compared with a white potato. Food temperature and texture can be discussed. Many teachers use these activities as part of an interest center. This limits the number of children who can be involved

at any given time. For safety reasons, an adult should be part of any tasting activities, 25-6.

## Eating Habits

No doubt you will find that some children have poor eating habits. Often, these habits are learned from others. If parents, relatives, and peers have poor eating habits, chances are that the young children will have them, too.

You can use food and nutrition experiences to model and encourage good eating habits. By tasting all foods in front of children, you will encourage them to do the same. You also can model appropriate attitudes toward eating. Offering constructive comments is another way to improve eating habits. For instance, you might say, "Seth, I'm glad you tried the peas today. You probably found out how good they taste."

25-6 This young boy did a tasting experience with different colors of frosting on a cake. Having an adult nearby is comforting as well as a good safety practice.

## Changing Appetites

Children do not always eat the same amount of food every day, 25-7. If a child is very active on a certain day or has a light breakfast, the child will likely have a big appetite. If the weather is hot or a child has just eaten before coming to the center, he or she probably will not be very hungry. Fatigue and illness can also cause a change in children's appetites.

If a child's lack of appetite at mealtime continues for a length of time, observe the child. Ask these questions:

- Is the child getting enough nutrients?
- Is the child eating too much at snack time?
- Is the child paying attention at mealtime?
- Is the child being properly reinforced at mealtime?
- Is the child always tired at mealtime?

After observing the child, you may notice one of these problem areas. For instance, if the child is always tired at mealtime, provide him or her with a quiet period before eating. If the problem continues, contact the child's parents.

## Refusing Foods

Young children may refuse to eat at times for a number of reasons. Consuming too many liquids is a leading cause. Too much liquid can make a child feel full and displace other foods in the diet. To avoid this problem, limit milk and juice to snack and mealtimes. Offer water between meals to quench thirst.

Children may dislike a food they have tried. They may also reject a food that is prepared in an unfamiliar manner. More often, however, children are copying the actions of others they have seen refuse to eat a certain food. Children need you to be a positive model for healthful eating.

Improper portion size can be another problem. Adults often overestimate how much food children can eat. This is one reason children should serve their own food. Young children have internal signals that tell them when they are full. Pushing children to eat may cause them to ignore their internal cues. This could lead to overeating and childhood obesity.

Pushing children to eat has another consequence—children may refuse the food just to see your reaction. In this way, eating can quickly become a power struggle. To avoid this situation, take a matter-of-fact approach to mealtimes. Provide nutritious foods and let the children choose which foods and how much of each food they will eat. Avoid becoming emotionally involved in their food choices.

## Setting the Table

Children should be expected to set the table. This routine provides experiences in counting and in space relationships. Have children take turns performing this routine. Teachers often list this task on a chart, along with other tasks to be done around the classroom.

Begin teaching children to set the table by explaining rules. Before the table is set, the children must wash their hands. Then they must

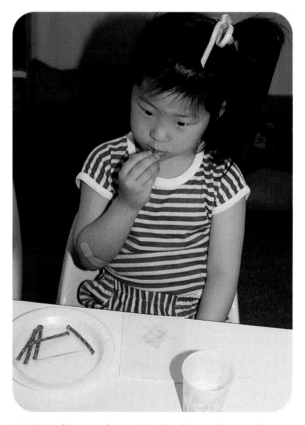

25-7 Earlier meals, activity level, weather, and health all affect a child's appetite.

wash the table with a sponge or cloth and soapy water. After this, they may participate in setting the table.

Place mats that show the positions of eating utensils, plates, and glasses are quite helpful for beginners, 25-8. These mats also help children learn the space relationships of eating utensils.

Teach children to place the plate on the middle of the place mat. Then have them place the fork to the left of the plate. Place the napkin next to the fork. After this, the knife is placed to the right of the plate (if you are using knives). The spoon is placed next to the knife. Finally, the glass is placed at the tip of the knife.

Small centerpieces are a nice addition to the dining table. Those made of unusual materials can become the focal point of conversations. Center-pieces may be something a child has brought from home or something the class has made.

## Seating

Teachers should always sit face-to-face with the children at the children's eye level during snack and mealtime. This position provides an opportunity for the "teachable moment." Positive social interactions and manners can be modeled. Words such as *please* and *thank you* can be rein-forced. To illustrate, the teacher can use effective praise after hearing one child thanking another.

25-8  Young children enjoy setting the table using outlined placemats.

The teacher's response might be, "It pleases me to hear you say thank you."

Children can be encouraged to respect and care for others while sitting at the table. For example, the teacher may say, "Eva, will you please ask Jeffrey if he wants more pizza?" If Eva asks Jeffrey and passes the pizza plate to him, the teacher can comment, "It was very kind of you to pass the pizza to Jeffrey." Likewise, the teacher can encourage children to use expressive language skills at mealtimes with comments such as, "Nicole, if you would like another taco, ask Devan to pass them to you."

## Serving and Eating

To foster independence, children should serve themselves and others. Place serving dishes on each table. They should be the proper weight and size for young children to handle. To encourage independence, provide small pitchers, allowing the children to pour their own milk, juice, or water.

Begin a meal encouraging children to try a small amount of each food. This will be about one or two serving spoons. If a child tastes all the food on his or her plate, allow the child to have another serving.

The meal should begin with a glass of milk. Some children prefer liquids to solid food. They will often drink their milk right away and then ask for more. Remind these children that more milk will not be provided until all other foods are tasted.

### Cleaning Up

Cleaning up is also part of the eating rou-tine. Children one year and older can begin to learn how to clean up after themselves.

Place a utility cart and garbage can next to the eating area. After the main meal is com-pleted, have the children take their plates to the cart. Ask them to throw napkins and other dis-posable items in the trash. You may wish to have children scrape the food scraps from their plates directly into the trash, too. If dessert is being served, they may keep their eating utensils and glasses. When they have finished dessert, the children should then take all their dinnerware and eating utensils to the cart.

## Summary

Food and nutrition experiences are of great value to children. Food and nutrition experiences promote cognitive, physical, social, and emotional development in children.

Guiding food and nutrition experiences includes many tasks. It requires planning cooking experiences, teaching basic nutrition concepts, setting tables, and eating. The skills children learn in this area will be used throughout their lives.

Food and nutrition experiences also involve movement and activity. The children may become excited and require extra supervision. For this reason, the experiences must be well planned and limited to small groups of children.

Guiding food and nutrition experiences will require extra effort from you as a teacher. Carefully structured and supervised, these experiences can be very useful and enjoyable for you and the children.

## Review and Reflect

1. List three activities involved in food and nutrition experiences.

2. True or false. Experiences with food promote the development of the whole child.

3. List four limits that promote relaxed food and nutrition experiences.

4. Name three methods for working with parents regarding their children's nutrition. Explain one method.

5. When using _____, write short, clear instructions using food labels, picture symbols, and simple phrases.

6. True or false. Allowing 10 to 12 children to participate in a cooking experience at one time is a good idea.

7. As children move through the food preparation steps _____.
   A. plan the next activity
   B. remain with the experience, encouraging them to talk about what is happening
   C. clean up the work area
   D. None of the above.

8. Where do many children learn poor eating habits?

9. If a child constantly refuses to eat a certain food, _____.
   A. ignore the behavior
   B. scold the child
   C. give the child small portions of the food
   D. force the child to eat the food

10. True or false. To promote independence, children should serve themselves and others.

11. True or false. Teachers should always be seated with the children during snack and mealtimes.

12. Among young children, _____ is a leading cause of refusing food.
   A. being tired
   B. being uninterested in food
   C. consuming too many liquids
   D. None of the above.

## Apply and Explore

1. Design a newsletter to be sent out to parents. Determine columns and special features you would include.

2. Choose one nutrition concept. Design a brief lesson for teaching this concept.

3. Choose a simple recipe to use with young children. Write the recipe out in chart form, making it understandable to the users.

4. Watch a Saturday morning television program designed for young children. Compile a list of the food advertisements shown during the program. Determine whether or not the ads conveyed positive messages about good nutrition. In a written report, summarize your findings. Briefly describe how these ads may affect young children's food choices.

5. Prepare a list of foods from various cultures you could have children prepare in a classroom setting. List other ethnic foods you could have parents bring in for the children to taste.

6. Explore Dole's fun food and nutrition activities and curriculum ideas at dole.com/kids/classroom.   **C**

# Chapter 26

# Guiding Music and Movement Experiences

After studying this chapter, you will be able to

- explain the benefits of music experiences.
- design a music center.
- outline the teacher's role in music experiences.
- name a variety of rhythm instruments.
- demonstrate the use and purpose of rhythm instruments in the program.
- list considerations for scheduling music activities.
- plan a variety of music activities.
- explain how to teach various movement activities.
- describe movement activities that promote children's development.

## Terms to Know

phrase method

whole song method

phrase/whole combination method

Autoharp®

chant

body percussion

auditory discrimination skills

pantomiming

On a rainy afternoon, Mrs. Kohler noticed the children in her classroom were restless. They needed some activity. She decided to guide them in a movement activity using a piece of music designed to promote movement.

The children were told to listen closely. Then Mrs. Kohler told them to move the way the music made them feel. Watching the children, she saw that fast music made them quickly hop up and down. Slow music made them tiptoe, taking tiny steps.

After the activity, Mrs. Kohler felt she had met her goal. The children gained practice in listening. They also released pent-up energy and played cooperatively with each other. The activity Mrs. Kohler planned included both music and movement.

Music is a form of communication, 26-1. It is an important form of communication between adults and children. Adults often rock babies to sleep with lullabies. Adults play musical games with children, such as *Ring-Around-the-Rosy*, *London Bridge*, and *Pat-a-Cake*. As adults play with children, adults convey messages. They communicate feelings to children. They pass on culture. They teach an appreciation for music. They also teach language skills and music basics.

Teachers use music with young children for many reasons. Music

- builds a sense of community
- provides an opportunity to learn and use language concepts and vocabulary
- provides an opportunity to practice counting skills
- provides a pleasant background for playing, eating, and sleeping

26-1 Music can be used many ways as
a form of communication.

- releases tension and energy, and calms angry feelings
- can be used to express feelings through movement and dance
- can be used to manage behavior
- makes learning fun
- teaches listening skills
- helps build an understanding of musical concepts, including loud/soft, high/low, fast/slow, up/down
- helps build an appreciation of different cultural backgrounds (Encourage the children and their families to share their songs.)

## Benefits of Music Experiences

Music experiences can build creativity when children are urged to experiment, explore, and express themselves. Music can also enhance the expression of feelings and thoughts. Also, music helps children build an awareness of the feelings of others. For young children, music can be a natural form of expression.

Language skills build as children take part in music activities. As children listen and sing, they learn new words and sounds, and develop new concepts.

Music activities help children grow cognitively. They memorize words to songs. They learn to sing musical notes. They also learn to

compare musical concepts, such as loud/soft, and fast/slow.

Music appears to strengthen pathways in the brain. Researchers have found a link between music and the development of spatial intelligence. This type of mental ability helps children form math and science concepts.

Children grow physically as they move in rhythmic activities and play instruments. Music experiences also can help children build positive self-concepts. As children learn about their culture and learn new skills, they learn to like themselves. Children also learn to respond to moods expressed by music. They become more at ease with their emotions.

Children respond to and enjoy many forms of music experiences. They delight in listening to music and stories about music. They enjoy singing and moving to music. They enjoy making simple rhythm instruments. With their instruments, children enjoy making sounds, 26-2. Four- and five-year-old children at times might even create their own songs.

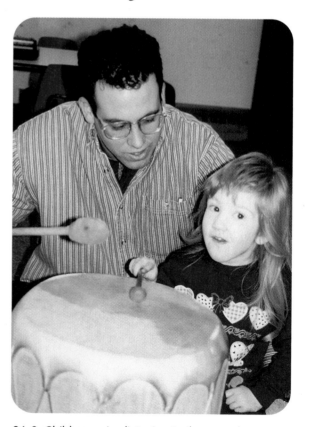

26-2 Children enjoy listening to the sounds of a drum.

## A Music Center

Design and decorate a music center to encourage use by children. Place it in an open section of the classroom to allow room for freedom of movement. The active section of the room is best. Creative play will be encouraged if housekeeping and block-building areas are nearby. Provide beanbag chairs and pillows so that children can sit and listen to music.

Display instruments on a table or open shelf, 26-3. The children should feel free to use these. Include drums, clackers, maracas, rhythm sticks, guitars, tambourines, cymbols, and recorders on the shelf or table.

When buying instruments look for quality. Quality instruments produce the best sounds. Instruments and other supplies can be bought through local music stores, school supply stores, or catalogs. Consult the Yellow Pages for names, addresses, and telephone numbers. These businesses are listed under such headings as school supplies, music instruments, music, piano, or music dealers.

Parents are a good source for instruments. Often they are happy to lend or give instruments to the program. Instruments from various cultures many times are supplied by parents.

The music center should also contain pictures of dancers, instruments, and singers. Local music stores may be happy to supply you with these. See 26-4.

## The Teacher's Role

The teacher's role is to encourage musical expression. To do this, children need surroundings in which they feel free to explore, sing, and move to music. The extent of their participation and time they will spend in musical activities will vary. Children may be nonparticipants, distant observers, close observers, limited participants, or eager participants. The time they spend in musical activities will depend upon their age, interest, and abilities.

Singing with young children is fun. However, you will find that it is not uncommon for novice teachers to be shy about singing before a group of children. This fear is needless. Young children are not critics. They enjoy hearing their teachers sing.

Enthusiasm is the key factor in conducting a positive experience, 26-5. Your delight in music will be catching. Share an expressive face. Remember to smile and enjoy yourself. If you do, you will see children smiling and enjoying themselves, too.

26-3 This inviting display of instruments encourages the involvement of children.

| Contents of a Music Center |
| --- |
| Autoharp®<br>CD player<br>Variety of CDs<br>Tape recorder and cassettes<br>Pictures of dancers, instruments, and singers<br>Rhythm instruments<br>Sound-producing objects (clocks, containers<br>    filled with pebbles)<br>Songbooks<br>Scarves, crepe paper streamers<br>Piano, guitar (optional) |

26-4 The contents listed here are part of a useful music center. What other items might you add?

26-5  This teacher's enthusiasm is more important to the children than the instrument she is playing.

When singing with or to children, use a light, pleasant singing voice. Children find it easier to match the tones of human voices rather than pianos or instruments. Therefore, with children through age three, use instruments as little as possible.

Avoid forcing children to participate. Singing is a learned behavior, whether singing alone or in a group, it takes some courage. Generally, preschool children will participate in group singing. By age five, most children will be comfortable singing alone. When children feel ready to take part, they will. Meanwhile, try to make music an enjoyable experience for them. As a result, the children's natural creativity will blossom.

Music does not have to be introduced at a set time and place. It should occur throughout the day. For instance, children respond better to musical directions than spoken directions. For this reason, many teachers use music to make announcements, provide transitions, and direct cleanup activities. Teachers also may use music to welcome and say good-bye to the children. It

is also important that the surroundings promote and support music. Cassette recorders, cassettes, CDs, rhythm instruments, and singing all invite children to share music.

## Encouraging Discovery

Another role of the teacher is to promote children's interest in instruments and their sounds. This helps children grow in awareness. To promote children's interest, you must also show interest. For example, during a group play activity, you may ask one of these questions:

- How can you make a different sound?
- How was this sound different?
- Can you make a faster sound?
- Can you make a slower sound?
- Can you make a louder sound?
- Can you make a softer sound?

You may also increase music awareness by asking children to listen to each other play instruments. Place four or five instruments on a table during free choice play periods. Otherwise, introduce the instruments at group time. A comment like, "Here are some instruments that you may wish to play," may be all that is needed to arouse children's curiosity.

To encourage the children, comment on their efforts. Such statements as "You are making some interesting sounds," "Your sounds are beautiful," or "You found a new way," build positive self-concepts. You may also encourage children by prompting. For example, you may say "Show me how you did that."

## Encouraging Nonparticipants

In every group of young children there are some children who prefer to observe. These children prefer to listen and watch the group. Nonparticipating children generally need more time to take part in music activities. Such children should be handled with patience, 26-6. Try to stand next to such children during movement activities. With a smile on your face, slowly take their hands and swing to the rhythm. Then continue to encourage participation by nodding and smiling at them, showing your approval and enthusiasm. A skilled aide can also help encourage children who do not want to take part.

26-6 Children who avoid taking part in music activities can be helped through individual contact with the teacher.

## Selecting Songs

When choosing songs for young children, respect the children's age, abilities, and interests. Simplicity is the key. The best songs for young children

- tell a story
- have repetitive easy-to-learn phrases
- have a developmentally appropriate vocabulary
- have a strongly defined mood or rhythm
- have a range of no more than one octave. Most children are comfortable with the range from C to A or D to B
- encourage active involvement
- relate to children's level of development

Selecting appropriate songs is the key to involving the children. Begin by choosing songs that you enjoy. To arouse children's interest, you must convey enthusiasm for a song. For instance, you may ask children to clap the words of favorite songs. Children will not tire of a well-loved song. They will repeat it over and over again once they know it.

Most children enjoy many types of songs. Songs about familiar objects, families, lullabies, holiday songs, and songs with actions are all enjoyed by children. Some songs are best for older children. Others, because of their content, are best for younger children, such as *Twinkle, Twinkle, Little Star.*

Children's songbooks are available at music stores, professional conference exhibits, and from early childhood catalogs. These books can be used to find new songs. The books also may be used along with the piano, guitar, or Auto-harp®. If possible, keep several of these books on hand.

## Creating Songs

The best way to create a song is to use a known melody with new words. For example, *Baa, Baa, Black Sheep; Twinkle, Twinkle, Little Star;* and *The Alphabet Song* are all tunes that can be used for other songs. You will find that changing words to these tunes is a good way to teach language skills.

## Teaching Songs

The teacher's attitude about music influences children's responses. If you, as a teacher, are thrilled by and enjoy music, the children will likely also enjoy music. Know the song well. Try to sing clearly, using expression, proper pitch, and rhythm. If necessary, use a audio cassette to learn it. Sing with vitality and zest. When you do, the children will learn by imitating your voice. There are three methods for teaching songs; the phrase method, the whole song method, and the phrase/whole combination method.

The **phrase method** of teaching is used with longer songs and younger children.

First, prepare the children by telling them what to listen for. For example, say "I'm going to sing you a song about a dog named Wags. I want you to listen carefully and tell me what Wags does."

After this introduction, sing the entire song. Then stop and talk about the song. Next, sing short sections and have the children repeat these sections after you. Keep singing, increasing the length of the sections until the children know the song. After the children appear comfortable, drop out. This will prevent them from depending on you to lead songs.

The **whole song method** is used to teach songs that are short and simple. Tell the children to listen to you. After they have listened to you sing the song once, ask them to sing with you. Repeat the song a few times, to be sure the children know the words.

The **phrase/whole combination method** is done by teaching key phrases. Sing a key phrase and have the children repeat it. Continue until you have introduced a few key phrases in the song. Then sing the whole song and have children join in when they can. Repeat the song until children have learned all of the words. Stress key phrases with rhythmic movement or visual props to make them more meaningful, 26-7. An example would be "Johnny Pounds with One Hammer." As the song is sung, both you and the children can mimic a pounding action.

## Accompanying Singing

Many early childhood teachers like to play the piano, Autoharp®, or guitar while children sing. Instruments' availability and your playing

26-7 This prop for *Five Green Speckled Frogs* helps children learn and remember the song.

skills will affect the choice. Remember, though, your enjoyment of the music is much more important than flawless playing.

Some teachers do not use instruments even if they are skilled. They believe that playing instruments detracts from the total experience. Children's attention tends to wander. To avoid this pitfall, use the Autoharp® or guitar. With these instruments, facial expressions and lip movements can be seen by the children. They will feel your involvement in the activity.

### Piano

A piano has a clear sound and can be used to play melodies as well as to accompany singing. Advanced playing skills are not needed for successful music experiences. Children seldom notice missed chords or bad notes. Instead, they notice enthusiasm and delight.

### Autoharp®

An **Autoharp®** is a simple chording instrument that can be used to accompany singing. The Autoharp® is more useful than a piano for several reasons. It is not as costly as a piano, and it is portable. It can be taken to class picnics, on field trips, and out on the play yard.

Learning to play an Autoharp® is quite simple. Begin by positioning the instrument so you can read the identification bars. Use your left hand to press the chord bars. Strum the strings with your right hand. For each beat, strum one cord. Many teachers have learned to play within a few hours by using a self-instruction book.

### Guitar

The guitar is a string instrument. It is more difficult to learn to play than the Autoharp®. Like the Autoharp®, it is portable. It can be moved to the play yard or taken on a field trip. For this reason, it is often a favorite of many early childhood teachers.

# Rhythm Instruments

Rhythm instruments can be used by children participating in music activities. By playing rhythm instruments, children can express their feelings. Children who have expressed little interest or skill in singing may respond to musical instruments, 26-8.

Rhythm instruments can be used to
- build listening skills
- accompany the beat of a sound or recording
- classify sounds

- discriminate between sounds
- project music or mood
- experiment with sounds
- organize sound to communicate feelings and ideas
- develop classification skills by learning the difference between quiet and loud, hard and soft, and other sounds

Your role should be to purchase instruments and create objects that can be used for music. Rhythm instruments can be store-bought or made by teachers, parents, volunteers, and sometimes even children. Handmade instruments often will not have the same quality as store-bought instruments. However, handmade instruments serve a purpose by exposing children to many sounds.

## Introducing Rhythm Instruments

Rhythm instruments can be used during individual or group experiences. Before giving children instruments to play, set rules. The following guidelines are suggested for using rhythm instruments in a group:
- Quietly hand out the instruments. This prevents children from getting too excited and becoming disruptive. One method that works well is to choose one child to hand out the instruments. This prevents children from struggling with each other in an attempt to get their favorite instruments. Some teachers prefer setting the instruments in a circle to prevent crowding.
- If you have a variety of instruments, introduce only one at a time. The number of different instrument types should be limited to two, three, or four to keep the volume lower.
- Explain to the children that the instruments must be handled with care. The instruments will be taken away from children who abuse them.
- After the children have instruments in their hands, allow them a few minutes to experiment. Most children will want to play their instrument right away. Use a signal such as beating a drum, raising your hand, or playing the Autoharp® to have the children stop.

26-8 Children can have fun with rhythm instruments without worrying about their musical talents.

- Rotate instruments after children have had time to experiment. This gives each child a chance to play all of the instruments.
- After the activity, have the children return their instruments to the box, table, or shelf where they belong.

## Building Rhythm Instruments

Some teachers have the time and resources to make rhythm instruments. Directions are included for making sandpaper blocks and sticks, bongo and tom-tom drums, rattlers and shakers, rhythm sticks and bells, and coconut cymbals.

### Sandpaper Blocks

Sandpaper blocks can be used by children of all ages. For this reason, they are often the first rhythm instruments used in the classroom. Some classrooms contain one pair of sandpaper blocks for each child.

Sandpaper blocks can be used for sound effects. They make a soft, swishing sound and are played by rubbing the two sandpaper blocks together. See 26-9 for instructions on making sandpaper blocks.

### Sandpaper Sticks

Purchase rough sandpaper and wooden doweling 1 inch wide and 12 inches long for each stick. To construct the sticks, wrap and glue sandpaper around each of the dowels. Leave a small section for use as a handle. Then sand the end of the sticks smooth. Direct the children to scrape the dowels back and forth across each other to make a sound. These sticks, like the sandpaper blocks, will need to have the sandpaper replaced from time to time.

### Bongo Drums

Bongo drums are a favorite of many preschool children. With a drum, they can create many tones by hitting the drumhead near the rim, in the center, and elsewhere.

To construct bongo drums, collect a pair of scissors, string, a piece of rubber, an empty coffee can with both ends removed, a hammer, and a large nail.

Use the plastic lid from the coffee can to trace two circles on the rubber. Allow an extra

| Sandpaper Blocks |
| --- |
| **Materials** |
| 2 blocks of soft pine, 4 by 3 by 1 inches in size<br>Several sheets of coarse sandpaper<br>Colored enamel paint<br>Thumbtacks or staples<br>Strong glue (epoxy based)<br>2 straps of leather or flexible plastic, 4 to 4½ inches long<br>Scissors<br>Hammer |
| **Procedure** |
| 1. Sand the wood to remove all rough edges.<br>2. Paint the blocks a bright color to make them attractive and to prevent the wood from becoming soiled.<br>3. Glue the handles to each block:<br><br>4. Cut the sandpaper to fit the bottom and sides of each block:<br><br>5. Attach the sandpaper to the blocks with thumbtacks or staples. (As sand is rubbed off the paper, replace with new sandpaper.) |

26-9 It takes just a little effort to make these inexpensive sandpaper blocks.

inch to pull over the edges. Cut the circles out. Take the hammer and large nail, and punch holes around the outside edge of the circle. After the holes have been punched, place each of the rubber circles over an end of the can. Then lace the rubber circles to each other using string.

### Tom-Tom Drums

Making tom-toms can be a group project for the children. You will need oatmeal boxes (with lids) and tempera paint, watercolor markers, or construction paper. One way to get all the empty oatmeal boxes needed is to ask parents to send them from home. To make the tom-toms, tell the children to tape the lid on the box. After this, give them tempera paint, watercolor markers, or colored construction paper and paste to decorate their tom-toms. A rhythm stick can be used for a drum stick.

Tin can tom-toms can be made with large empty coffee cans. Use the plastic top to cut three sheets of wrapping paper 2 inches larger than the top of the tin for each tom-tom. Glue the three sheets together. Stretch the glued paper over one end of the coffee can. Secure the paper with a large rubber band or string.

### Rattlers

Making rattlers is a simple activity in which the children can take part. To collect supplies for making instruments, ask parents to send a round salt box to school with their children.

To make the rattlers, give each child a handful of dry beans, corn kernels, or rice. Show the children how to pour them into the box. Then give each child a strip of tape to seal off the pour spout on the box.

After the box has been filled and the spout taped closed, the children can decorate their rattlers. Give the children tempera paint, washable markers, crayons, colored construction paper, and paste. After the rattlers have been decorated, put them on display. Encourage the children to explore the variety of sounds made by the different materials.

### Shakers

Collect empty toilet tissue and paper towel tubes. Tape one end of the tube shut with paper fastened by masking tape. Pour small pebbles, dried corn, dried beans, or rice into each tube. Tape the open end shut. If desired, cover each shaker with construction paper, gift wrap paper, or enamel paint.

Shakers are most useful with light, fast music. Show the children how to hold the shakers at face level. Then demonstrate how to shake them briskly. You will discover that the children delight in using shakers.

### Rhythm Sticks

Rhythm sticks are always made in matching pairs. Wooden doweling from ¾ to 1 inch in

diameter is needed. Cut the doweling into 12-inch lengths. Sand each end of the doweling. Add a protective coat of shellac or enamel paint.

Rhythm sticks can also be made from bamboo. This type of wood will produce a hollow sound. A good source for bamboo is a local carpet dealer. To make the rhythm sticks, cut the bamboo into 10- to 12-inch pieces. Tape each end of the stick with tape to prevent splinters.

Teach the children to play rhythm sticks holding one stick in each hand. One stick should be held steady while it is struck near the top with a second stick. See 26-10.

Jingle sticks are rhythm sticks with bells attached to each end. The bells can be attached with a small cup hook. After placing the bell on the hook, use a pliers to force the cup hook closed. You may wish to paint the sticks bright colors. This may make them appealing to children.

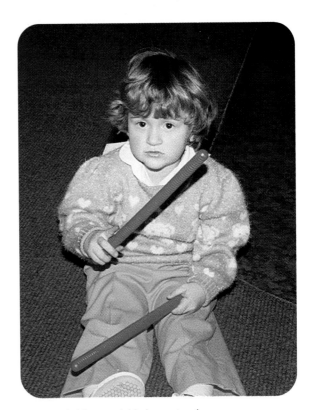

26-10  Children quickly learn to play rhythm sticks properly.

### Rhythm Bells

Materials needed to make rhythm bells include strips of elastic, ½ to ¾ of an inch wide and 5 inches in length. Five to six bells are needed for each strip of elastic. A needle and thread are needed to sew the bells to the elastic.

Sew the ends of the elastic together by overlapping the ends. This can be done by hand or on a machine. On one side of the loop, sew on five or six small bells. Vary the size of the bells on the loops for a variety of sound. The children will then learn that the sounds made by bells of different sizes vary.

### Coconut Cymbals

Cymbals made of coconut halves offer many sounds. They can sound like horses galloping when clapped together. They can also be hit with a rhythm stick to make fast, light music.

To make coconut cymbals, buy several large coconuts at the supermarket. Each coconut will make a pair of cymbals. Cut each coconut in half with a sharp saw. Drain the milk and remove all the meat. Sand the outside and inside edges of the shell until smooth. After this, shellac or paint both sides of the shell.

## Buying Rhythm Instruments

Many teachers do not have time to make all the instruments needed for their programs. As a result, some instruments will have to be bought.

Buy instruments that are sturdy, 26-11. For instance, buy maracas that are constructed in one piece. Otherwise the handles may come loose. Triangles should hang from sturdy holders. If the holder is not strong, the instrument may twirl around when a child is trying to strike it. Jingle bells should always be attached to elastic. This makes them flexible enough to use as either wrist or ankle bracelets. Check drum and tambourine heads to make sure they are durable and fastened firmly. The skins should be free from cuts or holes.

Try to buy instruments in a number of sizes. This allows for a good mix of tones. Usually, smaller instruments have higher tones. Larger instruments have deeper tones.

26-11 Center instruments get much use, so they need to be durable.

## Scheduling Music

Music should be scheduled throughout the day. It fits in well after a story, at the start of the day, after a snack, and during free playtime. It can be used during waiting times, such as the end of the day, a bus ride on a field trip, or before and after lunch. Music can be used to remind children of rules they may have forgotten. For instance, if Sam and Gail did not hang up their coats, you may sing "At school we hang up our coats, hang up our coats."

In addition to these impromptu uses, music should also be scheduled as a group activity for four- and five-year-old children. This should occur at the same time every day since children thrive on consistent schedules.

## Using Group Music

Group music activities are useful in building group feelings and pride. A group setting is a good way to introduce new songs and new instruments. These activities should focus on the group, not the individual.

Group time should be fairly brief. Schedule seven to ten minutes for two- and three-year-olds. You may later extend the period up to 15 minutes for four- and five-year-old children. Some centers schedule two short music periods. Child care centers may have to adjust their music time to meet the attention spans and developmental levels of the children.

### Suggestions for Group Music

You will need to be well-organized for a successful music period. The following suggestions may help:

- Always be prepared. Make sure you have collected all the instruments, music, and other accessories needed.
- Use the same signal for calling the children together for group music time. This signal may be a song, an Autoharp® chord, a beat on a drum, or a piano tune.
- Have the children sit in a circle or semicircle. Then the children can see you and you can see them. To help children sit in the proper places, mark the floor with chalk, tape, or carpet squares.
- Require all adults in the classroom to take part. Their support encourages children to join in, too. These adults can also sit on the floor by the children and help them learn words and responses to the music.
- Switch between active and quiet music activities. Children may become bored if they are always required to listen to music. Likewise, they may tire quickly from, or become too excited by, activities that involve a great deal of movement.
- Reward children for positive behavior. Tell them what type of behavior you expect: sitting quietly, waiting for their turns, holding instruments correctly, singing clearly at the proper volume. Ignore disruptive behavior if it is being used by only one child. If

the child continues despite being ignored, ask another adult in the group to remove the child. Children who act up when they sit together should also be separated during group time.
- Use familiar songs that include fingerplays every day. Such songs are favorites because children find it easy to take part.

## Using Individual Music

Group music activities tend to stress conformity. Children are not as free during these times to express their creativity. For this reason, individual music activities are also an important part of the music experience.

During self-selected play, encourage children to interact with the music. Play music during this period. Make rhythm instruments, the piano, and a tape recorder available throughout the day, 26-12. It is also a good idea to station a teacher or other adult in the music area. An adult's presence will encourage children to enter the area and engage in musical experiences.

## Music Activities

Listening, singing, playing rhythm instruments, and moving to rhythm are all music activities. A good program contains all of these activities.

### Listening

All music activities involve listening. The ability to listen is important for learning. Good listening skills help children build proper speech habits, an extended attention span, and reading readiness skills.

Listening to music can enrich the imaginations of young children. It also can help them relax and release pent-up feelings. Listening can take place when singing or when playing rhythm instruments, the piano, the CD player, or a tape player.

Children need to be taught how to listen. You, as a teacher, need to give them reasons for listening. For example, you may say, "Listen to this music and tell me how it makes you feel." After playing the music, let the children express their feelings. The games in 26-13 can help young children develop listening skills.

26-12  Many children love to spend time listening to taped music.

| Listening Games | |
|---|---|
| **What's the Sound?** | **Body Sounds** |
| Tape sounds from different parts of the home. These may include running water, flushing toilets, ringing telephones, closing doors, or sounds made by scissors, doorbells, washing machines, radios, and electric garage door openers. Play each sound back to the children and ask them to name the object making the noise. | Tell the children that you are going to play a body sound game. Tell them to close their eyes or cover them with their hands and listen carefully. Then stomp your feet, snap your fingers, slap your thigh, smack your lips, and clap your hands. Have the children guess how you are making the sounds. |
| **Instrument Sounds** | **Guess the Instruments** |
| Provide the children with a box or basket of rhythm instruments to explore. Then ask the following questions:<br>• What instrument sounds like jingle bells?<br>• What instrument sounds like a church bell?<br>• What instrument sounds like the tick of a clock?<br>• What instrument sounds like thunder?<br>• What instrument has a loud sound?<br>• What instrument has a quiet sound? | Let the children become familiar with the classroom instruments. Then, based on developmental level or age of the child, choose a few instruments to use in a game called "Guess the Instrument." With two-year-old children, choose only two instruments. These should have very different sounds. As the children progress, add more instruments. To play the game, tell the children to cover their eyes and listen to the sound made by the instrument you are playing. Then they can guess what instrument you are playing. After children are familiar with the game, older children may want to play the teacher's role. In this event, you, too, should cover your eyes and take part. |

26-13  Children have fun and develop their listening skills while playing these games.

## Fingerplays

Fingerplays are another useful method for teaching listening skills. Choose fingerplays based on developmental levels. For example, a fingerplay for two-year-olds should be short and contain simple words.

Teachers who enjoy fingerplays may wish to order their own fingerplay books. These books can be ordered through a local bookstore. Also, they can be bought in the exhibit area at a professional conference or from a local school supply store.

Some teachers prefer to file fingerplays under certain themes. For example, "Two Little Apples" could be filed with units on apples, fall, or nutrition. "Roll Them" could be filed under transitions, movements, or body concepts. Size concepts or numbers would be good themes for using "Here's a Ball." "Lickety-Lick," a childhood favorite, is often filed under science concepts. It is used for teaching these concepts during cooking experiences. See 26-14.

## Singing

Children's best musical instruments are their voices. Their voices are always with them. Even very young children make musical cooing and crying sounds. These tones vary in strength and pitch. Voice control is learned as children grow.

After children babble, tonal patterns emerge. By age two most children can sing. They often sing as they dress, eat, and play. By this time, singing is a meaningful activity.

Children's singing skills vary a great deal. In a group of two-year-olds, there may be children able to sing in tune and make up tunes. Other children may not be able to master these skills until they are three or four years old.

You may notice that children who stutter often sing clearly. Speech skills can be improved through singing, 26-15.

### Mouthing

Children's mouths can be used to make coughing, gurgling, sipping, kissing, and hissing sounds. Animal, train, plane, machinery, and traffic sounds can also be made with the mouth. As children compare these sounds, they will learn that some are fast, others are slow, some are

---

### Fingerplays

**Two Little Apples**

Two little apples hanging high in the tree. (Place arms above head.)
Two little apples smiling at me. (Look up at hands and smile.)
I shook that tree as hard as I could. (Make a shaking motion.)
Down came the apples. Mmmmmmm, so good. (Make a falling motion with arms. Hold hands to mouth pretending to eat.)

**Roll Them**

Roll them and roll them. (Roll hands.)
And give your hands a clap. (Clap hands.)
Roll them and roll them. (Roll hands.)
And place them in your lap. (Place hands in lap.)

**Here's a Ball**

Here's a ball (Make a small circle with thumb and index finger.)
And here's a ball (Make a large circle by using both thumbs and index fingers.)
A great big ball I see. (Make a huge circle with arms.)
Shall we count them? Are you ready? One, two, three.

**Lickety-Lick**

Lickety-lick, lickety-lick. (Make a big circle with the left arm by placing hand on hip. Place the right hand inside the circle.)
The batter is getting all thickety-thick. (Stir with the right hand.)
What should we bake? What shall we bake? (Gesture by opening hands.)
A great big beautiful cake. (Extend arms to show a big cake.)

26-14 How would you file these fingerplays?

---

loud, and some are quiet. Thus, exploring mouth sounds can add to knowledge. As children explore these sounds, they learn others. Joining a variety of sounds can produce unique music.

To encourage children to make sounds, bring pictures to a group activity. For instance, collect pictures of large, medium, and small dogs in a number of poses. The dogs might be barking, showing their teeth, or playing with their owners. Show the children each picture. Ask them to

26-15 Singing along to music helps many children correct speech problems.

mimic the sounds a dog would make in each instance. You can use pictures of other animals, people, machines, cars, trucks, and other objects. These activities will help children become sensitive to sounds.

### Chants

A **chant** is a group of words spoken with a lively beat. It is a song that has word patterns, rhymes, and nonsense syllables in one to three tones repeated in a sequence. "Teddy Bear, Teddy Bear, Turn Around" is a chant. Mother Goose rhymes are also chants. Chants are an important form of early childhood song. Children learn to speak together in unison by chanting.

Chanting is a beneficial activity for all children. They learn to share the joy of language. They also learn to cooperate. The rhythmic response to chants are useful for children who are learning English as a second language. Chanting is also good for children who speak non-standard English. Shy children can develop self-confidence and self-expression by chanting.

Like singing, you will need to model chanting for the children. Begin by repeating it aloud several times. When the children feel comfortable, encourage them to join you.

## Movement Experiences

For learning, movement is an important nonverbal tool. It provides opportunities to pretend. Children can walk like elephants, crawl like worms, or pilot an airplane. Children almost always enjoy these experiences, 26-16.

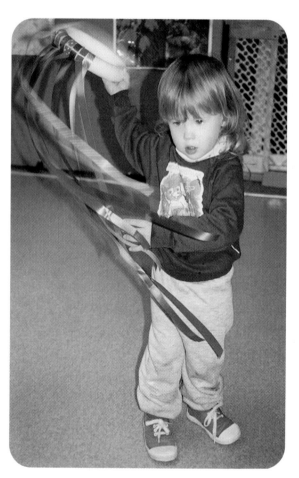

26-16 Children like to discover what their bodies can do through movement activities.

Movement activities should provide children with the chance to

- explore the many ways their bodies can move
- practice combining movement with rhythm
- discover that many ideas can be expressed through movement
- learn how movement is related to space

Some children will take naturally to movement activities. Other children may feel more self-conscious or embarrassed. To help these children, begin with some short, simple movement activities. Knowing what type of responses to expect can help you prepare.

## Children's Responses

Studies show that two- and three-year-old children's responses to movement vary. Most two-year-old children actively respond to rhythm, but at their own tempo. Their response may be to repeat the same basic movement through the entire activity. For example, a two-year-old may simply jump up and down during an entire song.

By age three, children have gained greater motor coordination. As a result, they have more control of rhythmic responses. Three-year-old children will likely use many responses. That is, they may circle with their arms, run, and jump during the same recording.

Between ages four and six, muscular coordination keeps improving. At the same time, their interest in movement and space increases. If you watch children at this stage, you will notice they skip, run, climb, and dance to music. These movements are now done to the beat of the music. If the beat is fast, their movements are fast. They move more slowly to slow beats.

## Teacher Preparation

To prepare for movement activities, first select your activity. Chart 26-17 lists many movements. Then stand in front of a full-length mirror and practice the movements. Do each movement in the activity. If possible, repeat the movements several times.

| Body Movements | | |
|---|---|---|
| **Finger Movements** | **Hand and Arm Movements** | **Whole Body Movements** |
| Cutting | Carrying | Bending |
| Folding | Circling | Bouncing |
| Holding | Clapping | Climbing |
| Patting | Dropping | Crawling |
| Petting | Grabbing | Creeping |
| Pinching | Lifting | Dancing |
| Pointing | Punching | Galloping |
| Poking | Pulling | Hopping |
| Pulling | Reaching | Jumping |
| Rolling | Shaking | Rocking |
| Rubbing | Slapping | Rolling Over |
| Smoothing | Stretching | Running |
| Snapping | Sweeping | Scooting |
| Tickling | Swinging | Shaking |
| Touching | Twisting | Shuffling |
| Typing | Waving | Skipping |
| Wiggling | | Sliding |
| | | Swaying |
| | | Walking |

26-17 These movements can be included in a variety of movement activities.

In the classroom, children learn best when they can see and hear. Rather than simply explain, you may have to act out certain movements. In the fingerplay, "Two Little Apples," for instance, during the line, "way up high in the sky," place your hands high above your head. Reinforcing the words with actions also adds interest.

## Teaching Movements

In most movement activities, children should be encouraged to explore and express their own way of moving. A tambourine can be used to capture children's interest before and during the activities. Tambourines are very useful. They can be played loud or soft, slow or fast. They can represent a galloping horse or a frightened kitten.

For successful movement activities, you will need to follow certain guidelines:

- Choose a time when the children are calm and well rested.
- Define space limits. There needs to be enough open, clear space. If space is

limited, move chairs and furniture to the side.

- Tell children they need to stop when the music stops.
- For variety in movement experiences, provide props such as paper streamers, balloons, balls, and scarves, 26-18.
- Use movement activities involving cassette tapes, rhythm instruments, and verbal instructions.
- Allow children to get to know activities by repeating many of the experiences.
- Stop before signs of fatigue appear.

You may want children to be involved in planning some movement activities. Ask the children to suggest movement activities and to bring in their favorite cassette tapes. After the group experience, cassettes can be placed in the music center. This will give children the chance to listen to the music again.

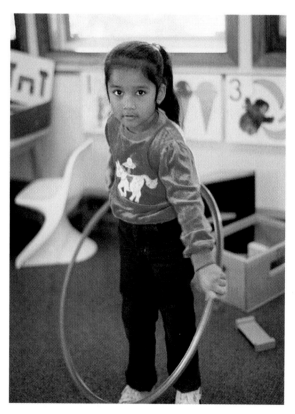

26-18 Using props adds a new dimension to movement activities.

## Body Percussion Activities

Early movement activities should be simple. Stomping feet, clapping hands, patting thighs, and snapping fingers are all simple movements. These are called **body percussion**. All of these movements involve using the body to make rhythm. Body percussion can be used to learn to do more than one movement at a time. Body percussion also helps children build **auditory discrimination skills**—the ability to detect different sounds by listening.

Stomping feet to music has always been a favorite action of young children. To stomp correctly, children should bring their legs back and stomp down and forward.

Children should be taught to clap with one palm held up steadily. You should refer to this palm as the instrument. The other hand serves as the mallet. Children should clap with arms and wrists relaxed and elbows out.

The thigh slap is easy to teach. Relax your wrist for modeling the thigh slap. With arms relaxed, move your hands to slap your thigh.

When teaching children to snap their fingers, hold your hands high. Tell the children to follow you. Snap once. Have the children repeat this action. After they have mimicked your action, have them do two snaps, and then three snaps. Keep this up as long as they are able to repeat your action.

After children have learned to stomp, clap, slap, and snap, you can have them combine two actions. They might "snap, snap, snap," and then "clap, clap, clap." Depending on the skills of the children, you may gradually introduce all four levels of body percussion during one experience.

## Movement Activities

Children learn to explore and express their imaginations through movement activities. One of the first movement activities should focus on listening to a drum beat. A drum is the only instrument needed for the activity. First, tell the children to listen to the drum and see how it makes them feel. For two-year-old children, provide one steady beat. With older children you may vary the rhythm: fast, slow, heavy, soft, big, small. Then ask them to respond. Encourage them to run, crawl, roll, walk, hop, skip, and gallop. After experiences using the drum, many more movement activities can be used with or without music. The key is to encourage the children to use their bodies to express themselves.

## Partners

This activity is best for four- or five-year-olds. Instruct the children to choose partners. You will also need a partner to demonstrate. With your partner, move under, over, and around each other. Then have the other children mimic your movements.

## Time Awareness

Use a drum to provide a beat that tells the children to run very fast. After they have done this well, tell them to run very slowly. Then tell them to jump on the floor quickly. Again, follow this request by having them jump slowly.

## Space Awareness

Have the children stand in front of you. Make sure that there is enough space between each child so movements can be made freely. Stress your instructions with actions as you tell them to do the following:

- Lift your leg in front of you.
- Lift your leg backwards.
- Lift your leg sideways.
- Lift your leg and step forward.
- Lift your leg and step backwards.
- Lift your leg and step sideways.
- Reach up to the ceiling.
- Reach down to the floor.
- Stretch to touch the walls, 26-19.
- Move your arm in front of you.
- Move your arm behind you.

## Weight Awareness

Children can learn differences between light and heavy using their own body force. To begin this activity, give verbal directions and demonstrate the actions. Tell the children to focus on the weight of their bodies as they make the movements. Give the following instructions:

- Push down hard on the floor with your hands.
- Push down softly on the floor with your hands.

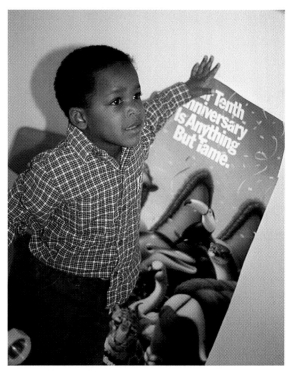

26-19  Reaching helps make children more aware of the space around them.

- Lift your arms slowly into the air.
- Lift your arms quickly into the air.
- Walk on your tiptoes.
- Stomp on the floor with your feet.
- Kick your leg as slowly as you can.
- Kick your leg as hard as you can.

## Organizing Movement into Dance

Combining time, space, and weight movements, children can learn to form movements into dance. To teach this concept, have the children do the following:

- Walk around quickly in a circle on the floor.
- Walk around slowly in a circle on the floor.
- Tiptoe slowly around the circle.
- Tiptoe quickly around the circle.
- Jump hard around the circle.
- Move your arms in a circle above your head.
- Move your arms in circles everywhere.

## Word Games

Word games can help children move in ways that express feelings. To play word games, tell the children to move the way the words you say might feel. Use such words as happy, sad, angry, sleepy, and lazy. After they have moved to these words, remind them to use their bodies and faces. Keep repeating the words. See 26-20.

## Moving Shapes

Four- and five-year-old children enjoy the moving shapes game. As with other movement activities, children will need ample space. Give children the following instructions:

- Try to move like something big and heavy: an elephant, tugboat, bulldozer, airplane.
- Try to move like something small and heavy: a fat frog, bowling ball, brick.
- Try to move like something big and light: a cloud, beach ball, parachute.
- Try to move like something small and light: a snowflake, flea, feather, butterfly, bumblebee.

## Pantomiming

**Pantomiming** involves telling a story with body movements rather than words. It is best for use with four-, five-, and six-year-olds. Begin by telling the children they are going to get imaginary presents. Tell them to show you the size of their box. The children should show you a shape made by outlining with their hands and arms. Continue with the following statements:

- Feel the box.
- Hold the box.
- Unwrap the present.
- Take it out of the box.
- Put it back into the box.
- Rewrap the present.

Another pantomime children enjoy is acting out an occupation. Tell the children to think about an occupation. Then have them show how the worker acts. Sometimes this is fun to do one by one. Have one child act out his or her occupation while the rest of the class tries to guess it.

## Pretending

Pretending is an activity best used with older children. Tell the children to pretend they are crying, singing, boxing, driving, cooking, laughing, typing, scrubbing, painting, playing an instrument, flying, playing cards, or building a house. There are many songs that children can act out as they sing. Classics include *Here We Go Around the Mulberry Bush* or *This is What I Can Do*. The music to *Peter and the Wolf* provides the same opportunity for drama.

Another pretending activity involves telling the children to imagine there is a box in front of them. Then tell them they are outside the box and they should crawl into it. After they have crawled into the box, tell the children to crawl out of it. Continue by telling them to crawl under and beside the box.

26-20 Older children can laugh to show how they move when they're happy.

# Summary

Music is a form of communication. It can be used to teach many skills. Through music experiences, children develop listening skills. They also learn about emotions and feelings, their culture, and sound. For these reasons, teaching music is an important part of an early childhood program. It nurtures the development of their minds, bodies, and emotions.

The music center in the classroom should be designed to encourage participation in music and movement activities. A variety of instruments can be made or purchased.

Music and movement activities should be planned with the age, ability level, and interest of the children in mind. Enthusiasm is the key factor in constructing a positive experience.

Movement provides children with opportunities to pretend and exercise. Movement activities can be easily combined with music activities for meaningful experiences.

# Review and Reflect

1. List four reasons teachers use music with young children.
2. True or false. Music experiences help children grow cognitively.
3. A music center should _____.
   A. be in a congested section of the classroom
   B. have instruments stored on high shelves or in a closet
   C. contain pictures of dancers, instruments, and singers
   D. None of the above.
4. Why is enthusiasm a key factor in conducting useful music experiences?
5. True or false. Nonparticipants should be pushed into taking part in music activities.
6. The best songs for young children should _____.
   A. have little or no repetition
   B. tell a story
   C. have a vocal range of two or three octaves
   D. All of the above.
7. Name three methods for teaching songs. Explain one method.
8. Why are the Autoharp® or guitar good instruments to use to accompany singing?
9. List four uses of rhythm instruments.
10. True or false. Music should be scheduled throughout the day.
11. _____ music activities are useful in building feelings of togetherness.
12. State five useful suggestions for conducting group music experiences.
13. True or false. All music activities involve singing.
14. _____ are songs that have word patterns, rhymes, and nonsense syllables used in sequence with one to three repeated tones.
15. List four objectives for movement experiences.
16. List three guidelines for successful movement activities.
17. _____ activities involve stomping feet and clapping hands.
18. What are auditory discrimination skills?
19. Combining time, space, and weight movements, children can learn to form their movements into _____.
20. _____ involves having children act out a story as it is told.

## Apply and Explore

1.  Observe a teacher during a music experience. Note the methods used to teach songs. Share these methods with the class.

2.  Design a music center. Start by reviewing equipment catalogs. Develop a budget for this center. Make a list of instruments and equipment to include.

3.  Select a movement activity and demonstrate it to your class.

4.  Select a song and teach it to your class.

5.  Construct two or three types of rhythm instruments. Plan a music activity using these instruments.

6.  Create two songs that could be used for daily transitions in the classroom.

7.  Search the Web site kaplanco.com for items early childhood teachers could include in a multicultural music curriculum.

# Chapter 27

# Guiding Field Trip Experiences

After studying this chapter, you will be able to

- describe the importance of field trips.

- explain points of consideration for first field trip experiences.

- list ways to promote safety on field trips.

- outline the process for selecting a field trip.

- explain the types and purposes of theme walks.

- plan a field trip from pretrip planning to follow-up activities.

## Terms to Know

theme walks

resource people

behavioral expectations

"Apples grow on trees," announced Karla after a recent field trip. Alberto replied, "I know that, and I know something else. Apples are grown in special places called orchards." Hearing the conversation, Robbie added, "Orchards can have red, green, or yellow apples." By going on a field trip, these children have expanded their concept of an apple.

Mr. Smith, after hearing the children's comments, promoted further learning by saying, "It sounds like you know a lot about apples." All the children agreed. Mr. Smith then suggested that they write a story about the trip.

From the field trip, the children learned many concepts related to apples. They learned about color, size, shape, and plant growth. When planning the field trip for the children, Mr. Smith had two main goals. The first was to expand the children's concepts of apples. The second was to introduce *orchard* as a new vocabulary word.

## The Importance of Field Trips

Young children have limited experience in understanding their world. Much of what they understand comes from books, pictures, television, and movies. Although these media help children learn about their world, they do not replace real experiences. To fully understand their world, young children need to connect with their community. They need to see, hear, feel, taste, and smell, 27-1. The more senses children use, the more they are likely to learn.

Children gain firsthand experiences during field trips. They are able to look at, listen to,

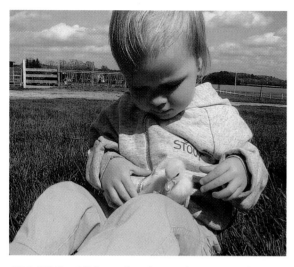

27-1 While children often learn about animals through books and videos, contact with live animals further enhances their learning.

smell touch, and feel their world. As children connect words and concepts with real objects people, and places, vague concepts become clearer to them. Field trips also help children

- build keener observation skills
- build vocabularies
- clarify concepts as new information is learned
- learn about their community

- take part in multisensory experiences
- gain new insights for dramatic play
- learn about their environment
- practice following directions in a group

## First Field Trips

For young children, field trips can be a very new experience. They may be unfamiliar with such activity. As a result, they may be anxious about what will occur. For this reason, first field trips should be short, nonthreatening, neighborhood events. For instance, a first trip could be a simple walk around the block, 27-2. Some children may be hesitant to leave the building. They may fear their parents will come for them while they are gone. Relieve them of their fears by reassuring them that this will not happen.

To provide security, remind children of their daily routine. Say, "First we are going to walk around the block. When we return, we will have a story. Then it will be snack time. After that we will play outside, and then it will be time to go home." Knowing a familiar routine will help prevent some fears.

After taking a few trips around the neighborhood, field trips may be taken to familiar places. A visit to a local grocery store is often a rewarding trip. Here, children can see and talk about things that are well known to them.

27-2 First field trips should involve familiar surroundings.

First field trips can build or hinder children's confidence. Therefore, first trips need to match children's developmental needs. Generally, two-year-olds do best with short mini-trips. Three-year-olds can take longer trips that may extend to an hour or so in duration. With longer field trips, allow plenty of time for walking slower and resting. Trips for four- and five-year-olds may be lengthened in time. Often these children can take trips that last several hours. Plan trips in which children will meet with success.

## Selecting Trips

The trips you select will depend on the ages of the children, location of the site, and the budget available. Centers located within walking distance of many potential sites will take more trips than those centers located in more isolated areas. Centers located in large cities have the option of using public transportation. Other centers may have their own vans to provide transportation.

Field trips are sometimes selected based on the season or weather. A trip to a pumpkin patch or an orchard can be taken in the fall. Trips that require walking, such as a trip to a zoo, should be taken during warm weather. Substitute days should be scheduled in case of bad weather.

Field trips are sometimes chosen based on the curriculum themes being studied. For instance, a trip to a farm may be chosen while children are studying about farms, food, or machinery. While learning about health, a trip to a dentist's office, doctor's office, or hospital may be chosen. Chart 27-3 lists many field trip suggestions based on themes.

### Theme Walks

Simple field trips involving walks near the center based on a theme are called **theme walks**. The center neighborhood contains many interesting and meaningful opportunities for children to learn about the world. Most children enjoy walking, and the exercise is good for their bodies. Theme walks also provide an opportunity to sharpen their observation skills.

Theme walks may center on many topics: numbers, colors, people, occupations, buildings, flowers, trees, or cars. For best results, focus on only one theme during each walk.

| Field Trip | Related Themes |
|---|---|
| Airport | Air transportation or airplanes |
| Animal shelter | Pets, dogs, cats |
| Aquarium | Fish, water, water animals |
| Artist's studio | Careers, art |
| Bakery | Foods, community helpers |
| Bird sanctuary | Birds |
| Bookstore | Reading, books |
| Butcher shop | Foods, careers, tools |
| Cafeteria | Nutrition |
| Car dealer | Transportation, car, truck, wheels |
| Car wash | Cars, trucks, water |
| Carpenter's shop | Careers, construction |
| Circus | Animals, careers |
| Construction site | Buildings, construction, tools |
| Dairy farm | Food, farm animals, machinery |
| Dance studio | Movement, communication, careers |
| Dentist's office | Health, careers, teeth |
| Doctor's office | Health, careers, "My Body" |
| Fire station | Community helper, fire safety |
| Garage | Tools, careers, machines |
| Greenhouse | Plants, spring, flowers, food |
| Grocery store | Food, community helpers |
| Hair salon | Health, "I'm Me—I'm Special" |
| Hatchery | Animals |
| Hospital | Health, careers, people and places |
| Laundry | Health, careers, clothing |
| Library | Community helper, books |
| Newspaper office | Books, careers, communication |
| Orchard | Nature |
| Park | Nature, My community |
| Pet shop | Pets, animals, careers |
| Photography studio | Communication, careers, art |
| Planetarium | The universe, planets |
| Police station | Community helper, safety |
| Post office | Community helpers, communication |
| Poultry farm | Food, farm animals, eggs |
| Print shop | Books, careers, communication |
| Radio or TV station | Communication, careers, listening |
| Retail store | Clothing, careers |
| Train station | Transportation careers |
| Veterinarian's clinic | Pets, animals, health, careers |
| Zoo | Animals, homes |

**Field Trip Suggestions**

27-3 In your community, there are probably even more field trip sites that can be related to a theme.

Before starting a theme walk, talk about what children might observe. If the theme is buildings, tell the children to observe types of buildings they see. They may see houses, apartments, offices, stores, and service stations.

Color is a good concept for a theme walk. Choose one or more colors the children should watch for throughout the walk. Two- and three-year-old children should be asked to look for only one color. Older children, especially five-year-olds, may enjoy looking for many colors. In fact, a fun walk for these children would be to record as many colors as they observe.

A shape walk is a way to teach children about shapes. Before leaving the classroom, review with the children what shape(s) they are to observe. As with colors, the number of shapes children are to observe depends on their ages.

Shapes are everywhere. Tires are round; most sidewalk slabs are square; doorknobs may be oval or round. Children encouraged to use their eyes to recognize shapes will also be busy using their minds.

Theme walks based on numbers and letters may also be useful learning experiences. As children walk, they will see numbers and/or letters everywhere. Numbers are seen on license plates, street signs, store windows, billboards, passing trucks, and houses. Determine the number of numbers or letters to observe based on children's ages, skills, and abilities.

People walks can teach many social concepts. The children will see that people may be tall or short and have different-colored hair and eyes. Children will also notice some people wear glasses or have beards or long hair.

Two-year-olds may be able to identify a baby, man, woman, boy, or girl. Three-year-olds may be able to distinguish differences among people based upon dress, hair color, and height. Four- and five-year-olds may be able to describe the actions of people they have observed.

During occupational walks, children observe what people are doing. They may see a bus driver, truck driver, bank teller, street sweeper, or house painter.

A building or architectural walk may be of special interest to older children. As you approach buildings, note their purposes. When children see a gas station-garage combination, discuss why large windows and large doors are part of the architecture. (Large windows are needed to see customers; large doors are needed for cars and trucks.) You may also encourage children to imagine what is inside the building.

To gain the most on these theme walks, carry a notepad and pencil, camera, or even a video recorder. Record observations that can be discussed when the children return to the classroom. These observations make good discussion topics for lunch, snack, or group time. Listening to the children's discussions, you will be able to note their interests.

## Resource People

To promote further learning, invite interesting people to class. Another option is take the children on field trips to visit the people. These guests or field trip hosts are called **resource people**, 27-4.

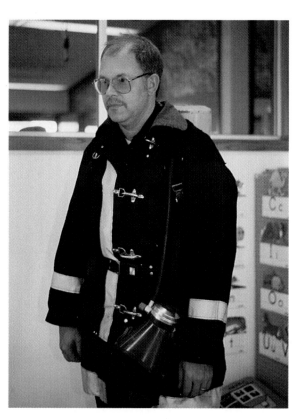

27-4 Firefighters are nearly always at the top of the list of interesting resource people.

Parents, grandparents, great grandparents, aunts, uncles, neighbors, siblings, and friends are some of the best resource people. Ask them what interests and hobbies, photos, crafts, clothing, and foods they would be willing to share. This can be done personally or through a questionnaire. Select only people who enjoy children. They should represent many cultural groups, both sexes, and people of different ages. Compile a list of these people, along with their interests and hobbies. During the year, select people from the list who complement your curriculum.

To be the most useful, resource people need an orientation before meeting the children. This is a necessary step for making the experience a success for both the children and resource people. Tell the resource people the number of children in your group, their interests, ages, and length of their attention spans. Suggest questions that they may ask the children. Let them know their presentation and words must be kept simple.

Warn the resource people that children often become very excited when they visit. They are proud of their guests, their classroom, and their classroom friends. Because of the stimulation, they may exhibit overly active behavior.

If possible, suggest to resource people that the children be allowed to have a "hands-on activity," 27-5. For example, if a grandmother is willing to demonstrate how she paints, encourage her to let the children try painting, too. If a person demonstrates playing the drums, ask that each child have the chance to hit the drum.

After a resource person has visited the classroom or hosted a field trip, always send a thank-you note or some other form of appreciation, 27-6. You may write a personal note, or children who can write may wish to express their own thanks. Younger children may choose to dictate thank-you notes to you. Other forms of thanking people include sending children's artwork or freshly baked cookies.

Appreciation may also take other forms. For instance, in February, handmade valentines may be mailed to all resource people who took part in the program during the year. Taped thank-you notes, songs on a cassette, and videotapes or photographs of the children at the site are other thoughtful ways to thank resource people.

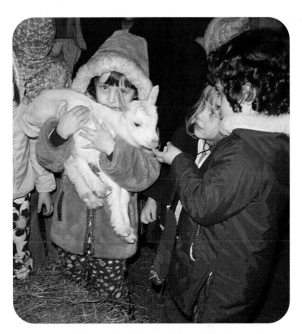

27-5 Hands-on experiences help make vague concepts more concrete for children. After holding this goat, the children will have a real experience to remember when they see goats in a book or hear about them in the classroom.

Dear Firefighter:

Thank you for showing us your fire truck. We enjoyed sitting in the truck. Thank you for showing us the truck's parts. Thank you for sounding the siren. Thank you for showing us a firefighter's clothing. We enjoyed trying it on, too.

Love,

Ron Smith's Class

27-6 Build a positive image of the center in your community with a thank-you note to resource people.

# Planning a Field Trip

Successful field trips for young children need to be carefully planned. Consideration should be given to appropriateness, costs, scheduling, adult-child ratio, behavioral expectations, educational goals, and the children's preparation. As a teacher, you need to think about all of these factors. A good way to do this is to take a pretrip to the site to prepare for the field trip.

## Pretrip

The success of any trip depends upon preparation, 27-7. After setting goals, always make a pretrip if you have never been to the site. This visit will give you a chance to

- describe the purpose of the trip to the tour guide
- explain the children's interests and their need to use a number of senses
- prepare the tour guide for the types of questions the children may ask
- locate bathrooms
- check for any potential dangers
- ask about parking (if necessary)
- observe for teaching opportunities
- revise trip goals, if necessary

Keep a field trip file. In some centers, teachers maintain their own files. In other centers, the director maintains a file for use by all personnel. This file may be a notebook, a folder, or an index card file box. As a rule, information to note for each trip includes

- name of site
- telephone number
- address
- contact person (tour guide)
- costs
- distance from center in blocks or miles
- dangers
- special learning opportunities
- location of bathrooms and water sources

Permission slips signed by parents or guardians must be on file for each child before a trip, 27-8. For convenience, many center directors use one form for all trips and walks. This form is filled in and signed at enrollment time. This saves the staff's time in obtaining permission slips for each trip. Busy parents will also benefit from this timesaving method.

27-7 The best field trips will be those the teacher has planned well.

Before the trip, plan your "trip bag." It should include the essential supplies that you will need to take along. Paper tissues, a first-aid kit, premoistened towelettes, a garbage bag, emergency telephone numbers, and coins for phone calls are a must. Many centers also require that you take a folder with copies of emergency forms and signed permission slips. Depending on the length of the trip and the weather, you may want to take snacks and refreshments for the children. For young children, diapers, bottles, and extra clothing might be a consideration. If available, also carry a cell phone in the event of an emergency.

In hot weather, children often become thirsty. Make sure water or some other nutritious drink is on hand. Insulated jugs are a good way to transport liquids.

Field trips involve added safety risks and responsibilities for child care centers. Before taking field trips, teach the children pedestrian safety. Practice taking short walks near the center. Before leaving the center, explain the rules the children must follow when crossing streets. When approaching a crosswalk, review these rules with the children. Be sure to observe traffic signals when crossing intersections. Make

**Brown's Child Care
Field Trip Permission Form**

Child's Name _____   Date _____

Parents' Names _____   Business Phone _____

Cell Phone _____

_____   Business Phone _____

Cell Phone _____

Home Address _____   Home Phone _____

Home E-Mail _____

In consideration of _____ 's
(child's name)

acceptance as an enrollee in Brown's Child Care Center, I hereby give
permission for my child to participate in any walks or field trips planned
and supervised by the staff. I understand that various modes of
transportation may be used for these trips, and I will be informed of each
trip before it occurs.

_____   _____
(Parent's Signature)                              (Date)

27-8  Permission slips from parents, such as this one,
are a necessity when planning a field trip.

sure you consistently enforce and follow the rules. This is important since children learn by experience and imitation.

## Suitability

Before choosing a trip, ask yourself "How appropriate is this trip for the children?" Consider the developmental level of the children. For five-year-olds, a trip to a television studio may be both fun and educational. This same trip would not be appropriate for two-year-olds. Two-year-olds are more interested in those things closer to

their immediate surroundings. For example, pets, animals, babies, mothers, fathers, and grandparents are topics that capture their interest.

Field trips for children under 24 months are often simple walks around the neighborhood. For safety purposes, use strollers for these children. Many centers purchase special strollers that hold up to six children. This allows one teacher to handle several children at one time, 27-9.

When planning field trips for young children, avoid crowds. Crowds may be overwhelming to some children. It is also difficult to watch children in a crowded setting. Trips to the zoo and the circus usually involve large groups of people. In these cases, during your pretrip ask what days are least crowded. When crowds cannot be avoided, ask for help from parents and other volunteers.

Choose trips that provide learning through participation. Children enjoy touching and doing things. When planning a trip to a farm, ask if the children can pet the animals, assist in milking the cows, and help collect the eggs. Likewise, a trip to a apple orchard could provide children with opportunities to pick and taste apples.

## Cost

When planning a field trip, always figure the costs. This helps you decide if the trip is the best use of your resources. You may feel that the cost of chartering a bus to the zoo is more than your budget allows. You may decide that the money needed for chartering a bus could be more wisely spent on classroom materials. If most of the children have already had this experience, you may want to use the money for some less costly trips. This would give the children new experiences.

Most field trips involve little or no expense, particularly if the site is within walking distance. In some cases, the only costs are admission and/or transportation. If there is an admission fee, call in advance and ask if group rates are available for child care centers. At times, you may get a generous discount or free admission.

27-9 Strollers such as this one make it possible for one adult to take several young children on a walk near the center.

## Transportation

Costs for transportation vary greatly, depending on the type used. For centers that own their own vans, the costs of most field trips are minimal. To cut costs, some centers ask parents and teachers to drive their own cars. This type of arrangement is not recommended. In case of an accident, legal problems could arise, and the driver and/or center could be sued for damages.

Public transportation, such as the city bus or subway, is often less costly than a chartered bus. However, there are disadvantages to public transportation. Trains can be crowded and noisy. This can be stressful for children. There is also the danger of children being hurt or lost during the course of the trip. Accidents often happen as children enter or exit buses or trains. This is why some teachers elect not to use public transportation for their children.

If you decide to use a chartered bus, call several reputable companies. Check to see that the company meets any state safety inspection guidelines. Explain where you intend to go, the length of your stay, the number of passengers, and request prices. Ask them to send you the price quote in writing. After you receive all the quotes, compare to find the company that will provide the best service for the least amount of money. By thoroughly checking costs for a field trip, you can get the most for your resources.

## Scheduling

Midmornings are the best time to schedule field trips. This time of day works best for several reasons. First, children are usually well rested. They often find it easier to listen, observe, and follow instructions. Second, children arrive at different times during the morning. Some parents may bring their children to the center at 7 a.m. Others may not bring their children until 8 or 9 a.m. If you schedule the trip too early, some children would be deprived of the experience. Also in colder climates, early morning temperatures can be too cool for children. This is a key consideration for trips that require walking, 27-10.

Afternoon field trips are also difficult to plan. Most preschool children need to take a nap at this time. Also, children may be deprived of the trip if their parents pick them up early in the afternoon.

Field trips should begin after a quiet activity. This helps children avoid excess excitement or overstimulation during the trip. Overstimulated children are very active and difficult to manage.

One question often asked is, "What is the best day for a field trip?" The answer to this question depends on the group and attendance. First, study the behavior and routine of the group. Some groups are always tired and restless by Friday. You may want to choose a day early in the week for such a group. Monday may not be a good day, depending on the program. The children may be tired as a result of weekend activities. Second, consider the days children attend. Some children may be deprived of trips if they are always scheduled for a day they do not attend.

The right day for a field trip may also depend on the site. If formal arrangements must be made, ask the contact person to suggest a day. Many resource people prefer midweek. This allows time to prepare for the visit.

Carefully plan around the children's needs, children's schedules, and resource person's schedule. This takes time. However, a well-planned field trip produces the greatest amount of learning and pleasure for the children.

## Adult-Child Ratio

To ensure safety and the success of the trip, provide enough chaperones. The most desirable adult-child ratio is based on the number of children in the group, the nature of the field trip, and the dangers involved, 27-11. Walks around the neighborhood can often be handled by the center staff. More adults may be needed for trips using public transportation or for visits to places with potential dangers.

Provide as many adults as possible to promote safety. For two-year-olds, it is recommended that there be one adult for every two children. An adult should be assigned to every four three-year-olds, five four-year-olds, and six five-year-olds for optimal safety. However, if some children need to be closely watched, this ratio should be adjusted. Many times, children are grouped based on their temperaments. For instance, if Sam and Frank behave badly when together, they should be separated. Place them in different groups. If there is a child who has a difficult time following rules, you may assign the child to one adult. Often, an "extra" adult is recruited who is not assigned any specific children. This adult can relieve a teacher to handle emergencies or give children one-to-one contact as needed.

27-10  Petting farm animals is most enjoyable in the warmth of late morning sunshine.

27-11 Field trips can have many hidden dangers. For this reason, extra adult supervision is required.

When more adults are needed for field trips, invite parents. Many programs maintain lists of parents and other volunteers interested in helping on field trips. When the need arises, give these people from one to several week's notice. Parent volunteers may have to make special arrangements at work. Prior to the trip, provide the volunteers with information regarding the trip. Time of departure, arrival at the site, length of stay at the site, planned events at the site, and arrival time back at the center should be included. In addition, volunteers should be told the behavioral expectations.

## Behavioral Expectations

**Behavioral expectations** need to be planned and discussed with children before the trip. Expectations for the children to follow will vary with the children and nature of the trip. Some expectations may apply to all trips. Regardless of the type of trip, expectations are most often the same in most early childhood programs.

For best results, state all expectations in a positive way. Tell the children exactly what they must do, 27-12. For example, tell the children to place their hands at their sides when they are in a store.

The first expectation for field trips is all children must wear an identification tag at all times. These tags should be durable so they can be reused. They should be worn on all field trips. The tag should include the program name, address, and telephone number. This information is helpful in case a child wanders from the group.

The second expectation for field trips is that children should speak softly. To ensure this, teachers need to set a good example. Speak in a low-key voice to avoid overstimulation.

The third expectation is that children must remain with their assigned group and adult supervisor on field trips. Then each adult will know the names of the children they are responsible for supervising.

Many teachers prefer to have children follow the "hold-your-partner's-hand" rule. However, this is not always useful. It is unfair to interested children to have partners whose attention is not focused on the learning experience. Also, constant physical contact can result in stress for some children.

Instead of holding hands children can hold on to a rope to keep them together as a group. To make this rope, purchase several 20-foot pieces of rope. With each piece of rope, loop and tie handles at 2-foot intervals. Show the children how to hold on to the handles and explain expectations during the trip.

## Educational Goals

For the most benefit on a field trip, educational goals must be carefully planned. For example, a trip to a local service station may have a number of goals:

- to observe mechanics at work
- to learn about the care of cars
- to see how machinery works
- to learn vocabulary words: *technicians, gas pump, nozzle,* and *hoist*

During the pretrip visit, these goals need to be discussed with the resource person.

## Children's Preparation

Preparation for children may begin a few days before the trip. Introduce the trip by putting up displays, reading a book, sharing a video, looking at the pictures, or simply talking about the trip.

27-12  These children can quietly watch the birds and listen to the speaker because their teacher shared these behavioral expectations with them ahead of time.

On the day of the trip, tell children what to observe (educational goals) and how to behave (behavioral expectations). Give an identification tag to each child. Assign children to their adult guides. After this, encourage children to use the bathroom. Explain that a bathroom is not always available on walks or some field trips.

## Parent Preparation

Parents should always be informed in advance of field trips. A newsletter, calendar, or notice posted on a bulletin board or classroom door are all useful methods, 27-13. E-mail can be used, too. Inform the parents of the date, location, address, and exact times you will be leaving and returning. This will help parents plan their schedules for dropping off and picking up the children.

You should also notify parents in advance if they are expected to pay any costs of the trip. Let parents know if you will need them to provide any special items, such as sack lunches or car safety seats.

Before leaving, post a sign on the classroom door. Note where you have gone and when you will return. This will also serve as a trip reminder for the parents and center staff.

Share trip goals with children's parents. This information may help them plan related home experiences such as discussions and books that compliment the trip.

## Follow-Up Activities

To help children clarify their learning, plan follow-up activities. Once you return to the

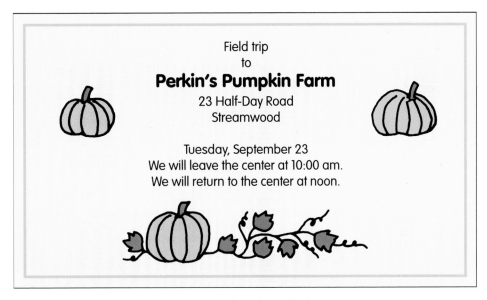

Field trip
to
**Perkin's Pumpkin Farm**
23 Half-Day Road
Streamwood

Tuesday, September 23
We will leave the center at 10:00 am.
We will return to the center at noon.

27-13  Placing this notice on a center bulletin board helps remind parents of an upcoming field trip.

center, talk about what they saw, heard, and experienced. Plan an activity that reinforces the learning that occurred on the trip. A class thank-you note could be a follow-up activity, 27-14.

Recall the classroom scene after the trip to the apple orchard described at the beginning of the chapter. Apples were discussed at lunch. Then the experience was used as a basis for writing a story. After a trip to a bakery, children could bake bread or cookies. Ice cream or butter could be made after a trip to a local dairy. See 27-15.

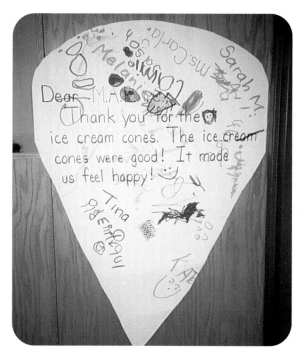

27-14 After a trip to an ice cream parlor, the children signed this thank-you note.

| Follow-Up Activities | |
|---|---|
| **Trip** | **Activities** |
| Apple orchard | • Taste a variety of apples.<br>• Make applesauce or apple muffins.<br>• Read stories about apple orchards.<br>• Serve apple butter, baked apples, or some other form of apple. |
| Fire station | • Place puzzles and stories related to the role of firefighters in the classroom.<br>• Read stories about firefighters.<br>• Place firefighters clothing in the dramatic play area.<br>• Act out fire safety procedures. |
| Print shop | • Provide rubber stamps, ink pads, and paper on which to print.<br>• Place a typewriter or computer in the classroom.<br>• Make games using alphabet letters. |
| Hair salon | • Provide a prop box containing hair rollers, combs, brushes, towels, and a hair dryer with the cord removed.<br>• Place dolls with hair and combs in the dramatic play area.<br>• Hang up a mirror and have children compare the ways they wear their hair. |

27-15 Follow-up activities based on field trips can be simple or complex.

## Summary

Field trips can be a concrete learning experience for children. Through field trips, children gain firsthand knowledge of the world around them. This learning can involve new experiences or enhance previous knowledge.

Field trips require planning. Children must be prepared for the experience. Their preparation includes pretrip talks and activities, rules to follow, and discussions.

The teacher must also be prepared. This preparation includes selecting a trip, taking a pretrip, setting goals, obtaining permission from parents, and arranging transportation. After the trip, thank-you notes should be sent to helpful individuals. Follow-up activities will also reinforce the value of the experience.

## Review and Reflect

1. List four benefits children experience from field trips.

2. For young children, first field trips should be _____.
   A.  long and unique
   B.  short and nonthreatening
   C.  at unfamiliar places
   D.  None of the above.

3. True or false. The location of the site and the budget are two factors that affect what field trips you will select.

4. True or false. For best results, focus on many topics during a theme walk.

5. How should resource people be selected?

6. List four opportunities a teacher is given by conducting a pretrip.

7. When planning field trips for young children, avoid _____.
   A.  crowds
   B.  hands-on activities
   C.  age-appropriate activities
   D.  All of the above.

8. What are the disadvantages of using public transportation to reach your field trip site?

9. Explain how to determine what the best day for a field trip would be.

10. True or false. More adults may be needed for field trips using public transportation or for visits to places with potential dangers.

11. List three basic rules for field trips involving young children.

12. What is the purpose of follow-up activities?

## Apply and Explore

1. Start a file of ideas for field trips that could be taken by young children in your community.

2. Compile a list of safety guidelines that should be followed on all field trips.

3. Make a list of follow-up activities for a field trip to a grocery store.

4. Interview a center director about successful field trips he or she has conducted.

5. Plan a field trip for your class. Go through the same steps you would when planning a field trip for a group of young children.

6. Brainstorm 10 possible local field trip sites. For each site listed, find out the address, phone number, Web page address, contact person's name, and price information. Use a computer's word-processing program to compile your information into a chart.

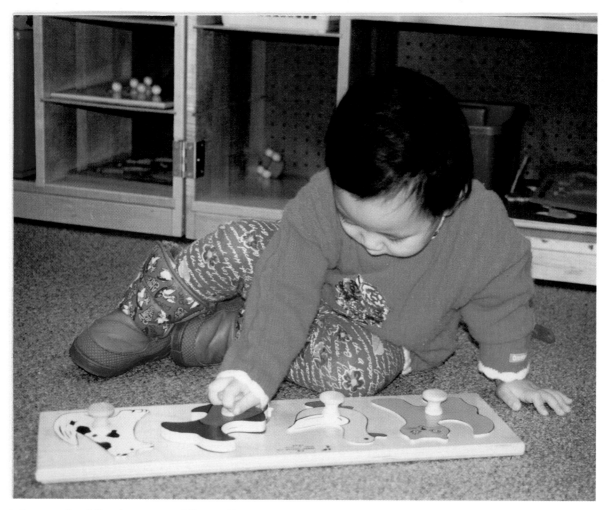

Infants and toddlers learn new skills quickly.

# Part 5

# Other People You Will Meet

Most early childhood programs are geared toward preschoolers. However, you may choose to work with younger children (infants and toddlers), school-age children, or children with special needs. In this part, you will discover what special qualities are needed by teachers in infant-toddler programs and school-age programs. You will learn special techniques for providing care and learning experiences for these children. This part also introduces you to the concerns of children with special needs. You will understand how such needs as speech disorders, health disorders, and giftedness may affect your role as a teacher.

Parents are very much involved with the care and guidance of their young children. You will want to keep them informed of everything that is happening at the center. Parent involvement can be the key factor in the success of a program.

A world of career possibilities is open to early childhood teachers. It's up to you to choose a career path that fits your goals and to find a job that will start you on your path. This part will help prepare you for your job hunt. You will read about how to prepare a resume and find available positions. You will also discover ways to make the best impression possible in an interview and land the job you really want.

The infancy and toddler stages are a time of exploration and discovery.

# Chapter 28

# Programs for Infants and Toddlers

After studying this chapter, you will be able to

- list the characteristics of a nurturing infant-toddler caregiver.
- state guidelines for proper infant-toddler care.
- design functional and developmentally appropriate infant and toddler environments.
- handle the routines of infants and toddlers.
- select toys that are safe and developmentally appropriate for infants and toddlers.
- plan the curriculum for infants and toddlers.
- maintain the environment to prevent illness.

## Term to Know

overfamiliarity

Ian is learning to walk. Hector has just said his first words and Pouneh has just begun exploring books. Working with infants and toddlers can be exciting and rewarding, 28-1. This is a unique and challenging stage in the life cycle.

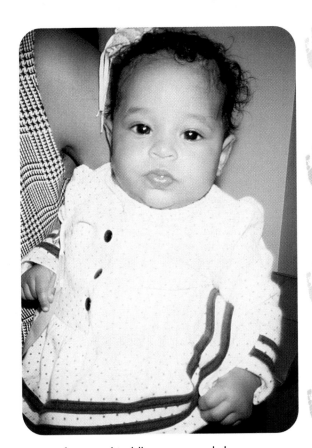

28-1 Infants and toddlers grow and change rapidly. They are constantly learning new skills, such as standing on their own.

Recent studies show brain development is more rapid from birth to age three than at any other period in life. As an infant-toddler caregiver, your nurturing and support play an important role in influencing brain growth during this most critical time. Providing a safe and stimulating environment promotes optimal brain development. Offering developmentally-appropriate activities can form and strengthen the connections in the brain, which increase lifelong learning power. As you watch a child learn and develop, you will feel satisfied knowing your efforts have made a difference. You can share in and enjoy each new accomplishment the child exhibits.

## Characteristics of Infant and Toddler Caregivers

As an infant-toddler caregiver, your behavior will influence the behavior of the children. Children will react based on the ways you treat them. If you are warm and loving, the children will be warm and loving. Touch, smile, make eye contact, and speak affectionately to the children. Cuddle them, rock them, talk and sing to them, and play with them. Likewise, be patient and accepting while working with them. Infants and toddlers need responsive caregivers. Trust, confidence, and self-esteem are promoted through caregiver responsiveness. See 28-2.

Young children are dependent on consistent relationships with their caregivers. You must have a high energy level, be healthy, and enjoy children. You must always be readily available to comfort and protect the children. You must also be able to handle many situations and understand feelings. Part of your responsibility includes helping children express feelings such as joy, love, anger, satisfaction, and sadness.

Infants and toddlers need caregivers who provide consistent guidance. To provide this consistent environment, all center staff must agree on what is acceptable behavior. In most cases, having only a few limits for children increases the chances that limits will be consistently followed.

Finally, you need to be aware of new research in the infant-toddler field. Read professional journals, books, and articles. Attend professional workshops and conferences. Another way to stay informed is to discuss your observations and needs with other infant-toddler caregivers.

## Guidelines for Infant-Toddler Care

In order to provide a quality infant-toddler program, consider the following general guidelines:

- Provide the children with a safe and healthy environment.
- Develop trusting relationships with the children and their families.
- Respect the cultures represented by the children and their families.
- Design a curriculum to meet the unique needs of each child.
- Care for each child affectionately.
- Respond to children's distress or discomfort signals immediately.
- Follow a consistent routine in providing for children's needs.
- Encourage curiosity by providing opportunities for the children to explore.
- Help children develop trust, respect, and a positive regard for their world.
- Avoid overstimulation. Too many new experiences at one time can overwhelm young children, particularly infants.
- Plan opportunities for infants and toddlers to master new skills.

28-2 All areas of this young child's development are nurtured by her affectionate, responsive caregiver.

# Infant Environments

Providing a quality infant environment cannot be left to chance. Such an environment should be attractive and comfortable for infants as well as caregivers. Environments for infants should address their daily routines. Areas for feeding, diapering, cuddling with a caregiver, sleeping, and playing should all be included.

The most convenient feeding area is near the entrance to the center. Parents arriving with baby food and bottles can place these items in the refrigerator at once. This area should be equipped with high chairs, feeding tables, a heat source, and comfortable, adult-sized chairs.

The diapering area should be located next to a sink. As in the feeding area, the floor surface needs to be washable. This allows for easy cleaning and disinfecting. To prevent back strain for adults, changing surfaces and storage areas should be waist high. Place a mirror on the wall next to the changing surface so children can look at themselves.

The sleeping area usually uses the most space because cribs take a large amount of floor space. The ideal location for this area is joining the diapering area. Do not worry about light. Infants do not need a dark room in which to sleep. However, a dimmer switch can be installed in this area to control lights used in the diapering area.

Infants also need their own play area, 28-3. They need to be safely out of the way of older children. To ensure safety, use low dividers to make a crawling area. A short pile carpeting should be on the floor for comfort and warmth.

# Toddler Environments

Balancing safety and health concerns is important in designing spaces for toddlers. Toddlers need more open areas than infants. When they are not sleeping, they are usually moving. Toddlers' needs can be met in several areas. Included are receiving, playing, napping, diapering, and eating areas. (Napping, diapering, and eating areas for infants can be shared by toddlers.)

The receiving area should be located near the main entrance. This area should contain a bulletin board for parent information and lockers or hooks to hold children's clothing. When standing in the receiving area, you should be able to have a clear view of all other areas, especially the play area. Provide interesting equipment in the room to encourage children to play and help ease separation anxiety.

Toddlers need a play area that allows them to move freely. To provide this, leave one-third to one-half of the total space open. In crowded areas, some children may find it hard to play. As a result, they are more inclined to cry and fight. If adequate space is not provided, the children will bump into each other.

Although a tile floor is easier to maintain, some teachers prefer a carpeted floor in the play area. Carpeting has two advantages. First, it provides a cushion for falls. Second, it is warmer for crawling children. If carpeting is used, it should have a tight weave and be washable.

In a section of the play area, there should be equipment that encourages toddlers' rapidly changing physical skills. Open areas and equipment for crawling, walking, and climbing should be available. Scaled slides and tunnels are two

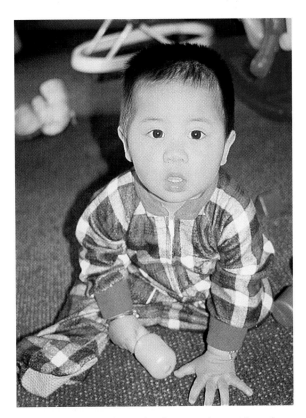

28-3 Infants need a safe place to play and explore their toys.

types of equipment that invite exploration and climbing, as well as carpeted platforms and low shelves. Cardboard boxes can also be fun for toddlers. Equipment should be arranged so all areas can be seen by the caregiver.

The outdoor play area should connect to the indoor play area. This outdoor area should have a large, grassy area for running and crawling. Grass, like carpeting, helps cushion falls.

# Caring for Infants and Toddlers

As you work with infants and toddlers, you will notice each child has his or her own rhythm. Some will go about their routines quickly. Others move slowly. As a caregiver, you must adjust your own rhythm to each child's rhythm.

All infants and toddlers, regardless of their differences, require their needs to be met promptly if they are to learn trust. A child who has been promptly and properly cared for is likely to be happy. To provide this attention to needs, you must provide consistent care. Through this care, children learn that they are special persons and develop trust.

## Crying as a Means of Communication

Infants often communicate by crying. They may cry to express needs, cope with frustration, or get attention. They may also cry when they feel lonely, uncomfortable, neglected or over-stimulated. Regardless of the reason, you should never ignore crying. Always remember that the crying has some meaning for the child.

Studies support the theory that an infant's crying should always be given prompt attention. According to these studies, when cries are answered promptly, the frequency of the crying will be reduced.

You will observe that babies have individual differences in their crying behaviors. Some babies cry more often and with greater strength. Other babies may seldom cry. All babies have various reasons for crying.

As a caregiver, you will have to learn the meaning of each child's cries. By listening to how a baby cries, you will soon learn his or her

needs. A short and low-pitched cry usually means the baby is hungry. A loud and sudden high-pitched shriek followed by a flat wail is a distress cry. Sometimes the types of cries overlap. For instance, a baby may wake up hungry and will cry for food. If you do not quickly respond to this need, the baby may then cry with rage. You will also learn which cries indicate fussiness, soiled diapers, boredom, or discomfort related to being too cool or warm.

Always respond to a child's crying by first trying to solve the problem. If the baby is wet, change him or her. Likewise, if the child is hungry, feed him or her. If you cannot find an obvious reason for the child's crying, check the baby's daily care record. (This record is described later in the chapter.) Perhaps the baby is sleepy, teething, reacting to medication, or catching a cold. A baby may also cry out of a feeling of loneliness or wanting to play or be cuddled.

Tired, crying babies can be comforted in a number of ways. Some enjoy being held; others love to be rocked. Often a child can be quieted simply by speaking or singing softly to him or her.

## Separation Anxiety

Between 9 and 18 months of age, some children will start experiencing separation anxiety. This is a feeling of fear and distress at being separated from a parent. It can include crying, protesting, clinging to the parent, withdrawing, or begging the parent not to leave. Many children experience separation anxiety. It is a sign they are learning and developing close relationships with their parents.

Separation anxiety is often strongest among children of this age who begin a child care situation for the first time. Children who start child care earlier can experience separation anxiety at this age, too. Their anxiety may be somewhat less severe, however, because they are already familiar with the surroundings and people at the center.

Feelings of separation anxiety are difficult for young children to handle. They need your acceptance and emotional support. Accept the child's feelings and describe them for him or her. Reassure the child the parent will return for him or her. Offer alternate activities, but be prepared for the child to refuse at first. In his or her own time, the child will join in. You might say, "You're sad

28-4 When a child shows separation anxiety, it's important to introduce new people and objects gradually.

because Mommy is leaving. She went to work, but she will come back for you this afternoon. Would you like to play blocks with me?"

You may notice the child may react strongly to strangers, sudden movements, noise, or strange objects. To help support the child, let him or her explore at his or her own pace. Allow the child to stay near you until these upset feelings have subsided. Meanwhile, gradually expose the child to new objects in the center, 28-4.

It can take several weeks or months for separation anxiety to fade. Throughout this time, continue to show support and understanding. You may find yourself feeling frustrated by the child's crying or other behavior at these times. Remind yourself that it will pass in time and your support is vital. It will help the child learn to depend on you and feel secure in the child care environment.

When children experience separation anxiety, it's difficult for their parents, too. Parents do not enjoy seeing their child in distress. They may feel

upset, sad, or guilty for having to leave their crying children. When their child begs them to stay, this can tug at their emotions. Remind parents that separation anxiety is normal and it will fade in time. Share with the parents any signs of progress you see. For example, if the child cries for less time or joins in with the others more quickly, let the parents know. This will help ease their minds.

## Handling Routines

With infants and toddlers, routines make up much more of the day than routines do with preschoolers. It is important that daily routines be predictable. This will help the children gain a sense of security. It will also help them know what to expect and the sequence of activities. Much of your day will be spent feeding, taking care of diapering and toileting needs, and preparing for nap time. See 28-5.

It is important to coordinate home and center schedules for infants. To do this, parents

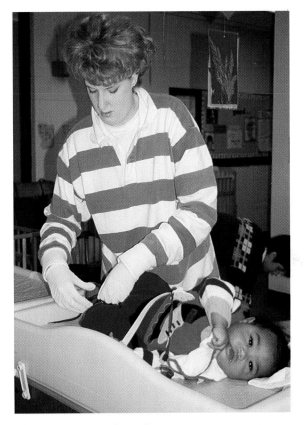

28-5 Routines such as diapering are an important part of caring for infants.

need to provide you with information daily. One effective method is to provide parents with a daily record to complete when they arrive each morning with their infants. Likewise, the caregiver also needs to record the infants' eating and elimination patterns during the day. Nap information and activities for the day can also be included. See Chart 28-6 for an example of an infant daily record.

## Feeding Infants

Nutrition is very important for infants. At no time do children grow faster than during their first year of life. If they don't get the nutrients they need, their growth and development can be hindered. This makes your task of infant feeding a high priority. It is a task you will handle several times each day.

Throughout infancy, babies rely mainly on either breast milk or iron-fortified infant formula. The majority of feedings will be by bottle. However, some mothers may come to the center to breast-feed their infants. If so, provide them a quiet, comfortable place to do this.

It's important to immediately label and refrigerate all bottles containing breast milk or formula. Bottles left at room temperature for more than two hours can start to grow bacteria. These bacteria multiply rapidly and can cause illness. Discard any bottle that has been out of the refrigerator two hours or more. Once a child has put his or her mouth on the bottle, bacteria from the mouth and saliva can enter the milk or formula. This causes it to spoil even more quickly. After one hour, discard any milk or formula remaining in a used bottle.

Many infants prefer their bottles at room temperature. When taking a bottle from the refrigerator, place it under a stream of warm running water. This will quickly bring the bottle to room temperature. Never place a bottle in the microwave. This is dangerous because the microwave heats unevenly. When part of the milk or formula is warm, another part might be hot enough to scald the baby's mouth. With breast milk, the excessive heat can also destroy the living substances and nutritional content of the milk. If you need to warm a bottle, use a pan of hot water or bottle warmer.

Starting at four to six months, infant cereals are often introduced as the first "solid foods." Be sure to feed cereals with a spoon rather than in a bottle. Putting cereal in the bottle does not give an infant the needed practice of eating from a spoon. It can also create a choking hazard.

Baby foods, such as pureed fruits, vegetables, and meats, will soon follow. While most parents use store-bought jars of baby food, others make their infants' foods at home. Your task will be serving the children the breast milk, formula, and foods provided by the parents. When serving baby foods, use a clean spoon to remove the desired portion from the jar or container. Put this into a small serving dish. Replace the lid and refrigerate the jar. Use within two to three days. Discard any uneaten food in the serving dish at the end of the feeding. This will keep the food from growing bacteria from the baby's saliva.

Talk with parents about feeding practices, preferences, and habits. Ask the parents which foods to offer as well as when to offer them. Try to follow the parents' wishes regarding feeding, unless safety is a concern. In this case, discuss with your center director how to proceed. The director can inform you of center policies and advise you how to handle the situation. It's often best to inform parents of the risks involved and suggest a more appropriate option. For instance, propping an infant's bottle is an inappropriate practice. It creates a choking risk and deprives the infant of the personal attention and social contact needed when eating. It also promotes ear infections. If parents ask you to prop their child's bottle, the director might advise you to gently explain your concern and tell the parents that center policy is to hold infants during feedings.

Meeting infants' nutritional needs will be a big part of your job as a caregiver. Very young infants express their hunger by moving their mouths, rooting, or crying. Older infants may cry for food, grunt and point at the food they want, or respond positively to a caregiver's offer of food. It's important to feed infants on demand rather than on a set schedule. Feed each child when he or she is hungry, not when it is convenient.

By the same token, do not force an infant to eat. Watch for cues the baby is full or doesn't want more. These include crying in response to the bottle or spoon, turning the head away, closing the mouth tightly, and stopping sucking from the bottle. If you see these or other signs of refusal, respect the baby's cues and end the feeding.

## Infant Daily Record

Infant's name: _____     Parent's name: _____

Day/Date: _____     Time of arrival: _____

Parent's signature: _____     Time of departure: _____

(filled in by parent)   (filled in by staff member)

---

Baby seems: ❑ Normal, typical
❑ Bit fussy
❑ Not acting as usual

Baby slept: ❑ Soundly
❑ Woke up several times
❑ Did not sleep well

Baby ate:

| Food/Drink | Amount | Time |
| --- | --- | --- |
| _____ | _____ | _____ |
| _____ | _____ | _____ |
| _____ | _____ | _____ |

❑ Nothing this morning

Bowel movement number: _____

❑ Regular              ❑ Irregular

Number of wet diapers: _____

Diet change for today: _____
_____

Special instructions: _____
_____
_____

Medicine taken today: _____

Time _____     Amount _____

Time _____     Amount _____

Medicine to be given today: _____
_____

Time _____     Amount _____

Time _____     Amount _____

(See medication form for details)

| Bottles: | Time | Food/Drink | Amount |
| --- | --- | --- | --- |
| | _____ | _____ | _____ |
| | _____ | _____ | _____ |
| | _____ | _____ | _____ |
| | _____ | _____ | _____ |
| | _____ | _____ | _____ |

| Foods: | _____ | _____ | _____ |
| --- | --- | --- | --- |
| | _____ | _____ | _____ |
| | _____ | _____ | _____ |
| | _____ | _____ | _____ |
| | _____ | _____ | _____ |

| Diaper checks and changes: | Time | Description |
| --- | --- | --- |
| | _____ | _____ |
| | _____ | _____ |
| | _____ | _____ |
| | _____ | _____ |
| | _____ | _____ |
| | _____ | _____ |

Medication given: _____

_____        _____
(Time)                    (Caregiver)

_____        _____
(Time)                    (Caregiver)

Activities, accomplishments, skills shown today:

_____
_____
_____

Caregivers' initials _____

---

28-6  An infant daily record can help to coordinate home and center schedules.

## Feeding Toddlers

Children's hand washing is important before and after eating. Many toddlers crawl on the floor and later use their hands to feed themselves. Before eating, always wash toddlers' hands. If child-sized sinks are not available, use a small pan of water at the table. In the beginning, you may have to assist the children in swishing their hands as well as wiping them on a paper towel or cloth. You may want to apply a small amount of liquid soap to a dampened towel and wipe the child's hands. Rinse the hands with a clean towel moistened with water. Finally, wipe the child's hands with a dry paper towel.

Whenever possible, toddlers should be served finger foods. These are easy for children to handle. Always provide many sizes and shapes so children can practice picking them up. Examples include cubes of pear, cooked green peas, chopped cooked eggs, banana pieces, and cheese.

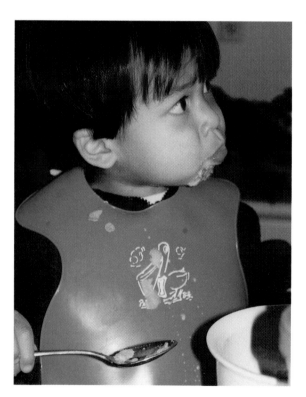

28-7 Toddlers can feed themselves with a spoon, but expect a mess. Use bibs to protect their clothing.

For feeding, toddlers can be seated in high chairs, at eating tables, or on low chairs placed in front of a low table, 28-7. They will need some table space on which to move their food. Children of this age love to explore their food. Before eating, toddlers may smell, touch, and push around their food. This behavior should be encouraged. Exploring food can give children important sensory experiences that foster cognitive growth.

## Diapering and Toileting

Changing diapers is a routine that a caregiver will repeat many times each day. For this reason, it should be a pleasant experience. Give the child all your attention. Look into his or her eyes. Smile, sing, and talk softly to the child. Stroke the child's hair. Diapering can be a wonderful time for personal interaction.

A diaper-checking routine is a useful policy to follow. Infants need frequent diaper changes because they eliminate often. For the infants' health and comfort, you need to change soiled diapers promptly. This prevents chaffing, diaper rashes, infections, and discomfort. Your center should have a specific diaper check routine. This might be checking each child's diaper once every hour or half-hour except when the child is sleeping. In addition to scheduled checks, diapers should be checked before each feeding and after each nap.

Most center policies state only disposable diapers may be used. Cloth diapers leak more often, causing more mess and the possible transmission of infection to others. Diaper pails for cloth diapers have a strong unpleasant odor and may present a drowning risk. Disposable diapers are more convenient and sanitary. In most centers, parents are responsible for supplying diapers. A few centers provide diapers for the children in their care.

When diapering, you may come into contact with many disease-causing germs. Thorough hand washing will greatly reduce the spread of these germs. Therefore, all staff should follow proper hand washing procedures before and after each diaper change. See Figure 28-8.

It is important to wash with warm water and use liquid soap. Liquid soap should be used

## Hand Washing Procedures for Diapering

1. Dispense enough liquid soap into the hand to provide a good lather.
2. Turn on the faucet. Add a small amount of warm water to the soap. Rub hands back and forth to produce lather. Lather over your wrists and clean under your fingernails. Scrub your hands for 20 seconds.
3. Rinse well with warm water, keeping your hands pointed down.
4. Turn off the faucet using your elbow or paper towels. (Do not touch the faucet controls with clean hands).
5. Dry hands thoroughly using paper towels. Discard used paper towels.
6. Apply gloves, if needed.
7. Change diaper and remove baby from changing area.
8. Disinfect changing area.
9. Remove gloves, if worn. Wash hands again, using steps 1 through 5.
10. Apply lotion to hands to prevent chapping.

28-8 Proper hand washing is vital to preventing the spread of disease from diapering.

because bar soaps, when wet and jellylike, harbor microorganisms. You will probably find that a soap dispenser is most convenient. Remember, though, that microorganisms may also grow in liquid soap. Therefore, clean the dispenser each time it is refilled.

In many centers, it is policy to use lightweight, disposable rubber gloves for all diaper changes. Other centers require these gloves only when there is a crack or cut in the skin of the hands. Rubber gloves will reduce the spread of infection from germs entering an open wound on the hand. Medical experts agree it is nearly impossible to prevent microorganisms from growing in an open wound in the skin.

Remove the soiled diaper and discard it. Clean the diaper area from front to back with a baby wipe or wet washcloth. Place a clean diaper under the baby. Avoid applying baby powder during a diaper change. If inhaled, the fine powder can harm the lungs of an infant or caregiver.

Next, check for signs of *diaper rash*. This is a skin rash that occurs in the baby's diaper area. It may result when the diaper is changed too infrequently. The wet, damp diaper promotes the growth of bacteria that can irritate and infect the skin in the diaper area. Itching, redness, and discomfort are common. If you notice any signs of diaper rash, notify the parents that same day.

Keeping the baby clean and dry will prevent many cases of diaper rash. Check infants' diapers often and change them promptly. If diaper rash does occur, the rash can be treated with a diaper rash ointment at every change. The parents would supply this ointment. To prevent diaper rash, some parents prefer to apply ointment with every change when no rash is present. Follow the parent's instructions on this matter. If a rash worsens or won't clear up, advise the parents to seek their doctor's advice.

After each change, spray the diapering table or changing mat with a disinfectant solution. Wash your hands. Then record diapering information on the daily record. The time of the check or change and whether the child urinated and/or had a bowel movement all need to be noted. If the child had diarrhea, this should be noted along with the amount, color, and consistency.

Do not be shocked if, as a child grows older, he or she objects to having a diaper changed. Many times this objection occurs because the child is having fun playing and does not want to be interrupted. When this occurs, there is no harm in waiting a few minutes. Wait until the child finishes with an activity, and then gently guide him or her to the changing area. Many times this transition is easier if the child is allowed to carry a toy into the changing area.

Some toddlers may be in the process of or showing an interest in toilet learning. For these children, it is important that the home and center coordinate their efforts. Discuss with the parents the toilet-learning process. Explain that it will be easier for the child if the home and center routines are consistent.

Like diapering, toileting policies must be used for health purposes. Children need to wash their hands after using the potty chair, 28-9. After each use, the seat of the potty chair needs to be sprayed with a disinfectant solution and wiped. The container under the chair must be emptied and rinsed with the solution. Finally, you will need to wash your hands with warm water and soap.

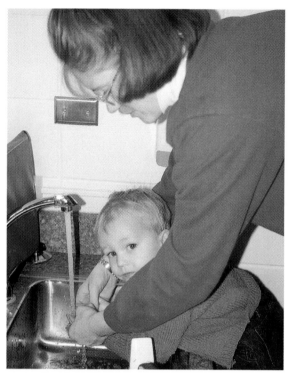

28-9  Young toddlers may need help washing their hands correctly.

28-10  Provide a safe, quiet, and comfortable sleeping area for infants and toddlers.

### Nap Time

All children need a certain amount of sleep. This amount varies from one child to another. Newborns sleep 16 to 20 hours a day, 28-10. Most infants need at least two naps a day ranging from one to three hours. Without adequate sleep, a child can become cranky and difficult to handle. When this happens, it can have a negative influence on other children in the center.

One consideration for planning a nap time schedule is to check parents' preferences. Some parents keep their infants up late and wake them early in the morning. They want their child to sleep at the center so he or she is awake and alert at the end of the day. Other parents, who may have to travel some distance to get home, prefer to have a sleepy baby at the end of the day. Their goal is to have the baby sleep on the way home.

Nap times may have to be staggered to meet the individual needs of the children. This type of scheduling will allow you time to feed and rock each child to sleep. Often this will require meshing individual needs with group needs.

Once a schedule has been developed that fits individual needs, it is necessary to be consistent.

## Toys for Infants and Toddlers

To meet the special needs of infants and toddlers, appropriate equipment is needed. Toys serve as sensory stimuli for young children. For instance, by positioning an infant's toys, you can create an incentive for the child to use his or her memory or locomotive abilities, 28-11. Even during the first few weeks of life, an infant can touch, see, and hear. As the child exercises these abilities, physical and mental development are fostered.

Toddlers need a range of equipment from soft blocks to puzzles. To promote language skills, include picture books, story books, audiotapes, dramatic play props, and puppets. The audiotapes can be used to promote music and movement. Sensory materials, including non-toxic crayons, markers, and play dough, should also be available.

When planning environments for toddlers, balance is important. You need to provide a sufficient quantity and variety of toys to encourage exploration. However, you must guard against overstimulation. Too many choices can overwhelm the children.

28-11 Crawling babies need a safe, appealing play area.

Many infant-toddler centers maintain a toy inventory that lists all the equipment available in the center. The inventory is subdivided into developmental sequences. See 28-12 for a sample toy inventory. This list is quite helpful when planning activities for children. Since it is important to frequently change toys, the list will help you keep a record of the toys already used and toys that are available. Another advantage of keeping a toy inventory is that it is helpful when ordering new toys.

## Safety Issues

When choosing toys for the infant or toddler, safety is the number one consideration. Check each piece carefully for sharp edges or points. To avoid splinters, all wooden toys should be smoothly sanded. Small toys or toys with small parts should be avoided. Objects smaller than $1^{1}/_{2}$ inches across and $1^{5}/_{8}$ inches in diameter could be swallowed or cause choking.

| Infant-Toddler Center Toy Inventory | | |
|---|---|---|
| **Looking**<br>• dog mobile<br>• farm animal mobile<br>• shape mobile<br>• plastic mirror<br>• cloth and cardboard books | **Squeezing/Manipulation**<br>• fish squeaker<br>• pretzel squeaker<br>• mouse squeaker<br>• bunny squeaker<br>• busy box<br>• plastic rings<br>• plastic rattles (various colors)<br>• snap beads<br>• chain of plastic discs<br>• activity mats | **Gross Motor**<br>• rubber balls<br>• push toys<br>• pull toys<br>• small, light wagon<br>• wheeled train<br>• wheeled lamb<br>• climbing tunnel<br>• small gym<br>• toy trucks big enough to ride<br>• activity saucer |
| **Reaching and Grasping**<br>• ring activity gym<br>• musical activity gym<br>• colored activity gym<br>• colored rattles | | |
| **Cuddling Toys**<br>• monkey<br>• black bear<br>• baby lamb (with chime)<br>• pink pig<br>• brown pony<br>• black puppy<br>• dolls | **Pull/Push**<br>• wooden train (makes a noise)<br>• wooden dog<br>• lawnmower<br>• wooden car<br>• wooden wagon | **Fine Motor**<br>• geometric form board<br>• snap beads<br>• small cards<br>• nesting cups and boxes<br>• shape sorting box<br>• strings of large beads<br>• sand or water toys<br>• stacking rings<br>• puzzles with large pieces<br>• plastic or foam blocks<br>• large crayons<br>• activity center |
| **Kicking and Hitting**<br>• large rubber beach balls<br>• colored foam balls<br>• bouncing clowns | **Sound**<br>• music box<br>• drum<br>• jingle bells<br>• CD or tape player and music<br>• xylophone<br>• squeaky animals | |

28-12  A toy inventory is useful for planning and buying.

To check whether an object is a choking risk, use a cardboard toilet paper tube. You could also buy a plastic safety tube for measuring small toys. Try to fit the object inside either of these tubes. If it fits, it's too small to be safe for an infant or toddler.

Each year many infants and toddlers accidentally swallow small toys or parts. This can cause suffocation from choking on the object. Also, a child may develop intestinal or respiratory problems as a result of swallowing a small toy. Unfortunately, most plastic toys do not show up on X rays. Toy companies, therefore, are now adding a special plastic to children's toys. This plastic is known as *nontoxic radiopaque plastic*. Toys made with this material will show up clearly on an X ray. When you choose toys, check the label or package to see if this material is included.

## Appropriate Toys for Infants

Mobiles make excellent first toys for infants. They provide visual appeal and require a minimum of physical interaction. Select mobiles carefully. Avoid mobiles that are not sturdy. If your center has such mobiles, hang them out of reach. For the young infant, place toys 7 to 24 inches from the eyes.

Between 1½ and 3½ months of age, infants will discover their hands. The hands then become a toy for the child. Infants will study their hands as they move them back and forth. Infants between three and six months of age will continue to watch their hands. Even when infants move objects to their mouths, they will continue watching.

Smiles begin to appear at about two months of age. Infants at this age also want to touch what they see. To provide stimulation for the child, place a mirror over the changing table. You will find it fun to watch the child smile at his or her reflections in the mirror.

Soon, infants begin touching objects within their reach. This behavior usually occurs between three and six months of age. As they do this, they gain information about the world and develop intelligence. Provide a variety of toys for the children to touch. These may include soft rattles and stuffed, furry animals.

To provide grasping exercise, infants need a variety of toys within reach, whether in the crib or on the floor. Since the child is likely to place these toys in his or her mouth, choose only safe toys. By placing objects in the mouth, babies learn about objects. Studies show that between 6 and 10 months of age, nerve endings in an infant's mouth are very sensitive.

Rattles are important for the infant's development. When a rattle is handed to an infant, he or she goes through a specific process. The first step is to locate the toy with the eyes. After this is done, the child will move his or her hand toward the rattle. Just before contact, the infant's hand will open. In this process the child will be persistent. He or she will repeatedly try to pick up a small toy.

Observations have shown that infants follow a progression of hand movement skills. First, there are raking motions which appear to be somewhat random. Next, scissor motions are made. The child uses the whole hand to pick up an object. Finally, the child develops the pincer grasp. Using this method, the infant is able to pick up objects using only the forefinger and thumb. A child using this method will usually shape the hand into the grasp before reaching for the intended object.

Toys will encourage the development of all these hand movement skills. A variety of toys such as cradle gyms can be used to encourage raking motions. Scissor motions can be encouraged by providing small balls or figures that will fit into the hand. Finger foods, such as dry, ready-to-eat cereal, can be used to practice the pincer grasp.

As the child develops, he or she begins to experiment with cause and effect. Up to this time, the infant has been more interested in watching the hands than the objects that were touched. By five to eight months, the child is more intent on watching the effects of his or her actions, 28-13.

Around this age, the child will enjoy dropping objects. He or she will often drop objects, including utensils and toys, from the high chair or feeding table. As the child does this, he or she will watch for the consequences of the actions. As the toy hits the floor, the infant may wince at the sound it makes.

At about the same time the child begins to enjoy dropping objects, he or she will become interested in simple gadgets in the environment. Electrical outlets appear to be appealing. For safety purposes, it is important that these all be

28-13 By using the toys on this avtivity saucer, this child can learn the effects of her actions.

capped. Other appealing objects include light switches, cupboard knobs, doorknobs, fringe on rugs, and locks. The manipulation of these objects gives the child a sense of magic.

## Appropriate Toys for Toddlers

Once the child begins to crawl or walk, he or she will want to continually explore the environment. To encourage this curiosity, make the environment safe. Maintain large, open areas where the child can pull or push toys, straddle large trucks, or roll large balls.

Toddlers love to climb. To meet their large muscle needs, provide them with small slides, jungle gyms, and sets of stairs. Make sure that you closely watch toddlers when they use the large muscle equipment. Some children may try to walk up the slide. When this happens, you need to take their hand and direct them back to the stairs. Once they learn how to use the equipment, it is not uncommon for children of this age to use the equipment over and over again. As they explore, they are growing physically and cognitively.

Small wagons, wheelbarrows, doll buggies, and strollers also appeal to toddlers. If you lack indoor space, limit the use of these toys to an outdoor area.

Toddlers love to play with water. Encourage this play by providing floating toys, spoons, sponges, and unbreakable cups in a water play area. Demonstrate how to pour water, sail a floating toy, and squeeze a sponge. For interest, add color to the water.

Books are also of interest to toddlers, 28-14. They enjoy stories about families, people, animals, and objects. Objects in the books should be recognizable. Toddlers love the surprise of flipping the pages in a book. Since they enjoy turning pages, select books with large pictures, thick pages that are easy to turn, and contain only a few words. Book bindings should be strong and sturdy.

Puppets also appeal to young children. Children enjoy puppets that are soft and recognizable. Puppets made of fabric, instead of plastic or rubber, are the easiest for the children to work. Before buying puppets, ask if they are washable.

The most time-consuming activity of toddlers is staring. Approximately one-fifth of their time is spent either sitting or standing and staring. They may stare at a picture, another child, a toy, or even at you. Therefore, keep the room visually stimulating.

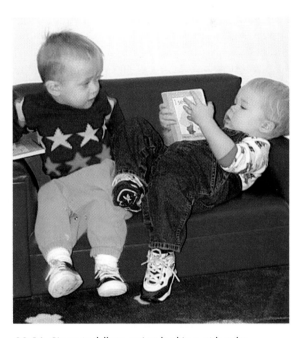

28-14 Since toddlers enjoy looking at books, provide a variety of age-appropriate and appealing books for them.

Some children will lack interest in a particular toy. This is a sign of **overfamiliarity**. Children who are given the same toy day after day may become bored. Once they are comfortable with a particular toy, they repeat the same actions over and over again. When this happens, new skills do not develop. It is time to provide a different toy that offers new challenges.

Young children like to have a variety of toys and need opportunities to make choices. Care must be taken, however, not to include too many choices. Toddlers need to feel a sense of control. As the teacher, you should change some toys every other day.

# Curriculum

A balanced curriculum is based on the needs of the children attending the center. It is also based on child growth and development principles.

Curriculum for infants or toddlers differs from that planned for older preschool children. Babies set their own goals. As the teacher, you support this growth. The curriculum consists of simple, basic activities. It includes physical activities: being fed, cuddled, held, bathed, rocked, diapered, and taken on walks. It involves both verbal and nonverbal communication: being sung to, talked to, and listened to. Curriculum for infants should include lots of materials, activities, and time for exploring and building fine and gross motor skills.

Curriculum for toddlers requires more planning. Much of their day will involve activities that promote physical, emotional, cognitive, and social growth. Most of these activities can take place in various activity areas within the center.

## Activity Areas for Toddlers

A developmentally appropriate environment promotes child-directed, age-appropriate learning. It supports the children's emotional well-being and challenges their motor skills. It also stimulates their social development. Toddlers need opportunities for seeing, touching, tasting, moving, and hearing.

The layout of the classroom needs to encourage play. The middle of the room should be open since motor development is critical to toddlers' development. This area can contain portable equipment such as tunnels, bolsters, and gyms. Toddlers also need some private space where they can rest and observe. This space may be included by introducing a small loft, a tunnel, a cabinet with a door removed, or even an enclosed corner of the room. The activity areas should be placed around the outer walls of the room.

Similar activities can be grouped into centers around the room. Each center should contain equipment and materials that offer the child a choice of activities. An interesting, well-equipped room invites children to take part. Areas that can be included in a toddler program include art, sensory, small muscle, large muscle, music, and language.

When planning the activity centers, ask yourself the following questions:

- Does the center encourage active exploration?
- Are the toys developmentally appropriate?
- Is there enough room for the children to play?
- Are the materials at the children's eye level and within their reach?
- Are the heavy toys stored on the bottom shelves?
- Are the children provided choices so they can pursue their own interests?
- Are a variety of toys presented including those for solitary play and those that support cooperative play?
- Are the toys safe and checked frequently for sharp edges, loose pieces, and small parts that could be swallowed?
- Are toys rotated so the children are exposed to new toys from time to time?

### Art

A center for art activities can be fun for toddlers. Plan the area to encourage freedom and creativity. Art activities provide good opportunities for promoting small muscle development. Chart 28-15 lists tips for art activities.

Finger-painting experiences are quite appealing and soothing to young toddlers. Tempera paint, shaving cream, and colored liquid soap can all be used for finger painting. As the children use these materials, they enjoy squeezing them through their fingers. During the

| **Tips for Art Activities** |
| --- |
| • Provide only nontoxic materials. Young children tend to put materials in their mouths.<br>• Allow plenty of space to prevent children from putting paint, chalk, or markers on each other.<br>• Cover the table and/or floor with a plastic cloth or newspapers to catch spills.<br>• Provide art smocks or large plastic bibs.<br>• Keep cloth or paper towels handy to clean children's hands as soon as they finish activities.<br>• Wipe spills as they occur to prevent children from slipping or getting soiled. |

28-15  Plan safe, healthy art activities. Then toddlers will not need to remember a large number of rules.

| **Sensory Materials** |
| --- |
| • Colored and/or scented water.<br>• Soap bubbles.<br>• Small plastic boats.<br>• Shaving cream, plain or with drops of food coloring.<br>• Dry or wet sand. Shovels, strainers, and/or small wheeled trucks.<br>• Wet or dry oatmeal.<br>• Snow.<br>• Ice cubes.<br>• Musical instruments such as drums, tambourines, bells on wristbands, and cymbals.<br>• Common foods with strong smells such as peanut butter, oranges, or lemons. |

28-16  You will find that toddlers are most interested in simple, everyday objects.

process, they learn to sense the different feel of each one.

Older toddlers also enjoy painting. Provide a variety of brushes for this type of experience. Regular art brushes, toothbrushes, small household brushes, and sponge staining brushes may all be used. You will need to mix paint with a thickener to help prevent dripping. Bentonite, starch, or a powdered laundry detergent usually work very well.

Toddlers also enjoy scribbling. At this age, they now make simple, random marks. Provide a variety of marking tools. Large crayons, chalk, and nontoxic markers can be used. To help children feel some control over their movements, give younger children larger tools. As their control improves, smaller tools can be used.

According to developmental principles, large muscle development precedes small muscle development. To accommodate large muscle movements, provide large sheets of paper for children to scribble or paint on. If paper is too small, drawings or paintings will run off the paper and onto the table or floor.

## Sensory

Sensory activities should stimulate many of the children's senses. Most activities involve at least seeing, hearing, and touching. Many teachers often add the sense of smell. Food flavorings and extracts with unique scents may be added to some activities at the sensory table.

Chart 28-16 lists sensory materials that can be used with toddlers. Small objects that can be

inhaled or swallowed should be avoided. Likewise, discourage toddlers from chewing or eating any of the sensory materials.

## Fine Motor

Most fine motor activities will revolve around toys. Stacking toys, building blocks, sorting boxes, puzzles, stringing beads, and play dough are all safe toys that promote fine motor development in toddlers. Most of these toys will also provide toddlers with problem-solving opportunities. These toys may also provide for hand-eye coordination and visual discrimination opportunities.

## Gross Motor

Gross motor activities can take many forms. These may involve indoor equipment, outdoor equipment, or simple movement. As children crawl, walk, and run, they are developing their gross motor skills.

Much space is needed for gross motor equipment, both indoors and outdoors. Plenty of free space is needed around it. Allow enough space for active use by several children.

Balls, slides, tumbling mats, pull toys, small wagons, and large blocks can all be used to promote gross motor development. The development of the children's large muscles can also be promoted by having them run, crawl, or even chase bubbles outdoors.

### Music

Young children love music. Background music from a tape or CD player is quite enjoyable and soothing for many toddlers. Some toddlers will even move to the music. If they do not, you may want to dance with them. The toddlers may also enjoy hitting drums with their hands or clapping their hands.

### Language

Although planned activities are not required, you should be encouraging language growth at all times. During play, speak to the children. Encourage them to respond. Avoid using baby talk with toddlers. Young children will often mimic your speech patterns. If they hear baby talk, chances are they will imitate it. It is also important to use complete sentences and introduce new words. Use adverbs and adjectives to create colorful descriptions.

Puppets, unbreakable mirrors, books, pictures, posters, and dolls can all be placed on shelves in the language area. These materials should be placed so the children can safely remove them from the shelves. See 28-17.

28-17 Encouraging children to play with dolls is one way to promote language development.

## Activity Files and Picture Collections

Many teachers maintain a file listing activities that have met with success. This will help you remember the best activities. Ask other infant-toddler caregivers to share their favorite activities. Observe other caregivers in your center. Make notes of useful interactions and activities.

You will also want to start your own picture collection. The best source for obtaining pictures is from calendars, children's books, magazines, and travel posters. Infants and toddlers enjoy large, simple pictures. People, animals, vehicles, and toys have the most appeal.

Before displaying a picture, mount it on a piece of colorful poster board. To frame each picture, leave at least a ½-inch border around the entire picture. Since young children enjoy touching pictures, protect the pictures by covering with clear contact paper or laminate.

## Parent Involvement

Communication with the families of infants and toddlers is very important. Keep the parents informed of how their child's day went. Also, encourage parents to provide you with the significant happenings in their home. When children are first enrolled, always find out their routines at home, food preferences, and favorite toys. You can use a form at enrollment time to record the information, 28-18. This information will help coordinate center and home activities.

To help you provide a quality experience for children, parents' goals and concerns need to be shared. It will also be helpful if any change in the home environment is shared. These changes, such as a death in the extended family, can cause stress for children. Other changes may cause pleasure. Examples include a new family pet or a grandparent visiting. Parents should also let the teacher know about such home routines as toilet learning.

From time to time, you may wish to share reading materials with parents. Information on topics such as toilet learning, separation anxiety, language development, and toy selection can be quite useful for parents. Parents also enjoy receiving information on developmental stages. Knowing and watching for stages of normal development can be reassuring to parents.

---

### Infant-Toddler Center Parent Information Sheet

Child's Name _____   Birth Date _____

Home Phone _____   Home Address_____

Mother's Name _____   Father's Name _____

Address _____   Address _____

Place of Employment_____   Place of Employment_____

Work Phone _____   Work Phone _____

Cell Phone _____   Cell Phone _____

E-mail_____   E-mail_____

If there are any special family circumstances such as divorce, separation, remarriage, parental death, or adoption, please indicate them.

_____

_____

In case of emergency, who should be notified?

Name _____   Phone _____

Name _____   Phone _____

Doctor or Clinic_____   Phone _____

**Environment and Experiences**

Names of others living in the home        Relationship

_____        _____

_____        _____

_____        _____

How does your child react when you leave him or her with someone other than a parent? _____

_____

List the name(s) of any previous child care center that your child attended. _____

_____

What was your child's response?_____

_____

---

28-18  Stress to parents the importance of the information on this form.              (Continued)

## Record Keeping

Record keeping is an important part of an infant-toddler program. Such records should track children's eating, sleeping, and eliminating routines. Also, keep track of new behaviors and skills as they occur and change over time.

Good records provide valuable information.

Parents will be especially interested in their child's daily eating, sleeping, and eliminating patterns. Unusual patterns may signal illness or a need to change the child's diet.

By maintaining a record of the child's skills and behaviors, you will be able to note the child's progress and the start of any problems. Early detection is important for the child's development.

When reporting the child's daily routines to the parents, be objective and factual. Do not be negative or judgmental. Try to state comments in a positive manner. For instance, avoid remarks such as "Mark was very crabby and difficult to be with today." Rather, say "Mark's new tooth was causing him some pain today." Whenever possible, provide the parent with comments in writing.

# Maintaining the Environment to Prevent Illness

As a staff member in a child care center, you will need to take steps to prevent illness. Disease-causing microorganisms grow in a damp, dirty environment. Play equipment, cribs,

---

**Physical Development**

Are there any special characteristics or problems which the school should know about in order to best help your child and your family? Include any vision, hearing, physical difficulties, and unusual abilities or disabilities of which you are aware.


**Toilet Learning**

Has your child completed toilet learning yet? _____

Does he/she usually stay dry all day? _____


**Eating Habits**

In general, describe your child's attitude toward eating.


What are his/her special food likes?


What are his/her special food dislikes?


Does your child have any food allergies, sensitivities, or foods that are excluded from the diet?


**Favorite Toys**

Describe your child's favorite toys.


**Favorite Activities**

Describe your child's favorite activities.

---

28-18 Continued.

changing tables, strollers, floors, tables, high chairs, and feeding tables—as well as the children's hands—all need to be cleaned.

Since infants and toddlers explore with their mouths, it is important that all toys be routinely cleaned. Saliva forms a film on the surface of toys. Microorganisms grow on this film. As a result, any toys such as rattles and teething rings that go into the infant's mouth must be cleaned on a daily basis or when used by a child. If your center has a dishwasher, use it. Most small toys are dishwasher safe.

Clean by hand the toys that cannot be washed in the dishwasher. First, wash the toys in a hot, sudsy detergent and rinse well. Then mix a disinfecting solution of one gallon of water with one tablespoon of chlorine bleach. Wipe or spray each piece of equipment with the solution. Air dry.

Depending on the frequency of use, cribs and strollers need to be cleaned daily or twice weekly. Likewise, floors, tables, high chairs, and feeding tables also need cleaning each day. Food left on any of these can grow microorganisms. This process should be similar to cleaning toys. Begin by washing each piece with warm, sudsy water. Rinse well. Wipe or spray with a solution of disinfectant. Air or sun dry.

Contaminated hands are a common cause of the spread of illness in child care centers. To prevent illnesses, it is most important that you follow proper hand washing procedures to keep your hands and the children's hands clean.

## Illness Policies

Sick children cannot be cared for in a center without endangering the health of other children. An environment for infants and toddlers needs to be healthy. As the teacher, it is your responsibility to maintain the best health conditions. In order to do this properly, you will need to have a center illness policy. This policy will help staff and parents decide whether a child is too sick to be brought to or remain in the center.

Prior to enrollment, every parent should be given a copy of the center's illness policy. At this time, it should be stressed that a primary objective of the program is to protect the children's health. Thus, center illness policy is always adhered to. An example of a center illness policy is shown in 28-19.

---

### Infant-Toddler Center Illness Policy

To protect all the children's health, you must keep your child home when he/she has:
- An oral temperature of 101 F or above or a rectal temperature of 102 F or above.
- Diarrhea.
- Vomiting that extends beyond the usual spitting up.
- Bronchitis symptoms, including hoarseness and/or cough.
- A severe cold that is accompanied with a fever and nose drainage.
- A rash that has not been diagnosed by a doctor.
- Impetigo, chicken pox, mumps, measles, scarlet fever, or whooping cough.

28-19 An illness policy helps avoid misunderstandings when infants and toddlers are ill.

## Summary

Infants and toddlers are at a special stage in their lives. They are just learning about their world and yet they learn and grow quickly. The care they receive at this stage is very important for brain development.

Caring for infants and toddlers requires skill in areas unique to the age group. Emphasis is shifted toward care of daily routines such as eating, diapering, and sleeping. However, infants and toddlers also require a developmentally supportive environment. The environment should balance safety and health concerns with developmental needs.

Infants often communicate by crying. As a caregiver, you will have to learn the meaning of each child's cries and respond promptly. Separation anxiety is also common between 9 and 18 months of age.

To meet the special needs of infants and toddlers, appropriate equipment is needed. Safety is again the number one consideration. Curriculum for infants and toddlers differs from that planned for older preschool children. Though the curriculum for infants consists of simple, basic activities, the curriculum for toddlers requires more planning. Activity areas should be provided to meet toddlers' needs.

## Review and Reflect

1. List three characteristics of a successful infant-toddler teacher.

2. What is the reasoning behind locating the feeding area near the entrance to the center?

3. Name the five major areas in the toddler space.

4. What portion of the play area should be left open for toddlers to move about freely?

5. All infants and toddlers require their needs to be met promptly if they are to learn to _____.

6. Always respond to a baby's crying by _____.
   A. ignoring the baby
   B. feeding the baby
   C. trying to solve the problem
   D. None of the above.

7. What is separation anxiety?

8. Describe how to feed an infant.

9. Should toddlers be encouraged to smell, touch, and push around their food before eating? Why or why not?

10. Why should liquid soap be used in the diapering area?

11. Name two advantages of keeping a toy inventory.

12. Why do infants seem to enjoy dropping objects from their high chairs?

13. In terms of curriculum, babies should set their own _____.

14. List five questions to ask yourself when planning activity centers for toddlers.

15. What should be your attitude when reporting the child's daily routines to his or her parents?

16. What is the purpose of a center illness policy?

## Apply and Explore

1. Collect and compare illness policies from three child care centers.

2. Design an infant space on a large piece of tagboard.

3. Design a pamphlet for infant caregivers regarding infant feeding using the information given in the chapter.

4. Collect daily care records from several centers. Discuss the contents of each.

5. Interview several parents. Ask them the type of characteristics they desire in an infant or toddler caregiver. Share your findings with the class.

6. For a toddler environment, design three private spaces.

7. Use the Zero to Three Web site (zerotothree.org/brainwonders) to look up activities for infants and toddlers that stimulate brain development.

# Chapter 29

# Programs for School-Age Children

After studying this chapter, you will be able to

- describe the three basic program models used in school-age child care.

- identify the characteristics of an effective teacher in a school-age child care program.

- discuss how to arrange indoor and outdoor space in a school-age child care environment.

- explain ways to assess children's interests for curriculum planning.

- list the components of a typical daily schedule in a school-age child care program.

## Terms to Know

child-centered program model

adult-centered program model

unit-based program model

There is a critical need for school-age child care. Two main factors account for this trend. First, the number of working parents with children between the ages of 6 and 12 has grown. Second, there are more single-parent families.

Due to cost or lack of quality programs, many school-age children are left to care for themselves. Felix, an eight-year-old, is an example. He returns home from school at about 3:40 in the afternoon. Felix carries a house key. When he arrives home, he unlocks the front door. Then he enters and locks the door behind him. Felix watches television until 6:00 p.m., when his mother returns home from work.

Felix's mother, like many others, cannot find affordable after-school care. Children like Felix are sometimes called *latchkey children*. This term refers to children left in self-care or in the care of a sibling under age 15. Many children are left in self-care for several hours each day.

Yolanda is another eight-year-old child. Unlike Felix who goes home to an empty apartment, Yolanda is fortunate. She attends a school-age child care program after school. Ricardo, her cousin who lives in the same community, also attends the program.

Parents need to decide on an individual basis about how old children should be before leaving them in self-care. State laws regarding self-care are an important consideration. In some states, it is illegal for a child under a set age (often 12) to stay home alone. If no such law exists in their state, parents can use age 12 as a good general guideline. However, parents may not feel comfortable leaving some immature 13- or 14-year-old children in self-care.

Even mature children can benefit from attending a school-age child care program. Studies show children who lack adult supervision tend to have a variety of problems. They are more likely to experience loneliness and unhealthy fears. They are also more likely to lack physical exercise and have poor nutritional habits. Attending a quality school-age program can help children avoid these problems.

Parents want more than custodial care for their school-age children. They want their children to do some of the following while in child care:

- broaden their education
- develop caring relationships with adults and other children
- acquire new skills
- receive tutoring
- study art and music
- perform community service

Studies have shown positive outcomes for children attending high quality school-age child care programs. These children tend to earn better grades and demonstrate higher academic achievement. They turn in higher-quality homework assignments and spend more time in the learning process. They have an increased interest and ability in reading. These children also have better school attendance records and lower dropout rates.

## Quality School-Age Programs

School-age children need challenges. They need to be independent. They need others to accept them for who they are. A quality school-age program will meet these needs. It will also provide companionship, supervision, a safe environment, and activities to promote children's development. A good school-age program has

- low adult-child ratios
- caring, well-trained staff members
- well-organized space with room for active play, quiet play, and interest centers
- curriculum based on the children's ages, abilities, interests, and needs
- parent involvement to achieve shared goals for the children
- flexible scheduling to allow a balance of individual, small group, and large group activities

Studies show that high-quality programs have common characteristics. These programs set goals and have strong leadership. They hire skilled staff and provide them with ongoing training. Quality programs also reach out to families.

## Types of Programs

Parents have a variety of options when choosing after-school child care. See 29-1. A nanny, an au pair, or a housekeeper can provide care in a child's home. Family child care homes and child care centers provide care outside the child's home.

Many for-profit child care centers provide school-age child care and transportation. These centers offer programs during the school year. Many have special summer programs, too. Parents who can afford the tuition often select this type of program. Often, children participating in these programs have attended preschool in the same facility.

Nonprofit organizations such as United Way, YMCA, and the Salvation Army offer school-age child care programs in some communities. Churches and synagogues may also provide school-age child care for their members.

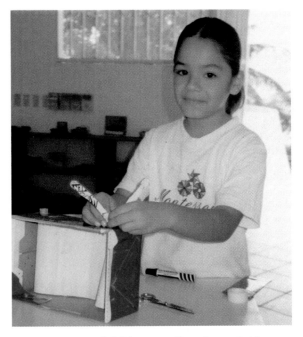

29-1 A variety of child care options is available for school-age children.

## Program Models

There are three program models used as curriculum formats in school-age child care programs. These are the child-centered, adult-centered, and unit-based models. A good program uses all three models to complement children's school and home experiences.

Several factors may influence the program model chosen. These include the ages, interests, and abilities of the children. Staff preferences and the amount of time children spend in the program can have an influence, too.

### Child-Centered Program Model

The **child-centered program model** is a curriculum format that allows children an opportunity to do self-selected activities. Staff members encourage children's involvement by serving as facilitators and resource persons. Together the staff and children plan the daily activities. Available resources and the children's interests help determine the activities. See 29-2.

### Adult-Centered Program Model

The **adult-centered program model** is a more structured curriculum format that includes a high level of adult direction. The curriculum includes recreation and tutoring programs.

29-2  Children in a child-centered program model may select activities that interest them.

Children may also have opportunities to take music and dance lessons.

### Unit-Based Program Model

The **unit-based program model** is a curriculum format that revolves around curriculum themes that reflect the children's interests. Frequently, these themes focus on special events and holidays. Staff members offer a variety of cooking, science, music, and art activities that relate to the theme. They choose children's literature and plan field trips, creative dramatics, and games to support the theme, too. Children can then choose many of the specific theme-related activities in which they will participate.

Regardless of the model used, school-age programs should focus on developing competence and self-confidence. Self-confidence contributes to an "I-can-do-it" attitude. It will help children master reading and writing skills. Self-confidence will also help children develop positive social relationships with their peers.

## Adult-Child Ratios

Program quality is enhanced when there are enough staff to meet the individual needs of children. Studies show that appropriate adult-child ratios and small group size improve program quality.

Children in school-age child care programs must be able to get adult help when they need it. Children will need assistance with homework. They will also need adults to serve as role models and provide emotional support and encouragement.

Having more adults available benefits staff as well as children. In this case, adults can provide the constant supervision needed to create a safe environment. While supervising, adults can use observation to gain information about the interests, needs, and abilities of each child.

Most states have laws addressing adult-child ratios for children's programs. These ratios vary from state to state. However, for children through six years of age, a minimum 1:10 ratio is usually recommended. For children seven years and older, a minimum 1:12 ratio is usually recommended.

## Characteristics of Staff

Who should care for school-age children? High-quality programs are staffed by well-trained personnel. These individuals understand child growth and development. They have age-appropriate expectations of the children's behavior and abilities. They are continuously seeking new ideas and learning new teaching techniques. These teachers also respect the cultural diversity of the children they teach.

Staff in school-age programs need to be understanding, patient, and warm. Moreover, they need to respond positively to each child's uniqueness and changing needs.

### Act as Facilitators

Staff in school-age programs act as facilitators. They ask the children to share thoughts and listen to the view of others. They assist the children in developing skills and abilities. They help by offering suggestions, providing encouragement, and recommending activities. They use demonstrations, explanations, and coaching to help children learn. Staff also ask thought-provoking questions that require children to use mental reasoning skills.

### Use Positive Guidance

School-age children are learning social expectations. They are learning to recognize the impact of their behavior on others. By experiencing consequences, children begin to understand what is acceptable and unacceptable behavior.

Skilled staff use positive guidance to help children achieve self-control. They encourage prosocial behaviors, such as taking turns, helping, cooperating, negotiating, and talking through interpersonal problems. Staff work with children to develop clear limits. When needed, staff remind children of the limits. After this, they redirect the children to more acceptable behavior.

### Involve Children

School-age children are learning to be independent. They want to solve problems. Staff of school-age child care programs need to involve children in daily problem-solving activities.

While developing limits, staff should involve the children in a discussion of expectations. This will help children make decisions related to their actions. Staff should also involve children by allowing them to help plan curriculum and make choices about activities, 29-3.

### Promote Respect for Cultural Diversity

As school-age children become more aware of the world around them, they begin to make social comparisons. Through this process, children not only define themselves, they also identify qualities in others.

Conscientious teachers help children appreciate cultural diversity. Children need to learn how others express beauty through art, literature, and music, 29-4. Teachers use toys, games, foods, and holiday celebrations to teach children about different cultures. They use storybooks, videotapes, posters, and puzzles to show people from all cultures in a variety of positive roles.

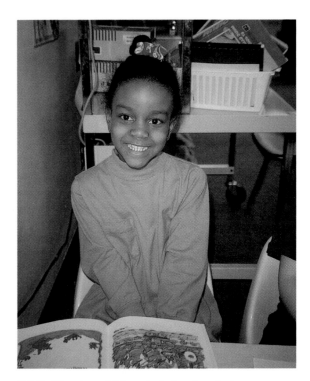

29-3 Allowing children to help plan their own activities promotes self-esteem and enjoyment of the program.

Seeing images of people who look like them helps children develop a sense of pride in their culture. Seeing images of people from other cultures helps children respect and value people's differences and similarities.

## Enjoy Physical Activities

School-age children thrive on physical activity. During a typical school day, they spend much time sitting in classrooms. When they arrive at after-school programs, they have pent-up energy to release. They want to move around, play games, run, and jump.

Teachers who are well suited for school-age programs enjoy physical activity. They do not have to be athletic. However, they need the energy and desire to join children in active play.

# The Environment

Throughout middle childhood, children need room to practice their emerging skills. A quality school-age child care environment should provide appropriate space, materials, and equipment. The environment needs to reflect the children's interests, ages, abilities, and needs. This environment will allow children to have fun, learn, and thrive as they move at their own pace.

The ideal environment is designed specifically for school-age programs. However, any facility with a large activity room and an outdoor play area can serve as a school-age program environment. Many programs are housed in libraries, cafeterias, gyms, and church basements.

When facilities are designed for other purposes, restrictions may apply. Providing an appropriate environment may be difficult. Teachers in these spaces often have only a limited time to prepare the environment. They must develop creative strategies for getting the room ready each day. They may use moveable carts to store games, art supplies, books, and other program materials, 29-5. They may have the children help by including setup and cleanup in the children's daily schedule.

## Indoor Space

The indoor space for a school-age program should be adequate for the number of children enrolled. Children need room for individual, small group, and large group activities. At least 35 square feet of space should be available for each child.

Children need a secure and safe environment. For them, a child care center is a home away from home. A quality school-age child care environment is informal and provides a homelike atmosphere. In this setting, the children can explore interests and develop one-on-one relationships.

Indoor space should be well designed and pleasing to the eye. Provide storage units for children's personal belongings that are separate from those used to hold classroom materials and supplies. Use pillows, pictures, posters, bean bag chairs, carpeting, couches, and curtains to help create a warm and inviting environment.

As a teacher in a school-age program, you will need to carefully plan how to use the space in your room. As in programs for preschool children, the room needs to include interest centers. You will also need to provide space for quiet activities. Create some open areas for group activities, too.

29-4 Teachers can plan activities to help children appreciate cultural diversity.

29-5 In a shared environment, staff can use wagons to store and transport art supplies.

### Interest Centers

Interest centers are a focus of quality school-age child care programs. Whenever possible, set up centers for hobbies, blocks, cooking, science, math, games, music, dramatic play, and arts and crafts. Try to provide bulletin boards or display areas near each center to show children's work.

Arrange interest centers to encourage independent use by the children. Place labeled open shelving units in the centers. These units will help children know where to acquire and return materials and equipment.

### Quiet Areas

Your room needs to include quiet areas. Children should be able to do homework, use computers, read, and relax in these areas. See 29-6. They should feel protected from the intrusion of others. Children often enjoy flexible quiet spaces that they can rearrange with movable furniture and privacy screens.

### Open Areas

Your room needs to include large, open areas. Children can use these areas for group planning times and special projects. They can enjoy movement activities, creative dramatics, and indoor games in open areas, too.

## Outdoor Space

Outdoor space is just as important in a school-age program environment as indoor space. Children need room for physical activity. At the end of the day, they need to make noise, play, and enjoy their friends, 29-7.

These activities require at least 75 square feet of outdoor space per child. Make sure this space is

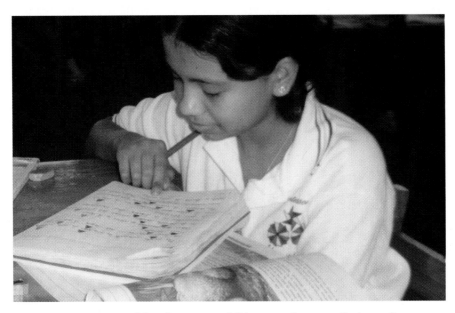

29-6 In a quiet area of the classroom, children can focus on their reading.

protected from unwanted visitors and traffic. Create separate areas for running, climbing, swinging, and organized sports. Also provide quiet outdoor play space.

# Planning Curriculum

Good planning allows you to offer an inviting and challenging school-age program. When you provide an appealing curriculum, everybody wins. You win because the children will enjoy participating. The children win because they have choices as well as opportunities to develop new skills and interests.

The question is, "Who should plan?" The answer is everybody—children, parents, and staff. Begin by finding out what is important to each of these groups.

Parents and staff are likely to have general goals for your program. They want you to provide a safe environment for school-age children during nonschool hours. They expect you to offer a variety of developmentally appropriate activities that allow children to develop new skills.

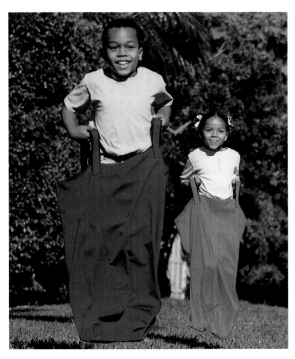

29-7 Children need plenty of safe outdoor space for physical activities, such as sack races.

These goals will help guide your overall planning. However, your specific day-by-day activity plans will be guided more by the interests of the children.

## Assessing Interests

No two school-age children are exactly alike. As a teacher in a school-age program, you must consider children's individual abilities and needs. You must also be aware of family backgrounds and special situations. This will help you plan personally meaningful curriculum built on what the children already know.

To plan a developmentally appropriate school-age program, you need to begin by assessing the children's interests. Children's interests are always changing. Therefore, you need to conduct assessment exercises on a continuing basis to improve teaching and learning.

Informally, you can assess children by observing their play and interacting with them individually and in small groups. You can also assess interests through get-acquainted interviews, group discussions, self-reports, and surveys.

### Get-Acquainted Interviews

Get-acquainted interviews can help you assess interests at the beginning of the year or when new children enroll. This assessment technique involves having a child ask a peer questions about himself or herself. Questions can focus on favorite hobbies, sports, foods, holidays, music, books, television programs, and vacation activities.

Because school-age children enjoy using technology, you may want to record the interviews on videotape or an audio cassette. You can share the tapes during group time to help all the children learn more about their classmates.

### Group Discussions

Group discussion is a useful method of determining individual interests of school-age children. Using this method on a regular basis can also help you keep up with changes in children's interests.

Group discussions are particularly effective with nonreaders. Begin the process by asking the following questions:

■   What are your hobbies?

- What new hobbies would you like to learn?
- What are your favorite sports?
- Are there any new sports you would like to learn?
- What are your favorite activities at school?
- What are your favorite program activities?
- What do you like least about the program?
- What else would you like to do in the program?

### Self-Reports

Another way to learn about children is through self-reports. These reports can take the form of either stories or pictures. Ask children to focus on a theme as they write or draw. Possible themes include "All About Me," "My Family," and "When I Grow Up." Invite children to share their stories and pictures with the class. Celebrate the children's diversity. Then display stories and pictures on a bulletin board or wall.

### Surveys

You can design a survey to assess children's interests. Children who are readers can complete the survey on their own. A staff member can ask questions and record the responses of non-readers. When designing the survey, keep it brief.

## Group Planning Sessions

After you have gathered information about children's interests, you are ready to begin making some specific plans. Group planning sessions are especially effective for planning themes, holidays, special events, and field trips. Begin by asking the children to brainstorm a list of ideas. Be sure to acknowledge each suggestion. You may want to record the ideas on a chalkboard or flipchart.

After children have presented all their suggestions, discuss each one. Explain your reasons for eliminating any ideas due to expense, location, safety, or lack of staff. When you have reviewed all the ideas, encourage the children to prioritize them as a group.

## Scheduling

Most school-age child care programs are open before and after school hours. Children may participate in these programs for up to five hours a day while attending kindergarten or elementary school. Some programs are available all day during vacation periods, holidays, and summer months.

As a school-age program teacher, you must carefully plan a daily schedule that meets children's needs for predictability. At the same time, your schedule should be flexible enough to allow for children's individual differences.

You will set up your daily program schedule between arrival and departure times. Your schedule will include times for children to eat and rest. It will include periods for children to participate in a variety of activities. It will also allow time for children to clean up. Figure 29-8 shows a typical schedule for a school-age child care program.

## Arrival and Departure Times

Arrival and departure times represent more than just the beginning and end of the daily schedule in a school-age program. These are valuable times to share information with children and parents. They serve as a bridge between home and the child care center. Use these moments to update parents about their children and to solicit parents' support for program activities. Also use these interaction times to gain insight about family values, roles, and events that may be affecting children.

When the children enter and leave your room, be available. Identify children by name. Give them warm greetings. Listen to their parting comments. Be sincere. Remember that the tone of your voice tells children how you feel about seeing them.

## Mealtimes

As you begin to plan your program schedule, think of your childhood. How did you feel when you arrived home from school? Chances are you were hungry. Like you, the children in your program will probably want something to eat when they arrive.

Mealtimes should be a learning experience. Mealtimes should also provide children with a

| School-Age Child Care Program Daily Schedule | |
| --- | --- |
| **6:00–8:30 a.m.**<br>• Arrival of children (Children will arrive at different times dependent on their parents' work schedules)<br>• Breakfast<br>• Self-selected indoor activities, such as games, blocks, sewing, crafts, pegboards, art materials, books, stories, discussions, hobbies, conversation, computers, card games, puzzles, and homework<br><br>**8:30–12:00 p.m.**<br>• Children attend morning kindergarten and area elementary schools<br><br>**12:00–12:30 p.m.**<br>• Lunch (morning kindergarten children return and afternoon kindergarten children go to school)<br><br>**12:30–1:00 p.m.**<br>• Group Time: Story, discussion, show and tell<br><br>**1:00–2:00 p.m.**<br>• Rest time | **2:00–3:00 p.m.**<br>• Self-selected activities, such as dramatic play, crafts, sand, water, checkers, card games, cooking, science, books, tapes, computers, and hobbies<br><br>**3:15–3:30 p.m.**<br>• Group Snack (afternoon kindergarten and elementary children return to program)<br><br>**3:30–5:30 p.m.**<br>• Outdoor Play: Field trips; organized sports; team games; mud, water, and sand play; gardening; jumping, skipping, hopping, climbing and other physical activities involving balls and jump ropes; music and dance lessons<br><br>**5:30–6:00 p.m.**<br>• Group Time: Discussion, program planning<br><br>**6:00–6:30 p.m.**<br>• Indoor individual and small group activities, outside and indoor cleanup in preparation for going home |

29-8  A comprehensive school-age child care program provides care 12 hours a day.

sense of responsibility and community. Children can learn how to measure and prepare foods. They can assist with planning the menus, setting and decorating the tables, serving, and cleaning up. They can use the time when they are gathered around the table to share the events of their day, too.

You can use mealtime as an opportunity to introduce multicultural foods. Invite children to share favorite family recipes. Ask them to help plan special meals for holidays, birthdays, and other events. For special events, you may want to have children invite a guest, such as a parent or grandparent.

## Rest Time

School-age programs sometimes include a daily rest time. The amount of time you schedule for rest will depend on the children in your program. Age, health, and activity level will affect a child's need for rest.

Some children, especially those who are younger, will want to sleep during rest time. Other, older children may simply enjoy low-key activities. You might encourage these children to

play quiet games, listen to music, or read books. The activities they choose should not disturb sleeping children.

Soft music may help some children relax during rest time. Other children find pleasure in having a teacher read to them.

## Activity Time

You are likely to devote the largest part of your daily school-age program schedule to activity time. You will notice fewer conflicts among children when they are all engaged in activity. Providing a variety of familiar and unfamiliar activities will ensure that all children can find something interesting to do. The specific types of activities you offer will depend on the length and time of your program.

Before-school programs should focus on quiet activities. Some children may need to spend the time before school finishing their homework. Other children may enjoy looking at books, constructing puzzles, or playing quiet games. They may also enjoy talking with friends.

After-school programs are generally longer than before-school programs, and they offer a wider variety of activities. After sitting in a classroom all day, many children enjoy physical activities that help release energy. They enjoy outdoor play, competitive sports, preparing snacks, and working on projects. They may want to participate in clubs, such as Cub Scouts, Boy Scouts, Brownies, and Girl Scouts. They may want to join book clubs and special interest clubs.

Other children need to find space to be by themselves after school to recharge their energy. For them, being with a group of people, following directions, and completing tasks all day may be stressful. They may simply want to listen to music, page through a book, enjoy quiet games, do homework, or rest.

### Balance of Activities

A good school-age program does not duplicate activities that take place during the school day. Rather, it complements the child's home and school experiences. The emphasis should be on recreational activities as opposed to academic ones, 29-9. The activities should be developmen-

29-9 Recreational activities, such as music, provide good balance for a full day of schoolwork.

tally appropriate and provide opportunities for skill development.

The schedule for a school-age child care program needs to include a balance of activities. Schedule separate times for child-directed and teacher-directed activities. Allow time for small group, large group, and individual activities. Plan for large motor activities, such as team sports and outdoor play. Also plan for fine motor activities, such as writing and drawing.

### Group Activities

Some school-age program activities will involve all the children. However, children in the middle childhood years also need opportunities to participate in small, self-selected peer group activities. Listening to a story, taking a field trip, and planning a project can all be group activities. Such activities help children communicate, develop friendships, and learn social skills.

Use different ways of dividing children into groups. You may group children according to age, interests, and needs. However, you may also group children according to such factors as favorite sports, recording artists, cars, foods, pets, and hobbies.

Mixed groups representing different developmental stages benefit children at all levels. Such groups reduce competition. These groups give older children an opportunity to develop leadership skills. Older children can help younger children with such activities as board games and crafts. The younger children learn by observing and interacting with the older children.

Groups may undertake special activities. For example, publishing a newsletter is a special activity for a group of children. The children can write, edit, and print it using a computer. They can decide who will be the editors, reporters, and production staff. Once the newsletter is published, children can share it with parents.

## Technology Use

Computers offer special learning opportunities for school-age children. As a result, school-age programs need to provide computers and developmentally appropriate software. Children of this age can use the computer for a variety of tasks. They can compose letters, practice keyboarding skills, complete homework, play games, or search for information on the Internet. Through these experiences, children improve their thinking skills by seeking information, making decisions, and solving problems.

Children need age-appropriate freedom to use the computers on their own, 29-10. This helps them develop self-confidence. Children must be protected from inappropriate content when using the computers, however. Programs must develop and enforce online safety limits. They should also investigate the use of filtering software and other technologies that keep children from accessing certain information. Supervision is also needed.

## Cleanup

Your school-age program needs to include scheduled time for cleanup. All children need to participate in cleanup activities. They have a responsibility for maintaining their environment.

Let children know your expectations for cleanup time. Tell them that they should return games and equipment to the proper storage units. Instruct them to place their personal belongings, projects, and art work in their lockers. Completing these tasks will help children develop a sense of pride.

29-10  Learning to use the computer independently is a valuable skill for school-age children.

# Summary

There is a critical need for school-age child care. Too many children are left alone to care for themselves. Parents should observe state laws regarding self-care for their school-age children. Within the limits of the law, they should decide about using self-care based on the child's age and maturity. A common guideline is 12 years old.

Parents have a variety of options when choosing after-school child care. These include in-home care, family child care homes, and child care centers. School-age child care programs follow any of three models: child-centered, adult-centered, or unit-based. High-quality programs are staffed by well-trained personnel. These individuals understand child growth and development. They have age-appropriate expectations of the children's behavior and abilities.

A quality school-age child care environment should provide appropriate space, materials, and equipment. The environment needs to reflect the children's interests, ages, abilities, and needs. This environment will allow children to have fun, learn, and thrive as they move at their own pace.

Parents and staff are likely to have general goals for the school-age program. They expect a variety of developmentally appropriate activities that allow children to develop new skills. Specific day-by-day activity plans will be guided more by the interests of the children.

Most school-age child care programs are open before and after school hours. Children may participate in these programs for up to five hours a day while attending kindergarten or elementary school. Some programs also operate all day during vacation periods and summer months.

# Review and Reflect

1. List four common problems of children who lack adult supervision.

2. List four positive outcomes for children who attend a school-age child care program.

3. Name and describe the three program models for school-age child care programs.

4. How do appropriate adult-child ratios benefit both the children and the adults?

5. Name five characteristics of staff members in high-quality school-age programs.

6. Describe a quality school-age child care environment.

7. In order to plan a developmentally appropriate school-age program, what must you do first?

8. Name four techniques you can use to assess children's interests.

9. In planning activities for school-age programs, the emphasis should be on _____ activities as opposed to _____ ones.

10. How do mixed groups representing different developmental stages benefit children at all levels?

# Apply and Explore

1. Visit two school-age child care programs that use different models. Write a report explaining how the programs are alike and different.

2. Interview a school-age child care provider about the characteristics that are important in his or her work. Share your findings in a brief oral report.

3. Measure the indoor and outdoor square footage at a school-age child care facility. Calculate how much space is available for each child enrolled in the program.

4. Discuss methods for including school-age children in curriculum planning.

5. Check the Web site gameskidsplay.net for an extensive list of children's game ideas. **C**

6. Visit yahooligans.com, the Web site Yahoo developed for school-age children. Which parts of the site do you think school-age children would find most interesting? **C**

# Chapter 30

# Guiding Children with Special Needs

After studying this chapter, you will be able to

- contribute to the development of an Individualized Education Plan for a child with special needs.

- develop individualized learning objectives and teaching strategies for a child.

- explain the role of the teacher in working with children who have special needs.

- describe methods for identifying and working with special needs that may be encountered in the early childhood program: hearing, speech, language, vision, physical, health, cognitive, and behavioral disorders.

- describe methods of integrating children with special needs into a typical program.

- explain the special needs of children who are gifted and how these needs can be met.

## Terms to Know

Individuals with
  Disabilities
  Education Act (IDEA)

inclusion

Individualized
  Education Plan (IEP)

Individualized Family
  Service Plan (IFSP)

referral

articulation problems

chronic health needs

giftedness

acceleration

enrichment

learning disability

Miguel, a lively four-year-old, has a hearing impairment. He can speak and understand only a few simple words. Rosie, an active five-year-old, is color deficient. She cannot identify the primary colors. Stephen has cerebral palsy. He needs special help to develop fine motor skills. Toby is a two-year-old who has taught herself to read. These are children who have special needs.

By federal law, children with disabilities must be provided with free, appropriate public education when they reach three years of age. The **Individuals with Disabilities Education Act (IDEA),** passed by Congress, requires that all states provide education for children who are developmentally delayed. Under this law, all three- to five-year-old children with disabilities that require special educational services must be provided with individual education programs. The same programs are available for children from birth to three years of age who are high risk or have significant developmental problems. Infants, toddlers, and preschoolers who might have a physical, sensory, cognitive, or emotional disability are guaranteed the right to a professional assessment under the Federal Education of Handicapped Children Act.

**Inclusion,** previously referred to as mainstreaming, means placing special needs children in regular classrooms. This process allows children to learn in the least restrictive environment. All children gain skills by interacting with each other. In this type of environment, children with disabilities have nondisabled children as role models. This interaction can lead to imitation. Inclusionary classrooms are frequently team-taught by regular and special education teachers.

There are many types of special needs. Communication needs are the most common. These usually fall into three categories: hearing, speech, and language problems. Visual, physical, and learning disabilites and chronic health problems are other types of special needs. Gifted children also have special needs, 30-1.

Assistants and volunteers can be most useful in inclusion. Instruct all staff members on the nature of the child's condition and how they are to help. Encourage adults to meet the special needs of the children in group settings, if possible. To do this, the staff may have to adapt classroom materials, change expectations, or give extra help when needed.

Nondisabled children can also assist in inclusion by helping a child with a disability adjust to the environment. The nondisabled child might introduce the other child to the classroom setting. At times, the nondisabled child can help the child organize his or her materials or practice a new skill. Nondisabled children also benefit from inclusionary classrooms. Children with disabilities frequently model unique adaptive skills and problem-solving abilities.

A word of caution is necessary when working with children who have with disabilities. Sometimes other children in the classroom will want to do too much for these children. They try to "help" by doing the disabled children's work for them or by helping them with self-help skills. Remind the children that assistance should be provided only when needed. Encourage staff, volunteers, and the other children to be patient and give extra encouragement to children with special needs.

## Individualized Education Plans

Federal law requires that an **Individualized Education Plan (IEP)** be written for each child with a diagnosed disability. The purpose of an Individualized Education Plan is to ensure that each child receives an appropriate education. By law, parents are allowed to take part in designing their child's program. This plan is jointly developed by the teacher, the parents or guardians, and experts on the particular disability. A copy of the plan is given to the parent(s). Some children with special needs will come to your center already identified. These children will already have an IEP. Usually an IEP is written for a 12-month period extending from October 1 to September 30. Children with a correctable disability or one that requires no special accommodations will not need an Individualized Education Plan.

Each IEP requires six components. These components are

- a description containing an assessment of the child's current level of performance and skill development
- annual goals for the child
- short-term educational objectives
- a statement outlining the involvement of the child in the regular educational program
- specific services that will be provided with a time line noting the dates services will begin and end

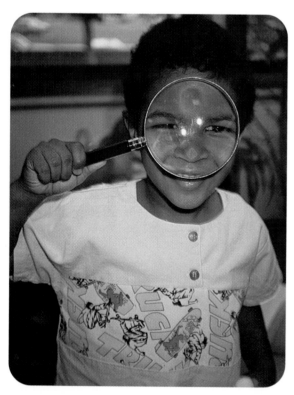

30-1 Children who are constantly curious and trying to figure out how objects work may be gifted.

■ evaluation criteria that will be used to decide if educational objectives are met

When a preschool age child is diagnosed as having a disability, an **Individualized Family Service Plan (IFSP)** is developed. The IFSP includes

■ the family's needs in regard to enhancing the child's development

■ goals for the child

■ services to be provided to the child and/or family, by whom and when

■ a plan for transitioning the child to other services and regular education

## Teachers' Roles

Teachers' roles have expanded since federal law first mandated including children with special needs in classrooms. Now teachers need to

■ take part in identifying children with special needs.

■ work with speech clinicians, school psychologists, health professionals, and other resource persons to design individual programs.

■ teach children who have special needs and nondisabled children in the same classroom.

■ share information with parents and make suggestions for referrals.

■ base program decisions on input from several resources including parents, other professionals, and personal observations.

■ encourage parents to participate in their child's education. This is their right. Find out what they are feeling as well as thinking. Be an equal partner with parents; keep them informed.

First, as a teacher, you will need to learn how to identify children with special needs. Then you will need to develop a basic understanding of the learning needs of children with hearing, visual, speech, physical, learning, behavioral, and health disabilities. With this knowledge, you can then adapt the curriculum and classroom environment to meet their special needs.

## Identification

Early identification of special needs is the key to promoting the child's successful development, 30-2. Children who are not identified early may go through years of failure. This failure, in turn, can create a poor self-concept that can compound the disability.

Many young children's special needs are identified after they enter an early childhood program. Often, identification is made by an adult who is not part of the family. You, as a teacher, may be the first to detect a speech, visual, or hearing problem. You also may be the first to note a cognitive, emotional, or physical disability.

To learn to identify special needs, you need to understand average development. When a problem is suspected, observe the child closely. Informal observation may be used for assessing a child's needs. These observations may be noted on cards or paper. When recording observations, mention those signs of behaviors that suggest a special need. Any unusual social, cognitive, emotional, or physical development could signal a possible special need.

For instance, you may suspect a certain child has a special need. Developmentally, there

30-2 Annual hearing tests are a vital tool for identifying hearing problems early.

appears to be far above or below average. In this case, you observe the child closely. Make notes about any unusual behavior. If Terry cannot identify primary colors after studying color concepts a number of times, observe him closely. Ask yourself "Could Terry be color deficient?" Consider a child's behavior in comparison to his or her usual behavior and in comparison to his or her peers.

A number of techniques can be used to collect data. You might study a child's work, 30-3. Photographs and video tapes are also useful. Scales or checklists that name skills children of certain ages should be able to perform can be helpful.

After you have made and confirmed your findings, alert the center director. The director may wish to confirm your observations. He or she may give other tests to measure the child's abilities. After this, a conference will likely be scheduled with the child's parent(s).

Begin the conference by introducing the suspected problem. Share your observations. Provide parents with examples from your observations. Ask the parents if they have noticed any of these behaviors at home. If their observations confirm yours, suggest a formal diagnosis.

Some parents may not share your concern. If this is the case, keep making your observations and schedule more conferences. It sometimes helps to ask the parents to take part in structured observations in the home and school. Remember,

any delay in diagnosis can hinder the child's development.

## Referrals

When the parent(s) agree a problem may exist, direct them to the needed service. Your role as a teacher is to help them see a need for their child's treatment. Once this has been done, obtain a diagnosis. Public schools are responsible for planning and paying the costs associated with the diagnosis of a disability unless parents choose to have their own assessment conducted. In that case, school staff are obligated to consider the results. You may be able to suggest a professional parents can take their child to see. This is called a **referral**. Vision or physical problems may first be referred to a county or school health nurse. Hearing, language, or speech problems may be referred to a speech clinician. Learning and behavioral problems are most often referred to a school psychologist or local agency. Depending on the state, a referral may be made to the Department of Social Services.

## Hearing Disorders

A child who is *hearing impaired* can often be identified by his or her lack of vocabulary and overall delays in language development compared to nondisabled children. This child may

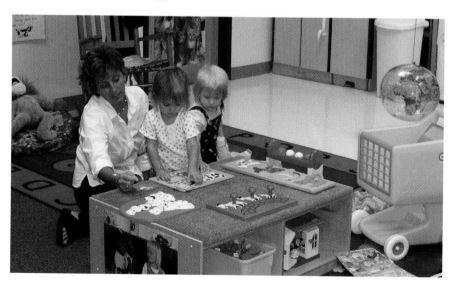

30-3 Closely observing children's skills allows teachers to note behavior that might indicate a special need.

only speak a few simple words. Before you begin to alter your program, learn the extent of the child's hearing loss. This information can only be learned through a professional.

The child's hearing loss may range from mild to profound. With a mild hearing loss, the child's vocabulary will not be as large as that of his or her peers who have normal hearing. This child might also have difficulty during large group activities, stories, and field trips. He or she may appear inattentive and distracted. The child may miss as much as half of what is being communicated.

A child with a moderate hearing loss will also have trouble in large group situations. This child has a limited vocabulary. To understand the child's speech, you should stand face-to-face. This will allow you to read the child's lips.

Children with severe, or profound, hearing loss often have little understandable speech. These children must rely largely on their vision, body language, and contextual clues to communicate.

To make up for alleviate hearing losses, many children will wear either a hearing aid in their ear or a Y-shaped hearing aid over their chests. The advantage of the ear hearing aid is that it can be adjusted to compensate for the hearing loss in each ear. The Y-shaped aid is the most popular. It has one hearing aid with tubes going to both ears.

It is important that you understand the type of hearing aid used by a child. Ask the parents to tell you about it. If it falls out of the child's ear during program hours, you will need to replace it. You should also know how to check the batteries. Keep a ready supply on hand.

The purpose of the hearing aid is to amplify and magnify all sounds. It will not perfect a child's hearing. In fact, most hearing aids are only useful within a 10-foot radius. Seat children who use hearing aids away from distracting noises. Hearing aids amplify close sounds.

## Teaching Suggestions

When approaching a child who is hearing impaired, get down to the child's eye level, 30-4. Then get the child's attention before speaking. Sometimes this can be done by lightly touching the child's hand or arm. With practice, you will learn how close you must stand in order to be understood.

30-4 The key to working with hearing impaired children is to modify your teaching methods to meet the needs of the child.

You should also follow these suggestions:

- Speak in a normal volume and speed.
- Use the same sentence structure as you would for other children.
- Pause and wait for a response after you speak.
- If the child does not understand you, repeat, rephrase, or demonstrate.
- Encourage other children to imitate you when they communicate with the child. That is, they need to get the child's attention, look into his or her eyes, and speak at a normal volume and speed.
- Whenever needed, use gestures and facial expressions to reinforce the spoken word.
- In a group situation, let the child sit in front of you. This will encourage him or her to watch your body language and lips as you speak.

In addition to using these teaching strategies, adapt the curriculum for the hearing impaired child. Before you begin making these changes, however, you may wish to consult a language and speech clinician. This person will likely offer you suggestions for working with the child.

Visual skills are important for children who are hearing impaired. Finely tuned visual skills help compensate for their lack of hearing. However, hearing impaired children do not automatically acquire acute visual skills. To provide for their needs, stress visual activities.

- Use concrete materials to demonstrate abstract concepts. For example, if you are talking about pumpkins, use a real pumpkin or a picture of a pumpkin. (Avoid drawing on the chalkboard as you are talking. These children need to see your face as you communicate with them.)
- Provide a variety of classification games and puzzles for the children to practice visual perception skills.
- Label classroom furniture and materials.
- Select books with simple, large, and uncluttered illustrations. These children will rely more on vision than hearing during story time.
- Teach safety by using traffic signals with the wheeled toys in the play yard.
- Teach daily routines and transitions using a light switch. Flash the light to get the children's attention.
- Use a picture poster to point to the upcoming activity.

Some children with hearing impairments are taught to communicate manually through finger spelling and sign language. An oral approach, emphasizing lip reading and speaking, is used with other children. Some parents feel very strongly about using one approach over the other even though most professionals today recommend a combined or eclectic approach with children who have hearing impairments.

# Speech and Language Disorders

A child in your center may refuse to talk. Another child may speak but may be inarticulate (cannot be understood by teachers or peers). Still another child may not be able to recall sentences correctly. These children have speech and language disorders.

## Identification

Before programs can be altered, you must identify the problem. Informal observations are the most common method used to identify speech and language problems. Chart 30-5 contains a checklist to use when observing for these problems. You will need to listen carefully as the child speaks. Listen to both sounds and content.

When a child is having trouble pronouncing words, record those sounds causing the difficulty. Young children find the consonants *p, b, m, w,* and vowels the easiest to pronounce. *Cr, bl, sh, ch, th, j, r, 1,* and *z* are more difficult sounds to pronounce and take longer to learn. Chart 30-6 contains the approximate ages at which most children use certain sounds.

Observe and listen to children in a variety of settings: on the play yard, in the housekeeping area, during lunchtime, and as they converse with others. As you identify the problem, make notes and continue observing to collect information.

Based on repeated observations, you may conclude a child likely has a speech problem. Share your observations with your director.

| Speech Observation Checklist |
| --- |
| • Do the sounds the child makes match those listed for his or her age group on a developmental chart? |
| • Is the rate and fluency of the child's speech appropriate for his or her age group? |
| • Is the child's speech understandable? |
| • Does the amount of talking done appear to be average? |
| • Does the child recall and repeat sentences correctly? |

30-5 If you suspect a speech disorder, observe the child, paying close attention to the items listed.

| Developmental Order for Speech Sounds | | | | | |
| --- | --- | --- | --- | --- | --- |
| **Age** | **Sounds** | | | | |
| 1½ to 3½ yr. | p | m | h | n | w | b |
| 2 to 4 yr. | k | d | t | n | g | |
| 2½ to 5½ yr. | f | y | | | | |
| 3 to 6 yr. | r | l | s | | | |
| 3½ to 7 yr. | ch | sh | z | | | |
| 4½ to 8 yr. | j | r | | | | |

30-6 Keep these parameters in mind when observing a child you believe may have a speech disorder.

The director will determine whether a parent conference should be scheduled. The child may then be referred to a speech therapist for assessment.

## Articulation Problems

The terms *lazy tongue* and *baby talk* are frequently used to describe articulation problems. These terms imply that the child's tongue or developmental level is the problem. Neither is true. **Articulation problems** are most often omissions, distortions, or substitutions of vowels or consonants or both. It is possible for a child to have one or more of these problems.

Certain speech sounds are left out in an omission error. This results in only a part of a word being said. For example, a child may say "oat" for "boat." The child may say "had" for the name "Thad."

A child with a distortion problem sometimes has trouble identifying and producing the intended sound. For example, instead of pronouncing an *s*, a child may suck air in between his or her teeth.

Substitutions involve speech patterns such as "thome" for "some" or "tate" for "cake." The most common sound substitutions include *f* for *th*, *t* for *k*, *b* for *v*, *th* for *s*, *k* for *t*, and *w* for *i* or *r*. One common substitution problem is referred to as a *lisp*. It involves substituting *th* sound for the letter *s*.

After a child has been diagnosed as having an articulation problem, a speech clinician should be consulted. This professional will provide direct therapy and/or advise you. Ask for advice on how to help the child.

As a teacher, your reaction to the child with articulation problems has a great effect. To help a child feel secure, always react positively. Ensure that the other children do, too. If the child does not respond verbally, do not demand a response. Instead, provide the correct answer for him or her.

Model good listening skills and speaking skills with all the children. Give the children your total attention. Look directly into their faces as they speak. Verbally respond with interest to what the children are saying. If you do not understand, ask the children to repeat what they have said.

Children with articulation problems need to be encouraged to talk. Set an example by feeding in language as they take part in activities. To illustrate, you may say to a child "You are placing a large red block in the square hole" as he or she plays with a sorting box.

Use language that is proper for the child's developmental level. For example, the child may point to a large red car and say "far." You should then say "That is a large, red car." This technique is called expansion. It involves taking the child's mispronounced words and correctly expanding them into sentences.

Some children are more comfortable talking about things that are special to them. One technique you can use is to have the child bring something special from home. Then have him or her tell everyone about the item.

Always provide a variety of activities in your classroom. The wider the variety, the more the children will have to talk about. Try to relate classroom activities to children's home experiences and cultural backgrounds.

Demand communication from all children, including those with articulation problems. Do this by asking open-ended questions. Instead of asking "Did you like the book?" ask "What did you like about the book?"

## Voice (Phonation) Disorders

Voice characteristics include pitch, loudness, flexibility, and quality. The lowness or highness of the voice is the *pitch*. It is not uncommon for some children to use a pitch that is too low or too high.

*Loudness* is related to the amount of energy or volume used when speaking. The voice may be strong or weak. A strong voice will be loud and can be disturbing. A weak voice may be hard to hear and can also hinder communication.

A good speaking voice during routine conversation uses a variety of pitches and loudness levels. This is referred to as *voice flexibility*. Changes in pitch and loudness often reflect the emotions of the speaker.

Harshness, hoarseness, breathiness, and nasality are all *voice-quality disorders*. The harsh voice is often louder than normal. Hoarseness may indicate a problem in the throat. A breathy voice sounds like a whisper. It is weak and not clearly phonated. Nasality is a condition in which sound passes through the nasal cavities instead of the throat.

To help prevent or correct voice disorders, promote voice control:

- Encourage children to use the correct voice volume during indoor play. You may need to say "Teddy, you need to use your indoor voice in the building."
- Discourage children from screaming or yelling too much during outdoor play.
- Model good voice characteristics. Your own voice should be the proper pitch, loudness, quality, and flexibility.

## Stuttering

Stuttering in young children is often characterized by repetition, hesitation, and prolongation. Few young children stutter all the time. It is often only under certain conditions that some children stutter.

In the early stages of language development, many children experience stuttering. This most often occurs when they feel pressured, 30-7.

Children function best in a warm, noncritical classroom. This type of environment helps all children speak with confidence.

If you have a stuttering child in your classroom, focus on creating good speaking conditions.

- Plan activities so all children will experience success. Praise the children.
- Provide children with enough time to say what they have to say.
- Listen closely to what the children are saying, as opposed to focusing on the stuttering.
- Avoid rushing children through a task. Do not complete a word or sentence for them.

Unfortunately, many well-meaning people try to provide directions to a stuttering child. "Stop and think," "Start over," and "Speak slower" are common examples. These suggestions often make the child feel even more fearful. A child's difficulty could continue as a result of this fear. An environment free of pressure is important. When stuttering is severe, speech therapy may be necessary.

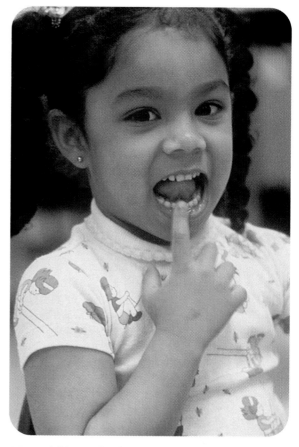

30-7 Children who feel pressured are more likely to stutter than children who are relaxed.

## Vision Disorders

One of the smallest groups of children with special needs is the visually impaired. Common vision problems include amblyopia, nearsightedness, farsightedness, and/or a color deficiency. Physically, children with visual impairments are similar to children with normal vision. However, this disability can limit their motor abilities as they take part in some physical activities. See 30-8.

To understand visual impairments, you need to understand how a healthy visual system works. Despite young children's thinking, the eye does not actually see. The purpose of the eye is to take in light. After it has taken in light, the eye transmits impulses to the brain through the optic nerve. The brain then decodes the visual

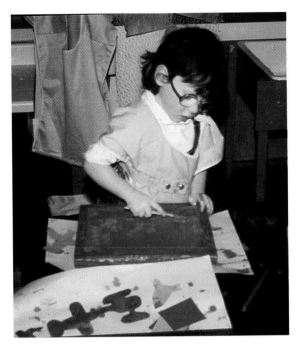

30-8 Children with visual impairments often lack small muscle coordination. They need to experiment with an art medium to build these skills.

stimuli, and "seeing" takes place. Most defects of the eye itself are correctable. If the brain or the optic nerve is damaged, however, the impairment is not correctable.

## Early Identification

Early identification of a visual impairment is important. Many child care centers have a volunteer from the National Society for the Prevention of Blindness, a county health nurse, or some other professional conduct a visual screening each year. Children who appear to have problems are given a referral for a complete exam by an eye specialist.

Classroom staff need to observe children closely to identify vision problems. Certain symptoms may suggest problems
- excessive rubbing of the eyes
- clumsiness and trouble moving around the classroom
- adjusting the head in an awkward position to view materials
- moving materials so they are close to the eyes
- squinting
- crossed eyes
- crust on eye
- swollen, red eyelids

## Types of Visual Disabilities

There are several common visual impairments that young children may have. Amblyopia is a disorder you might note in your classroom. You may also find children with glaucoma, nearsightedness, farsightedness, a color deficiency, and some uncorrectable conditions.

### Amblyopia

*Amblyopia* is often called lazy eye. This disorder is the result of a muscle imbalance caused by disuse of an eye. It is one of several visual conditions that can be corrected if found during early childhood. To force the use of the weaker eye, a patch is placed over the stronger eye. If this does not work, surgery may be required. If treatment of amblyopia is not done by age six or seven, the child's vision may always be poor.

### Glaucoma

*Glaucoma* is a condition caused by failure of the eye fluid to circulate in the proper way. This results in increased pressure on the eye. Over time, this pressure can destroy the optic nerve. This problem can be treated with medicated eyedrops if diagnosed early. This can prevent loss of vision.

### Nearsightedness

Some children may be unable to see things that are far away. These children are *nearsighted*. The medical term for this visual disorder is *myopia*. It results when the eye focuses in front of the retina.

### Farsightedness

Children who have a difficult time seeing objects that are close to them are *farsighted*. The medical term for this visual disorder is *hyperopia*. It is caused by having the visual image focus behind the retina.

### Color Deficiency

*Color deficiency*, or *color blindness*, as it is sometimes called, is the inability to see a color.

This problem is hereditary. It mostly affects males and is caused by a recessive gene. You should be able to quickly identify children with color deficiencies. They are not able to recognize one or more primary colors.

### Uncorrectable Conditions

There are several visual disorders that cannot be corrected by glasses, surgery, or other means of treatment. Any damage to the optic nerve by disease or trauma is an example. After damage, signals do not get to the brain to provide the child with sight.

## Teaching Suggestions

You may need to make changes in your classroom depending on the visual needs of the children. The following teaching suggestions may be helpful:

- Always create a need to see. For instance, if farsighted children refuse to wear their glasses, provide them with materials that have fine detail and print. The children will then realize the importance of wearing their glasses.
- Include a study unit on sight to help all the children understand vision.
- When ordering chalkboards, purchase those with a dull finish. Use yellow chalk on chalkboards. Use colored, rather than black, markers on white boards. Glare can be very tiring for partially-sighted children.
- Hang children's work at their eye level.
- Safety is always important. To ensure a safe environment, blocks, cars, and other items should be picked up right after play.
- Auditory clues are important for children with visual impairments. Provide a comfortable environment by keeping the noise level low.
- In the reading area, always have a number of large print books with clear, simple pictures.
- Provide many tactile (touch), olfactory (smell), and auditory (sound) clues to structure the environment for the child. For instance, use a piece of shag carpeting in the story area and a bubbling aquarium or fragrant flowers in the science area.
- Use auditory reminders for transition times. These may include singing a song, beating a drum, playing a piano, or hitting tone bells.
- During activities, always encourage children to describe what they remember using their senses.

Remember that children with visual impairments may need to learn some skills children with normal vision already have. For instance, children with normal vision acquire eating, toileting, and dressing skills by watching others. A visually impaired child, however, may not possess these skills when he or she comes to the center. You will need to teach these skills. You will also need to teach the child the classroom areas. Do this by repeatedly guiding the child from one area to another.

## Physical Disabilities

Most preschool children can crawl, walk, run, climb, and move their bodies in different ways. A child with a physical impairment may have a limited range of motion. Due to this limitation, his or her experiences may vary from those of his or her peers.

## Types of Physical Disabilities

Children who are physically impaired are grouped based on their ability to function. Disabilities are classified as severe, moderate, or mild. Children with severe impairments usually cannot move independently. Typically, they have to be carried, pushed, or moved about using a wheelchair. Children with moderate impairments can do more for themselves, but they still require much help from staff members. Due to their need for accessible facilities and adaptations, children with severe or moderate physical impairment are not often enrolled in nonadapted child care centers.

Children with mild physical impairments can often do what most other children do, 30-9. These children may need to use walking aids or other devices to help them move about. As can be expected, they will need more time to move about or to do tasks.

30-9 Children who use a wheelchair can often use the playground equipment with a little help from teachers.

The children you will meet in the typical child care center will be *ambulatory*. They will be able to move from place to place. You may elect, however, to work in a center that caters to children with special needs. In these centers, you will observe a higher staff-to-child ratio. This is necessary to meet the special needs of these children.

## Cerebral Palsy

*Cerebral palsy* results from damage to the brain. This damage can be caused by an infection or improper nutrition during pregnancy, physical injury to the brain during birth, or lack of oxygen during birth. It can also be acquired during the developmental years as a result of a tumor, head injury, or brain infection. Cerebral palsy is characterized by lack of control of voluntary movements.

Speech problems are often found in children with cerebral palsy. These problems are caused by the inability to control the muscles used to make speech sounds. If a child in your group has a speech disorder, consult with the parents and a speech clinician. A child with severe cerebral palsy may benefit from use of an *augmentative communication device* such as a board containing pictures of commonly referred to objects. Thus, the child can point to a picture of a glass of milk when he or she is thirsty.

Children with cerebral palsy also often lack fine motor skills. Many of their self-help skills are impaired. Eating utensils and other equipment may be difficult for them to use. An occupational therapist and the child's parents can best advise what type of eating utensils, crayons, and other items are most useful. Modifications may be needed on equipment. For example, you may want to glue large wooden knobs on puzzles so the child with cerebral palsy can remove and insert the pieces. A wide range of adapted toys and personal care devices are available. Consult your nearest rehabilitation technology center for suggested adaptive aids.

## Spina Bifida

*Spina bifida* is a condition in which the bones of the spine fail to grow together. The nerves are left exposed. This results in paralysis. This is a *congenital* (caused before birth, but not hereditary) problem. The cause of spina bifida is unknown. Children with this problem often lack bowel and bladder control. They often cannot tell when they have eliminated because of lower body paralysis.

In order for a child with spina bifida to focus on learning activities, he or she needs to feel comfortable. You may need to ask such questions as "Are you comfortable?" or "Do you want to sit another way?" To provide the best environment for this child, discuss positions with the parents and physical therapist. They may suggest positions that will provide the child with a sense of balance. Specific questions you may want to ask them include "Should learning activities be on the floor or table?" and "Should the classroom tables be modified?"

## Amputation

At some point, you may have a child in your classroom who is missing a hand, arm, or leg. Perhaps the severed limb resulted from an accident or cancer. Sometimes the limb is missing from birth. A child who is missing a limb is often fitted with an artificial limb called a *prosthesis*. Research has shown that young children adjust to an artificial limb quite easily.

In order to use a prosthesis, it must fit and be cared for properly. To avoid frustrating the child, you, as a teacher, will need to know how the artificial limb works. Parents usually welcome a teacher's questions related to the device. In fact, these questions assure them of your interest in providing the best care for their child. Other children will model their teacher's matter-of-fact acceptance of a prosthesis.

## Teaching Suggestions

Although it is difficult for some, movement is important for all children. Children with physical disabilities may have to crawl or move with special equipment such as wheelchairs and walking aids. As a result, they need more time and energy to do fine and gross motor tasks. It takes them longer to use the bathroom or finish a project. To allow for this, you will need to provide time in your schedule. You may also have to make some adjustments in the facility.

- Modify chairs to accommodate the child.
- Provide space for a child's wheelchair, crutches, cane, walker, or cart.
- Provide ramps so the child has access to the classroom.
- Raise tables so wheelchairs fit under them.
- Glue knobs on puzzle pieces so the pieces are easy to remove and replace.
- Secure all carpeting or area rugs to the floor so the child does not slip or trip on them.
- Provide two-handled mugs and deep-sided bowls rather than plates.
- Serve finger foods as often as possible at snack time.

## Health Disorders

Some children have more illness than others. These are often the children with chronic health needs. A **chronic health need** can be defined as an illness that persists over a period of time. For some children, a problem may last a lifetime, while for others, it may last a few months.

Children with health problems often have cycles of good and poor health. Since health needs are the most common type of special needs, it is vital that you be aware of a variety of these disorders.

## Allergies

The most common health problem of young children is allergies. Studies note that up to 50 percent of all people have mild or severe allergies. An allergy may begin at any age. Studies also note that only a small percentage of children with allergies have been diagnosed.

An allergy is a reaction of the body to a substance in the environment. The offending substance is called an allergen. Exposure to the allergen may cause rashes, swelling, sneezing, or other reactions, 30-10. There are four categories of allergenic substances: inhalants, ingestants, contactants, and injectables. *Inhalants* are airborne substances that are inhaled. *Ingestants* are foods, drugs, or anything taken through the mouth. *Contactants* are things that make contact with the body through touch. *Injectables* are chemicals or drugs injected into the body.

Animal dandruff, dust, feathers, fungi spores, molds, and plant pollens are all types of airborne allergenic substances. If a child in your classroom has a severe allergy to animal dandruff, you may have to remove any hamsters, gerbils, guinea pigs, or rabbits.

Beans, berries, chocolate, cinnamon, citrus fruits, corn products, cola drinks, eggs, fish, shellfish, milk, tomatoes, nuts, and wheat are typical foods to which the body reacts. Fabric dyes and fragrances or colorings added to soaps and shampoos

30-10 An allergic reaction to an insect bite may cause swelling and skin irritation.

are contactants that may also cause reactions. Aspirin, penicillin, and sulfa drugs are common drugs that are offenders. It is important that you ask parents at the time of enrollment whether their children have any known allergies.

If a child has food allergies, you will need to plan accordingly. Try to plan menus that avoid foods to which the child is allergic. At times, you may have to offer the allergic child food substitutes. For instance, if a child has an allergy to milk, you will have to supply a substitute beverage. Many times parents will provide the substitute to make sure their child is not tempted to have cow's milk.

Cosmetics, some detergents, wool, and starch are all substances that may cause an allergic reaction when they come in contact with the skin. Common reactions include a red rash and itching. These symptoms are a warning for the child to avoid contact with whatever substance caused the problem.

Some substances cause a reaction when they enter the body through the skin. Examples include the drug penicillin and the venom from bee or wasp stings. You need to be keenly aware of insect bites. For some children, these bites can be fatal.

Bee or wasp stings usually result in redness and swelling around the wound. This indicates only a mild allergy. With a severe allergy, the child may swell all over the body and have trouble breathing. If this should occur, promptly seek medical attention. Death can result if treatment is not received immediately.

Some symptoms of allergies may be related to the season. For example, a child who is allergic to tree pollens may sneeze often in the spring. There are three major pollen seasons: early spring with tree pollens, late spring or early summer with grass pollens, and late summer and fall with weed pollens.

You may be the first to suspect allergies in a young child. Allergy symptoms are listed in 30-11. If you suspect that a child has an allergy, discuss it with his or her parent(s).

You may be responsible for some aspects of treatment for children with allergies. There are three basic treatment methods for people with allergies. The sensitive person may avoid the offending item. For instance, if a child is allergic to chocolate, foods with chocolate should be taken out of the diet.

If the person cannot avoid the irritant, he or she may be *desensitized*. In this process, a doctor injects small amounts of the allergen into the body over a period of time. This builds immunities so the person is eventually able to withstand the irritant.

Finally, medication may be used to treat the symptom. For example, a person who has nasal congestion and blockage could use a medication to control this symptom.

## Arthritis

*Arthritis* is a condition brought on by inflammation that produces swelling of the joints and surrounding tissues. The most common form of juvenile arthritis is called *rheumatoid arthritis*. General fatigue, loss of appetite, fever, aching joints, and a stiffness of joints as they become tender from swelling are the first signs of the disease.

| Allergy Symptoms | |
|---|---|
| **Eyes** <br> • pink and puffy <br> • red from being constantly rubbed <br> • dark circles underneath <br> • burning feeling and much tearing <br> • lids may appear glued together by dry mucus | **Nose** <br> • inability to smell <br> • nasal discharge <br> • frequent sneezing <br> • itchy nose <br><br> **Skin** <br> • frequent rashes <br> • lesions <br> • redness and swelling <br> • itching and hives |
| **Mouth** <br> • constant dry hacking cough <br> • mouth breathing more common than nose breathing <br> • wheezing <br> • canker sores | **Throat** <br> • tickling <br> • enlargement of lymph nodes <br><br> **Body** <br> • chills <br> • fever <br> • sweating <br> • abdominal cramps <br> • vomiting <br> • headache |

30-11 Allergies are quite common in young children. As a result it is vital that you recognize symptoms of more common allergies.

After 10 years, 60 to 70 percent of affected children are free from juvenile arthritis. Adults who acquire the condition have a much smaller chance of recovery.

Children with arthritis often find it difficult to remain in one position for long periods of time. They also may require more time to move from one place to another. They may need adapted toys, utensils, and clothing. Activities requiring fine motor dexterity, such as cutting paper or stringing beads, are particularly troublesome. Rheumatoid arthritis is typically most acute in the morning and subsides somewhat during the day. Regular, but moderate, activity is best. When the disease is in its active stage, the child will need more rest.

## Asthma

Asthma is a chronic inflammatory disorder of the airways. Symptoms include coughing, wheezing, rapid or labored breathing, shortness of breath, and chest tightness. When symptoms occur, this is called an asthma attack. It may last minutes, hours, or even weeks. Some children outgrow asthma as they get older, but others never do.

An asthma attack occurs when the airways are inflamed, or swollen and irritated. This is most commonly caused by exposure to an allergen. Attacks can also be caused by exposure to extremely cold or hot weather. Overexertion or excessive exercise can cause attacks, too. Asthma attacks are treated with medication. This is usually given in a fast-acting inhaler or nebulizer machine, 30-12. If the inhaled medicine does not provide relief or the child stops breathing, this is a medical emergency. You must call 911 or rush the child to the nearest emergency room.

Depending on the severity of the disease, some children also take daily medications to reduce inflammation of the airways. These medications might be a pill or an inhaler. Their purpose is to prevent attacks. Once an attack has begun, these medications provide little or no relief.

As the teacher, your role might be to administer medications and to monitor the child's breathing. Try to teach the child to let you know when symptoms occur. If the child doesn't seem to be breathing well, take action immediately.

Keep calm during the attack, and help the child to stay calm, too.

Ask the parents what triggers their child's asthma and try to prevent these conditions. For example, if exposure to dust is a big trigger, be sure to keep your classroom as dust-free as possible.

## Cystic Fibrosis

*Cystic fibrosis* is a hereditary disease that occurs almost from birth. This chronic condition involves persistent and serious lung infections; failure to gain weight; and loose, foul-smelling stools. Some of these symptoms are caused by a thick mucus produced by the sweat glands. This mucus interferes with the digestive and respiratory systems.

Seldom do children with cystic fibrosis enroll in early childhood programs. This is because they cannot risk developing lung infections, such as pneumonia. Moreover, these children must be treated under the close supervision

30-12  A nebulizer is a machine that turns liquid medicine into a fine mist. A person with asthma can inhale the mist through the tube and mask.

of a doctor. If children with cystic fibrosis are enrolled, they need frequent rest and a lot of fluids. They may also need to urinate frequently. The teacher should consult with the child's doctor and parents for specific care plans.

## Diabetes

Juvenile diabetes is a hereditary disease. Common symptoms of diabetes include frequent urination, loss of weight, constant hunger, itching (especially around the groin), and slow healing cuts and bruises. However, it is also possible that some affected children will not show any obvious symptoms.

With juvenile diabetes, insulin is not produced by the pancreas to burn or store foods as energy. This causes the body's sugar content to increase which, in turn, increases the sugar level of the blood. When the blood passes through the kidneys, the sugar is excreted in urine. This loss of carbohydrates is damaging to the body over time. If diabetes is not controlled, it can be fatal.

A careful diet is extremely important. A balance of proteins, fats, carbohydrates, vitamins, and minerals is necessary.

In most cases of juvenile diabetes, children need insulin injections. These are prescribed by a doctor and are usually given by the parents. Blood sugar levels may need to be checked with special medical equipment. This keeps the parents informed so they can better control the child's health.

To maintain blood sugar levels, it is necessary to balance physical activity, insulin, and diet. The child's parents and doctor can devise a plan for this. Follow this plan as closely as possible. If an imbalance occurs, this is called an *insulin reaction*. It may include trembling, dizziness, headache, confusion, sweating, fatigue, and weakness.

In an insulin reaction, the body needs sugar right away to keep it from slipping into shock or a coma. For this reason, keep fast sources of sugar, such as orange juice or candy, with you at all times in case an insulin reaction occurs. If the child passes out as the result of an insulin reaction, call 911 or rush the child to the emergency room. This is a medical emergency.

Several teaching suggestions are important when diabetic children are enrolled in the program. These are given in 30-13.

---

### Suggestions for Teaching Diabetic Children

- Ask the parents how to handle emergencies. Have them put these recommendations in writing. Place this information in the child's file.
- Schedule snack and lunch at the same time each day.
- Make sure diabetic children follow eating, medication, and activity plans each day.
- Keep quick sugar sources, such as candy bars, soda, or orange juice, on hand in case an insulin reaction occurs.
- Take the child immediately to a hospital emergency room if she/he becomes unconscious.

30-13 Follow these suggestions to assure that a diabetic child receives proper care in your program.

## Epilepsy

Epilepsy is a convulsive disorder caused by damage to the brain. It affects about one percent of the population. As a result of this disorder, the electrical rhythms of the central nervous system are disturbed. Epilepsy is not a disease.

Epilepsy can cause varying degrees of reactions or seizures. Two major types are petit mal and grand mal. Petit mal seizures result in reactions that many times go unnoticed. Often, the only visible signs are the fluttering of the eyelids, frozen postures, staring, and a temporary stop in activity. This type of seizure may only last five to ten seconds.

As a teacher, you may not always notice a petit mal seizure. You may notice the child's behavior is strange or he or she may not be paying attention. During the seizure, the child may have only a brief lapse of consciousness. Most of these seizures do not require medical attention.

Grand mal seizures are much more pronounced. During a grand mal seizure, a child will lose consciousness. He or she may also jerk, thrash, or become stiff. The child may also be injured by hitting objects or biting the tongue.

When the child regains consciousness, he or she may be confused. In fact, the seizure will not be remembered. Instead, the child may get up and continue with classroom activities.

Epilepsy is treated primarily with drugs. These drugs will either prevent or reduce the frequency of the seizures. Unfortunately, many drugs for epilepsy cause serious side effects, such as restlessness and lethargic behavior.

There may be times when you, as a teacher, may have to control a seizure. If a child falls, you should

1. let the child remain on the floor, clearing the area to provide him or her with ample room to thrash
2. remain calm
3. cradle the child's head in your lap. Avoid restraining movement. If possible, turn the child's body to the side, allowing saliva to drain from the mouth. This should help keep the child from choking. Never place your finger or other object in the child's mouth.
4. If the convulsion does not stop within two minutes, call for emergency medical help.
5. After the child has regained consciousness, allow him or her to remain lying down. Place a blanket over the child and allow him or her to sleep.
6. Call the child's doctor and parents to inform them of the seizure and ask for advice regarding further actions.

## Hemophilia

*Hemophilia* is a genetic blood disease in which the blood cannot clot normally. Extreme *internal* (under the skin) bleeding and deep bruising may result from simply bumping against something. This causes joint problems and extreme pain that may require a stay in the hospital. The real threat, however, is death caused by internal bleeding of vital organs or by blood flowing into air passages.

With the help of the parent(s), decide what equipment is safe for the child to use. You should also

■ tag the outdoor and indoor equipment the child can use
■ ask the parent(s) what to do if the child is injured
■ carefully watch the child's play to prevent accidents

## Leukemia

*Leukemia* is a form of cancer that affects the blood-forming organs and the blood. There is a sharp increase in the number of white blood cells in the bloodstream. Moreover, the number of healthy white blood cells decreases. Other signs and symptoms include bleeding, bruising, fever, infection, and weight loss.

Leukemia can be fatal. It is unlikely that a child with leukemia would enroll in a child care center. You may find, however, that a child currently enrolled may develop the disease. This child will have to be treated in the hospital. When the disease is in remission, the child may want to come back and visit friends at the center. If the parents elect to have a child with leukemia attend the center while the child is in remission, you will need to discuss the disease with them. Find out what goals the parents have for the child as well as implications of the disease.

## Learning Disabilities

Although children who have learning disabilities are in almost every classroom, their disabilities can be hard to define. Generally, a **learning disability** means having a problem with one or more basic skills of learning.

Children with learning disabilities model some common traits. They may have trouble following directions or have poor memory skills. After listening to a story, some children cannot remember it. They may have problems storing, processing, and producing information. Others have problems identifying or making numbers and letters. Poor hand-eye coordination skills may be another trait.

These learning disability traits may occur in varying patterns. As a teacher, you will need to carefully observe all children for signs of possible learning disabilities. Remember, there are marked differences in young children.

Likewise, there are marked differences within a normal range of development. You may find that children who have disabilities in one area of development are developing normally in other areas.

## Attention Deficit Disorder

Five to ten percent of school-age children have trouble focusing and staying on task. They are easily distracted. These children have an *attention deficit disorder (ADD)*. Many children with this disorder are also overactive, restless, and impulsive. This condition is called *attention deficit hyperactivity disorder (ADHD)*. Often such children become hostile and fail to follow classroom limits.

Attention deficit hyperactivity disorder affects more boys than girls. For every girl, there are five boys affected. The cause of ADHD is not known. However, children identified as having ADHD are usually treated with drugs that have a calming effect. Many of these children also receive behavior therapy.

# Integrating Children with Special Needs

The number of children with special needs who can be accommodated in a center classroom varies. Several factors must be considered: the teachers' training and experience, the ratio of adults to children, and the specific needs of the children.

Regardless of a child's needs, he or she should be grouped with others based on developmental level, not age. This requires careful observation of the child before grouping.

It is important for children with special needs to enjoy the center, 30-14. Some of these children have not had a full range of home and neighborhood experiences. Others receive painful medical treatment. For these children, the center will provide a chance for companionship and education.

At times, to meet the individual needs of the children properly, you must ask for help from a specialist. For example, if a child has a speech problem, a speech therapist can be most valuable. The therapist can also help you plan helpful activities for the child.

If the parent does not remain with a child on a first visit, provide the parent(s) with feedback on the progress of that time. Parents will be most interested in their child's adjustment to the school setting. Some teachers make a habit of

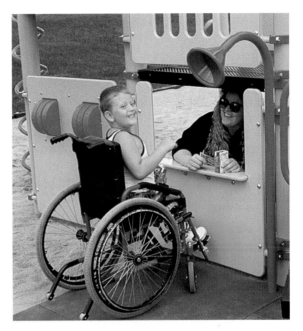

30-14 Encouraging a child with special needs to try new experiences may help the child enjoy being at the center.

either verbally sharing some positive experiences or writing a short note each day during the child's first week or two.

The children in your classroom should be prepared for a child with special needs. Explain any changes that will need to be made in the classroom. As you talk to the children, be positive and focus on strengths. This will help your group of children focus on positive expectations.

Inform the other children about this child. Some children are afraid of children with special needs. They fear the disorder or illness is contagious. Create an open climate in which children are free to ask questions and discuss differences, 30-15. The older preschooler should be encouraged to educate classmates about his or her disability. Sometimes children's parents influence their attitude toward a classmate who has a disablity. Respond to parent's concerns or fears while maintaining the right to privacy of the child with special needs.

Develop a few simple rules for classroom behavior. Stress to the children that the child with special needs should be encouraged to be independent. Young children may want to be overly helpful. This type of behavior can cause dependence and prevent a child from developing to his

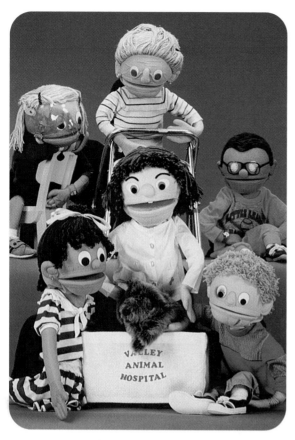

30-15  Puppets that represent people with disabilities may help prepare children for classmates with special needs.

Remember that parents are the primary teachers of their children. Therefore, it is vital that parents take part in planning useful, proper learning experiences. Parents should always be involved in planning for the child's individual needs, as well as planning for complementary opportunities in the home.

## Gifted Children

No one had prepared Yvonne Libby, an early childhood teacher, for all the children she would meet in her first teaching position. Thad, a two-year-old child enrolled in the program, had taught himself to read. By 10 months of age, this same child had spoken in complete sentences. Thad is a minority in Ms. Libby's classroom. He is a child who is gifted, and he needs help.

Often, gifted children's unique educational needs are neglected in traditional education. They often spend time doing things they already know. Only a small number receive instruction at the appropriate level for their needs or abilities. These children need programs and services dif-

or her fullest potential. As children become more independent, they feel better about themselves.

As a teacher, your attitude toward the child with special needs will set the classroom tone. To make yourself feel comfortable, study the disorder or illness  before the child begins at the center, 30-16. If the child is already enrolled and the condition has just become known, learn as much as you can about it. This will help lessen any fears that you may have.

After you have learned about the disorder, arrange to have the child visit the classroom for a short period of time. This visit will reduce the fears of the child, the other children in the classroom, and perhaps the parents.

Parents of the child with special needs may wish to remain with the child for the first, brief visit. This practice usually reduces the separation anxiety the child and parents may feel.

30-16  You will feel more comfortable working with a child with special needs if you study the need in advance.

ferent from those provided in the average classroom. This is vital since gifted children's skills vary more than other groups with special needs.

## Giftedness

**Giftedness** can be defined in many ways. Traditionally, giftedness was based only on intelligence quotient scores (IQ). Today scholars argue that there are many forms of giftedness.

People who are gifted can be defined as having exceptional skill in one or more of six areas:

- creative or productive thinking
- general intellectual ability
- leadership ability
- psychomotor ability
- specific academic aptitude
- visual or performing arts

About three to five percent of young children could be gifted. These children may become political leaders, artists, dancers, and scientists. These children need to be identified so they can receive the education they require.

## Identification

Identifying children who are gifted is difficult. No single test, checklist, or observation will point out all types of giftedness. During the preschool years, observations are commonly made by parents and teachers.

A child's parents are often most familiar with his or her development, interests, and abilities. Because of this, they may be better able to identify their children as gifted.

Teachers are more aware of how the child's behavior compares with that of his or her peers. However, identification of children who are gifted by the teacher is not always the best method. Studies found that teachers who identified giftedness chose about one-third of the children incorrectly. In addition, over half the children who are actually gifted were not identified by their teachers.

There are certain characteristics that can be used to identify the gifted. Many children who are gifted have a constant curiosity about many subjects. Their social and emotional behavior equals or exceeds that of children the same age. They also are more independent and motivated. Chart 30-17 lists other characteristics of children who are gifted.

### Characteristics of Children Who Are Gifted

- Early speech
- Advanced vocabulary for age
- Keen observation skills: see more on field trips, in films, or pictures than other children
- Attention span is unusually long for age
- Inquisitive nature: constantly asking questions
- Flexible: adapt easily to new situations
- Persistent
- Responsible for age
- Self-critical
- Strive toward perfection
- Good memory
- Aware of other's feelings

30-17 Early identification of children who are gifted will promote further growth.

## Teaching Suggestions

The needs of a preschool child who is gifted can be met by including acceleration and enrichment in the program. **Acceleration** is a process in which a gifted child is assigned to a class with older children. The objective is to move the child through activities at a faster pace than children with average ability. After spending a year with older children, the child who is gifted may be ready for even older children.

In **enrichment** the range and depth of experiences is broadened to provide the child with a special curriculum. This process will help the child identify areas of interests.

Children who are gifted often receive enrichment through individual or small group instruction. You or a volunteer may use audiovisual materials, games, and field trips to promote learning. The key to a useful program for these children is to build educational experiences around student interests.

Provide open-ended learning activities for creative children. They prefer loosely structured activities that give them the chance to express ideas and inquire and discover on their own, 30-18.

Children who are gifted in a certain area, such as reading, should have instruction designed to match their skills. They should be provided a variety of books related to their special interests. It also helps to have an adult who will take the time to listen to the child read and tell the child about the story.

Many small group activities should be planned to build leadership skills. These activities provide children with opportunities to learn to plan, organize, and make decisions.

As a teacher of children who are gifted, you need to understand the problems these children face. These children tend to be self-critical. As a result, they tend to be too hard on themselves. To help them, you will need to provide guidance so they learn to accept failure.

Sometimes, because of a critical nature, a child who is gifted will not involve himself or herself with other children. You will need to help the child learn to be considerate of others. This will help improve his or her social skills.

30-18 During the science theme *Plants and Flowers,* a teacher could extend learning for a gifted child by asking her to videotape plants and flowers around the building during outdoor play time.

## Summary

All children, including those with special needs, are entitled by law to an appropriate education. As a result, you may have children with special needs in your center.

Children with special needs require Individualized Education Plans. As a teacher, you will need to know how to identify a child with special needs. You then must work to provide the child the most effective education possible. Teachers must be able to accommodate special needs of children with hearing, speaking, language, vision, physical, health, cognitive, and behavioral disorders. These children must be integrated into a typical program. Teachers must also be able to identify and meet the needs of children who are gifted.

## Review and Reflect

1. _____ needs are the most common special needs.

2. _____ is the term used to refer to a regular educational setting in which children with and without special needs are integrated.

3. Each Individualized Education Plan needs six components. Name them.

4. A child who is _____ impaired can often be identified by his or her lack of vocabulary and overall delays in language development compared to nondisabled children.

5. What four consonants are easiest for children to pronounce?

6. Articulation problems usually take the form of _____, _____, and _____ of vowels or consonants or both.

7. _____ is the result of a muscle imbalance caused by disuse of the eye.

8. What is the difference between nearsightedness and farsightedness?

9. What actions might you need to take if a child with cerebral palsy is enrolled in your program?

10. _____ is a condition in which the bones of the spine fail to grow together.

11. List four teaching suggestions for working with children who are physically disabled.

12. The most common health problem of young children is _____.

13. _____ is a genetic blood disease.

14. List six characteristics of a child who is gifted.

15. List four signs of a possible learning disability.

## Apply and Explore

1. Interview a speech therapist about stuttering.

2. Discuss the disadvantages of labeling children's special needs.

3. List items found in a child care center that may cause an allergic reaction in children.

4. Contact your state's Department of Education. Request information on early childhood programs for children with special needs.

5. Go to the Web site for the National Information Center for Children and Youth with Disabilities at NICHCY.org. Click on your state to obtain the *State Resource Sheets*.   **C**

6 Check the Web site for the National Association of Gifted Children (nagc.org) for information on teaching gifted children.   **C**

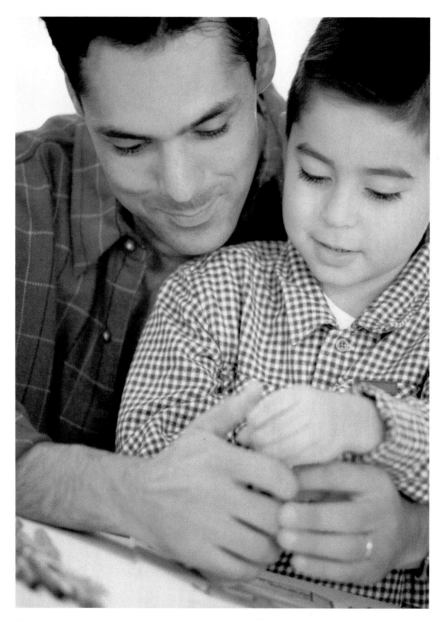

Parent involvement is crucial to the success of any child care program.

# Chapter 31

# Parent Involvement

After studying this chapter, you will be able to

- list objectives for parent involvement.
- cite advantages and disadvantages of various methods for involving parents in the center.
- describe the importance of a positive caregiver/family alliance.
- design a center newsletter.
- write a letter to parents.
- plan, conduct, and follow up on a parent-teacher conference.
- explain how to conduct a discussion group.
- describe the process of recruiting and orientating parent volunteers.

## Terms to Know

parent involvement
newsletters
letters
daily news flash
traveling backpack
problem-solving file
sunshine calls
theme bags

Frequent, two-way communication between teachers and parents creates an environment that welcomes families. The teacher-parent relationship is vital. Parents need caregivers for reassurance and emotional support. Caregivers need to learn from family members to create an environment that reflects the children's home experience. To do this, they need to learn the parenting beliefs and culture of the family. This can only occur by building partnerships between child care teachers and parents.

**Parent involvement** refers to patterns of participation in educational programs by parents. There is no one model of parent-program interaction. Parent involvement activities may include assisting in the classroom, helping with fund-raising activities, home teaching, supplying classroom resources, and attending parent education classes. Parent involvement can be the key factor in the success of a program, 31-1.

It is unfortunate, then, that little information has been written about the parent-teacher relationship. At times, staff and parents fail to view each other positively. Historically, teachers have neglected to contact parents to praise the child's efforts and accomplishments. Likewise, parents have neglected to express their appreciation of the teachers' roles.

The relationship between parents and teachers needs to be one of mutual support and learning. Often, teachers are surprised to learn that parents want unhurried time to experience relating with them. Parents want to learn more about their children's experiences, interests, and development. They may also want advice on how to work with their children at home. To provide this support, teachers and parents need to become partners in teaching young children.

As a teacher, you will need to build positive relationships with parents. To do this, set aside time to communicate with parents, particularly at the beginning or end of the day. During these causal conversations, share your observations and knowledge of early development behaviors. Parents also enjoy learning of their children's preferences and ways of responding to people and things. Communicate a child's strengths to the parents. Parents will then be more accepting when you have to share a child's weaknesses.

Always welcome parents to the center. Whenever possible, include them in program functions. Parents may be observers, resource people, volunteers, or guests at special celebrations. They can share a hobby or interest, as well as ethnic traditions. Studies show that teachers who are confident of their skills and abilities are more inclined to include parents in program functions. Likewise, studies show that good relationships with parents affect a teacher's feelings of self-esteem and competence as a teacher.

## Objectives

The purpose of parent involvement is to promote an exchange of ideas and information. Parents can gain by

- developing an understanding of child growth and development
- gaining confidence in their parenting roles
- learning about their children's experiences at the center
- understanding their children by observing other children
- learning new ways of positively interacting with children, 31-2
- becoming informed about community resources
- fostering the children's and parent's ability to interact with each other
- extending learning from the center into the home
- understanding how a partnership between center and home can promote the children's development

31-1 A parent's involvement in a child's school program reaps many benefits for both child and parent.

31-2 Being exposed to other parents and children means adults can find new ways to work with children.

Parent involvement can be encouraged using several methods. Some of these include written communication, class videos, parent-teacher conferences, and discussion groups. When parents see how their involvement can benefit their children, they are more likely to participate.

# Written Communication

Three popular forms of written communication are newsletters, letters, and daily news flashes. **Newsletters** most often include information concerning a variety of subjects. They are shared on a regular basis. **Letters** most often address only one subject and are sent out as needed. A **daily news flash** contains bits of news that parents can discuss with their children. These forms of communication are often written or printed on paper. However, e-mail is also an option that parents and teachers can use for effective communication.

Written communications are popular for one important reason. These forms of communication require less time and energy for the teacher than meetings or multiple telephone calls. If a letter is sent out regarding an upcoming event, the teacher need only compose one letter and then print copies of that letter for all parents.

Parents also like written communication for the same reason. A newsletter can be read over a weekend, during lunch hour, or while commuting. This saves parents time and energy, also.

Use the active, not passive, voice when you write newsletters. The active voice states the subject did something. The passive voice says the subject was acted upon. For example, the active voice would say "Reza read books and painted pictures." The passive voice would say "Reading books and painting pictures were Reza's main activities."

Keep your communications short, clear, and simple for all parents. Short messages are appreciated by busy parents. Simple, clear writing prevents misinterpretation of the message.

## Newsletters

A newsletter serves as a link between home and center. In most centers, the newsletter is produced and sent out on a regular basis, 31-3. A center might send out newsletters on the first Monday of each month. Other centers, depending on budgets and resources, might send out newsletters on a biweekly basis. If most parents have e-mail accounts, programs can send newsletters by e-mail to lower their costs.

A newsletter may include the following:
- review of special activities
- special activities for children to do in the home
- guidance tips
- upcoming special events at the center
- short articles of interest
- summaries of books or articles related to parenting
- nutritious recipes
- child development information
- a want-ad section
- a help-wanted section asking for parent volunteers

31-3  A newsletter can be written quickly using a computer.

- upcoming community events of interest to young children and their families
- a "meet the staff" section
- recognition for parent contributions
- a parent exchange section
- reminders of center policies

The design of a newsletter can also allow for a blank section. This section can be used by the teacher to write a brief, personal note. This should be a positive note about the child. For instance, a teacher may write, "I'm so pleased with James; he has learned how to tie his shoes."

---

Dear Parents,

Our curricular emphasis next week is "Eating Well: Foods for Good Health." This will be a continuation of our Self-Awareness unit. We have previously explored how our bodies work and the importance of exercise.

The children will be involved in a wide variety of experiences. We will play "fruit basket upset," make collages of healthy foods that are good for us, play "grocery store," participate in having a "pickle party," paint with onions and potatoes, and enjoy tasting a variety of fruits. Thursday will be a very special day—our trip to Connell's Orchard! The children will watch apples being washed, dried, sorted, bagged, and boxed. We will taste "Connell Reds" and drink some delicious apple cider. After the trip, we will write a language experience chart.

**Center Activities**

Our learning experiences will focus on "Foods for Good Health." Activities will include

- preparing and eating mini-pizzas (with smiley faces of pepperoni and green peppers)
- creating mosaics of eggshells
- having a play restaurant in our dramatic play area
- acting out a "Good Breakfast" version of *The Three Bears* (we heard it last week)
- making applesauce
- mixing colors with eyedroppers
- reading "Bread and Jam for Frances"

**At-Home Activities**

Activities you can do at home to reinforce the concepts learned at the center include

- visiting a grocery store, identifying foods in the Food Guide Pyramid for Young Children: grains; vegetables; fruits; meats; milks; and fats and sweets
- looking through old magazines, cutting out pictures, and making a collage of "Good Foods" for the whole family
- reading labels with your child, especially focusing on fat and sugar (in their many forms) content within certain foods
- encouraging your child to try new foods (you can, too)
- allowing your child to help in the kitchen
- involving your child in planning what to eat for a meal

Here's to healthy eating!

Sincerely,

Miss Judy

31-4 Use detailed, descriptive language when writing a parent letter. It is an inexpensive way to keep all parents informed.

Another section could also be provided for parents. After reading the newsletter, the parents might write their comments and/or thoughts. Perhaps they could respond to the newsletter or submit ideas or information for future issues. This way, the newsletter can be a two-way communication tool.

## Letters

Letters are another useful written communication tool. Letters can be used to touch base with one parent or an entire group of parents. Letters are often one page long and sent as needed. Parent letters can serve as a supplement to newsletters.

The first letter sent to parents should introduce the teachers and staff. This letter can also address classroom goals, rules, and expectations. The first letter should also welcome parents to observe and/or take part in center activities.

After the first letter, subsequent letters should include the current theme. Special center activities should be noted, along with the goals. New songs and fingerplays should be written out with the accompanying music or actions that go with them. Field trip sites, dates, and times should be included. Parents should also be thanked for any favors. Home learning activities for the parents to do with their child should be shared. Include with these activities a rationale for their use. This will make parents feel involved in their child's education. An example of a parent letter is shown in 31-4.

At times, you may choose to send home a special letter during the week. This letter should outline something special the children did on a special day. It may be an event, such as a field trip, or an activity within the classroom, 31-5. This letter can promote a learning experience between parents and children.

## Daily News Flash

Parents and teachers may be too busy for daily in-depth, face-to-face communication. A daily news flash can be an effective tool for communicating with parents. The flash may contain news about special occasions or interesting events such as the following:

- We made blueberry muffins today.
- Erica lost her tooth today during lunch.
- Mrs. Huth is the new center cook.
- Henry is the name of the center's pet gerbil.
- Toby has a new brother named Ivan.

The daily news flash may be posted at the center's main entrance, on a classroom door, or on a bulletin board. Some teachers even use a computer screen to share this information on a daily basis. Others have been successful in videotaping classroom experiences and sharing them using a television monitor.

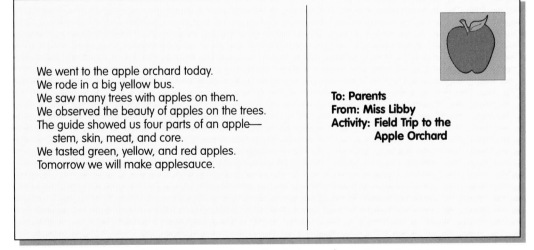

We went to the apple orchard today.
We rode in a big yellow bus.
We saw many trees with apples on them.
We observed the beauty of apples on the trees.
The guide showed us four parts of an apple—
    stem, skin, meat, and core.
We tasted green, yellow, and red apples.
Tomorrow we will make applesauce.

To: Parents
From: Miss Libby
Activity: Field Trip to the
    Apple Orchard

31-5  This letter is intended to promote discussion between parents and children.

## Class Videos

Prepare videos of the children involved in activities that can be checked out and shared with families. You may want to tape special days such as birthdays and other holiday celebrations. Tapes of favorite fingerplays and stories can also be interesting. Parents enjoy tapes of children participating in theme-related activities. Tape them in the dramatic play area acting out stories, building with blocks, preparing foods, and experimenting with creative media.

## Parent-Teacher Conferences

Parent-teacher conferences are one way to involve parents in their children's center program. Conferences help parents and teachers understand the children. Parents will share what children are like at home. Teachers will share what children are like at the center. When these two viewpoints are shared, everyone gains, especially the children, 31-6. Plans can then be made to better meet the needs of the children.

Parent-teacher conferences can be a way to bridge a culture gap between home and center. Parents from other cultures may be unfamiliar with the American approach to early childhood education. They may not understand what is expected of their children or how to help the children succeed. To help these parents, teachers can explain the program goals, schedule, and competencies the children will gain. Parents can explain how their culture views the role of early childhood education. Teachers can use this information to better understand the family and make learning experiences more culturally relevant for the children.

There are three phases to parent-teacher conferences. The first phase is planning. The second phase is the individual conference. The final phase is the follow-up.

### Planning

Planning includes setting basic rules that will help you work successfully with the parents. Before the conference, spend time planning. A good conference does not just happen. It needs to be carefully planned if you are to win the respect

31-6 Through parent-teacher conferences, the parent can gain insight into how best to work with a child at home.

of the parents. The responsibility for the success of the conference lies largely on you as the teacher.

Conferences provide an opportunity to review each child's progress. This time should provide an objective review of the child's total development. Begin the planning phase by gathering developmental data on the child. Gather records on the child's emotional, social, cognitive, and physical development. This information can most often be obtained from developmental checklists and from anecdotal records.

Some teachers use planning sheets to prepare for conferences. After reviewing all anecdotal records and developmental records, this information is recorded on the planning sheet. Included are the following:

- daily routines
- types of play
- activity preferences
- fine motor skills
- gross motor skills
- social-emotional development
- relationships with children and adults
- cognitive development
- language development

- eating habits
- sleeping habits

The planning sheet is divided into sections. For instance, one section might cover these routines: dressing, cleanup, rest patterns, eating, and toileting, 31-7.

Be prepared to share children's portfolios with their parents. Begin by collecting notes, developmental assessments, and observations. Then continue by collecting some of the children's artwork to share with the parents. Make sure that the child's name and date are on each piece. Photographs, tape recordings, and notes can also be useful. If developmentally appropriate, ask each child to tell you a story about a picture. Record the story as the child speaks.

Video recordings are also becoming popular for use in parent-teacher conferences. A week or two before a conference, videotape each child engaging in classroom activities. Allow three to five minutes per child. Review the tape before the conference, and note the start and stop numbers for each child.

## Parent Availability

A brief newsletter can be sent home explaining the purpose of the parent-teacher conference. Include in the newsletter the date(s) the conferences will be held.

These dates should accommodate parents' schedules whenever possible. Before you begin scheduling parents for specific time slots, ask about their availability on the scheduled date(s).

Try to schedule conferences for the times parents find most convenient. Your teaching schedule may also make it difficult to find times for conferences. You might try scheduling conferences

- during nap time (teachers can alternate conferences and supervising nap time)
- before or after program hours
- by hiring a substitute teacher for one day each month
- by hiring a substitute teacher for lunchtime if working parents can come at this time
- by dismissing center activities for a day every two to three months (this may not be a desirable option if parents cannot find alternate care)

Generally, each conference should last about half an hour. Allot 10 minutes between conferences. This will give you a chance to record any needed information. It will also provide time if a conference runs longer than planned. If families have two or more children at the center, it is considerate to schedule consecutive conferences. When evening conferences are scheduled, provide child care for the children.

Another option is to schedule parent-teacher conferences in the family's home. Dual-worker or single-parent families may find this appointment most convenient. Teachers can learn more about the child's home environment from this visit. This scheduling is most costly because it involves time and expense for the teacher to travel to the homes. As a result, not many centers offer this alternative.

A scheduled home visit can be valuable for the teacher. Seeing the child's home environment can provide a better understanding of the child. The teacher can observe parent-child interactions as well as the home environment.

## First Impressions

The first impression you make with children's parents is important. Be prepared. Have your notes outlined, including what you would like to discuss. Use your notes during the conference. This will show the parents you are well prepared.

As you think through the conference, keep in mind you will set the tone for it. If you are nervous and anxious, parents will likely feel the

---

**Routines**

Dressing:
_____ needs   _____ some   _____ much help
no help

Cleanup:
_____ accepts   _____ helpful   _____ needs
encouragement

Nap time:
_____ accepts   _____ resists

Eating:
_____ good   _____ fair   _____ finicky eater

Toileting needs:
_____ needs   _____ some   _____ much help
no help

31-7 If you use a planning sheet, you may wish to divide notes into sections.

same way. If you are calm, parents will likely be calm, too. Your goal is to set the proper tone for a successful meeting.

### Questions

You may ask parents questions during the conference to help them think. For instance, invite them to share how their children act at home and what their children's interests are. It is best to plan your questions before the meeting.

Ask open-ended questions if you want more than a yes or no answer. The "w" questions are many times the most successful. These include why, what, how, when, and where. Make sure to provide parents opportunities to share and ask questions.

### The Setting

The conference setting can greatly influence success. Find an area in the center that is private. No interruptions should occur during the conference. To ensure this, place a sign on the door that

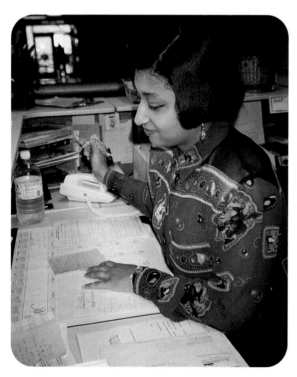

31-8 Many parents will sign up eagerly for parent-teacher conferences. For others, a phone call might be necessary to set up an appointment.

states a parent-teacher conference is in session and must not be interrupted. If the conference is scheduled in an office, take the telephone off the hook or arrange for messages to be taken.

When an office is used, set chairs in a grouping that will help create a feeling of a partnership. Likewise, avoid sitting behind a desk. This places you in the position of authority. This will decrease the feeling of a partnership.

## The Conference

Always begin and end the conference with a positive comment. Parents always enjoy hearing something positive about their child. As you share the comment, try to be relaxed. If you are tense, the parents will be aware of it.

Avoid making general statements. "Tommy is doing fine" or "Jodi is doing well in school" does not give parents much information. Rather, be specific. For instance, you might say, "Travis has really improved in the area of routines. He no longer needs assistance with his clothing when preparing to go outside. At transition time, he takes care of his personal needs in the bathroom. At nap time, he accepts the center's rest pattern. Likewise, he no longer needs encouragement to help during cleanup. In fact, I am so pleased, for he is even encouraging other children to assist."

Watch how you word your comments. As you speak, put yourself in the parents' place. Try to imagine the effects of your remarks. You must evaluate the child's progress without being critical. To do this, always try to use a positive expression. See 31-9.

During the meeting, watch for signs of emotion. These signs may include gestures, changes in tone of voice, or expression. If the parent appears uncomfortable, provide reassurance that all information will be kept confidential.

### Questions Parents Ask

"How is Divina doing?" "Does Kelly behave at the center?" "Is Kris ready for kindergarten?" All these questions are common for parents to ask. Each question can have several answers. When planning for the conference, be prepared for these questions. Questions may be phrased differently, but they basically include

- Is my child happy in child care?
- How can I help at home?

| Language Expressions | |
|---|---|
| **Negative Expressions** | **More Positive Expressions** |
| troublemaker ____ | disturbs others at story time |
| below age ____ | performs at his own level |
| lazy ____ | is capable of doing more |
| stubborn ____ | insistent in having his own way |
| mean ____ | finds it difficult to get along with others |
| clumsy ____ | is not physically well coordinated |
| selfish ____ | needs to learn to share with others |
| show-off ____ | tries to get others' attention |

31-9 Practice using positive phrases when talking to others. Such phrases are much more acceptable than negative phrases.

- Does he or she get along with others?
- Does he or she respect others' property rights?
- How long does he or she nap?
- Does he or she eat a nutritious diet?
- Is he or she making progress in all developmental areas?
- With whom does he or she play?
- Does he or she have any special abilities or needs?

Be prepared to answer these questions with positive comments. Instead of labeling a child based on behavior, explain actions using positive expressions.

## Listening

Most people can listen to 400 words per minute but only speak 131 words. Based on this difference, a good listener does not jump ahead of the speaker. Give parents time to finish their stories or thoughts.

While a parent is talking, show interest and alertness. Avoid preparing an answer while listening. The parent's last sentence may be a source of new information. This may put an entirely different slant on what was previously shared.

Never interrupt a parent. Also, avoid quibbling over words. Instead, focus intently on what the parent is trying to say. Also focus on areas of agreement. This will encourage more friendly, open communication from the parent.

## Working with Parents

Some parents are more difficult to work with than others. For example, a timid parent may be speechless at the start of a meeting. To reassure this parent, be friendly. As you speak, provide this parent with several sincere compliments. Second meetings are often much easier for timid parents.

The worried parent always needs reassurance. This parent can often be identified by hand twirling, handkerchief twisting, or finger drumming. If the parent expresses concern regarding the child's developmental progress, provide reassurance. Often parents are unaware of unevenness of a child's development. They may also be unaware of the "spurts" that can occur in a short period of time.

A parent who is egotistical often enters feeling self-confident and smiling. The parent will want to talk about what a wonderful child he or she has and what a wonderful parent he or she is. With this parent, it is very important to remember the ego is a precious possession and to comment on the parent's skills.

The critical parent can be hard to work with if not handled properly. This parent has expert opinions on teaching the children in the center. Be accepting. That is, do not show disapproval or surprise as the parent talks. Never argue with this parent or any other. Arguing only arouses resistance and bad feelings. Arguments will not benefit the child. Successful conferences depend on your relationship with parents.

## Professional Behavior

Always model professional behavior. If a parent makes a negative comment about another teacher, ignore it. Your attitude should always be positive toward your colleagues. Do not bring up or respond to negative comments about other children or parents.

## Ending a Conference

Just as a conference should begin on a positive note, it should also end on one. Summarize major areas that have been discussed. Begin by repeating positive comments made at the beginning of the conference. Note areas that may need attention, including the agreed upon goals and action. Then restate your goals at the center as well as what the parent(s) can do at home. End the conference by again making a constructive, pleasant comment. Let the parents know how appreciative you are of having an opportunity to share their children's progress with them.

Invite the parents to visit the center any time. Thank them for sharing. Stress the importance of shared information and common goals. Then walk them to the door. Leave them with a statement of encouragement or reassurance.

## Follow-Up

The follow-up involves touching base again with the parents to make sure actions agreed on in the conference are being followed. It should also include a report of the progress made since the conference. A parent-teacher conference should allow for sharing of information. Just as parents will learn, so will you, the teacher. Specifically, you may learn answers to the following:

- the child's reaction to the center, including likes and dislikes
- how the child spends time outside the center
- what home responsibilities the child has
- special interests the child has shown at home
- the status of the child's health
- who the child prefers to play with in the home as well as in school

Record conference notes in the child's folder. Make a point of calling or sending a note to parents, sharing any progress the child has made. Some teachers schedule time each week to contact parents. Each week they contact a few parents by phone or with a brief note. Over the course of a month, each parent hears from the teacher regarding his or her child.

# Discussion Groups

Another method for involving parents in their children's education is group discussion. Through discussion, parents become familiar with child growth and development concepts. They also learn to notice some crisis points in the family cycle and learn to understand their own roles better.

When conducting discussions, remember that adults

- need to integrate new information with what they already know
- tend to take errors personally
- prefer self-designed learning experiences
- like straightforward "how-to" approaches
- must be physically comfortable
- learn a great deal from interacting with others
- enjoy learning when many senses are used

Group discussions are useful for studying new ideas. Discussions allow several people to take part. Through discussion, individual thinking is challenged. As the group exchanges experiences during discussion, individuals have the chance to study and review their own experiences. They are made to think through their positions. Chart 31-10 lists techniques for helping parents relax in a discussion group.

Group discussion also has disadvantages. First, it most often takes a long time. Other methods, such as a film or lecture, are generally faster. If the group is not handled properly, the discussion may wander. See 31-11.

## Preparation

Arrange the room so parents can easily talk face to face. A circle or horseshoe arrangement is usually best. Coffee, tea, punch, and/or water should be available for parents when they arrive. If all the parents do not know each other, hand out name tags. These tags should include the child's name under the parent's name. This will allow parents to identify parents of their children's friends. You may also ask parents to introduce themselves before the discussion begins. To encourage the parents to talk, you may want to begin with a short filmstrip or cassette tape addressing the subject to be discussed.

Several problems may arise. Some parents may not feel comfortable taking part. When this happens, ask a question that requires a response. For example, you may ask, "John, how do you feel?" Also, you can build on a previous comment by saying, "John, earlier you said you were

| Techniques to Help Parents Relax |
| --- |
| • Place items of interest on the walls for parents to look at. |
| • Provide refreshments for parents to eat and drink. |
| • Play soft background music. |
| • Provide name tags on which parents can write their name as well as their child's name. |
| • Arrange the chairs in a circle. |
| • Greet parents individually as they enter. |
| • Introduce parents to each other. |

31-10 Parents are not immune to being nervous when visiting the school. Listed here are several methods for helping parents relax prior to a group discussion.

| Advantages and Disadvantages of Discussion |
| --- |
| **Advantages** |
| • Ideas can be carefully studied. |
| • Many people can take part. |
| • Parent educators can note if parents understand the discussion. |
| • People are forced to think through their problems. |
| • Disagreement is clarified or agreement is reached. |
| **Disadvantages** |
| • It is time-consuming. |
| • Parents may pool misinformation. |
| • Parents expecting to be told what to do may dislike this method. |
| • Parents can come to the wrong conclusion. |
| • Tension and emotions may be aroused. |

31-11 Before you decide to schedule a group discussion, study the advantages and disadvantages. Will your concerns be best addressed by such a discussion?

opposed to physical punishment. Why do you think you feel this way?"

Another problem that occurs quite often is that small groups begin debating among themselves. If this happens, you will need to redirect the group's attention by asking them to share their comments with the whole group.

# Other Methods of Involvement

There are many other ways to involve parents in their children's educations. These other methods are not as detailed as meetings and discussion groups. However, they are useful in their own way. These methods include a lending library, traveling backpack, problem-solving file, bulletin boards, sunshine calls, and theme bags.

## Lending Library

A lending library is one way to share parenting information, 31-12. If space is not available for a parent library, a few shelves in the director's office can be used. Current books and magazines that relate to parenting should be included in the library. Available reading materials can be mentioned during daily parent contacts, at conferences, in newsletters, and/or on the parent bulletin board.

## Traveling Backpack

Another method for involving parents in their children's education is the **traveling backpack.** On a rotating basis, the children can choose their favorite books, music cassettes, puzzles, or games. Some teachers even encourage them to include paper and writing tools. When

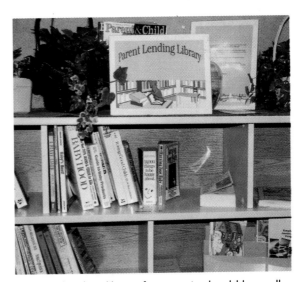

31-12 A lending library for parents should be well-organized and inviting.

the children take home the backpack, they can share these items with their parents.

## Problem-Solving File

Some child care directors use a **problem-solving file** to help parents. This file contains information on problems parents may face. Reading materials such as journal articles and newspaper clippings related to each problem are filed in folders. Topics you may wish to include in a problem-solving file are listed in 31-13. The file can be publicized through newsletters and at parent meetings.

## Bulletin Board

Making a parent bulletin board is a convenient way to communicate with parents. Post meeting dates, newspaper clippings, and other center information, 31-14. Inform parents of local events, library resources, and educational television programs. Offer tips for choosing toys, books, and nutritious snacks. Attach a pocket for

handouts on childhood diseases, immunizations, safety, and child development issues.

Hang the bulletin board in the most visible and well-traveled area of the center. Cover it with paper or attractive fabric. Change the background color often. This alerts parents to updated information on the board.

## Sunshine Calls

Sunshine calls create positive parent-teacher relationships and foster two-way communication. A **sunshine call** is a telephone call made by a teacher to a parent to communicate praise and support for the child. The purpose of this call is to share with parents something outstanding or interesting the child has done recently. It also informs the parents of the teacher's interest in and knowledge of their child. For instance, Mrs. Barr may call Mr. Ross to let him know his child has just learned to ride a tricycle, jump rope, or tie shoelaces.

Some parents have had poor school experiences. When these parents were in school, a call from the teacher usually meant they had done something wrong. Such calls often focused on a social or learning problem. As a result, these parents may be alienated.

| Topics for a Problem-Solving File | |
|---|---|
| Allowance | Language |
| Behavior problems |    development |
| Biting | Lying |
| Child abuse | Nightmares |
| Childhood diseases | Nutrition |
| Children's products | Play |
| Cognitive development | Safety |
| Crying | School readiness |
| Death | Selecting toys |
| Disabilities | Self-esteem |
| Discipline | Separation anxiety |
| Diversity | Sibling relationships |
| Divorce | Single-parent families |
| Emotional | Speech problems |
|    development | Stepfamilies |
| Fine-motor skills | Stress |
| Friendships | Teething |
| Giftedness | Technology |
| Gross-motor skills | Television |
| Guidance | Thumbsucking |
| Handedness | Toileting issues |

31-13 Today, parents are concerned about many topics that affect their children. A problem-solving file is a useful resource.

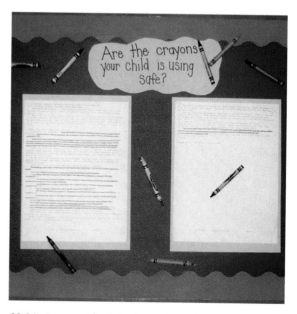

31-14 A parent bulletin board can be set up outside the classroom door to announce topics of interest and messages to parents.

Done well, sunshine calls can help dispel some of these negative attitudes and help build good feelings toward the teacher and center. The goal of sunshine calls should be to build feelings of cooperation.

Sunshine calls are valuable for the parent, teacher, and child. For the teacher and parent, the value of sunshine calls lies in the two-way communication that occurs. For the child, the call is a pleasant event. The teacher has taken a personal interest in him or her. A sunshine call, however, should not replace regularly scheduled parent-teacher conferences.

There are several guidelines that must be followed when using the telephone.

■ Plan the conversation by carefully choosing what to say.

■ Keep the call to about five minutes in length.

■ Begin the conversation by asking the parent if it is a convenient time to talk. If it is not, arrange a time to call back.

■ Put the parent at ease immediately by telling the reason for the call.

■ Share positive statements about the child.

■ Whenever possible, also give the parent a word of praise or thanks.

Some adults are at ease with a telephone conversation. Thus, the conversation may be quite relaxed. Also, many teachers and parents are more at ease on the phone than when they talk face-to-face.

## Theme Bags

For teaching parents how to promote children's learning at home, some teachers use **theme bags** to involve parents. These bags are in the form of a traveling backpack. Included for the parent is a letter of introduction that includes the purpose of the bag along with the contents. The specific value of the activities are described in terms of the child's development. The letter also includes specific suggestions for successfully involving their children in the activities.

Games, puppets, storybooks, songs, and charts can all be included. You may even send home a tape recorder to have the parents record their children's favorite stories. Be creative. Study your theme and brainstorm a list of related activities that can be shared at home. Then determine which ones would be the most successful for parents to introduce.

## Volunteers

Parents want to be involved in their children's education. Many parents feel a need to develop a sense of connection with their child's classroom. This is why teachers and directors need to make an effort to involve parents. One way to do this is through volunteer programs.

Some teachers hesitate to include parents in their program plans. Their objections include:

■ Parents may not have the time needed to devote to volunteer efforts.

■ Parents may criticize the program.

■ Parents may not have effective child guidance skills.

■ Parents may want to take over classroom responsibilities.

■ Children may act up when their parents are present.

■ Parents may discuss confidential information outside of school.

These concerns are all worthwhile. However, most can be addressed by carefully recruiting and then training volunteers. Each volunteer, in turn, will gain a great deal, including

■ personal satisfaction

■ a better understanding of child development and child guidance

■ an understanding of how children learn

■ an understanding of what activities are appropriate for young children

■ an understanding of his or her own child by observing him or her playing with other children

■ an experience of being part of a teaching team

### Recruiting

The best volunteers are those who have an interest in working with young children. Perhaps they would have enjoyed teaching as a profession. Still others are interested in presenting the best experiences to their children. These people are interested in supporting the center and learning more about young children. Many parents have talents or interests that could be useful to your program. A letter that can be used

**To: Parents**
**From: Cindy Mirro, Director**

To help us provide a quality early childhood program, volunteers are needed from time to time. If you are interested, please check those tasks with which you would like to assist.

_____ Repairing books

_____ Repairing toys and equipment

_____ Coordinating and assisting with field trips

_____ Assisting with holiday celebrations

_____ Assisting with public relations activities

_____ Supervising art experiences

_____ Cooking with the children

_____ Newsletter editor

_____ Reading stories to children

_____ Sharing a musical hobby or vocation

_____ Organizing the fall family picnic

_____ Organizing the spring family picnic

_____ Making puppets, doll clothes, and/or dramatic play costumes

_____ Serving on a parent advisory board

_____ Librarian

_____ Secretarial aide

_____ Other (specify):_____

_____

Please return this note to the basket in my office. If you have any questions, please contact me.

_____     _____
Parental Signature                              Date

31-15 Written communication is effective when recruiting volunteers for the center.

to recruit parents is shown in 31-15. Parent volunteers are usually interested in what the job entails and what they need to know. Finally, they are interested in the day or dates they are needed, the time, and for how long.

Parent volunteers must be dependable, fond of children, and healthy. In order to take part in a program, parents need some type of orientation.

## Orientation

To get the most from volunteers, plan a training session. During this session, share staff expectations of them, including classroom limits and state licensing rules. As you discuss these duties, make the parents feel welcome. In addition, prepare a list of guidelines for parent volunteers as shown in 31-16.

If you have not met parents before the orientation session, be prepared to make a good impression. Studies show that first impressions are lasting impressions. The tone for an entire relationship is often set in the first four minutes.

First, begin by making the parents feel comfortable. Welcome them. Offer them chairs. Begin the orientation by explaining how important volunteers are in a center.

Parents feel good when you remember their names. As you meet each parent, pay attention to his or her name. If you do not hear it, ask the person to repeat it. Say the name to yourself. Memory experts claim that by repeating the name to yourself, you will improve recall by 30 percent. See 31-17.

Whenever possible, use the parent's name in conversation. Through repetition, you will engrave the parent's name in your memory. Studies show people recall faces better than names. Another way to recall parents' names is to observe their faces. Concentrate on one trait such as the nose, eyes, or cheekbones. Then associate the names to their faces. By remembering the parents' names, you will make them feel important.

---

### Suggestions for Parent Volunteers

**General participation.** Remember the children always come first. Share your interest in the children in the following ways:
- Provide praise with such statements as "I like your painting," "Thanks for hanging your coat on the hanger," or "You are good at helping with cleanup."
- State your suggestions positively by telling what the child should do. For example, instead of saying "Don't put the puzzle on the floor," tell the child where to place the puzzle. Say "Place the puzzle on the table."
- When talking with the children, get down at their level by squatting or sitting. As the child speaks, give him or her your full attention.
- Speak with other adults only when necessary.
- Avoid doing for a child what he or she can do for himself or herself. That is, always stress independence. Let children put on their own coats, boots, etc. Assist only when absolutely needed, so the children gain independence.
- Avoid discussing the children outside the center.

**At story time**
- Sit in the circle with the children.
- Allow interested children to crawl on your lap.
- Show your interest in the story by listening attentively.
- If you are asked to read, hold the book so all the children can see.

**At the easel**
- Children need to wear a smock while painting.
- Only one child should use each side of the easel at a time.
- Encourage the children to replace the brushes in the proper container. (There is one brush for each container of paint.)
- Show an interest in the children's work, but do not interpret it for them. Do not ask children what they have made.
- After children finish painting, print their names in the upper left-hand corners of their work. Capitalize only the first letter of each name.
- Hang finished paintings on the drying rack.
- At the end of the day, encourage the children to take their artwork home.

**At music time**
- Participate with the children.
- Reinforce the head teacher's actions.
- Show your enjoyment of the music.

31-16 Parent volunteers need guidance when they begin their work at the center.

31-17 Parents and teachers both benefit by wearing name tags. These help everyone learn names more quickly.

## Schedule

Parents will only return to the classroom if they feel needed. Post a parent helper schedule such as the one shown in 31-18. This will help detail your expectations. Also ask volunteers if there are any questions you can answer.

## Thank-You Notes

Send each parent a thank-you note after he or she has volunteered. This gesture will show your appreciation. It will also encourage parents to volunteer again.

| | Parent Volunteer Schedule | | | |
|---|---|---|---|---|
| **Time** | **Teacher—Judy Tenario** | **Teacher—Lisa Sung** | **Parent—Rita Ulesich** | **Parent—Georgia Suski** |
| **Before class** | Set up equipment for special free play activities. Welcome volunteers. | Set up equipment for activities other than dirt-and-water play; special, and paint activities. | Place paper on easels. Put out paint. | Fill water table. |
| **9:00** | Welcome children. Supervise free choice of activities. | Welcome children. Supervise free choice of play activities. | Supervise painting. | Supervise water table. |
| **10:00** | Serve snack. | Supervise handwashing. | Put away easels and join snack table. | Put away dirt-and-water play equipment and help with handwashing. Assist with snack. |
| **10:30** | Help with equipment or story as needed. | Read story. | Assist Judy in putting away equipment. | Assist with story and quiet time. |
| **10:45** | Help with special activity, or on alternate days, introduce it. | Introduce special activity, or on alternate days, help with it. | Assist with special activity. | Help with special activity. |
| **11:00** | Supervise movement activity. | Put away equipment from special activity. | Assist with movement activity. | Assist with movement activity. |
| **11:15– 11:45** | Do dishes and pick up classroom. | Supervise play yard. | Supervise play yard. | Supervise play yard. |

31-18 Have duties outlined for parent volunteers for the days they work.

## Summary

An alliance between teachers and parents is important. Parents play the key role in the physical, emotional, cognitive, and social development of their children. They are the children's primary teachers, as well as partners with the center staff. Involving them in the early childhood program, then, makes sense.

Involve parents in their children's school program by keeping in touch with the parents. Set aside time to communicate with them, particularly at the beginning and end of the day. Conduct parent-teacher conferences during which you can get to know parents one-on-one. Hold discussion groups so all parents can share ideas and get to know one another. Communicate often using these methods: telephone, newsletters, letters, informal contacts, and e-mail (if it is available).

Parents can assume many roles in the classroom as volunteers. With their help, new activities that are impossible without adult assistance can be introduced.

## Review and Reflect

1. What is needed to establish and maintain an alliance between parents and caregivers?

2. List four objectives for involving parents in the center program.

3. Name two points to consider when developing a writing style.

4. Newsletters should _____.
   A. include a review of special classroom activities and upcoming events
   B. be negative in nature
   C. be long and detailed
   D. All of the above.

5. What are the three phases of the parent-teacher conference?

6. True or false. About five minutes should be allowed for each parent-teacher conference.

7. The "w" questions are often the most successful for getting information from parents. What are these questions?

8. What is the purpose of scheduling a 10-minute break after each parent-teacher conference?

9. True or false. Always begin a parent-teacher conference with a positive comment.

10. Rewrite the following negative expressions as more positive expressions.
    A. Selfish.
    B. Show-off.
    C. Lazy.
    D. Clumsy.

11. When talking with a parent, avoid preparing a(n) _____ while listening.

12. During a conference, worried parents always need _____.
    A. to be ignored
    B. refreshments
    C. reassurance
    D. None of the above.

13. True or false. Adults tend to take errors personally.

14. List two advantages of group discussions.

15. Disadvantages of group discussions include _____.
    A. too many people can take part
    B. the discussion may wander
    C. parents will take over the discussion
    D. All of the above.

16. What is the purpose of a lending library?

17. A _____ file contains information on difficulties parents with children may face.

18. A sunshine call _____.
    A. is made by a teacher to a parent
    B. is made to share with parents something positive about their children
    C. can help dispel some negative feelings parents may have about school
    D. All of the above.

19. Who makes the best volunteer?

20. Send each parent a _____ after he or she has volunteered.

## Apply and Explore

1.  Interview several early childhood teachers and find out the strategies they use for developing alliances with parents.

2.  Make a list of questions that parents most often ask teachers. Design answers for these questions based on the contents of this chapter.

3.  Discuss ways you might build a positive relationship with
    A.  a shy parent
    B.  a worried parent
    C.  an angry parent
    D.  an unconcerned parent

4.  Write a parent letter about an upcoming field trip to an ice cream factory. Use the active voice.

5.  Collect parent newsletters from several centers. Analyze their design and content. Then, based on your analysis, design a newsletter for the A-B-C Learning Center.

6.  Interview a child care teacher about parent-teacher conferences. Share your findings in an oral report.

7.  Brainstorm a list of discussion topics for a parents' group.

8.  Identify two advantages for child care teachers who work as partners with parents.

9.  Develop a list of materials that could be included in a portfolio for a four-year-old child.

10.  Role-play parent-teacher conferences with each type of parent described in the chapter.

11.  Review the information provided for parents and people who work with parents on the Web site for the National Parent Information Network (npin.org). **C**

12.  Visit the Web site for the National Coalition for Parent Involvement in Education at ncpie.org to learn more about fostering relationships between home and school. **C**

# Chapter 32

# A Career for You in Child Care

After studying this chapter, you will be able to

- explain how interests, abilities, personal priorities, and family responsibilities affect career choices.
- compile your resume.
- write a cover letter.
- list various methods for seeking employment.
- list questions to ask during an interview.
- prepare a teaching portfolio.
- explain the basic interviewing process.
- describe illegal questions and how to respond to them.
- describe the rights and responsibilities of employees and employers.
- summarize the importance of finding balance among family, work, and community roles.

## Terms to Know

self-assessment

personal priorities

professional priorities

resume

cover letter

hidden job market

networking

teaching portfolio

attitude

confidentiality

role

role strain

Preparing for your future is both rewarding and exciting. Choosing a career and job hunting are important, challenging tasks. To be successful, it must be approached in a thoughtful manner. Successful candidates often treat job hunting as a full-time job. They commit themselves to the process 100 percent. They approach the hunt with a plan.

Many child care teachers have been successful using several types of job searching techniques. One method has been to apply directly to the employer or center director. This contact may be in the form of a request for an application, a visit to the center, or a telephone call. Usually people make these contacts just before their courses to meet state licensing guidelines or early childhood certification are completed.

Answering newspaper ads is one more way to seek employment. Check the want ads on a daily basis. If you notice an appealing position, contact the center director at once. If a telephone number is listed, a call can be made. Many times, positions need to be filled immediately. Therefore, do not waste any time in making a contact.

## Choosing a Career

Choosing your life's work is a challenging responsibility. As you begin the process of selecting a career, you may be thinking, "What do I want to do with my life?" Only a few people seem to know from an early age what career they will pursue. Most people find this a difficult question to answer. It is a decision best made with much care and thought, 32-1. People often begin choosing a career by doing a self-assessment.

**Self-assessment** is the process of examining your interests and abilities, as well as personal and professional priorities. As you consider these factors, you will gain important self-knowledge for use in choosing a career. You will ask yourself many questions, and your answers will help you determine whether a career working with young children is for you.

## Interests

Interests usually play a large role in career choices. For the most part, people seek to prepare themselves for a career they will enjoy. The Chinese philosopher Confucius offered important advice concerning career decisions. He said if you choose a job you love, you will never need to work a day in your life. You will feel fulfilled and believe you are doing something worthwhile.

Determining what work you will enjoy can be challenging. Begin this process by analyzing your interests. Start by asking yourself the following basic questions:

- How do you spend your time? What are your hobbies?
- Do you enjoy learning? Which courses in school have you found most interesting?
- Do you prefer working independently or working with others?

- Do you prefer working with people, information, or objects?
- Which career fields do you find most exciting?

Gaining experience in a career field can help you make or confirm a career decision. For example, volunteering, working part-time, or doing an internship can help you explore early childhood as a career option. As a result of this experience, you might decide you are not suited to be a child care teacher. On the other hand, you may feel more strongly than ever that working with young children is a good career option for you.

You can also assess your interests by learning more about other careers. Research a few careers you are considering. What responsibilities does each job entail? Are these tasks you would enjoy? Interview a professional employed in the field to learn more. You might be able to arrange a job shadowing experience, where you can spend an entire day with an employee at his or her job. This experience can give you an overview of the job duties and rewards.

## Abilities

A second part of self-assessment is analyzing your abilities. Abilities have a direct influence on job performance—you are more likely to succeed in a job you can do well. Having interests and abilities in similar areas is not uncommon. You are more likely to be interested in tasks you are good at, and you may work harder to develop abilities in areas that interest you. It is also possible to have abilities that differ from your interests.

What abilities do you have? Perhaps you are well aware of your abilities. These may be areas in which you have always excelled. Other abilities may seem less obvious. You might discover these abilities through tests given by a guidance or career counselor. Common names for these tests are *aptitude tests* and *skills assessments*. Taking these tests can help you identify careers for which you might be suited.

You can also ask close friends and trusted adults for their insight. They may comment, "You're so good with children," "You relate to people so easily," or "You solve problems well." These comments can help you identify areas of strength.

32-1 Many teens spend a great deal of time reflecting on the future and what careers they will pursue.

Developing a solid foundation of basic skills will help you in any career. This foundation includes skills in human relations, teamwork, leadership, communication (writing, speaking, and listening), computers, mathematics, problem solving, decision making, time management, stress management, and planning. With these basic skills, chances are you will become a successful employee in your chosen career, 32-2.

In addition, you will need some career-specific abilities. These relate more closely to the demands of a particular job. Effective early childhood teachers need the abilities that will help them carry out their responsibilities as described in earlier chapters of this book. Some of these abilities include the following:

- planning developmentally appropriate themes, lessons, activity areas, schedules, and routines
- leading group activities and assisting children in activity areas as needed
- matching guidance and communication techniques to children's developmental ages
- setting and enforcing needed limits for children's health, safety, and healthy development

- providing comfort, nurturance, affection, and effective praise
- offering constant supervision to all children throughout all daily activities
- demonstrating appropriate physical care techniques (such as diapering, feeding, dressing, toileting, and hand washing) to keep children safe and healthy

Abilities needed by professionals in other child-related careers may differ somewhat from those that teachers need. For example, a child care director needs budgeting, recordkeeping, planning, organizing, leading, and supervising abilities. Learning more about particular careers will help you find out what career-specific abilities are needed.

How do the abilities you have now compare to those you will need in your chosen career? You may have many of the needed abilities already, but there may be others you still need to develop. If a career deeply interests you, it may be worthwhile to identify ways to build the needed skills. Taking additional classes to learn more about the subject can help. Ask a teacher, guidance counselor, supervisor, or other trusted adult to help you identify other ways to develop the needed abilities.

## Personal and Professional Priorities

First, you will want to take a look at your **personal priorities**. These are your beliefs, feelings, and ideas about what is important. Personal priorities influence your decisions and actions. Each person is an individual with unique thoughts, feelings, experiences, and beliefs. These differences are often reflected in the priorities people hold. For example, some people desire popularity, wealth, and material possessions most. Others find education, career, family life, or friendships more meaningful. Each person can value any combination of priorities in any order of importance. That is what makes personal priorities truly personal.

As you examine your personal priorities, you will better understand the importance of various people, objects, and ideas in your life. Choosing a career that aligns with your personal priorities greatly increases your chances of happiness and career success. Such a career will

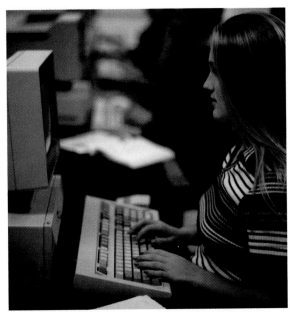

32-2 Developing your computer skills will make you a more valuable employee in almost any career you choose.

enhance your life by allowing you to focus on what matters most to you.

Closely related to personal priorities are **professional priorities**. These are global aspects of work that are important to a person's satisfaction. Which of the following are professional priorities for you?

- helping or providing service to others
- feeling a sense of accomplishment
- working as a team member
- having a leadership role
- gaining recognition
- earning a high salary
- being competitive
- working independently
- making a contribution to society through your work

In addition to these professional priorities, what others can you identify? When you think of a fulfilling career, what characteristics come to mind? List your professional priorities on a sheet of paper. Compare your list to those commonly found among workers in your chosen career field. Figure 32-3 shows professional priorities commonly shared by successful child care teachers.

Professionals in child-related careers other than teaching may have professional priorities

---

**Professional Priorities of Child Care Teachers**

Successful child care teachers commonly share the following professional priorities:

- **Independence**: working on their own
- **Creativity**: trying out their own ideas
- **Responsibility**: making their own decisions and solving problems
- **Achievement**: gaining a feeling of accomplishment
- **Relationships**: providing service to others and working with coworkers in a friendly noncompetitive environment
- **Sharing** knowledge: teaching and guiding young children to learn new concepts

32-3 How do your professional priorities compare to those of early childhood teachers?

---

that differ somewhat. For example, successful directors are likely to list managing, organizing, and leading among their priorities.

Examining your personal and professional priorities will help you determine whether working with young children will be a satisfying career choice for you. This part of self-assessment can also help you narrow the objective *to work with young children* into a more specific career goal. With a specific career in mind, you can seek the needed education, training, and experiences to qualify you to work in that career.

# Resumes

To prepare for your job search, first prepare a resume. A **resume** is a brief summary of your qualifications, skills, and experience. It should be tailored to the type of job for which you're applying. The purpose of a resume is to secure an interview and/or inform a potential employer of your qualifications and experience. If your resume is effective, you will receive invitations to interview from potential employers.

Resumes also serve many other purposes. First, a resume may serve as your own self-inventory. Having an objective list of your background and skills can be quite helpful when looking for a job. It can also serve as a starting point in an interview. A well-written resume will give the employer information on which to base the interview. After the interview, your resume will help the employer recall your experiences as well as the interview.

## Preparing a Resume

A well-prepared resume plays an important role in your job search. First, it instantly creates a favorable impression of you. Second, it creates a desire on the part of the employer to meet you. In many cases, it is your ticket to a job interview.

All resumes contain key information about the applicant: name, current address, and telephone number are always included. If you are applying for jobs outside your hometown, include the area code with your telephone number.

Remember, your resume represents you. Be accurate and neat. Use simple words and write in a clear, concise manner. Include your educational background, paid and volunteer work experience, professional activities, and other qualifications. Organize the experience section so your strongest experience comes first even if it was not the most recent. Always be descriptive. For instance, if you want to share that you are a hard worker, create a statement that will deliver that message: "Worked 20 hours per week during the past two semesters."

Using a resume as a tool, your goal should be to present yourself as an active, well-rounded person. The resume should have an easy-to-read format. An example of a resume is shown in 32-4.

## Helpful Hints

Directors will quickly look at a resume to find out if you have enough educational background and experience to qualify for the position. If your experience appears to meet the requirements of the job description, the resume is read more closely. At this time, most employers will look for gaps in your employment dates, the amount of space given to earlier jobs, and the emphasis on education.

Are there gaps in your job history? These gaps may make directors wary of problems in your job history. They may signal that you were unemployed between jobs. You may choose to leave out a job on your resume because it does not apply to the position you seek. Perhaps you were unemployed for a legitimate reason, such as returning to school. Be sure to explain such gaps in your cover letter.

When you give the time of your employment, be sure to specify the month and year of the starting and ending date of each job. Listing only years can be confusing to directors. Such a listing can also give the impression that gaps in employment are being concealed. Be honest in your resume. Center directors are experienced at dissecting resumes. Avoid omitting facts.

A good resume should reflect progress in a career over the years. Also, directors are more interested in an applicant's most recent accomplishments. Therefore, the most recent job experience should be emphasized. Some resume writers devote more space to an earlier teaching position. This usually means one of two things. It may simply be due to poor judgment. It could mean the applicant has updated

an old resume by simply adding a few lines about the new job. Overall, these errors convey a lack of ambition and/or poor planning on the part of the applicant. These errors may not always rule out an applicant from an interview. However, they do signal that the applicant needs to be closely reviewed during this process.

The director will also review a resume to see if there is too much stress on education and non-job factors. When an applicant has been out of school for several years, the resume should stress work experience. Applicants who stress post-secondary honors may be focusing too much on the past. If the applicant stresses more non-job factors, this may indicate where his or her real interests lie.

Students who are recent graduates have a special challenge. How can you stress work experience if you have little or none? Do not overlook any previous unpaid work experience. Any practice teaching or volunteer work in your field of study can be included on your resume. Any involvement in professional organizations related to your field of study such as an affiliate of the National Association for the Education of Young Children (NAEYC) may also be included. You may wish to explain any leadership roles you assumed, or any skills you developed that will help you on the job.

Poor computer or writing skills and grammatical errors will always reflect badly on the applicant. Basic mistakes may cripple your job search. In fact, some highly qualified applicants have failed to obtain interviews because of poor writing skills. It is always wise to ask a friend who has outstanding writing skills to proofread any resumes before you send them to an employer.

## Cover Letters

A **cover letter** is a letter of introduction that is usually included when sending a resume. The main purposes of the letter are to capture the employer's attention and to request an interview. This letter is important. A mistake some job applicants make is putting too little effort into writing the cover letter.

Remember the basics while preparing your cover letter. Follow a business letter format. As

# Sharon Kaminski

*University Address:*
University of Wisconsin-Stout
Tainter Hall
Menomonie, WI 54751
(715) 555-1111

*Home Address:*
109 Liberty Street
Valders, WI 54362
(414) 555-4422

## Education

*University of Wisconsin-Stout*
- Graduating June, 20xx with a Bachelor of Science in Early Childhood Education.
- 3.83 (out of 4.0) cumulative grade point average.
- Dean's List: 20xx-present.

*Valders High School*
- Graduated June, 20xx.
- Activities: member of National Honor Society and school band, and president of women's volleyball team.

## Experiences

*Wee Care Child Care Center,* Atlanta, Georgia, June, 20xx-September, 20xx
- Assisted head teacher with all program activities during the summer session.
- Created new teaching aids for art, science, music, and social studies activities.
- Supervised adult volunteers.

*Course Assistant, Early Childhood Department at University of Wisconsin-Stout,*
September, 20xx-June, 20xx
- Coordinated teacher education resource room: maintained files, ordered materials, and designed room layout.

*Valders Public Schools,* September, 20xx-June, 20xx
- Assisted kindergarten teacher with special activities: coordinated and supervised holiday parties, prepared teaching aids, and maintained classroom centers.

## Activities

*International Relations Council,* University of Wisconsin-Stout
- Delegate to State Model United Nations.

*Dean's Student Advisory Council,* University of Wisconsin-Stout
- Advised Dean on students' activities. Coordinated special school events including Parents Weekend.

*Student Ambassador,* University of Wisconsin-Stout.
- Visited community high schools to recruit students for the University of Wisconsin-Stout.

## Interests

Alpine and cross-country skiing, reading, gourmet cooking.

References available upon request.

32-4 Resumes should be neatly organized and evenly spaced.

with the resume, use proper grammar and punctuation. Write each cover letter separately. Avoid writing one generic cover letter that can be used to apply for any job. This gives the impression you're not interested enough to write a tailored letter. It also fails to stand out to the reader.

Keep in mind no one in the early childhood community is called *Sir, Madam,* or *Whom It May Concern.* Find out the name of the center director or the person responsible for hiring. Address the cover letter to this person.

Your cover letter is an opportunity to "sell yourself" to the employer. The cover letter should not be a summary of your resume. It should convince the person hiring to read and consider your resume.

Keep the cover letter short. A few paragraphs should be enough. Tell how you learned of the opening or how you are familiar with the center. Explain why you want to be considered for the position. Describe your interests, aptitudes, and abilities related to the job. Close by telling the employer what action—for instance, a phone call or interview—you would like him or her to take. Be polite in your request, and thank the person for reviewing your cover letter and resume. Sign the letter *Yours truly,* or *Sincerely,* and your name.

Reread your letter several times for content, typing, and grammatical errors. Have several other people proofread the letter for you, too. In one study, seventy-six percent of recruiters said they would not consider an applicant whose resume contained errors. A mistake could make a poor impression of you. See 32-5.

# Avenues for Seeking Employment

Early childhood job seekers may use a number of methods to find employment. These methods include mailing cover letters with resumes and placing or answering ads in the newspaper. Career fairs and networking provide other opportunities to search for positions. Successful applicants also do not overlook the hidden job market.

Make sure your cover letter and resume are forwarded to the proper person. Find out the name of the individual who is responsible for hiring and address your letter to that person.

## Newspaper Ads and the Internet

Answering newspaper ads and responding to announcements on the Internet can be helpful when looking for work. As a job seeker, make a habit of reading the ads every day, 32-6. Newspaper ads are alphabetized. Ads for child care center staff may be listed under different areas. Therefore, study the entire section. Examples of titles related to child care include child care teacher, infant teacher, toddler teacher, preschool teacher, child care teacher, early childhood teacher, school-age child care teacher, program coordinator, curriculum specialist, and activities director. If you are looking for an administrative position, look closely for descriptions such as director, administrator, or coordinator.

If an ad appeals to you, respond according to the instructions given in the ad. Some ads contain telephone numbers. In this case, do not wait; call right away. Telephone numbers are most often included when a position must be filled as soon as possible.

If a phone number is not given, send your resume with a cover letter to the address or post office box listed.

If an advertisement does not ask for your salary requirements, do not mention them in your letter. By including a salary figure, you could be screened out and not have the chance to interview. Some ads state the exact salary or range they will pay. For instance, an ad might note the exact dollar figure per hour or a range of several thousand dollars. Many times when a range is provided, the ad might state that salary is open "based on experience" or "based on educational background." See 32-7.

### Internet Job Search

Have you ever thought about knocking on doors using the Internet? By using an Internet browser, you can search for a job. Job hunting on the information superhighway can be fun and rewarding. Although you may begin with a goal in mind, chances are you may encounter better contacts than you expected. On the Internet, there are thousands of Web sites that will offer you assistance. A Web site will provide you addresses.

615 Market St.
Menomonie, WI 54362
August 1, 20xx

Alex Briones, Director
Child Development Center
1318 Hillcrest Road
Springfield, MA 56789

Dear Mr. Briones:

While searching for job positions on the Internet, I read your advertisement for a teacher. I am interested in obtaining a position in the child care field and in relocating to Springfield, Massachusetts.

I hold a certificate in early childhood education. My interest in early childhood education as a profession started while I was in middle school. Since then, I have babysat, assisted with the preschool program at my church, and worked in an after-school program in a local center. These experiences convinced me of my interests, skills, and enthusiasm for working with young children.

My resume is enclosed for your consideration. You will see that both my experience and education match the qualifications outlined in your advertisement.

Thank you for considering me for a position in your center. This is exactly the type of opportunity I am seeking. If you would like to schedule an interview or have any questions, please call me at 789-555-5748 or e-mail me at chak@uwstout.edu.

Sincerely,

*Kim Cha*

Kim Cha

32-5 Include a cover letter with your resume when responding to newspaper ads.

Joining a chat room (discussion group) in your field is another way to find a job. Some professional associations sponsor list servers, message boards, and use net news groups.

## Placing Ads

Newspaper ads, ads in professional journals, or ads on the Internet can help you make your availability known. They are quite helpful if you are moving to another area. For example, you may want to work as a child care teacher in New

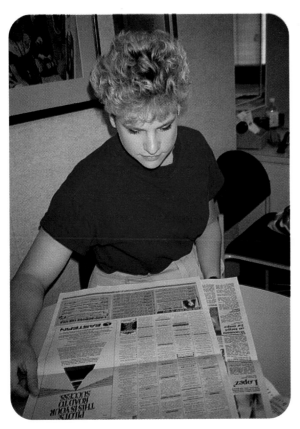

32-6 Many new child care teachers find their first jobs through newspaper ads.

York City after graduation, but you live in Chicago. You could place an ad in the *New York Times* in the positions wanted section of the paper.

Before placing an ad, write, e-mail, or call to find out the cost. The cost of placing an ad varies depending on the city, circulation of the paper, size of the ad, and the number of days it will run. Often, charges are either on a per word or per line basis. Depending on your budget and

Head Teacher at the Sheboygan Early Childhood Center. Applicant must hold a two-year certificate from an accredited institution of higher learning. Salary range from $2,200-$3,000 per month.
Call 1-414-555-4598 or e-mail: eccenter@sheboygan.edu

32-7 Newspaper ads give a short summary of the open position.

the costs of advertising, you may have to limit the length of your ad.

Placing a position wanted ad is a passive job search technique. It requires employers to seek you out. However, most employers will actively pursue only the most qualified candidates. Therefore, this method works best for those people who are experienced. It is best to also use active job search techniques.

## College or School Placement Offices

Most early childhood certificate and degree programs provide a placement service. The purpose of this service is to find positions for graduates. Placement offices are usually located on campus. Employers are encouraged to call in, send, or e-mail job information for the office to post, 32-8. Likewise, employers are given help finding qualified graduates when they contact the office.

As a student, you will be asked to prepare a file concerning yourself. This file may be on paper or on a computer disk. Regardless of the format used, this file will usually include a standard form prepared by the college or school placement service. The form lists your current address, schools attended, degree earned, and past work experiences. In addition, your file will contain your resume and letters of recommendation from faculty and/or previous employers.

## The Hidden Job Market

Many job candidates are most successful when they focus their efforts on the **hidden job market**. These are jobs advertised informally through personal contacts. Many child care positions are never listed in help wanted ads, in early childhood journals, or with placement offices. Rather, these jobs are filled through word of mouth. To find out about such openings, you as a job seeker should contact center directors personally. This can be done through a letter, a telephone call, or e-mail. Some candidates have met with success by arranging a visit to the center and then asking about job openings. Even if no position is open at the time of the visit, some applicants have been called later when jobs become available.

---

**Position:**
Head Teacher, Child Care Program
Full-Time Position
Yearly contract renewal for a maximum of three years.

**Date Available:**
August, 20xx

**Job Responsibilities:**
Head Teacher in child care center. Plan and implement a developmentally appropriate curriculum for three- and four-year-old children. Supervise a teacher's aide and volunteers from a local community college. Assist Director in applying for accreditation. Plan and implement parent meetings, conferences, and related activities.

**Qualifications:**
- B.S. degree in Early Childhood Education is required, graduate work preferred.
- Must be certified to teach preschool in Texas.
- Experience in assessment, curriculum development, and program evaluation.
- Demonstrated excellence in teaching young children for a minimum of three years.
- Demonstrated ability to interact positively with people and work cooperatively with other staff members, parents, students, volunteers, and children.
- Must be able to organize and coordinate activities with volunteers.
- Must be able to motivate children in a creative environment.
- Must be able to demonstrate initiative and continuous professional development.

---

32-8 Notices posted in school placement offices often give a comprehensive summary of the open position.

Get to know early childhood staff workers in the community. One way to do this is to join the local chapter of the NAEYC. When you attend meetings, try to meet as many people as possible. Always let them know of your job search and when you will be available. In addition, become active in the organization. Volunteer for committees. Show the membership you are willing to work and are professionally motivated.

## Networking

**Networking** is a process of building relationships with people who can help you. It is an important skill to develop. Networking is the job-seeker's most powerful tool. Almost 80 percent of positions are found through some type of networking with others.

One way to have your resume considered is to have recommendations from respected people in the field. To find these people, you need to go where they are. Attend meetings of early child-

hood organizations, workshops, conferences, seminars, open houses, job fairs, and center tours. Since networking is a process, it usually takes several contacts to build a relationship. These contacts may be person-to-person meetings, phone conversations, e-mail contacts, voice mail, letters, and notes.

## Maintaining a Filing System

Keep a file of all the centers or schools you have contacted, 32-9. Make a photocopy of each cover letter you send or maintain copies on a computer disk. You may also prepare index cards or a file on your computer for each contact. If you get a call from a director, you should quickly be able to retrieve the information and refresh your memory on the open position. To assist in this process, always keep a record of the school's name, address, telephone number, contact person, and date the contact letter was mailed.

If you have answered an ad, you may want to attach a copy of the ad to your cover letter or index card. When you receive a response (whether negative or positive), record this on your cover letter or index card. Make notes of interviews, thank-you notes, and other contacts on each letter or card as well.

# Preparing for an Interview

Job offers only happen during or after an interview. Interviews are the single most important aspect of a job search. When preparing for an interview, think positively. Picture yourself walking into the interview confident and relaxed. Get in the habit of being enthusiastic. Remember, enthusiasm is catching. It indicates appreciation and interest. Often, if you are enthusiastic, the interviewer will also share this feeling.

Employers want to hire self-directed people with a wide range of skills. They want people who are dependable, enthusiastic, and committed to the child care profession. They also want people who work hard and learn fast. They want people who manage their time well and who look for extra work when their work is done. In order to run a quality center, directors need to hire people who are resourceful.

Chart 32-10 outlines traits employers seek when hiring people to work in early childhood centers. In preparation for an interview, read the statements and check those that match qualities you would be able to bring to a position. Completing this task will bolster your own self-image. The exercise will help you get a clear picture of your skills. It will also prepare you to make a persuasive presentation during an interview.

## Preparing Your Questions

In nearly all interviews, applicants are given the opportunity to ask questions. Thus, smart applicants always prepare questions for an interview. Learn everything you can about the center. You might form questions by talking to teachers who have taught at the center or asking questions of parents who have children attending the center. You can get general information about the center from the local Chamber of Commerce. Some questions you may wish to ask during an interview include

- What is the educational philosophy of your center?
- To what extent may I implement my own ideas?

32-9  Keeping your job search information organized and up-to-date is important.

| Positive Traits of Early Childhood Workers | |
|---|---|
| • Flexible | • Positive |
| • Energetic | • Resourceful |
| • Self-confident | • Dependable |
| • Enthusiastic | • A good planner |
| • Mature | • Committed to |
| • Willing to do extra | teaching |
| work | • Open to new ideas |
| • Patient | • Self-disciplined |
| • Cooperative | • Dedicated to hard |
| • Easy to get along | work |
| with | • Motivated |
| • A fast learner | • Self-reliant |
| • A good time man- | • Thorough |
| ager | • Self-directed |
| • Creative | • Friendly |
| • Cheerful | • Nurturing |

32-10  Deciding which of these traits fit you will help you focus on your best traits and skills during an interview.

- Is the staff encouraged to attend conferences? If so, how often may a staff member attend, and who pays the fees?
- What audiovisual equipment is provided by the school?
- How often are parent conferences scheduled?
- Does the center send home a weekly parent letter or monthly newsletter? If so, who is responsible for writing and editing them?

Asking questions tells the interviewer you are serious about a job. Take time to practice your questions, eye contact, and posture.

## The Interview

When you go to a job interview, remember to take your driver's license or state ID card, Social Security card, resume, portfolio, and list of questions for the interviewer. Give special thought to your appearance. You want to make a good impression. Make sure your hair is well groomed and attractively styled. Choose conservative jewelry, accessories, and shoes. For females, makeup should be applied lightly. Be sure your clothes are clean and neat. Choose clothes that are one step above those you would wear on the job. Avoid overdressing, but don't wear a T-shirt and jeans, either. Let your appearance tell the interviewer you are professional and can fit into the workplace.

At the interview, make eye contact, smile, and greet the employer with a firm handshake. Many interviewers begin an interview simply by introducing themselves and welcoming you to the center. This is usually followed by small talk that might include the weather or a center activity. After this, you will probably be told information about the job. The interviewer may then ask you structured questions concerning your education or experience. Be enthusiastic and provide full, focused answers. Avoid answering a question with "no" or "yes." Instead say "no, but" and "yes, and." After all questions have been answered, the interviewer will ask you if you have any questions. At this point, you can ask those questions you prepared beforehand. Avoid asking questions about vacation time, benefits, and breaks. The interviewer may think your main concern is with nonwork functions.

Follow the lead of the interviewer. Throughout the interview, listen with an intelligent, intent look on your face. When necessary, ask questions that will help you better understand the job. Other tips for successful interviewing are listed in 32-11.

Be careful not to volunteer negative information about your former employer or yourself. Employers are seeking positive people to work for them. If you were not happy in a previous job or jobs, you may not be happy with this job either. Thus, it is vital not to mention anything negative. Focus on the position.

Throughout the interviewing process, you will need to sell your positive qualities. When asked what you did during your practicum, student teaching, or last job, do not recite the daily schedule or curriculum. Instead, state specific things you did to improve the center or classroom. For example, you might tell about how you made protective education part of the curriculum. Perhaps you revised the format for parent letters and reorganized the children's library.

### Interview Questions

Prospective employers usually decide before the interview what information they need to share with you about a job. Job expectations, duties, and benefits are often included. Specific questions that you may be asked are also recorded, 32-12. The following questions are often included:

- Will you please share your educational background?
- What philosophy of education did that center have?
- What type of course work did you have?
- Do you have previous job experience? If so, describe your positions.
- Why are you looking for a new job?
- What are the most important characteristics of a teacher of young children?
- How would you describe your teaching style?
- Where do you see yourself professionally 10 years from today? Describe that job.
- Why are you interested in this job?

In addition, any of the following questions may also be asked:

## Tips for a Successful Interview

- Be on time.
- Present your best appearance.
- Extend your hand to greet the interviewer with a firm handshake.
- Use the interviewer's name and smile as you speak.
- Bring your resume and teaching portfolio with you.
- Remain relaxed and friendly.
- Listen carefully.
- Convey a positive attitude.
- Show your enthusiasm.
- Stress your strengths.
- Use active verbs while speaking.
- Personalize your questions.
- Respond to questions carefully.
- Be truthful; if you do not know an answer, say so.
- Provide more than a "yes" or "no" response to questions, but be concise.
- Thank the interviewer for his or her consideration at the end of the interview.
- Send a thank-you note.

32-11 The interview is your chance to make a good impression. Following these tips will help you.

32-12 Interviewers often prepare questions for the applicant ahead of time. They may record the applicant's answers during the interview.

- What is the value of children's play?
- How would you handle a child that is always hitting others?
- How would you plan a developmentally appropriate curriculum?
- How do you think your references described you when they were contacted?
- How would you handle transitions?
- How would you relate to parents?
- What is most annoying about children?
- On what basis do you plan curriculum for young children?
- What would you do if a child kicked you and said "I don't like you"?

Employers who have had training in interviewing techniques may ask the following questions to find out more about your performance in your previous position:

- What disappointments did you face in your last teaching position?
- In what areas did your supervisor criticize you?
- In what areas did your supervisor compliment you?
- For what things did you need guidance or help from your supervisor?

Questions will also be asked to determine your level of motivation.

- Why did you select teaching young children as a career?
- Why did you apply for this job?
- What is your long-term career objective?
- What are you looking for in this position that you have not had in past positions?
- What type of position would you like to hold in three years? Ten years?

It is not unusual for an interviewer to ask "What are your weaknesses?" If this happens, sit quietly for a moment. It is always a mistake to quickly answer a question off the top of your head. Give each question some thought, then form a response in your mind. Then respond carefully and positively. Do not put yourself down while answering this question. Rather, share your growth by saying something like "I have really developed skills in classroom control" or "My parent interaction skills really grew during the last few weeks of my student teaching." Or express your weaknesses in a positive way: I care too much about the children, I take my work too seriously, I try too many new ideas, etc.

## Teaching Portfolio

Bring along your teaching portfolio to demonstrate your growth and success. Your **teaching portfolio** tells a story. It should serve as a professional snapshot of your efforts, progress, and achievements. Your portfolio should contain evidence of your competence. Chart 32-13 contains the contents of a teaching portfolio.

Offer to share your teaching portfolio. You may say "I brought along my teaching portfolio. I would like to share the contents with you." While sharing the contents, use descriptions to support your materials. Explain why you chose each piece to include in the portfolio.

Exercise care so that your portfolio does not take the form of a scrapbook. This type of portfolio should include your philosophy of teaching. One way to organize a portfolio is to have a table of contents with two major subheadings. The first subheading could be labeled "Background Information." Your resume and background information on your teaching experience could be included. Also include information on your teaching goals, letters of recommendation, and teachers' evaluations of your work.

The second subheading could be labeled "Teaching Artifacts." This section of the portfolio should focus on the actual process and outcomes of teaching. Lesson plans, unit and theme plans, videotapes, parent letters, and examples of teacher-made materials could be included.

## Legal Problems in Interviewing

At both the state and federal level, it is illegal to discriminate on the basis of age, sex, national origin, race, or religion. Most employers do not intend to use information obtained from an interview in order to discriminate. However, such information could affect the hiring decision. Therefore, it is illegal for an employer to ask questions about an applicant's race, national origin, or religion.

| **Teaching Portfolio** |
|---|
| Table of contents |
| Resume |
| Official transcripts |
| Copies of certifications, licenses, or CDA Credential certificate |
| Letters of recommendation |
| Anecdotal records |
| Critical incident journals |
| Photographs of bulletin boards and room arrangements you designed |
| Parent letters |
| Sample lesson plans and block plans |
| Curriculum units and themes you have developed |
| Photographs of activities with descriptions |
| Teachers' evaluations |
| Videotapes of a good teaching lesson |
| Teacher-made materials |
| Statement of educational philosophy and teaching goals |
| Extracurricular activities |

32-13 Keep the contents of your portfolio updated to reflect the progress of your career.

Interviewers are limited in the questions that can be asked. For example, a parent of small children cannot be asked how the children will be cared for while he or she is working. Likewise a parent cannot be asked about a spouse's employment or salary.

Women cannot be asked if they are planning to have a family or are currently pregnant. Interviewers are also forbidden to ask applicants their marital status or the number of children they have. Chart 32-14 lists questions that may be asked. To prevent discrimination, all applicants for a job should be asked the same questions during an interview.

Despite the fact that they are illegal, you may still find yourself being asked some of these questions. Some prospective employers may purposely ask such questions to discriminate. Others, however, may simply ask them in an effort to get to know you better or make you feel at ease. These interviewers may not even know that the questions they ask are illegal.

If you are ever asked an illegal question, it is up to you to decide what the intent of the interviewer was. Based on your judgment, use discretion and tact to handle the situation. You may decide to simply answer the question. If you believe the person's intent was to discriminate, and then you are offered the job, you may ask why the question was asked. If the person's answer concerns you, you may decide to decline the job offer.

You may also choose to not answer the question. Do not accuse the person of discrimination. Instead, you may say simply and calmly "I am sorry, but I am not required to answer that question."

## Ending the Interview

An interview can be ended with words and/or through actions. Verbally, the interviewer may thank you for coming to signal the end of the interview. Nonverbally, the interviewer may sit up straight or stand up. This gesture means the interview is over. At this point, the interviewer has obtained all the information from you that is needed. Respond by thanking the interviewer for his or her time. See 32-15.

Many people are disappointed when they learn they were not successful in getting the position. If you feel this way, do not think something is wrong with you. It is not unusual to feel depressed or feel a slip in your self-esteem. These feelings will pass.

## Thank-You Notes

Always write a brief note thanking the people who interviewed you. Sending a thank-you note will make you stand out. This simple

| Interview Questions | |
|---|---|
| **Subject** | **Legal Inquiries** |
| Age | Only a question to determine if you meet state licensing requirements related to age.<br>Date of birth |
| Arrest record | Nothing |
| Marital status | Nothing |
| Convictions | Only convictions that would affect the job position. |
| Education | Only questions related to training and experience related to the position. |
| Family | Only questions related to meeting work schedule. |
| Disabilities | Only questions about disabilities that would affect job performance. |
| National origin | Only questions about ability to read, speak, and write the language the job requires. |
| Organizations | Only questions about participation in professional organizations related to your ability to perform the job. |
| Pregnancy | Only questions about anticipated absences from work. |
| Religion | Only questions about anticipated absences from work. |

32-14 Interviewers are not allowed to ask questions that may result in discrimination.

32-15 Be sure to leave the interviewer with a positive impression of you.

courtesy is observed by as few as 10 percent of job seekers. In the letter, mention the secretaries, if appropriate. Also, your letter will serve as a reminder to those you met. Even if you are not hired for that position, the interviewer may remember you for future openings. He or she may even pass your name to someone else who is searching for a child care employee.

More people are sending thank-you notes to interviewers by e-mail. In today's era of electronic communication, this is quite acceptable to most employers. Whether you use e-mail or regular mail, the key is to be prompt. Always send your thank-you note within two days of the interview.

# Employee Rights and Responsibilities

As an employee, you have certain rights that are protected by law. You also have other rights that are granted by your employer through personnel policies. Rights come with responsibilities, however. Some of a child care teacher's responsibilities are defined by law. Others have

been set by NAEYC in the *Code of Ethical Conduct*. (See the Appendix at the back of this book for more information about the *Code of Ethical Conduct*.)

Knowing your employee rights helps you ensure those rights are respected. Employees desire a work environment in which their rights are honored. Similarly, being aware of your responsibilities helps you to be the best employee possible. When you understand what is expected of you, you can comply with all program policies and state child care licensing requirements. Following these guidelines will ensure that your work contributes to the quality of the program and builds the program's reputation.

In many ways, your employee rights parallel responsibilities your employer has to you. For example, it is your employer's responsibility to make sure your right to a safe workplace is met in accordance with federal and state laws. Likewise, your employee responsibilities parallel rights of your employer. For example, your employer has the right to receive a full day's work in exchange for a full day's pay. It is your responsibility as an employee to provide this work in a manner that meets the employer's expectations.

## Employee Rights

Employers have an ethical responsibility to create a quality workplace. The employer should strive to offer a supportive early childhood environment where both children and adults can reach their potential. This type of environment will encourage you to focus on your work and find satisfaction in it, 32-16.

In addition, your employer's policies may grant you other rights. When you begin a new position, ask for a copy of the employee handbook or other personnel papers. This information should outline your employee rights and responsibilities as defined by the employer. These are in addition to any rights and responsibilities protected by law.

Most importantly, you are entitled to be treated fairly by your employer as outlined in the handbook. All employees should be treated equally according to the terms set forth by the

32-16 Early childhood teachers are happiest and most effective in a quality work environment.

employer. Make it a point to familiarize yourself with the handbook so you can obtain all the benefits to which you are entitled and adhere to the employer's rules and expectations.

Early childhood programs have an ethical responsibility to provide a job orientation program for new hires. *Job orientation programs* are activities designed to acquaint you with the workplace. You should receive an overview of the program, its policies and procedures, and your employer's expectations of you. Any other training needed for your position should be part of the orientation period.

Another ethical practice is supportive supervision for employees. Your supervisor should assist you by answering questions, solving problems, and recommending areas for improvement. Early childhood programs should provide ongoing training to meet licensing requirements and improve the quality of the program. Workshops or classes that may be offered include curriculum, technology, parent involvement, health, safety, and communication skills. Supervision and ongoing training promote professional growth and job satisfaction.

In addition to employer-granted rights, many employee rights are protected by federal and state laws, 32-17. Employers have an obligation to understand and adhere to these laws.

Your employer has a legal responsibility to observe all federal and state labor laws. In addition, all applicable federal and state payroll, wage, and income tax laws must be followed. You have legal rights regarding some aspects of employee benefits and insurance. Federal laws give you the right to work in an environment free from discrimination and sexual harassment. You have the right to a safe work environment. In specified medical and family situations, your employer must allow you to take up to 12 weeks unpaid leave per year and hold your job (or an equivalent job) until your leave ends. These are only a few examples—you have many other employee rights that are protected by law.

## Employee Responsibilities

When you accept an early childhood teaching position, you agree to fulfill certain responsibilities. You agree to do the job for which your employer is paying you. First and foremost, you are responsible for complying with all center policies and state childcare licensing requirements. You must also adhere to the ethical standards of the profession, as set forth in NAEYC's *Code of Ethical Conduct*.

An early childhood teacher's role is to provide the children with developmentally appropriate, responsive care. Your employer has a

---

| **Employee Rights Protected by Law** |
| --- |
| • Labor, pay, tax, and benefit administration procedures in accordance with laws |
| • Equal pay for equal work regardless of gender |
| • Freedom from workplace discrimination |
| • Freedom from sexual harassment |
| • Safe workplace |
| • Reasonable workplace accommodations for disabled workers |
| • Right to take specified unpaid leave to attend to covered family and medical conditions |

32-17  This list is only a sampling of the many employee rights that are protected by state and federal laws.

responsibility to create a quality work environment. You have a responsibility to maintain and contribute to the quality of the program. To do this, you must have good attendance and be punctual. You should also have a professional appearance, model a positive attitude, and maintain confidentiality. When necessary, you are also responsible for seeking help from your supervisor.

## Attendance and Punctuality

Your employer has the right to expect a full day's work from you in exchange for the pay you earn. You have a responsibility to maintain good work attendance and be punctual. The director, staff members, and parents count on you to be at work everyday. You should arrive a few minutes early each day or at least be on time.

Being even a few minutes late also causes extra work and stress for your coworkers and director. State licensing rules and regulations specify required adult-child ratios at all times. This means the director must try to make other arrangements to cover your classroom in case you are absent or late. If no one can cover for you, this places your program at risk for noncompliance. The center can receive a licensing violation for being understaffed. Legally, the center can also be at risk if a child is seriously injured when required ratios are not met. Repeated violations can cause a center to lose its license. In addition to legal responsibilities, you have an ethical obligation to the families and children you serve, as well as to your coworkers and director.

For these reasons, repeated absenteeism or tardiness is a serious performance problem. Many programs have attendance and tardiness policies. If you fail to follow these policies, you are likely to be fired from your job. Even if no written attendance policies are in place, you can lose your job as a result of repeated attendance problems.

## Professional Appearance

You have an ethical obligation to your employer to maintain a professional appearance. You must represent your program in a professional manner. In large part, parents, children, visitors, and coworkers will base their initial impressions of you on your appearance. To illustrate, parents may feel a teacher wearing a casual two-piece outfit is more intelligent and nurturing than a teacher wearing blue jeans. People may equate your grooming and dress with how seriously you take your work. These assessments may not be accurate, but nevertheless they occur.

Looking professional requires good grooming and avoiding extremes in hairstyles and clothing. Being well groomed involves both cleanliness and neatness, 32-18. Follow good hygiene practices, such as showering or bathing daily. Keep your hair clean, groomed, and simply styled. If you have long hair, try to keep it out of your face. Tying your hair back while working with young children will prevent children from pulling it. This also prevents loose hair from falling into the children's faces.

When you work with young children, you will need comfortable, washable clothing that allows for easy movement. Avoid tight or restrictive clothing in which it is difficult to move. Your clothes should be clean and neat. Clothing should not be wrinkled, frayed, stained, or ripped.

Male and female teachers alike often prefer washable slacks because these are comfortable yet convey a professional appearance. Most early childhood programs consider jeans, sweatpants, shorts, and spandex leggings unacceptable. Females can wear skirts or dresses, but skirts and dresses can be less comfortable for playing with children outside or on the floor.

Sweaters or shirts should be washable, casual business attire. T-shirts are often considered inappropriate, especially those with crude sayings or graphics. Tube, halter, sleeveless, cropped, and low-cut tops are always inappropriate for the early childhood workplace.

For directors, more dressy business attire may be appropriate, depending on the program. Directors interact more with parents, visitors, and teachers than directly with children. Male directors might wear dress slacks, shirt, and tie, with a jacket for more formal occasions. Female directors might wear dresses, skirts, and pantsuits.

## Positive Attitude

Much of your success as a child care professional will depend on your attitude. Your

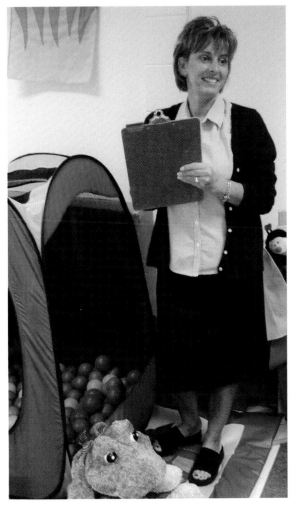

32-18 Child care directors should present a neat, clean, appearance with their dress and grooming.

**attitude** is your outlook on life—the ways in which you think about or act toward others. Finding great pleasure in teaching requires a positive attitude. This attitude enables you to see the potential in any child, parent, staff member, situation, or idea. Instead of seeing limitations, you seek opportunities.

People with a positive attitude want to do well. They take responsibility for their decisions. Teachers who have a positive attitude view working with young children as a chance for continuous learning. They seek knowledge about child development, guidance, and curriculum. These teachers are easy to recognize on the job.

They welcome suggestions on improving their skills for working with young children. Employers enjoy workers who demonstrate a positive attitude.

## Confidentiality

As a teacher of young children, you will have access to a wide range of privileged information. You may see personal records and learn private information about others. For example, you may know which children do and do not receive child care tuition assistance. Daniel's parents may share with you personal information about their divorce to help you work with Daniel in the most understanding way. You may know that Juana's mother has cancer, and Kevin may tell you about his father leaving the family.

In most cases, you must keep sensitive personal information private. This is called keeping **confidentiality**. It means not sharing this information with others beyond what is required by your work. Keeping confidentiality protects children, families, coworkers, and the program itself.

Confidentiality does have some limits. For example, you can and should share information about children and families with certain coworkers for reasons relevant to the job. For example, you should inform other staff members who work with a child about the child's special medical, physical, or learning needs. This information helps the staff provide appropriate care and learning experiences. Likewise, you may need to inform your director about the unethical practices of a coworker after you have tried unsuccessfully to resolve the matter with that person. This information helps the director keep the children healthy and safe.

Child abuse and neglect present another exception to confidentiality. The law requires that cases of abuse and neglect be reported to the proper state agency. If you suspect neglect or abuse, follow your program's policy for making this report. Your legal responsibility as a mandated reporter outweighs your responsibility to keep private information. In this case, you are required by law to break confidentiality.

In most other cases, it is unacceptable to break confidentiality. For example, you should not gossip with your coworkers, friends, or family members about the children and families at the center. Do not talk to parents about other families or children in the program. Avoid discussing the personal matters of coworkers. These practices are unethical. If parents learn you have broken confidentiality, they may feel betrayed. Their resulting suspicion could cause long-term damage to the reputations of you and your program. Broken trust can strain coworker relationships and undermine teamwork.

Some centers ask their employees to sign confidentiality agreements. These agreements protect the confidentiality of a program's families, children, and fellow employees. A confidentiality agreement should specify with whom various types of information can and cannot be shared. If an employee violates this agreement, the employee loses his or her job.

At times, knowing which information to keep private can be challenging. It is always best to err on the side of caution. When considering whether to share personal or private information about other people, always ask yourself the questions in Figure 32-19. Base your decision on your answers to these questions.

## Terminating Employment

You will have many jobs during the course of your lifetime. Job changes are common today. Employee turnover is high for all age groups.

There are many reasons why people leave their jobs. Some of these reasons include the following:

- desire for better pay or fringe benefits
- desire for better working conditions or hours
- seeking more opportunities for advancement
- looking for new challenges and responsibilities
- making better use of personal skills and abilities
- a conflict with supervisors or coworkers at current job
- transportation problems
- company layoffs, restructuring, downsizing, or closings

A change in their personal lives can lead to a job change. For example, a person may need to change jobs if a spouse is transferred to another

| Deciding When to Share Private Information |
| --- |

- What is my purpose for sharing the information? Does my disclosure help the child or family in any important way?
- With whom am I sharing the information? Does this person have a need or right to know?
- Whose privacy is involved? How might this person feel about me sharing this information with others? If I am unsure, have I asked him or her?
- How would my supervisor feel about me sharing this information? If I am unsure, have I asked him or her?
- How might sharing this information negatively affect my current position and my career? Is the disclosure legally or ethically important enough to take these risks?

32-19 Answering these questions can help you decide whether it is a good idea to share confidential information you possess.

city. A family move can lead to a job change. Marriage, divorce, death, or the birth of children can create new job requirements. Others leave their jobs to further their education. Sometimes health problems can dictate a job or environment change.

Before a job change is made, it is important to think through your options. Is this the best course of action at this time? Carefully weigh the pros and cons of leaving your current job for another job.

If you decide a job change is needed, resist the urge to leave your old job immediately. Instead, start looking for a new job before leaving your current job, if at all possible. Be sure you have enough money set aside to carry you over to your next paycheck. If you do not have enough money in savings, you may want to keep your current job until you find a better one.

### Guidelines for Leaving a Job

There is a right way to leave your job. You want to leave under the best possible circumstances. Inform your employer before you tell your coworkers. Do so at least two weeks prior to your leaving. This allows your employer time

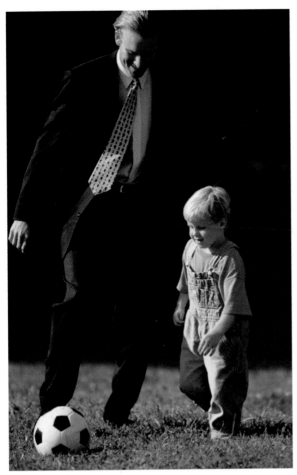

32-20 When working parents come home, they often find their children are eager to spend time with them.

to find your replacement.

Give notice to your employer in person, but also provide a written letter of resignation. A resignation letter is appropriate in most situations. This letter should state your last day of work and why you are leaving. It can be brief, but it should be positive. Thank your employer for the opportunity to work there. Describe how you have benefited from your job. You might offer to train your replacement, if appropriate.

During the two weeks before you leave, continue to do your job as you always have. If you work directly with children, prepare them for your departure. Be pleasant to your coworkers as you may work with them again in a different job. Do not complain about your current job, nor brag about your new one. Thank them for their help and friendship.

## Balancing Multiple Roles

One of the most challenging tasks for workers is to balance their many roles. A **role** is a set of responsibilities that accompanies a position you hold in life. Each person has several roles. For example, some of these roles include wage-earner, spouse, parent, son or daughter (and other family relationships), friend, citizen, and volunteer. Every role has demands and responsibilities. Achieving harmony among various roles is challenging, but important.

Many adults feel **role strain**, a type of stress created by being unable to successfully balance multiple roles. Anyone can feel role strain, but it is most common in single-parent and dual-career families. In these families, parents arrive home from a day's work and must assume home-care and parenting tasks in the evening, 32-20. Errands must also be squeezed into evening and weekend hours. Working parents often feel they are juggling too many responsibilities with too little time to devote to them.

Even as a young person, you have several roles. You are a son or daughter, student, friend, community member, and perhaps also a worker or volunteer. As a family member, you may be expected to help with family tasks, attend family events, and spend quality time with the family (such as evening meals). As a student, you have homework, tests, and projects to complete. Extracurricular activities, such as clubs or sports, bring additional roles. Friends will want you to spend time with them.

Making time for all these roles can be an enormous challenge. Learning to manage your time is a valuable tool. Planning can help you meet your most important duties. Although you might like to, you will not always be able to say *yes* to everything. Being able to set priorities will help you decide which things to let go.

Staying healthy will help you meet your many obligations. Getting adequate rest, nutrition, and physical activity will allow you to feel your best. You also need personal time to relax, think, and plan. Strengthening relationships will promote your social and emotional development.

To succeed in a child care career, you will need to strike a balance among your many roles. The way in which you do this will likely be as unique as you are. However, finding this balance matters more than exactly how you achieve it.

# Summary

Choosing a career involves a process of self-assessment. As part of this process, you must examine your interests and abilities, as well as personal and professional priorities. Your answers to many important questions can help your childhood position decide if you are well suited to a career in teaching.

Searching for an early childhood career is a rewarding, but sometimes frustrating, experience. During your search for a position, you can learn a great deal about yourself. A well-organized search is never boring!

While each person's search differs, there are some general guidelines to follow. Start with a resume. Include a cover letter. Use your resume when you meet with or talk to prospective employers.

When you obtain an interview, be prepared. Bring your teaching portfolio. Prepare yourself for the interviewer's questions. Also write questions of your own to ask the interviewer. Conduct yourself in a professional manner and show your enthusiasm for the child care field. Send a thank-you note after the interview.

Once you are hired for a position, you gain employee rights and responsibilities. It is important for you to fully understand both your rights and your responsibilities. Knowing your rights helps you receive the full benefits to which you are entitled. Understanding your responsibilities allows you to do your work as your employer expects.

Balancing multiple roles is challenging but important. Many conflicting demands will arise, but you can prioritize which demands to fulfill and which to let go. Many skills can help you in this process. Achieving a healthy role balance will promote your success as a child care professional!

# Review and Reflect

1. Why are interests and abilities important considerations in choosing a career?
2. Explain the differences between personal priorities and professional priorities

3. If you notice an ad for an appealing position, _____.
   A. wait a few weeks and then contact the center director
   B. contact the center director at once
   C. place your own ad in hopes that the center director will contact you
   D. None of the above.

4. A _____ should include a list of your qualifications, skills, and job experience.

5. True or false. Some highly qualified job applicants may not obtain job interviews because of poor writing skills.

6. How can a recent graduate stress job experience on his or her resume?

7. What is the major disadvantage of placing a position wanted ad?

8. What is the hidden job market?

9. What steps might you take to learn about job openings through the hidden job market?

10. When preparing for an interview, _____.
    A. think positively
    B. put the interview out of your mind until the time it is scheduled
    C. it's best if you are nervous
    D. None of the above.

11. Asking questions about a job shows the interviewer you are _____ about the position.
    A. desperate
    B. serious
    C. undecided
    D. None of the above.

12. True or false. For a job interview, you should always dress for the job for which you are applying.

13. If an interviewer asks you what your weaknesses are, you should _____.
    A. answer quickly
    B. think for a moment before answering
    C. refuse to answer
    D. None of the above.

14. Your teaching _____ tells a story about your efforts, progress, and achievements.

15. True or false. It is illegal to discriminate on the basis of an applicant's religion.

16.  Why should you write a thank-you note to your interviewer following a job interview?

17.  How do employee rights relate to employer responsibilities?

18.  List four employee rights and four employee responsibilities.

19.  Explain why keeping confidentiality is important for professionals in early childhood.

20.  What does it mean to balance multiple roles?

## Apply and Explore

1.  Prepare a resume. When you finish, ask your teacher for suggestions on how you might improve it.

2.  Prepare a teaching portfolio. Practice describing the contents to a friend.

3.  Attend a meeting of a local chapter of NAEYC. Talk with a variety of the members to learn about their work.

4.  Role-play a job interview with a classmate.

5.  Write a cover letter to accompany your resume.   **C**

6.  Search hotjobs.com to compare various early childhood positions. Compare educational requirements and job responsibilities of various jobs.   **C**

7.  Visit the Web site of the American Job Bank (ajb.org), which is sponsored by the Department of Labor. Search the database for early childhood jobs.

Getting along with staff members is as important to job success as working well with children.

# Appendix A

## Principles from the Code of Ethical Conduct
## National Association for the Education of Young Children

### Section I: Ethical responsibilities to children

- Above all, we shall not harm children. We shall not participate in practices that are disrespectful, degrading, dangerous, exploitative, intimidating, emotionally damaging, or physically harmful to children. This principle has precedence over all others in this Code.

- We shall not participate in practices that discriminate against children by denying benefits, giving special advantages, or excluding them from programs or activities on the basis of their race, ethnicity, religion, sex, national origin, language, ability, or the status, behavior, or beliefs of their parents.

- We shall involve all of those with relevant knowledge (including staff and parents) in decisions concerning a child.

- For every child we shall implement adaptations in teaching strategies, learning environment, and curricula, consult with the family, and seek recommendations from appropriate specialists to maximize the potential of the child to benefit from the program. If, after these efforts have been made to work with a child and family, the child does not appear to be benefiting from a program, or the child is seriously jeopardizing the ability of other children to benefit from the program, we shall communicate with the family and appropriate specialists to determine the child's current needs; identify the setting and services most suited to meeting these needs; and assist the family in placing the child in an appropriate setting.

- We shall be familiar with the symptoms of child abuse, including physical, sexual, verbal, and emotional abuse, and neglect. We shall know and follow state laws and community procedures that protect children against abuse and neglect.

- When we have reasonable cause to suspect child abuse or neglect, we shall report it to the appropriate community agency and follow up to ensure that appropriate action has been taken. When appropriate, parents or guardians will be informed that the referral has been made.

- When another person tells us of a suspicion that a child is being abused or neglected, we shall assist that person in taking appropriate action to protect the child.

- When a child protective agency fails to provide adequate protection for abused or neglected children, we acknowledge a collective ethical responsibility to work toward improvement of these services.

- When we become aware of a practice or situation that endangers the health or safety of children, but has not been previously known to do so, we have an ethical responsibility to inform those who can remedy the situation and who can protect children from similar danger.

# Section II: Ethical responsibilities to families

- We shall not deny family members access to their child's classroom or program setting.
- We shall inform families of program philosophy, policies, and personnel qualifications, and explain why we teach as we do, which should be in accordance with our ethical responsibilities to children (see Section I).
- We shall inform families of and when appropriate, involve them in policy decisions.
- We shall involve families in significant decisions affecting their child.
- We shall inform the family of accidents involving their child, of risks such as exposures to contagious disease that may result in infection, and of occurrences that might result in emotional stress.
- To improve the quality of early childhood care and education, we shall cooperate with qualified child development researchers. Families shall be fully informed of any proposed research projects involving their children and shall have the opportunity to give or withhold consent without penalty. We shall not permit or participate in research that could in any way hinder the education, development, or well-being of children.
- We shall not engage in or support exploitation of families. We shall not use our relationship with a family for private advantage or personal gain, or enter into relationships with family members that might impair our effectiveness in working with children.
- We shall develop written policies for the protection of confidentiality and the disclosure of children's records. These policy documents shall be made available to all program personnel and families. Disclosure of children's records

beyond family members, program personnel, and consultants having an obligation of confidentiality shall require familial consent (except in cases of abuse or neglect).
- We shall maintain confidentiality and shall respect the family's right to privacy, refraining from disclosure of confidential information and intrusion into family life. However, when we have reason to believe that a child's welfare is at risk, it is permissible to share confidential information with agencies and individuals who may be able to intervene in the child's interest.
- In cases where family members are in conflict, we shall work openly, sharing our observations of the child, to help all parties involved make informed decisions. We shall refrain from becoming an advocate for one party.
- We shall be familiar with and appropriately use community resources and professional services that support families. After a referral has been made, we shall follow up to ensure that services have been appropriately provided.

# Section III. Ethical responsibilities to colleagues

## Responsibilities to co-workers

- When we have concern about the professional behavior of a co-worker, we shall first let that person know of our concern, in a way that shows respect for personal dignity and for the diversity to be found among staff members, and then attempt to resolve the matter collegially.
- We shall exercise care in expressing views regarding the personal attributes or professional conduct of co-workers. Statements should be based on firsthand knowledge and relevant to the interests of children and programs.

## Responsibilities to employers

- When we do not agree with program policies, we shall first attempt to effect change through constructive action within the organization.
- We shall speak or act on behalf of an organization only when authorized. We shall take care to acknowledge when we are speaking for the organization and when we are expressing a personal judgment.
- We shall not violate laws or regulations designed to protect children and shall take appropriate action consistent with this Code when aware of such violations.

## Responsibilities to employees

- In decisions concerning children and programs, we shall appropriately utilize the education, training, experience, and expertise of staff members.
- We shall provide staff members with safe and supportive working conditions that permit them to carry out their responsibilities, timely and nonthreatening evaluation procedures, written grievance procedures, constructive feedback, and opportunities for continuing professional development and advancement.
- We shall develop and maintain comprehensive written personnel policies that define program standards and, when applicable, that specify the extent to which employees are accountable for their conduct outside the work place. These policies shall be given to new staff members and shall be available for review by all staff members.
- Employees who do not meet program standards shall be informed of areas of concern and, when possible, assisted in improving their performance.
- Employees who are dismissed shall be informed of the reasons for their termination. When a dismissal is for cause, justification must be based on evidence of inadequate or inappropriate behavior that is accurately documented, current, and available for the employee to review.
- In making evaluations and recommendations, judgments shall be based on fact and relevant to the interests of children and programs.
- Hiring and promotion shall be based solely on a person's record of accomplishment and ability to carry out the responsibilities of the position.
- In hiring, promotion, and provision of training, we shall not participate in any form of discrimination based on race, ethnicity, religion, gender, national origin, culture, disability, age, or sexual preference. We shall be familiar with and observe laws and regulations that pertain to employment discrimination.

# Section IV: Ethical responsibilities to community and society

- We shall communicate openly and truthfully about the nature and extent of services that we provide.
- We shall not accept or continue to work in positions for which we are personally unsuited or professionally unqualified. We shall not offer services that we do not have the competence, qualifications, or resources to provide.
- We shall be objective and accurate in reporting the knowledge upon which we base our program practices.
- We shall cooperate with other professionals who work with children and their families.
- We shall not hire or recommend for employment any person whose competence, qualifications, or character makes him or her unsuited for the position.
- We shall report the unethical or incompetent behavior of a colleague to a supervisor when informal resolution is not effective.

- We shall be familiar with laws and regulations that serve to protect the children in our programs.
- We shall not participate in practices which are in violation of laws and regulations that protect the children in our programs.
- When we have evidence that an early childhood program is violating laws or regulations protecting children, we shall report it to persons responsible for the program. If compliance is not accomplished within a reasonable time, we will report the violation to appropriate authorities who can be expected to remedy the situation.
- When we have evidence that an agency or a professional charged with providing services to children, families, or teachers is failing to meet its obligations, we acknowledge a collective ethical responsibility to report the problem to appropriate authorities or to the public.
- When a program violates or requires its employees to violate this Code, it is permissible, after fair assessment of the evidence, to disclose the identity of that program.

©1998 National Association for the Education of Young Children. These excerpts from an official position statement of the National Association for the Education of Young Children are reprinted by permission.

# Appendix B

| Developmental Traits of Children from Birth to Age 12* | |
|---|---|
| **Birth to Two Years** | |
| **Motor Skills** | |
| **1 Month** | Moves reflexively.<br>Does not control body movements.<br>Needs support for head. Without support, head will flop backward and forward.<br>Lifts head briefly from the surface in order to turn head from side to side when lying on tummy.<br>Twitches whole body when crying.<br>Keeps hands fisted or slightly open.<br>May hold object if placed in hand, but drops it quickly. |
| **2 Months** | Can keep head in midposition of body when lying on tummy.<br>Can hold head up for a few minutes.<br>Can turn head when lying on back.<br>Cycles arms and legs smoothly.<br>Movements are mainly reflexive, but may begin to become voluntary.<br>Grasps objects in reflex movements, but grasps are becoming voluntary.<br>May hold object longer, but still drops object after a few seconds.<br>Uses improved vision to look at objects more closely and for a longer time. |
| **3 Months** | Shows active body movements.<br>Can move arms and legs together.<br>Turns head vigorously.<br>Can lift head when lying on tummy.<br>Can sit briefly with support.<br>Follows moving objects with eyes. |
| **4 Months** | On tummy, can lift head and chest from surface using arms for support.<br>On tummy, may roll from side to side.<br>Can maintain a sitting position for several minutes if given proper support.<br>Begins to use mitten grasp for grabbing objects near the hands.<br>Looks from object to hands to object.<br>Swipes at objects, gradually improving aim. |
| **5 Months** | On back, can lift head and shoulders off surface.<br>Can roll from tummy to back.<br>When supported under arms, stands and moves body up and down, stamping feet alternately.<br>Helps when being pulled to a sitting position.<br>Can sit supported for 15 to 30 minutes with a firm back.<br>Reaches for objects such as an activity gym with good coordination and aim.<br>Begins to grasp objects with thumb and fingers.<br>Grabs objects with either hand.<br>Transfers objects from one hand to the other, dropping objects often. |
| **6 Months** | Rolls from back to tummy.<br>On tummy, moves by pushing with legs and reaching with arms.<br>Gets up on hands and knees, but then may fall forward.<br>Is able to stand while supported. |

*The items listed are based on average ages when various traits emerge. Many children may develop certain traits at an earlier or later age.

| Motor Skills (Continued) | |
|---|---|
| **6 Months** (continued) | May be able to sit for short periods of time.<br>Reaches with one arm and grasps object with hand, then transfers the object to other hand, then reaches for another object.<br>Learns to drop an object at will.<br>Holds an object in both hands.<br>Sits in a tripod position using arms for support. |
| **7 Months** | Crawls awkwardly, combining movements on tummy and knees.<br>Likes to bounce when in standing position.<br>May be able to pull self to a standing position.<br>Can lean over and reach while in sitting position.<br>Has mastered grasping by using thumb in opposition to fingers.<br>Holds an object in each hand.<br>Brings objects together with banging noises.<br>Keeps objects in hands most of the time.<br>Fingers, manipulates, and rattles objects repeatedly. |
| **8 Months** | Sits alone steadily for longer periods of time.<br>Crawls.<br>Achieves sitting position by pushing up with arms.<br>Learns pincer grasp, using just the thumb and forefinger.<br>Is able to pick up small objects and string. |
| **9 Months** | Sits alone.<br>May try to crawl up stairs.<br>May be able to move along furniture, touching it for support.<br>Uses index finger to point, lead, and poke. |
| **10 Months** | Likes to walk holding caregiver's hands.<br>Climbs on chairs and other furniture.<br>Stands with little support.<br>Can release grasped object instead of dropping it. |
| **11 Months** | Stands alone.<br>Is able to stand and pick up objects.<br>Likes to grasp feeding utensils and cup.<br>May carry spoon to mouth in feeding attempt.<br>Takes off shoes and socks. |
| **12 Months** | Climbs up and down stairs.<br>May show preference for one hand.<br>May be able to take off clothes.<br>Walks with one hand held. |
| **13 to 15 Months** | Builds a tower consisting of 2 one-inch cubes.<br>Turns pages in a book 2 or 3 at a time.<br>Walks without assistance.<br>While walking, cannot maneuver around corners or stop suddenly.<br>Scribbles vigorously. |
| **16 to 18 Months** | Walks up steps.<br>Walks well while carrying or pulling a toy.<br>Hurls a ball.<br>Can place 6 round pegs in pegboard. |

| **Motor Skills** (Continued) | |
|---|---|
| **19 to 22 Months** | Walks up stairs independently, one at a time. <br> Completes a 3-piece formboard. <br> Places 4 rings on post in random order. <br> Rolls, pounds, squeezes, and pulls clay. <br> Kicks backward and forward. <br> Jumps in place. |
| **22 to 24 Months** | Attempts to stand on balance beam. <br> Builds tower of 6 cubes. <br> Runs without falling. <br> Pedals a tricycle. <br> Kicks a large ball. |
| **Cognitive Skills** | |
| **1 Month** | Prefers to look at human faces and patterned objects. <br> Listens attentively to sounds and voices. <br> Cries deliberately for assistance, also communicates with grunts and facial expressions. <br> Is comforted by the human voice and music. |
| **2 Months** | Coordinates eye movements. <br> Shows obvious preference for faces to objects. <br> Makes some sounds, but most vocalizing is still crying. <br> Shows some interest in sounds and will stop sucking to listen. |
| **3 Months** | Is able to suck and look at the same time, thus doing two controlled actions at once. <br> Discovers hands and feet as an extension of self. <br> Searches with eyes for sounds. <br> Begins cooing one syllable, vowel-like sounds—*ooh, ah, aw.* <br> Laughs out loud. |
| **4 Months** | Likes to repeat enjoyable acts like shaking a rattle. <br> Enjoys watching hands and feet. <br> Looks at an object, reaches for it, and makes contact with it. <br> Makes first consonant sounds—*p, b, m, l.* <br> Smiles and coos when caregiver talks to him or her. <br> Explores toys by grasping, sucking, shaking, and banging. |
| **5 Months** | Recognizes and responds to own name. <br> Smiles at self in mirror. <br> Can recognize people by their voices. <br> Babbles spontaneously. |
| **6 Months** | Grabs at any and all objects in reach. <br> Studies objects intently, turning them to see all sides. <br> Varies volume, pitch, and rate while babbling. <br> Acquires sounds of native language in babbles. |
| **7 Months** | Anticipates events. <br> Enjoys looking through books with familiar pictures. <br> May begin to imitate an act. <br> May say *mama* or *dada* but does not connect words with parents. <br> Produces gestures to communicate. Points to desired object. |

| **Cognitive Skills** (Continued) | |
|---|---|
| **8 Months** | Likes to empty and fill containers.<br>Begins putting together a long series of syllables.<br>May label object in imitation of its sounds, such as *choo-choo* for train.<br>Finds objects that are totally hidden. |
| **9 Months** | Responds appropriately to a few specific words.<br>Likes to look for contents in a container. |
| **10 to 12 Months** | Speaks first recognizable word.<br>Links specific acts or events to other events.<br>Can point to body parts.<br>Likes to look at pictures in a book.<br>Puts nesting toys together correctly.<br>Begins to find familiar objects which are not in view but have permanent locations (looks for cookies after being told he or she can have one).<br>Waves good-bye. |
| **13 to 15 Months** | Identifies family members in photographs.<br>Gives mechanical toy to caregiver to activate toy.<br>Has an expressive vocabulary of 4 to 10 words; most refer to animals, food, and toys. |
| **16 to 18 Months** | Demonstrates knowledge of absence of familiar person (points to door, says "gone").<br>Enjoys cause-effect relationships (banging drum, splashing water, turning on TV).<br>Has expressive vocabulary of 10 to 20 words. |
| **19 to 24 Months** | Sorts shapes and colors.<br>Mimics adult behaviors.<br>Points to and names objects in a book.<br>Points to body parts upon request.<br>Has expressive vocabulary of 20 to 50 words.<br>Refers to self by name. Recognizes self in photo or mirror. |
| **Social-Emotional Skills** | |
| **1 Month** | Reacts to discomfort and pain, by crying for assistance.<br>Recognizes a parent's voice.<br>Is comforted by the human face.<br>Makes eye contact. |
| **2 Months** | Is able to show distress, excitement, contentment, anger and delight.<br>Can quiet self by sucking.<br>Looks at a person alertly and directly. Prefers to look at people over objects.<br>Quiets in response to being held.<br>Shows affection by looking at a person while kicking, waving arms, and smiling. |
| **3 Months** | Shows feelings of security when held or talked to.<br>Senses that the hands and feet are extensions of self.<br>Whimpers when hungry, chortles when content.<br>Communicates with different sounds and facial expressions.<br>Responds with total body to a familiar face.<br>Tries to attract attention of caregiver.<br>Watches adults' facial expressions closely. |

| Social-Emotional Skills (Continued) | |
|---|---|
| **4 Months** | Expresses delight.<br>May form an attachment to one special object.<br>Responds to continued warmth and affection.<br>Shows increased pleasure in social interactions.<br>Enjoys social aspects of feeding time.<br>Becomes unresponsive if left alone most of waking hours.<br>Laughs when tickled. |
| **5 Months** | May begin to show fearful behavior as separateness is felt.<br>Distinguishes between familiar and unfamiliar adults.<br>Builds trust when cries are answered; becomes anxious and demanding when cries are unanswered.<br>May be able to play the peek-a-boo game. |
| **6 Months** | Enjoys playing with children.<br>Responds to affection and may imitate signs of affection.<br>Likes attention and may cry to get it.<br>May begin clinging to a primary caregiver. Desires constant attention from caregiver.<br>Laughs when socializing.<br>Smiles at familiar faces and stares solemnly at strangers. |
| **7 Months** | May show more dependence on caregiver for security.<br>Has increased drive for independence but senses frightening situations.<br>Shows desire for social contacts.<br>Thoroughly enjoys company of siblings.<br>Begins to have a sense of humor.<br>Expresses anger more dramatically. |
| **8 Months** | Exhibits fear of strangers.<br>May anticipate being left and become disturbed.<br>Values quick display of love and support from caregiver.<br>Likes to explore new places, but wants to be able to return to caregiver.<br>Enjoys playing with own image in a mirror.<br>Definitely prefers caregiver to strangers.<br>Is more aware of social approval or disapproval. |
| **9 Months** | May show fear of heights; may be afraid to crawl down from a chair.<br>May show a fear of new sounds.<br>Shows interest in play activities of others.<br>Likes to play games like pat-a-cake.<br>Recognizes the social nature of mealtimes.<br>Performs for others, repeats act if applauded. |
| **10 Months** | Cries less often.<br>Expresses delight, happiness, sadness, discomfort, and anger.<br>May be able to show symbolic thought by giving love to a stuffed toy.<br>Is more aware of and sensitive to other children.<br>Enjoys music and may mimic movements others make to music.<br>Fears strange places. |
| **11 Months** | May not always want to be cooperative.<br>Recognizes the difference between being good and being naughty.<br>Seeks approval and tries to avoid disapproval.<br>Imitates movements of other adults and children.<br>Likes to say no and shake head to get response from a caregiver.<br>Tests caregivers to determine limits.<br>Objects to having his or her enjoyable play stopped. |

| | Social–Emotional Skills (Continued) |
|---|---|
| **12 Months** | May reveal an inner determination to walk.<br>Begins to develop self-identity and independence.<br>Shows increased negativism. May have tantrums.<br>Enjoys playing with siblings.<br>Likes to practice communication with adults.<br>Continues to test caregiver's limits.<br>May resist napping. |
| **13 to 15 Months** | Shows pride in personal accomplishments.<br>Likes to exhibit affection to humans and to objects.<br>Prefers to keep caregiver in sight while exploring environment.<br>Demands personal attention.<br>May show fear of strangers.<br>Shows negativism. Becomes frustrated easily.<br>Enjoys solitary play.<br>Shows preference for family members over others.<br>Demands personal attention. |
| **16 to 18 Months** | Is emotionally unpredictable and may respond differently at different times.<br>Is unable to tolerate frustration.<br>May reveal negativism and stubbornness.<br>May exhibit fear of thunder, lightning, large animals, and strange situations.<br>Is very socially responsive to parents and caregivers.<br>Responds to simple requests.<br>May punch and poke peers as if they were objects.<br>Is unable to share. |
| **19 to 21 Months** | May become possessive of toys, hiding them from others.<br>Likes to claim things as "mine."<br>Gives up items that belong to others upon request.<br>Begins to show empathy for another child or adult.<br>Continues to desire personal attention.<br>Indicates awareness of a person's absence by saying "bye-bye."<br>May enjoy removing clothing and is not embarrassed about being naked.<br>Reveals a sense of trust in adults.<br>Plays contentedly alone if near adults.<br>Likes to play next to other children, but does not interact with them.<br>Is able to play some simple interacting games for short periods of time. |
| **22 to 24 Months** | Displays signs of love for parents and other favorite people.<br>Is easily hurt by criticism.<br>Shows the emotions of pride and embarrassment.<br>May show some aggressive tendencies, such as slapping, biting, hitting.<br>May assume an increasingly self-sufficient attitude.<br>Wants own way in everything.<br>May dawdle but desires to please adults.<br>Is more responsive to and demanding of adults.<br>Still prefers to play alone, but likes to be near others.<br>Engages in imaginative play related to parents' actions.<br>Uses own name in reference to self when talking to others.<br>Is continually testing limits set by parents and caregivers.<br>Likes to control others and give them orders. |

| Two- and Three-Year-Olds | |
|---|---|
| **Gross Motor Skills** | |
| **24 to 29 Months** | Runs without falling.<br>Pedals a tricycle.<br>Kicks a large ball.<br>Jumps in place.<br>Plays on swings, ladders, and other playground equipment with fair amount of ease.<br>Throws ball without falling.<br>Bends at waist to pick up object from floor.<br>Walks up and down stairs, both feet on step, while holding onto railings.<br>Stands with both feet on balance beam. |
| **30 to 36 Months** | Walks on tiptoes.<br>Performs a standing broad jump 8½ inches.<br>Attempts to balance on one foot.<br>Walks to and picks up a large ball.<br>Balances on one foot for 5 seconds.<br>Catches a large ball with arms.<br>Walks up stairs with alternating feet.<br>Rides a tricycle.<br>Performs 1 to 3 hops with both feet together. |
| **37 to 48 Months** | Walks toe-to-heel for four steps.<br>Balances on one foot for 8 seconds.<br>Catches a beanbag while standing.<br>Performs 1 to 3 hops on one foot.<br>Catches a bounced ball with hands. |
| **Fine Motor Skills** | |
| **24 to 29 Months** | Inserts key into lock.<br>Turns pages in a book one at a time.<br>Strings large beads.<br>Copies a vertical line.<br>Copies a horizontal line.<br>Builds a tower consisting of 6 to 7 cubes.<br>Uses two or more cubes to make a train.<br>Uses one hand consistently for most activities.<br>Holds scissors correctly.<br>Opens and closes scissors. |
| **30 to 36 Months** | Builds a tower consisting of 8 cubes.<br>Copies a circle.<br>Imitates building a three-block bridge.<br>Snips paper with scissors. |
| **37 to 48 Months** | Pours liquid from a pitcher.<br>Copies a cross.<br>Builds a tower of 9 to 10 cubes.<br>Completes simple puzzles.<br>Wiggles thumb.<br>Folds paper twice (in imitation).<br>Draws a person with three parts.<br>Cuts a 5-inch piece of paper in two.<br>Traces a diamond.<br>Cuts along a 5-inch line within ½ inch of the line. |

| Self-Help Skills | |
|---|---|
| **24 to 29 Months** | Cooperates in dressing.<br>Removes shoes, socks, and pants.<br>Pulls on simple garments.<br>Unzips zipper.<br>Unsnaps snap.<br>Verbalizes toilet needs.<br>Usually remains dry during the day. |
| **30 to 36 Months** | Seldom has bowel accidents.<br>Unbuttons large buttons.<br>Closes snaps.<br>Sits on toilet without assistance.<br>Puts on shoes.<br>Pours well from a pitcher.<br>Uses a knife for spreading. |
| **37 to 48 Months** | Washes and dries face and hands.<br>Unbuckles belt.<br>Usually remains dry at night.<br>Turns faucet on and off. |
| Expressive Language Skills | |
| **24 to 29 Months** | Combines two or more words (boy hit).<br>Yes/no questions marked only by intonation (Mommy go? You see me?).<br>*No* and *not* used to negate entire sentence (No eat; Mommy no; No sit down).<br>Preposition *in* used (Go in house; Ball in box).<br>Uses plural (More cookies; cats). |
| **30 to 36 Months** | Uses negative elements *no, can't,* and *don't* after subject (I can't eat; Mommy, don't go).<br>Use of different modifiers: qualifiers (some, a lot, all); possessives (mine, his, hers); adjectives (pretty, new, blue).<br>Overgeneralization of regular past with an *ed* (He eated it; I woked up). |
| **37 to 48 Months** | Preposition *on* used (book on table; sit on chair).<br>Possessives used (mommy's coat; daddy's car).<br>*When* questions appear.<br>Negatives *cannot* and *do not* appear.<br>Uses double negatives with a negative pronoun (*nobody, nothing*) or adverb (*never, nowhere*). Examples include "I can't do nothing" or "I don't never get to go."<br>Joins sentences with two clauses (Then it broke and we didn't have it anymore). |
| Language Comprehension Skills | |
| **24 to 29 Months** | Child answers routine questions (What is that? What is your name? What is he doing?).<br>Points to six body parts on doll or self.<br>Provides appropriate answers to yes/no questions that deal with the child's environment (Is mommy sleeping? Is daddy cooking?).<br>Comprehends pronouns: *I, my, mine, me.* |
| **30 to 36 Months** | Follows two-step directions.<br>Provides appropriate answers for *where* (place) questions that deal with familiar information (Where does daddy work? Where do you sleep?).<br>Comprehends pronouns: *she, he, his, him,* and *her.* |

| **Language Comprehension Skills** (Continued) | |
|---|---|
| **37 to 48 Months** | Provides appropriate answers for *whose* questions (Whose doll is this?).<br>Provides appropriate answers for *why* (cause or reason) questions (Why is the girl crying?).<br>Provides appropriate answers for *who* (person or animal) questions (Who lives at the North Pole?).<br>Understands the pronouns *you* and *they*.<br>Provides appropriate answers for *how* questions (How will mother bake the pie?). |
| **Math Readiness Skills** | |
| **30 to 36 Months** | Gives "just one" upon request.<br>Comprehends concepts *light* and *heavy* in object manipulation tasks.<br>Comprehends size concepts *big* and *tall* in object manipulation tasks.<br>Comprehends spatial concepts *on, under, out of, together,* and *away from* in object manipulation tasks. |
| **37 to 48 Months** | Gives "just two" upon request.<br>Distinguishes between *one* and *many.*<br>Understands the quantity concept *empty* in object manipulation tasks.<br>Understands *smaller;* points to smaller objects. Understands *largest.*<br>Counts while correctly pointing to 3 objects.<br>Understands quantity concepts *full, more,* and *less* in object manipulation tasks.<br>Comprehends spatial concepts *up, top, apart,* and *toward* in object manipulation tasks.<br>Comprehends spatial concepts *around, in front of, in back of, high,* and *next to* in object manipulation tasks. |
| **Social Skills** | |
| **24 to 29 Months** | Likes to play near other children, but is unable to play cooperatively.<br>Becomes a grabber, and may grab desired toys away from other children.<br>Does not like to share toys.<br>Has not learned to say please but often desires the toys of other children.<br>Likes to give affection to parents.<br>May pull hair or bite before giving up a desired possession. |
| **30 to 36 Months** | Continues to have a strong sense of ownership but may give up a toy if offered a substitute.<br>May learn to say please if prompted.<br>Has increased desire to play near and with other children.<br>May begin cooperative play.<br>Distinguishes between boys and girls.<br>Likes to be accepted by others.<br>Enjoys hiding from others.<br>Likes to play with adults on a one-to-one basis.<br>Enjoys tumble play with other children and caregivers. |
| **37 to 48 Months** | Is learning to share and take turns.<br>Follows directions and takes pride in doing things for others.<br>May act in a certain way to please caregivers.<br>Makes friends easily.<br>Seeks status among peers.<br>May attempt to comfort and remove cause of distress of playmates.<br>Seeks friends on own initiative.<br>Begins to be choosy about companions, preferring one over another.<br>Uses language to make friends and alienate others. |

| | **Emotional Development** |
|---|---|
| **24 to 29 Months** | Continues to be self-centered.<br>May exhibit increasing independence one minute and then run back to security of parents the next.<br>Likes immediate gratification of desires and finds it difficult to wait.<br>May exhibit negativism.<br>Continues to seek caregiver approval for behaviors and accomplishments.<br>Displays jealousy.<br>May develop fear of dark; needs reassurance. |
| **30 to 36 Months** | May display negative feelings and occasional bad temper.<br>May exhibit aggressiveness.<br>May dawdle but insists on doing things for self.<br>Likes to dress self and needs praise and encouragement when correct.<br>Feels bad when reprimanded for mistakes.<br>Desires caregiver approval.<br>Wants independence but shows fear of new experiences.<br>May reveal need for clinging to security object.<br>Needs an understanding, orderly environment.<br>May have trouble sleeping if the day's events have been emotional. |
| **37 to 48 Months** | Is usually cooperative, happy, and agreeable.<br>Feels less frustrated because motor skills have improved.<br>May still seek comfort from caregivers when tired or hungry.<br>Learns more socially acceptable ways of displaying feelings.<br>May substitute language for primitive displays of feelings.<br>May show fear of dark, animals, stories, and the "bogeyman." |
| | **Four- and Five-Year-Olds** |
| | **Gross Motor Skills** |
| **4 Years** | Catches beanbag with hands.<br>Hops on one foot.<br>Walks down stairs with alternating feet.<br>Throws ball overhand.<br>Carries a cup of liquid without spilling.<br>Rides bicycle with training wheels.<br>Balances on one foot for 10 seconds.<br>Skips with alternating feet.<br>Walks backward toe-to-heel for four consecutive steps.<br>Builds elaborate structures with blocks. |
| **5 Years** | Marches to music.<br>Jumps from table height.<br>Climbs fences.<br>Attempts to jump rope.<br>Attempts to skate.<br>Walks forward, backward, and sideways on balance beam.<br>Catches ball with hands. |
| | **Fine Motor Skills** |
| **4 Years** | Builds a 3-block bridge from a model.<br>Completes a 6- to 8-piece puzzle.<br>Folds paper diagonally (three folds).<br>Copies a square.<br>Paints and draws freely. |

| Fine Motor Skills (Continued) | |
|---|---|
| **5 Years** | Copies a triangle. <br> Prints first name. <br> Prints simple words. <br> Dials telephone numbers correctly. <br> Models objects with clay. <br> Colors within lines. <br> Draws recognizable people, houses, and vehicles. |
| **Self-Help Skills** | |
| **4 Years** | Laces shoes. <br> Buckles belt. <br> Cuts with knife. <br> Dresses and undresses with supervision. <br> Distinguishes front and back of clothing. <br> Zips separating zipper. |
| **5 Years** | Dresses and undresses without assistance. <br> Washes self. <br> Puts shoes on correct feet. <br> Unbuttons back buttons. |
| **Language Skills** | |
| **4 Years** | Understands has/doesn't have and is/is not. <br> Identifies penny, nickel, and dime. <br> Follows three commands in proper order (clear the table, wash the table, and get ready to go outdoors). <br> Understands the pronoun *we*. <br> Uses irregular verb forms (ate, ran, went). <br> Uses regular tense (ed) verbs. <br> Uses third person present tense verbs (runs, shops). <br> Speaks fluently with a 1500-word vocabulary. <br> Forms sentences of 4 to 8 words. <br> Asks many *when*, *why*, and *how* questions. <br> Tells simple jokes. |
| **5 Years** | Uses third person irregular verbs (He has a ball.) <br> Uses compound sentences. (I went to the grocery store and I went to my grandmother's.) <br> Uses descriptions in telling a story. <br> Uses some pronouns correctly. <br> Uses words to describe sizes, distances, weather, time, and location. <br> Asks the meaning of words. <br> Recalls the main details of a story. <br> Recognizes some verbal absurdities. <br> Tells original stories. <br> Has a 2000-word vocabulary. |
| **Math Readiness Skills** | |
| **4 Years** | Understands the concepts *beside*, *bottom*, *backward*, and *forward* in object manipulation tasks. <br> Understands size concepts *short*, *fat*, and *thin* in object manipulation tasks. <br> Counts 1 to 4 chips and correctly answers questions such as "How many altogether?" with cardinal number. |

| Math Readiness Skills (Continued) | |
|---|---|
| **4 Years** (Continued) | Says correct number when shown 2 to 6 objects and asked "How many?"<br>Can rote count 1 through 9.<br>Understands the concepts of *triangle* and *circle*.<br>Understands the concepts *tallest* and *same size*. |
| **5 Years** | Understands *square* and *rectangle*.<br>Understands the concept of *same shape*.<br>Understands the position concepts *first* and *last* in object manipulation tasks.<br>Understands position concept *middle*.<br>Rote counts 1 through 20.<br>Recognizes the numerals 1 through 10.<br>Writes the numerals 1 through 5.<br>May count 1 to 20 objects correctly. |

| Social-Emotional Development | |
|---|---|
| **4 Years** | May seem less pleasant and cooperative than at age 3.<br>May be more moody, tries to express emotions verbally.<br>Strives for independence; resents being treated like a baby.<br>May be stubborn and quarrelsome, at times.<br>Resents directions; may think he or she knows it all and can do it all.<br>Learns to ask for things instead of snatching things from others.<br>Is increasingly aware of attitudes and asks for approval.<br>Needs and seeks parental approval often.<br>Has strong sense of family and home.<br>May quote parents and boast about parents to friends.<br>Becomes more interested in friends than in adults.<br>Shares possessions and toys, especially with special friends.<br>Suggests taking turns but may be unable to wait for his or her own turn.<br>Likes to play with friends in cooperative play activities. |
| **5 Years** | Shows increased willingness to cooperate.<br>Is more patient, generous, and conscientious.<br>Expresses anger verbally rather than physically.<br>Is more reasonable when in a quarrel.<br>Develops a sense of fairness.<br>Likes supervision, accepts instructions, and asks permission.<br>Has a strong desire to please parents and other adults.<br>Still depends on parents for emotional support and approval.<br>Is proud of mother and father.<br>Delights in helping parents.<br>May act protective of younger siblings.<br>Shapes ideas of gender roles by watching parents' behavior.<br>Is increasingly social and talkative.<br>Is eager to make friends and develop strong friendships.<br>May pick a best friend.<br>Prefers cooperative play in small groups.<br>Prefers friends of same age and gender.<br>Stays with play groups as long as interests hold.<br>Learns to respect the property of friends. |

| Six to 12 Years of Age | |
|---|---|
| **Physical Development** | |
| **6 Years** | Body becomes more slender with longer arms and legs; babyhood physique continues to disappear.<br>Loses baby teeth, which are replaced by the first permanent teeth.<br>Is constantly active.<br>Prefers running over walking.<br>May have frequent minor tumbles and scrapes. |
| **7 to 8 Years** | May look lanky due to thin body and long arms and legs.<br>Becomes better coordinated; movements become more fluid and graceful.<br>Develops improved sense of balance and timing.<br>Enjoys sports, especially boisterous games.<br>Enjoys skating, skipping, and jumping rope.<br>Able to handle simple tools.<br>Girls are developing faster than boys. |
| **9 to 10 Years** | Continues to improve coordination.<br>Improves sense of balance and timing.<br>May develop particular physical skills.<br>Enjoys organized games.<br>Can run, kick, throw, catch, and hit.<br>Further refines fine motor skills.<br>Is able to use hands skillfully in building models, learning handcrafts, or using tools.<br>Enjoys drawing.<br>Spends a lot of time and energy playing physical games.<br>Girls may start adolescent growth spurt. |
| **11 to 12 Years** | Likes to test strength and daring.<br>Becomes very conscious of overall appearance.<br>Boys may grow little in height.<br>Girls may experience growth spurt.<br>Girls may begin menstruation. |
| **Cognitive Development** | |
| **6 Years** | Asks more complex questions and wants detailed answers.<br>Concentrates on doing one activity for longer period of time.<br>Has improved memory.<br>Has better understanding of the concept of time.<br>Is inquisitive and eager to learn in school.<br>May begin to understand concepts of seriation, conservation, reversibility, and multiple classification.<br>Usually can distinguish between fantasy and reality.<br>Can understand and follow rules.<br>Begins reading, writing, and math at school. |
| **7 to 8 Years** | Accepts idea of rules and knows harm might result if rules are not followed.<br>Understands concept of time.<br>Has longer attention span.<br>Understands value of money and may be ready for an allowance.<br>Favors reality; is less interested in fairy tales.<br>Beings to show interest in collectiing certain objects.<br>Likes to help teachers.<br>Enjoys reading animal stories and science fiction stories.<br>May show interest in stories about children of other countries.<br>Refines concepts of seriation, conservation, reversibility, and multiple classification.<br>Begins to understand cause and effect. |

| Cognitive Development (Continued) | |
|---|---|
| **9 to 10 Years** | Is able to consider more than one conclusion to problems or choices.<br>Understands more about truth and honesty.<br>Likes to act in a more adult manner.<br>Is still enthusiastic about learning.<br>Likes games that involve mental competition.<br>Enjoys quizzing parents and impressing them with new facts.<br>Shows increasing capacity for self-evaluation.<br>Enjoys mysteries and secrets.<br>May show less interest in TV programs.<br>May continue to show interest in collecting certain objects.<br>Has vocabulary of about 5400 words.<br>Has better use of language and is able to converse well with adults.<br>Uses more abstract words. |
| **11 to 12 Years** | Is able to detect problems in daily situations and work out solutions.<br>Grasps math concepts and applies them to daily activities.<br>May like group projects and classes based on cooperative effort.<br>Likes active learning, reading aloud, reciting, and science projects.<br>May allow peer relationships to affect schoolwork.<br>Has vocabulary of about 7200 words.<br>May enjoy lengthy conversations with teachers.<br>May enjoy long periods of solitude to think or to work on projects like building models.<br>May show interest in reading; mysteries, adventure stories, and biographies are favorites.<br>Understands concepts of seriation, conservation, reversibility, and multiple classification.<br>Applies logic to problem solving.<br>Uses language to discuss feelings. |
| Emotional and Social Development | |
| **6 Years** | Becomes more socially independent; chooses own friends.<br>May feel less jealous of siblings as outside interests become more important.<br>Is still egocentric, but is becoming interested in group activities.<br>May still have a hard time waiting and taking turns.<br>Wants desperately to be right and to win.<br>Tattles often to check sense of right and wrong.<br>Wants all of everything, making choices is difficult.<br>May have nightmares.<br>Often expresses sense of humor in practical jokes and riddles.<br>Begins to see other's point of view.<br>Learns to share and take turns. |
| **7 Years** | May seem withdrawn and moody.<br>Likes to spend time alone or in the background.<br>May feel that everyone is against him or her.<br>Wants and needs approval of adults and peers.<br>Is very conscientious; strives hard to please.<br>Is sensitive and hurt by criticism. |
| **8 Years** | Shows more spirit; is willing to try just about anything.<br>May turn to tears and self-criticism upon failure, but recovers quickly.<br>Is able to get along well with others.<br>Chooses companions of same gender and age.<br>Is very sensitive to what others think.<br>Shows intense interest in groups. |

| Emotional and Social Development (Continued) | |
|---|---|
| **8 Years** (Continued) | Wants to look and act like peers.<br>Enjoys group activities in organizations and in own secret clubs.<br>Chooses a best friend, but may change best friends often. |
| **9 Years** | Is relatively quiet.<br>Worries about everything.<br>Is sensitive to criticism.<br>Forms groups with others of same gender.<br>Complains a lot.<br>Has definite likes and dislikes.<br>Begins a new drive for independence; resents being "bossed" by parents.<br>Knows right from wrong; will accept blame when necessary, but offers excuses.<br>Shows increased interest in friends and decreased interest in family.<br>Is interested in group activities and concerns.<br>Often competes with others. |
| **10 Years** | Is happy with life in general.<br>Likes people and is liked by others.<br>Is dependable and cooperative.<br>Obeys adults easily and naturally.<br>Likes to accept responsibility and tries to do things well.<br>Likes praise and encouragement.<br>Still has strong group spirit, but it may be diminishing.<br>May begin to show more loyalty to a best friend than to the group, especially girls.<br>May enjoy being part of a team.<br>Likes teacher attention and approval. |
| **11 to 12 Years** | Is less self-centered.<br>May express great enthusiasm.<br>Likes to plan and carry out activities with a group.<br>Is willing to reach out to others for friendship.<br>Has improved social skills.<br>May show more tact, especially with friends.<br>Is patient and friendly with younger children.<br>If puberty has begun, may become moody and show signs of emotional turmoil.<br>Has strong desire to conform to peers in dress and behavior.<br>Likes team games.<br>Is becoming interested in opposite gender; girls more interested than boys. |

Adapted from *Parents and Their Children* by Verdene Ryder, Goodheart-Willcox Company, Inc., 2000.

# Acknowledgments

Through the long months of revising this manuscript, there were many individuals whose encouragement, support, and expertise helped me immeasurably. My sincere thanks to all of them.

First, I would like to dedicate this book to my grandchildren, Jeffrey and Eva Herr. They are fascinating and constantly remind me just how much young children know and learn.

To my husband, Dr. James Herr, who has supported and nurtured me throughout this process.

To my sons, John and Mark, who by their development and accomplishments have reinforced the value of the book's content and the importance of nurturing young children. They have more than earned all the credit and appreciation that I can give them; both have become independent, productive, and fascinating young adults.

To May and Molly Herr, my daughters-in-law, who share my love of young children.

To Carolee Samuels and Billie Hainsey, my editors, who have provided stimulating insights and ideas as well as continuous support and encouragement throughout the development of the manuscript and supplements.

To Dr. Judy Jax, who saw a need for this textbook.

To Deb Hass, Vicki Weber, Shirley Gebhart, and Betsy Hartford, my secretaries, who so ably transcribed my writing.

To Deanna Applehans, Sandy Duncan, Karen Maggio, and Sue Unger for their professional support and friendship.

To Mary Hopkins-Best, who provided editorial assistance on the Special Needs chapter.

To Sue Dunkley, who allowed me to photograph in her centers.

To Julia Lorenz, Kathy Pruesse, Jamie Lynch, Heidi Weber, Julie Scharlau, Travis Young, and Patti Kettenacker for providing photography and allowing me to photograph in the center.

To Andrew Farrar, Tanya Jones, Nicole Stopera, Marian Marion, Dawn Tenneyson-Grimm, Terri Swim, and Robin Muza. Paula Noll, Connie Weber, Karen Benkowski, Carla Ahman, Gina Schafer, Megan Shaw, Dr. Esther Fahm, Dr. Janice Coker, Dr. Mary Thompson, Donna Dixon, Eileen Zenk, Margaret Brunn, Judy Gifford, Paula Noll, Peg Saienga, Lori Register, Patti Herman, Janet Massa, Teresa Mitchell, Rita Devery, Dr. Priscilla Huffman, Candy Jordon, Carla Ahmann, Dianne Carriveau, Linda DeMore, Dr. Karen Zimmerman, Dr. Joan Herwig, Elaine Staaland, Janet Mafet, Cari Parent, Joanne Fruit, Kari Merritt, Dr. Penny Warnert, Nancy Graese, Nan Olson, Angela La Bonne Kaiser, Paulette Fontaine, Paula Iverson, Jeannette Daines, Sally Olm, Phyllis Barilla, Lori Pioske, Elizabeth Kaster, Jill Behnke, and my parents, Melba and Herb Knutsen, for their support and encouragement throughout this process.

To Yvonne Libby, a former colleague and coauthor on other publications.

To Chancellor Charles Sorensen, Vice Chancellor Robert Sedlak, Associate Vice Chancellor Julie Furst-Bowe, and John Wesolek, Dean of the College of Human Development, for their continuous support of the early childhood program.

To Martin Springer and Kathy Rucker Schaffer for assistance with photography.

To Gladys Earl, Assistant Professor in the Food and Nutrition Department, who contributed recipes for use in the text.

Finally, to all the early childhood majors at the University of Wisconsin-Stout and the children in the Child and Family Study Center who have facilitated my thinking for this book.

# Photo Credits

# Glossary

## A

**abrasion.** A scrape that damages a portion of the skin, such as a skinned knee, scratched arm, or rope burn. (12)

**acceleration.** Process in which a gifted child is assigned to a class with older children. (30)

**accredited.** Having a certification that states a set of standards has been met. (2)

**acoustic material.** Material used to deaden or absorb sounds. Carpets, drapes, bulletin boards, pillows, stuffed toys, and sand are examples. (8)

**active listening.** Listening to what is said, then repeating it. (13)

**activity patterns.** Levels of movements in infants. (4)

**Acquired Immune Deficiency Syndrome (AIDS).** A disease caused by the human immunodeficiency virus. The virus breaks down the body's immune system, leaving the body vulnerable to disease. (12)

**adult-centered program model.** A structured curriculum format for school-age child care that has a high level of adult direction. (29)

**allergy.** A reaction to a substance, possibly causing rashes, swelling, sneezing, or other reactions. (11)

**amblyopia.** The result of a muscle imbalance caused by disuse of an eye. Often called *lazy eye*. (30)

**ambulatory.** Being able to move from place to place. (30)

**anecdotal records.** Notes kept by the teacher concerning children's play. (3)

**animal stories.** Books giving animals some human qualities. Usually, the animal has some unusual success or ability. (19)

**anaphylactic shock.** Extreme allergic reaction that causes shock symptoms and possibly death. (11)

**arthritis.** Condition brought on by inflammation that produces swelling of joints and surrounding tissues. (30)

**articulation.** The ability to speak in clearly pronounced sounds. (6)

**articulation problems.** Omissions, distortions, or substitutions of vowels or consonants or both. (30)

**artificial consequences.** Those that are deliberately set up by an adult to show what will happen if a rule is broken. (13)

**assessment.** A process that involves observing, recording, and documenting children's individual capabilities over time. This information is the basis for curriculum decisions when planning for one child or groups. (3)

**asthma.** A respiratory disease that causes labored breathing, gasping, coughing, and wheezing. (30)

**attachment.** The strong emotional connection that develops between people. (4)

**attention deficit disorder (ADD).** Condition in which a child has an unusually short attention span; is considered a learning disability. (30)

**attention deficit hyperactivity disorder (ADHD).** Form of ADD that includes hyperactivity and impulsiveness; is considered a learning disability. (30)

**attitude.** Your outlook on life; the way in which you think about or act toward others. (32)

**audiovisual board.** A smooth wall board that serves as a bulletin board, chalkboard, and movie screen. (8)

**auditory discrimination skills.** The ability to detect different sounds by listening. (26)

**auditory learner.** A child who learns best through hearing. This child is the first to hear a fly in the classroom or a snow plow outdoors. (17)

**auditory signals.** Informing children of a change through the use of sound, such as a bell, timer, Autoharp®, tambourine, or piano. (16)

**augmentative communication device.** Device designed to help facilitate communication with a child who is unable to speak understandably. (30)

**au pair.** A person from a foreign country who lives with a family and provides child care in exchange for room, board, and transportation. (1)

**Autoharp®.** A simple chording instrument used to accompany singing. (26)

*Note: Numbers indicate the chapter in which the term is defined.*

# B

**behavioral expectations.** Limits that children are expected to follow. (27)

**behaviors.** Refers to any visible activities done by the child. (17)

**bentonite.** A clay product used as a thickening agent for powdered tempera paint. (18)

**block plan.** A written overall view of the curriculum. (17)

**body percussion.** Musical movement activities such as stomping feet, clapping hands, patting thighs, and snapping fingers. (26)

**bridging.** A process of placing two blocks vertically a space apart, then adding a third block. (18)

**burn.** An injury caused by heat, radiation, or chemical agents, generally classified by degree or depth. (12)

# C

**cautious.** Slower to make decisions. (17)

**cephalocaudal principle.** Principle of development stating that development tends to proceed from the head downward. According to this principle, the child first gains control of the head, then the arms, then the legs. (4)

**cerebral palsy.** Condition resulting from damage to the brain and characterized by lack of control of voluntary movements. (30)

**chalk painting.** Art activity in which chalk is dipped into water and used to draw on construction paper. (18)

**chalk talk.** Storytelling method using drawings on chalkboard, tagboard, or newsprint. (19)

**chant.** Song that has word patterns, rhymes, and nonsense syllables in one to three tones repeated in a sequence. (26)

**checking-in services.** Program assigning workers to call children in self-care to make sure there are no problems. (2)

**checklist.** Form of assessment designed to record the presence or absence of specific traits or behaviors. (3)

**child care centers.** Full-day child care facilities that focus on basic nutritional, social, emotional, intellectual, and physical needs. (2)

**child-centered program model.** A curriculum format for school-age child care that allows children an opportunity to self-select activities. (29)

**Child Development Associate (CDA) Credential.** A national credential that requires postsecondary courses in child care education and a minimum number of hours of child care experience. To be eligible for this credential, a person must be eighteen years of age and have a high school diploma. (1)

**chronic health needs.** Needs for special care caused by an illness that persists over a period of time. (30)

**chronological age.** Age determined by a birth date. (9)

**classification.** The process of mentally grouping objects or ideas into categories or classes based on some unique feature. (7)

**closed wound.** An injury to the tissue directly under the skin surface but not involving a break in the skin, such as a bruise. (12)

**closed-ended questions.** Questions requiring few decision-making skills and most often answered with yes or no. Also referred to as *single-answer questions*. (23)

**closure.** How an activity will end. (17)

**coaching.** Teaching skill that provides children with ideas for difficult situations. (20)

**cognitive development.** Growth in the mental processes used to gain knowledge, such as thought, reasoning, and imagination. (4)

**collage.** Selecting and mounting materials on a flat surface. (18)

**color blindness.** The inability to see a color. This problem, also referred to as color deficiency, is hereditary. (30)

**color deficiency.** The inability to see a color. This problem, also referred to as color blindness, is hereditary. (30)

**communicable diseases.** Illnesses that can be passed on to other people. (12)

**compassion.** Being aware of others' distress and wanting to help them (7)

**concept.** A generalized idea or notion. (17)

**concrete operations**. The use of logic based on what has been experienced or seen. (7)

**conditions of performance.** List of tools a child will use, including puzzles, paper, scissors, beads, or any other materials and/or equipment found in early childhood settings. This list can also include what the child will be denied. (17)

**confidentiality.** The keeping private of sensitive personal information involving other people. (32)

**conflict.** Two or more forces that oppose each other. (20)

**congenital.** A condition caused before birth but not hereditary. (30)

**consequence.** A result that follows an action or behavior. (13)

**conservation.** Concept that change in position or shape of substances does not change the quantity. (7)

**consumable supplies.** Supplies that, in most cases, cannot be used again. (9)

**contactants.** Objects that make contact with the body through touch. (30)

**content and process-centered approach.** A teaching philosophy in which learning is seen as a constant process of exploring and questioning the environment with hands-on curriculum stressed. (17)

**cool colors.** Colors, such as blue and green, that make a room appear larger and create a feeling of openness. (8)

**co-op.** Group of people or groups who unite so they have more buying power. (9)

**cooperative play.** Type of play in which two or more children interact with one another. At this stage socio-dramatic play begins. (20)

**cover letter.** A letter of introduction that is usually included when sending a resume to a prospective employer. (32)

**crawling.** A skill in the motor sequence occurring shortly after the infant learns to roll onto the stomach. It occurs when the infant's abdomen is on the ground. (4)

**creeping.** Movement in which infants support their weight on their hands and knees, moving their arms and legs to go forward. (4)

**cubbies.** Top sections of lockers used to store finished artwork, library books, parent letters, and other valuable items. (8)

**culture.** A group's ideas and ways of doing things—such as traditions, language, beliefs, and customs—that become a learned pattern of social behavior. (24)

**custodial care.** Type of child care that focuses primarily on meeting the child's physical needs. (2)

**cystic fibrosis.** A chronic hereditary disease that involves persistent and serious lung infections; failure to gain weight; and loose, foul smelling stools. (30)

**D**

**daily news flash.** A written communication tool used by centers to inform parents about program or center news. Parents can use this news to bring about verbal interaction with their children. (31)

**dawdling.** Eating slowly or having a lack of interest in food; sometimes used as an attempt to gain attention. (16)

**deferred imitation.** Watching another person's behavior, then acting out that behavior. This occurs between eighteen and twenty-four months. (4)

**desensitized.** A process in which a doctor injects small amounts of an allergen into the body over time building immunities to an irritant. (30)

**development.** Change or growth in a human being. Development is usually measured in terms of physical, intellectual, social, and emotional growth. (4)

**developmental age.** A child's skill and growth level compared to what is thought of as normal for that age group. (9)

**developmental norms.** Characteristics and behaviors considered normal for children in certain age groups. (3)

**diabetes.** A disease in which the body cannot properly control the level of sugar in the blood. (11)

**direct guidance.** Physical and verbal actions, such as facial and body gestures, that influence behavior. (13)

**direct learning experience.** Learning experience planned with a specific goal in mind. (17)

**dramatic play.** A form of play in which a child imitates others. (20)

**draw and tell.** Storytelling method using drawings made on chalkboard, tagboard, or newsprint. Also called *chalk talk*. (19)

**E**

**early childhood.** The period of life from birth to nine years of age. (1)

**ecology.** Study of the chain of life, focusing on water, land, air, grass, trees, birds, and insects. (24)

**egocentric.** Quality of people believing everyone thinks as they do. (5)

**elimination.** Bowel or bladder release. (16)

**emetic.** A substance used for emergency poisonings. When swallowed, it will induce vomiting. (10)

**emotional abuse.** Abuse of a child's self-concept by parents or guardians through such acts as providing insufficient love, guidance, and/or support. (10)

**empathy.** The ability to understand the feelings of others. (7)

**empty set.** A set without any members, such as a set of tables without legs or a set of children with beards. (22)

**encouraging.** A guidance strategy teachers use to recognize a child's efforts and improvements. (13)

**enrichment.** A process to broaden the range of experiences with special curriculum. (30)

**entrepreneur.** A person who starts his or her own business. (1)

**epilepsy.** A convulsive disorder caused by damage to the brain causing a person to have periodic seizures. (12)

**ethics.** A guiding set of moral principles, either those held personally or those determined by a professional organization for its members. (1)

**expansion.** Technique that involves taking a child's mispronounced words and correctly expanding them into sentences. (5)

**expressive language.** The ability to produce language forms; used to express a person's thoughts to others. (5)

**F**

**fairy tales.** Books having a theme of achievement. The characters or heroes of these stories must perform difficult tasks in order to succeed. (19)

**family child care.** Child care that is provided in a private home. (2)

**family life stories.** Books containing the theme of social understanding. (19)

**farsighted.** Able to see objects in the distance more clearly than those that are close. (7)

**feeding-in.** A strategy where a teacher helps a child learn language by providing the child's language for him or her. (5)

**feely box.** A box with a circle cut in it large enough for children to put their hands into and identify different objects and materials placed inside by touch. (23)

**felt board.** A board covered with felt or flannel that is used as a background for placing felt characters and props to tell a story. (19)

**field-independent.** Children who are more independent and prefer to work on their own. They enjoy competition as well as individual recognition. (17)

**field-sensitive.** Children who are more interactive with others; volunteering, assisting, and helpful, they also try to gain attention. (17)

**fine motor development.** The ability to coordinate the small muscles in the arms, fingers, and wrists to complete tasks such as grasping, holding, cutting, drawing, and writing. (4)

**first-degree burn.** Burn to the top layer of skin. It is the least severe of all burns. Signs include redness or mild discoloration, pain, and mild swelling. (12)

**flannel board.** A board covered with felt or flannel that is used as a background for placing felt characters and props to tell a story. (19)

**flexible limits.** Limits that can be adapted to the needs of an individual or a situation. (15)

**flipcharts.** Stories drawn on large tagboard cards used for storytelling. (19)

**flowchart.** Drawn chart that outlines major concepts related to a theme. (17)

**foodborne illness.** An illness caused by eating food that contains harmful bacteria, toxins, parasites, or viruses. (12)

**Food Guide Pyramid for Young Children.** A model used to make food choices for children ages two to six years. Made of six groups, the Pyramid shows how groups work together to form a nutritious diet. It also shows the recommended number of daily servings for each group. (11)

**frustration.** Feelings of defeat or discouragement causing tension. (14)

**functional stage of play.** Second stage of material use. During this stage, a child will use a prop as it was intended while playing with other children. (20)

# G

**gender roles.** Behaviors expected of girls or boys. (5)

**gerontology.** Study of the aged. (24)

**giftedness.** Having exceptional skills in one or more of six areas: creative or productive thinking, general intellectual ability, leadership ability, psychomotor ability, specific academic aptitude, and/or visual or performing arts. (30)

**glaucoma.** Condition caused by failure of the eye fluid to circulate in the proper way, resulting in increased pressure on the eye. Over time, this pressure can destroy the optic nerve. (30)

**grand mal seizure.** A reaction, or seizure, caused by epilepsy. During a grand mal seizure, a person will lose consciousness, jerk, thrash, or become stiff. (12)

**gross motor development.** Improvement of the skills involving arms, legs, and whole body movements. Examples include running, jumping, throwing, and climbing. (4)

**guidance.** Direct and indirect actions used by an adult to help children develop socially acceptable behavior. (13)

# H

**hand-eye coordination.** Muscle control that allows the hand to do a task in the way the eye sees it done. (21)

**head lice.** Small bugs that make their homes on the hair and scalp and feed on human blood. (12)

**Head Start.** A program developed by the federal government to strengthen the academic skills of children from low-income homes, and designed mainly for four- and five-year-olds. (2)

**hearing impaired.** Term that describes a person who has at least some degree of hearing loss. (30)

**hemophilia.** Genetic blood disease in which the blood cannot clot normally. (30)

**hidden job market.** Jobs advertised informally through word of mouth. (32)

**hitching.** Movement that occurs after an infant is able to sit without support. From this position, infants move their arms and legs, sliding their buttocks across the floor. (4)

**human immune deficiency virus (HIV).** A virus that breaks down the body's immune system, eventually causing the disease AIDS. (12)

**hyperopia.** Difficulty in seeing things that are close. Also referred to as farsightedness. (30)

# I

**ignoring.** Avoiding an acknowledgment to a child's inappropriate behavior if the behavior is not dangerous. (13)

**imaginative stage of play.** The third and final stage of material use. Children in this stage do not need real props; they are able to think of substitutes. (20)

**I-message.** A verbal statement that explains the effect of a child's behavior on others without placing blame. (13)

**impulsive.** Quick to make decisions. (17)

**incest.** Sexual abuse by a relative. (10)

**incidental learnings.** Learning experiences that happen during the course of the day. (24)

**inclusion.** Term used to refer to an education setting in which children with and without special needs are integrated. (30)

**indirect guidance.** Outside factors influencing behavior, such as the layout of the center. (13)

**indirect learning experience.** Learning experience that occurs on the spur of the moment. (17)

**individual transition.** Quietly informing a particular child of a change, such as cleaning up or going to the snack table. (16)

**Individualized Education Plan (IEP).** A written strategy for learning designed to ensure that each child with special needs is educated in the most appropriate manner for him or her. (30)

**Individualized Family Service Plan (IFSP).** Strategy developed when a preschool age child is diagnosed as having a disability. It includes the family's needs in regard to enhancing the child's development, goals for the child, services to be provided to the child and/or family, and a plan for transitioning the child to other services and regular education. (30)

**Individuals with Disabilities Education Act (IDEA).** Federal law requiring all states to provide education for children who are developmentally delayed. (30)

**induce.** To produce on purpose. (16)

**infant.** Term used to refer to a child from birth through the first year of life. (4)

**ingestants.** Foods, drugs, or anything taken through the mouth. (30)

**inhalants.** Airborne substances that are inhaled. (30)

**initial assessment.** An assessment done when a child enrolls or at the beginning of the year to determine what skills children have mastered or where they are in their development. (3)

**injectables.** Chemicals or drugs injected into the body. (30)

**insulin.** A hormone that is needed to keep sugar in the blood at a proper level. As insulin is released into the body, the blood sugar level drops. (11)

**insulin reaction.** Occurs in a person with diabetes when the amount of insulin is not properly adjusted. (30)

**internal.** Under the skin. (30)

**irritability.** Tendency to feel distressed. (4)

**isolation area.** Special room or space in the center for children who become ill or show signs of a communicable disease. (8)

## L

**laboratory schools.** Schools located on a post-secondary or college campus with a primary purpose of training future teachers and serving as a study group for research. (2)

**language comprehension.** An understanding of language. Sometimes referred to as receptive or inner language. (5)

**latch-key children.** Term used to describe children left in self-care; also refers to children left in the care of a sibling under age 15. (29)

**lazy eye.** An eye disorder that is the result of a muscle imbalance caused by disuse of the eye. The correct name is *amblyopia*. (30)

**learning disability.** Problems with one or more basic skills of learning. Poor memory skills, trouble following directions, or poor coordination may be signs. (30)

**learning objective.** Outcome of an activity that is used to plan teaching strategies. (17)

**lesson plan.** A written plan outlining specific actions and activities that will be used to meet goals. (17)

**letters.** Written communication most often addressing only one subject and sent out on an "as needed" basis. (31)

**leukemia.** A form of cancer that affects the blood-forming organs and the blood. This cancer can cause a sharp increase in the number of white blood cells in the bloodstream. (30)

**level of performance.** States the minimum standard of achievement and how well one might want the child to do. (17)

**licensing specialist.** A person employed by a state to ensure that the state's child care rules and regulations are followed. (1)

**limits.** Guides to actions and behaviors that reflect the goals of the center. (10)

**listening.** Giving full attention to another person or people. (13)

**loudness.** Relates to the amount of energy or volume used when speaking. (30)

## M

**malnutrition.** A lack of proper nutrients in the diet that happens when a nutrient is absent or lacking from the diet; caused by an unbalanced diet, poor food choices, or the body's inability to use certain nutrients properly. (11)

**manipulative stage of play.** First stage of material use. Children in the manipulative stage will screw and unscrew a bottle cap. (20)

**manuscript writing.** A simple form of calligraphy not requiring the sustained muscle control that cursive writing does. This writing involves unconnected letters made of simple, separate strokes. (21)

**matching.** A form of classification involving putting like objects together. (22)

**maturation.** Sequence of biological changes in a child giving the child new abilities. (4)

**middle childhood.** The span of years between ages six and twelve. (7)

**modeling.** Verbal and nonverbal actions by one person, setting an example for others. (13) Showing the children the appropriate behavior to use during their socio-dramatic play. (20)

**molestation.** Sexual contact made by someone outside the family with a child. (10)

**mono painting.** Art activity in which a piece of paper is placed over a finger painting. The two papers are patted together, then pulled apart. (18)

**Montessori approach.** Schools provide children freedom within limits by a rather structured approach, and a fixed method in which materials are presented. (2)

**moral development.** Process of acquiring the standards of behavior considered acceptable by a society. (7)

**morality.** Understanding and using accepted rules of conduct when interacting with others. (7)

**motivation.** In a lesson plan, a method of gaining children's attention. (17)

**motor sequence.** Order in which a child is able to perform new movements. Motor sequence depends on the development of the brain and nerves. (4)

**multicultural.** Representing a variety of racial and ethnic groups. (9)

**myopia.** Visual difficulty in seeing things that are far away. Also referred to as *nearsightedness*. (30)

## N

**nanny.** A child care worker who usually provides care in the child's home and may receive food and housing in addition to wages. (1)

**National Association for the Education of Young Children (NAEYC).** One of the most respected professional organizations for people who work with young children. (1)

**natural consequences.** Experiences that follow naturally as a result of a behavior. (13)

**nearsighted.** The ability to see close objects more clearly than those at a distance. (7)

**neglect.** Form of child abuse in which the child is not given the basic needs of life. Neglected children may be deprived of proper diet, medical care, shelter, and/or clothing. (10)

**networking.** A process of building relationships with people who can help you. (32)

**newsletters.** Written communications most often including information concerning a variety of subjects. (31)

**nonaccidental physical injury.** Physical abuse inflicted on the child on purpose; the most visible type of child abuse. (10)

**numerals.** Number symbols, each of which represents an amount. (22)

**nutrients.** Chemical substances found in foods that are needed for growth and maintenance of health. (11)

**nutrition.** The science of food and how the body uses it. (11)

**nutrition concepts.** Basic concepts that will help children develop good lifetime healthy eating habits. (25)

## O

**obesity.** A major health problem caused by overeating. A condition in which the body weight is 20 percent above the normal weight for a given height. (7)

**object permanence.** An understanding that objects continue to exist even if a person cannot see them. (4)

**omission.** Implication that some groups have less value than other groups in our society caused by not mentioning or including a group in teaching. (24)

**one-to-one correspondence.** The understanding that one group has the same number as another. (22)

**ongoing assessment.** Type of assessment after an initial assessment that measures a child's continuing progress or development. (3)

**onlooker.** Describes a person who watches others' behavior but does not participate in it. (14)

**open wound.** An injury involving a break in the skin, such as a cut or scrape. (12)

**open-ended questions.** Questions promoting discussion and requiring decision-making skills. (23)

**operation.** The manipulation of ideas based on logic rather than perception. (7)

**overeating.** The intake of more food than is needed by the body to function properly, often causing health and emotional problems. (11)

**overfamiliarity.** Lack of interest in a particular toy shown by children who are given the same toy day after day. (28)

**overstimulated.** Overexcited. (14)

# P

**pantomiming.** Telling a story with body movements rather than words. (26)

**parallel play.** A type of play in which children play by themselves but stay close by other children. All the children may be involved in similar activities, but play between and among the children does not exist. (20)

**parent cooperatives.** Child care programs that are formed and run by parents who wish to take part in their children's preschool experience. (2)

**parent involvement.** Patterns of program participation by parents in early childhood settings that are related to their parenting roles. Volunteering in programs, home teaching, and helping with fundraising are examples. (31)

**parquetry blocks.** Geometric pieces that vary in color and shape used to teach shape concepts. (22)

**participation chart.** A tool used to gather information on specific aspects of children's behavior. (3)

**passive voice.** Sentence in which the object of the sentence is placed before the verb. (6)

**passivity.** Term for describing the level of involvement with a child's surroundings, such as withdrawing from a new person or event. (4)

**perceptions.** Ideas formed about a relationship or object as a result of what is learned through the senses. (24)

**personal priorities.** Your beliefs, feelings, and ideas about what is important. (32)

**personification.** Giving human traits to non-living objects, such as dolls or puppets. (20)

**persuading.** Encouraging children to act or behave in a certain way by appealing to their basic wants and needs. (13)

**petit mal seizure.** An epileptic condition in which the person may have a few muscles twitch briefly or may become confused with the surroundings. These seizures are milder than grand mal seizures. (12)

**phrase method.** Method of teaching songs using short sections of a long song, having children repeat these sections. These sections are increased until the children know the entire song. (26)

**phrase/whole combination method.** Method of teaching a song stressing key phrases with rhythmic movement or visual props. (26)

**physical age.** Age determined by a birth date. (9)

**physical development.** Physical body changes in a growing individual, such as changes in bone thickness, size, weight, vision, and coordination. (4)

**pica.** A craving for nonfood items such as paper, soap, rags, and toys. (16)

**picture books.** Books having single words or simple sentences and simple plots. (19)

**pitch.** The lowness or highness of a speaking voice. (30)

**Plasticene®.** An oil-based, commercially manufactured modeling compound available in many bright colors. (18)

**policy.** A course of action chosen that controls future decisions, such as a center's health policy. (12)

**portable kitchen.** Kitchen created in the classrooms by placing the ingredients, tools, and other equipment on a low table so all children can watch. Also, portable appliances such as an electric skillet or a hot plate are used rather than a stove. (25)

**portfolio.** A collection of materials that shows a person's abilities, accomplishments, and progress over time. (3)

**positive reinforcement.** Molding children's behavior by rewarding positive behavior. (13)

**practical life experiences.** Experiences in the Montessori curriculum that stress independence for children. (2)

**praising.** Giving children recognition for their accomplishments. (13)

**preschooler.** Term referring to children ages three to six years. (4)

**principle of proximodistal development.** Principle noting that development of the body occurs in an outward direction. The spinal cord develops before outer parts of the body; arms develop before hands; hands develop before fingers. (4)

**privacy law.** A law designed to protect children. It states that a child's records cannot be given to anyone other than parents without the parents' permission. (10)

**privately sponsored programs.** Child care programs sponsored by a house of worship, hospital, charitable organization, or an individual. (2)

**problem-solving file.** File containing helpful information on problems parents may face. (31)

**professional priorities.** Global aspects of work that are important to a person's satisfaction. (32)

**program goals.** Broad statements of purpose that reflect the end result of education. They state what is important. (17)

**projection.** A type of play allowing children to place feelings and emotions they feel onto another person or an object, such as a puppet. Through this play, a child may share his or her inner world. (20)

**prompting.** Making a verbal or nonverbal suggestion that requires a response; used either to stop an unacceptable action or start an acceptable one. (13)

**props.** Items that relate to the story and would attract children's attention. (19)

**prop box.** Box containing materials and equipment needed for certain roles in sociodramatic play. (20)

**prosocial behaviors.** Acts of kindness that benefit others, such as helping, sharing, and cooperating. (13)

**prosthesis.** An artificial limb, such as an arm, a hand, or a leg. (30)

**publicly sponsored programs.** Child care programs funded by the government, school district, and/or division of social services. (2)

**puppetry.** Using puppets in play. (20)

**puppets.** Figures designed in likeness to an animal or a human, used to enact stories, actions, or thoughts. (20)

## R

**rabies.** A disease caused by a viral infection of the nervous system and brain. Rabies is transmitted through the saliva of a rabid animal. (12)

**rating scale.** Tool used to record the degree to which a quality or trait is present. (3)

**rational counting.** Attaching a number to a series of grouped objects. (22)

**recognizing.** The ability to relate past and present experiences and classify items; made possible by using the senses to learn from repeated experiences. (22)

**redirecting.** Diverting or turning a child's attention in a different direction. (13)

**referral.** Directing a parent to obtain a diagnosis from a professional when a problem exists with a child. (30)

**reflex.** An automatic body response to a stimulus. At birth, an infant's physical abilities are limited to reflexes. (4)

**rehearsal.** The repetition of information after it is used. (7)

**resource people.** Center guests or field trip hosts. (27)

**resume.** Brief summary of a person's qualifications, skills, and job experience. The purpose of a resume is to secure an interview and/or inform a potential employer of a person's qualifications and experience. (32)

**reviews.** Lists and descriptions of books, which can be found in public libraries. (19)

**rheumatoid arthritis.** Common form of juvenile arthritis that can also strike adults. General fatigue, loss of appetite, aching joints, and a stiffness of joints are the first signs of the disease. (30)

**role.** A set of responsibilities that accompanies a position you hold in life. (32)

**role-playing.** A type of play allowing children to mimic the actions of others, such as wife, husband, mommy, daddy, doctor, or police officer. (20)

**role strain.** A type of stress created by being unable to successfully balance multiple roles. (32)

**rote counting.** Reciting numbers in their proper order. (6)

**routines.** Everyday experiences such as dressing, undressing, eating, napping, toileting, and changing activities. (16)

## S

**salt painting.** Art activity using salt mixed with colored tempera in shakers. (18)

**school-age child care programs.** Programs often sponsored by schools, houses of worship, or child care centers that provide care for children before and/or after school. (2)

**school-age years.** Another name given to middle childhood. (7)

**science.** The study of natural processes and their products. (23)

**science table.** A table used to display items related to the science area. (23)

**second-degree burn.** Burn causing damage to underlying layers of skin, requiring medical treatment. This burn is marked by pain, blistering, swelling, and discoloration. (12)

**self-assessment.** The process of examining your interests and abilities, as well as personal and professional priorities. (32)

**self-concept.** Qualities a child believes he or she possesses. A result of beliefs, feelings, and perceptions a child has of himself or herself as part of the world. (5)

**self-esteem.** The belief that you are worthwhile as a person. (7)

**sensory table.** Table in the sensory area that gives children practice in social situations. Also known as a water or sand table. (8)

**sensory training.** Learning from impressions received from the five senses. (2)

**separation anxiety.** A child's difficulty in separating from parents, often occurring between 9 and 18 months of age. (4)

**seriation.** The ability to arrange items in an increasing or decreasing order based on weight, volume, or size. (7)

**set.** A group of objects that are alike in some way and, therefore, belong together. (22)

**sexism.** Any action, attitude, or outlook used to judge a person based only on the sex of that person. (19)

**sexual abuse.** Abuse that involves adults using children for their own sexual pleasure, including rape, fondling, incest, pornography, and indecent exposure. (10)

**shape.** The outline of an object. (22)

**single-answer questions.** Questions requiring few decision-making skills and most often answered with yes or no. Also referred to as close-ended questions. (23)

**skywriting.** Demonstrating the correct way to make a letter by writing it in the air. (21)

**social comparison.** Process where people define themselves in terms of the qualities, skills, and attributes they see in others. (7)

**social-emotional development.** Growth in the two related areas of social and emotional skills. Social development involves learning to relate to others. Emotional development involves refining feelings and expressions of feelings. (4)

**socio-dramatic play.** Social play in which several children play together as they imitate others. (20)

**solitary play.** Independent play. (20)

**sorting.** A form of classification involving the process of physically separating objects based on unique features. (22)

**specific task assessment.** Giving children set activities to determine skill and/or needs. (22)

**spectator toys.** Toys requiring little action on the child's part, such as battery-powered cars and talking dolls. (9)

**spice painting.** Art activity in which children spread glue on a piece of paper, and then shake spices onto the paper. (18)

**spina bifida.** A condition in which the bones of the spine fail to grow together, resulting in paralysis. (30)

**spiral curriculum.** A curriculum based on the fact that as children grow, their circle of interests becomes larger. (17)

**staff room.** Room in a child care center provided for staff to spend work-related time away from the classroom. (8)

**stationary equipment.** Permanently installed equipment in the play yard, such as jungle gyms, slides, and tree houses. (8)

**statute.** Formal document drawn up by elected officials. (10)

**stereotypes.** Preset ideas about people based on one characteristic such as sex, ethnicity, age, or religion. (19)

**storybooks.** Books that contain pictures but have more complex plots than picture books. (19)

**storytelling.** Reciting a story or reading aloud from a book. (19)

**stress.** The body's reaction to physical or emotional factors, often taking the form of tension. (14)

**string painting.** Type of art activity in which heavy yarn or string is dipped in paint and pulled across a piece of paper. (18)

**stuttering.** Speech disorder that is often characterized by repetition, hesitation, and prolongation. (6)

**suggesting.** Placing thoughts for consideration into children's minds. (13)

**sunshine calls.** Telephone calls made by teachers to parents to communicate praise and support for children. (31)

**T**

**teaching portfolio.** A collection of materials that tell a story about your efforts, progress and achievements. (32)

**telegraphic speech.** Two-word phrases used by toddlers when they first learn to combine words. (4)

**temperament.** Quality and intensity of children's emotional reactions to their environment, such as passivity, irritability, and activity patterns. (4)

**texture painting.** Using liquid tempera paints mixed with sand, sawdust, or coffee grounds. (18)

**theme.** One main topic or concept around which the classroom activities are planned. (17)

**theme bags.** A child's backpack filled with games, puppets, story books, songs, and charts and including a letter of introduction for the parents. (31)

**theme walks.** Simple field trips taken in and around the center based on a theme. (27)

**third-degree burn.** Burn that destroys the skin layer and nerve endings, requiring prompt medical attention. (12)

**time out.** A guidance technique used when a child's behavior cannot be ignored. It involves excusing the child from interacting with others so he or she can calm down and gain self-control. (13)

**toddler.** Term used to refer to a child from the first year until the third birthday. The term is used because of the awkward walking style of children in this age group. (4)

**traffic pattern.** The way in which people move through the classroom area, affecting its arrangement. (8)

**transitions.** Changing from one activity to another and/or moving from one place to another. (16)

**traveling backpack.** A backpack in which children take home their favorite books, music cassettes, puzzles, or games to share with their parents. (31)

## U

**undernutrition.** Not eating enough food to keep a healthy body weight and activity level. (11)

**unit-based program model.** A curriculum format for school-age child care that revolves around curriculum themes that reflect the children's interests. (29)

## V

**vendors.** People and companies who sell products and supplies. (9)

**visual learner.** A child who depends a great deal on the sense of sight. This child will notice small visual changes in the environment. (17)

**voice flexibility.** Good speaking voice during routine conversation using a variety of pitches and loudness levels. (30)

**voice-quality disorders.** Disorders in which the quality of a speaker's voice is affected; includes harshness, breathiness, nasality, and hoarseness. (30)

## W

**warm colors.** Colors including red, yellow, and orange that make a room appear smaller. (8)

**warning.** Reminding children to follow classroom rules, stating the misbehavior and the consequences. (13)

**whole song method.** Method used to teach short, simple songs by having the children listen and then sing along. (26)

**wound.** Damage to the surface of the skin or body tissue. (12)

# Index